LINCOLN
AND HIS WORLD

THE
EARLY
YEARS

LINCOLN
AND HIS WORLD

THE
EARLY
YEARS

Birth to Illinois Legislature

RICHARD LAWRENCE MILLER

STACKPOLE
BOOKS

Published by
STACKPOLE BOOKS
5067 Ritter Road
Mechanicsburg, PA 17055
www.stackpolebooks.com

Printed in the United States

First edition

10 9 8 7 6 5 4 3 2 1

Library of Congress Cataloging-in-Publication Data

Miller, Richard Lawrence.
  Lincoln and his world / Richard Lawrence Miller.—1st ed.
    p. cm.
  Includes bibliographical references and index.
  ISBN-13: 978-0-8117-0187-7 (hardcover)
  ISBN-10: 0-8117-0187-5 (hardcover)
  1. Lincoln, Abraham, 1809–1865. 2. Lincoln, Abraham, 1809–1865—Childhood
and youth. 3. Lincoln, Abraham, 1809–1865—Political career before 1861.
4. Legislators—Illinois—Biography. 5. Illinois—Politics and government—To 1865.
6. Presidents—United States—Biography. I. Title.

E457.3.M55 2006
977.3'03092—dc22

                                                          2006006080

✤ CONTENTS ✤

⇒ ACKNOWLEDGMENTS ⇒

Help from several individuals went far beyond the call of duty. Marjorie R. Miller provided financial assistance that speeded completion of this book, a factor of importance at any time, but particularly when an author is creaking through his sixth decade of life. While Jeff Mueller was acting president of Springfield College in Illinois, he demonstrated his commitment to the lost world of collegial scholarship by letting me rent a student apartment for months. Without Jeff's generosity, I don't know how I could have afforded an extended research visit to various archival and library holdings in Springfield. Connie Butts routinely provided me with transportation in Springfield, and after my stay ended, she responded to my occasional requests to double-check confusing points in my notes. Gary Davis let me hitch a ride with him one day from Springfield to Chicago, allowing me a valuable research visit to the Chicago Historical Society (and yes, I did eventually do more research there). James Gunn arranged for a brief but valuable stay in a student dormitory at the University of Kansas, allowing me several days of intensive examination of journals and books. Doug Wilson posed acute and helpful questions. Doug Schroeder and David Hunker furnished unstinting technical assistance. Siegfried Ruschin, who was run out of Germany by Hitler and has a keener appreciation for the value of democracy than some Americans do, generously translated German-language materials into English. Bob Sanders and Fred Whitehead provided years of encouragement. Nancy Clark's supportive aid was amazing, but of course, she is an amazing gal.

⪥ PREFACE ⪥

This volume takes Lincoln's story to 1834. Subsequent volumes cover his years in Illinois politics and his emergence as a national figure.

This book reconstructs the hidden world of Abraham Lincoln. Much of his world is irretrievable—the primeval wilderness he grew up in, fear of threats presented by Native Americans, fetid smells of a town square. Words of participants still exist, however, even though the speakers are dead. Just as an archeologist can reassemble pot shards and draw inferences about the civilization that produced it, I've examined a mass of verbal chunks left by Lincoln and persons around him. I've sorted jumbled piles of fragments, restored them, and pieced them together in a way that reveals the speakers' world. That world has not been lost, but has remained hidden in a jungle of interviews, letters, diaries, newspapers, handbills, legislative proceedings, and court records.

My goal is to reconstruct fragments so meticulously, and display them so skillfully, that someone viewing them in the display case (this book) can comprehend the civilization by viewing the reassembled vessel itself, without having to read explanatory captions (my personal opinions). Still, in choosing which shards to assemble and which to discard, I offer a very personal portrait of what Lincoln was all about.

This book opens a window to the past. Readers eavesdrop on actual words of Lincoln and his contemporaries, revealing their hopes, plots, confusion, and reactions. What was it like to spend a snowy winter's night in a cabin, eating meager fare and listening to Lincoln read aloud? A participant's memory is here. What was it like to have a flatboat take in water while Lincoln and his crew desperately waded through the river with their cargo? Eyewitness accounts give impressions. What was it like for Lincoln to fall in love with another man's fiancée? Villagers who saw it happen give their memories. What was it like to go on a drunken chase after Indians? Lincoln and his troops offer recollections.

I strive to lift layer after layer of gauze applied by legend, stripping bare the raw reality of Lincoln's world. I usher readers to a window, and what they see through it depends on where they look. I offer a world for readers to move around in. What would you have thought, had you been there? This book allows readers to have such a vicarious experience. I don't say something is good or bad, moral or immoral. I don't tell readers what they should think. I avoid becoming a character in the narrative. My function is to minimize obstructions to seeing reality beyond the window. I present a world, not a point of view and not a drama. The inquiring reader will be challenged to reach conclusions about what the book's characters say and do. Different readers will reach different conclusions.

If I cite an authority in the text, that means I believe the authority gives reasonable support for an assertion. I do not necessarily believe everything the authority says about other topics. A knowledgeable person can, in good faith, be correct about some things and mistaken about others. I may accept a sometimes questionable source, such as Slicky Bill Greene, Mentor Graham, or Leonard Swett, when the testimony is plausible and isn't discredited by what we otherwise know. Readers deserve to know what was said by people who were on the scene. Problems with eyewitness testimony are familiar, but sometimes memories are the only evidence we have.

Denny Hanks, cousin of Lincoln's mother, is one of the most prolific sources of information about Abraham's early years. The two young men spent so much time together, said another relative, that "the impression here among the old people is that Hanks and Abe were half brothers" (Charles Friend to William H. Herndon, Feb. 22, 1866, H-W Papers [transcript available in Wilson and Davis, *Herndon's*, 219]). Denny, however, was a notorious truth stretcher, and I am always judicious in using him as an authority.

While studying Lincoln and his world, I discovered numerous examples of incorrect reporting by persons who participated in events. I have evaluated accounts carefully, and from my knowledge of personalities and the era, I conduct readers through that jungle without bothering to point out false paths that continually invite the unwary. Often I can justify the path I take; that is one reason why I offer source notes. As to why I accept some sources and reject others, basically it's a question of where accounts support or contradict one another, and then whether accounts are plausible and how they tie in with any objective evidence. Sometimes contradictory accounts have external factors to grasp, such as chronology, geography, or an incident supported by another report. Sometimes they don't. Sometimes my decision on credibility simply comes down to experience. Typically I know who is reliable about something and who is not. If I don't know, my experience may still allow me to take us on what should be the right path. Yet I know that the best guides can make dreadful mistakes.

Newspaper sources are particularly challenging. I've been involved with numerous public events. I recall only one instance of accurate newspaper reporting of an event in which I participated and am unconvinced that newspapers of Lincoln's time were better in that regard. They are an important record of his world, however, and we simply need to remember that what they say is a portrait of a subject, with each rendition differing—just as portraits of the same subject rendered by different artists will differ. An image by Norman Rockwell differs from one produced by Lucian Freud, but the difference doesn't mean that neither is trustworthy; they simply reveal different things about the same subject. That, however, assumes an artist strives to reveal truth, an assumption that doesn't necessarily apply to newspapers.

With quotations, my normal preference is to reproduce a passage exactly—warts and all. Two factors persuaded me to do otherwise in this book. First, in quotations, my responsibility is to help the dead speak as they intended, which can involve silent correction of typos and modernizations of spelling and punctuation. Passages riddled with *sics* and brackets can be tough even for scholars. My approach here is no different from editing out stutters and "uhs" from audiotapes, eliminating distractions from what someone is saying. The second factor impelling me to take this approach was practical. When taking notes, by necessity I routinely abbreviated words because I did my research without assistants, typing hundreds of pages. Working alone, it was impractical for me to go back to all quoted sources, including those in distant archives, to double-check them. Anyone needing to study nineteenth-century American English and typography, rather than what the writers were intending to communicate, will simply have to consult the original sources as I did.

Occasionally I present quotations that reproduce someone's accent or a region's local English. My intent in transcribing such passages is to enable the reader to hear a person's voice more authentically.

If I have examined both an original manuscript and a published version, I generally prefer to cite the published version, on the grounds that it is more accessible to a reader. When I say a transcript of a document is available in a printed source, my silently modernized version of the document doesn't necessarily duplicate the transcript. For example, if a transcript shows a document's misspelled word, I typically correct the spelling silently. The main exception to this policy is law; I do strive for exact reproduction of passages from nineteenth-century constitutions, statutes, court decisions, legislative resolutions, and official transcripts of legislative debate. I also strive for exact reproduction of words from twentieth- and twenty-first-century authorities, though not, as explained above, from transcripts of manuscripts printed in such volumes.

A more fundamental question can be what a handwritten scrawl says, and deciphering flawed microfilm images of nineteenth-century newspaper pages can be as challenging as reading nineteenth-century penmanship. Someone with better bifocals than mine may interpret a smudge differently. Being aware of my own fallibilities, I normally refrain from criticizing other Lincoln authors. Having been there, I know what they face.

When reading someone's recollection of a conversation, particularly if a long time has passed between earlier speaking and later memory of it, we should expect that such memory is faulty. Such a problem, however, doesn't mean that the person is misreporting the gist of an oral comment.

I accept William H. Herndon's interview notes as renditions of what people told him. These notes aren't verbatim; occasionally words allegedly spoken to him sound like his sort of phrasing. Nonetheless, in the Herndon materials, I have followed the practice of attributing interview quotations to the person interviewed, even though Herndon was not a stenographic reporter and was not necessarily trying to reproduce exact language in his personal note taking. Much the same can be said about quotations from various other sources, accepted at face value, which is not necessarily the gold standard.

Name spellings can be puzzling. The U.S. Senator from Illinois signed his name as both Stephen A. Douglass and Stephen A. Douglas. Which version is correct? Such decisions become harder with lesser-known individuals. I leave ultimate answers to other students.

Many state and federal officials have similar titles, such as senator or representative. My practice is to capitalize titles of federal officials and agencies.

Especially for the Kentucky period, so much of the Lincoln story is based on memories, so little on documentary evidence. Accounts may support or contradict one another, and either way, evaluation of their plausibility is necessary. That latter judgment may have the benefit of objective evidence, such as a signed document, but sometimes a decision must rely simply on experience with the material. Some parts of the Lincoln story involve possibilities; some involve probabilities; some rest upon fact. I believe readers deserve to know that entire range. Proving something right or wrong may be impossible; historians are sometimes more in the role of a judge than a scientist. I believe everything I offer to readers is reasonable but, particularly with the Kentucky years, I cannot claim that everything I offer is proven, even though I may cite authorities for what I say. Lincoln scholars will readily distinguish among authorities I cite, seeing where my story is limited by its underlying sources. For nonspecialist readers, I have tried to signal uncertain aspects of the Lincoln story in the text by using qualifiers such as "reportedly" or "allegedly." My book's bibliographic list of cited sources occasionally has cautions about particular authorities. Rather than withhold doubtful information that I know, I offer it with a warning label.

Respected authorities have produced contradictory accounts of Tom Lincoln and Nancy Hanks up to the time of their marriage, complicated by the Hanks family's notoriously treacherous genealogy involving more than one Nancy Hanks who lived in the same region at about the same time. I have done my best to provide a safe path through the perilous forest.

CHAPTER 1

KENTUCKY

Father Abraham was Kentucky-born. His was a world of wonders long lost to us. He came to life near the Sinking Spring, where, as one chronicle said, "rocks curved inward, making a sort of cave or ledge beneath which people could stand, and in the center was a never-ending flow of clear, cool water. It was a fairy-like place, with moss over the rocky sides."[1] A reliable supply of fresh water was much coveted by settlers. This particular supply was hidden. It didn't flow on the ground's surface, but instead stayed inside the cave and disappeared into untraced nether regions.[2] Here was a country of hollows and strange conical hills, where even visitors who had traveled much might feel unease. Before Lincoln was born, someone stood atop a hill near the Sinking Spring and declared it "a steep and lofty mountain that forms a kind of amphitheatre." He went on to describe the surroundings: "From its summit the neighboring country presents the aspect of an immense valley, covered with forests of an imperceptible extent, whence . . . nothing but a gloomy verdant space is seen, formed by the tops of the close-connected trees, and through which not the vestige of a plantation can be discerned. The profound silence that reigns in these woods, uninhabited by wild beasts, and the security of the place, forms an *ensemble* rarely to be met with in other countries."[3]

Whites chose to settle in that strange region because they were brave enough to overcome their fears or desperate enough to tolerate them. A few settlers appeared to exploit that special advantage arising from control, or at least manipulation, of spirits that ruled the land. Afflictions of man or beast succumbed to chants and ceremonies of faith doctors. Wizards found water and other underground treasures by holding a forked stick. Hunters learned that rifles could be bewitched: "I was so unlucky as to afford what was considered an incontestable proof of the truth of witchcraft," said one visitor to Western settlements. "I thought I saw . . . some part of the body of a deer. . . . Got within eighty yards of the spot. . . . I saw two deer standing. . . . Having taken deliberate aim, fired at the one nearest me, which fell, as I thought, plump down on the spot." The hunter saw two more deer and shot toward one. "I heard the bullet play thump on his ribs, and off he bounded." Upon going to the spot where the first deer had fallen, he found that "there was no deer—not blood—not even the slightest trail in the grass!"[4] To remove a spell, an image of the responsible witch might have to be prepared and shot with a silver ball.

Attempting such manipulations was harder than avoiding their necessity. Perhaps a dog had simply crossed the path of the hunter who had the mysterious encounter with deer, and he neglected to hook his little fingers together and pull until the dog could no longer be seen. Obedience to the moon, that all-powerful controller of the earth, was essential. Putting in a fence was hard enough, but the labor was wasted unless done during the light of the moon. Even trees cut to make fencing had to be cut down in that moon phase. Soap had to be made in that phase also, stirred in one direction only and by one person alone. Potatoes and other roots had to be planted in the three days preceding a new moon. Obedience to the calendar was imperative. People had to know when Friday arrived, lest they began a new task on that day and thereby doom it to failure.[5] Such things weren't just a Kentucky phenomenon, but existed everywhere. A New Yorker named William H. Seward (whose life would intertwine with Lincoln's) grew up amid reports of witches haunting a forested cliff in Orange County by day and doing their work by night in a country schoolhouse attic at the cliff's foot.[6] Newspapers contained reports of marvels:

> On Tuesday the 24th ult. the inhabitants of this town and neighborhood were astonished much at the appearance of leaves, small pieces of limbs, bark, &c. falling apparently from the clouds. The day was mild, except a breeze now and then from the southwest with a few flying clouds, but no rain, nor was there the least appearance of any extraordinary commotion in the heaven. . . . Accounts from various quarters for more than forty miles around state that the same appearance was observed.[7]

Someone who lived in Lincoln's time looked back on the experience: "Even to the ear of the most practical of mankind, there is an awesome solitude in unexplored forest wilderness; and the sighing of the winds, the roar of night-growling animals, the hollow murmur of distant streams, and the indescribable hum that goes up continually from the hidden life of the forest are ever after in the memory of those who have spent much of their childhood in scenes like these."[8]

How much of this world was real and how much was a dream I cannot say. Reports about deep forests, barren knolls, and assorted wildlife come from the same persons who obeyed the moon and feared encounters with witches.[9] People lived as if all were real and serious. As that time recedes ever farther from us, we are tempted to view it as a simpler era. Yet its inhabitants had many more rules to follow than we do, spirit rules with dire consequences far surer than befell violators of a Kentucky statute. Law violations could be hidden from agents of the state or evaded in court, but the moon and birds and witches knew all and couldn't be deceived. And rules imposed by spirits weren't written like statutes, but had to be learned orally from generation to generation. Survival among nature spirits required respect for knowledge of elders and close attention to things ignored in later centuries. Such was the world Lincoln entered when he was born.

Abraham Lincoln's introduction to Kentucky was not the famed bluegrass, not the salons of Lexington with a personal slave to attend every want, though eventually he would become a welcome visitor in such domains. No, the Kentucky that Lincoln first saw was country more barren than lush, where survival—let alone prosperity—was a hardscrabble business.

One description of the territory called it "a desolate spot,"[10] and another likened it to the stony soil of New England, with clay instead of soil, a barren grassland infested with underbrush every bit as hard to remove as forest trees.[11] "Barren grassland" is a term reflecting pioneer opinion that the fertility of land was proven by thickness of forest: The sparser the trees, the poorer the soil. This was incorrect, and to someone without such opinion, the land around Sinking Spring could have grandeur. A few years before Lincoln's birth, a traveler through the area discovered that prior descriptions didn't match what he saw: "I conceived I should have had to cross over a naked space, sown here and there with a few plants. . . . I was agreeably surprised to see a beautiful meadow, where the grass was from two to three feet high."[12]

As obedience to the moon and spirits died away, the land sickened. Barely half a century after white farmers arrived, a visitor found the Sinking Spring area dismal:

> There were narrow valleys along the streams, where two to three families to the mile could have their little garden and truck patches. But as the timber was cleared off, and the clay soil washed in and filled up these small fields, they became less and less productive, until the land was soon "worn out." And it remains poorer to-day than when it had the game and fish which the early settlers found there, and hunted and fished for until they were well-nigh exterminated.[13]

In 1862, one old resident said:

> It war n't allus so pore. Afore they cut down and hauled off most of the trees, and kiled and druv out the birds and the squirls and all the

game, and when they tuk away the timber and shade, arter that the
sun kinder dried up the clay hills, and the winter and the spring
storms and floods filled up the little cricks with gravel and rocks and
clay. So now we have these dried-up clay and stony bottoms whar the
pretty little cricks used ter run, and the birds and game as war n't
killed or starved have found water and shade and sumthin' to live on
whar they take better keer of thar timber and thar rivers and cricks
and medders fur paster. We know that we are pore, porer than we war
when I war a young man.[14]

In 1866, another resident declared that the Sinking Spring vicinity had
"some very good land as much so as river bottom—then some as poor as need be.
In some cases it changes within a few rods. I might say from first to fourth
rate. . . . The place on which Abe was born is rather poor yet it would sell for say
twenty dollars per acre, but it would take a man a long time to get his money out
of it."[15] That same year, the owner of the old Lincoln place described it a little
more generously, as "barren land but can all be cultivated with the plow. It is
divided into basins, hills, and hillsides. The basins occupy about one-third of the
land and are very rich. The hills and hillside are less productive. . . . A description of this farm is a very good description of all the country around."[16]

Lincoln's parents resided there as a result of choices made by them and by
others, choices that would eventually drive the parents not only from their farm,
but from the entire region after they had invested years of labor in improving
their land. Here is what happened.

A few years before Lincoln's birth, the surrounding district was sparsely
populated. A traveler then noted, "On the road where the plantations are closest
together we counted but eighteen in a space of sixty or seventy miles."[17] The Lincolns weren't yet among those outlying settlers, however. Instead, Abraham
Lincoln's parents, Thomas and Nancy, were townspeople. Both knew wilderness
intimately, knew that the lack of neighbors could turn deadly.

Tom was a child of the Revolution, born about 1776. His Virginian father had
sufficient means to acquire thousands upon thousands of prime acres in Kentucky. One day, young Tom and his father were minding their own business on
the vast family estate when a Native American guerrilla band saw opportunity to
demonstrate what they thought of Lincoln's real estate deeds. While Tom's father
reportedly was concentrating on fence building, one of the hidden partisans was
concentrating on careful enough rifle aim to drop the elder Lincoln with one
shot. The marksman then dashed to Tom and scooped him up. Becoming an
Indian captive was feared perhaps even more than death, and it was one of the
most potent terror tactics available to them. Tom pleaded with his captor. Few
children can put up sufficient fight to stop a ruthless adult from doing anything,
but from a distance, Tom's older brother Mordecai was watching the struggle
closely over his rifle's barrel, later declaring that a silver moon trinket on the

Indian's chest "was the prettiest mark he held a rifle on." The bullet's impact hurled the guerrilla into the air. No one knows whether punching a bullet into the attacker instead of Tom was due more to skill or to luck. Reports vary on whether the Indian died instantly, but he abandoned Tom. One report says Mordecai shot two more, who died on the spot.[18] In the 1850s, Abraham Lincoln said the story was "more strongly than all others imprinted upon my mind and memory."[19] His law partner, Billy Herndon, heard him relate the tale many a time, and it was well known to friends and neighbors of the Lincoln family, some of whom got the story from Abe Lincoln himself.[20]

Years later, Tom would marry Nancy Hanks, reportedly a woman also brushed by results of Indian combat. A story is told that while traveling across Kentucky, the immediate family of Nancy's ten-year-old cousin Sarah Mitchell was attacked by Native American defenders. They snatched the girl and carried her off while the father was tending to the fatally wounded mother. Later, the father set off to find his daughter but drowned while crossing a river. Sarah's grandmother appealed to Kentucky's governor, Isaac Shelby: "As you have frequent opportunity of writing Governor Blunt I beg of you to mention the matter to him as he once promised to use his best endeavor to gain intelligence of her. . . . I am now old and very frail and cannot be contented without trying every method in my power for her redemption from captivity."[21] "Governor Blunt" was surely William Blount, governor of the Tennessee country, who was serving simultaneously as President Washington's Superintendent of Indian Affairs. Shelby already had experience in Indian diplomacy and would gain more. Whatever the two governors did, if anything, Sarah was eventually tracked down, and the Indians released her after several years of captivity. Although we don't know what happened during her sojourn among Indians, a large body of captivity narratives implies that the experience could not have been good. Not everyone who lived through such an ordeal was able to resume a comfortable life in white society. For several years after her return, however, Sarah supposedly had the good fortune of close contact with her cousin Nancy Hanks, who reportedly helped her relearn the language and customs of white America. A tradition asserts that the two girls became like sisters. Sarah later named one of her daughters Nancy Hanks Thompson, and Nancy named her first child Sarah.[22]

Such was frontier life, or part of it anyway.

Shock and grief aside, the killing of Tom Lincoln's father had a permanent practical effect on the boy. Although the man was a large property owner, he had never drawn up a will for the division of his property. Authorities say the old British requirement for such cases governed the outcome, giving two-thirds of all the thousands of acres, two-thirds of all the livestock, two-thirds of all the farm equipment, and two-thirds of all other personal property to brother Mordecai, with the remaining third going to the boys' mother.[23] Such a settlement would transform Tom from the status of eventual landed proprietor into a young man with no financial means at all. Abraham Lincoln declared, "I have often said that

Uncle Mord had run off with all the talents of the family,"[24] and it appears that he ran off with the family's money as well.

That scenario puts the case too harshly, however. We know this because of the affectionate regard in which relatives held Mordecai until his death and beyond, affection that would have dimmed considerably if they had felt cheated. Indeed, surviving family anecdotes about Mordecai lack even a whisper about the money.

Still, cut off from his father's estate, young Tom was no longer destined to be among Kentucky's gentry. When old enough to be employable, he began hiring out. During George Washington's presidency, teenager Tom was laboring alongside slaves, all doing the same hard manual work at a Hardin County mill site. Slaves earned three shillings a day for their masters, and Tom received the same slave wages. As one chronicler delicately phrased it, the free workers' slave competitors had "a tendency to keep wages down."[25] Slavery thoroughly permeated working conditions throughout the South.

> "I wish to hire fifteen likely healthy negro men, to work at the Little Sandy salt works, the present year, and will bind myslf to clothe them well and pay high wages to their owners."
>
> —Alfred W. Grayson, *Lexington Kentucky Gazette and General Advertiser*, February 20, 1809

> "Two hundred dollars reward. Ranaway . . . from the subscriber at the Cumberland Furnace, Dickson County, state of Tennessee, a dark mulatto fellow called Billey. . . . His countenance indicative of discontent. . . . He was guilty of crimes previous to his elopement, for which he expected punishment. Any person apprehending him will iron him in the most secure manner, paying no regard to any promises he may make."
>
> —Montgomery Bell, *Vincennes Western Sun*, November 17, 1807

> "300 Dollars Reward. Ranaway from the subscriber at Cumberland Furnace, Dickson County. . . .
> "Fifty Dollars Reward. Runaway from me at the same place . . . a young negro fellow named Bob . . . his middle toes on both his feet contracted by corns. . . . If caught neither will acknowledge to whom they belong but will try to make their escape if not securely ironed."
>
> —Montgomery Bell, *Vincennes Western Sun*, July 13, 1816

Employer records indicate that Tom was one of the mill's most reliable workers; he could be depended on to show up. Although some free laborers took their wages in whiskey, Tom drew cash.[26] No master snatched Tom's pay away from him, but eventually he left this situation. In the words of Abraham Lincoln, Tom became "a wandering laboring boy" who descended into "poverty."[27] His wandering wasn't aimless, however. He headed south and east, hundreds of miles, past the Cumberlands toward the Holston Mountains and Watauga Valley. In a piece of Tennessee surrounded by Virginia and North Carolina, he found his uncle Isaac Lincoln. Isaac was a prosperous planter, owning slaves whose numbers eventually, if not already, reached into the dozens. He could afford to hire a nephew to work with them. Later, Tom would often tell Abraham about the experience.[28]

After perhaps a year with Uncle Isaac, Tom made his way back to the Hardin County area of Kentucky he had left. About the time President John Adams took office, Tom Lincoln entered adulthood at age twenty-one. The young man began switching from pick and shovel jobs to rough carpentry.[29] Evidently he was thrifty enough to save a portion of his wages year by year until, perhaps through those savings or perhaps with the assistance of brother Mordecai, Tom had £118 to buy about 240 acres near Mill Creek,[30] the area where his two sisters lived with their husbands.[31] This was good land he could farm, where in theory he could work for himself, just as his father had done—on a much smaller scale, to be sure, but a wage slave no longer. I say "in theory," because apparently he didn't farm it himself, but instead leased it to one sister's husband.[32] This was a close family arrangement; Tom's mother lived with that couple then and long after.[33] Tom was a little past twenty-five years old when he acquired this property.

This acquisition raised his social status. He may now have been liable for taxes on his land, but being a taxpayer was something of an honor in that era. Landowners were also both privileged and obligated to serve on juries, a task that Tom began to fulfill, judging conduct of fellow citizens.[34] The community began assigning him other duties as well, guarding prisoners[35] and serving with a handful of picked men as a patroller. Normally patrollers would prowl Hardin County looking for slaves who were absent without leave from their owners or who had unauthorized possession of property.

"ONE HUNDRED AND FIFTY DOLLARS REWARD. Runaway from the subscriber . . . a negro man named Bill . . . has some spots on his neck and collar bone occasioned by a burn, some stripes on his back towards his right side under his shoulder blade, occasioned by whipping, may have some scars on his legs near his ankles, occasioned by being ironed."

—Richard Wells, Broke County, Virginia,
Vincennes Western Sun, November 19, 1808

"Twenty Dollars Reward. Ran away from the subscriber . . . a
mulatto man named Anthony . . . branded R on each cheek . . . he is
crafty and cunning."

—Jacob Gray, Nashville, Tennessee,
Vincennes Western Sun, December 24, 1808

"Fifty Dollars Reward. Ran away from the subscriber living in Madison County, Mississippi Territory, near Huntsville . . . a mulatto man
named David, has since at Shawneetown called himself James
Veach . . . a scar on one of his legs, many on his back and shins, and
two under one of his breasts."

—William Thomason, *Vincennes Western Sun*,
June 22, 1816

"Fifty Dollars Reward. Ran away from the subscriber living on
Floyd's Fork, Jefferson County, Kentucky . . . a negro man named
Harry . . . his four fingers on the right hand partly perished away and
drawn under; has a slight brand on his left cheek, thus TB, but will
not be perceived without close examination. . . . This is the second
time he has attempted to pass for a freeman, which caused him to be
branded."

—Thomas Buckner, *Vincennes Western Sun*,
October 5, 1816

Patrollers were also supposed to help discourage revolts by breaking up illegal meetings of slaves. With permission from the patrollers' captain, they could
administer summary punishment for any of the preceding offenses, stripping
slaves' backs bare and laying on ten lashes from a whip. Whether Tom participated in such discipline is unknown, but such was the routine.[36] Possibilities for
mayhem and murder from slaves generated continual undercurrents of fear
among whites. When Tom's three-month term as a patroller expired, conditions
were such that the county authorities increased the size of patrols.[37]

"Mr. Tibbatt's negro Jack, charged with setting fire to his master's
bake house, has been found guilty, and sentence of death was passed
on him by the Fayette County Court, on Thursday last. The day of
execution is fixed for the 18th of March."

—*Lexington Kentucky Gazette*,
February 18, 1809

"A most horrid murder was committed on the body of a Mr. Chapman of Adair County a short time since, by three of his negroes. After repeatedly striking him with a handspike, they carried his body some little distance, and built a large log heap on it, which they consumed by fire. The negroes have since been apprehended, and confessed their guilt."

—*Mirror*, clipped in *Vincennes Western Sun*, June 24, 1809

"Apprehended insurrection of the blacks. The editors of the *Boston Patriot* have received from a correspondent in Augusta, Georgia, the following copy of a letter from Gen. Thomas Blunt of North Carolina to the Hon. J. Milledge, of Georgia. Mr. M. spread the information, and it excited much alarm and occasioned great preparations for security. The communication says, 'the letter of Capt. James is but a small evidence of the disposition of the blacks in this part of the country.'"

—*Vincennes Western Sun*, June 9, 1810

While performing these civic tasks, Tom lived in the community of Elizabethtown. He settled there about the time he bought the farm he leased out. Whether that lease generated income for him is unclear—understandings among family members aren't always documented. For sure he earned money as a skilled carpenter. He worked on his own dwelling and others; his craftsmanship on one residence was still in good shape six decades later.[38] His skill with carpentry developed far enough that he became a cabinetmaker, producing quality furniture.[39] Surviving examples from his hands over the years include corner cupboards, a hutch, a chest of drawers, a desk, and a bookcase. He used cherry, black walnut, white oak, and white ash, adding decorative scrollwork and inlays that survived decades of handling.[40] His pieces show fine control and are works of art that anyone with good taste would be pleased to own. Surviving business records demonstrate that tradesmen considered him a customer in good standing.[41] In addition to being a homeowner, he prospered enough to obtain horses,[42] and store accounts indicate he dressed well.[43] A neighbor said, "I remember thinking as I would pass by the place and see them out, that they [Tom and son] had the appearance of a dignified man and boy."[44] A casual acquaintance of later years said of Tom, "His manners were what might be termed backwoodsish, yet they were easy, so much so that I almost would say they were polished."[45] Tom was respected by the town and respectable in appearance. In later days, people who never knew Tom would call him uncouth, shiftless, and lazy—a portrayal inconsistent with official records and informal recollections of acquaintances.

Tom's brother Mordecai lived some miles east of town in Washington County. Tom had also resided in that vicinity during childhood and after his wanderings as a laboring boy, before moving into Elizabethtown. For years, the two Lincolns were neighbors to Nancy Hanks.[46] It would seem likely that Tom got to know Nancy before he moved to town, and he maintained contact afterward. Yet Abraham told of a dream Tom had:

> My father . . . dreamed that he rode through an unfrequented path to a strange house, the surroundings and furnishing of which were vividly impressed in his mind. At the fireside, there was sitting a woman whose features he distinctly saw. She was engaged in paring an apple. That woman was to be his wife. He could not shake off the vision. It haunted him incessantly, until it compelled him to go down the unfrequented way. He quietly opened the door of what he recognized to be the house, and saw, at a glance, that it was where he had been in his dream. There was a woman at the fireside engaged in paring an apple.

The woman was Nancy Hanks.[47]

Nancy's home situation appears to have been unorthodox. Abe believed she was the illegitimate daughter of a Virginia planter.[48] Accounts suggest that she was taken to Kentucky by her mother and then abandoned. Her maternal grandparents took her in, but that arrangement ended with the death of her grandfather. Her mother seems to have married by then, but she evidently tolerated Nancy in the home only until she was able to ship her daughter off to other relatives in the Washington County area. Finding hearts generous enough to adopt an unwanted girl may have taken a while, but finding relatives was almost as easy as a visit to the next cabin. One of Lincoln's successors in the White House noted: "It is sometimes difficult for non-Southerners to understand how stable the population of rural Southern communities had been since European settlers moved into these areas five or six generations earlier. . . . Intermarriages and blood kinships in the neighboring towns were extensive and intricate. Rosalynn was one of the few female residents in Plains who was not related to me, at least within the last 120 years or so."[49] That situation described by Jimmy Carter certainly applied to Tom Lincoln and Nancy Hanks. Nancy was part of a kinship group extending throughout the region, a clan whose disregard for sexual proprieties was demonstrated by illegitimate offspring. Billy Herndon said that Lincoln had told him "his relations were *lascivious*, *lecherous*, not to be trusted."[50] Vigorous tracing of genealogy could produce faint whiffs almost reminiscent of incest. Relationships traced by one distinguished authority showed Tom and Nancy to have been first cousins, though an equally distinguished authority staunchly denied such a close relationship.[51] Settlers routinely possessed kinship ties well known to themselves although unapparent to strangers.[52]

Tom Lincoln and Nancy Hanks were officially married on June 12, 1806. Apparently they had become sexually intimate some time earlier, at least by later calculations of a physician who said the couple must have been sexually active before marriage or their first child, Sarah, would have been too premature to survive.[53] The marriage ceremony was performed at the home of Nancy's Washington County relative Richard Berry. Although the couple would set up housekeeping in Elizabethtown over in Hardin County, they had enough friends and relatives in Washington County to justify a celebration there. Rev. Jesse Head did the honors. Like Tom, the reverend worked as a cabinetmaker, but on a larger scale, with employees and apprentices. The red-haired preacher's long nose poked into many other secular areas. Reverend Head served as a postmaster and president of town trustees in Springfield, Kentucky. As justice of the peace, he had tried a case involving Tom's brother Mordecai. Described as a "good fighter," Head was a fine example of the preacher-politician familiar to that era.[54] Tradition says that circuit court was adjourned for the day so officials and people having business at court could attend the wedding. If true, that would be yet more indication of the community's esteem for Tom and for others associated with the nuptials. And in fact, we do know that Richard Berry, brother Mordecai, Jesse Head, and several of Nancy's kin had business scheduled before the circuit court on Thursday, June 12; yet for reasons evidently unstated officially, court was canceled that day but held Wednesday and Friday.[55]

Both Tom and Nancy were mature in age for a newly married couple of that era, Tom being about thirty, Nancy about twenty-three. They had a good start to married life in Elizabethtown. They apparently owned their own home, furnished with domestic implements from needles to a basin, and dishware with knives, forks, and spoons. The couple's purchases included tools and a bridle, calfskin, and silk.[56] The married pair didn't have to make whatever they needed, but instead could afford to buy store goods. Tom was an established "mechanic," as many artisans were then called. Nancy had typical skills of Western wives; her spinning and sewing abilities reportedly admirable.[57] A visitor who came through the area about this time noted: "The women seldom assist in the labors of the field; they are very attentive to their domestic concerns, and the spinning of hemp or cotton, which they convert into linen for the use of their family. This employment alone is truly laborious."[58] Nancy's physical appearance is lost; tall or short, fat or thin, color of hair or eyes—all are forgotten.[59] We do know what Tom looked like: black hair, gray eyes, height almost six feet, a stout build.[60] "He was built so compact," said a relative, "that it was difficult to find or feel a rib in his body—a muscular man, his equal I never saw."[61]

Physical appearance, however, tells little about impressions that Lincoln's parents made on people. They remembered Nancy as calm and imperturbable, with little formal education but much good judgment and even shrewdness. She seemed more inclined toward spiritual concerns than material ones, showed appreciation for acts of small kindness, exuded affection and generosity tinged with melancholy.[62] In his mature years, Abraham Lincoln described her as an intellectual,[63] an appellation he wouldn't have used lightly. She was drawn toward a manly and decent husband. Like his wife, Tom lacked thirst for material possessions. His goal was an estate large in happiness. He was sociable and good-humored, earned a reputation for jokes and jolly stories, and urged neighbors to look at the bright side of life. Yet like his wife, he had quiet and reflective moments that people noticed and commented on.[64] In 1862, someone near Elizabethtown told a visitor:

> Thomas Lincoln was a real nice, agreeable man, who often got the "blues," and had some strange sort of spells, and wanted to be alone all he could be when he had them. He would walk away out on the barrens alone, and stay out sometimes half a day. Once when he was out thar, one of my boys, what he did n't see, hearn him talkin' all alone to hisself about God and his providence and sacrifices, and how thar war a better, more promised land, and a whole lot of things what my boy knowed nothin' about, in the Scripture. This was when they lived over thar on Nolin's Crick, on the [Sinking Spring] farm. Some of us was afear'd he was losin' his mind.[65]

Tom's step-granddaughter reflected:

> He had the old Virginia notion of hospitality—liked to see people sit up to the table and eat hearty, and there were always plenty of his relations and grandmother's willing to live on him. Uncle Abe got his honesty, and his clean notions of living and his kind heart from his father. Maybe the Hanks family was smarter, but some of them couldn't hold a candle to Grandfather Lincoln, when it came to morals. I've heard Grandmother Lincoln say, many a time, that he was kind and loving, and kept his word, and always paid his way, and never turned a dog from his door.[66]

He appeared to enjoy children. A neighbor girl recalled sitting on his lap often;[67] he joshed about young Abe's toddling around;[68] and he bought a toy truck wagon, surely for his son.[69] He was aware of the influence an admired adult could have on children and tried to conduct himself accordingly. Nancy's cousin Denny Hanks remembered: "One day his baby girl picked up a foul oath and was bruisin' the bitter morsel in her sweet lips, when Nancy called 'Thomas!' and said 'Listen, husband.' He stopped that habit thar; never swore agin."[70] He treated horses with more consideration than many pioneers did.[71] He took liquor but was no drunkard.[72] He was also no brawler, but ready for a friendly fight. Denny Hanks still remembered such an encounter fifty years afterward, recalling that Tom "was a man of uncommon endurance. Mr. Lincoln's friends thought him the best man in Kentucky, and others thought that a man by the name of

Hardin was a better man—so the two men through the influence of their friends met at a tavern in Hardinsburg, Kentucky. There the two men had a long and tedious fight, and Lincoln whipped Hardin without a scratch. They did not fight from anger or malice but to try who was the strongest man—to try manhood."[73]

People who knew Tom and Nancy in Kentucky found them happy together, faithful partners in a life they were building. In a land where sexual shenanigans were rampant and rumors thereof possibly even more so, a survey of Tom's and Nancy's acquaintances found no juicy gossip about either spouse.[74]

Elizabethtown was the county seat. In addition to cabins, there were brick and frame houses, one having three stories. The town was big enough to attract theatrical exhibitions and other amusements. Small industry operated there: hide tanning, brickmaking, liquor distilling. Businessmen included a cobbler, tailor, gunsmith, blacksmith, and storekeepers offering both necessities and frills. One merchant was a fellow named John J. Audubon, who found fame as a scholar of bird life. Another was Duff Green, who would become a senior adviser to President Andrew Jackson. The Hardin County bar had almost two dozen attorneys. Brother Mordecai's lawyer Felix Grundy was then a state legislator and became a justice of the state supreme court about the time Tom and Nancy married; Grundy would later be a U.S. Senator and Attorney General. Hardin County lawyer John Pope was then a Kentucky legislator and soon to be a U.S. Senator. Thomas Reed would become a U.S. Senator. Then there was Ninian Edwards, who would soon become Kentucky's chief justice, later governor of Illinois and U.S. Senator (Lincoln would marry into the Edwards family).[75]

Elizabethtown may have been a frontier town, scarcely a village by standards of later centuries, but it was no backwater. It was a place where men who went on to prominence crossed paths. And it was a sensible home for a carpenter and cabinetmaker such as Tom Lincoln.

He had seen a bit of the world as a wandering labor boy, and now he saw a bit more when, just before his wedding, he joined a crew taking a flatboat to New Orleans for some Elizabethtown businessmen. The cargo apparently included lard, steer, pork, corn, potatoes, and a small quantity of hemp (thirty-eight pounds, hardly enough to bother with). Perhaps hats and venison hams were on board. The merchants sponsoring the trip seem to have purchased some of the pork and beef from Tom, which may have been products he received from the Mill Creek farm he had leased to relatives.[76] New Orleans was a real city. An old Elizabethtown resident later recalled:

> There war a lot of our folks work'n on the river . . . an' they did see
> lots an' lots of things that we folks never dreamed on, an' got to be
> reel smart men, some of 'em. Some of our folks went 'way down the
> river on the big boats two or three times, 'way down on the biggest
> river to New Orleans before Abe's folks moved to the big woods, an'

they declared there war more houses thar then there war in the state
of Kaintucky, and houses, four of 'em bilt, one right on top of t'other,
an' boats, big and little, they raly did say, up an' down the river, as
close as they could tie 'em, for mor'n ten mile, as it 'pear'd like.[77]

Tom's visit to New Orleans must have been memorable for him, but there is
little mention of the experience other than the £30 ($150) he netted, a substantial
sum for the era.[78] The man who much later married Tom's stepdaughter said that
Tom made two New Orleans voyages during his Kentucky years, walking home
both times.[79] One of these trips was made with Isaac Bush,[80] son of the slave
patrol captain under whom Tom had served and brother of Sarah Bush, a woman
of whom we shall hear much more.

Tom did well enough as an artisan to own a town lot a year after he married
and acquire another in 1808.[81] Evidence exists that he had even become a small
money lender.[82] A bad incident, however, gave a sour taste to town life. A big
farmer, a justice of the peace and a pillar of the community, hired Tom to produce timbers for a mill. The job was demanding and lengthy, and at its end, the
rich guy alleged not only that the quality of the work was too inferior to merit the
agreed-upon compensation, but that Tom should pay him $100 for losses caused
by bad performance. The two men sued each other more than once, with the
court deciding in Tom's favor each time. He prevailed, but spending years in litigation to collect for labor cannot have been rewarding.[83] Such conditions promoted a societal malaise that received public comment:

"An almost *incurable lassitude* has seized all ranks and descriptions
of people in this country. Laws are passed; but how are they executed? Officers are appointed; and do they not *doze* and *nod* at their
posts? People complain of ill health; and yet they will suffer horses,
dogs, and what not, to *rot* at their doors! . . . Farmers complain of
the *hardness of the times*; and few of them make anything to sell;
and for what they have to dispose of, they ask two or three times its
value, and if they cannot get it, they will leave it to waste on their
farms. Merchants complain of the *small profits* they make, when
they sell their goods at an advance of from 50 to 150 per cent on the
Lexington prices; and yet they will not take an article of our surplus
produce for exportation. . . . Who are they who consume . . .
immense quantities of whiskey that are brought annually to this
place? Is there not something *rotten* at the bottom of all this?"

—editorial, *Vincennes Western Sun*,
September 3, 1808

In mid-1808, Tom, his pregnant wife, and their daughter Sally left town and
evidently moved to the so-called Plum Orchard farm in what was later Larue

County. Rather than plums, the trees were crab apples, and it wasn't a cultivated orchard, but a natural grove. In blossom time, settlers reportedly would come from afar, cut branches laden with flowers as bouquets, and carry them away on horseback, with the riders virtually disappearing among the petals. There the Lincolns lived as tenants for one crop season, while Tom did carpentry and agricultural labor for the squatter owner. That was just a stopover while Tom arranged to buy a farm of their own, where they moved late in the year. This $200 cash transaction (no loan needed) was for the three-hundred-acre Sinking Spring farm, where Abraham Lincoln was born.[84]

Stories of the birth vary, but all treat it as a routine pioneer event. One or more midwives attended.[85] One declared, "The baby was born just about sunup, on Sunday morning." Tom had "that sort of a hang-dog look that a man has, sort of guilty like, but mighty proud, and he says to me, 'Are you sure she's all right, Mis' Walters?' And Nancy kind of stuck out her hand and reached for his, and said, 'Yes, Tom, I'm all right.'" The midwife added, "You can tell whether folks wants the baby or not, and whether they love or hate each other on account of it. . . . I never saw a prouder father than Tom Lincoln; and I never saw a mother more glad than Nancy was to know that her baby was a boy."[86]

According to one person, much later Nancy's cousin Denny Hanks supposedly recalled getting the news of the baby:

> Tom an' Nancy Hanks Lincoln lived on a farm . . . about two miles from us, when Abe was born. I ricollect Tom comin' over to our house, one cold mornin' in Feb'uary an' sayin' kind o' slow an' sheepish: "Nancy's got a boy baby."
>
> Mother got flustered an' hurried up her work to go over to look after the little feller, but I didn't have nothin' to wait fur, so I jist tuk an' run the hull two miles to see my new cousin. Nancy was layin' thar in a pole bed lookin' purty happy. Tom'd built up a good fire and throwed a b'ar skin over the kivers to keep 'em warm, an' set little two-year-old Sairy on the bed, to keep 'er off the dirt floor. Yes, thar was only a dirt floor in the cabin. Sairy always was a say-nothin' little gal with eyes like an owl's, an' she set thar an' stared at the new baby, an' pinted 'er finger at him.
>
> You bet I was tickled to death. Babies wasn't as plenty as blackberries in the woods o' Kaintucky. Mother come over an' washed him an' put a yaller flannen petticoat an' a linsey shirt on him, an' cooked some dried berries with wild honey fur Nancy, an' slicked things up an' went home. An' that's all the nuss'n either of 'em got.[87]

Denny also said of his new relative:

> I guess I was on hand purty early, fur I rickolect when I held the little feller in my arms his mother said, "Be keerful with him, Dennis, fur

you air the fust boy he's ever seen." I sort o' swung him back and forth; a little too peart, I reckon, fur with the talkin' and the shakin' he soon begun to cry and then I handed him over to my Aunt Polly who wuz standin' close by. "Aunt," sez I, "take him; he'll never come to much," fur I'll tell you he wuz the puniest, cryin'est little young-ster I ever saw.[88]

The child was named Abraham in honor of Tom's father, killed by Indians so long ago.[89]

Nancy had close ties to several relatives in the vicinity, but apparently little else was appealing about the Lincoln homestead. Surrounding acreage was later characterized as of such poor quality that it hardly merited being called a farm.[90] A visitor in 1862 described the property as "a small valley farm, with not more than twelve to fifteen acres of any kind of tillable land."[91] Two of Abraham's later associates called it "barren hillocks and weedy hollows, covered with stunted and scrubby underbrush." In their judgment, "the ground had nothing attractive about it but its cheapness."[92] Living off the land was brutal. Denny Hanks allegedly recalled: "It was mighty ornery land. . . . Choppin' trees, an' grubbin' roots, an' splittin' rails, an' huntin' an' trappin' didn't leave Tom no time to put a puncheon floor in his cabin. It was all he could do to git his fambly enough to eat and to kiver 'em. Nancy was turrible ashamed o' the way they lived, but she knowed Tom was doin' his best, an' she wasn't the pesterin' kind nohow."[93]

Struggling against the land was hard enough, but on top of that was struggle against the lawyers. A war of attrition began almost as soon as Tom arrived at Sinking Spring, a two-front war involving legal title to the acreage and conflict about identifying the acreage the farm comprised. During his White House years, Lincoln recalled that in Kentucky, "They used to be troubled with . . . mysterious relics of feudalism, and titles got into such an almighty mess with these pettifoggin' incumbrances turnin' up at every fresh tradin' with the land, and no one knowin' how to get rid of 'em, as this here airth never saw."[94] The feudal relics referred to here were metes and bounds, an English surveying technique describing property lines by reference to other property lines, landscape, and plants,[95] such as "sixteen and one-third rods northeast of crooked oak tree near bottom of hill at eastern boundary of Lord Smith's land." That system worked well enough for seldom-traded parcels in a limited district, but applying it to numerous and continually fluctuating real estate transactions of the Kentucky frontier produced chaos in a situation already confused by incompetent surveying and inaccurate record keeping.[96] For example, because of clerical error in the records, Tom lost forty acres of his Mill Creek property, the farm he had leased to a relative.[97] In 1837, long after the Lincolns had departed, American surveying principles showed that although Tom thought he was buying 300 acres at Sinking Spring, the tract actually contained 348½ acres.[98]

As to legal title, the Sinking Spring property had been snipped from 15,000 acres in the hands of a Hardin County landowner. The first fellow who bought the Sinking Spring parcel was an Elizabethtown blacksmith who earned a reputation for unreliability and was apprehended for stealing after he ran off on his spouse and children.[99] The blacksmith failed to pay the full amount he had promised for Sinking Spring, thereby leaving the big landowner with a lien on the property. The blacksmith sold his interest to Isaac Bush, who had once gone to New Orleans with Tom. Bush, in turn, sold his interest to Tom. The big landowner then sued Bush and Tom to get the rest of the compensation promised by the blacksmith. That remaining compensation was a barter deal, not cash. Tom said he had already consented to fulfill the blacksmith's promised barter, although he hadn't yet furnished the barter, and he characterized the landowner's suit as an effort to obtain cash instead of barter. Tom argued that a deal was a deal, and the landowner should furnish him with a valid deed in exchange for the barter. After years of fussing, the court sold Sinking Spring to a third party from whom the landowner could get cash. Tom had the necessary money to save the farm, but by that time, he no longer cared to maintain his claim. He sued Bush to get back the $200 plus interest and legal expenses. Tom won, but whether Bush paid is unclear.[100]

So after three crop seasons, Tom gave up on the Sinking Spring property. Some might view his decision as showing a quitter's mentality; others might see a rational evaluation of the costs and benefits of further struggle and a decision to invest his energy in property less prone to attract trouble.

Knob Creek was only about a dozen miles away, but the terrain cut off easy communication with Elizabethtown. That didn't mean, however, that the Lincolns were cut off from civilization. Their cabin was only a few dozen feet from the Louisville and Nashville highway, also called the Cumberland road, a main thoroughfare of the West. This same road passed by the Sinking Spring cabin as well.

The Knob Creek farm included bottomland where soil washed down from the hills, a farm more fertile than Sinking Spring. "My earliest recollection . . . is of the Knob Creek place," Abe Lincoln said. "I remember [it] very well."[101] Denny Hanks called Knob Creek "knobby as a piece of land could be, with deep hollows, ravines—cedar trees . . . as thick as trees could grow. Lincoln's house was in a hollow. High, tall, and peaky hills . . . stood up against the sky all around."[102] Sugar Camp Hollow, it was called, just a couple miles from where Nancy had spent her girlhood with her grandparents.[103]

A pioneer reminisced that in 1811, when the Lincolns settled at Knob Creek, "a comet, large and brilliant, appeared in the fall of this year, in the southwest section of the heavens. This comet was believed by many to be a true harbinger of war, and stories were afloat amongst the people, that the roar of battle, the reports of the cannon and small arms were heard in the skies."[104] As foretold in the heavens, war did come in 1812. In earlier years, Tom had served in active militia duty against Indians, and he didn't enlist for the new war. He was, after all, a family man in his late thirties. American soldiers traveling on the highway came by the Lincoln cabin, where, according to Denny Hanks, Tom "fed and cared for them by companies, by strings of them."[105] Abe Lincoln himself remembered: "I had been fishing one day and caught a little fish which I was taking home. I met a soldier in the road, and, having been always told at home that we must be good to the soldiers, I gave him my fish."[106] Surely the Lincolns' support of troops and the war effort was heartfelt. People whose sympathies were questioned could suffer untoward consequences. A Western merchant accused of pro-British sympathy published this notice: "I will pay five hundred dollars for discovering and convicting the white skinned but vile and black hearted incendiary or incendiaries who placed the fire in my new house on Wednesday night. The reward shall be paid without exposing the informer, if conviction can otherwise be effected."[107]

The Lincoln family raised corn, supplemented by potatoes and onions. Before the boy was old enough to handle a plow, Abe assisted in "corn dropping," forming small hills of soil and sticking in a few seeds, a chore common to farm children of the era.[108] By the time he was seven, he was plowing. Daniel Drake, to whom Abraham Lincoln would appeal for help many years later, recalled such work: "To sit bareback on a lean and lazy horse for several successive hours, under a broiling sun, and every now and then, when you were gazing at a pretty bird, or listening to its notes, or watching the frolic of a couple of squirrels on the neighboring trees, to have the plow suddenly brought to a dead halt by running under a root, and the top of the long hames to give you a hard and unlooked for punch in the pit of the stomach, is no laughing matter, try it who may!"[109] Many years later, Lincoln recalled a scene of neighborly cooperation:

> I remember that old home very well. Our farm was composed of three fields. It lay in the valley surrounded by high hills and deep gorges. Sometimes when there came a big rain in the hills the water would come down through the gorges and spread all over the farm. The last thing that I remember of doing there was one Saturday afternoon; the other boys planted the corn in what we called the big field; it contained seven acres—and I dropped the pumpkin seed. I dropped two seeds every other hill and every other row. The next Sunday morning there came a big rain in the hills, it did not rain a drop in the valley, but the water coming down through the gorges washed ground, corn, pumpkin seeds and all clear off the field.[110]

Long afterward, severe flooding was still known at the cabin site.[111]

In addition to planting and plowing, the boy apparently took the family's corn to Robert Hodgen's mill for grinding. Decades afterward, Abe Lincoln still remembered and asked about a large stone house on the mill road, where young folk had dances. A White House visitor from the county was amazed at the President's detailed recollections of "every house and farm, hill, creek, and family that lived here when he was a boy."[112]

Such were Abe Lincoln's memories of Knob Creek. And what were the memories of people who knew him then? Some are simply small vignettes common to many childhoods, of interest simply because of the child involved. Rebecca Redmon West lived atop a major hill near the Lincoln place and would come down to play with Abe's sister, Sally. Once they saw him tumble into a water-filled tub and yanked him out by his shirttail, a shirt being the only clothing he was wearing.[113] He used moccasins, but such footwear has been dismissed as only "a decent way of going barefoot." Someone claimed that Denny Hanks recalled:

> It didn't seem no time till Abe was runnin' 'round in buckskin moccasins an' breeches, a tow-linen shirt an' coonskin cap. Yes, that's the way we all dressed them days. We couldn't keep sheep fur the wolves, an' pore folks didn't have sca'cely any flax except what they could git tradin' skins. We wasn't much better off'n Injuns, except 't we tuk an intrust in religion and polytics. We et game an' fish, an' wild berries an' lye hominy, an' kep' a cow. Sometimes we had corn enough to pay fur grindin' meal an' sometimes we didn't, or thar wasn't no mill nigh enough. When it got so we could keep chickens, an' have salt pork an' corn dodgers, an' gyardin sass an' molasses, an' have jeans pants an' cowhide boots to wear, we felt as if we was gittin' along in the world. But that was some years later.
>
> Abe never give Nancy no trouble after he could walk except to keep him in clothes.

Along that line, Denny supposedly mentioned:

> I ricollect how Tom joked about Abe's long legs when he was toddlin' round the cabin. He growed out o' his clothes faster'n Nancy could make 'em. . . . Most o' the time we went b'arfoot. Ever wear a wet buckskin glove? Them moccasins wasn't no putection ag'inst the wet. Birch bark, with hickory bark soles, stropped on over yarn socks, beat buckskin all holler, fur snow. Me 'n' Abe got purty handy contrivin' things thataway. An' Abe was right out in the woods, about as soon's he was weaned, fishin' in the crick, settin' traps fur rabbits an' muskrats, goin' on coon-hunts with Tom an' me an' the dogs; follerin' up bees to find bee-trees, an' drappin' corn fur his pappy.[114]

Another Kentucky acquaintance told of chasing a groundhog with Abe. After their dogs ran the groundhog into a hiding place in a cliff, he said, "We worked some four or five hours in trying to git him out. I gave it out. Lincoln then went off about a quarter of a mile to a blacksmith shop and got the blacksmith to make an iron hook and fasten it on a pole. The blacksmith went with young Abe and hooked the groundhog out of the rocks."[115] Whether the youngster would have been trusted with firearms, which were neither plentiful nor cheap, is uncertain, but Denny Hanks remembered Abraham going to Knob Creek, where he would "shoot fish in puddles and holes washed by the water. Killed a fawn—Abe was tickled to death."[116] Long afterward, people in the Knob Creek area said he "had a fondness for fishing and hunting with his dog and axe. When his dog would run a rabbit in a hollow tree he would chop it out."[117] His older playmate, Austin Gollaher, told of hunting pheasants with Lincoln, with the younger boy nearly drowning in a creek before Gollaher could rescue him—a misadventure they concealed from their mothers.[118]

Although the Lincolns were able to coax crops from the Knob Creek farm, Tom also worked as a carpenter locally and over in Bardstown,[119] just as he had supplemented his Sinking Spring earnings with carpentry.[120] Coffins apparently were a routine assignment. To children, coffin manufacturing was an invitation to fun. Abraham and his sister Sally enjoyed playing with the shavings. They were good for more than romping. Two girls passing by on horseback dismounted while Tom was working. Each picked up a long shaving, extended her arm, closed her eyes, and spun around three times. She then tossed it over her left shoulder and examined where it fell. If an alphabet letter could be discerned in the shaving's curves and twists, that revealed the initial of the man who would one day marry the girl. Little Sally wasn't husband hunting, but she enjoyed trying to read letters in shavings.[121]

A store clerk remembered young Abraham as "a slender, well behaved, quiet boy."[122] Another townsman described him as a small "shirttail boy" who stayed nearby his mother in town.[123] Long afterward, folks still said, "He always appeared to be very quiet during play time. Never seemed to be rude. . . . Was rather noted for keeping his clothes cleaner longer than any others."[124] His mother's cousin John Hanks said Abraham "was known among the boys as a bashful, somewhat dull, but peaceable boy."[125] Someone asserted that Denny Hanks agreed: "He was mighty good comp'ny, solemn as a papoose, but interested in everything. An' he always did have fits o' cuttin' up. I've seen him when he was a little feller, settin' on a stool, starin' at a visitor. All of a sudden he'd bust out laughin' fit to kill. If he told us what he was laughin' at, half the time we couldn't see no joke."[126]

Like sociable Tom, the boy also occasionally withdrew from company. One resident noted that years later, people still remarked that the lad "seemed to have a liking for solitude."[127] In 1862, an elderly black woman told a visitor to this Kentucky district, "Abe moped round an' had spells, an' we all got mighty feared that he was losin' hissef, but he did n't. He was all right agin in a day or two, and peart as ever."[128] The racial status of this informant may be significant, indicating an opportunity to observe the child in a different context. In addition, Abraham's melancholy wasn't so generally known in 1862, thus this comment from an African American woman acquaintance is of particular interest, noting that this aspect of his personality was present in childhood before the loss of his mother, of Ann Rutledge, or the suffering of other traumas to which his melancholy is sometimes attributed. Also in 1862, an Elizabethtown acquaintance shrewdly commented: "Abe war a querish sort of a boy then, so consid'rn' and old like for a six or seven year ole chap. . . . Some of 'em said Abe went mopin' round, and had spells like his father; but then they war mistak'n about him, just like they war about Thomas. Abe did n't have spells. It was just the way his face 'peared when he was sober and thinkin' like and a-studyin', what he allus did when he could get a book; and it did set everybody a-wonderin' to see how much he knowed, and he not mor'n seven."[129]

The mill where Lincoln's family had their corn ground was a natural gathering place for boys, if for no other reason than the necessity to wait around for hours as the miller dealt with each batch of grain. A participant remembered Abe as shy and retiring. The boys would challenge one another's prowess in fights, but Lincoln was left alone until one day a bigger boy struck him by surprise. Years later, a witness recalled that Abraham not only defeated the first attacker, but went on to beat two others and then called for more. No one took him up on his offer, then or later.[130] A person who asked around in the 1860s was told the lad "was considered brave but had few if any difficulties."[131] His reputation was not that of a fighter, but of a peacemaker. Years later, people in the Knob Creek vicinity said he "was the one to adjust difficulties between boys of his size. When appealed to his decision was the end of the trouble."[132] Denny Hanks remembered good Abraham as occasionally having a "somewhat wild nature."[133] Abe relished pranks and merrily asked a White House visitor from the old Kentucky home:

> Where is my old friend and playmate Austin Gollaher? . . . I would rather see Gollaher than any man living; he played me a dirty trick once, and I want to pay him up. One Sunday Gollaher and another boy and myself were out in the woods on Knob Creek, playing and hunting around for young squirrels, when I climbed up a tree and left Austin and the other boy on the ground. . . . Gollaher shut his eyes like he was asleep. I noticed his hat straight with the reverse side up. I thought I would shit in his hat. Gollaher was watching, and when I let the load drop he swapped hats, and my hat caught the whole charge.[134]

Though Abraham was generally well behaved toward both parents, his mischievousness occasionally leaked over. "Sometimes Abe was a little rude," Denny Hanks recalled. "When strangers would ride along and up to his father's fence, Abe always, through pride and to tease his father, would be sure to ask the stranger the first question, for which his father would sometimes knock him a rod." Denny seems to be speaking here in the context of Kentucky days, as Tom is unlikely to have been able to knock the brawny Abe of Indiana very far. But Denny may not have been speaking literally regarding the force of Tom's blow—

an important consideration, given that most published claims of Tom routinely striking his son with great force seem traceable to the preceding remarks by Hanks, who may well have spoken casually, leaving an incorrect impression without intent to deceive. For example, consider this variant allegedly given by Hanks, which has an Indiana feel:

> Sometimes a preacher, 'r a circuit-ridin' jedge 'r lyyer, 'r a stump-speakin' polytician, 'r a school teacher'd come along. When one o' them rode up, Tom'd go out an' say: "Light, stranger," like it was polite to do. Then Abe'd come lopin' out on his long legs, throw one over the top rail and begin firin' questions. Tom'd tell him to quit, but it didn't do no good, so Tom'd have to bang him on the side o' his head with his hat. Abe'd go off a spell an' fire sticks at the snow-birds, an' whistle like he didn't keer. "Pap thinks it ain't polite to ask folks so many questions," he'd say. "I reckon I wasn't born to be polite, Denny. Thar's so darned many things I want to know. An' how else am I goin' to git to know 'em?"[135]

Lincoln's Kentucky playmate Austin Gollaher commented that Nancy Hanks administered corporal punishment to her son,[136] which is certainly plausible, even though question exists about Gollaher's reliability as an informant. Denny remembered other corporal punishment: "Abe, when whipped by his father, never bawled, but dropped a kind of silent unwelcome tear."[137] Yet in reply to the question "Did Thomas Lincoln treat Abe cruelly?" Denny replied simply, "He loved him."[138]

His mother loved him, too, a bond that was fully reciprocated. More than once he is quoted saying something like "All I am or shall ever hope to be I owe to my loving angel mother, God bless her!"[139] As an adult, Lincoln marked this stanza of William Cowper's poem "On Receipt of My Mother's Picture"[140]:

> Oh that these lips had lang! Life has passed
> With me but roughly since I heard thee last.
> Those lips are thine own sweet smile I see;
> The same that oft in childhood solaced me.

Abraham and his stepmother said that Tom felt handicapped by a lack of education and wanted better for his son.[141] From an 1801 document, we know that Tom could sign his name before he married, so Nancy didn't teach him how to do that.[142] Being able to write one's name and puzzle out words in the Bible, however, doesn't mean one is literate. For example, over the years, Tom switched back and forth between signing documents with his name and his mark,[143] a vacillation that no literate person would show. Acquaintances agree that Tom's skills in reading and writing were so deficient as to make him illiterate for all practical purposes.[144] His son declared flatly, "He never did more in the way of writing than to bunglingly sign his own name."[145] Tom's second wife said he "could read a little and could scarcely write his name."[146] Seemingly knowledgeable authorities disagree on whether Nancy could write.[147] She signed documents with her mark, and her signature has never been found.[148] Being unable to write, however, doesn't mean she was unable to read. Indeed, Abe said she read the Bible to him.[149] Denny Hanks agreed.[150]

According to Denny Hanks, Nancy used a Webster's spelling book to teach her children the alphabet (which isn't the same as teaching them to write), and she taught Abe to read.[151] Denny also claimed to have taught Lincoln to read, spell, and write.[152] If so, Abe certainly surpassed Denny's skills. Said one mutual acquaintance, "The idea that he taught Lincoln to read and write is to me preposterous."[153]

In addition to what Lincoln learned at home, his parents sought to make formal education available to him, and to his older sister Sally as well. No public schools existed on the Western frontier, but itinerant schoolmasters would pause in an area long enough to hold classes in exchange for tuition payments. An 1817 Hardin County contract may be typical of the era. The instructor agreed to teach reading, writing, and arithmetic at $4 per child for a term of six months, five days a week. Subscribing settlers agreed to furnish a "comfortable" schoolhouse and boarding.[154] Many decades later, someone observed that the prime qualification for teaching was a physical presence hefty enough to overawe older country boys whose plans didn't include university careers.[155] An example was recounted by John Sherman, who, along with his army officer brother, would later be well known to Lincoln.

> [The teacher] called me to the blackboard and directed me to demonstrate some problem in my lesson of Euclid. I went, and, as I believed, had made the drawing and demonstrated the problem. He said I had not, that I had failed to refer to a corollary. I answered that he had not required this in previous lessons. Some discussion arose, when, with the ferule in his hand, he directed me to hold out mine. I did so, but as he struck my right hand, I hit him with all the force I could command with my left.[156]

A later friend and colleague of Lincoln's who lived near St. Louis in the 1820s recalled, "These people were without schools, except as an occasional drunken deserter from the U.S. Army could be picked up and enthroned in some miserable log hovel, occupied by the children in the day time and by the pigs at night."[157] As one traveler noted, a typical instructor was "anything but that object of reverence which becomes his office."[158] Not much had changed by the 1830s, when someone noted that "the schoolmaster of a country village is the most miserable being on earth."[159]

Conditions in Abe's schools were better than the above observations would imply, however. We have no reason to believe his log schoolhouse, about two miles from his home, did double duty for livestock storage. Schoolmasters were known for drifting from one locality to another, but the two who taught Lincoln in Kentucky were longtime area residents.

His first teacher, Zachariah Riney, lived on the old Joseph Hanks farm (Nancy's grandfather) and was a friend of the Lincolns. Earlier, Riney resided near a short-lived colony of Trappist monks close to the Knob Creek place. He was a Roman Catholic, and his lessons included religious instruction and some ceremonies, from which Protestant children were excused. Long afterward, Riney became an informal member of the Trappist Abbey of Gethsemani, monks known locally for their efforts to educate children of the poor. Unlike many schoolteachers of the era, Riney was a mature man, about forty-five years old when he taught Lincoln. At some point, he was also a slaveowner.[160]

Caleb Hazel's school wasn't far from the Knob Creek place. He was a member of the Hanks clan, and his farm adjoined the Lincolns'.[161] He was a real estate trader[162] who apparently supplemented farming with tavern keeping and reportedly once was prosecuted for selling liquor by the drink without a license.[163] Such conduct is unlikely to have shocked the community. A boy remembered: "In the harvest field . . . I then first noticed that . . . men sweat more than boys; but the circumstances were not precisely the same for the former drank more whiskey than the latter and it contributed to the sudorific effect. I was, however, more sparing than many other boys."[164] A farm next to the Sinking Spring property ran a still, and the Knob Creek cabin was less than two miles from a distillery called the world's biggest. The general district was famed for its distillery operations.[165] Like Zachariah Riney, Hazel was a mature man—indeed, nearly ancient at the age of fifty-five, when he kept the school attended by Abraham and Sally.[166]

Hazel appears to have had at least the writing and grammar talents needed by a teacher.[167] A man who in his boyhood knew the Lincolns and Hazel mused that Hazel "could perhaps teach spelling, reading, and indifferent writing, and perhaps could cipher to the rule of three—but had not other qualifications of a teacher except large size and bodily strength to thrash any boy or youth that came to his school."[168]

Playmate Austin Gollaher was also a schoolmate. Someone who spoke with Gollaher in later years reported:

> He said Lincoln attended very little. All the boys at the time used to wear just one long garment in the summer time: . . . the boys wore long tow shirts. But in school, trousers were expected, and Austin said Abe had his first pair of pants when he went to school. But he said Abe did not have a hat. Hats were about the hardest garments to get. Coonskin caps were common, but the boy who had a wool hat was in style, and Gollaher was quite certain that when Abe first came

to school he was shy a hat. His impression was that Abe had no schoolbook of his own; but that was not uncommon.[169]

These memories about clothing further demonstrate that although the Lincolns lived in physically primitive conditions, they cared about social proprieties.

Schools that Lincoln attended were what's known as "blab" schools, in which students read their lessons aloud, typically all speaking simultaneously in a din. A veteran of such education described it thus:

> 1st Children are naturally prone to speak or utter audibly when they are learning. . . . May . . . improve their speech and . . . impress the matter upon them through the medium of a second sense—their own hearing.
>
> 2d In silent study, an active and diligent child does not sit the more listless; but in audible study it does. When a boy would raise his voice and become more intense and rapid, others would do the same, and they would extend the impulse further, until the high excitement would be spread throughout the whole school. Master Beaden, the while, looked on with the satisfaction of one who sees his work going on with becoming energy.
>
> 3d The scholars, when accustomed to this mode of study, do not interrupt each other. They merely hear a noise, as Charlie hears the noises in the street, in front of Miss Bennett's schoolroom. They do not apprehend what is said by those around them. Now, there is an advantage of a permanent kind in becoming accustomed in early life to do "head work" in the midst of noise.[170]

Lincoln retained such reading methods the rest of his life, much to the annoyance of his officemate, Billy Herndon, who had trouble concentrating on his own law work while Abe was reading aloud. When asked about the habit, Lincoln gave the same explanation as above—that simultaneously seeing and hearing the words made their comprehension easier for him.[171]

Schooling was one of the few activities in which genders mixed. Someone who had the experience reflected: "The union of boys and girls within and without a country school house is not free from objections, but it is natural; and if the latter hear some things which they should not, and form some habits not befitting their sex, they become better prepared for the rough and tumble of life, in which the most favored may be involved. Their constitutions are hardened; and their knowledge of the character of the other sex increased; while the feelings and manners of the boys are to some extent refined by the association."[172]

John Hanks recalled that the young student Lincoln was "not a brilliant boy, but worked his way by toil. To learn was hard for him, but he walked slowly but surely."[173] Schoolmate Austin Gollaher thought just the opposite, remembering that Lincoln was "an unusually bright boy at school, and made splendid progress in his studies. . . . Though so young, he studied very hard. He would get spice-wood bushes, hack them up on a log, and burn them two or three together, for the purpose of giving light by which he might pursue his studies."[174] Certainly by the age of seven, he was a good reader.[175]

A standard Kentucky schoolbook at that time was Murray's *English Reader*, a volume explaining how to read different sorts of writing, using classical and modern examples. Lincoln's later antagonist, Horace Greeley, called it "solid . . . but not well adapted to the instruction of children of eight to fourteen years."[176] Lincoln, who would disagree with Greeley on so many things, declared that "Murray's English Reader was the greatest and most useful book that could be put in the hands of a child in school," praise that gives us excellent reason to believe he used it himself.[177] Given that praise, his intelligence, his appreciation for poetry, and his retentive memory, we can wonder about the impact of this book's selection from William Cowper:

> He finds his fellow guilty of a skin
> Not colour'd like his own; and having pow'r
> To enforce the wrong for such a worthy cause
> Dooms and devotes him as his lawful prey.[178]

Given that Lincoln attended school in Kentucky for barely three months, broken into two different sessions, even mentioning his schooling may well exaggerate its importance. Perhaps the importance lies in what a person can achieve in life without benefit of formal education.

All was not labor, and adults occasionally played too. Some adult pastimes were simple, such as singing or shooting marbles. Some were tests of skill that paid in prestige, such as Christmas shooting matches, which also paid in prizes of turkeys or cattle. "We have observed that persons are in the habit of shooting at marks &c. in this town, to the eminent danger of the personal safety of those who are passing the streets as well as those who are in their houses."[179] Horse racing was frowned on by some Baptist circles, but it was important enough that a racetrack was built a few miles from the Lincoln place. Elections then were held at county seats over a three-day period, allowing plenty of time for drunken exhibitions and rowdiness. Lincoln genially recalled:

> When I was a little boy, I lived in the state of Kentucky, where drunkenness was very common on election days. At an election . . . in a village near where I lived, on a day when the weather was inclement and the roads exceedingly muddy, a toper named Bill got brutally drunk and staggered down a narrow alley where he laid himself down in the mud, and remained there until the dusk of the evening, at which time he recovered from his stupor. Finding himself very muddy, [he] immediately started for a pump (a public watering place on the street) to wash himself. On his way to the pump another

drunken man was leaning over a horse post. This, Bill mistook for the pump and at once took hold of the arm of the man for the handle, the use of which set the occupant of the post to throwing up. Bill, believing all was right, put both his hands under and gave himself a thorough washing. He then made his way to the grocery [barroom] for something to drink. On entering the door one of his comrades exclaimed in a tone of surprise, "Why, Bill, what in the world is the matter?" Bill said in reply, "I G——d you ought to have seen me before I was washed."[180]

An old resident said that men "settled all their difficulties out of the court-house. . . . Old fashioned Kentucky knock down was the order of the day. Get up, drink, make friends, and all went on well. The man that came off second best must find someone that he could whip. Unless a man could boast of whipping somebody he was not taken up in the best of society." Corn shucking was a classic social occasion, in which two teams would compete to see which could shuck a vicinity's harvest faster; one old Kentucky resident recalled, "A general wrestle, and sometimes a fight would ensue—generally good-humored." There would be community suppers and hoedowns with entertainment from slave musicians.[181]

Organized religious activities were important to many pioneers. Lincoln's district of Kentucky had a strong Roman Catholic presence. His schoolteacher Zachariah Riney was Roman Catholic. Uncle Mordecai married into a family so devout that some of his descendants joined the Sisters of Charity convent, a dozen or two miles from the Knob Creek homestead, and other family members reportedly found formal Roman Catholic vocations as well.[182]

"For sale at this office, *The Real Principles of Roman Catholics* by a French clergyman, in reference to God and the country, a new edition, carefully revised and elucidated with notes."

—*Vincennes Western Sun,* May 6, 1809

During the Knob Creek years, relatives and other neighbors of the Lincolns attended the South Fork Church. About the time of Abraham's birth, that church split over the slavery question.[183] Antislavery preacher William Downs, a powerful orator and debater, was declared to be in disorder, and South Fork members were forbidden to have him preach in their homes. Church records show that Nancy Hanks's uncle Jesse Friend was expelled for "joining a disorderly set of people who call themselves Separate Baptists," known for their antislavery sentiments. About this time, a Western newspaper noted "'The Infamous Slave Trade.' Under this head the *Richmond Enquirer* . . . remarks—'Humanity shudders at this abomination. The spirit of the age denounces it in the voice of thunder. The Almighty has no attribute which can take side with such an atrocious heresy.'"[184] Abraham's teacher Caleb Hazel was another South Fork Church member who left, apparently joining the Little Mount Church of antislavery Separate Baptists.[185] In 1816, Tom joined Little Mount, baptized in Knob Creek by William Downs.[186] Tom was a Bible reader and would say grace before family meals, typically "Fit and prepare us for life's humblest service, for Christ's sake, Amen."[187] Separate parson and antislavery advocate David Elkin was a frequent visitor at the home.[188] Tom's wife, Nancy, was also a Baptist who joined Little Mount.[189]

The family observed the Sabbath.[190] One account says that when they couldn't attend a church service on Sunday, Nancy would read the Bible to the family, a duty in which Abraham and Sally participated after they learned to read.[191] The account's silence about Tom implies that his reading ability wasn't good enough for such a task.[192] Nancy would sing Bible passages while she worked, from which her boy learned some.[193] He enjoyed Bible stories she told and learned the Ten Commandments from her.[194] After Abraham's son Willie died in 1862, he conversed with a nurse who watched over children in a hospital. "He spoke of his mother . . . with tenderest recollections. 'I remember her prayers,' said he, 'and they have always followed me. They have clung to me all my life.'"[195]

In addition to regular local church services, occasional camp meetings occurred where persons from far and wide thronged for days. Pioneers met together to revive religious spirit and for other purposes. The "jerks" were common; one witness said, "It seemed an involuntary exercise, and made the victims sometimes dance and leap until they were entirely exhausted, and would fall down helpless on the ground. When they were in these furious motions the parties would generally shout, and cry aloud on the Lord."[196] Another witness related, "The first jerk or so you would see those fine bonnets, caps and combs fly, and so sudden would be the jerking of the head that their long loose hair would crack almost as loud as a wagoner's whip."[197] An Elizabethtown resident had vivid memories of such gatherings.

> I was at a camp meeting . . . about 1816 when a general shout was about to commence. Preparations were being made; a young lady invited me to stand on a bench by her side where we could all see over the altar. To the right a strong athletic young man about twenty-five years of age was being put in trim for the occasion—which was done by divesting him of all apparel except shirt and pants. On the left a young lady was also being put in trim in somewhat the same way so that her clothes would not be in her way and so that when her combs flew out her hair would go into graceful braids. She, too, was young, not more than twenty, perhaps less. The performance commenced about the same time by the young man on the right and the young lady on the left. Slowly and gracefully they worked towards the center. Singing, shouting, hugging, and kissing generally their own sex until

at last nearer and nearer they came. The center of the altar was reached, and the two closed with their arms around each other. The man singing and shouting at the top of his voice, "I have my Jesus in my arms. Sweet as honeycomb and strong as bacon ham."

The witness added, "There were very few who did not believe this [was] true religion inspired by the holy spirit, and the man that could not believe it had better keep it to himself or be off, for we had our bullies to keep order at such places. The Hankses were the finest singers and finest shouters in our country. The only drawback on them was that some nine months after these interesting meetings some of them were likely to have babies."[198]

Now come the lawyers. When Tom paid for Knob Creek, apparently he obtained a written contract turning over the land to him but didn't receive a deed that could be registered at the courthouse. In other words, he had a document establishing a right to be on the property, but nothing establishing ownership. Such an arrangement was an invitation to litigation, but it was standard in that era. Tom wasn't being careless; he was doing what most Kentucky settlers did.[199] And he thereby suffered a standard fate. Big land operators, one or more of whom resided in Philadelphia, sued him. They claimed that the man Tom had paid for the land was simply a squatter and they owned the land on which Tom had created a farm. The aristocrats demanded that he depart forthwith, thereby allowing them to collect not only the acreage, but also the years of improvements he had to leave behind. Moreover, they seized part of his harvest, claiming he owed them rent for farming their land. Tom didn't like their attitude and mounted a defense in court. One nice touch was that he had been paying the taxes assessed on the land; if the aristocrats were the owners, why weren't tax bills being sent to them? In 1818, the court finally judged Tom as the legal owner, a decision of little practical consequence, as he had sold out and left not only Knob Creek, but the state of Kentucky in 1816.[200]

In addition to land titles, slavery apparently was becoming an annoyance to Tom and Nancy. They were familiar with the institution. The slave population of Hardin County numbered above one thousand.[201] Tom had worked side-by-side with slaves and served as a patroller assigned to hunt them down. A Sinking Spring neighbor used a slave to deliver small comforts to Nancy,[202] and surely slave gangs under supervision trudged along the highway near both Lincoln cabins. This road was a primary route used by Kentucky slave breeders who were delivering slaves to cotton producers.[203] Abraham said he watched operations at the Atherton ferry near the Knob Creek home, and the ferry used slave labor.[204]

"Twenty-Five Dollars Reward. Ranaway from the subscriber . . . in Sumner County, Tennessee, a very large negro man . . . named Sam, his left leg a good deal smaller than his right, a large scar on his left chin, and two on his forehead. . . . I tracked him into the Indiana territory, and into the neighborhood of Vincennes."

—Elisha Green, *Vincennes Western Sun*,
January 7, 1815

"One Hundred Dollars Reward. Ranaway from the subscriber . . . a negro man named Sam Carr . . . he is one of the greatest hypocrites and liars perhaps in the world. . . . Professes to be a Methodist, prays regularly night and morning. . . . I purchased him out of jail at $560 at this place, of Elisha Green, of Tennessee, from whom he ranaway. He has with him a rifle gun, brass mounted, tomahawk, and butcher knife."

—B. V. Beckes, *Vincennes Western Sun*,
September 6, 1817

Before Tom and Nancy married, but while both were living in Elizabethtown, a highly publicized incident occurred there in which a slave was hired out to someone who viciously whipped him for alleged unauthorized possession of a ball of soap. The owner sued the whipper because the slave was damaged so badly as to diminish his commercial worth. Upon seeing the slave's back, one witness at the trial declared, "I would not have had him scarred so for fifty pounds if he was my negro—no, not for one hundred pounds." As it turned out, the disciplinarian's wife had given the soap to the slave.[205]

We know Tom and Nancy disliked slavery enough to join a church organized by opponents of slavery. That was no trivial matter. This area of Kentucky was experiencing some of the most vigorous debate in the West about slavery, and churches were the driving force in this debate.[206] Some people opposed slavery for moral reasons, some disliked having to compete with slave labor, and those two feelings weren't mutually exclusive. Not everyone in the Lincoln family had Tom's aversion to the institution, however. His uncles Isaac and Thomas and his brother Mordecai were slaveowners.[207]

By any measure, Tom's life in Kentucky had been one of success. Indeed, in money alone, he ranked number fifteen among the ninety-eight property owners listed in county records for 1814.[208] Two years later, he was appointed to a small but important political office, in charge of maintaining repairs on a six-mile stretch of public road.[209] But Tom decided he had had enough of the slave wages, slaveowners, land aristocrats, and lawyers of Kentucky. As his son put it, "This removal was partly on account of slavery, but chiefly on account of the difficulty in land titles in Kentucky."[210] A decision to move yet again to unimproved land couldn't have been made lightly. Pioneer John McConnel once asked, "What motives could induce men to leave regions, where the axe had been at work for many years—where the land was reduced to cultivation, and the forest reclaimed from the wild beast and the wilder savage . . . seeking a new home in an inhospitable wilderness, where they could only gain a footing by severe labor, constant strife, and sleepless vigilance?" Such a move was generated by grim determination. McConnel declared of his brethren, "A check enrages him more than a decided failure."[211] Such appears to have been the mood of Tom Lincoln.

His brother Josiah was now located in Indiana and may have told him about the good land there.[212] Recommendation may have come from Austin Lincoln, a relative who resided near the very spot Tom chose for his Indiana homestead.[213] Regardless of any personal testimonials, Tom knew that in Indiana he could buy public land straight from the U.S. government with a perfect title. No one could throw him off such a farm after he had spent years improving it. Whatever he achieved from the labor he invested would be his to keep.

And so Tom Lincoln decided to take his family to Indiana.

CHAPTER 2

INDIANA

The autumn season of 1816 was progressing toward winter. No time was left to clear land in Indiana and sow crops. For months, the family would have to rely on hunting and whatever victuals they could bring from Kentucky. Tom's and Nancy's unwillingness to wait for spring indicates how urgently they wanted to get out of Kentucky. To avoid privation that would result if the family arrived without preparation at the start of winter, Tom decided to make a preliminary expedition. He would go alone into Indiana with family property, including tools and domestic items; locate a homestead site; establish a supply base; and ideally, erect a temporary shelter.

Tom had experience with river conveyance, and family members later said he transported the property on "a kind of flatboat" he built from yellow poplar logs (which sounds more like a raft), launched where Knob Creek empties into Rolling Fork,[1] a water route eventually leading into the Ohio River forty miles or so downstream. Rafts were efficient and common, though an Ohio pioneer remembered that such craft were normally constructed in winter and used when rivers were running high in springtime. (Tom's defiance of that seasonal custom is more evidence of urgency he felt.) The Ohio pioneer declared: "Sometimes several rafts would be joined together, till they could cover an acre of space, or even more. On these were built shanties for the men." He added:

> Families were constantly leaving for the countries down the river, and they made these rafts available as the means of moving. . . . The movers could build themselves a comfortable shanty of loose lumber, a shed for their horses or cows, if they wanted to take them along, and be quite at home during a journey. . . . I have seen the shanties of

two or three families, with wagons, horses, cows, and even poultry, all snugly situated, with room for the children to play outside. Often I have seen the women washing, and a clothesline hung with the linen, as if in the dooryard they had left.[2]

Tom's floater was not that elaborate, carrying furnishings for just one small family, and it started out on waterways considerably more constricted than the Ohio River. Midway, the craft tipped over, with many tools and some additional cargo going overboard.[3] This loss crippled plans to establish a comfortable base, but Tom continued voyaging ahead until he reached Thompson's Ferry on the Ohio River in Perry County, Indiana, a couple miles or so from where the town of Troy developed. Ashore, he left his cargo with a fellow named Francis Posey and headed inland to find a farm location.[4] Posey's father was lieutenant governor of Kentucky when Abraham Lincoln was born and was finishing service as governor of Indiana Territory as the Lincolns arrived there.

Tom walked back to his family in Kentucky.[5] Doubtless they were no more pleased than he was about the loss of household supplies, but at least Tom's carpentry skills meant that some replacements could be constructed in Indiana. Nancy's enthusiasm about the move surely helped keep up the family's spirits. An old Elizabethtown resident declared in 1862, "Nancy got joyful like, mor'n any of 'em; for her and John Hanks war the fust that wanted to go." The old neighbor explained that Indiana was "whar they all could make so much better livin', whar they had the big woods full of deer and all kinds of game and fish, and nice little openin's 'tween the thickets, whar they could have thar truck and gardenin' patches."[6]

As departure from Kentucky neared, on some autumn day Nancy took her children Sally and Abraham to the gravesite of her third child, their brother, who had died after being with the family barely three days. Little is known about the infant; even his name is uncertain, though Denny Hanks said the boy was named Thomas. The child did not live long enough to receive mention in the family Bible, but he was not forgotten by Abraham, who mentioned him long afterward. Rather than have the body buried in the Knob Creek hollow, which was routinely swept by floodwater, supposedly a neighbor carried the little corpse for burial atop a nearby hill.[7]

Preparing for departure, Tom sold off everything the family couldn't carry. The Mill Creek farm (which he had leased out) he had already sold a couple years earlier.[8] Reportedly Tom got $300 in cash and bartered goods for the Knob Creek farm,[9] but the cabin wasn't much. It was an example of typical pioneer housing, structures notable for smallness and congestion. A schoolmaster of that era spoke of boarding in a sixteen-foot-square, one-room cabin occupied by a husband, wife, ten children, three dogs, and two cats.[10] When the Lincolns moved away, their Knob Creek cabin was used as a cattle shed.[11] The birthplace cabin at Sinking Spring had even less value; its logs were simply pulled down for use as firewood.[12]

Tom borrowed two packhorses for the move. Reportedly, Denny Hanks recalled that preparations for the move were simple: "Nancy emptied the shucks out o' the tow-linen ticks, an' I piled everything they had wuth takin' on the backs o' two pack hosses. Tom could make new pole beds an' puncheon tables an' stools, easier'n he could carry 'em."[13] Family tradition says that in addition to bedding and clothes, a few cooking utensils were packed.[14] That was it. Denny said the Lincolns took "no dogs, cats, hogs, cows, chickens, or such."[15] The overland migration began sometime between mid-November and Christmas.[16] According to Denny, "Abe rode with his mother, and Sally with her father."[17] The trek has been glibly described as an easy five days over ninety miles of well-marked trail with convenient lodging.[18] "Marked trail," however, is not the same as "improved highway." One distinguished authority noted that roads were "mere openings through the woods" and that "in southern Indiana the roads were so indistinct that travellers often were lost."[19] Still, long afterward, Abe Lincoln indicated that the family made good progress through Kentucky, implying that at least once, by starting at sunrise, they had gone "some thirty miles" before stopping for the day.[20]

Arriving at Posey's Indiana place, Tom rented a wagon and team and loaded the belongings he had left there.[21] The migration party cut, chopped, and hacked its way through dense forest toward the homestead of Thomas Carter, whom Tom had long known.[22] A Western newspaper item described such territory: "T'other evening, I heard a loud cracking and crashing among the trees. I looked to see what it was, and I'm darned if it warn't the moon trying to get through the branches, but it was so tarnation thick she couldn't do it, so down she set again, and I had to come home in the dark."[23] Abe said he never made a tougher trip than the seventeen miles or so inland from the Ohio River.[24] The emigrants finally arrived at their new home, with little more than bedding and kitchen implements.[25]

Controversy exists about whether the Lincolns resided in a "half-faced camp" during their first months in Indiana. The Lincolns used such a camp, but the question is how long they did so. A half-faced camp was a quickly built three-sided hut, with one side fully exposed to the elements. Walls and roof were typically poles, branches, and leaves. Such a structure is sometimes called a "hunter's camp," a description referring to the shelter's temporary nature. The term also had a derogatory connotation; in the social scale of that era, hunters (full-time stalkers, as opposed to settlers who hunted) hovered around the status of Indians. Of hunters, one observer said: "Their women never sit at a table with them; at least, I have never seen them. I cannot speak in high terms of the manners or of the virtue of their squaws and daughters. Their houses contain but one room, and that used as a sleeping room as well by strangers as by the men of the family, they lose all feminine delicacy, and hold their virtue cheap."[26] Said another observer:

> The hunter is always poor, and in some measure despised by his more
> industrious neighbors; and when a man once acquires the habit of

wandering in the pathless wilderness in search of game, it takes such hold of him that he rarely shakes it off; indeed, the occupation requires a vigilance so absorbing, as speedily to characterize his whole manner. The old hunter's eye is never at rest; meet him where you will, in the forest or within the walls of a house, and whilst he is conversing with you, his eye will be wandering, slowly and intently, from object to object; and if on his feet, he will be constantly shifting his position, and, with his head and shoulders depressed with habitual caution, will repeatedly sweep the entire circle of vision.[27]

That any settler would tolerate half-faced camp quarters for more than a few days, and then only while something superior was under construction, is almost beyond belief. Yet according to an alleged interview with a very elderly Denny Hanks, the Lincolns lived in a half-faced camp for several months. In definitely authentic commentary, Hanks can be interpreted as saying the same.[28] Additional accounts by seemingly knowledgeable persons agree but may well be traceable back to Denny.[29] His story has been used to illustrate hardship suffered by the Lincolns and as evidence of slothfulness on Tom's part.

Denny is known to have been wrong about several aspects of the Lincolns' move to Indiana, mixing up details of their 1816 arrival with his own at the same site a few months later. That doesn't mean, however, that he was wrong about everything. Nonetheless, authentic accounts are uncommon about pioneers living in a half-faced camp for extended periods. Two pioneers in Sangamon County, Illinois, reminisced about their autumn 1819 arrival, "Our father built a camp, which we lived in until winter."[30] When one settler and his wife came to Sangamon County in August 1820, "they lived four weeks in a tent, while their house was building."[31] A tent in August was arguably superior to a half-faced camp, and four weeks was not a whole season. One person's ancestors came to Indiana a few years before the Lincolns and used "temporary shelters of poles and rails roofed with wild grass, in front of which fires in the open air consumed real heaps of logs." The family spent a winter headquartered in such accommodations but had an abandoned cabin available as well—an important point.[32] Referring to half-faced camps, an expert on Sangamon County's history said, "In such as this the early settlers spent the first few years of their sojourn in the new country,"[33] and an Indiana historian declared, "Most of the first settlers, for a few years lived in what was called in that day, a half-faced camp";[34] but those general assertions do not seem founded on pioneer accounts. A most distinguished historian of conditions in Sangamon County, however, does cite two specific instances of settlers wintering in a half-faced camp.[35] The most plausible reason for any delay in cabin construction was that a settler was supposed to provide sufficient logs cut to the right lengths, along with any needed boards, before asking neighbors for help in raising the cabin. Community help was for assembly of prepared materials, not for their preparation.[36] We have evidence, however, that carpenter Tom Lincoln began such preparation immediately: Abe wrote, speaking of himself in the third person, that "A[braham], though very young, was large of his age, and had an axe put into his hands at once."[37] Surely in late December he was felling trees first for a cabin rather than simply clearing a patch of ground for spring planting and leaving logs where they fell.

Common sense also dictates against the extended use of a half-faced camp. Although the Lincolns were in a wilderness forest, they had neighbors in the district, some of whom were relatives. The Lincolns' arrival and destination were known in Posey's river settlement and by Tom Carter in the interior. Word had to have spread. Neighbors in a district routinely gathered together to help a newcomer build a cabin, and December was hardly a peak time for activities such as sowing or reaping that could have interfered with swift help. An Indiana settler of that time declared: "Most always there was a neighbor or two with their boys willing to help a newcomer. With a good crew of men it wasn't such a big job."[38] A settler in southern Indiana left a record of arriving on a Tuesday, felling logs the next day, and building the cabin on Thursday.[39] A pioneer who came to Illinois in the winter of 1821–22 said that neighbors instantly aided in raising a cabin: "We invited in the whole neighborhood, far and near, and got the services of six women and four men. The men kept up the corners and the women lifted the logs up to them, and we did an admirable job. We put the walls cabin fashion, weighted down the clapboard roof with poles, cut openings for door and fireplace, all in one day."[40] Given that such help was routine, one can scarcely imagine circumstances in which it would have been withheld, let alone in winter. And if it were withheld, one can scarcely imagine Tom and Nancy failing to add a fourth wall to a hut if they weren't planning to build a better cabin instantly.

In one interview, Denny Hanks said the camp was merely "serving a momentary purpose" and referred to the Lincolns quickly moving to a cabin that took only a day to construct and was later replaced by a bigger one.[41] An 1860 biography of Lincoln stated that a cabin was quickly constructed. In one copy of the book, Abe placed marginal notes and corrections but left no objection to that cabin statement, though of course he was then a busy man and may have considered the point too small for comment.[42] That same year, however, he had enough time to write, again referring to himself in the third person, "A few days before the completion of his eighth year, in the absence of his father, a flock of wild turkeys approached the new log cabin, and A[braham] with a rifle gun, standing inside, shot through a crack, and killed one of them."[43] Lincoln knew a half-faced camp differed from a cabin, and his words show that within two months of their arrival, if not sooner, the Lincolns were living in a regular cabin.[44]

"It was pretty pinching times," Lincoln said decades later, "at first in Indiana, getting the cabin built, and the clearing for the crops; but presently we got reasonably comfortable."[45]

Much of the motivation in moving to Indiana was to secure perfect title to land by buying it from the U.S. government. Denny Hanks recalled that Tom settled on the Indiana tract and started improving it before going to the U.S. land office in Vincennes to buy the acreage.[46] Such conduct was typical. Pioneers commonly took physical possesion of acreage and began converting it to farmland long before they got around to seeking title from the government. Denny and his son-in-law reported that Tom bought the Indiana property from the government on the installment plan.[47] Tom took the minimum allowable purchase of 160 acres. After making installment payments for a while, he arranged a deal with the government to relinquish half the acreage in return for final title to the rest.[48]

After the Lincolns arrived in Indiana, lawyers threw Nancy's aunt and uncle Thomas and Betsy Sparrow, who also were her stepparents, off their Kentucky homestead.[49] In autumn 1817 they came to live with the Lincolns, and Denny Hanks came with them.[50] Another aunt, Nancy Hanks Hall, soon arrived with her husband, Levi Hall, and their children.[51]

In addition to the pleasure of his company, Denny Hanks, like the other new arrivals, brought a welcome set of hands for the hard physical labor of transforming a forested area into a farm. "We all hunted pretty much all the time, especially so when we got tired of work, which was very often I will assure you. We did not have to go more than four or five hundred yards to kill deer, turkeys, and other wild game. We found bee trees all over the forests."[52] A list of birds and mammals hunted by settlers would sound like a passengers manifest for Noah's ark, and that doesn't even consider varieties of fish.[53] Seven-year-old Abraham had been entrusted with a rifle when the family took a ferry raft across the Ohio River, keeping the weapon dry and in good enough condition that the boy later was able to shoot a turkey hen at the home site, an incident mentioned by Lincoln. Wild turkeys, said a visitor to the West, "are the shyest of game, and, to hunt them with success, requires experience and dexterity. . . . Great care is necessary lest the slightest movement, click of a lock, or rustle among the leaves be made, as on any such occurrence the bird makes off at a speed which defies pursuit."[54] Denny Hanks supposedly said the boy was proud of the kill: "He couldn't stop talkin' about it till Tom hollered to him to quit."[55] Reportedly the boy even talked about it in his sleep.[56] Later, Abe and a neighbor walked over to Vincennes and together bought a rifle, which they shared for hunting.[57] Another neighbor said, "There was a great many deer licks, and Abe and myself would go to those licks sometimes and watch of nights to kill deer, though Abe was not so fond of a gun as I was."[58] Lincoln also hunted turkeys and raccoons, although companions did not consider him a hunter.[59] An observer described an outing typical for the territory:

> A *coon hunt* affords capital sport for the boys, who, when night has fairly set in, sally forth with the dogs, which are generally well trained to the business. On arriving at a cornfield, whilst the hunters stand on the outskirts, the curs are silently directed to range, when, if they find, they instantly start full cry after the game, which makes for the woods, and ere long takes to a tree; a circumstance of which the hunters become aware from the peculiar bark of the dogs. As the

darkest nights are selected for the sport, tumbles and other mis-
chances are frequent in the rush made towards the spot indicated.
When the tree is reached, materials are collected for making a fire.
The flames soon gather strength and dispel the darkness, which
seems only to have retreated, and to have added to the deepness of
the shadows. And now many an anxious face and peering eye is
directed towards the limbs of the tree in search of cooney, who, at
length, is discovered perhaps huddled into some crotch. If the hunt is
possessed of a rifle, poor cooney soon has his *flint fixt*; but if the axe
is the only weapon, his fate is not quite so soon decided, for the tree
may be large, and when cut down, he sometimes will escape through
the melée, and succeed in gaining another. Four or five are sometimes killed in a night.[60]

One excursion, involving Abe's stepbrother John Johnston, went awry. Lincoln related the story to a friend, who passed it on to posterity:

He [Abe] used to be very fond of coon hunting, and his father used to
oppose their hunting. But he would slip out of a night after the old
man had gone to bed and take a hunt. But they had a small fice dog
that would detect them when they would return. So one night they
took the fice along. They caught a coon and skinned him, and then
stretched it over the little dog and sewed him up, and turned him
loose and put the other dogs on the track; and they ran him home and
caught him the yard; and the old man jumped up and hissed the dogs
on the fice, thinking it was a coon; and they killed the fice. They
[Abe and John] couldn't come up to his relief. The next morning
when the old man went to examine the coon it was the little dog.
They were called up and was both thrashed. But the little dog never
told on them any more when they went a coon hunting.[61]

Turkeys and raccoons were by no means the only animals prowling about.
Abe recalled how "the panther's scream filled night with fear."[62] More troublesome were bears, which liked to snack on pigs. Bears were numerous and bold
enough to grab pigs in daylight hours.[63] Lincoln wrote that at the first squeal, settlers would turn out with guns, horses, and dogs to hunt down the predator. The
hounds would circle around, sniffing at the pig-kill site, then dash off as their
masters followed. The forest would be in an uproar, with dogs baying, men calling, horses leaping. A rider might be unhorsed as another lost his firearm. At that
point, Lincoln said, "the world's alive with fun." When the dogs caught up to the
bear, they'd circle around yelping, as settlers arrived and called out to them:
"Whoop! Take him Tiger. Seize him Drum." Crushing some dogs, the bear would
rear up while rifles fired, the beast's furious eyes fading as his blood poured out
from multiple wounds. Then argument would begin about who was entitled to the

bearskin. Etiquette awarded the trophy to whoever drew first blood from the bear, but when disagreement arose about who fired first, the hunt's alliance of settlers would dissolve into bickering, with an intensity that Lincoln once likened to courtroom argument in murder cases. Such is one vignette he left of his Indiana days.[64] These excursions could be robust.

> The dogs drove the bear into a swamp and brought him to bay, and when Mr. Rhodes came up, the animal climbed a tree, the dogs hanging to him until he was ten feet high. The bear's jaw was broken by a shot and he came down when the dogs pitched into him. Mr. Rhodes joined in the melee, and struck the bear in the forehead with a tomahawk. The weapon stuck fast and the bear raked Rhodes's arm from the shoulder down. He succeeded in loosening it and struck again, when it again stuck fast, and he received another rake from the shoulder down. Then a hunter, who was looking on, called out: "John, a little lower," and Mr. Rhodes struck the bear just above the eyes, which killed it.[65]

Indiana was a fat country. About the time Lincoln arrived, in 1817 a visitor declared, "Indiana is a vast forest, larger than England, just penetrated in places, by the backwood settlers, who are half hunters, half farmers."[66] Some years earlier, a traveler through the country said: "There is something which impresses the mind with awe in the shade and silence of these vast forests. In deep solitude, alone with nature, we converse with God." The traveler gave an example: "We often stopped to admire the grapevines in these forests, which twine among and spread a canopy over the summits of the highest trees. Some are nine inches in diameter. They stretch from the root, which is often thirty and forty feet from the trunk of the tree, and ascend in a straight line to the first high limb, thirty and even sixty feet from the ground. How they have reached such an height, without the help of intermediate branches, is unaccountable."[67] In addition to grapevines "matted together so that . . . you could drive a butcher knife up to the handle in it," Denny Hanks remembered the big woods having black walnut, black oak, white oak, jack oak, hickory, elm, and dogwood.[68] In addition to poplar, sweet gum, maple, box elder, plum, crab apple, redbud, and ash trees, Indiana neighbor Elizabeth Crawford remembered the wildflowers: blue and yellow flags (irises), butterfly weed, honeysuckle, pink lady's slipper, sweet william, and wild roses.[69] Decades later, she could still list wild fruits that surrounded settlers: wild cherry, fox grape, winter grape, blackberry, gooseberry, persimmon, raspberry, strawberry, and more.[70] Neighbor David Turnham recalled, "The country was very rough, especially in the lowlands, so thick with brush that a man could scarcely get through on foot."[71]

In cold weather, the woods could be just as awesome; a traveler left this account of 1818 conditions in Indiana: "The trees were covered with ice, so transparent and so brilliant, that the boughs looked like glasswork, and threw on the eye a confused splendor, which was bounded only by the distant hills. The boughs and fretwork of ice, that intercepted the rays of the sun, were faintly tinged with prismatic colors. At our feet were rapid torrents, which gushed from the caverns above us, sparkled in light, and then leaped into the darkness of the abysses below." [72] An Indiana settler from Lincoln's time declared: "As for the woods itself there wasn't a lonesome spot in it. There was plenty of wild life at all times to keep a feller company. . . . There was a bigness and a certain mouldy or woodsy smell to a forest that's hard to describe, but to us it was mighty sweet and satisfyin'." [73]

Improved farmland exhibited the same lushness. A few years before the Lincolns arrived, a Vincennes newspaper gloated: "A gentleman in the neighborhood of this place the last season, measured and put up in cribs, upwards of eleven hundred bushels of good corn, from eleven acres of ground. The above fact must silence every rumor of the barrenness of our soil." [74] Credible information exists that the Lincolns raised corn, wheat, and potatoes, along with sheep and cattle. [75]

The Lincoln farm site was close to Little Pigeon Creek, less than two miles from where Gentryville grew up. Yes, there were pigeons in the area, lots of them. Soon after Lincoln arrived in Indiana, a traveler wrote of them:

> [The pigeons would roost in] woodland or barrens, from four to six miles in circumference. The screaming noise they make when thus roosting is heard at a distance of six miles; and . . . they fly . . . in immense flocks, hiding the sun and darkening the air like a thick passing cloud. . . . They roost on the high forest trees, which they cover in the same manner as bees in swarms cover a bush, being piled one on the other, from the lowest to the topmost boughs, which so laden, are seen continually bending and falling with their crashing weight, and presenting a scene of confusion and destruction, too strange to describe, and too dangerous to be approached by either man or beast. When the living birds are gone to their distant dinner, it is common for man and animals to gather up or devour the dead, then found in cartloads. When the roost is among the saplings, on which the pigeons alight without breaking them down, only bending them to the ground, the self-slaughter is not so great; and at night, men, with lanterns and poles, approach and beat them to death without much personal danger. But the grand mode of taking them is by setting fire to the high dead grass, leaves, and shrubs underneath, in a wide blazing circle, fired at different parts, at the same time, so as soon to meet. Then down rush the pigeons in immense numbers, and indescribable confusion, to be roasted alive, and gathered up dead next day from heaps two feet deep. [76]

John James Audubon, who ran an Elizabethtown store while the Lincolns resided nearby, spent time around Pigeon Creek studying the birds after the Lincolns moved there. [77]

Even in the deep woods, though, unsettling reminders existed of a civilization Tom Lincoln had tried to leave behind:

"Fifty Dollars Reward . . . for the apprehension and safe delivery of a negro man slave called Frisby, to either of the following persons, Mr. David Apperson of Shawneetown, Illinois Territory, or to Maj. A.R. Woolly, Pittsburgh, Pennsylvania. . . . Said negro was going from Pittsburgh to New Orleans, and absconded at the mouth of Pigeon Creek, Indiana."

—Oliver C. Johnson, *Vincennes Western Sun*, December 14, 1816

Denny Hanks allegedly once said the farm site "was good land, in the timber whar the women could pick up their firewood, an' on a crick with a deer-lick handy."[78] Little Pigeon Creek, however, wasn't all that close to the Lincoln farm. Later students of the topic noted that lack of spring water was a significant drawback.[79] Abe would walk a mile to bring water back to the homestead.[80] Despite the accessibility of Little Pigeon Creek, Denny and another relative said the Lincolns dug a hole for water and that in warm weather, the supply was so noxious that they strained it.[81] Hanks once described the vicinity as "swampy."[82]

Perhaps life was good in Indiana, but it was hard. Nancy's body showed the strain. Abraham later wrote of her "withered features . . . wrinkles . . . want of teeth, weather-beaten appearance in general."[83] Her experience was typical for frontier women, about whom one person observed: "Last came the mother, prematurely old, with that woebegone expression which I noticed upon the faces of most of the wives and mothers whom I met in my subsequent travels through the West. It is they who feel most severely the labors and privations of frontier life. Their work is never intermittent. With no help until their children are old enough to help them, without proper medical attendance when ill, with a great deal to annoy and very little to encourage them, they are old before they have reached middle age."[84] A traveler through Illinois in 1818 wrote, "People are not so long-lived here as in England, and they look old sooner. . . . Their lean carcasses, their pale and eager countenances, early in life marked with wrinkles."[85]

In autumn 1818, bilious fever and milk sickness hit Little Pigeon Creek. Both afflictions were common and feared. Entire villages were almost wiped out.[86] Bilious fever acted rather like yellow fever. One nineteenth-century authority described milk sickness as "fixed in the stomach; a fiery, burning sensation is felt in the lower region of the stomach, accompanied with a constant desire to puke—the glands are affected; and as the bowels become torpid from the poisonous matter making a lodgement on the stomach and destroying not only the coats of the stomach, but affecting all the digestive powers, it is almost next to impossibility, in an advanced state of the disease, to procure passage from the bowels."[87] Milk sickness's cause was debated for decades; settlers knew only that it seemed somehow associated with their cows and that some districts were more prone to it (thus people could move away from it). As late as 1838, an Illinois newspaper carried this notice: "MILK SICKNESS. The legislature of Kentucky has offered a premium of two thousand dollars for the discovery of the cause of that fatal disease."[88] Eventually the cause was shown to be consumption of milk or meat from cattle that ate poisonous plants. One authority reported: "Whole families were prostrated in a week, from using the milk of one cow. Sometimes they would drag around like living skeletons, and finally succumb."[89]

Thomas and Betsy Sparrow came down with milk sickness. The closest physician was thirty or more miles away.[90] Whether a doctor of that era could have made any difference is doubtful; remedies were available, such as whiskey, baking soda, and enemas,[91] but no one seemed to be aware of their effectiveness. Nancy did what nursing she could to comfort her stepparents, but both died. Tom Lincoln made their coffins; indeed, he made coffins for all the fatalities. "There was scarcely enough will in the neighborhood that fall to bury those that died," said one of Lincoln's relatives.[92] Abraham's mother also nursed the wife of Peter Brooner. When Mrs. Brooner said death seemed near, Nancy suggested the possibility that Mrs. Brooner might well outlive her; but the hesitant prophecy was not fulfilled.[93]

Then Nancy came down with milk sickness. "I sat up with her all one night," neighbor William Wood recalled. Wood suspected that she was already ill with some other affliction and milk sickness simply finished her off.[94] Some said she suffered from consumption.[95] The previous year, a traveler through the Ohio River country thought that protracted forest dwelling itself was unhealthy and was appalled by "the effect on the complexion produced by the perpetual incarceration of a thorough woodland life," noting that one family he met was "tall and pale, like vegetables that grow in a vault, pining for light."[96] Nancy "struggled on . . . day by day," Denny remembered. "She knew she was going to die and called up the children to her dying side and told them to be good and kind to their father, to one another, and to the world. Expressing a hope that they might live as they had been taught by her, to love men, love [and] reverence and worship God."[97] Denny reportedly declared:

> O Lord, O Lord, I'll never furgit the mizry in that little green-log cabin in the woods when Nancy died!
> Me 'n' Abe helped Tom make the coffin. He tuk a log left over from buildin' the cabin, an' I helped him whipsaw it into planks an' plane 'em. Me 'n' Abe held the planks while Tom bored holes an' put 'em together, with pegs Abe'd whittled. . . . 'Pears to me like Tom was always makin' a coffin fur some one. We laid Nancy close to the deer-run in the woods. Deer was the only wild critters the women wasn't afeerd of. Abe was some'er's 'round nine years old, but he never got over the mizable way his mother died. I reckon she didn't have no sort o' keer—pore Nancy![98]

He added, "Abe's said many a time that Nancy'd lived to be old if she'd had any kind o' keer, an' I reckon she must 'a' been strong to 'a' stood what she did." [99]

Henry Brooner said, "I remember very distinctly that when Mrs. Lincoln's grave was filled, my father, Peter Brooner, extended his hand to Thomas Lincoln and said, 'We are brothers now,' meaning that they were brothers in the same kind of sorrow. The bodies of my mother and Mrs. Lincoln were conveyed to their graves on sleds." [100]

Long afterward, Lincoln wrote to a child grieving for her father:

> In this sad world of ours, sorrow comes to all; and, to the young, it comes with bitterest agony, because it takes them unawares. The older have learned to ever expect it. . . . Perfect relief is not possible, except with time. You can not now realize that you will ever feel better. Is not this so? And yet it is a mistake. You are sure to be happy again. . . . I have had experience enough to know what I say. . . . The memory of your dear father, instead of an agony, will yet be a sad sweet feeling in your heart. [101]

David Elkin, the antislavery preacher who had found welcome in the Lincoln home back in Kentucky, dropped by a year or so after Nancy's death and conducted a memorial service. On the frontier in that era, such a delay between demise and funeral was not uncommon. A story got up that Elkin came in response to a letter from Abe, but Denny Hanks said the minister simply responded to a visitation request from Little Pigeon Baptist Church. "Parson Elkin," said Denny, "was a good, true man, and the best preacher and finest orator I ever heard. I have heard his words distinctly and clearly one fourth of a mile." [102] Nancy's corpse was buried next to her stepparents' bodies. The graves were unmarked, and eventually their location was forgotten, [103] though later investigators were convinced that they had found the site. A traveler in Lincoln's time wrote of such a locale:

> I was one day wandering through the woods in search of deer, when, in a lonely spot, overshadowed by some large oaks, I stumbled on five graves. There was no enclosure, nor anything to indicate the presence of a burial ground, beyond the unequivocal shape of the mounds, and a few split rails arranged over each, to prevent an attack of the numerous bands of hogs, which roam at large, or of wild animals. A feeling of awe came over me. . . . There was a sense of complete seclusion— a silence befitting the last repose. There was nothing pertaining to existence to distract the attention; the face of the earth, beyond the mere graves, was still under the dominion of nature; there was no busy hum of voices . . . not even the sound of an axe, whose stroke is heard far through the silent woods, whilst the light shed through the thick foliage of the lofty trees was in perfect keeping with the whole. [104]

The three Lincolns and Denny Hanks struggled along. Denny moved into the Lincoln cabin after Nancy and the Sparrows died. "Tom, he moped 'round. Wasn't wuth shucks that winter," Denny reportedly said. "Sairy was a little gal, only 'leven, an' she'd git so lonesome, missin' her mother, she'd set by the fire an' cry. Me 'n' Abe got 'er a baby coon an' a turtle, and tried to git a fawn but we couldn't ketch any."[105] Sally did the cooking.[106] "We still kept up hunting and farming," Denny related. "Abe's father was a cabinetmaker and house joiner etc. He worked at this trade in the winter at odd times, farming it in the summer. We always hunted. It made no difference what came, for we more or less depended on it for a living, nay for life. We had not been long at the [newer] log cabin before we got the usual domestic animals . . . driven out from near the Ohio River or hauled in a cart pulled by one yoke of oxen."[107] At some point, Abraham planted an orchard.[108]

Denny Hanks said that during the autumn of 1819, the Lincoln clan began felling timber to construct what he called "our new grand old log cabin," a one-story structure that had a sleeping loft and one unglazed window. Rather than use a ladder to get upstairs, they inserted pegs in the log wall. Denny remembered "the pegs creaking and screeching" when he and Abe would climb up to bed.[109]

In addition to whatever feelings of loneliness he had, Tom Lincoln was wise enough to notice that certain standards were declining in the absence of a woman's touch. A distinguished biographer of Lincoln wrote, "From trustworthy accounts of better conditioned families in the same wilderness, it can only be believed that for the Lincolns 1819 was a year of squalor."[110] Judging from descriptions by travelers, such dismal conditions were nothing unusual. Around 1818, one person noted, "Though the houses near Henderson [Kentucky] are bad, there are good gardens and icehouses; and cleanliness, which strongly contrasts with the dirty Ohio houses, and the Indiana and Illinois pigsties, in which men, women, and children wallow in promiscuous filth."[111] Said another Western visitor: "Saving two comfortable plantations, with neat log-houses . . . I saw nothing between Vincennes and Princeton, a ride of forty miles, but miserable log holes, and a mean village of eight or ten huts or cabins, sad neglected farms, and indolent, dirty, sickly, wild-looking inhabitants. Soap is nowhere seen or found in any of the taverns, east or west. Hence dirty hands, heads, and faces everywhere."[112]

In November 1819, Tom left the children on their own long enough to go to Elizabethtown on a mission to bring back a wife. "We knowed what he went fur," Denny allegedly said, "but we didn't think he'd have any luck, bein' as pore as he was, and with two children to raise."[113] Tom, however, had a plan.

Years earlier, he had courted Sarah Bush,[114] daughter of his slave patrol captain Christopher Bush and sister of Isaac Bush, from whom Tom later purchased the Sinking Spring farm. The Bush family was well off financially; Denny Hanks said Sarah "had been raised in Elizabethtown in somewhat a high life."[115] She enjoyed eating and had a light complexion and blue-gray eyes. She was tall, "straight as an Indian," a granddaughter said, "sprightly, talkative, and proud [*sic*] wore her hair curled."[116] Another relative described her as "a woman of great energy, of remarkable good sense, very industrious, and saving, and also very neat and tidy in her person and manners."[117] An Elizabethtown resident who knew her said that when Sarah was a girl, "Her mother thought she was too proud, simply because the poor girl tried to make herself look decent and keep in the fashion of that early day."[118]

The seventeen-year-old Sarah Bush married Daniel Johnston in 1806, the same year that thirty-year-old Tom Lincoln and Nancy Hanks married. Tom gave Sarah a wedding present. After their marriage, the Johnston couple's finances headed ever downward. Their account with an Elizabethtown merchant contains the notation "An empty vessel makes the most noise." Except for a horse one year, Daniel had no taxable property after he married. He began borrowing money, was unable to pay, and apparently lacked property that creditors could attach. Her brothers paid some debts. All this must have been quite an experience for Sarah, who came from a financially comfortable background, but perhaps the couple found better rewards than money in their marriage. A financial respite occurred in 1814, however. Both the Bush and Johnston families were politically active, with the men holding various low-level offices, and in that year Daniel became county jailer. Sarah took on the duties of jail cook, and both spouses did janitorial tasks in the courthouse.

Two years later, Daniel Johnston died in an epidemic that killed thirteen persons in a day's span in Elizabethtown, and Sarah became a single parent with three children. How they survived in Elizabethtown is unclear. She was, however, able to buy a residence and lot, sent one of her daughters to a fine private academy of a quality far above country schools, and had excellent—and fairly expensive—furnishings in her home.[119]

According to a nephew of Sarah's, when Tom Lincoln came from Indiana and showed up at her place, he got straight to the point. He noted their past acquaintance and present circumstances, and then proposed marriage.[120] Being a single mother in that era was no easier than it is now, nearly two centuries later, and Sarah's friends urged her to accept Tom's proposal.[121] That she would consider such a proposal from someone she hadn't seen in years suggests that she and Tom did indeed have a past history of congenial acquaintance. She told him, however, that she couldn't marry and leave Kentucky until she paid off some debts; she did not want to leave unfinished business behind. Tom got the names of her creditors and paid everything Sarah owed. One report says the total indebtedness was $2.50.[122] This time Tom and Sarah married. To call her wealthy would be an exaggeration—after all, she had been unable to pay the debts Tom took care of for her—but she had far more household possessions than the Lincolns did. Enough that Tom urged her to sell some of the furniture, said one relative, on grounds that "it was too fine for them to keep, but this she refused to do."[123] Tom needed to hire a wagon and team from his brother-in-law Ralph Crume to haul everything into Indiana.[124]

"We was all nigh about tickled to death when Tom brung a new wife home," Denny supposedly said. "She had three children of 'er own, an' a four-hoss wagon-load o' goods—feather pillers an' homespun blankets, an' patchwork quilts an' chists o' drawers, an' a flax-wheel an' a soap kittle, an' cookin' pots an' pewter dishes—lot o' truck like that 'at made a heap o' diffrunce in a backwoods cabin."[125] There was even a pet cat.[126] In a supposed interview, one can almost hear the admiration in Denny's voice: "Aunt Sairy sartinly did have faculty. I reckon we was all purty ragged and dirty when she got thar. The fust thing she did was to tell me to tote one o' Tom's cyarpenter benches to a place outside the door, near the hoss-trough. Then she had me 'n' Abe 'n' John Johnston, her boy, fill the trough with spring water. She put out a big gourd full o' soft soap, an' another one to dip water with, an' told us boys to wash up fur dinner. You jist naturally had to be somebody when Aunt Sairy was around."[127] That was just the start. She repaired their clothes.[128] "She had Tom build 'er a loom, an' when she heerd o' some lime burners bein' 'round Gentryville, Tom had to mosey over an' git some lime, an' whitewash the cabin. An' he made 'er an ash-hopper fur lye, an' a chicken-house nothin' could git into. . . . Cracky, but Aunt Sairy was some punkins!"[129] Denny allegedly added:

> Maybe it was somethin' she tuk comfort in to have a man that didn't drink an' cuss none. She made a heap more o' Tom, too, than pore Nancy did. Before winter he'd put in a new floor, he'd whipsawed an' planed off so she could scour it; made some good beds an' cheers, an' tinkered at the roof so it couldn't snow in on us boys 'at slep' in the loft. Purty soon we had the best house in the kentry. Thar was eight of us then to do fur, but Aunt Sairy had faculty an' didn't 'pear to be hurried or worried none. Little Sairy jist chirked right up with a mother an' two sisters fur comp'ny.[130]

A garden appeared in front of the cabin.[131] Under his wife's prodding, Tom fruitlessly sought a water source nearby. He dug enough holes to turn the hill into a honeycomb. A witch offered to find water for a payment of $5, but "Old Man Lincoln couldn't believe such stuff," Denny said. Tom refused the offer, saying he could do as well with a forked stick as the witch could.[132]

In the delicate phrase of one biographer, Sarah Bush Johnston Lincoln "must have felt some contrast between his [Tom's] readiness in Elizabethtown to produce money and pay off her small indebtedness and the manifest poverty of the [Indiana] home as she found it."[133] Relative A. H. Chapman confirmed that she was "astonished to find that there was no floor or door to the house of her husband, no furniture of any kind, no beds or bedding, or scarcely any."[134] But years later, she made no complaint, saying, "When we landed in Indiana Mr. Lincoln had erected a good log cabin, tolerably comfortable. . . . I dressed Abe and his sister up, looked more human." She did remember, however, that "the country was wild and desolate."[135] Someone recalled an 1823 Indiana incident illustrating one type of wildness: "I was riding through a dense forest when I encountered a terrific storm. Black clouds drifted rapidly across the sky, and heavy peals of thunder mingled with the noise of the wind in the timber. I dismounted from my frightened horse and stood holding him by the bridle, seeing no way to seek safety. It became very dark, tall trees fell crashing in every direction, and the lightning ran in streams along the prostrate timber."[136]

Simple stories of farm life reveal elements of Abraham Lincoln's character. He recalled an instance when he and his stepbrother were plowing, "I driving the horse, and he holding the plough. The horse was lazy; but on occasion rushed across the field so that I, with my long legs, could scarcely keep pace with him. On reaching the end of the furrow, I found an enormous chin fly fastened upon him, and knocked him off. My brother asked me what I did that for. I told him I didn't want the old horse bitten in that way. 'Why,' said my brother, 'that's all that made him go!'"[137] A young neighbor once admitted to coveting watermelons from Abe's patch. "Some of us boys lit into the melon patch accidentally. We got the melons, went through the corn to the fence, got over. All at once to our surprise and mortification Lincoln came among us, on us. Good naturedly said, 'Boys, now I've got you.' Sat down with us, cracked jokes, told stories, and helped to eat the melons."[138] "Once in a while my mother used to get some sorghum and ginger and make some gingerbread," Lincoln remembered.

> It wasn't often, and it was our biggest treat. One day I smelled the gingerbread and came into the house to get my share while it was hot. My mother had baked me three gingerbread men. I took them out under a hickory tree to eat them. There was a family near us that was a little poorer than we were, and their boy came along as I sat down.
>
> "Abe," he said, "gimme a man?"
>
> I gave him one. He crammed it into his mouth in two bites and looked at me while I was biting the legs from my first one.
>
> "Abe," he said, "gimme that other'n."
>
> I wanted it myself, but I gave it to him, and as it followed the first I said to him, "You seem to like gingerbread?"
>
> "Abe," he said, "I don't suppose there's anybody on this earth likes gingerbread better'n I do." He drew a long breath before he added, "and I don't suppose there's anybody on this earth gets less'n I do."[139]

A neighbor told of an ordinary evening at the Lincoln place. The account shows something about Tom Lincoln's personality and also reveals the homestead to be more than a simple cabin. Wesley Hall was a lad bringing his family's grist home from the miller when a heavy snowstorm and approaching nightfall persuaded him to seek shelter at the Lincoln place.

> Bye and bye I heard the door begin to creak on its wooden hinges, and then through the storm I saw old Tom a shadin' his eyes with his hand a tryin' to see who I wuz. . . . He leaned back and laughed a big

broad laugh, and then a startin' out to where I wuz he says, says he: "Is that you Wesley? You get down from thar and come in out of the weather." So I commenct to git ready to slide off my sack and by the time I got ready to light, old Tom wuz there and helped me down. Then a turnin' around lookin' towards the cabin, he calls out a time or two, big and loud: "Abe! O, Abe! Abe!" And he aint more'n called till I seen Abe a comin' through the door, and when he asked what wuz wanted, and seein' who I wuz at the same time, old Tom says: "Come out here and git Wesley's grist while I put his hoss in the stable. Wesley's mighty nigh froze I reckon." Then he laughed again. Well, I wuz cold I c'n tell you for I hadn't had anything to eat ceptin' parched corn since mornin'. Well, as I say, old Tom told Abe to come and get my sack, and I noticed as Abe come out to where I wuz he hadn't but one shoe on. . . . I saw Abe was a walkin' on the ball of his heel so's to hold his big toe up which wuz all tied up, and by this time I reckon there wuz mighty nigh six inches of snow. . . . When I asked him what was the matter with his foot he told me he'd split his big toe open with an ax out in the clearin' that day. . . .

I set down in front of the fireplace and commenct to thaw out, and in a little bit old Tom come in, and a settin' down by me a slappin' his hands together and then a rubbin' em so, like he allus' done, he says, says he: "Wesley, you got purty cold I reckon, did you?" And when I commenct to say I did, Mrs. Lincoln come in and she says, after we'd passed the time of day, she says, says she: "Wesley, I reckon you're hungry." And I told her I wuz; and then I told her about the parched corn. And she says: "We haint got no meal to bake bread. We're out just now," but a pointin' to the big bank of embers that I'd already noticed in the fireplace and of course knowd what it meant, she says, says she, "we've got some potatoes in thar a bakin' and we'll git a bite for you purty soon." At that I spoke up and I says, says I: "Mrs. Lincoln, just help yourself out of my sack thar." And so she done as I told her.

Well, old Tom and Abe and me went on a talkin' and purty soon I heard a funny grindin' noise back of me, and I looked around to see what it wuz, and it wuz Mrs. Lincoln a hollerin' out a big turnip.

She stuffed lard and a wick into the hollowed turnip, which then served as a disposable lamp.

She handed it to me, and a butcher knife to Abe, and she says: "Boys, go out and get me some bacon.". . . So Mrs. Lincoln went on with gittin' supper, and bye and bye she says: "Supper's ready." So when we set down to it we had corn cakes, baked potatoes, and fried bacon. After the supper dishes was washed up old Tom, a slappin' his hands together and a rubbin' em like I say, he says, says he: "Now, Abe, bring out your book and read fer us." Old Tom couldn't read himself, but he wuz proud that Abe could, and many a time he'd brag about how smart Abe wuz to the folks around about. Well, Abe reached up on a shelf where he kept his books and then a stirrin' up the fire on the hearth with some dry stuff he had piled in one corner by the jamb, he commenced to read.

After hearing about Benjamin Franklin's life for a while, the household went to bed.[140]

Vocal music was another simple amusement. "Could Lincoln sing?" Billy Herndon asked. "Can a jackass whistle or sing?"[141] Daniel Burner, who knew Abraham in Illinois, said, "Lincoln couldn't sing any more than a crow."[142] The teenager was neither a singer nor connoisseur of music but occasionally belted out songs. "Anything that was lively," Denny Hanks said.[143] Sometimes hymns, sometimes popular ditties, sometimes songs of Lincoln's own creation.[144] Doing field labor, he would sing a parody of "Hail Columbia, Happy Land": "Hail Columbia, happy land / If you ain't broke / I'll be damned."[145] Denny said, "Our little smutty songs I won't say anything about. Would not look well in print."[146] We do know that Lincoln enjoyed singing "None Can Love like an Irishman," a traditional ballad about how a hundred wives can't exhaust the capacity of an Irishman.[147]

By request, neighbor David Turnham would sing "The Romish Lady" for Abe and Tom Lincoln: "There was a Romish lady brought up in popery, / Her mother always taught her that the priest she must obey; / O pardon me dear mother, I humbly pray thee now / For unto these false idols I can no longer bow." The remainder of the song tells of the lady's devout mother reporting the daughter to the priests, who take her to trial and have her executed for reading the Bible.[148] Abe would sing "William Riley," about a poor man who ran off with a wealthy businessman's daughter, only to be hunted down, jailed, and exiled to Botany Bay despite his sweetheart's testimony.[149] From Dupuy's *Hymns and Spiritual Songs*, Abraham and Denny Hanks would sing "The Morning Trumpet," also called "Bound for Canaan" ("Oh, when shall I see Jesus and reign with Him above / And shall hear the trumpet sound in that morning"), and "How Tedious and Tasteless," also called "Greenfields" ("How tedious and tasteless the hours / When Jesus I no longer see; / Sweet prospects, sweet birds and sweet flowers, / Have all lost their sweetness to me").[150] Hymns of Isaac Watts impressed the boy. In his homemade arithmetic exercise book, he recorded these lines from Watts:

> Time, what an empty vapor 'tis!
> And days, how swift they are!
> Swift as an Indian arrow flies,
> Or like a shooting star.

> The present moments just appear,
> Then slide away in haste,
> That we can never say, "They're here,"
> But only say, "They're past."[151]

Similar sentiments are found in poetry that appealed to Lincoln throughout his life. Moreover, the technical construction of that Watts hymn—its rhyme and meter—would be the model he used in his own poetry. Indeed, next to this excerpt in his exercise book is the word "meter," suggesting that as a teenager he was analyzing methodology of poetry. Schoolmate Nat Grigsby pointed out that "essays and poetry were not taught in the school. Abe took it up of his own accord."[152] Lincoln's close familiarity with Watts can be seen in his adult years. His controversial 1842 speech advocating temperance includes a couple lines from Watts: "While the lamp holds out to burn, / the vilest sinner may return."[153] He also referred to Watts in conversation. Said one acquaintance, "I have heard him say over and over again about sexual contact, 'It is the harp of a thousand strings.'" "Harp of a thousand strings" is a line from Watts, although Lincoln used it in a context mischievously different from what the writer intended.[154]

And Abe did have a streak of mischief reported in a story traditionally ascribed to Denny Hanks:

> Aunt Sairy often told Abe 'at his feet bein' clean didn't matter so much, because she could scour the floor, but he'd better wash his head, or he'd be a rubbin' dirt off on her nice whitewashed rafters.
>
> That put an idy in his head, I reckon. Several of us older ones was married then, an' thar was always a passel o' youngsters 'round the place. One day Abe put 'em up to wadin' in the mud-puddle by the hoss-trough. Then he tuk 'em one by one, turned 'em upside down, an' walked 'em acrost the ceilin', them ascreamin' fit to kill.
>
> Aunt Sairy come in, an' it was so blamed funny she set down an' laughed, though she said Abe'd oughter be spanked. I don't know how far he had to go fur more lime, but he whitewashed the ceilin' all over agin.[155]

Denny Hanks revealed more of this side of Abe's personality in an interview: "He was a tricky man, and sometimes when he went to log house raising, corn shucking, and such like things, he would say to himself and sometimes to others, 'I don't want these fellows to work anymore,' and instantly he would commence his pranks, tricks, jokes, stories. And sure enough all would stop, gather around Abe and listen, sometimes crying and sometimes bursting their sides with laughter. He sometimes would mount a stump, chair, or box and make speeches."[156] In the guise of such mischief, the teenager was learning how to make men do his bidding. "He naturally assumed the leadership of the boys," Nat Grigsby recalled. "He read and thoroughly read his books whilst we played. Hence he . . . became our guide and leader."[157] Denny Hanks remembered, "Up to 1830 when our intimacy ended . . . he was ambitious and determined, and when he attempted to excel by man or boy his whole soul and his energies were bent on doing it."[158]

One incident perhaps revealed as much about Lincoln's friends as it did about him. While Lincoln and a group of friends were going home on a freezing cold night, they found an unconscious drunkard. Lincoln was urged to leave the man where he was to allow him to suffer the consequences of his behavior. But fearing the man would die outdoors, Abe picked him up and carried him until they reached a building where the man could be revived near the fireplace's warmth. In a later era, such an act might have been considered normal, but in Lincoln's community, it was unusual enough to cause comment. The drunkard himself was quoted as saying, "It was mighty clever of Abe to tote me so far that cold night."[159] Not all tipplers had such good luck.

> "A man was found *dead drunk*, near Edwardsville, on the 10th inst. He had got drunk, and fallen asleep, and was frozen to death. Will drunkards never be warned of their peril?"
>
> —*Vandalia Illinois Intelligencer,*
> February 28, 1829

> "[They] frequently fall down in the streets and lie out all night—sometimes they freeze their limbs and sometimes perish."
>
> —Address by Galena, Illinois, Temperance Society,
> May 10, 1836, in the *Galenian*, May 17, 1836

Reliable testimony indicates that Lincoln was a light user of beverage alcohol. "Sometimes we spent a little time at grog," Denny Hanks said.[160] John Hanks watched Lincoln mix some honey into whiskey, take a sip, and declare, "Den, that tastes pretty good."[161] Nat Grigsby noted: "He did drink his dram as well as all others did, preachers and Christians included. Lincoln was a temperate drinker."[162] More evidence comes from neighbor David Turnham: "Sometimes he took his dram as everybody did at that time."[163] Perhaps the most interesting comment is from William Wood: "Abe once drank as all people did here at that time."[164] This is interesting because Wood helped publish a temperance essay written by the young Lincoln. Rev. Peter Cartwright, with whom Lincoln would later have unfriendly interactions, recalled:

> From my earliest recollection drinking drams, in family and social circles, was considered harmless and allowable socialities. It was almost universally the custom for preachers, in common with all others, to take drams; and if a man would not have it in his family, his harvest, his house-raisings, log-rollings, weddings, and so on, he was

considered parsimonious and unsociable; and many, even professors of Christianity, would not help a man if he did not have spirits and treat the company. . . . I have often seen it carried and used freely at large baptizings, where the ordinance was administration by immersion.[165]

Alcohol abuse and what to do about it were growing issues throughout the United States, and Lincoln was already a temperance man. One of his favorite songs that he cried out was "John Adkin's Farewell," a religious parody of a popular Western drinking song. "Much intoxication my ruin has been" went the parody, in which a drunkard told of murdering his wife and the lawful penalty he had to pay.[166] Different approaches existed within the temperance movement, just as there were different denominations and sects within Christianity. Eventually close ties would develop between the temperance and abolition movements, both seeking to liberate people from types of slavery.

Ironically for a temperance man, Lincoln substituted for his stepbrother John Johnston, who had been hired to work "a small still house, up at the head of a hollow," as Lincoln described it. He wrote up the employment contract between Johnston and the owner.[167] Distilling was a lucrative way to market corn crops. A bushel of corn that sold for a quarter dollar as grain sold for a full dollar as beverage alcohol.[168] We don't know Lincoln's brand of temperance during his Indiana years (though later we shall see his approach in Illinois). All we can say is that in Indiana, he was a light drinker and argued against alcohol abuse. In such argument, he had plenty of company.

> "Our country pays or loses at the rate of *one hundred and twenty millions of dollars per annum, by intemperance*! This sum is five times as large as the revenue of the United States government [and] it would pay off our national debt in six months!"
>
> —*New York Observer*, clipped in *Vandalia Illinois Intelligencer*, October 18, 1828

A settlement of idealists dedicated to women's rights, emancipation of slaves, and a communist lifestyle influenced Lincoln's district of Indiana and apparently attracted his attention. Newspapers to which he had access had much to say about the experiment.

> Harmony, Indiana. The land held by them in Pennsylvania, from the increase of their numbers, being too small for them, they purchased a large and beautiful tract on the Wabash, in the new state of Indiana, and removed to it just about three years ago. . . . They already have many good houses, large workshops, and extensive barns . . . a steam

mill driving two pair of stones; a very large brick house in the shape of an L, for Mr. Rapp, with an excellent and highly ornamented garden . . . ; they have 1500 Merino sheep, whose wool they manufacture into excellent broadcloths, with a large stock of cattle, hogs, &c., and carry on almost every trade and manufacture . . . among them are tin workers, shoemakers, saddlers, joiners, carpenters, hatters, stocking and other weavers, tanners, blacksmiths, &c. &c. They have many acres planted . . . 200 in wheat, 40 in rye, 30 in barley, 30 in oats, 50 with meadow grass, and 500 enclosed in pasture fields. All these things have been done in three years. This society is numerous, amounting, we believe to nearly 300 families, who have all things in common; are among the most industrious and economical people in the world, and very harmless and inoffensive.[169]

The story of the settlement called New Harmony is way beyond the scope of this book. Suffice it to say that German reformer George Rapp and English reformer Robert Owen established a colony where people sought to implement a way of life differing in important ways from traditional American ideals. For example, in April 1829, Owen debated for eight days in Cincinnati with Rev. Alexander Campbell, "denying the truth of all religions in general" and arguing (from a newspaper report, not necessarily Owen's own words): "We are the 'effects' of our 'circumstances' as strictly as inanimate matter obeys its laws. Therefore, we are not subjects of reponsibility, praise or blame. We can neither think, act, love, hate, marry, become fathers, eat, drink, sleep, or die, other than as we do." People act from involuntary compulsion, not from altruism, let alone by influence from a divinity. A couple months later, an Illinois newspaper commented, "There never was a more demoralizing, and anti-social doctrine, than that contained in the heartless philosophy of Mr. Owen." We have good reason, however, to believe that the philosophy appealed to Lincoln; it was virtually a secular version of predestinarian teachings in his family's Indiana church that God has foreordained all, and humans can do nothing about it. We shall see evidence of that philosophy's appeal in what Lincoln said on more than one occasion in Illinois. And for the Indiana years, we have purported evidence from Denny Hanks:

When Abe was about seventeen, somethin' happened that druv him nigh crazy. Thar was a feller come over from England,—Britisher, I reckon—an' spoke in Congress about a settlemint he was goin' to lay out on the Wabash, buyin' out some loony Dutch [i.e., German] religious fellers that had mills an' schools thar. Now, mebbe you think 'at us folks livin' in the backwoods didn't know what was goin' on in the world. Well, you'd be mighty mistaken about that. . . .

So when this furrin feller spoke in Congress about that gyarden o' Eden he was goin' to fence in on the Wabash, we soon heerd about it. Boats brung news every week. An' one day arly in the winter, a big keel-boat come down from Pittsburg over the Ohio. They called it "the boatload o' knowledge," it had sich a passel o' books an' machines an' men o' l'arnin' on it. Then little rowboats an' rafts crossed over from Kaintucky, an' ox teams an' pack-hosses went through Gentryville and struck across kentry to—to—plague on it! Abe'd tell you in a minute—

Here the interviewer prompted Hanks by asking if he referred to New Harmony.

That's it! Thar wasn't sca'cely anything else talked about fur a spell. I reckon some folks thought it was New Jerusalem, an' nobody'd have to work. Anyway, thar was a lot o' wuthless cusses lit out fur that settlemint. Abe'd a broke his back to go, an' it nigh about broke his heart when he couldn't.

"Denny, thar's a school an' thousands o' books thar, an' fellers that know everything in creation," he'd say, his eyes as big 'n' hungry as a hoot-owl's. The schoolin' cost only about a hundred dollars a year, an' he could 'a' worked out his board, but Abe might jist as well 'a' wished fur a hunderd moons to shine at night. I was married to one o' the Johnstone gals by then an' had hard grubbin' to keep my fambly, or I'd 'a' helped him. Tom didn't set no store by them things. An' thar it was, only about sixty miles west of us, an' Abe couldn't go! The place petered out after awhile, as it was sartin to do, with all them ornery fellers in it, livin' off the workers. But I reckon it lasted long enough fur Abe to 'a' l'arned what he wanted to know. Well, I reckon Abe put it out o' his mind, after awhile. . . . But things'd ben easier fur him if he could 'a' gone to that school.[170]

If, as alleged, Lincoln yearned to attend school in New Harmony, such ambition must have met sympathy from his stepmother. She had already sent his stepsister Elizabeth Johnston to the Elizabethtown Academy, where instruction included English, geography, algebra, geometry, and trigonometry, though she may not have taken all those classes. The faculty included someone with Transylvania University training, and the academy was run by Duff Green,[171] brother-in-law of Illinois governor Ninian Edwards (whose son would marry the sister of a woman named Mary Todd). Such training for a young woman in the early nineteenth century was extraordinary. If Sarah Bush Johnston Lincoln supported such schooling for her daughter, surely she wanted no less for her stepson. But such was not to be.

Lincoln later mused that he "was never in a college or academy as a student" and that he felt the lack.[172] Instead of receiving higher education, Abraham once again intermittently and briefly attended country schools, what he called "A.B.C. schools,"[173] where the kind of teaching differed substantially from what was available in New Harmony. He later declared, "There was absolutely nothing to excite ambition for education" in these local schools. He noted: "There were some schools, so called; but no qualification was ever required of a teacher beyond *'readin, writin, and cipherin.'* . . . If a straggler supposed to understand Latin happened to sojourn in the neighborhood, he was looked upon as a wizard."[174]

Teacher Andy Crawford was no straggler. Sometimes confused with the farmer Josiah "Blue Nose" Crawford, Andy was a justice of the peace. Apparently he taught Lincoln in the summer and autumn of 1820. Andy earned a place in local memory by teaching his pupils manners, having a student leave the schoolhouse and then be greeted by another student at the door, who would then escort the "visitor" from bench to bench, making socially proper introductions. A student in another school recalled such etiquette training:

> When the scholars arrived, after the master had taken his seat, the boys were required, on entering the door, to take off their hats and make a bow—the girls to curtsy. In *some* schools, the same was commanded on leaving the house in the evening. . . . It was further inculcated on them to take off their hats and bow and curtsy to all whom they met, either coming or going. Even during play hours, if a man or woman rode near the groups, it was regarded as a duty to give the salutation. Thus I have often run to the roadside with other boys to make my bow; and when a dozen of us or more might be returning together, if a man overtook or met us, we all stepped aside, stopped in a row, took off our hats and made our bows as near as possible at the same time.[175]

Abe's schoolmate Katie Roby remembered a gentle incident:

> One day Crawford put a word to us to spell. The word to spell was "defied." Crawford said if we did not spell it he would keep us in school all day and night. We all missed the word. Couldn't spell it. We spelled the word every way but the right way. I saw Lincoln at the window: He had his finger on his *eye* and a smile on his face. I instantly took the hint that I must change the letter y into an i. Hence I spelled the word. The class let out. I felt grateful to Lincoln for this simple thing.[176]

Appreciating young Lincoln's interest in reading, Andy loaned him Weems's biography of Washington,[177] a book Abraham spoke about forty years later: "Away back in my childhood, the earliest days of my being able to read, I got hold of a small book . . . 'Weems's Life of Washington.' I remember all the accounts there given of the battlefields and struggles for the liberties of the country. . . . I recollect thinking then, boy even though I was, that there must have been something more than common that those men struggled for."[178]

Lincoln's second Indiana schoolteacher was James Swaney. Fellow student John Oskins noted that the school was four and a half miles from the Lincoln cabin, with the walk eating up so much of Lincoln's day as to be a hardship.[179]

Around 1826, Azel Dorsey taught Lincoln for a while. Dorsey was an old Kentucky neighbor of the Lincolns, and in Indiana he became a merchant who was elected to county offices. He was also the guardian and teacher of James Swaney. This school was the only public school Lincoln attended, its expenses paid by the government instead of by parents, with a teacher who had to pass qualification exams. Young Abraham made a deep enough impression on Dorsey that he gave this recollection years later, even before Lincoln was a presidential candidate: "Abraham Lincoln was one of the noblest boys I ever knew and is certain to become noted if he lives." Dorsey spoke of the lad's studiousness, his buckskin attire and coonskin cap, and an arithmetic book that he brought to school. Few students on the frontier had their own arithmetic books, so that Lincoln had one implies strong support of education from his family. It was from this school that several pages of Abraham's school writings have been preserved.[180] He wrote out a homemade book of arithmetic exercises, some pages of which still exist, and in a copybook he wrote out excerpts from literary works that struck him. None of the literary copybook has survived.[181] Jefferson Davis, who would later lead the Confederate States, recalled:

> Instruction in these old log school-houses was very simple. It consisted solely of a long copybook—the qualifications required of the teacher being that he should be able to write at the head of each page the pot-hooks, letters, and sentences which were to be copied by the pupil on each line of the paper.
>
> As the pupil advanced, he was required to have a book for his sums. He worked out the examples in the arithmetic, and, after a sufficient amount of attention, he was required to copy this into a book, which, when it was completed, was the evidence that he understood arithmetic. After some time a bright boy could repeat all the rules; but if you asked him to explain why . . . he could give the rule, but no reason for it. And I am not sure that, as a general thing, the teacher could have explained it to him.[182]

The wife of Blue Nose Crawford noted that speeches were part of schooling then. "I have a book called *The Kentucky Preceptor*, which we brought from Kentucky and in which and from which Abe learned his school orations, speeches, and pieces to recite. School exhibitions used to be the order of the day. . . . Abe attended them, spoke and acted his part, always well free from rant and swell."[183] Sometimes students would give public presentations on gentle topics such as bees and ants or compare the power of water and that of wind. The topic for discussion might be more formidable, however, such as examining whether Indians had more grievances against white civilization than blacks did.[184] *The Kentucky*

Preceptor itself covered such matters. In "The Desperate Negro," the *Preceptor* told of an obedient slave driven to suicide by whippings. "Disguise thyself as thou wilt, still slavery!" shouted a *Preceptor* piece about liberty. "Still thou art a bitter draught, and though thousands in all ages have been made to drink of thee, thou art no less bitter on that account."[185]

"He was always at school early and attentive to his studies," schoolmate Nat Grigsby said. "He lost no time at home. When he was not at work he was learning his books. He pursued his studies on the Sabbath day."[186] A neighbor boy recalled, "He was exceedingly studious."[187] According to another neighbor, "He read and re-read, read and studied thoroughly."[188] Nat Grigsby said: "When he went out to work anywhere [he] would carry his books with [him] and would always read whilst resting. . . . Whilst other boys were idling away their time Lincoln was at home studying hard. Would cipher on the boards. . . . Had a slate sometimes, but if not handy would use boards. He would shave boards bright and cipher on them, dirty them, re-shave them."[189] His stepmother also mentioned this practice: "He ciphered on boards when he had no paper or no slate, and when the board would get too black he would shave it off with a drawing knife and go on again."[190] Schoolmate David Turnham admitted, "I was older than he was by six years and further advanced, but he soon outstripped me."[191] John Hanks, who lived at the Lincoln homestead for four years, recalled, "He went to school but little whilst I was there, say one or two months, and his father has often told me he [Abraham] had not gone to school one year in all his life."[192] "The little advance I now have upon this store of education," Lincoln declared, "I have picked up from time to time under the pressure of necessity."[193] Speaking in the third person, he said, "He regrets his want of education, and does what he can to supply the want."[194] Even in his Indiana days, he was picking up enough to amaze neighbors. Neighbor Katie Roby remembered:

> One evening Abe and myself were sitting on the banks of the Ohio. . . .
> I said to Abe that the moon was going down. He said, "That's not so.
> It don't really go down; it seems so. The earth turns from west to east,
> and the revolution of the earth carries us under, as it were. We do the
> sinking as you call it. The moon as to us is comparatively still. The
> moon's sinking is only an appearance." I said to Abe, "Abe, what a
> fool you are." I know now that I was the fool, not Lincoln.[195]

His interest in astronomy would be long-standing. "One night he [Lincoln] said to me, 'Gilbert, you have to stand at your printer's case all day and I have to sit all day, let us take a walk.' As we walked on the country road out of Springfield, he turned his eyes to the heavens full of stars, and told me their names and their distance from us and the swiftness of their motion. He said the ancients used to arrange them so as to make monsters, serpents, animals of one kind or another out of them."[196]

⊹⇌ ⇌⊹

An institution that Abraham attended more than school was church. He and Tom Lincoln helped build the Little Pigeon Baptist Church, where Tom held various posts of trust.[197] Evidence exists that Abe may have been sexton there, but this possibility is unproven.[198] Nat Grigsby said flatly, "He never made any profession [of faith] while in Indiana that I know of."[199] Elizabeth Crawford said likewise.[200] Still, John Hanks reported that "Abe went to church generally, not always."[201] His religious beliefs at that time are less apparent than his outward conduct. He was happy to ask a trick question about the Bible. Denny Hanks recalled: "One day when Lincoln's mother was weaving in a little shed Abe came in and quizzically asked his good mother, 'Who was the father of Zebedee's children?' She saw the drift and laughed, saying, 'Get out of here you nasty little pup, you!' He saw he had got his mother and ran off laughing."[202] Membership in Little Pigeon Baptist Church was basically adults only and virtually limited to married adults (Abraham's sister Sally was not accepted as a member until shortly before her marriage),[203] marital status thereby providing a socially acceptable reason for Abe's nonmembership. Apparently Little Pigeon Baptist Church didn't provide child care; at least, the Lincoln-Johnston children were left at home when their parents went to church. Abraham's stepsister Tilda recalled:

> When they were gone, Abe would take down the Bible, read a verse, give out a hymn, and we would sing. We were good singers. Abe was about fifteen years of age. He would preach, and we would do the crying, sometimes he would join in the chorus of tears. One day my brother John Johnston caught a land terrapin, brought it to the place where Abe was preaching, threw it against the tree—crushed the shell, and it suffered much, quivered all over. Abe preached against cruelty to animals, contending that an ant's life was, to it, as sweet as ours.[204]

Abe's stepmother noted that "he loved animals generally and treated them kindly."[205] Years later, neighborhood folks still remembered that Lincoln even wrote "essays on being kind to animals and crawling insects."[206] He was willing to kill animals when necessary but respected their lives. Such an attitude was hardly universal in his time. "One of the farmers' favorite amusements at log rollings, William McLaren recalled with delight, 'was to round up a chip-munk, a rabbit, or a snake, and make him take refuge in a burning log-heap, and watch him squirm and fry,' or, at communal hunts, 'to skin a wolf alive and watch its "antics." ' "[207]

"The Bible puzzled him, especially the miracles," Denny Hanks said. "He often asked me in the timber, or sittin' around the fireplace nights, to explain Scripture."[208] Putting such questions to Denny was reasonable; he may have known the basics as well as any frontier preacher. In the West, college-trained clergymen were rare, and respect for them rarer. Indeed, apparently Little Pigeon Baptist Church was hostile to such.[209]

Lincoln's interest in astronomy had the potential of distancing him from the church, though no dispute on that ground is remembered. A backwoods resident of later years noted the potential trouble:

> I knew that I was not an infidel, even though I parted company with my friends in the Baptist ministry in my belief that the earth was round. . . . I count it a privilege to have lived with earnest and intelligent people who believed the earth flat, and to whom that belief was an important article of Christian faith. But I saw intelligent young men who had come to another opinion concerning some of these matters who accepted without protest the names that overzealous mountain preachers applied to them and who, believing themselves to be infidels, in time became so.[210]

According to an alleged report, another element of Lincoln's knowledge also portended conflict with fundamentalists, and that knowledge came from the simple act of writing his name: "'Denny,' he sez to me many a time, 'look at that, will you? *Abraham Lincoln!* That stands fur me. Don't look a blamed bit like me!' An' he'd stand an' study it a spell. 'Peared to mean a heap to Abe."[211] If reported correctly, that simple comment from Denny Hanks shows that at an early age, Lincoln understood the difference between a word and what it stood for, that words were symbols for something else. We should not infer too much from Lincoln's realization. Nonetheless, his native ability to grasp the concept shows that he had the capability to see that stories (groups of words) could stand for something else (act as metaphors). Such an understanding easily leads to interpreting religious writings in a way profoundly different from fundamentalist preachers. We don't know whether Lincoln ever viewed religious writings as metaphorical, but we do know (and shall see later in his political career) that Christian fundamentalists sensed something about his attitude that set him apart from them, even though he could—when he wished—profess something that sounded almost like orthodoxy.

Still, Denny mused, "I thought he never believed it."[212] John Hanks was more explicit: "Lincoln was as much of an infidel as anyone could be. I wouldn't like to say how much."[213] Abraham's stepmother declared that during the Indiana years, "Abe had no particular religion, didn't think of that question at that time, if he ever did. He never talked about it."[214] At least, not to her. But like Denny, Nat Grigsby remembered such conversations: "He talked about religion as other persons did, but I do not know his views."[215] He was so skilled at self-expression that leaving his listeners ignorant about his views after repeated conversations had to be deliberate. By implication, something about his religious beliefs would not have pleased his fundamentalist community.

When he was old enough to attend church, "for a man to preach a sermon he would listen to with great attention," Denny said.[216] Intently enough, stepsister Tilda said, that Abraham could "get up on a stump and repeat almost word for word the sermon he had heard the Sunday before."[217] His stepmother said likewise.[218] A neighbor recalled that church sermons were not milquetoast affairs. "The preacher would then take his stand, draw his coat, open his shirt collar, and commence service by singing and prayer, take his text and preach till the sweat would roll off in great drops."[219] Lincoln heard one Baptist minister preach often enough that he instantly made the family connection when introduced to the clergyman's son in 1861.[220] And what were these Baptists preaching? The Little Pigeon Church brand of Baptists was strong for predestination,[221] that God had long ago decided what happens in the world, and what we experience is part of a motion picture already filmed, whose scenes and ending we cannot change. Moreover, God had chosen the saved and the damned before birth; humans might strive to become reconciled to their fate but could not change it. Whatever Lincoln's level of Christian orthodoxy, he was permeated with the fatalism of predestination.

Church services were as social as they were religious. A Lincoln neighbor reminisced:

> Thought it nothing to go eight or ten miles. The old ladies did not stop for the want of a shawl or cloak or riding dress or two horses in the wintertime, but they would put on their husbnd's old overcoats and wrap up their little ones and take one or two of them up on their one beast, and their husbands would walk. . . . They would go to church and stay in the neighborhood till the next day and then go home. The old men would start of out of their fields from their work, or out of the woods from hunting with the guns on their shoulders, and go to church. Some of them dressed in deerskin pants and moccasins, hunting shirts with a rope and leather strap buckled around them. Come in laughing, shake hands all round, and set down and talk about their game they had killed or some other work they had done, smoke their pipes together with the old ladies. If in warm weather, would kindle up a little fire out in the meeting house yard to light their pipes. If in wintertime, they would hold church in some of the neighbors' houses. At such times they were always . . . treated with the utmost of kindness. A bottle of whiskey, pitcher of water, sugar and glass, or a basket of apples or turnips, or some pies or cakes. . . . Sometimes potatoes were used as a treat. I must tell you that the first treat that I ever received in old Mr. [Tom] Lincoln's house . . . was a plate of potatoes washed and pared very nicely and handed round. It was something new to me. . . . People seemed to enjoy religion more in them days than they do now. They were glad to see each other and enjoyed themselves better than they do now.[222]

Frequent trips to a mill were necessary to grind the family's grain, as mold made long-term storage impossible. Abraham took the family's grain to a watermill down by Posey's place toward the Ohio, a round-trip of about thirty-five miles, and to a closer, horse-powered mill about two miles from the Lincoln farm.[223] Not everyone enjoyed such a chore. A pioneer looking back on his childhood complained: "I'd have what I called mill pains, I dreaded it so. I was always worried for fear that big homemade linen bag, with the corn held in either end, might catch on a limb or snag and rip open, or the horse would stumble and throw me and the bag off. I wasn't big enough to hoppus the bag up on my shoulder and throw it across the horse's back. Then there was the brush swipin you in the face, and the shyin and snortin of the horse at every wild thing that moved."[224] Lincoln, however, welcomed mill trips.[225] "Abe'd come home with enough news an' yarns to last a week," Denny allegedly said.[226] He definitely noted that "the mill was a poor concern. It was a little bit of a hand horse mill, the ground meal of which a hound could eat as fast as it was ground."[227]

One day Lincoln suffered a nearly fatal accident there. The mill was powered by a horse that walked around and around in a circle, attached to the mill apparatus, with its speed of walking determining the speed of milling. There was no mill horse per se; mill customers provided their own horsepower. Nine-year-old Abraham hooked up his mare, which had already traveled the distance to the mill, and began urging it along with a stick or whip administered with a frequent cry of "Get up, you lazy old devil." Apparently the horse objected to Lincoln's prodding, eventually kicking him in the forehead as he said, "Get up," cutting off his command and inflicting a terrible injury that rendered him unconscious and bleeding. He later said that he was "apparently killed for a time." Tom Lincoln was sent for, and he brought his son home in a wagon. After a few hours, Abe awoke with a jerk, finishing the sentence he had been speaking when kicked.

The injury left a skull malformation readily evident to a physician who, many years later, examined life masks made of the adult Lincoln. The physician attributed subsequent differences in eye and facial muscle functioning on the left and right sides to this injury and noted, "Electronic recording has now shown that an appalling amount of damage to the brain, heretofore unsuspected, follows from blows on the head, at the point of impact and from hydrostatic repercussion (contra-coup), and through the production of numerous, small (petechial) internal hemorrhages as well as subdural blood clots, without external evidence of fracture." Lincoln found the experience fascinating and in later years routinely discussed it with Billy Herndon.[228]

When Thomas returned to the Indiana homestead with his new wife and her three children, the combined family now amounted to eight persons (including Denny Hanks) who had to live off the land and from what income they could earn through odd jobs in the district. Over the years, some cabin residents married and moved out, and Denny's half-brother John moved in.[229] Authorities disagree on how many relatives resided in the cabin,[230] but at times it was crowded.

As in Kentucky, farming didn't yield enough income. Denny Hanks described the farm as about twenty cultivated acres producing barely enough for the family and generally no surplus that could be sold.[231] A family member recalled a day with "nothing for dinner but roasted potatoes. After Grandpa [Tom] Lincoln got through returning thanks (which duty he never neglected—if he only had dry bread or potatoes he would ask the same blessing when he sat down to eat). So this time Uncle Abram put on a long face, and looked up at his father and [said], 'Papa, I call these (meaning the potatoes) very poor blessings.'"[232]

Tom Lincoln continued to work as a carpenter and cabinetmaker.[233] Denny Hanks purportedly declared: "Thar wasn't sca'cely any nails in the kentry an' little iron, except in knives and guns an' cookin' pots. Tom's tools was a wonder to the hull deestrict."[234] Neighbor Samuel Crawford remembered, "Mr. Thomas Lincoln was a good carpenter, and made the cupboard, mantels, doors, and sashes in our old home."[235] According to neighbor William Wood: "Thomas Lincoln often and at various times worked for me, made cupboards and other household furniture for me. He built my house, made floors, run up the stairs, did all the inside work for my house. Abe would come to my house with his father and play and romp with my children."[236] Abraham did carpentry as well.[237]

Financial necessity required cabin inhabitants, male and female, to hire out whenever feasible. Of such work, Lincoln said with a resentful tone: "I was given the subjects which only a man should undertake at fifteen. I was as well able and as strong for any labor as I have ever been at nineteen."[238] We have excellent reason to believe that money earned by Abraham's labor went to his father. In that era, a father had legal claim on his children's earnings until they reached the age of twenty-one. Indeed, loss of earnings that a father could have received from a daughter's employment was classic grounds in suing a male for having had sexual intercourse with an unmarried minor who became pregnant.[239] The importance of a father's claim on a minor's earnings cannot be overemphasized in a biography of Lincoln. Abe's earnings, mostly through the hardest kind of physical labor, passed to his father. Resentment over this may well have colored their relationship. Such resentment may have helped make Lincoln's hatred of chattel slavery visceral rather than simply moral. When the time came, he probably relished the opportunity to strike blows against the institution. In 1864, he declared: "If slavery is not wrong, nothing is wrong. I cannot remember when I did not so think, and feel."[240]

Elizabeth Crawford recalled when Lincoln would come over to work for her husband, Blue Nose: "He would stop at the door, raise his hat, make a bow, and speak politely; and when invited, step in and set down if not in a hurry to go to work. If so, he would pass compliments in a plain but polite and friendly way and go to his work. He was no hand to pitch in at work like killing snakes, but he would take hold of his work as calmly and pleasant as his manner was." Elizabeth saw the two men engage in horseplay: "Sometimes my husband would trip him as he would walk out, and then they would have a scuffle in the yard before they would go to work, and it was a tight scuffle. Sometimes Lincoln would throw Mr. Crawford, and sometimes Crawford would get the best of him. They were always joking or playing some prank on each other when they were out together."[241] Women on farms where Lincoln labored noted that he would, unasked, fill a bucket with water or bring along some firewood when he came in for the noon or evening meal.[242]

As a teenager, Abe Lincoln was physically formidable, better proportioned than in his Illinois years. "Physically he was a stout and powerful boy," Denny said, "round, plump, and well made."[243] Lincoln's stepmother noted that "he was more fleshy in Indiana than ever in Illinois," and added, "He always had good health, never was sick."[244] Nat Grigsby said likewise: "He was always in good health, never was sick, had an excellent constitution and took care of it."[245] According to a neighbor, "He was quick and moved with energy."[246] Abe engaged in sports that tested his mettle as much as his skill, such as wrestling and maul tossing.[247] By stature, he was a natural for earning money through hard labor that might intimidate even the hardy pioneers of that time. "Abe could sink an axe deeper in wood than any man I ever saw," remembered one Indiana neighbor. "He could strike with a maul a heavier blow than any man."[248] Denny Hanks declared, "If you heard him fellin' trees in a clearin' you would say there were three men at work."[249] Another neighbor recalled a particular incident: "We had a corn crib put up, of large round logs. The building was so arranged that it required large posts . . . and they lay some distance off. . . . Some of the men commenced preparing sticks to carry them. But young Lincoln told them that if they would assist him to get them on his shoulder he would carry them to the place, which he did to the astonishment of all present."[250] The same neighbor watched him "carry a chicken house made of poles pinned together and covered that weighed at least 600" pounds.[251]

Despite his excellent physical condition, Abe apparently disliked physical labor. "Abe was awful lazy," a neighbor declared. "He worked for me, was always reading and thinking—used to get mad at him. . . . Didn't love work but did dearly love his pay. . . . Lincoln said to me one day that his father taught him to work but never learned him to love it."[252] Lincoln's stepmother shrewdly observed, "He didn't like physical labor—was diligent for knowledge—wished to know, and if pains and labor would get it, he was sure to get it."[253] Unlike some of his associates, she understood that the boy was not at all lazy; his work was a kind of labor that went unrecognized by neighbors[254] and, for now, involved no financial remuneration. An Illinois resident described the situation in one home around 1822:

> I looked to see if there were any books—an old almanac, begrimed and greasy, hanging against the wall, was all the literature offered. But Jesse and Peggy "didn't want books"; did not think it was of "any use to be allus reading"; "didn't think folks was any better off for reading, an' books cost a heap and took a power of time"; "twant so bad for men to read, for there was a heap of time when they couldn't work out, and could jest set by the fire; and if a man had books and keered to read he mought; but women had no business to hurtle away their time, case they could allus find something to du, and there had

been a heap of trouble in old Kaintuck with some rich men's gals that had learned to write. They was sent to school, and were high larnt, and cud write letters almost as well as a man, and would write to the young fellows, and, bless your soul, get a match fixed up before their father or mother knowed half about it." Such were Jesse's honest sentiments, and such was the standard of at least nine-tenths of the inhabitants that were our neighbors.[255]

In a comment revealing as much about herself as about her stepson, Sarah Bush Johnston Lincoln said, "He was the best boy I ever saw. He read all the books he could lay his hands on."[256] Testimony conflicts on whether Tom Lincoln was supportive of this endeavor. Denny told of Tom's "having sometimes to slash him for neglecting his work by reading."[257] A neighbor saw the contrary: "When Abe was reading his father made it a rule never to ask him to lay down his book. No difference what was to do, but let him read until he saw fit to lay it by himself."[258] Abe's stepmother reported: "Mr. Lincoln never made Abe quit reading to do anything if he could avoid it. He would do it himself first. Mr. [Thomas] Lincoln could read a little and could scarcely write his name. Hence he wanted, as he himself felt the uses and necessities of education, his boy Abraham to learn; and he encouraged him to do it in all ways he could."[259]

Long afterward, Lincoln's attorney colleague Leonard Swett recalled, "He said to me that he had got hold of and read through every book he ever heard of in that country for a circuit of about fifty miles."[260] Not literally true perhaps, but true enough. Denny Hanks described Lincoln as "hungry for books."[261] Hungry enough that a promise of access to a book could motivate him into doing work he would otherwise prefer to avoid.[262] "He read diligently," his stepmother said. "Studied in the daytime, didn't after night much. Went to bed early, got up early and then read. . . . Abe read all the books he could lay his hands on, and when he came across a passage that struck him, he would write it down on boards if he had no paper and keep it there till he did get paper. Then he would rewrite it, look at it, repeat it."[263]

The same process happened in face-to-face encounters. According to his stepmother: "Abe, when old folks were at our house, was a silent and attentive observer—never speaking or asking questions till they were gone, and then he must understand everything, even to the smallest thing, minutely and exactly. He would then repeat it over to himself again and again, sometimes in one form and then in another. . . . Sometimes he seemed pestered to give expression to his ideas and got mad almost at one who couldn't explain plainly what he wanted to convey."[264] Years later, someone reported a conversation with Lincoln that confirmed what his stepmother said:

> I remember how, when a mere child, I used to get irritated when anybody talked to me in a way I could not understand. I don't think I ever got angry at anything else in my life. But that always disturbed

my temper, and has ever since. I can remember going to my little bedroom, after hearing the neighbors talk of an evening with my father, and spending no small part of the night . . . trying to make out what was the exact meaning of some of their, to me, dark sayings. I could not sleep, though I often tried to, when I got on such a hunt after an idea, until I had caught it; and when I thought I had got it, I was not satisfied until I had repeated it over and over, until I had put it in language plain enough, as I thought, for any boy I knew to comprehend. This was a kind of passion with me, and it has stuck by me, for I am never easy now, when I am handling a thought, till I have bounded it north and bounded it south and bounded it east and bounded it west.[265]

And what did he read? "Abe read the Bible some," his stepmother reported, "though not as much as said. He sought more congenial books, suitable for his age."[266] Denny Hanks, John Hanks, stepsister Tilda, and others remembered Lincoln reading Aesop's fables, *Pilgrim's Progress*, *Robinson Crusoe*, a biography of Henry Clay ("Harry of the West," whose destiny was always to almost be President), and Weems's biography of Washington—and having a retentive memory for what he read.[267] According to one account, Denny Hanks supposedly remembered Abe reading *Sinbad the Sailor* out loud:

[It was] about a feller that got near some darned fool rocks 'at drawed all the nails out o' his boat an' he got a duckin'. Wasn't a blamed bit o' sense in that yarn. . . . Abe'd lay on his stummick by the fire, an' read out loud to me 'n' Aunt Sairy, an' we'd laugh when he did, though I reckon it went in at one ear an' out at the other with her, as it did with me. Tom'd come in an' say: "See here, Abe, your mammy kain't work with you a botherin' her like that"; but Aunt Sairy always said it didn't bother her none, an' she'd tell Abe to go on. I reckon that encouraged Abe a heap.

"Abe," sez I, many a time, "them yarns is all lies."

"Mighty darned good lies," he'd say, an' go on readin' an' chucklin' to hisself, till Tom'd kiver up the fire fur the night an' shoo him off to bed.[268]

Perhaps above all else, young Abraham Lincoln sought newspapers. "Abe was a constant reader of them," his stepmother said.[269] In 1824, the *Vincennes Western Sun* was strong for the presidential candidacy of U.S. Rep. Henry Clay, printing copious quantities of his speeches. Was that coverage connected with Lincoln's decision to read a Clay biography? Denny reportedly said, "We'd git holt of a newspaper onct in a while, an' Abe'd l'arn Henry Clay's speeches by heart."[270] The boy frequently borrowed the *New York Telescope* from a neighbor,[271] a newspaper emphasizing religion, with a smattering of literature and current events. John Hanks recalled: "[When] Abe and I returned to the house from work, he would go to the cupboard, snatch a piece of cornbread, take down a book. Sit down on a chair, cock his legs up as high as his head and read."[272] Denny purportedly declared: "I've seen many a feller come in an' look at him, Abe not knowin' anybody was 'round, an' sneak out ag'in like a cat, an' say: 'Well, I'll be darned!' It didn't seem natural, nohow, to see a feller read like that. Aunt Sairy'd never let the children pester him."[273]

Abe would read books owned by neighbor Blue Nose Crawford. According to Blue Nose's wife: "When he worked for us he . . . would sit up late in the night, kindle up the fire, read by it, cipher by it. We had a broad wooden shovel on which Abe would work out his sums, wipe off and repeat till it got too black for more. Then he would scrape and wash off, and repeat again and again."[274] She remembered, "Whenever he would get hold of a new book he would examine it, and if he thought it a good work and would be an advantage to him to read it, he would do so; but if not, he would close it up and smile and say, 'I don't think this would pay to read it,' or words to that amount, and get something else."[275] Blue Nose once loaned David Ramsay's biography of Washington. The book got wet from rain in the Lincoln cabin. How much damage it suffered is uncertain, but it was enough to be noticeable. Abraham pulled fodder for about three days to pay for the book, at the rate of 25 cents' credit per day.[276] One neighbor asserted that "Lincoln I know felt wronged" by the amount of labor demanded by Blue Nose, and a Lincoln relative concurred.[277] Supposedly Lincoln wrote some verse in retaliation, calling Crawford "Old Blue Nose," a rhyme enjoyed so much by the neighborhood that the nickname stuck.[278] Denny, however, put it in a genial context, calling it "a piece of humorous rhyme on his friend Josiah Crawford that made all the neighbors, Crawford included, burst their sides with laughter."[279] Indeed, another version of the book incident says that although Lincoln had paid in full for the volume, he wanted to do more—not in compensation but in gratitude, because he cherished the book. Having heard Elizabeth Crawford say that she would like to have a corner cupboard, he got Tom's assent to fabricate one for her. Working together, father and son crafted a seven-foot-tall piece of furniture, solid walnut, hefting over three hundred pounds, with paneling and decorative carving.[280] Abraham also fashioned for himself a small cabinet of walnut and poplar, about two feet high and not quite a foot and a half wide, wherein he could store his books and writings safe from cabin leaks.[281]

In Gentryville, Abe would borrow books and newspapers from merchants William Jones and James Gentry (Gentry helped Tom Lincoln acquire government-guaranteed title to the Lincoln farm).[282] Young John Lamar and his father encountered Abraham in town or nearby (the story has several versions), reading or ciphering so intently that he did not notice the two pass by. Duly impressed, the father declared: "Son, look at that boy. He will make a mark in the world. He either works or reads. He never wastes a minute!"[283] John Lamar reflected, "There was one thing about the man that anybody could see, and that is he was determined to make something of himself."[284] "The ambition of the man soared above us," Nat Grigsby said.[285] Neighbor Absolom Roby reminisced: "I predicted in 1827, if not sooner, that Abe would cut a figure in this world, chance or no chance. I thought this, taking what he was, what he said and did, etc."[286] Blue Nose Crawford's wife recalled: "Abe Lincoln was one day bothering the girls—his sister and others playing yonder—and his sister scolded him, saying, 'Abe, you ought to be ashamed of yourself. What do you expect will become of you?' 'Be President of the United States,' promptly responded Abe."[287] Such comment may have been good-humored, but some old acquaintances said it was not facetious.[288] Later, in the White House, Lincoln remarked to Ward Hill Lamon, "You know better than any man living that from my boyhood up my ambition was to be President."[289]

Young Lincoln did not keep his learning to himself, but began expressing his thoughts in oral communication that arrested the attention of hearers. His step-mother told of "speeches such as interested him and the children. His father had to make him quit sometimes, as he quit his own work to speak, and made the other children, as well as the men, quit their work."[290] Stepsister Tilda also reported, "His father would come and make him quit."[291] Abe may simply have been choosing times when a ready-made audience was available, but I wonder whether he enjoyed flexing a power that made others stop what they were doing. Denny Hanks reported that the teenager "could hear a sermon, speech, or remark, and repeat it accurately. He would go home from the church, say to the boys and girls that he could repeat the sermon—got on stumps, logs, fences—and do it well and accurately. Old people have heard him do it o'er and o'er again. . . . Lincoln would frequently make political and other speeches to the boys. He was calm, log-ical, and clear always."[292] John Hanks and others said likewise.[293] Abe would repeat sermons, courtroom addresses, political stump speeches. His mimicry of speeches he had heard was precise not only in content, but also down to a speaker's accent and even the way he moved his eyes.[294]

He also began expressing himself in writing that he shared with the public. There was the rhyme about Blue Nose Crawford. At possibly the age of fourteen, he wrote a composition he prized so highly that he kept it for years. His Illinois friend William Greene remembered Lincoln reading it to him in the 1830s: "It was full of wit, and I pronounced [it] a good thing."[295] According to Indiana neighbor William Wood: "Abe wrote poetry a good deal . . . [including] one piece which was entitled the 'Neighborhood Broil.' Abe always brought his pieces, prose or poetry, to me straight."[296] He also wrote a satirical poem about a ribald comment made by a male neighbor to a woman, a comment to which the woman's husband took enough offense that a church trial resulted.[297]

From a biographical standpoint, one of his most interesting writings was, paradoxically, a story he never wrote. On a lazy, rainy day in Springfield, with his feet propped on a windowsill, he turned to a friend and asked:

> Did you ever write out a story in your mind? I did when I was a little codger. One day a wagon with a lady and two girls and a man broke down near us, and while they were fixing up, they cooked in our kitchen. The woman had books and read us stories, and they were the

first I had ever heard. I took a great fancy to one of the girls; and when they were gone I thought of her a great deal, and one day when I was sitting out in the sun by the house, I wrote out a story in my mind. I thought I took my father's horse and followed the wagon, and finally I found it, and they were surprised to see me. I talked with the girl and persuaded her to elope with me, and that night I put her on my horse, and we started off across the prairie. After several hours we came to a camp; and when we rode up we found it was the one we had left a few hours before, and we went in. The next night we tried again, and the same thing happened—the horse came back to the same place; and then we concluded that we ought not to elope. I stayed until I had persuaded her father to give her to me. I always meant to write that story out and publish it, and I began once; but I concluded that it was not much of a story.[298]

That tale's dreamlike quality invites psychological analysis. One examiner found the story to demonstrate Abraham's self-reliance while still respecting Tom Lincoln's authority. Evidence was also seen of free communication between mother and son, and that the son had a persuasive ability over his sister—and his father as well. The analyst concluded, "With all their hardships, the Lincolns were a happy, peaceful family."[299]

The teenager did serious writing as well. Neighbor Wood recalled "a piece on national politics, saying that the American government was the best form of government in the world for an intelligent people, that it ought to be kept sound and preserved forever. That general education should be fostered and carried all over the country. That the Constitution should be saved, the Union perpetuated, and the laws revered, respected, and enforced." Wood showed the piece to a circuit-riding attorney who was spending the night at Wood's house. "He read it carefully and asked me where I got it. I told him that one of my neighbor boys wrote it. He couldn't believe it." The attorney declared, "'The world can't beat it.' He begged for it. I gave it to him and it was published." The young lawyer, John Pitcher, would later start loaning law books to the teenager. Wood wrote of another incident:

I took newspapers. . . . One of these papers was a temperance paper. Abe used to borrow it, take it home and read it and talk it over with me. He was an intelligent boy, a sensible lad I assure you. One day Abe wrote a piece on temperance and brought it to my house. I read it carefully over and over, and the piece excelled for sound sense anything that my paper contained. I gave the article to one Aaron Farmer, a Baptist preacher. He read it. It struck him. He said he wanted it to send to a temperance paper in Ohio for publication; it was sent and published. I saw the printed piece.[300]

Even general periodicals opened their columns to such material by various authors. Mimicking a runaway slave ad, one Indiana newspaper item said:

> 1000 Dollars Reward. Ranaway from the subscriber, within a few years, his whole estate; consisting of houses, lands, &c. They gradually and almost imperceptibly stole away after being put in motion by the magic art of INTEMPERENCE, who lived in the vicinity. Any person who will put me in possession of said estate, shall be entitled to the above reward.
>   Toper.
>   ☞All persons are cautioned to beware of said Intemperance, who, as I am told, has established several places of rendezvous through the country, where numbers of the incautious are daily seduced.[301]

Neighbors routinely came to the boy, asking him to write correspondence for them.[302] A friend reported that Lincoln said he "learned to see other people's thoughts and feelings and ideas by writing their friendly confidential letters."[303] Neighborhood folk considered Abraham a fine penman. One admiring lad asked for a sample, and Abe wrote out for him, "Good boys who to their books apply/ Will all be great men by and by."[304]

Lincoln began going to court trials, at both the lowest level, the justice of the peace court, and the next-higher level of county circuit courts. An observer in one Indiana court recalled, "As I entered the court-room, the judge was sitting on a block, paring his toenails, when the sheriff entered, out of breath, and informed the court that he had six jurors tied, and his deputies were running down the others."[305] A prosecutor recalled that at Fall Creek, Indiana, "The court was held in a double log cabin, the grand jury sat upon a log in the woods, and the foreman signed the bills of indictment which I had prepared, upon his knee; there was not a petit juror that had shoes on—all wore moccasins, and were belted around the waist, and carried side-knives used by the hunter."[306]

Whatever the physical environs, circuit courts had formal dockets. One month's docket for a district in that era listed two cases for selling horses that did not belong to the seller, one rape, one adultery, two bigamy, two divorce, two assault and battery, and one slander, as well as twenty-five prosecutions for profanity.[307] These were typical, but an occasional case of greater import would arise. Supposedly young attorney John Brackenridge noticed Abraham's intent observation of a murder case the lawyer was handling, but apparently he was unable to be as gracious as he might have been in accepting a compliment afterward from such a rustic-appearing youth. Many years later, they crossed paths in the White House, where Lincoln told Brackenridge: "It was the best speech that I, up to that time, ever heard. If I could, as I then thought, make as good a speech as that . . . my soul would be satisfied." The story goes that Abraham declared that the trial had persuaded him to become a lawyer.[308] Brackenridge reportedly was not the only person who noticed the lad's rapt attention at trials.[309]

Attendance at court was a common recreational pastime for rural folk, but Lincoln did more than just attend. He began reading statute texts, an uncommon activity indeed among his neighbors.[310] The edition of Indiana statutes he used also contained the Declaration of Independence, Ordinance of 1787, and U.S. Constitution,[311] three documents that would eventually intertwine intimately with his life. He sought to study law with John Pitcher, the lawyer who had been so impressed by Abraham's essay on national politics, but Tom Lincoln told him he was needed too urgently for other tasks.[312] Nonetheless, by the age of seventeen or eighteen, Abe was informally representing neighbors and winning cases at justice of the peace trials,[313] where regulations were relaxed enough to allow appearance by someone not admitted to the bar. Whether he was getting fees for such work is less certain, as accepting compensation might have opened him to punishment for practicing law without a license.[314]

According to one story, in his very earliest cases he exhibited a trait that would be noticed and commented on during his years as an Illinois lawyer—a preference to discourage litigation and settle disputes out of court. Two neighbors went to court over ownership of a goose worth 25 cents, and a good crowd turned out for the trial. Before proceedings commenced, Lincoln arose and argued that everyone had more to lose than to gain by proceeding with a trial that was bound to cement hard feelings; instead, the two disputants should pause and consider the paltry sum at issue and simply shake hands and stop any more fussing. The litigants took the advice and dropped the matter before trial.[315] Such courtroom work must have been a godsend to an intellectual youth otherwise condemned to hard manual labor. I wonder whether Tom Lincoln's veto of law studies deepened whatever resentments a teenage boy felt toward his father.

If a person read a lot, uneducated persons of that era tended to ascribe the activity to laziness.[316] For example, Denny Hanks, whose love for Abraham is unquestioned, said, "Lincoln was lazy, a very lazy man. He was always reading, scribbling, writing, ciphering, writing poetry."[317] Someone familiar with those general times noted: "Anyone who was given to idleness was called a lazy hound and was looked upon with contempt. In fact it was such an odium to be called an indolent, lazy body that the ones so inclined were soon frozen out or talked out and moved away."[318] This did not happen to Lincoln, however. Quite the contrary. Part of the reason may have been the kind of books he would read to the boys in the woods, away from the grownups and womenfolk. One such volume was *Quinn's Jests*, with jokes already old in that era, but including ribald humor of apparently everlasting interest to men.[319] "It is not strange to me that Mr. Lincoln should have such a great passion for dirty stories," an Illinois friend said. "It was his early training by the Hanks boys."[320]

Abraham was well liked anyway, but such demonstrations of the value of reading surely helped establish him as a person worth listening to, whether the topic was light or serious. In Gentryville, "when he appeared in company," Nat Grigsby recalled, "the boys would gather and cluster around him to hear him talk. . . . Mr. Lincoln was figurative in his speeches, talks, and conversation. He argued much from analogy, and explained things hard for us to understand by stories, maxims, tales, and figures. He would almost always point his lesson or idea by some story that was plain and near, as that we might instantly see the force and bearing of what he said."[321] Neighbor Katie Roby said, "He took great pains to explain, could do it so simply."[322] Her father Absolom similarly stated, "He understood a thing thoroughly and could explain so clearly."[323] When Lincoln started talking, Denny Hanks said, "all the people in town would gather around him. He would keep them there till midnight or longer telling stories, cracking jokes, and running rigs [i.e., bantering], etc. I would get tired, want to go home, cuss Abe etc. most heartily."[324]

Denny was struck by Lincoln's rigid truthfulness, "speaking it at all times and never flinching therefrom."[325] The phrase "never flinching" is revealing. Years later, in courts and in the great political discussions he led, again and again he stated conclusions impelled by logic no matter how unpalatable they might be. For Lincoln, this dedication was not a question of morality, but of facing realities rather than pretending they didn't exist. He acted as if he believed that recognizing and acting upon truth gave people an advantage in confronting life's challenges. "Never evaded," his stepmother said. "Never equivocated, never dodged."[326] Neighbors recognized such honesty; one noted, "Men would swear on his simple word."[327]

Probably due in part to his routine expressions of commonsense logic, he became a peacemaker in Indiana just as he had been in Kentucky. "He scarcely ever quarreled," companion Nat Grigsby said.[328] John Hanks asserted that Lincoln "settled the disputes of all the young men in the neighborhood, and his decisions were always abided by."[329] The wife of Blue Nose Crawford said that "while other boys would quarrel he would appear to be a peacemaker."[330] And according to Denny Hanks, "All the family disputes were referred to Abraham."[331]

The whiffs of incest in the Hanks clan of Kentucky continued in Indiana. In 1821, Denny Hanks, who was a cousin to both Abe and Abe's mother, Nancy Hanks, married Abraham's fifteen-year-old stepsister Elizabeth Johnston. Prior to that marriage, Denny and Elizabeth had been living in the Lincoln cabin's close quarters for quite some time.

When Abraham was an older teenager, exuding manliness and hormones, his sixteen-year-old stepsister Tilda reportedly began exibiting more than sisterly interest in him. I say "reportedly" because Billy Herndon's notes of his conversation years later with Tilda are inconsistent with his subsequent personal notes on the topic, and those later notes (along with Weik's version in the biography he coauthored with Billy) have been extrapolated upon. The topic merits examination here.

In an 1865 conversation in the home of Abraham's stepmother, and in the stepmother's presence, Tilda said, "Once when he was going to the field I ran, jumped on his back, cut my foot on the axe." Period.[332] Billy Herndon's undated, but obviously subsequent, personal notes are much richer in detail. Where that detail came from is unknown. From Tilda? From another family member? From details of the Tilda conversation that he remembered but didn't write down at the time? From plausible guesswork that drew on what he knew to be fact? Although he had a fondness for writing suppositions about Lincoln, Herndon's writings normally distinguish between what he believed and what he personally witnessed. He is known for mistakes, but not for lies. Here is what Billy said to himself in his personal notes:

> Mrs. Lincoln, a good old lady, and mother of 'Tilda, began to think that the two young ones should not run so wild in the forests together and alone; and therefore, to stop all possible tattle in the neighborhood, she told 'Tilda that she must not any more go into the forests to carry Abraham his usual dinner, that she must cook his dinner before she [*sic*, he?] went into the woods and hand it to him when he started out for his day's work. . . . 'Tilda soon grew tired of her restraint. Abraham one morning ground his ax sharp and keen, put the maul and ax on his shoulder, and taking his dinner in the basket on his arm and so marched on into the forests with the maul, ax, and wedges, full of life and fun, not dreaming of 'Tilda's intentions. He wended his way southward down the cattle, hog, and deer paths to his place of cutting and felling trees preparatory to the making of the rails. 'Tilda that morning was determined to go into the woods and have a good long chat and a wild romp with Abraham. When Lincoln had traveled some three or four hundred yards from the house, 'Tilda ran quickly along the path in a silent and somewhat stealthy manner, and, all at once and unexpectedly to Abraham, she bounced [*sic*] on his back like a panther, putting her knees in the small of Abraham's back and locking her hands around his neck, and then threw Abraham down on his back, his face to the sun and his spine to the ground. In the fall of Abraham the pole of the ax fell on the ground and the sharp keen edge upward. In pulling Abraham backward, 'Tilda fell on the sharp keen edge of the ax and cut herself badly and quite severely; he was astonished at the bound and trick of the girl but he quickly saw that his sister had cut herself severely and seriously, if not fatally. Abraham and 'Tilda were both frightened. Abraham tore off the tail of his undergarment, for it was all he had to tear or use on that occasion. By Abraham's good sense, care, and attention, and a little skill, he closed the wound and staunched the blood. The wound was a deep wide gaping wound in the thigh near an artery.[333]

Such a story is so entertaining that I'd like to believe it. I wonder if Tilda related what Lincoln told her about his thoughts as he walked into the woods. I wonder whether a woodsman as experienced as he would not have heard someone running up behind him. I wonder if he wore an undergarment. I wonder about other aspects of the narrative as well. Weik's version adds details not found in Billy's and locates the wound on her ankle.[334] The story as told by Herndon and Weik has been used to read a component of sexual attraction into the encounter.[335] The story as told by Tilda is simply a brief mention of adolescent stupidity, followed by a discussion between her and Abraham about what to tell Sarah Bush Johnston Lincoln. Tilda said she was in favor of massaging the truth, but Abe insisted on saying exactly what happened.[336] Ah, if only *we* knew exactly what happened! In 1826, Tilda married Denny Hanks's half-brother Squire Hall.[337]

Women found Lincoln attractive, but supposedly he was not interested in them.[338] His brother-in-law Nat Grigsby may have inadvertently explained that reputation by saying, "He also attended places of amusements but not places of vice."[339] In other words, he did not go whoring. The robust crowd he ran with may well have misinterpreted his aversion to promiscuity as aversion to women. Although his stepmother said that "he was not very fond of girls,"[340] actually he routinely escorted young women to various gatherings.[341] "He was not a timid man in this particular," John Hanks said, "but did not seek such company."[342] Neighbor Katie Roby said he thought girls were "too frivolous."[343] Abe's stepmother commented that while her own boy John Johnston was attending dances, Abraham was attending to his studies.[344]

During a political excursion to Indiana in the 1840s, Lincoln reminisced about a teenage experience in Princeton. "I rode there from my home across the country on a flea-bitten gray mare, with a bunch of wool which my mother had sent along to have carded. . . . While waiting for the wool carder I strolled about the village and happened to pass on the street a very beautiful girl—the most bewitching creature it seemed to me I had ever seen. My heart was in a flutter. The truth is, I was so thoroughly captivated by the vision of maidenly beauty that I wanted to stop in Princeton forever." He was interested enough to find out her name, Julia Evans, before he returned to the carding operation, where he asked more about her. There he learned she was the niece of the carding operation's owner. The owner's brother, though Lincoln may not have learned this, wrote articles for the New Harmony newspaper. "When I finally overcome [*sic*] my passionate yearning and set out on the long journey homeward it was with the fixed purpose to return," Lincoln reminisced. He did not return, "but so deep an impression had the Princeton girl made on me I remember it was several years before her image was effaced from my mind and heart."[345] Which is not to say he was pining away.

Abraham's older sister Sally was growing up. "Short built," John Hanks said, "eyes dark grey, hair dark brown."[346] In the eyes of their old Kentucky playmate Austin Gollaher, "She was a very pretty girl."[347]

One neighbor declared that "Sarah Lincoln had a good mind."[348] Another neighbor recalled: "Sally was a quick-minded woman and of extraordinary mind. She was industrious, more so than Abraham. Abe worked almost alone from the head, whilst she labored both. Her good humored laugh I can see now, is as fresh in my mind as if it were yesterday. She could, like her brother Abe, meet and greet a person with the very kindest greeting in the world, make you easy at the touch and word."[349]

In that era, the basic outline of a typical frontier girl's life was apparent from birth, but Sally Lincoln's parents sought to give her as much formal education as Abraham received.[350] The amount was modest even by standards of that time, but she received as much as her younger brother did. She did not, however, share his thirst for learning. Denny Hanks allegedly observed that Abe "tried to inter*est* little Sairy in l'arnin' to read, but she never tuk to it."[351]

Sally supplemented family income by hiring out to Blue Nose Crawford's household. His wife, Elizabeth, described her as "a good, kind, amiable girl."[352] Crawford's son Samuel recalled: "One day I ran in calling out, 'Mother! mother! Aaron Grigsby is sparking Sally Lincoln; I saw him kiss her!' Mother scolded me, and told me I must stop watching Sally, or I wouldn't get to the wedding."[353]

Aaron Grigsby was the son of a prominent farmer, member of the district's upper social circle.[354] Sally was marrying "up," as might be said. Whatever disparities existed between the Lincolns and the Grigsbys, their membership in the Little Pigeon Baptist Church shows that they shared some common values, not just Christianity, but also points of doctrine that were hotly disputed among various sects. Sally was nineteen years old, a mature bride for that era.

At the August 1826 wedding, the Lincoln family sang a little song, apparently attributed to Abraham by some in the neighborhood, but it probably was not an original composition.[355] The title was "Adam and Eve's Wedding Song," and it told of the need for a wife to avoid bossing her husband and the husband to avoid mistreating his wife.[356] The little performance had to have been in good cheer; I can't imagine the Lincoln clan doing anything intended to spoil Sally's big day. The couple had a traditional infare dinner,[357] a formal reception given to newlyweds at the residence of the groom's father the day after a wedding. Given the prosperity of the bridegroom's father, the infare must have provided a good spread. A pioneer of that era wrote:

> Weddings, commonly in the day time were scenes of carousal, and of mirth and merriment of no very chastened character. The "infare" of the following day presented on the winding road through the green woods a long and picturesque cavalcade, in which the cavalier and his "lady love" were paired off with the groom and bride in the van. At the house of *his* father the scenes of the preceding day were re-enacted, with such new accompaniments as new members of the company could suggest, or the inventions of a night of excited genius had brought forth.[358]

Relations remained close between Abe and his sister. He would go over to Sally's home and start shenanigans when some of the Grigsby boys were around.

She would scold him and get the reply, "Oh, you be good yourself, Sally, and Abe will take care of himself."[359]

How the marriage seemed to outsiders is unclear. One person spoke of Aaron's "cruel treatment"[360] of Sally, but that comment came from someone born twenty years after the fact and is uncorroborated. Nonetheless, something happened that was bad enough to cause public hard feelings between the Lincolns and the Grigsbys, although we don't know the source of the feud.[361]

In January 1828, Sally took to bed to give birth to her first child. The experience did not go well. An attending midwife, apparently Sally's mother-in-law, Nancy Grigsby, became overwhelmed by complications. Nancy's niece recalled: "My mother was there at the time. She had a very strong voice, and I heard her calling father. He awoke the boys and said, 'Something is the matter.'" The Grigsbys decided to bring in a doctor to whom the Lincolns objected, a doctor who reportedly was so drunk when he arrived that he had to be put to bed. One of the Grigsby men then headed off through an intense rain in the night, across Little Pigeon Creek to bring back another physician who was four miles away. Rising creek waters forced the two men to dodge around, looking for a crossing, adding more miles and time to the return trip. The infant was stillborn, and Sally was dead by the time the second doctor arrived. Nancy Grigsby's niece declared, "They let her lay too long." The niece's husband said, "This was a hard blow to Abe, who always thought her death was due to neglect."[362] Sally was twenty years old.

During the crisis, Abraham knew what was happening, realized he could do nothing to help his sister, and went to a smokehouse. Word was brought to him there. He sat down with his hands over his face, tears leaking through his fingers while his body shook.[363] Sally was remembered as a devout Baptist, and her body was interred in the Little Pigeon Baptist Church cemetery.[364] "Abe used to say he was glad Sairy had some good times," Denny puportedly said. "She married purty young an' died with her fust baby. I reckon it was like Nancy [Hanks Lincoln], she didn't have no sort o' keer."[365] The acute pain of loss must have gradually receded for Lincoln, but did memory of her ever bring him joy? Billy Herndon rarely heard him speak of her.[366]

Supposedly the experience with the drunken doctor further fueled Lincoln's interest in temperance.[367] Said someone in the *Vincennes Western Sun*:

> We say the times are grievous hard,
> And hard they are 'tis true;
> But drunkards, to your wives and babes
> They're harder made by you.[368]

In 1829, when two of Aaron's brothers married on the same day, the Lincolns were pointedly excluded from the infare.[369] Betsy Ray Grigsby, one of the brides, later recalled: "There was a big crowd and we did not finish eating until after dark. We played all that evening 'Old Sister Phoeby' and other kissing games."[370] After the infare, the couples spent that night in the father's residence, and reportedly Lincoln arranged for the two grooms to be sent to the beds of each other's bride, a switch that was quickly corrected but caused excitement.[371] Years later, one of the alleged victims, Betsy Ray Grigsby, genially asserted that the incident never occurred: "They said my man [Reuben Jr.] got into the wrong room, and Charles got into my room. But it wasn't so. Lincoln just wrote that for mischief. . . . Abe and my man often laughed about that."[372] Maybe they laughed together, and maybe they didn't.

What Lincoln wrote was "The Chronicles of Reuben." It made a big impression in the neighborhood. Said one resident, "This poem is remembered here in Indiana in scraps better than the Bible."[373] Forty years afterward, Elizabeth Crawford (who was a Grigsby in-law) was able instantly to recite part of it to Billy Herndon. Blushing, she stopped and said, "The poem is smutty, and I can't tell it to you." For the sake of history, though, she said she would recite it to her daughter-in-law, who would tell it to Elizabeth's son, who indeed sent it to Herndon. She did not claim to reproduce it perfectly in every detail but felt that she had it close enough.[374] We have reason to believe her claim, because she additionally gave her memory of a temperance song she called "John Adkinson's Lamentation." It is also known as "John Adkin's Farewell," and if her memory of the "Chronicles" is as good as her memory of "John Adkin's," her version is reliable.[375]

The chronicled Reuben Sr. was the Grigsby boys' father. The tale started out in a parody of King James Bible language. The narrator told of Reuben's great wealth and his sons' desire to find wives. The sons' reputation, however, was such that they had to travel to where they were unknown in order to find brides. Achieving success, they returned home to a great feasting with a multitude of guests. Music included Josiah (Blue Nose Crawford) blowing his bugle (which could mean either his horn or his nose, depending on how a reader chose to interpret the passage). When festivities ended that night, banquet waiters escorted the brides to their separate bedchambers. Then other waiters escorted the bridegrooms but in the darkness inadvertently deposited each with the other's bride. Talking with the waiters afterward, the bridegrooms' mother discovered the mistake and, dashing to one chamber, shouted to Reuben Jr., "You are in bed with Charles's wife!" Consternation and confusion erupted. There was also a poem, considered a subsequent chapter of the "Chronicles," that took on Aaron's brother Billy. In the following excerpt, keep in mind this is the recollection of someone forty years later, not a direct quotation from the original:

> . . . Reuben and Charles has married two girls
> But Billy has married a boy.
> The girls he had tried on every side
> But none could he get to agree.
> All was in vain. He went home again,
> And since that he is married to Naty.

So Billy and Naty agreed very well,
And Mama's well pleased at the match.
The egg it is laid, but Naty's afraid
The shell is so soft that it never will hatch.
But Betsy she said, "You cursed ball [bald?] head
My suitor you never can be.
Besides your low crotch proclaims you a botch
And that never can answer for me."

The poem's reference to homosexuality is extraordinarily rare for that era. Lincoln reportedly dropped the manuscript at a spot where one of the Grigsbys would find it.[376] The item was anonymous, but authorship was instantly attributed to him, as he had both a local literary reputation and some grievances.[377] He was known for writing similar pieces,[378] and there were no other likely suspects. Samuel Crawford, son of Blue Nose and husband of Aaron Grigsby's sister Nancy, carried the "Chronicles," including the poem, over to Gentryville and publicly read them. He recalled that Aaron's brother Red Grigsby "being present got very mad over it, but Naty who married Billy being present affirmed the same to be facts."[379]

Fussing grew intense enough to require a fistfight for the defense of honor. The countryside turned out to watch. "Strong men came, bullies came," recalled Aaron Grigsby's brother Nat. Lincoln was slated to settle matters with Billy Grigsby, but objection arose that the difference in their size precluded a fair match. Abe's stepbrother John Johnston then stepped in to handle Billy. One version says Lincoln served as second for Johnston, William Bolen as second for Grigsby; another account lists different names, but those details are small. "Seconds" made sure that rules of such an encounter were observed—partisan referees, as it were. Feelings were hot enough that Lincoln and Bolen got into an altercation, resulting in a dislocated shoulder for Bolen. One version says the principals, Johnston and Billy Grigsby, fought to a draw. Another version says Grigsby gave Johnston a beating described as "savage." Still another version says that as Johnston was getting the worse of it, Lincoln pulled Grigsby off, threw him into the crowd, "waved a bottle of whiskey over his head" and "swore he was the big buck at the lick," resulting in a general free-for-all.[380] Afterward Lincoln told Billy that though he might have been able to defeat Johnston, Lincoln could whip Billy. Billy suggested a match between the two but, to even the odds, proposed that they use pistols instead of fists. Now Lincoln backed off, saying the dispute wasn't worth getting killed. There the activity ended, regardless of whatever animosities lingered.[381] Anyone who achieved a standoff with the Grigsby clan was wise to call that outcome good enough. Someone named Grigsby in Spencer County encountered an

Old bear and a cub which seemed to be trying to move a heavy [tree] limb that had fallen. He shot at the bear, but only hit her in the top of the shoulder, not disabling her. Before he could reload, she came rushing at him. His dog caught the bear by the hind leg, but only stopped her for a moment, and then she came at the hunter with all the fury that a wounded bear could. The hunter clubbed his gun and there was a battle royal for some time, the dog doing his best to help his master in the fight.

Finally, the bear knocked the dog down and attempted to catch him by the throat with her mouth, when the hunter thrust his hunting knife into her heart.[382]

In addition to encountering death, Abraham Lincoln encountered madness. Matthew Gentry was a bright youth, son of James Gentry. Matthew suddenly went berserk, mutilating himself, attacking his father, and trying to murder his mother. Alarmed by the commotion, neighbors came on the run and helped tie him up. Still he struggled, screaming protests, uttering profanity, and laughing wildly, while fixing the crowd in his gaze. As the crisis and time passed, both the danger and Matthew's intellect lessened. In wonder, Lincoln would listen to Matthew at night, singing sadly, "far-distant," Lincoln said, "sweet, and lone; the funeral dirge it ever seemed of reason dead and gone." To Lincoln, this inexplicable loss of intelligence and communication, with a human being reduced to a mere animal, was more disturbing than death.[383] "O death!" Lincoln wrote, thinking of Matthew, "why dost thou tear more blest ones hence, and leave him ling'ring here?"[384]

Around 1826, at the mouth of Anderson's River on the Ohio River, Lincoln found some escape from farm labor. A visitor en route to Illinois recalled "Anderson's river, from fifty to sixty yards wide." Nearby, "the soil was so rich that the Indian corn was the largest I have ever seen. . . . I should judge the highest of it was from fourteen to sixteen feet. There were great quantities of beans, pompions, and melons, running on and between the corn, all very luxuriant."[385] Here was a depot for river traffic, a landing for steamboat fueling and for loading corn and pork. Here was a little interaction, at least, with part of the larger world.

James Taylor ran a ferry operation across Anderson's stream there, along with produce shipping, a store, and a mill. He hired Lincoln for $6 a month and board. Abe later described the labor as, in Jesse Weik's words, "the roughest work a young man could be made to do." Apparently he had already made himself known in the vicinity as an efficient cutter of wood for steamboat fueling, earning 25 cents a cord, paid in cloth yardage instead of cash. In addition to physical labor, Lincoln did clerical work for Taylor. The ferryman's son Green Taylor was duly impressed with Lincoln's reading deep into the night.[386] Steamers might tie up at night, with passengers and crew going ashore. An Indiana traveler on the Ohio about this time wrote of such a stop, featuring the roasting of a beef ashore, climaxed with setting a tree afire for sake of the spectacle.[387]

During a genial White House evening, Lincoln later reminisced about building a small boat at Taylor's ferry:

A steamer was going down the river. We have, you know, no wharves on the Western streams, and the custom was, if passengers were at any of the landings, they were to go out in a boat, the steamer stopping and taking them on board. I was contemplating my new boat, and wondering whether I could make it stronger or improve it in any part, when two men, with trunks, came down to the shore in carriages, and looking at the different boats, singled out mine, and asked, "Who owns this?" I answered, modestly, "I do." "Will you," said one of them, "take us and our trunks out to the steamer?" "Certainly," said I. I was very glad to have the chance of earning something, and supposed that each of them would give me a couple of bits. The trunks were put on my boat, the passengers seated themselves on them, and I sculled them out to the steamer. They got on board, and I lifted their trunks and put them on the deck. The steamer was about to put on steam again, when I called out, "You have forgotten to pay me." Each of them took from his pocket a silver half-dollar and threw it on the bottom of my boat. I could scarcely believe my eyes as I picked up the money. You may think it was a very little thing, and in these days it seems to me like a trifle, but it was a most important incident in my life. I could scarcely credit that I, the poor boy, had earned a dollar in less than a day; that by honest work I had earned a dollar. The world seemed wider and fairer before me; I was a more hopeful and thoughtful boy from that time.[388]

That payment for probably less than an hour's work was all the more awesome considering that Lincoln was then earning $6 a month from ferryman Taylor. The story also illustrates the youth's strength and agility. Evidently Lincoln began taking more passengers to steamers midstream in the Ohio River.

Unfortunately, that kind of work ran him afoul of the law and, worse yet, afoul of the Dill brothers, John and Len. Lincoln was working for the Taylor ferry, running across the Anderson River, which emptied into the Ohio. The Dills ran a ferry across the Ohio River from the Kentucky side. The law granted them a monopoly on the trade, and they felt Lincoln was cutting in on their business. According to one plausible but not entirely reliable account, one of the brothers shouted across the river to attract Abe's attention, pretending to need transportation. Abe reportedly rowed over and, on alighting, was ambushed by both brothers. As the story goes, Lincoln quickly established that he was able to overpower them and suggested that the matter be settled in court rather than on the riverbank. The law gave Kentucky jurisdiction in such a river dispute, so the rivermen went before a Kentucky justice of the peace.

In court, Abe argued that his rowing from the Indiana side had cost the Dill brothers no business, because in each instance, their ferryboat was on the Kentucky side, and steamboats would not wait for their ferry to cross to passengers waiting on the Indiana side and then back again midway into the river where the steamers were pausing. This was a good point in equity, but the justice decided the case on a point in law. The statute giving the Dill brothers a monopoly spoke of transportation *across* the river, from one shore to the other, not of transportation *midway* into the river as Lincoln had been doing. The judge found him innocent.[389] Supposedly, and certainly plausibly, this case increased Lincoln's interest in the law.[390]

River duties gave Abe at least an occasional escape from farmhand labor, but he was not entirely spared such work, which included fencemaking, plowing, and hand-grinding corn. Once he and Green Taylor were shelling corn for milling. Frustrated by Lincoln's superiority at the task, Taylor struck him with an ear of corn. "Cut him over the eye," Taylor said. "He got mad."[391] Abe also helped with hog killing. This occupation earned him 31 cents a day, using the traditional clubs and barrels of boiling water.[392] A distant writer recalled, "We usually killed from six to eight in December, and the impression which that slaughter left upon my youthful mind was far more profound than any account I have yet read or heard of the carnage at the siege of Santiago."[393] Another nineteenth-century writer remembered:

> "Hog killing time" meant even more than Christmas did to us. It came in December, when the weather was sharply cold. The slaughtering was usually done on the river beach, where a great bonfire was made. . . . As the bonfire was lighted about four o'clock in the morning, while it was still dark, and as we boys were always permitted to get up in time to see it lighted, the occasion took upon itself in our eyes the character of a mad revel. Then, too, the farmhands who did the killing and dressing always gave us the tails of the hogs, and we roasted them in the coals of the bonfire.[394]

Around 1827, Abe and his stepbrother John Johnston helped construct the Louisville and Portland Canal to bypass some falls on the Ohio River, the type of internal improvement so strongly advocated by Harry of the West (Henry Clay). "Internal improvements" were projects to improve transportation and thereby promote commerce. River improvement—clearing obstructions, deepening channels, and the like—and building canals, roads, and railroads were typical projects. None of the pick-and-shovel work was easy, and canals were built by tough characters. Lincoln and Johnston got their pay in silver dollars.[395] An eyewitness to canal construction in Ohio at this time remembered: "This afforded work and money to the men who could do it during the winter, at prices they seemed glad to get and thought they were doing well to take. Hands were paid eight to ten dollars a month for chopping, digging, etc., receiving board and lodgings in addition; but every wet day was counted out, the laborer losing his time. . . . In this way, it would take all winter to make about two months time. It was hard earned money, but it was esteemed worth the labor."[396]

More than one story is told of Abe Lincoln making river voyages to sell cargoes of produce from the family farm,[397] but the only generally accepted one is about his trip as a crew member on a flatboat to New Orleans. He was hired in 1828 at $8 a month to accompany James Gentry's son Allen; the deal included return deck passage for the two youths on a steamer.[398] The flatboat cargo included produce grown "chiefly by my labor," said Lincoln. [399] Abraham's stepmother was not at all keen about him making the trip but finally consented.[400] Physical dangers were not the only kind in such a voyage. David Turnham mentioned that he "worked on the river fitting up a flatboat with him [Lincoln] where the surrounding influence was very bad."[401] The character of Ohio River boatmen in 1818 was described like this:

> Some incorrigble scoundrels among them; and their conversation and manners are only to be equaled in the sinks of London; but should you take a respectable young woman on board a boat, especially if it be your own, you will not hear a word to offend you. But I would advise all travellers going alone down the river, to get one man at least that they can depend upon, and to wear a dagger or a brace of pistols; for there are no desperadoes more savage in their anger than these men. Give them your hand, accost them with a bold air, taste their whisky—and you win their hearts. But a little too much reserve or haughtiness offends them instantly, and draws upon you torrents of abuse, if not a personal assault. They are a dauntless, hardy set; thoughtless, and short lived from intemperance.[402]

A traveler described boat crews as "a rough set of men, many given to drinking whisky, fighting and [eye] gouging."[403] Allen's pregnant wife, Katie (the same Katie who had listened skeptically to Abraham's explanation of the moon's apparent motion), said she watched the flatboat drift off into the Ohio with her husband and Lincoln in April.[404] Another traveler on the Ohio recalled:

> Near midnight, one of the men and myself being up, we discovered something near us, which we took for a log, and began pulling from it, when we found our mistake; it was a bear swimming in the river; he came close to that part of the boat where I was standing, and then made off up the river in great haste. We could hear him blow in the water longer than we could see him. Made this day sixteen or seventeen miles. We continued floating till near two o'clock, when we stuck on the top of a fallen tree, and we were obliged to cut off a bough before we could extricate.[405]

In *The Adventures of Huckleberry Finn*, Mark Twain evoked the atmosphere of raft and flatboat trips down the Mississippi to New Orleans, describing weather, currents, scenery, pacing, and other river craft. In memoirs from Lincoln's time, one steamer passenger speaks of "a huge bell tolling in the fog to warn every flatboat to get out of the way" and the startling size of waves during a thunderstorm.[406] A later chronicler noted, "There was no end to the almost circular twists of the wandering river."[407] The two young men encountered bustling river towns and drifted past elegant mansions. En route, the men occasionally moored and traded at towns, farms, or plantations. The nature of that trading is unclear, but some flatboatmen both sold cargo and acquired new items via cash or barter, hoping the new inventory could be sold profitably farther downriver.[408]

Often flatboats traveled in groups of eight or ten,[409] but this one went alone. There was safety in numbers. "When my husband and Lincoln went down the river," Katie said, "they were attacked by negroes. Some say Wade Hampton's negroes, but I think not. The place was below that called Madame Busham's [Duchesne's?] plantation six miles below Baton Rouge. Abe fought the negroes, got them off the boat, pretended to have guns (had none). The negroes had hickory clubs. My husband said, 'Lincoln, get the guns and shoot,' the negroes took alarm and left."[410] Neighbor John Romine said likewise: "Lincoln was attacked by the negroes, no doubt of this. Abe told me so. Saw the scar myself."[411] Riverman John R. Dougherty asserted: "Gentry has shown me the place where the niggers attacked him and Lincoln. The place is . . . about six miles below Baton Rouge."[412] Abraham wrote an account of the event, referring to himself in the third person: "The nature of part of the cargo-load, as it was called, made it necessary for them to linger and trade along the Sugar Coast—and one night they were attacked by seven negroes with intent to kill and rob them. They were hurt some in the melee."[413] Jesse Weik said Allen and Abe switched to the offensive during the attack, chasing the blacks into the countryside.[414] After beating away the attackers, Allen and Lincoln shoved off and put some miles between them and the plantation.[415]

That year, 750 steamers and more than 1,000 flatboats arrived in New Orleans.[416] It was some town. For "a boy brought up in the woods, and seeing, as it were, but little of the world," as Lincoln described himself,[417] the impact must have been tremendous. A visitor to the city that year left this account:

New Orleans is built very like an old French provincial town; the same narrow streets, old fashioned houses and lamps suspended by a chain across the road. Many of the houses, however, are picturesque, with their large projecting roofs and painted sides and windows. . . . The population including blacks is upwards to 40,000 the greater part of which are still French, or speak only that language. The whole place has quite the air of a French town.

There are two Catholic churches and one Presbyterian church for the whole population. I should suppose that New Orleans like the small town of Natchez is not famous for its morality or religious feeling. Those who come here on account of trade think only of making money as fast as they can. . . .

There is a public ball here two or three times a week, which includes all of the colored ladies of the place known by the name of quadroons. Many I have seen are really very beautiful girls; their blood is a mixture of Indian, African and French. There was a play Sunday evening at the French theatre. Sunday is one of the regular days of performance.

I observed in walking through the streets several large rooms fitted out as slave markets and generally filled with unhappy blacks dressed up for the occasion. The men and women are ranged on opposite sides of the apartments where they may traffic for human beings with the same indifference as purchasing a horse.[418]

In 1860, Lincoln reportedly said, "When a boy I went to New Orleans on a flatboat, and there I saw slavery and slave markets as I have never seen them in Kentucky, and I heard worse of the Red River plantations."[419] A settler in the Lincoln vicinity of Indiana reminisced about stories from flatboat crews:

These river-men, as they were called, brought us strange accounts of the countries in the far South. They told us of the magnolia, the cypress, the live-oak, of the fields of cane and cotton, and of the large and populous plantations which they visited on their route, where the overseer would buy almost a whole boat-load of supplies. They had seen also the negro slaves, men and women, working on the plantations, and the guards armed with guns and whips, who watched the hands at their labor. They told us, in an undertone, that this was very hard to look at; that it was all wrong, but that the law allowed these things.[420]

Financial profit in the trip is hard to guess. The New Orleans market was notorious for its fluctuations, and the amount of trading the two young men did en route along the rivers is unclear.[421] About a dozen years later, someone summarized a flatboat expedition from Illinois to New Orleans thus: "The adventurers lost all their time, and some of their capital; but *they have gained experience*, and this will lead them to remain at home for the future and engage in no similar speculations."[422] An exasperated observer in that era declared that a flatboat operator normally was fleeced in New Orleans and "returned to a desolate farm which had been neglected whilst he was gone. One crop was lost by absence and another by taking it to market. This kind of business was persevered in astonishingly for several years to the great injury and utter ruin of a great many people."[423]

The steamboat trip upriver was probably not as exciting as the flatboat trip down, but steamer travel was always an adventure. You never knew when a snag might run through the hull and sink the vessel or a boiler might explode and clear the decks.

"I have to inform you of one of the most indescribable accidents by steam that has ever been witnessed. . . . The *Grampus* was coming up [the Mississippi] . . . when an explosion took place which has left her a complete wreck. Her boilers, six in number, were blown to atoms, with both her decks."

—*Vandalia Illinois Intelligencer*, September 13, 1828

"The steamboat *United States*, which left this city at 4 o'clock this afternoon, for New Haven, burst its boiler. . . . Twelve hats were picked up, four of which are recognized."

—*Connecticut Courant*, September 14, 1830, clipped in *Vandalia Illinois Intelligencer*, October 9, 1830

A more dependable hazard was for deck passengers to be treated as auxilliary crew members, expected to perform heavy labor, such as bringing wood aboard during fueling stops, and subject to brutal treatment from steamboat crew bosses.[424] We don't know whether that happened to Lincoln. In talking about one of his two steamboat trips from New Orleans, he was intrigued that a horseshoe bend penninsula that the flatboat had to be guided around had been transformed into an island by the river's current, allowing the steamboat to travel across what had been dry land a few weeks earlier.[425] Katie Roby Gentry said the two men returned in June.[426]

Flowing waters pulled at some people. The father of one of Abe's later associates said: "I often watched them [river travelers] from the bank of the river with longing envy. To think of being always on the river, where there was no confinement to close quarters, and where you could stand on the water's edge and fish, and watch the passing shore, with all its changes of scene, to me was enchantment."[427] After the New Orleans trip, according to the memory of William Wood: "Abe came to my house one day and stood around about, timid and shy. I knew he wanted something. I said to him, 'Abe, what is your case?' Abe replied, 'Uncle, I want you to go to the river (the Ohio) and give me some recomendation to some boat.' I remarked, 'Abe, your age is against you. You are not twenty-one yet.' 'I know that, but I want a start,' said Abe. I concluded not to go for the boy's good. . . . In 1829, this was."[428] Years later, during an alleged conversation, Denny Hanks said: "Tom owned Abe's time till he was twenty-one an' didn't want him to go. He was too vallyble fur chores."[429] Once again, an ambition of Abraham's was thwarted by owing his labor to his father.

The Lincoln homestead was only a mile or so from Gentryville, a village close enough to become a common destination for Abe after he finished a day's labor. In the Gentryville store of William Jones, where Lincoln became popular for stories and debating, he made a good enough impression on Jones to be hired as a clerk. He read all of Jones's books—a collection possibly above average, as Jones had attended Vincennes University. The merchant also subscribed to the *Terre Haute Register.* In addition to other talents, Lincoln brought his academic experience in commercial arithmetic, such as figuring interest on loans, a skill highly relevant to storekeeping, which was typically conducted on a credit rather than cash basis. His duties at the Jones store were not exactly what would later be called white-collar work, but they were far removed from agricultural labor as a means of making money for the family. This store employment was during his last Indiana year.[430] An associate of Jones's recalled: "Jones often said to me that Lincoln would make a great man one of these days. . . . Said so as far back as 1828–9."[431]

Jones is worth additional mention because Denny Hanks and Nat Grigsby said the merchant was a major factor in transforming Lincoln's politics.[432] Abe is known to have had warm regard for Jones.[433] "We were all Jackson boys," Nat Grigsby said.[434] According to Denny, Abraham had staunchly supported Andrew Jackson of the Democratic Party, but toward the end of the Indiana years, he switched his loyalties to Harry of the West (Henry Clay) and the Whig Party.[435] (What those two statesmen and their supporters stood for will be discussed later in this book.) Nat Grigsby recalled attending political meetings with Lincoln, and afterward they thoroughly discussed what they heard.[436] Denny said he and Lincoln "went to political and other speeches and gatherings. . . . We would hear all sides and opinions, talk them over, discuss them, agreeing or disagreeing. Abe, as I said before, was originally a Democrat after the order of Jackson, so was his father, so we all were. Abe turned Whig in 1827–8."[437] That date is approximate. Blue Nose Crawford's wife remembered Abraham singing a ditty that could be from either the 1824 or 1828 presidential campaign, to the tune of "Auld Lang Syne":

> Let auld acquaintance be forgot
> And never brought to mind
> And Jackson be our President
> And Adams left behind.[438]

Four news items illustrate an undercurrent running through Lincoln's world, so obvious to his neighbors that little mention is recorded from them:

> "Riot in Cincinnati. . . . On the 15th instant a large number of the inhabitants turned out and collected together, with the determination of forcing out of the city, the free negroes. . . . The houses of the blacks were attacked and demolished, and the inmates beat and driven through the streets till beyond the limits of the corporation. During the affray, one of the assailants, a young man of respectable character, was killed."
>
> —*Louisville Adv.*, clipped in *Vandalia Illinois Intelligencer*, September 19, 1829

"The jail of this county (Stewart [TN]) was discovered last night to be on fire, and what is indeed most shocking, the alarm was given by a poor negro who was confined in it. . . . His cries were now most heart-rending. But human efforts were of no avail, and the all-devouring element soon put a period to his existence. He was a runaway slave."

—Unidentified clip in *Vandalia Illinois Intelligencer*, October 24, 1829

"The President of Mexico has issued a decree abolishing slavery throughout the whole extent of the republic."

—*Vandalia Illinois Intelligencer*, January 2, 1830

"The emperor of Brazil has declared his intention to suppress the slave trade."

—*Vandalia Illinois Intelligencer*, August 7, 1830

In the autumn of 1829, Tom Lincoln was satisfied enough with his Indiana life to start building a new house with the help of his son's labor. The new house was to be a big step up from a log cabin, constructed of plank lumber. By year's end, however, Tom had decided to leave for Illinois. I think there were two reasons.

"We were perplexed by a disease called milk sick," Denny Hanks said. It struck again in 1829, killing an uncle and aunt of Abraham's mother.[439] Cattle were also affected. Denny, who lived near the Lincoln Indiana homestead, lost four cows to milk sickness in one week. "When we left it was on account of the milk."[440] Billy Herndon aptly observed:

Men of capacity, integrity, and energy—for such are the generality of pioneers in the West—emigrate to this new land from their old homes, not because they are inefficient men, men unable to grapple with the home conditions, but rather *because they refuse to submit to the bad conditions at home.* . . . The spirit of pioneering is not a spirit of *shiftless discontent* . . . but is the creating spirit, a grand desire, wish, and will to rise up in the scale of being. . . . Good men and women do not, from the spirit of shiftless discontent, quit the sacred ashes of the dead loved ones, and wildly rush into a cold, damp, uncleared, gloomy, unsettled, wild wilderness, where they know they *must struggle* with disease, poverty, nature, the wild wolf and wilder men, and the untamed and ungeared elements of nature, that sweep everywhere unconfined. They do not go for game, nor sport, nor daring adventure.[441]

I think refusal to submit to milk sickness was the primary reason for Tom's decision to leave Indiana. What, however, was the reason for selecting Illinois as a destination?

John Hanks had moved in 1828 from Kentucky to Illinois, near Decatur, and told Tom Lincoln about the area.[442] Simeon Francis, who would become a close associate of Abraham, was also hearing good things: "I am inclined to think we shall all be pleased to go where Josiah would have us. He likes Illinois: He says it is the country for poor men—rich in soil, healthy, and pleasant."[443] Denny Hanks decided the Decatur area sounded good. He made arrangements to sell out and move to Illinois. His wife's mother, Sarah Bush Johnston Lincoln, "could not think of parting with her," Denny said, "and we ripped up stakes and started to Illinois."[444] He supposedly mused: "Linkhorns an' Hankses an' Johnstons, all hangin' together. I reckon we was like one o' them tribes o' Israel that you kain't break up, nohow."[445] The migration party consisted of Tom Lincoln and his wife, Sarah; Abraham; Denny Hanks and his wife, Sarah (daughter of Tom's wife, Sarah); the four children of Denny and Sarah; Squire Hall and his wife, Matilda (daughter of Tom's wife Sarah); their infant son; and John Johnston (son of Tom's wife, Sarah). Nephews and a niece of Sarah Bush Johnston Lincoln resided east of Decatur, over in Coles County, Illinois,[446] and the Lincoln clan was also moving closer to Hanks kin. Joseph Hanks (uncle of John) had settled near Decatur, as had John's father, William, who was a man of some importance around Decatur. Indeed, together with his real estate partner, Jesse Fell, he owned part of the town.[447] (Three decades later, Fell would develop and act on an idea that helped make Lincoln President.)

As the Lincolns prepared to head for Illinois, they had to choose what to leave behind. Abe gave his little book cabinet to friend and neighbor John Lamar, whose father had praised Lincoln's studiousness.[448] Land obviously had to be left behind. In September, Tom and his wife traveled to Elizabethtown, where she sold some city real estate for about $125.[449] Next, Tom sold his eighty-acre tract to Charles Grigsby for $125. Neighbor John Romine may have bartered a horse to obtain the other tract, of twenty acres, but soon enough James Gentry had ownership of the smaller parcel.[450] Like the other log cabins Abraham lived in, the Indiana one disappeared.[451] The planks he had sawed from timber he felled for the new house were sold to Blue Nose Crawford.[452] David Turnham said he paid a dime a bushel for Tom's four hundred or five hundred bushels of corn and also bought all Tom's hogs, maybe a hundred of them.[453]

A not unimportant detail of departing Indiana was the request Tom and Sarah made to their church for a letter of dismission, a document certifying their good standing in the church and allowing them to transfer membership to an Illinois church without having to go through the rigorous investigation that might otherwise be necessary for new members of a congregation. The letter was granted but then revoked at the request of Aaron Grigsby's mother, Nancy. After investigation, the letter was reissued. Aaron's mother then laid charges of lying against Elizabeth Crawford, wife of Blue Nose. Tom Lincoln was on the committee appointed to investigate.[454] Results are unclear, but his participation demonstrates good standing in the congregation.

As the moment of departure neared in early 1830, Abe Lincoln and John Johnston dickered with Peter Brooner, whose wife had died in the same milk sickness outbreak that had killed Abraham's mother. "John did all the talking," Brooner's son Allen said. "If anyone had been asked that day which would make the greatest success in life, I think the answer would have been John Johnston."[455] Eventually the three struck a deal in which Brooner traded a yoke of oxen for a horse,[456] oxen being desirable draft animals to haul the Lincoln party's wagons. The migrants built their wagons themselves.[457]

The night before departure, Abe supposedly bought about $35 worth of small goods—needles, combs, and the like—from storekeeper William Jones. Abraham peddled them on the trip to Illinois, later saying that he doubled his money.[458] That would have been a major boost to the family's capital. (Among them, the three Lincolns had about $500 cash when they began traveling to Illinois.[459])

Folks who watched the Lincoln clan's departure agreed about Abraham's appearance: He wore moccasins, buckskin trousers not long enough for him, a coonskin cap with tail.[460] As the clan headed off, he ran up a hill for a last visit to his mother's grave. Tom shouted for him to hurry up, and Abraham returned to the trek, crying.[461]

Lincoln's farewell to Indiana was also farewell to his childhood. What did his first two decades mean to him? Two students of the topic said the experience was "shrouded in the darkness of his reticence."[462] But reticence is not silence. Friend Joseph Gillespie remembered, "He was never ashamed of the poverty and obscurity of his early life."[463] Absence of shame, of course, doesn't imply presence of pleasure. According to a neighbor in Springfield, Illinois, "He said to me on one occasion, 'I have seen a good deal of the back side of this world.'"[464] John L. Scripps, who had Lincoln's cooperation in preparing a biography, said:

> The chief difficulty I had to encounter, was to induce him to communicate the homely facts and incidents of his early life. He seemed to be painfully impressed with the extreme poverty of his early surroundings—the utter absence of all romantic and heroic elements, and I know he thought poorly of the idea of attempting a biographi-

cal sketch for campaign purposes. "Why Scripps," said he, on one occasion, "it is a great piece of folly to attempt to make anything out of my early life. It can all be condensed into a single sentence, and that sentence you will find in Gray's Elegy:

'The short and simple annals of the poor.'

That's my life, and that's all you or anyone else can make of it."[465]

"I can remember," he told Leonard Swett, "our life in Kentucky; the cabin, the stinted living, the sale of our possessions, and the journey with my father and mother to southern Indiana."[466] And yet Swett listened to Lincoln talk of those days "as the story of a happy childhood. There was nothing sad or pinched, and nothing of want, and no allusion to want in any part of it. His own description of his youth was that of a joyous, happy boyhood. It was told with mirth and glee, and illustrated by pointed anecdote, often interrupted by his jocund laugh."[467] Persons who knew Lincoln in Indiana described him as follows: "naturally cheerful and good natured," "a cheerful boy, a witty boy, was humorous always," "always jovial and full of innocent jokes," "always appeared cheerful and not gloomy," "he was or seemed to be always cheerful and happy. I never discovered any sadness or melancholy in his appearance."[468] Tom Lincoln had opportunity to see his son's dark side, but Tom's step-granddaughter said, "I have often heard Grandpa Lincoln tell what a jovial fun loving boy Abram was."[469] We should consider a reminiscence that Denny Hanks sent to Billy Herndon: "We had to work very hard [to] clear ground for to keep soul and body together, and every spare time that we had we picked up our rifle and fetched in a fine deer or turkey. . . . I tell you, Billy, I enjoyed myself better then than I have ever since."[470]

Following a visit to Indiana in the 1840s, however, Lincoln wrote an account with a tone unlike the one Swett heard:

> My childhood-home I see again,
>   And gladden with the view;
> And still as mem'ries crowd my brain,
>   There's sadness in it too.
>
> O memory! thou mid-way world
>   'Twixt Earth and Paradise
> Where things decayed, and loved ones lost
>   In dreamy shadows rise.
>
> And freed from all that's gross or vile,
>   Seem hallowed, pure, and bright,
> Like scenes in some enchanted isle,
>   All bathed in liquid light.

As distant mountains please the eye,
    When twilight chases day—
As bugle-tones, that, passing by,
    In distance die away—

As leaving some grand water-fall
    We ling'ring, list its roar,
So memory will hallow all
    We've known, but know no more.

Now twenty years have passed away,
    Since here I bid farewell
To woods, and fields, and scenes of play
    And school-mates loved so well.

Where many were, how few remain
    Of old familiar things!
But seeing these to mind again
    The lost and absent brings.

The friends I left that parting day—
    How changed, as time has sped!
Young childhood grown, strong manhood grey,
    And half of all are dead.

I hear the lone survivors tell
    How nought from death could save,
Till every sound appears a knell,
    And every spot a grave.[471]

+=== CHAPTER 3 ===+

ILLINOIS

For 225 miles, the migration party rode its wagons and trudged alongside the oxen and horses. Traveling conditions in March were icy. Illinois newspaper items like these appeared at the time of the trip: "On Saturday morning the mercury in Fahrenheit's thermometer was at 27° below zero"[1]; "A man was found dead, by Mr. Fenamore, on Thursday the 18th ult. about 20 miles this side of Prairie du Chien, supposed to have frozen to death."[2] Freezing temperatures were compounded by hard rains: "Considerable rain fell on Thursday night and Friday last, and Fever River has swollen to some height since."[3] After passing through Vincennes, the migrants had to cross the flooded Wabash River. Then they nearly lost everything crossing the upper Kaskaskia River.[4] In Illinois, even the roads were flooded. Thirty years later, Abraham Lincoln noted that "the low prairie was covered with water a half mile at a stretch, and the water covered with ice."[5] The travelers would break through the thin layer of ice that formed overnight and slosh through the icy water. How they succeeded in hauling wagons through such territory is bewildering. Many years later, Lincoln bemoaned a mishap:

> We were not as warmly clad as people are these days; but our work kept us warm usually by keeping us busy. In an accident . . . I lost my trousers, which were so torn as to be useless. . . . I had no other pair. . . . I was shivering, with the torn ones not half covering my limbs. My good mother ransacked the wagon, and found an old pair of my father's. They were better than the torn ones, and were drawn on over them. The legs of the old ones were cut off below the knees, and that was the best that could be done. . . . My legs were only half clad. My father was almost a foot under me in height, and his legs

were shorter in proportion. His trousers came only a little below my knees. My shoes were low, and though I had good, warm, woolen socks of my mother's knitting, my shanks were thin and the socks were loose and large.

I walked often through tangled brush along the roadside as I drove the oxen. The trousers were of little use as covering below my knees, and the socks slipped down on my ankles, and my long shins were neutral, neutral [undefended] ground in the frosty . . . air.[6]

The migrants struggled through Purgatory Bottom, where the roadway was so notorious that it still merited newspaper comment three years later: "We are sorry the legislature did not cause the road 'through Purgatory' to be improved."[7] Six years after that statement, the road's condition was a matter of joking in the general assembly,[8] but the Lincoln party was probably not amused while traveling. After passing through Purgatory Bottom, the group slogged toward Paradise, Illinois. Somewhere between Purgatory and Paradise, another mishap occurred. The families were pushing along a corduroy road through a swamp. A corduroy road was made of logs laid across the pathway. The effect was like a road made entirely of chuckholes, a horrible experience in vehicles lacking pneumatic tires, shock absorbers, and other suspension elements. Some years later, a voyager described it thus: "A corduroy road . . . is made by throwing trunks of trees into a marsh, and leaving them to settle there. The very slightest of the jolts with which the ponderous carriage fell from log to log was enough, it seemed, to have dislocated all the bones in the human body."[9] Another person familiar with such roadways declared, "of all infernal roads for roughness, they bangs the beater."[10] In normal times, travelers at least could have the consolation of not sinking through swamp muck, but on this trip, flooding meant the corduroy road was underwater. The only way Abe could distinguish the road from a bottomless (for practical purposes) swamp was to watch for posts or stakes erected here and there at the road's edge. Oxen ordinarily are low-maintenance and placid, pulling a burden as long as a driver wants, but under these conditions, they balked. A person who spoke with Lincoln about the experience reported: "He swung his long ox lash around and around over the oxen high in the air and brought the lash down, cutting open the hide. The oxen at last went on the thin ice," breaking through the ice layer as each step hit the corduroy logs hidden below the water's surface.

About halfway across the swamp, Abe's "fice dog" leaped from the wagon in which it was riding, perhaps believing that walking would be preferable to the horrible jostling. The dog instantly broke through the ice, crying in fear and agony as it struggled. Lincoln "stopped the oxen, pulled off his shoes, rolled up his pants, got out of the wagon, jumped into the cold water, the sheets of ice hitting his shins." "I could not bear to lose my dog," he said, "and I jumped out of the wagon and waded waist-deep in the ice and water, got hold of him and helped him out and saved him." Lincoln put the dog back in the wagon, where it stayed at the feet of Sarah Bush Johnston Lincoln. After the migrants finished their slog across the swamp, Abe could not persuade the dog to leave the wagon. He pulled the dog out and put it on dry ground, where it cut joyous capers and kept coming back to him, lying at his feet momentarily and then running around again. "I guess that I felt about as glad as the dog," Lincoln said.[11]

When the migration party reached Decatur, they made an overnight camp on the village square. The town wasn't much at that time, fewer than a dozen log houses, but it must have seemed like civilization after the long, wet journey. The next day, they moved on. Finally, about two weeks after they had started in Indiana, the migrants reached their new home in Macon County, Illinois, a few miles from Decatur on a high bluff overlooking the Sangamon River. "It tuk us two weeks to git thar," Denny Hanks allegedly recalled, "raftin' over the Wabash, cuttin' our way through the woods, fordin' rivers, pryin' wagons an' steers out o' sloughs with fence rails, an' makin' camp. Abe cracked a joke every time he cracked a whip, an' he found a way out o' every tight place while the rest of us was standin' 'round scratchin' our fool heads. I reckon Abe an' Aunt Sairy run that movin', an' good thing they did, or it'd 'a' been run into a swamp an' sucked under."[12] Such a party of migrants was probably nothing unusual. While traveling southeast from Springfield, Illinois, someone recalled: "I met a great many new settlers coming into the country with their wagons, horses, cows, cattle, dogs, furniture; in short, their whole moveable property. These prodigious assemblages regularly bivouac in the prairie. The cattle and livestock feed at large. The human beings eat and sleep in the wagons."[13]

While the whole party lived in a camp made with wagon sheets, Abraham helped construct a cabin for Tom and Sarah. John Hanks, who lived in the area, had already felled logs; Abe hauled them in a dry sled; Denny Hanks prepared them. No doubt other members of the party helped as well. Then neighbors assembled and raised the cabin. Abe also helped open the ground for planting, pitching in on splitting enough rails to enclose ten acres.

Making fence rails was a substantial job. "I remember," John Hanks said, "when we set out together in the cold winter to cut and maul rails on the Sangamon River in Macon County . . . to enclose his father's little home, and from day to day kept at work until the whole was finished and the homestead fenced in."[14] A pioneer recalled mauling rails: "This was generally done in winter, and, although a most laborious work, I took delight in it and still recollect it with pleasure. . . . When I got a tough log the wedges and 'gluts' would fly out on being struck a hard blow. Gentle taps were necessary to get them well entered. I have often observed since that many failures occur, in the enterprises of human life, from want of patience in giving the gentle taps which are necessary in beginning them."[15] A traveler noted urgency in such a task: "Fencing the farm is an operation requiring speedy attention, as without it no crop is secure from the depredations of cattle and horses, which roam over the prairies and through the woods at will; all land which is not enclosed being common. The almost universal fence is the zig zag or worm fence, which is constructed of split rails."[16] An immigrant from Switzerland watched Illinois settlers in amazement:

It is almost unbelievable what an American worker can do. He splits 150 to 200 wooden fence rails a day. These are made 11 feet long and 3 to 4 inches thick. For this he first has to fell the trees in the forest. All deciduous trees that are seldom more than two lengths, and mostly only one length, are useful. For this he has an ax, an iron wedge, and in the forest some wooden mallets and blocks. . . . The wage for making 100 rails is 62½ cents without meals and 50 cents with meals.[17]

As in Indiana, Abe made money as a farmhand. But unlike the situation in Indiana, he now had legal claim to his wages, having reached the age of twenty-one. John Hanks recalled Lincoln breaking prairie for persons in the vicinity; Lincoln himself spoke of helping a member of the Hanks clan.[18] He was willing to barter his labor; seeking a new pair of pants, he split rails for another Hanks clan member at a rate of one yard of homespun brown jean cloth for each 400 rails.[19] Illness hindered such labor. In the autumn, the entire party was laid low by ague and fever, common and devastating afflictions of pioneer life. "We had fever'n ager turrible," Denny purportedly said. A store account shows the Lincolns bought substantial quantities of a remedy made from whiskey and Peruvian bark.[20] "After the fever went down you still didn't feel much better," said one nineteenth-century Illinois writer.

You felt as though you had gone through some sort of a collision, threshing machine, or jarring machine, and came out not killed, but next thing to it. You felt weak, as though you had run too far after something, and then didn't catch it. You felt languid, stupid and sore, and was down in the mouth and hell and partially raveled out. Your back was out of fix, your head ached and your appetite crazy. Your eyes had too much white in them; your ears, especially after taking quinine, had too much roar in them, and your whole body and soul were entirely woe-begone, disconsolate, sad, poor and good for nothing. You didn't think much of yourself and didn't believe that other people did either; and you didn't care.[21]

Another victim reported:

I fell sick, and indeed throughout the settlement there were more sick than well. . . . My fever reduced me to a state of extreme weakness, but my nurse, by constantly supplying me with cornmeal gruel and chicken broth prevented me from sinking under the violence of my disorder.

The fever soon became a regular intermittent, of which I was soon cured by bark and laudanum.

These intermittent fevers are the scourges of new settlements in the Western Country.[22]

Still another firsthand account said:

> A friend residing in that part of the country which is watered by the Sangamo, a district almost proverbial for its fertility, and which is fast rising into importance, writes:—"In this country, life is at least fifty per cent. below par in the months of August and September. I have often thought that I ran as great a risk every season which I would spend here as I would in an ordinary battle. I really believe it seldom happens that a greater proportion of an army falls victims to the sword during a campaign, than there has of the inhabitants of Illinois to disease, during a season that I have been here."[23]

State elections were coming on in August 1830, and some Decatur precinct voters wanted the polling place changed. In May, Abe Lincoln and some of his relatives in the migration party signed a petition asking the Macon County Court to do this. County courts were executive bodies administering the county government, as opposed to circuit courts, which were judicial bodies holding trials. Other than Lincoln's signature, the petition's main notoriety was that neither he nor any of his migration party had yet qualified as voters. None had resided six months in Illinois, as required by the state constitution, but all claimed otherwise. It was a small lie, and probably no one cared, but it was a lie nonetheless. The county court granted the request.[24]

In Illinois elections of that era, candidates would not only do individual campaigning in their district, but also make joint appearances. Traditionally the first day of a circuit court session was adjourned so that those gathered in the county seat for trials could hear what candidates had to say. Quite possibly such a court day was occurring when, by one account, Lincoln heard huzzas from the Decatur public square while he was plowing nearby. The account says he stopped the oxen and went over to the scene, where John Posey, a Democratic candidate for state representative, was mounted on a wagon and laying into the Whigs. Macon County being strong Democrat territory, he had an enthusiastic audience. Also speaking was a state political star, Democrat William Lee Davidson Ewing from down in Fayette County. Ewing was then clerk of the Illinois house of representatives, appointed by Democratic legislators, and soon to become speaker of the house after being elected to the legislature in August. In the summer of 1830, Ewing's father-in-law, Col. Elijah C. Berry, was state auditor, another office filled by vote of state legislators. The crowd was a little grumpy because Posey had failed to treat the throng to free drinks of whiskey. As one politician of the era explained, "In many counties the candidates would hire all the groceries [saloons] at the county seats and other considerable villages, where the people could get liquor without cost for several weeks before the election."[25]

John Hanks thought Posey's speech "was a bad one, and I said Abe could beat it." Custom allowed a bold onlooker to address such a gathering, taking a turn after an official speaker finished. "I turned down a box or keg," John Hanks said, "and Abe made his speech." Lincoln, though a newcomer, was an experienced public speaker and made an impromptu rebuttal to Posey and Ewing that delighted the crowd, which at such gatherings typically appreciated a good contest regardless of who came out ahead. Concerning Posey, "Abe beat him to death," Hanks said. Fellow rail-splitter George Close said Lincoln "made the best speech of the day." Abe spoke mainly about navigation of the Sangamon River. This was one of the hottest political topics. We don't know what Lincoln said, but we do know that Whigs staunchly advocated government sponsorship of "internal improvements," projects to improve navigation of rivers and construct canals, highways, and railroads. Democrats tended to view such projects as improper for government and corporations, though permissible for private partnerships responsible for all expenses.

The Sangamon River was the region's outlet to the Illinois River and the port at Beardstown, and from thence to the mercantile depots of St. Louis and New Orleans on the Mississippi River, so the question of making the Sangamon more navigable was important to voters in Macon County and elsewhere in the region. In 1830, Springfield minister John Bergen publicly proclaimed, "Two thousand dollars expended in clearing the fallen timber from this stream will make it navigable for steamboats." As Denny Hanks allegedly put it, "We was all tuk up with the idy that they could run steamboats up to our cornfields an' load."

John Hanks recalled that Posey "after the speech was through, took Abe aside and asked him where he had learned so much. . . . Abe explained, stating his manner and method of reading and what he had read. The man encouraged Lincoln to persevere." Ewing also complimented Lincoln, saying "he was a bright one."[26] A native of Kentucky, Ewing was known for suave manners.[27] Someone who attended political meetings that year declared: "The present race of politicians are the most polite and palavering set of mortals on earth. They are like Lanbro, the pirate: 'They are the mildest mannered men that ever scuttled a ship or cut a throat. . . .' I never see one of these sleek looking rascals, with a smirk on his countenance, and an obliging and familiar conversation, without thinking of a trap covered with flowers."[28] After Posey won this election, he got the Illinois house of representatives to pass a resolution for the internal improvements committee to look into making the Sangamon navigable as far upstream as Decatur.[29] A rhyme expressed popular opinion about politicians:

> He greets the woman with courtly grace,
> And kisses the babies' dirty face;
> He calls to the fence the farmer at work,
> And bores the merchant, and bores the clerk;
> The blacksmith while his anvil rings,
> He greets. And this is the song he sings:
>   "Howdy, howdy, howdy do?
>   How is your wife, and how are you?

Ah! it fits my fist as no other can,
The horny hand of the working-man."[30]

+≔ ≕+

The first document we have indicating community respect for Lincoln is dated December 1830, in which he appraised the value of a horse found wandering through the countryside; the valuation and description would then be noted by a justice of the peace and advertised so the owner could make claim. Such civic duty was minor indeed, but being chosen for it was a mark of respect.[31] Lincoln's environment wasn't at all gentle, and not all citizens enjoyed the respect he earned.

> "Look Out for Horse Thieves & Counterfeit Money. . . . A man who calls himself Retherford, and a youth of this county, viz. Greene County, Illinois, his name is Pirce Costley. These fellows got two horses of an industrious poor youth, for which they gave him $100 of counterfeit money. . . . $20 reward will be given to any person that will deliver the above described men to the sheriff of Greene County."
>
> —*Vandalia Illinois Intelligencer*,
> August 21, 1830

> "Mr. Kinney, of Mercer County, was *shot dead* a few days since, by his neighbor and guest for the evening, a Mr. Lane, who perpetrated the act under the influence of insanity."
>
> —*Commentator*, clipped in *Vandalia Illinois Intelligencer*, September 11, 1830

> "A clock pedlar is stated to have been lately murdered, not far from Mount Vernon, in this state. He was found suspended by his heels, with his head severed from his body!"
>
> —*Vandalia Illinois Intelligencer*,
> October 16, 1830

> "Stolen from my wagon, on the night of the 31st, $200 in specie, and a rifle gun, branded J. Ferguson, by a man named Andrew Stepleton. . . . I will give ten dollars reward for him, if taken in this state, or $20 if taken out of the state."
>
> —Benjamin Royse, Hillsboro, Illinois, *Vandalia Illinois Intelligencer*, November 6, 1830

"$50 Reward. Stop an old atrocious Murderer. A man of the name of John Pollin, after having butchered a negro in Virginia, where he left a wife, and butchered another in Warren County Kentucky, with circumstances of the most wanton cruelty, had escaped in Tennessee, where he tried to murder a white man, whence he was obliged to escape up the stream of Missouri, to shelter among the new settlements of the north of that state, or the adjoining ports of the Illinois. . . . He went up the Missouri with . . . his second wife (for he has two alive) by the name of Betsy, and a widow woman by the name of Nancy Samuel, with two female children, Martha and Rany.

"He has with him two rifles, and a butcher knife, and was about St. Louis last July. . . . I understand he was lately about Jonesborough."

> —John B. A. Thevenot, *Vandalia Illinois Intelligencer*, October 30–November 13, 1830

"$150 Reward. . . . It has been represented to me, that Uriah Downs, of the county of Clinton, is charged with the murder of his brother, William Downs: Now, therefore, I, John Reynolds, Governor of said state, by virtue of the powers in me vested by law, do offer a reward of one hundred and fifty dollars to any person or persons, who will apprehend the said Downs."

> —*Vandalia Illinois Intelligencer*, January 8, 1831

In the winter of 1830–31, Abe was a rail splitter for Sheriff William Warnick. Accounts vary on how many thousand rails were split, but the total was a lot. Lincoln recalled a rail-splitting accident: "One day, while I was sharpening a wedge on a log, the ax glanced and nearly took my thumb off, and there is the scar, you see." Whether that mishap occurred on the Warnick job is unknown, but such labor required vigilance.[32] "Mr. Thomas Shores, of this neighborhood, on Monday last went out to make rails, and in felling a tree a part of the top of another tree was thrown upon his head, and killed him instantly."[33] In February 1831, quite plausibly while engaged on the Warnick job, another accident nearly left Lincoln crippled. Weeks of subzero temperatures had made the Sangamon River well frozen, but somehow, while walking across the ice, Abe broke through. The shallow depth put him in no danger of drowning, but soaking his feet and shoes in such weather was a crisis. By the time he slogged two miles through snow to the Warnick place, his feet had become severely frostbitten. Mrs. Warnick immediately set to work with pioneer remedies, but the damage was so bad that the patient needed to stay in the cabin for four weeks to recover. He spent much of his time reading Sheriff Warnick's copy of Illinois statutes.[34]

This was the Winter of the Deep Snow, whose survivors were ever afterward known as Snow Birds. The season began gently enough that a snowfall on Christmas Day 1830 was cheery.[35] Four days later, a blizzard dumped three feet. Rain added a crust of ice, followed by more snow—nineteen additional snowstorms by February 13. Eventually snow covered the landscape four to six feet deep, with drifts higher. For weeks, overnight temperatures dropped to twelve degrees below zero, or colder.[36] Over toward New Salem, McGrady Rutledge (Ann's cousin) observed that the situation "was hard on the wild game, it starved the deers, turkeys and prairie chickens. . . . Two deers come to father's feed lot and stayed, fed with the cattle and sheep."[37] Not all experiences were so gentle. One Snow Bird had a couple dozen pigs trapped for six weeks in a small area along Panther Creek. About half the drove remained when the settler reached them; the survivors were in good condition, the bigger hogs having eaten the smaller ones.[38] Deer, which run by taking one leap after another, quickly crashed through the ice crust under the top layers of snow when they attempted to flee predators and became mired, allowing lighter-running wolves or dogs or humans to catch up and devour them at leisure.[39] "That winter nearly cleaned out the deer," reported one authority.[40] Noted another, "They never became plentiful afterwards."[41] The same was said of other game.[42] Animals were not the only victims; fruit trees perished along with cotton plants. Indeed, the Deep Snow ended cotton cultivation in Illinois.[43] A Springfield Snow Bird spoke of "snow within, snow without, snow everywhere, cold cutting the face, drifts blinding the eyes, horses rearing and plunging."[44] At least Springfield had adequate food on hand.[45]

But like many other Snow Birds, the Lincolns faced a dire food shortage. A mild autumn portended no hurry for corn harvesting, and rains interfered as well. Now much of the region's crop was lost.[46] Abe Lincoln and John Hanks crossed the Sangamon River with a quantity of corn to grind at a mill. The mill owner was going through a cornfield with a sled pulled by oxen, grabbing what ears he could find above the snow cover. He asked whether the other side of the Sangamon was doing as poorly. "Yes," Lincoln replied, looking at the miller's sled operation. "We have to do worse than that, for we have used up all our corn, and now have to go to our neighbors for assistance."[47]

Settlers desperate to break out of being snowbound would somehow pass the word, and everyone in an area—young and old, male and female—along with hounds, horses, and oxen, would turn out. Struggling together, they would wallow through the snow, tramping and tramping until a path was made. Come springtime, noted one chronicler, "The muddy-white foundations of these rural roads remained, unmelted, to stretch across the black soil of the prairies."[48] Said another writer in the 1800s: "The season following the winter of the deep snow was a very late one, and frost came every month in the year. The crops were poor . . . and the corn did not ripen."[49]

Soon after Lincoln's feet recovered from frostbite, John Hanks asked him to come over to Decatur and meet Denton Offutt.[50] Offutt would eventually earn renown as a horse whisperer, a man with such understanding about animals and power over them that within minutes he could tame the wildest of horses, whispering words of persuasion into the beast's ears. Harry of the West—Henry Clay himself—attested to Offutt's power in that regard.[51] Seemingly Offutt had the same talent in relations with human beings.

He had just arrived in Decatur from life among Kentucky's slavocracy gentry.[52] Despite such an advantageous background, however, Offutt was not only uneducated, but also indifferent to learning.[53] We're not talking about fancy learning, but basics such as being able to write a coherent letter. Although he circulated well enough in Lexington parlors to know Henry Clay and other notables of the region,[54] Offutt was robust enough that he had gone flatboating down to New Orleans personally.[55] One Illinois acquaintance called him "a wild, harum-scarum kind of a man."[56] Another remembered him as "wild, reckless, careless."[57] Still another called him an "unsteady—noisy, fussy, rattlebrained man, wild and unprovidential."[58] Yet another described Offutt as "gassy, windy, brain rattling."[59] A few years later, while he was on the run after escaping from jail, the pursuing sheriff said he was "very talkative and wishes to pass for a gentleman."[60]

His current enthusiasm was Illinois and its opportunities to make money. At that time, Illinois farmers wanting to sell produce in New Orleans typically had to take it there themselves.[61] Offutt was trying to make money as a middleman who bought produce from farmers and took it to New Orleans, a service that not only eliminated farmers' shipping risk, but also opened the city's market to farmers who were not boatbuilders or who wanted to send less than a full boatload. In Decatur, he was trying to raise a flatboat crew to run a cargo from Beardstown to New Orleans and had learned that John Hanks was an experienced riverman. Handling a flatboat took both brawn and familiarity with river lore in order to avoid perils leading to shipwreck. For example, at least a half mile's travel downstream might occur while moving the craft a hundred feet across a river; thus a need to swerve around obstacles had to be perceived well in advance. And the boat couldn't be stopped simply by tossing a rope around a tree as the craft passed by; multiple tons of the vessel's inertia would break the cable in an instant.[62] Hanks wanted Lincoln and John Johnston on the crew, and according to Hanks, the three men agreed to hire on for about $60 for the trip plus an additional 50 cents a day, to be divided among the three boat hands, all four men agreeing to meet in Springfield when the spring thaw came.[63]

A nineteenth-century writer described the Deep Snow thaw: "The face of the country was covered with water. The little creeks became great rivers, and all intercourse between the settlers stopped; for people could have traveled better with steamboats than with ox teams." Thwarted in overland travel, at the beginning of March the three young flatboatmen bought a canoe and headed down the Sangamon River toward Springfield. They ran the canoe ashore a few miles from Springfield and walked the rest of the way. In Springfield, they found Offutt at the Buckhorn Tavern. The proprietor's son recalled: "The sign was a fine fat buck with fine horns pointed. He was painted proudly standing and, as it were, stamping. . . . The boys one night shot the deer full of bullet holes—he looked as if he ought to be dead, yet he stood on the sign and swung." Offutt had planned on buying a flatboat, but that arrangement had fallen through.[64]

He now hired the three Macon County men to build a flatboat, paying them $12 a month for that job. A few miles down the Sangamon from Springfield, they began cutting trees. "Suppose it was on Congress land," Hanks said. A safe supposition. A property owner was unlikely to permit free harvest of trees from his land, so people needing free timber typically went to "Congress land," a term for acreage owned by the U.S. government and not yet for sale to settlers or speculators. Such theft of government property was illegal and reduced the land's value, but the custom was common. Noted one Illinois visitor, "Settlers have . . . in defiance of the law, ransacked all the government lands within reach; never cutting a stick of their own for any purpose so long as there is any suitable that can be stolen from U.S. or Uncle Sam as they facetiously term the United States government."[65] Locals exhibited none of the visitor's concern. An 1833 Sangamon County newspaper advertisement announced: "The subscribers offer for sale, on good terms . . . twelve acres of land, with its improvements. . . . The country around abounds with excellent Congress timber."[66] Dispute could arise between interlopers on Congress land, ignoring that none of them had a right to steal the timber: "A murder was committed in Bond County, on Thursday last, by William Wilmington, on the person of Joseph Gillispie. A dispute arose between them about making rails—they both lived on Congress land, and . . . Wilmington told him he should not make any there, and if he did, he would kill him; Gillispie remarked that he reckoned not—whereupon Wilmington raised a rail and knocked him down, and broke his skull in one or two pieces."[67]

John Hanks recalled that the flatboat builders needed two weeks to steal enough trees. After making the logs into a raft, the crew floated them down to Sangamo Town, between Springfield and New Salem. (The terms "Sangamon" and "Sangamo" were used interchangeably in the era.) "Sangamo Town was then quite a place," John Roll remembered. "There were two stores, a steam saw mill and a gristmill, a tavern and a carding mill. I have seen fifty horses hitched there of a Saturday afternoon." At Sangamo Town, the crew had the logs cut into planks at a mill and assembled the craft. The men built a little shanty to live in during this stage of the enterprise, Lincoln acting as cook. Caleb Carman watched the operation and played cards with the men: "Played seven-up in the camp after dark," Carman said. "Abe played a good game." "He taught me how to play cards," a New Salem resident said. Having such skill was fortunate in that country; according to Illinois governor John Reynolds, "A person who could not, or would not play cards, was scarcely fit for genteel society."[68] A New Salem resident wryly noted the value placed on cards: "I locked up Shakespeare in a trunk with some other articles, among which was a few packs of cards. It was afterwards broken open. Shakespeare was not disturbed, and I have him yet. But the cards were among the missing."[69]

The Macon County men occasionally went into the village of Sangamo Town. John Hanks remembered Lincoln attending a juggler's exhibition. "I saw Abe at a show one night at Sangamo Town," Carman recalled. "The showman cooked eggs in Abe's hat. Abe, when the man called for the hat said, 'Mister, the reason why I didn't give you my hat before was out of respect to your eggs, not care for my hat.'" Villagers occasionally lounged at the boat construction site, and evidently some locals helped fabricate the vessel. Years later, when Lincoln was a well-known politician but before he was a national figure, Roll and a friend were joking that Roll's help with the flatboat construction ought to entitle him to a patronage job if Abe ever became President. During that conversation, Lincoln passed by and laughingly promised such a reward. "But I never got it," Roll later said.

Erastus Wright recalled Lincoln's appearance while building the flatboat: "boots off, hat, coat and vest off. Pants rolled up to his knees and shirt wet with sweat and combing his fuzzy hair with his fingers as he pounded away on the boat." "Abe was full of jokes during all this time," John Hanks said, "kept us alive." "He was funny," Caleb Carman recalled, "joky, humorous, full of yarns, stories, rigs [kidding], etc. He was frequently quoting poetry, reciting prose like orations." Carman also recalled that Lincoln "talked about politics considerable. He seemed to have the run of politics very well. He was a John Q. Adams man." From start to finish, the flatboat construction took about a month. The craft had below-deck as well as top-deck storage, and the crew slept below.[70]

While this construction project was under way, Lincoln signed a petition asking the Sangamon County Court to fill a constable position that had been vacant for some time. Such a document is barely worth mention, except for showing that a signature from someone just passing through was good enough for county petitions in that era. Lincoln also signed the names of John Hanks and John Johnston, further demonstrating the looseness of standards in such documents[71] (already seen in the Decatur polling-place petition). A couple years later, Lincoln wrote out a petition to the county court asking that an insane man be supported by county funds. Almost all the twenty-seven signatures were in Lincoln's handwriting.[72] Knowledge of such standards may well have influenced his later reactions to petitions arriving at the state legislature.

Offutt became more and more impressed with Lincoln. Coleman Smoot, who knew both men, said:

> Offutt seemed to think that with Lincoln as pilot or captain there was no such thing as fail in the navigation of the Sangamon. While building his flatboat he determined on their return from down the river to build a steamboat for the Sangamon. His friends remonstrated with him on account of the lowness of the river for a large part of the season and frozen over for months. Offutt said he intended to build it with rollers underneath so that when it came to a sandbar it would roll right over, and runners underneath for to run on the ice. For when Lincoln was captain, by thunder she would have to go.[73]

George Harrison remembered the loading of cargo, that Abe "attracted the farmers engaged in hauling corn to load the boat, by his profusion of anecdotes and jokes."[74] Caleb Carman said fifteen hundred bushels of corn were loaded, at a dime a bushel, to be sold for five times that price in New Orleans.[75] Whether Carman was right on those points is unclear; corn had to have been in short supply that spring, after Deep Snow privations. In mid-April, Offutt and his crew at last shoved off.

The river journey had been under way only a few miles when the boat hung up on a milldam at New Salem, a structure made of wooden cribs filled with stone. Exactly what happened is unclear. Lincoln said the river depth was neither exceptionally high nor low, but "was lower than it had been since the breaking of winter in February, or than it was for several weeks after." Billy Herndon's cousin Row Herndon similarly observed, "There was but one rise that come that spring to let a boat over, and that one was when the first breakup of snow" came. John Roll said, to the contrary, "The river was very high, fairly 'booming.'" Maybe the crew hoped the river current's power would carry the boat far enough across the dam that the craft's bow end would tilt down, allowing the boat's stern end to slide across the dam's top and down its face, just a foot or two high, by force of gravity with no dependence on the current. The journey would then continue. Before reaching the dam, perhaps the crew shifted cargo a bit toward the stern in order to lift the prow up and thereby give the boat a "running start" across the dam before the hull started scraping on the dam's top, friction that would slow the boat exactly when it needed to keep up speed. If the bow were not tilting into the air, the boat would simply crash head-on into the dam. Assorted accounts indicate that the flatboat got partway across the dam, but not far enough for the prow to tilt back down. Instead, it may have been left tilted somewhat upward in the air, with some portion of the hull resting on top of the dam, forcing the stern downward and the bow upward. At any rate, apparently the stern began taking in water belowdecks.

While not life threatening, the situation promised a chance of destroying the boat or dam or both, so a good throng turned out to watch the show. Onlookers included William G. Greene, known as "Slicky Bill": "There for the first time I saw Abraham Lincoln. . . . He was endeavoring to pry the boat over the dam. Whilst straining every nerve to push the boat off the dam, Mr. Lincoln having noticed by his quick river eye that the river was falling, remarked to Offutt, 'We will have to get the boat to the shore and unload it, or it will sink.'" The crew borrowed a boat from shore and began ferrying cargo from the flatboat to dry ground in order to lighten the craft. Eventually it became light enough that barrels still on board could be rolled forward, providing enough shift in weight to push the bow down and stern up. The scene was rather like a teeter-totter, with the flatboat as the board and the milldam as the fulcrum. When the bow tilted down enough for the belowdeck water to run forward to bow end, supposedly Lincoln bored a hole in the forward area to let the liquid out. After plugging the hole, more weight may have been transferred to the front, allowing the boat to slide down the dam as originally hoped. Descriptions are a little indefinite, but the preceding scenario seems reasonable. The boat was stuck at the dam for a portion of one day and overnight.[76]

Legality of the dam, incidentally, was in dispute. The state legislature had forbidden construction of dams or other obstructions to navigation on the Sangamon River from a few miles west of Decatur all the way to the river's mouth. Litigation involving a flatboat that sank after hanging up on a Sangamon River dam would be one of the first law cases handled by Lincoln after he became an attorney.[77] As early as 1830, a grievant had called the New Salem dam an obstruction to navigation; the legislature had given permission for construction, but apparently the Sangamon County Court ordered modification of the original structure in response to complaint.[78] In retrospect, Lincoln seemingly dismissed the milldam incident, saying, "The principal difficulties we encountered in descending the river were from the drifted timber,"[79] but he may have been referring to the Sangamon River trip as a whole. He made that statement in the context of what needed to be done to improve the channel.

Although he was only pausing—and involuntarily at that—in New Salem, Lincoln would date his residence in the village as starting now. Slicky Bill Greene and his brother Nult Greene long remembered how Abe "used to say to the boys and young men that they might always know when he came to New Salem by the high water in the spring after the Deep Snow, that he came down with it as a kind of 'driftwood.'"[80]

A little farther downstream from New Salem, the Offutt flatboat stopped to pick up a load of thirty or so live hogs that Offutt had bought to take down to New Orleans. Unsurprisingly the animals were uncooperative in being herded to the flatboat. Frontier pigs of that era were at least half wild, as farmers let them roam in the woods. "The breed of hogs in this part of the country is very bad; they are long-nosed, thin creatures, with legs like greyhounds; and, like the greyhound among dogs, seem to be the kind formed for speed and agility among swine, as they think nothing of galloping a mile at a heat, or of clearing fences which a more civilized hog would never attempt."[81] A pioneer later recalled: "The pigs of that day were a kind of wild beast. The breed was very different from anything we have now, they were active, enterprising, and self-reliant; and all they asked for was a free range of the woods. . . . In their habits they were ravenous to an extreme, and even ferocious; their voracity knew no bounds, and they would kill and eat up the young poultry and lambs on a farm without any scruple."[82] Humans were by no means safe around pigs:

During the night after the Johnson family moved into their cabin, they heard their dog barking and fighting with the hogs. The cabin had no door to it. A hole had been cut out for entrance, and also another for a fireplace. In the latter a large fire was burning, and some green sticks were near by. Mr. Johnson jumped up and grasped a long, green stick and met the hogs, about seventy-five in number, in the doorway as they were attempting to come in. He fought them there for life, while Mrs. Johnson prevented them from coming in at the fireplace by throwing fire at them. Mr. Johnson fought until he was exhausted completely. He battered their heads; he struck powerful blows, and at last knocked off the snout of one of the hogs, which ran squealing away to Funk's Grove, followed by the whole drove.[83]

One visitor declared, "It is true pork in this country costs nothing, and the way it is raised it is good for nothing." Such pigs were "the meanest that I have ever seen." Getting them to go somewhere was a little akin to herding cats, and taking hold of the hogs involved risk. The attempted solution reported by Lincoln might be dismissed as unbelievable if the story came from any other source—but John Hanks and Coleman Smoot backed him up on it. "Caught them," Hanks said, "Abe held the head of them, I the tail, and Offutt sewed up their eyes" to make the animals more cooperative. I have put medicated drops into the eyes of domestic cats and cannot imagine successfully sewing shut the eyes of one conscious ten-pound tame cat, let alone thirty larger and fiercer beasts. Perhaps the flatboaters had no concern about piercing eyeballs. Abe Lincoln and John Hanks said that after the sewing was completed, the animals wouldn't go anywhere, so they had to be trussed up and heaved aboard carts that took them to the flatboat. On board, the sewing was clipped so the pigs could open their eyes. Abe described the incident simply as "ludicrous."[84] The scene impressed witnesses. When Lincoln first ran for the state legislature, some locals remembered him as "the man who went to Orleans on a hog boat."[85]

The boat proceeded downstream on the Sangamon to the Illinois River. Travel along the Illinois must have been slow. A few years earlier, a traveler described the river:

> It presents to the eye a smooth and sluggish current, bordered on each side by an exuberant growth of aquatic plants, which, in some places, reach nearly across the channel. We found the water tepid and unpalatable, and oftentimes filled with decomposed vegetation to a degree that was quite offensive. . . . We moved upon so calm and smooth a surface, that sometimes it became a subject of debate whether there was any apparent current. . . . We came to a part of the river, which was covered for several hundred yards with a scum or froth of the most intense green colour, and emitting a nauseous exhalation, that was almost insupportable.[86]

A little ways after entering the Illinois River, Lincoln and his companions reached Beardstown, and from there made their way down the Illinois to the Mississippi and thence toward New Orleans. John Hanks said they made stops at Memphis, Vicksburg, Natchez, and elsewhere.[87] A nineteenth-century chronicler wrote that Natchez "was then noted as the hardest place on the Mississippi River. Many murders were committed there every day and human life was held very cheap."[88] From the south Mississippi River, a flatboat crew about this time reported "every night the voices of panthers and alligators." Gator "voices were

sometimes as numerous as the croakings of frogs in a pond."[89] Lincoln said John
Hanks left the flatboat crew at St. Louis, feeling the need to return to his family
because the trip was taking longer than expected.[90] John said otherwise—that he
went all the way to New Orleans and the crew split up in St. Louis on the *return
trip*.[91] Certainly the return would be a more likely occasion for Hanks to feel that
the trip seemed to be taking too long. We don't know why two such conflicting
stories were told, and most people tend to accept Lincoln's version. The point is
seemingly small and apparently not the only trivial difference in the two men's
memories of the trip,[92] but as we shall see, it is a factor in evaluating Hanks's testimony about what happened in New Orleans.

An 1830 visitor to New Orleans wrote:

> There are some 1,500 flatboats lying at the sides of the levee at a
> time, and frequently at the same moment 5,000 or 6,000 boatmen.
> Steamboats are arriving every hour. I have seen fifty steamboats at
> one point. No city contains a greater variety of population. Inhabi-
> tants from every state in the union, and from every country in
> Europe, mixed with the Creoles, and all the shades of the colored
> population, form an astonishing contrast of manners, languages, and
> complexions.[93]

A Pennsylvania newspaperman and canal contractor named Simon Cameron
hit New Orleans the same year Abe did and observed:

> I like the city exceedingly, the people are kind and hospitable. . . . The
> shipping now along the wharves far exceeds that of Philadelphia. . . .
>
> Everybody makes money here. Raw materials are all cheap and
> labor of every kind dear. The whole western world must come here
> and they do come and leave their money which is generally picked
> up by Yankees but they are clever Yankees.
>
> Next Saturday I shall go to a masquerade if I have time. On Sun-
> day perhaps to the French Theatre. All matters of pleasure are
> attended to on Sunday and many of the stores are open on that day.[94]

A foreign traveler in the city noted, "The object of all seems to be to make
money, and to spend it."[95] While visiting there a few years later, an amazed Illinois Democrat named Adam Snyder remarked: "I never yet saw as extravagant a
place. . . . Where in the name of God all the money comes from I cannot tell."[96]
Eventually Lincoln would become well acquainted with Cameron and Snyder,
and also with Illinois attorney Leonard Swett, who gave this colorful description:

> The boatmen also form a distinct feature among the people of
> Orleans. They live an aquatic life, spending most of the year upon the

river in their ill-constructed crafts and perhaps not improperly have been styled a brother to the alligator whose domains they inhabit. As they walk along the levee, they may be easily distinguished from the crowd, by that peculiar swagger and independent air which can never be counterfeited. . . . Woe to the man who provokes the boatman's wrath, for the darts of death are not more deadly and sure than the stroke of his revenge. . . .

The farmers along the rivers, raising much produce which would afford him [sic] profit if marketed, built him a "flatboat" or a box about ten feet wide and perhaps twenty long and covered with a lid so as to be capable of containing several tons. Filling this with the fruits of his labors he literally casts himself and his bread to the waters, without sails or any locomotive force, he fearlessly trusts to the current alone to impel him onward. In a month perhaps if he escapes the snags, he arrives at New Orleans. [Illegible] he sells his cargo and boat, the latter being worthless except for wood. . . .

Little can be said in favor of the morals of New Orleans, on the contrary habits and amusements are countenanced which are wicked and deplorable. . . . Perhaps nowhere in the world is gaming practiced so extensively as here. . . . The drinking houses are numerous and well patronized. In some of the streets I have taken notice and more than half of the rooms are grog-shops. . . .

The police and watchmen deserve some notice. . . . The watchmen are the robust men and the city so divided between them that each one shall have his separate walks. They are "armed to the teeth" and not at all afraid to use their weapons. They are [illegible] over town thick as bees and the least disturbance will collect them by twenties.

From fifty to an hundred boats may be seen at one time at the levee, and more ships and other vessels than will be found in any harbor in the Union.[97]

A visitor in New Orleans not long before Abe arrived observed: "Only a few of the streets are paved. The cleaning of the streets is performed under the direction of overseers, by slaves chained together, with hardly any clothes on their backs, sent for the purpose, at the discretion of their masters, as a punishment for some delinquency, whether real or supposed. Even females are frequently employed in this way. The masters generally receive about a shilling sterling per day for each slave thus employed." He added: "There is a corps of mounted *gen d'armes*. In this respect, in the appearance of an armed police, Charleston and New Orleans do not resemble the free cities of America; but the great number of blacks, and the way in which they are treated by the whites, render this precaution . . . indispensably necessary."[98] Not all whites, however, perceived oppression and danger. An 1831 Illinois magazine contained this tourist's report:

In Charleston, the stranger will not fail to remark, that he is in a country, where the negro . . . seems to be well at ease, and comfortable, if not rising in the world. The stranger . . . must admit, that the evils of slavery are softened by humane treatment. . . .

I have never seen elsewhere, and I fear I never shall, such an outgushing of affection as I have seen on the arrival of "young master" or mistress. I have even had a share of it myself, in my relation of cousin to the young heir apparent. A hundred sable arms were extended to hug him, and he was patted, petted, and thrice blessed. This is a feeling that you can hardly conceive in New England, for it cannot subsist between a man and his cattle; but in Carolina it raised my estimation of the master and sympathy for the slave. The slave . . . is kind and cheerful, and he is never better pleased than when he can contribute to the pleasure of a white man. In riding, I have often known boys of fifteen and upwards, run by my side for miles to open the gates, and the happiness of any negro is complete when he is permitted "to take his pleasure," that is, when hunting or fishing. . . .

The slaves have their own private fields, poultry and swine, and can often purchase delicacies; and I believe, that one, very prudent, might, in twelve years, collect enough to purchase his freedom.[99]

That song of the South was contradicted by an article reprinted in the Springfield, Illinois, newspaper regarding slave revolt. Southerners "dare not speak freely on this subject at a dinner table when a slave is within hearing. Such conversation is obscure or in whispers." The article continued: "They do not go to bed at night with the same ease and freedom that we do. They call their military to their aid, and keep their slaves under martial law. The citizens of Richmond, Charleston, and Savannah, keep up a military guard. No small portion of the white population must watch under arms, while the other portion sleeps. . . . John Randolph hardly exaggerated when he described the Richmond mother as more tenderly pressing her infant to her bosom, at each sound of the clock or toll of the bell at night."[100] The year before Lincoln traveled to New Orleans, the Louisiana legislature decreed: "Whoever shall write, print, publish or distribute any thing having a tendency to produce . . . insubordination among the slaves therein, shall on conviction thereof . . . be sentenced to imprisonment, at hard labor for life or suffer death," and "Whoever shall make use of language in prvivate discourses or shall make use of signs or actions, having a tendency . . . to excite insubordination . . . shall on conviction . . . suffer imprisonment at hard labor, not less than three years nor more than twenty-one years, or death."[101] A happy populace cannot be roused.

New Orleans slave auctions were something of a tourist attraction. In 1831, auctions were advertised daily. One week, dealers received 371 slaves, mostly from Virginia and South Carolina.[102] A few years after Lincoln and the other two Macon County boys walked the streets of New Orleans, Adam Snyder wrote, "Every day here you see negroes set up on a stand and sold, droves of them chained and driven along to the cotton and sugar plantations, miserable, half clothed, and starved-looking beings."[103] John Hanks said: "We saw negroes chained, maltreated, whipped and scourged. Lincoln saw it. His heart bled. Said nothing much, was silent from feeling, was sad, looked bad, felt bad, was thoughtful and abstracted. I can say knowingly that it was on this trip that he formed his opinions of slavery. It ran its iron into him then and there."[104] The account Jesse Weik ghosted for Billy Herndon said:

> One morning in their rambles over the city the trio passed a slave auction. A vigorous and comely mulatto girl was being sold. She underwent a thorough examination at the hands of the bidders; they pinched her flesh and made her trot up and down the room like a horse, to show how she moved, and in order, as the auctioneer said, that "bidders might satisfy themselves" whether the article they were offering to buy was sound or not. The whole thing was so revolting that Lincoln moved away from the scene with a deep feeling of "unconquerable hate." Bidding his companions follow him he said, "By God, boys, let's get away from this. If ever I get a chance to hit that thing, I'll hit it hard." This incident was furnished me in 1865, by John Hanks. I have also heard Mr. Lincoln refer to it himself.[105]

Reference to a "room" in which the girl's sale took place suggests it was one of the higher-toned auction operations, as opposed to an outdoor sale of common laborers. And sexual implications were obvious not only in the bidders' conduct, but also in referral to the slave as a "vigorous and comely mulatto girl." According to Hanks, Abe was angry enough about the scene that his comments continued and eventually became indiscreet: "His talk agin slavery right down thar amongst it. . . . We were afeared of gettin' into trouble about his talkin' so much, and we coaxed him with all our might to be quieter-like down thar, for it wouldn't do any good nohow."[106] Hanks apparently said of Abe's comment at the auction: "It was his stepbrother he made that remark to. . . . I was not at the sale at the time."[107] Distinguished authorities have implied or outright asserted that Hanks and Herndon fabricated that story, on grounds that neither was present in New Orleans and therefore could not have heard the remark.[108] Uncertainty exists about whether John Hanks was in the city, although we can be certain that Billy Herndon was absent. A person doesn't have to be present at an event, however, in order to know it happened. No reason exists for skepticism, let alone rejection, of Hanks's and Herndon's testimonies that they heard Lincoln talk about the incident.

No reason exists, either, to think that Lincoln's reaction to slavery was widely shared in Illinois. Admittedly his feelings weren't unique, as shown by these 1831 resolutions passed by the Shoal Creek Meeting House, Bond County:

Resolved, That in the opinion of this meeting, the buying, selling, or holding slaves for the purpose of gain, convenience, ease, or honor, is a scandal to the Presbyterian Church.

Resolved, That every attempt to justify it by the Bible is a slander on that holy work.

Resolved, That to honor any man as a fit person for the gospel ministry, as a worthy member of the Christian Church, as a philanthropist, as a good and honest citizen, or even as a republican, who holds slaves, or vindicates the practice of slavery, is contrary both to the precepts of the Christian religion, and the spirit of our civil institutions.[109]

Such an attitude, however, was advanced for the era. A likely expression of community consensus can be found in Illinois statutes that rewarded residents for hunting down fugitive slaves. Blacks had to have certificates proving they weren't slaves: "Every black or mulatto person who shall be found in this state, and not having such a certificate as is required by this act, shall be deemed a runaway slave or servant," and "If any person shall harbor such negro or mulatto . . . not having such certificate . . . or shall hire, or in any wise give sustenance to such negro or mulatto, not having such certificate of freedom . . . shall be fined . . . five hundred dollars, one half thereof to the use of the county, and the other half to the party giving information thereof."[110] Just before Lincoln went to New Orleans, the Illinois legislature passed a law saying, "No black or mulatto person shall hereafter be permitted to come and reside in this state" without first giving a $1,000 bond guaranteeing good behavior and economic self-suffiency. Illinois law also forbade anyone to bring slaves into the state with the intention of freeing them.[111]

Lincoln's New Orleans sojourn lasted about a month. John Hanks said all four men left New Orleans in June and went to St. Louis by steamboat. Gustave Koerner, with whom Lincoln would later become well acquainted, recalled an 1833 visit to St. Louis:

Nearly one-half of the people we met on the streets were black or mulattoes. . . . The Americans were almost to a man from the Southern States. Passing the court-house, we saw colored men, women and children sold at auction. We were also shown a sort of prison, where refractory slaves were confined at the request of their masters or were whipped at their masters' cost, by men regularly appointed for that purpose. . . . From the second story of our residence we could see into the yard of a neighboring house, where we once saw what appeared to be an American lady, lashing a young slave girl with a cow hide.[112]

About the time Lincoln left St. Louis, a Northern immigrant wrote: "I don't feel much at home in St. Louis. This is a slave state and the inhabitants are haughty and arrogant."[113] John Hanks said it was on this return trip (not on the downward trip as Lincoln said) that the party split up in St. Louis. The three hired hands crossed to Illinois and walked about twenty-five miles to Edwardsville. From there Hanks went on to Springfield or Decatur, and the other two to Coles County, where Tom Lincoln and the rest of the Indiana migration party had moved from Macon County, Illinois.[114]

While Abe was returning to Illinois, his father was leaving. A nineteenth-century chronicler noted:

> The year 1831 was particularly celebrated for the fever and ague. A great deal of rich soil was turned over for the first time, and the vapors and exhalations made the climate unhealthy. Mr. Esek Greenman says that out of twenty-four persons belonging to three families, twenty-three had the ague. It was as much to be expected as harvest or the changes of the seasons. It was a disease to be dreaded because of its effect upon the mind as well as upon the physical system. It induced a feeling of despondency, and took away that spirit of enterprise and that strong will, which bore up the settlers under misfortune. For many years the fever and ague was the scourge of the West.[115]

Attorney Stephen T. Logan recalled: "I came to Springfield on the 16th of May 1832. . . . Very soon after I came I began to get the symptoms of the chills and fever, and then I wished I had never left Kentucky. But then I couldn't get away; I would have left if I could have done so. In those days I have often seen ten wagons going back to where I saw one coming this way."[116]

A year of fever and deep snow was enough to convince Tom Lincoln that he had made a mistake, and he and the rest of the migration party (except the two young men returning from New Orleans) began heading back to Indiana. En route from Macon County, Illinois, they paused in Coles County at the homestead of a fellow named Sawyer. Assorted friends and relatives of Tom's also resided nearby. Perhaps their combined influence encouraged him to stop there instead of continuing on.[117] He and Sarah stayed and would spend the rest of their lives in Coles County. From now on, their lives had little to do with Abraham's, as he was now out on his own.

During the flatboat enterprise, Abe had accepted a further employment offer from Offutt, who was establishing himself as a merchant in New Salem and wanted Lincoln as an assistant. So after a visit with his family in Coles County, Abe headed west to New Salem, where he arrived in July.[118]

He already had local notoriety from rescuing the boat on the milldam, and villagers were pleased to discover a winning personality. Robert Rutledge, son of the town's old tavern keeper, remembered that when Abe settled in New Salem, he "was all life and animation, seemed to see the bright side of every picture."[119]

"Uncle Jimmy" Short recalled: "On coming into New Salem at that time, Mr. Lincoln was pointed out to me by my sister . . . whom Mr. Lincoln had before that time employed to make him a pair of pantaloons. . . . Without the necessity of a formal introduction we fell in together and struck up a conversation. . . . He made a favorable impression upon me . . . through his intelligence and sprightliness."[120] Royal Clary said, "He was humorous, witty and good natured, and that geniality drew him into our notice so quick."[121] Lincoln himself stated that he "rapidly made acquaintances and friends."[122]

Although New Salem had about a hundred residents in a couple dozen cabins, the usual family interconnections meant the town had only a dozen or so families. The place was a mercantile center where a larger outlying population could obtain assorted services, with stores, milling, blacksmithing, barrel making, and the like.[123]

In July, Offutt was back in Sangamon County, but Abe arrived in New Salem before the store merchandise did,[124] so Lincoln was temporarily unemployed. Apparently in that summer of 1831, he was hired by Reuben Brown to work on a Sangamon County farm that Brown was renting from William Butler. As told by someone who reported a conversation with Mrs. Brown, she recalled:

> [Abe] worked all the season, and made a crop of corn, and the next winter . . . they hauled the corn all the way to Galena, and sold it for $2.50 per bushel. . . . One evening a right smart looking man rode up to the fence, and asked my old man if he could get to stay overnight. "Well," said Mr. Brown, "we can feed your crittur, and give you something to eat, but we can't lodge you unless you can sleep on the same bed with my hired man." The man hesitated, and asked, "Where is he?" "Well," said Mr. Brown, "you can come and see him." So the man got down from his crittur, and Mr. Brown took him around where, in the shade of the house, Mr. Lincoln lay stretched at full length . . . on the green grass with an open book before him. Pointing to him, "There," said Mr. Brown, "he is." The stranger gazed on him a moment, and said, "Well, I think he'll do."[125]

The stranger explained, "A man who reads a book as hard as that fellow seems to, has got too much else to think of besides my watch or my small change."[126]

Farm owner Butler was on hand one day when Rev. Peter Cartwright stopped by. Reverend Cartwright might well be considered the most prominent Methodist minister in the multistate region, and he had been acquainted with Jesse Head, who performed the Thomas Lincoln–Nancy Hanks wedding ceremony.[127] Though Sangamon County voters had recently forced Cartwright to take a break from service as an Illinois legislator,[128] he remained one of the state's more important Democratic politicians. Butler remembered that Reverend Cartwright was "dressed as became his station" and Lincoln "was awkward and very shabbily dressed." On this occasion, the reverend preached the Democratic gospel for a while, with Brown a friendly listener but Butler and Lincoln more skeptical. Abe decided to join in. "A discussion soon arose between him and Cartwright," Butler recalled, "and my first special attention was attracted to Lincoln by the way in which he met the great preacher in his arguments, and the extensive acquaintance he showed with the politics of the state—in fact he quite beat him in the argument."[129]

An election came off on August 1, 1831, and Abe voted in New Salem. Tradition says he served as a polling-place clerk, but poll records show otherwise. No secret ballot existed. A man (women couldn't vote) walked up to poll officials and publicly announced his vote, which was then written down next to his name. Lincoln was one of the later voters that day, so onlookers knew the precinct's trend when he declared his preferences.[130]

His unpopular choice for U.S. Congress was a former Tennessean, Gen. James Turney. In Illinois, any claim to military title helped pull votes, but Turney's claim was a stretch, originating from his service as Illinois attorney general. An acquaintance described Turney as "commanding eloquence, and of a very majestic appearance." An example of his eloquence is preserved by an attorney of that time, who recalled the end of a murder trial:

> The judge then said, "Mr. Green, the court gives you until this day four weeks, at which time you are to be hung." The case was prosecuted by James Turney . . . who here interposed and said: "May it please the court . . . on solemn occasions like the present when the life of a human being is to be sentenced away for crime by an earthly tribunal it is usual and proper for courts to pronounce a formal sentence, in which the leading features of the crime shall be brought to the recollection of the prisoner, a sense of guilt impressed upon his conscience, and in which the prisoner should be duly exhorted to repentance, and warned against the judgment in a world to come." To this the judge replied: "O! Mr. Turney, Mr. Green understands the whole matter as well as if I had preached to him a month. He knows he has got to be hung this day four weeks. You understand it in that way, Mr. Green, don't you?" "Yes," said the prisoner; upon which the judge ordered him to be remanded to jail and the court then adjourned.

Like Abe Lincoln, Turney was a follower of Henry Clay—the great opponent of President Jackson. Or at least Turney was at the time; apparently he ran as a Jackson elector in 1824, when some say Turney was secretly pledged to vote for William Crawford in the Electoral College. During the 1830 election campaign, a critic of Turney's wrote:

> [Ninian Edwards,] while a Senator in Congress, stated at Belleville, in Mitchell's store, that he had a damned notion to resign his office

as Senator, and return to Madison County, and become a candidate for the legislature, for the express purpose of impeaching Judge John Reynolds and James Turney, for corruption in their offices, as judge and attorney general: that property was no longer safe in the country where the laws were administered by such men: that Mrs. Edwards was compelled to have his horses led through his parlor or passage every night, and kept in the backyard, to keep them from being stolen. . . . Judge Reynolds talked about cutting off the damned old rascal's ears—but the matter *died away*—Edwards has his ears still on his head.

Ninian Edwards had lived in Hardin County, Kentucky, when Abe's parents lived there. The critic also said of Turney:

As attorney general, he is reported by the cashier of the branch bank at Edwardsville, as a defaulter to that branch, for notes placed in his hands for collection, for a sum over six thousand dollars! This fact was communicated officially to the legislature during the last session, and a suit brought against him ten or twelve months afterwards, by the present attorney general [George Forquer], too late to be tried by the last supreme court. He is now making speeches in favor of John Reynolds; and lately told a gentleman in Springfield (whose name can be given if required) that he was to be appointed secretary of state by John Reynolds, if [Reynolds was] elected.

John Reynolds, nicknamed "the Old Ranger," was elected governor in that August 1830 balloting but didn't make such an appointment. Alexander Pope Field continued to be secretary of state under the Old Ranger and was running against Turney for Congress in 1831, when Lincoln voted. Reynolds wasn't fastidious about keeping promises, so maybe the story was right or maybe it wasn't. Supposedly Reynolds denied the story, which admittedly wasn't from a disinterested source. It came from the brother of incumbent Congressman Joseph Duncan, and Joseph defeated Turney, Field, and two other candidates for Congress in the August 1831 election. Alexander Trent, however, attested to the story's accuracy:

I am assured by David Batterton, a respectable citizen of this county, that James Turney told him that he supported the election of Reynolds because Reynolds had promised to make him (Turney) secretary of state. Judge Reynolds, at the last circuit court in this county, made a bargain of a similar nature with Capt. Bowling Green, who was then a candidate for a seat in the legislature. He told Green that they had been old rangers, and if he would decline as a candidate, and use his influence for him (Reynolds) that he (Reynolds) would give him (Green) an office worth more than the office of representative: in consequence of which proposition Green did decline, and is now one of the most active supporters of John Reynolds.

This statement of the bargain between Green and Reynolds, was told by Green himself to Allen Richardson, William Green, and others.

. . . I live in Sangamon County, Illinois, and hold myself at all times responsible for the truth of what I write.

That last sentence invited a duel if any of the men Trent referred to were offended enough; dueling was illegal in Illinois, so language about such matters required discreet phrasing. Bowling Green immediately issued a handbill denying Trent's story. After the 1830 election, Green had enough clout in the legislature to be chosen doorkeeper of the Illinois house of representatives, and Governor Reynolds soon appointed Bowling Green to a plum job, that of Illinois canal commissioner, a position of great statewide political influence and equally great potential for personal financial gain through insider knowledge and manipulation of contracts.[131]

In August 1831, however, Bowling Green was running for justice of the peace in New Salem and received Lincoln's publicly declared vote. Green won that local election. Constables were also elected that day, and Lincoln's votes helped elect Henry Sinco and Bowling Green's half-brother Jack Armstrong. John Rutledge and Bennett Abell were defeated in their bids for the constabulary. Abe would soon acquire an up-close-and-personal acquaintanceship with Armstrong. Rutledge was the town's senior merchant and father of Ann, a young woman with whom Lincoln would become well acquainted. He would also become well acquainted with Abell's sister-in-law Mary Owens.[132]

At the election, Abe was among the later voters, and Billy Herndon's cousin Row Herndon offered this memory of the occasion:

In the afternoon, as things were dragging a little, Lincoln, the new man, began to spin out a stock of yarns. One that amused me more than any other he called the lizard story. "The meeting house," he said, "was in the woods and quite a distance from any other house. It was only used once a month. The preacher—an old line Baptist—was dressed in coarse linen pantaloons, and shirt of the same material. The pants manufactured after the old fashion, with baggy legs and a flap in front, were made to attach to his frame without the aid of suspenders. A single button held his shirt in position, and that was at the collar. He rose up in the pulpit and with a loud voice announced his text thus: 'I am the Christ, whom I shall represent today.' About this time a blue lizard ran up underneath his roomy pantaloons. The old preacher, not wishing to interrupt the steady flow of his sermon, slapped away on his legs, expecting to arrest the intruder; but his efforts were unavailing, and the little fellow kept on ascending higher and higher. Continuing the sermon, the preacher slyly loosened the central button which graced the waist line of his pantaloons and with a kick, off came that easy fitting garment. But meanwhile Mr. Lizard had passed the equatorial line of waist band and was calmly exploring that part of the preacher's anatomy which lay underneath the back of his shirt. Things were now growing interesting, but the sermon was still grinding on. The next movement on the preacher's part was for the collar button, and with one sweep of his arm off came the tow linen shirt. The congregation sat for an instant as if dazed; at length one old lady in the rear of the room rose up and glancing at the excited object in the pulpit shouted at the top of her voice: 'If you represent Christ then I'm done with the Bible.'"[133]

Such a story would have offended some among the pious. That Lincoln felt comfortable poking public fun at a minister tells us something about him and shows that the men of New Salem appreciated such ridicule.

In New Salem, Denton Offutt was setting up his store. A resident recalled, "Offutt brought some goods, wares, and merchandise up from Beardstown, and Lincoln put them up, unboxed them and put them up on shelves." Already, that era was bureaucratic enough that Offutt had to get a store license, the $5 fee implying that he began with a $1,000 inventory.[134]

As September started, Offutt got a deed, witnessed by Abe Lincoln and Slicky Bill Greene, for a New Salem lot. One authority says this is where he put up his store; another says Offutt rented a structure. We have proof he was borrowing money from a Whig politician at an interest rate of 60 percent.[135] Around the middle of September 1831, his store seems to have been ready for business.[136] Apparently Lincoln earned $15 a month as chief clerk.[137] Slicky Bill Greene worked with him: "Mr. Lincoln and I clerked together for Offutt about eighteen months and slept on the same cot, and when one turned over the other had to do likewise. He was an attentive, kind, generous, and accommodating clerk, and was then as much a center of attraction as he was when President of the U.S., though not quite so grand a one."[138] Jack Armstrong's brother-in-law said Lincoln "was a good obliging clerk and an honest one. He increased Offutt's business much by his simplicity. Open, candid, obliging, and honest. Everybody loved him."[139] Mentor Graham watched Abe in action: "He was among the best clerks I ever saw: He was attentive to his business, was kind and considerate to his customers and friends and always treated them with great tenderness, kindness, and honesty. He in fact superintended and managed Offutt's whole business."[140] Rather than wait for a customer's next trip to the store, Lincoln walked three miles to correct a 6¼-cent error in making change. He made a similar journey to deliver four ounces of tea to someone who had been shorted by a mistake in scale weights. Supposedly such occurrences really happened and were extraordinary enough to be talked about and remembered.[141]

He also protected customers in other ways:

> [Charlie Revis] was in the habit of coming to Salem about every other day and would . . . sit and spin out his yarns to the men who would gather around him. As he had at one time been a hand on a keel-boat he had contracted the habit of using profane language. He could swear by note. In fact, almost every other word was an oath. He was so in the habit of swearing that he scarcely knew when he did swear.
>
> One day he came into the store while a couple of ladies were in the store doing some trading, and getting their mail. Charlie was sitting on a dry goods box telling his stories to his companions and almost every word he would utter one of his big oaths.
>
> Lincoln noticed that the ladies were very much shocked at his profanity, and after they had left Lincoln walked up to Revis and said to him: "Now Charlie Revis, I have admonished you a number of times about swearing in this store before ladies and you have paid no attention to it and now I am going to punish you so you will recollect it." So he took him by the arm and led him out a short distance from the store to a vacant lot where there was a large patch of smart weed.
>
> He threw him on his back and put his foot on his breast and commenced to gather smart weed. He then commenced and rubbed his face, eyes and mouth with it till Revis began to yell and he promised Mr. Lincoln if he would let him up he would never swear in the presence of ladies again. Lincoln told him to promise that he would never swear before anybody again and Charlie promised. Mr. Lincoln let him up and a complete reformation was made in the language of Charlie Revis, and from that day his most intimate friends said that they never heard an oath escape his lips.[142]

Offutt's was not the only general merchandise store in town. All scrambled to survive. Frontier folk vacillated in their feeling toward such a business. It served somewhat as a broker. Customers could run up a tab and bring in farm produce as barter to pay off the debt. The store owner would then ship off the produce and sell it for cash in a distant market; Offutt already started that sort of thing with the New Orleans flatboat before he opened his store as a steady source of produce to ship. A later chronicler said Offutt traveled through the area "urging the production of bigger and better crops. . . . He would prove the Sangamon navigable. . . . He would buy all the grain and pork the farmers . . . could raise, process what was needed for their family use at his mill, settle their accounts at his store with part of it, and sell the excess in New Orleans. These were to be . . . links in a chain of integrated enterprises which . . . would make every participant a . . . fortune."[143] Some years before Offutt set up, a traveler noted, "There is a class of men throughout the western country called 'merchants,' who, in the summer and autumn months, collect flour, butter, cheese, pork, beef, whiskey, and every species of farming produce, which they send in flats and keel-boats to the New Orleans market. The demand created by this trade, added to a large domestic consumption, insures the most remote farmer a certain market. Some of these speculators have made large fortunes."[144] Such operations provided a market for local produce and allowed people to acquire goods without having to use cash.

Normally on the frontier, cash was in short supply. Storekeepers were glad to accept it, of course, but tended to send the cash to their wholesale suppliers rather than circulate it around the local community. So stores were viewed as draining off cash needed by frontier settlements. Frontiersmen were well aware of a barter economy's limits, and many felt that progress in their territory was hindered by anything that drained away cash. Stores often ran up tabs with their wholesale suppliers, and when those suppliers insisted on receiving their money, storekeepers had to squeeze their debtor customers for cash, using personal persuasion or court-ordered debt collection enforced by sales of confiscated personal property. Successful store owners easily developed reputations as heartless. The kinder ones went out of business.

Abe Lincoln did more than stand behind a counter. Mentor Graham recalled: "Hands being scarce, Lincoln turned in and cut down trees and split enough rails for Offutt to [build] a pen sufficiently large to contain one thousand hogs. . . . Offutt had purchased a great deal of corn and had it at, in, and about the mill. The hogs were purchased to eat the corn, so that [they] would become good, well fed and fattened hogs for market."[145] Fattening hogs in a pen, instead of having them run wild in the woods where they found their own food, was a new practice. John Cameron and James Rutledge owned the saw- and gristmill where the flatboat had hung up but now rented it to Offutt. A New Salem physician said that Abe "used to unload sacks of wheat from farmers' wagons, measure out and settle with them for the same."[146] Rutledge's son Robert remembered, "Mr. Lincoln was ever ready to work with his stalwart hand, and to assist in constructing or repairing the dams or mill, raising houses in the village, etc.; and this, too, when he had no personal interest in the success of the enterprise."[147]

By September 1831, New Salem folk began routinely calling on Lincoln to sign their legal documents as witness.[148] Such service may simply signify that he could write and was conveniently available to sign his name, but a person held in low esteem would not have been sought out for such purpose. So we know fellow townsmen quickly considered him a solid citizen.

A gang known as the Clary's Grove Boys now called on him in order to determine how solid he was in another context. That encounter was basically Offutt's doing. He was impressed with his clerk, roaring to New Salem folk, "By God, Lincoln will yet be President of these United States."[149] That kind of bragging was harmless, but Offutt started claiming that Lincoln could whip anyone in athletic competition or in personal combat.[150] That sort of brag attracted attention among New Salem's red-blooded element.

Thus far we've been considering the higher- and midtoned New Salem folk. There was also a noticeable percentage of rougher characters. Jimmy Short, often called "Uncle" Jimmy, noted that "New Salem and the surrounding country was settled by roughs and bullies, who were in the habit of winning all the money of strangers at cards, and then whipping them in the bargain."[151] A substantial contingent of such folks lived a few miles from New Salem, over toward the neighboring Clary's Grove district. Like a twentieth-century motorcycle gang, the Clary's Grove Boys would ride into New Salem and take it over. They "pretty much had their way," John Potter recalled.[152] If you could stay out of their way, you were okay. But they were kind of hard to avoid. You then did your damn best to avoid frustrating them about anything. Their frustration threshold lowered as whiskey intake rose. "Neat clothing, correct speech, and gentlemanly bearing were often a sufficient provocation."[153] A survivor recalled:

> They trimmed the manes and tails of horses, cut bridles so that but a little remained to break at the first pull; cut girths, put stones under saddles so as to cause riders to be thrown mounting. Right here in front of Offutt's store they rolled James Jordan down that hill. You see it goes down at an angle of forty-five degrees. Then it reached down to the river 200 feet. . . . He used to come here for whisky fifteen miles, and he would get his fill. When drunk the Armstrongs headed him up in a hogshead. He was a large, fat fellow, and nearly filled it. Then they sent it rolling down the hill. It went with increasing velocity, threatening to go into the river, when it was caught under a leaning white oak, and their victim liberated. Lincoln was here, surrounded by tough fellows of this stamp.[154]

Daniel Burner remembered: "This same crowd called up an old man with a wooden leg and made him a prisoner. They then built a fire around the wooden leg, and held the man there until the wooden leg was consumed."[155] Uncle Jimmy Short said, "The stories about Armstrong and others cooking [a] live pig etc. may be true."[156] James Taylor said there was no doubt about it, "The roughs of New Salem and surrounding country did cook a live pig in a tin plate stove."[157] Someone who spoke with Slicky Bill Greene reported that the "magistrates were afraid to issue process against 'Clary's Grove Boys.'"[158] And since any such writs were served by the constable, and newly elected constable Jack Armstrong was the leader of the Clary's Grove Boys, success in serving writs was doubtful. In their territory, the Clary's Grove Boys pretty much held sway. Similar bands were the Island Grove Boys, Sangamon River Boys, and Sand Ridge Boys,[159] but accounts indicate the Clary's Grove Boys ruled.

Robust incidents were part of town life. Lincoln recalled one:

> A certain rough, rude, and bullying man in our county had a bulldog, which was as rude, rough, and bullying as his master. Dog and man were the terror of the neighborhood. Nobody dared to touch either for fear of the other. But a crafty neighbor laid a plan to dispose of the dog. Seeing Slocum and his dog plodding along the road one day, the dog a little ahead, this neighbor, who was prepared for the occasion, took from his pocket a junk [*sic*] of meat in which he had concealed a big charge of powder, to which was fastened a deadwood slow-match. This he lighted, and then threw it into the road. The dog gave one gulp at it, and the whole thing disappeared down his throat. He trotted on a few steps, when there was a sort of smothered roar, and the dog blew up in fragments. . . . The head of the dog lit on the porch, the fore-legs caught astraddle the fence, the hind-legs fell in the ditch, and the rest of the dog lay around loose.

I wonder whether the fuse would have kept going long enough inside the dog to fire the charge, but the story *is* told by Honest Abe.[160]

Gander pullings were popular. A gander would be tied upside down from a tree limb, with its neck greased, and horsemen would pay to ride fast under it while grabbing for the neck. Whoever yanked off the head won.[161] Someone who watched a gander pulling wrote, "The protracted torture to which the poor bird was subjected for half a hour—the agonized writhings and convulsions—the blood starting from every pore of his lacerated skin, from the body to the head, and streaming out of his eyes—and, finally, the shock, when his neck was broken, and the mercy of death granted to him—may have afforded 'sport' to those who were engaged in it—but filled me with pain and disgust."[162] Such were the sportsmen who admired Abe Lincoln and whose companionship Abe enjoyed. Reportedly Lincoln had enjoyed cockfights since his Indiana days and was selected to judge them in New Salem[163] and to decide horse races as well,[164] where the winner might be less obvious than at a gander pull. An Illinois pioneer noted: "Quarter races were the most common, and at which the most chicanery and jugglery were practiced. In quarter races, more depends on fast judges than fast horses."[165] A horse-race official declared: "Lincoln is the fairest man I ever had to deal with. If Lincoln is in this county when I die I want him to be my administrator, for he is the only man I ever met with that was wholly and purely and unselfishly honest."[166] According to Abe's best friend, Josh Speed, Lincoln's fairness in judging such competitions won him the nickname "Honest Abe."[167]

Lincoln had the personality and physique to hold his own in such surroundings. Ann Rutledge's brother Robert said: "I have seen him frequently take a barrel of whiskey by the chimes and lift it up to his face as if to drink out of the bunghole. This feat he could accomplish with the greatest ease."[168] Daniel Burner similarly reported, "I have often seen him pick up a barrel of whisky, place it on the counter, and then lower it on the other side."[169] Slicky Bill Greene lost some small bets to a confidence man, but on Lincoln's advice, he beat the confidence man with a substantial bet that Abe could lift a forty-gallon whiskey barrel and drink from the bunghole. Part of the sting on the confidence man was evidently that the bet didn't specify how the barrel would be lifted. Lincoln squatted, rolled the barrel along his thighs until he could reach the bunghole with his mouth, and slightly stood, lifting with his legs rather than his arms.[170] Row Herndon declared: "He was by far the stoutest man that I ever took hold of. I was a mere child in his hands, and I considered myself as good a man as there was in the country until he come about. I saw him lift between 1,000 and 1,300 pounds of rock weighed in a box."[171] Uncle Jimmy Short remembered Lincoln hoisting "1,000 pounds of shot by main strength."[172] Hardin Bale didn't see it but was convinced that "he made a box in the mill, put stones in it and raised 1,000 [pounds] by throwing straps across his shoulders, he getting on some logs. I saw the box, rocks, and straps; and it is said by good men and true that he lifted the thousand pounds."[173] Slicky Bill Greene said he saw it: "I saw him lift one thousand and twenty-four pounds. He was harnessed with straps in the New Salem mills."[174]

A feat like that was surely impossible, but such was Lincoln's reputation around New Salem. And such may have been nearly the reality until his death. On meeting a Canadian editor, the President "extended his hand and shook mine kindly, but rather loosely, as if he was afraid of hurting it."[175] An army sergeant declared, "He had a grip on him like a vise, and I felt my whole hand would be crushed."[176] The President spent a lengthy time visiting and shaking hands with each wounded soldier in a hospital, perhaps five to six thousand men. Afterward, "the surgeon expressed the fear that the President's arm would be lamed with so much handshaking, saying that it certainly must ache. Mr. Lincoln smiled, . . . stepped out at the open door, took up a very large, heavy axe which lay there by a log of wood, and chopped vigorously for a few moments, sending the chips flying in all directions; and then, pausing, he extended his right arm to its full length, holding the axe out horizontally, without its even quivering as he held it. Strong men who looked on—men accustomed to manual labor—could not hold the same axe in that position for a moment."[177] A cabinet member was astonished by the muscularity of Lincoln's body as he lay dying.[178]

New Salem residents were already well aware of Lincoln's robustness, so Offutt's bragging had credibility. He went further, according to villagers, and proclaimed he had $5 or $10 that said Lincoln could outwrestle Jack Armstrong.[179]

Lincoln enjoyed wrestling,[180] but the business with Armstrong involved more than a friendly trial of manliness. The issue was whether Abe could hold his own with the leader of the Clary's Grove Boys. Neither Armstrong nor Lincoln had sought the encounter, but its outcome could easily decide whether Abraham could continue residing in New Salem. Thank you, Denton Offutt.

This combat with Jack Armstrong was professional, not personal. After all, Abe had recently made a public demonstration of friendship by helping elect Armstrong constable. Their friendship is attested to by Abner Ellis's memory of a scene "shortly after his flatboat disaster at or near Salem dam," at "corn planting time," when Ellis was collecting back taxes on behalf of Sheriff James D. Henry:

> I went from the tavern down to Jacob Bales's old mill, and there I first saw Mr. Lincoln. He was setting on a saw log talking to Jack and Royal Armstrong and a man by the [name of] Hohimer. I shook hands with the Armstrongs and Hohimer and was conversing with them a few moments when we was joined by my old friend and former townsman George Warburton, pretty tight as usual. And he soon asked me to tell the old story about Ben Johnson and Mrs. Dale's blue dye, etc., etc., which I did. And then Jack Armstrong said, "Lincoln, tell Ellis the story about Governor Ticknor, his city-bred son, and his negro Bob." Which he did with several others, by Jack's calling for them.[181]

No grievance was involved in the wrestling match; it was simply a test to settle curiosity about who had more mettle. Those conditions meant that rules had to be followed. In a fight of passion, anything was allowed. In a test of skill, however, contestants competed within perimeters designed to show who was more proficient, not who was more tricky or ruthless. Uncle Jimmy Short described Lincoln as a "scientific wrestler,"[182] meaning he liked to win by following rules, so that when he and his opponent limited themselves to agreed-upon techniques, Abe's win meant that everyone recognized he was truly the better wrestler.

The two contestants met outside Offutt's store. Robert Rutledge described Armstrong as "in the prime of life, square built, muscular and strong as an ox."[183] Uncle Jimmy Short noted that "Armstrong was a regular bully, was very stout, and tricky in wrestling."[184] The Clary's Grove Boys argued for lenient rules, allowing Armstrong to use his forte of twisting an opponent's limbs. Armstrong's brother-in-law said Lincoln insisted on stricter limitations, which were agreed to. The men took side holds and had at it.[185] Such a start portended well for Lincoln. His friend James Gourley said, "His specialty was side holds; he threw down all men."[186] Apparently Abe was ahead in the contest when onlooker Bill Clary shouted for Armstrong to throw Lincoln any way he could. Armstrong then resorted to an illegal move that downed his opponent.[187] Commotion ensued, provoked partly by Armstrong's conduct, but probably more fired by the issue of whose bets were won or lost. Robert Rutledge said his father, who had just lost the constable election to Armstrong, "ran into the crowd and through the influence which he exerted over all parties, succeeded in quieting the disturbance and preventing a fight."[188]

How the bet collection wound up is unclear; some testimony says that the Clary's Grove Boys claimed the stakes, but Abe made them back off from that claim. According to Nult Greene: "Offutt was inclined to yield, as there was a score or more of the Clary's Grove Boys against him and Mr. Lincoln and my brother W. G. [Slicky Bill] Greene. But Lincoln said they had not won the money and should not have it."[189] Nonetheless, everyone seemed to recognize that the match was basically a draw. Lincoln had been thrown, yes, but only because Armstrong had resorted to a technique that both men had agreed to avoid. "Abe got up pretty mad," said one apparent eyewitness. "He didn't say much, but he told somebody that if it ever came right he would give Bill Clary a good licking."[190]

Testimony by New Salem residents is conclusive that Armstrong and his Clary's Grove Boys thenceforward accepted Lincoln as one of them.[191] As Jason Duncan put it, "Many men sought and made his acquaintance who were not of the most refined and quiet dispositions, yet he so managed with that class as to obtain complete control over them; for there was a clan in that vicinity who prided themselves on their manhood and ready to measure steel with anyone who could be induced to enter the contest or trial of manhood."[192] His membership in the nineteenth-century equivalent of a motorcycle gang did not, however, mean he engaged in rowdy behavior. As Abner Ellis said, "Salem in those days was a hard place for a temperate young man like Mr. Lincoln was, and I have often wondered how he could be so extremely popular and not drink and carouse with them."[193] Membership in the Clary's Grove Boys demonstrated his extraordinary knack at winning acceptance from the whole range of his community's citizens. Two men who later knew him well said: "The verdict of Clary's Grove was unanimous that he was 'the cleverest fellow that had ever broke into the settlement.' He did not have to be constantly scuffling to guard his self-respect, and at the same time he gained the goodwill of the better sort by his evident peaceableness and integrity."[194]

People began turning to Abe Lincoln not only to witness legal documents, but also to prepare them. In November 1831, he prepared a real estate sale contract involving acreage a hundred miles away down in St. Clair County, complicated because it was being sold by the husband of a wife who had inherited it.[195] A couple months later, Abe prepared the document by which John Ferguson sold his rights in the New Salem river ferry to Alexander Trent.[196] Any such document must be prepared with care. In this case, Lincoln also had to consider the parties involved. Ferguson was "a great fighter. He would fight any man just to show how good a man he was."[197] He once defeated Jack Armstrong.[198] Trent was the fellow apparently willing to engage in an illegal duel regarding Governor Reynolds's election promise to Bowling Green.

Daniel Burner and Mentor Graham remembered Abe preparing legal documents,[199] and Caleb Carman recalled him occasionally handling cases in justice of the peace court.[200] Jason Duncan explained: "As there were no attorneys nearer than Springfield, his services were sometimes sought in suits at law, and he frequently consented to appear before Esquire Bowling Green's court to argue cases. . . . Bowling Green permitted him to speak at first more for amusement than anything else, but in a short time was led to pay great respect to his powers of mind in a forensic point of view."[201] Slicky Bill Greene talked about such court appearances as well.[202] Duncan, Graham, and Greene noted that Lincoln performed such services free of charge, a policy perhaps less motivated by charity than by the possibility of being punished for practicing law without a license.[203] The documentary proof we have of Lincoln's paralegal work, supplemented by villagers' memories, demonstrates that he was indeed acquainted with the law by this time and was already interested in that profession while he was still a store clerk for Offutt.

When store clerk duties slacked off, Abe Lincoln and Slicky Bill Greene spent time studying. Slicky Bill was preparing to enter Illinois College, a couple dozen miles away at Jacksonville. "I told him [Lincoln] I had a grammar and surveying books at home. . . . He went down with me and got them and instantly commenced his studies."[204] Lincoln also heard from Mentor Graham that farmer John Vance, about seven miles north of town, had a grammar book. Lincoln, Graham said, "was then at breakfast, ate, got up and went on foot to Vance's and got the book."[205] Graham and Greene's older brother Nult said they helped Lincoln in the grammar effort.[206] Another clerk in the store, Charles Maltby, recalled that Abe was studying grammar hard.[207] Jason Duncan said he helped Lincoln study grammar at this time as well: "His application through the winter [1831–32] was assiduous and untiring; his intuitive faculties were surprising. He seemed to master the construction of the English language and apply the rules for the same in a most astonishing manner."[208] After a while, Abe boasted to Slicky Bill, "If that is what they call a science I'll subdue another."[209] Charles Maltby acknowledged the careful study but noted, "His correct mastery of the language was acquired more from reading and writing than from study."[210]

Lincoln's application to the study of grammar is evidence of higher ambition. Mentor Graham recalled: "Mr. Lincoln spoke to me one day and said, 'I had a notion of studying grammar.' I replied to him thus, 'If you ever expect to go before the public in any capacity I think it the best thing you can do.'"[211] A careful student has suggested that Lincoln's application to grammar could indicate he was planning for a career in law or politics.[212] Unquestionably, good grammar was a skill unnecessary for most aspects of frontier life but advantageous in law and politics, and Lincoln wasn't known for close study of a topic simply to kill time. Indeed, Maltby said outright, "He had already desires for public recognition, and aspirations for political distinction."[213] Slicky Bill asserted the same.[214] Slicky Bill's brother Nult Greene said that while studying grammar, Abe told him "all his folks seemed to have good sense, but none of them had become distinguished, and he believed it was for him to become so—had talked with men who had the reputation of being great men, but could not see that they differed from other men."[215] Lincoln's later friend Orville Browning declared, "I have no doubt that even in his early days he had a strong conviction that he was born for better things than then seemed likely or even possible." Browning added: "I think he all his life more or less believed in presentiments. . . . While I think he was a man of very strong ambition, I think it had its origin in this sentiment, that he was destined for something nobler than he was for the time engaged in."[216]

Abe sought to learn more and more. "I don't think I ever saw Lincoln idling any time away," Caleb Carman said. "He had but few books, but those few were always near him, and in going to and from his work, would read."[217] Abe may have owned few books, but he had access to private libraries owned by the fair number of intellectuals around New Salem, including a number who had attended college.[218] William McNeely noticed, "When at work he was in the habit of carrying a book about with him, and when stopping to rest would devote the time to reading, and what he read he remembered."[219] Ann Rutledge's brother recalled the tall store clerk studying "grammar, philosophy, astronomy, etc. . . . While clerking for Offutt as . . . an opportunity would offer, he would apply himself to his studies. If it was but five minutes' time, would open his book, which he always kept at hand, and study, close it, recite to himself, then entertain company or wait on a customer in the store."[220] "Philosophy" here means science and economics. We have seen testimony that he was studying surveying while clerking for Offutt; New Salem schoolmaster Mentor Graham (a neighbor of young Abraham Lincoln in Kentucky) and fellow clerk Charles Maltby remembered that Lincoln borrowed Blackstone's *Commentaries*, a basic law book, from a justice of the peace at the same time.[221]

Hardin Bale recalled, "When his associates would return in the evening to their various homes he would go to his reading, and in the morning he would read till his associates would come back."[222] Maltby said, "Most of the evenings . . . were, from eight to eleven o'clock, employed by Lincoln in reading and study; a short time was then spent in reviewing the reading of the evening."[223] Rutledge remembered: "His practice was, when he wished to indelibly fix anything he was reading or studying on his mind, to write it down. Have known him to write whole pages of books he was reading."[224] Another witness asserted, "I have . . . known him to write a proposition in three different forms in order to state the meaning as clearly and simply as possible—and to spend half a day doing so."[225] Caleb Carman recalled: "He read sitting, lying down, and walking in the streets. He was always reading if he had time."[226] Fellow clerk Charles Maltby noted, "Lincoln's studious habits and his close attention to his books and to all the appliances within his reach, for advancement, tended to bring him into notice and attraction, and many were the favorable comments relative to his present efforts and future success."[227] Mentor Graham said, "In New Salem he devoted more time to reading . . . and to the acquisition of knowledge of men and things than any man I ever knew, and it has been my task to teach in the primary school forty-five years."[228] Denny Hanks wasn't in New Salem but summed it up well: "Abe couldn't have knowed more of what he read and studied unless he could have lived without any sleep."[229]

That same winter, James Rutledge established a debating club, meeting in an unused storeroom.[230] In addition to a money job, paralegal work, and a private program of intense study, Abe now took up public speaking. Jason Duncan reminisced, "The first time I ever heard him attempt to speak in public was at a polemic society meeting in an underground room of a rude log cabin." Duncan was impressed by the speaker's "very earnest and able manner."[231] Daniel Burner said: "He was a good debater. He couldn't be beat by anyone in those parts."[232] The club president's son Robert Rutledge described Lincoln's first speech there:

As he arose to speak his tall form towered above the little assembly. Both hands were thrust down deep in the pockets of his pantaloons.

A perceptible smile at once lit up the faces of the audience, for all anticipated the relation of some humorous story. But he opened up the discussion in splendid style. . . . He pursued the question with reason and argument so pithy and forcible that all were amazed. The president [James Rutledge] at his fireside after the meeting remarked to his wife that there was more to Abe's head than wit and fun. . . . From that time Mr. Rutledge took a deeper interest in him.[233]

Denny Hanks supposedly noted that Abe's stepmother "always said he'd oughter go into polytics, because when he got to argyin' the other feller'd purty soon say he had enough."[234] The same principle would apply to the law profession.

According to a fellow Offutt store clerk, Charles Maltby, at Lincoln's suggestion the club debated this question: "Are the principles and policy of African slavery so unjust, and the evils thereof of such magnitude as to make the colonization and emancipation of the enslaved colored race in the United States necessary and desirable for the welfare of the American people?"[235] We have no compelling reason to disbelieve Maltby's claim. About a year later, the Tyro Polemic and Literary Club over in Farmers' Point debated "whether slavery has been beneficial to the W. Continent, or not," deciding slavery was advantageous.[236] One debating society in New Salem's vicinity discussed slavery three times,[237] and the Sangamon County Lyceum dealt with the topic in 1833.[238] According to Maltby, a big crowd, including women, listened as Abe, teachers, doctors, and preachers discussed the issue. Maltby said Lincoln argued that slavery caused free workers to be held in contempt by slaveholding aristocrats, thereby harming the position of free workers in slaveholding society. Moreover, this attitude encouraged talented workers to leave the South, draining away talents that the region needed for economic development. A growing antislavery agitation was promoting hostility between North and South, and the sooner slaves were removed from the country, the better the chance of improving good feeling between the regions.[239] Maltby's account of Lincoln's argument is so convenient as to be questionable, but the topic was current among debating societies, and the argument reported by Maltby is consistent with what we know of Lincoln's thinking.

In this era, debating clubs were common features of frontier society, and they discussed topics of current interest. Around New Salem, the groups were considering whether to improve navigation of the Sangamon River, whether to link the New Salem area with Beardstown via canal, whether land or water transportation was preferable, and the question of internal improvements in general.[240] John Allen and Nult Greene said Abe would walk six miles to participate in such discussions.[241] His views on civic issues were becoming publicly known.

CHAPTER 4

POLITICS OF 1832

As election season arrived in early 1832, John Rutledge prodded Lincoln to run for state representative. Part of the suggestion was motivated by friendship, but as a founder of New Salem and the town's senior businessman, Rutledge had to be familiar with the legislature and its members. He surely saw that Lincoln's views were congenial to promoting the town's prosperity and that Lincoln had the necessary people skills to be effective at the state capital down in Vandalia. Rutledge wasn't the only person to press this candidacy.[1] Apparently William Butler, who owned the farm where Lincoln had debated Reverend Cartwright, was involved as well.[2] Row Herndon remembered that Whigs and Democrats alike asked Lincoln to run, being less interested in his politics than his ability to promote the interests of New Salem.[3]

Lincoln hesitated, not from coyness or reluctance to hold office, but because he thought success was unlikely. State representatives in Sangamon and other counties, rather than being elected from small districts, were elected at large by all county voters. At that time, Sangamon was about forty or fifty miles square, with an additional region jutting another fifteen or twenty miles like a panhandle up in the county's northwest area. Although Abe Lincoln was well known around New Salem and was acquainted with folks from the surrounding countryside from working at the store and mill, he would have to run as a stranger among voters elsewhere, who were well acquainted with some of his competitors. Long afterward, one of those competitors recalled, "Lincoln was new then—very few people knew him."[4] Circulating around that entire area while needing to earn a living was challenging enough, but the problem ran deeper than publicity. A shrewd observer in the Illinois political scene noted how these campaigns worked. Candidates could be divided into various classes, rated as to the importance of the office sought. First class was the level of governor or U.S. Congress; second class was state legislature; third class was the main county offices; and fourth class was smaller county offices. Lincoln was starting near the top, which wasn't a problem per se, but he had to confront fourth-class aspirants—the "little big men":

> The candidate goes round in the first place, and secures the *little big men* of each town and neighborhood, by flattering their vanity, and cooperating with them in their own little views of ambition. Many of the candidates have complete lists of all the *little big men* in the state or district of country in which they are a candidate. The *little big man* speaks to his *moccasin boys*. . . . No man can run upon his own independent merit.[5]

Moccasin boys, also known as butcher knife boys, were persons whose votes a little big man could control by passing out favors. The moccasin boys looked to their little big man on how to vote for higher offices. If you were running for higher office, you had to offer something to little big men. An unknown first-time candidate like Abe Lincoln had nothing to offer, nor could he expect to rally enough independent voters to overcome organized platoons commanded by little big men, who in turn were coordinated by company commanders. Thus we can see why Lincoln hesitated. If he were well known, he might have had a fighting chance as an independent candidate; but if he started without notoriety across the county, a dismal outcome was certain.

Lincoln's friends argued that even if he didn't win this time, the campaign would introduce him to the county's voters, providing the notoriety he needed and thereby positioning him to win in 1834. The point wasn't to win in 1832; the goal was 1834. He agreed to run.[6] He was twenty-three years old.

As he officially started his campaign in early March, an event unfolded that perhaps brought him to the attention of a wider electorate. That event was the steamboat *Talisman*'s ascent of the Sangamon River.

Denton Offutt was not the only mercantile promoter in the vicinity. Vincent Bogue had been talking big about running a steamboat on the Sangamon River past New Salem and clear up to Springfield. In January, Springfield's newspaper declared: "We have strong confidence that the undertaking will succeed. We will not now undertake to state the benefits that would result to this village and county from the complete success of the experiment. It would be worth more to us than a dozen railroads."[7] A couple weeks later, the paper said: "It would be folly, perhaps, ever to anticipate for our village advantages from steamboat navigation equal to those which St. Louis has derived from that source. Yet such an anticipation cannot be deemed more chimerical than was the project of running steamboats from the mouth of the Ohio to St. Louis in 1817."[8] Bogue was now in Cincinnati arranging to charter a "splendid upper cabin steamer" with "superior accommodations"[9] and wrote home with the following request:

that I should be met at the mouth of the [Sangamon] river by ten or twelve men, having axes with *long* handles, under the direction of some experienced man, and that one of the men should be one of those who has most often descended the river with flatboats (to shew the course of the stream) and that the merchants should reserve all the produce they may have for the St. Louis market, for the boat's return trip. I intend to freight the boat to Springfield myself—if not, I shall deliver freight from St. Louis at the landing on the Sangamo River, opposite the town of Springfield, *for thirty-seven and a half cents per* 100 *pounds!*[10]

Fees for shipping by wagon were more than twice that rate,[11] so Bogue was promising a substantial boost to regional commerce—increasing the profit margins of farmers who exported crops and allowing merchants to cut prices on transported inventory and still make the same profit. "Arrangements," the *Sangamo Journal* reported, "are being made to furnish him with all the assistance he requires."[12] A meeting at William Miller's tavern coordinated plans for assistance, including financial aid. Meeting leaders included Dr. John Todd and Gershom Jayne.[13] (Lincoln eventually became well acquainted with Jayne's future son-in-law Lyman Trumbull and Todd's niece Mary.) Two candidates for the state legislature, Thomas M. Neale and Edmund D. "Dick" Taylor, would help supervise the clearing of channel obstructions as the boat progressed up the Sangamon River.[14] When the *Talisman* arrived at the Sangamon's mouth, onlookers could see one reason why Bogue wanted a crew to help clear the way on the river. The vessel was almost too large for the Sangamon. Neale said the boat was three times the size of any that should attempt such a navigation; the *Sangamo Journal* indicated the river could handle a craft half the *Talisman*'s size; state senatorial candidate George Forquer split the difference.[15]

On the Sangamon, the *Talisman*'s progress wasn't like a Mark Twain sternwheeler going up the Mississippi, but more like the *African Queen* plodding through a tunnel of trees overhanging a narrow, twisting channel with fast current but at times blocked by ice.[16] "The northwest winds continue to blow with a chilliness that would give credit to a Canadian March. On Saturday morning, the seventeenth, we understand that the thermometer was eight degrees below zero."[17] The *Talisman*'s sidewheeler design increased its width and invited constant collision with obstructions on either side of the channel. Said one contemporary observer, "The boat experienced some difficulty from drifts and leaning timber on shore, which made her trip somewhat tedious."[18] Another contemporary observer noted "obstructions frequently made by stooping trees on the wheels and wheelhouses."[19]

Reportedly Lincoln was among the axemen who hacked away timber to open room for the boat's passage. Some accounts indicate he also acted as pilot, directing the craft around obstacles while keeping it in the navigable part of the river.[20] Whatever the extent of his role, he was conveniently available because Denton Offutt's business operations were failing and almost dead. Having no employment, and anticipating a thriving river traffic once the *Talisman* proved the practicality of steamboating on the Sangamon, Lincoln and fellow ex-clerk Charles Maltby bought a New Salem building that could be used for a warehouse and shipping business.[21] This was the type of business that Offutt had unsuccessfully projected, but Maltby and Lincoln apparently felt prospects were improved by the steamboat factor. Wrote an early-twentieth-century chronicler: "Salem was then the first town after leaving Beardstown and many air castles were built, and Salem was to be a great river port. This incident gave a boom to Salem and most of the building in the town was the result of the visit of this boat."[22] William H. Herndon recalled, in the phrasing of a ghostwriter, "All the land adjoining each enterprising and aspiring village along the river was subdivided into town lots—in fact, the whole region began to feel the stimulating effects of what, in later days, would have been called a 'boom.'"[23]

Bogue's vow to bring a steamer to Springfield was a formidable promise. The previous year, someone else had attempted the feat from Alton. The Alton boat's journey went well enough until reaching the New Salem milldam. Water was high, and the boat could almost run up and over the dam, but not quite. The craft hung up on the dam and became stuck, rather like the situation with Lincoln's flatboat in the same river season. The Alton cargo had to be unloaded, a cable was attached between the vessel's capstan and a tree, and then the boat was winched up and over the dam by brute force. The unloaded cargo next had to be reloaded, and the Alton vessel proceeded.[24] Not the smoothest kind of river shipping.

The *Talisman* deposited part of its cargo of liquor, clothing, food, and goods in New Salem at the Lincoln and Maltby warehouse; tore away some of the milldam to get past; and proceeded to Bogue's mill at Portland landing, where it stopped. This was about five miles short of Springfield but apparently as far as the vessel dared go. William H. Herndon's memory of the occasion was presented by ghostwriter Jesse Weik: "After having passed New Salem, I and other boys on horseback followed the boat, riding along the river's bank as far as Bogue's mill, where she tied up. There we went aboard, and lost in boyish wonder, feasted our eyes on the splendor of her interior decorations." Herndon was thirteen years old. "It was my first sight of a steamboat, and also the first time I ever saw Mr. Lincoln."[25] Upon docking, Capt. J. M. Pollock refused to let Bogue unload. A good guess is that Bogue had failed to pay Captain Pollock for bringing the vessel from Cincinnati. Whatever the reason, Bogue had to get a court order forcing release of the cargo.[26] But such details were ignored by Springfield. The *Sangamo Journal* proclaimed:

> Her arrival at her destined port was hailed with loud acclamations and full demonstrations of pleasure.

When Captain Bogue located his steam mill on Sangamo River, twelve months ago, and asserted his determination to land a steamboat there within a year, the idea was considered chimerical by some, and utterly impracticable by others. . . . This county owes a deep debt of gratitude to Captain Bogue for getting up the expedition, and his never-tiring and unceasing efforts until the end was accomplished. . . .

The result has clearly demonstrated the practicability of navigating the river by steamboats of a proper size; and by the expenditure of 2,000 dollars in removing the logs and drifts and standing timber, a steamboat of 80 tons burthen will make the trip in two days from Beardstown to this place. . . .

Springfield can no longer be considered an inland town. We have no doubt but within a few months a boat will be constructed for the special purpose of navigating the Sangamo River.

The results which must follow the successful termination of this enterprise to our county, and to those counties lying in its neighborhood, it would be impossible to calculate.[27]

Springfield held a ball to celebrate. With a population of fourteen hundred, the town was big enough to host such a fancy social event, although a visitor from the East that year was unimpressed with the residences, "a considerable proportion of them being log cabins, the whole town having an appearance of dirt and discomfort."[28] Only after the *Talisman*'s arrival did the town government pass an ordinance prohibiting anyone to "leave a dead carcase in any of the public streets, alleys, branches, or on any lot in said town."[29] A traveler on the *Talisman* noted, "When I landed in the town of Springfield the whipping [post] stood on the public courthouse square." That traveler was H. E. Dummer, who said, "The citizens gave Pollock a good reception, got up a ball, danced in the old courthouse."[30] The event was distinguished enough to receive favorable notice in St. Louis. "The collection of ladies," said the *St. Louis Missouri Republican*, "was greater than on any other occasion . . . there was as much beauty and taste exhibited in the specimens as ever I have witnessed in the Western Country."[31] The following verse was written at the time of the ball:

> There was a ball at night, I guess
> For the ladies' sakes it couldn't be less—
> And twenty bachelors they say,
> Were strung in Hymen's noose that day.
> To such a height their courage went,
> So tired were they of Love's long lent![32]

Decades later, someone spoke with a woman who was present:

"Such excitement as its landing caused. You see we all thought if a boat could come up the Sangamon we'd have a direct waterway to Cincinnati. Such hopes as we built upon that project! . . . It was a great triumph. . . . All the town was on the riverbank, waving and shouting when the boat landed. That night we had a fine ball at the hotel in celebration."

"Were you at the ball?"

"I peeped in," she confessed, "You see I was a church member and dancing was not looked upon with favor. Just for standing there in the doorway and watching, I was called before the minister to explain my conduct."

"Was Lincoln there? Did he dance?" . . .

The old lady's spine grew even stiffer. "Only gentlemen and ladies were present," she said.[33]

John Lightfoot recalled another aspect of the occasion: "Mrs. Pollock, the mistress of Pollock, got tipsy and played the devil. . . . The elite and cultured ladies of the city were in high dudgeon—highly offended."[34] Dummer described Mrs. Pollock as simply "a whore."[35] Springfield's attitude about public sexual decorum is indicated by an ordinance passed in April "relating to the indecent exhibition of horses," forbidding mares to be mounted by stallions within city limits.[36]

By the time the *Talisman* started its return journey, the river level was quickly getting lower, increasing the trip's hazard. Indeed, the river had fallen so much that the boat couldn't turn around and had to back the whole way down the Sangamon. Row Herndon claimed that, being an experienced Sangamon riverman, he was summoned when the boat was about a dozen miles upstream from New Salem. Row said he acted as pilot, with Lincoln as assistant pilot—a job of some celebrity. The boat made about four miles a day, a rate of travel well demonstrating the journey's difficulty. Row Herndon said the pace was determined partly because Captain Pollock was getting paid by the day, but Charles Maltby noted another reason why Pollock would want to go slow: "The steamer was continually running into the banks of the river and into the tops of trees that grew on and over the banks of the river, and the result was that the cabin and upper parts of the boat were badly broken and injured." A Springfield resident of the time remembered, "The boat in going out of the river was nearly torn to pieces." Row recalled encountering the New Salem milldam: "When we struck the dam she hung. We then backed off and threw the anchor over the dam and tore away part of the dam, and raised steam and run her over the first trial."[37] Lively discussion reportedly occurred between the steamboaters and millers about whether the millers had a right to block a navigable stream, and the dam was immediately repaired.[38]

After passing New Salem, Bogue's involvement was done and Pollock was on his own.[39] Charles Maltby said: "From New Salem the steamer floated down the river, with long oars on stern and bow to keep her as near as possible in the middle of the river. After several days, with difficulty the steamer reached Beardstown, badly injured, and the enterprise was abandoned. The failure of the steamboat undertaking carried with it the warehouse enterprise of Lincoln."[40] According to Row Herndon, Lincoln received $40 for *Talisman* piloting work,[41] a hefty sum in that vicinity. A few weeks, later a St. Louis newspaper reported an end to the craft's career: "Fire broke out from the S.B. *Talisman*, which threatened the total destruction of the middle ward. When the steamboat was discovered to be in flames she was lying near the office of the American Fur Co. One of the crew made an ineffectual attempt to scuttle her; and then cast her adrift. She floated down to the wharf, in front of the store of John Lee & Co. where she remained until entirely consumed."[42]

Although five years later a book promoting Illinois cited the *Talisman* as proving the Sangamon River's navigability for steamboats from Beardstown to Springfield,[43] the proof was so costly that the experiment was repeated by only one craft. A witness succinctly described that 1834 confirmation: "The *Utility*, a sternwheeler, came up and laid at the Salem mill for a week or ten days. I was old enough to remember the *Utility*. It attracted great attention. Farmers came for miles around to see it. The river began to fall," preventing the craft's return to the Illinois River. "It was dismantled at Petersburg, and its machinery was put in the first mill, while the pine lumber used in its construction was used in building houses in Petersburg."[44]

By the end of March 1832, Lincoln reported, "Offutt's business was failing—had almost failed."[45] Throughout April, Offutt ran an announcement, dated March 8, in Springfield's *Sangamo Journal* that he had thousands of bushels of seed corn en route and invited farmers to pay in advance to assure themselves of a share.[46] While that ad was running, however, an editorial notice in the newspaper declared, "We solicit the attention of our farmers to Mr. Manning's advertisement of seed corn."[47] Manning operated in Lower Alton. In May an editorial notice said, "SEED CORN.—'If you want a thing done, do it yourself.' This is a sound maxim, and may be well applied to those who want seed corn. There is plenty of this article at Alton. If you will ☞ go after it yourself!"[48] When a newspaper urges readers to patronize a merchant ninety miles away instead of a local merchant who runs a steady ad, something is wrong with either the editor or the merchant. That spring, Offutt closed his New Salem business operations, left town, and never came back.[49] The loan he had taken at 60 percent interest remained unpaid.[50]

Lincoln's announcement of candidacy for state representative was dated March 9, 1832, as the *Talisman* excitement was building, and included a detailed statement of his stance on issues.[51]

He had been studying grammar intensely the previous winter and was a well-read man. That background shows in the campaign platform's smooth phrasing, although he may have sought advice on composition from a New Salem businessman who was then engaged to Ann Rutledge.[52] Lincoln's statement was lengthy compared with circulars published by other candidates so far and some later. He was also specific about his stance on assorted issues, giving details of his intentions. Some other candidates spoke only of being honored and intending to serve the public. Such candidates probably had little big men working for them and therefore had no need to say anything about issues. Lincoln, however, had to say enough to attract "independent" voters weren't controlled by anyone and knew nothing about him.

The bulk of his platform dealt with ways to improve transportation, a topic known as "internal improvements." He introduced the topic with a statement on finances: "It is folly to undertake works of this or any other kind, without first knowing that we are able to finish them—as half finished work generally proves to be labor lost. There cannot justly be any objection to having railroads and canals . . . provided they cost nothing." This last comment about getting something for nothing may seem odd, but some internal improvement promoters argued that state-sponsored projects need cost taxpayers nothing—an argument that eventually devastated the state government's finances. In those later years, as state finances worsened, Representative Lincoln would generally vote to continue and even increase internal improvement projects at public expense rather than cut losses by abandoning partly finished works and thereby lose everything already invested. That stance was foreshadowed in his very first public statement on the topic in 1832.

Lincoln went on to endorse a proposal to build a railroad connecting the Illinois River, Jacksonville, and Springfield. He praised railroads as the best means of transportation, unaffected by river levels or ice. "Yet . . . however high our imaginations may be heated at thoughts of it—there is always a heart appalling shock accompanying the account of its cost." He noted this railway's estimated expense at $290,000, "the bare statement of which . . . is sufficient to justify the belief that the improvement of Sangamo River is an object much better suited to our infant resources" (state treasury receipts for the previous year totaled scarcely $290,000[53]). Here are two attitudes that became important when Lincoln later helped lead the state's internal improvement drive. First, he felt that railroads were a better transportation mode than rivers or canals. Second, he felt that state financial resources were meager, and therefore state-sponsored projects had to be modest—a stance he would later change, with disastrous consequences.

Lincoln proceeded to argue the practicality of improving the Sangamon River enough to allow thirty-ton vessels—vessels one-fifth the *Talisman*'s size[54]—to navigate much of it for six months a year. He was hardly alone in this stance; a couple weeks earlier, the county's biggest newspaper had declared, "We seriously believe that the Sangamo River, with some little improvement, can be made navigable for steamboats for several months in the year."[55] Lincoln said the key factor was river depth. "It is probable that for the last twelve months I have given as particular attention to the stage of the water in this river as any other person in the country. In the month of March, 1831, in company with others, I commenced the building of a flatboat on the Sangamo, and finished and took her out in the course of the spring. Since that time, I have been concerned in the mill at New Salem. These circumstances are sufficient evidence that I have not been very inattentive to the stages of the water." As we shall see shortly, candidates gladly proclaimed any connection with the *Talisman*. Lincoln's silence raises the question of how much he was involved with that project.

He saw two primary obstacles to navigating the Sangamon. One was drift-wood in the channel, but he regarded the removal as simple. The driftwood problem related to the second obstacle, the river's particularly winding course in the final thirty-five miles before reaching the Illinois River near Beardstown. Because that stretch wound through flat prairie, Lincoln thought a cut could be made straight across the prairie soil, allowing the river to be diverted into the cut and thereby straightening its course in a way that would shorten the trip by a couple dozen miles. He also thought the straighter course would reduce driftwood problems by providing fewer places for the wood to hang up and increasing current velocity, thereby flushing driftwood out of the river. Higher up the river, he recommended cutting through the necks of peninsulas jutting into the Sangamon, as he had noted natural forces slicing through Mississippi River peninsulas on his trip back from New Orleans. This would provide the same benefits expected from the big prairie cut closer to Beardstown.

His general idea had public support. A couple weeks after publishing Lincoln's campaign platform, the *Sangamo Journal* noted that when the *Talisman* went up the Sangamon, "the citizens of Beardstown manifested great interest for the success of the enterprise. . . . They proposed the cutting of a communication or canal from the bluffs to their landing, whereby seventy-five miles of navigation may be saved; and offered 1,000 dollars to assist in completing it. It is to be hoped that the next legislature will afford some aid in making the river safe and pleasant in its navigation."[56] Someone in an article that summer said:

> The important subject of internal improvement . . . seems to absorb all others in most of the adjoining states. Why should the people of Sangamo County remain inactive, when they have every advantage presented to them in a natural point of view? . . . Having had some knowledge of the Sangamo River, both in high and low water, the height of its banks, and the depth of its channel, I feel justified in saying that its channel ought to be so improved as to render the navigation practicable at least four months in the year. The expense would be quite trifling compared with the inestimable advantages which would result from such navigation. . . .
>
> There are many bends in the Sangamo River, through which if the channel were cut in low water, the whole current would flow, thereby displacing the sand and making the bottom on a level with that of the natural bed of the river—which would supersede the necessity of

cutting down the trees which stood over the channel of the river in all the bends. It would require but little labor to effect this.[57]

In Lincoln's campaign platform, he admitted, "What the cost of this work would be, I am unable to say," but asserted, "I believe the improvement of the Sangamo River to be vastly important and highly desirable to the people of this county." Lincoln pledged to support any sensible proposals introduced in the legislature to improve the Sangamon. Curiously, he refrained from pledging to introduce any such legislation himself. Thus, after making a case for the importance of such river improvement, he backed away and indicated his role in such enterprise would be passive, supporting proposals introduced by others, rather than initiating any himself. But given his interest in the subject, perhaps he and everyone else thought no pledge of activism was necessary. Perhaps.

Other candidates also made friendly noises about internal improvements. State senate candidate George Forquer declared, "The spirit of public improvement is abroad in the land, and shall the people of the far famed and greatly favored Sangamo, stand idle spectators of its magical influence upon the prosperity of their neighbors?"[58] He said that improving the river was feasible technically and financially:

The fine country watered by this stream and its tributaries, already contains about 25,000 inhabitants, and at no distant period is destined to contain at least five times that number. A measure necessary to advance the interest of such a population, would command the attention of any government, and the legislature would doubtless be willing to afford any assistance in their power to improve the navigation of this stream. The recent experiment made by the steamboat *Talisman*, in ascending the river to the Springfield landing, has disclosed how far its navigable capacities may be improved. . . . It is believed by the most practical men that a judicious expenditure of a few thousand dollars, would enable steamboats of from fifty to eighty tons burden, for about five months in the year, to run from Beardstown to this place in twenty-four hours, and return in less time. This done, and the Sangamo would add as much to our commercial facilities as a canal from here to the Illinois [River]. To accomplish this desirable object, it is true, is a task more difficult to execute than to discover its great utility. It should not be done by adding to the taxes of the people, and to rely upon voluntary contribution, will only produce disappointment. The means, therefore must come from some other source.[59]

Forquer suggested the river project could be financed by money from sale of state-owned saline lands, commercially valuable for salt manufacturing. He favored a modest program of internal improvements "to the extent of our means," including "good roads, bridges, and such local improvements as are most promotive of the daily transaction of business." After these were done successfully, a larger program could be considered.[60]

Justice of the Peace Thomas M. Neale, running for state representative, said:

> The experienced and observant part of the community have looked to the Sangamon River as a fruitful source of wealth to our growing and flourishing part of the state. Their anticipations in part have been realized by the successful attempt of the steamboat *Talisman* to navigate the river as high up as Bogue's mill. This boat was nearly three times as large as should ever attempt its navigation—a circumstance which has sufficiently demonstrated to the most incredulous its future usefulness. Having been one of the committee who superintended the navigation of the river last spring (an opportunity I had long wished for) from my own observations, together with information derived from different sources, and especially from the officers of the boat, I can most confidently say that, with an appropriation judiciously applied, of 2,000 dollars, by an experienced waterman, our river may be made navigable for steamboats of sixty tons burthen at least four months in the year, and whenever there is eighteen inches of water on the shoals. In this opinion I am confirmed by the most sanguine expressions of the captain and pilot of the *Talisman*— the last of whom, for several years past, has been engaged, as superintendent, in clearing out some of the tributary streams of the Ohio River.[61]

Whether Row Herndon had been spending recent years supervising work on the Ohio's tributaries is questionable, a doubt that challenges his account of piloting of the *Talisman*.

Former representative Edward Robison, who was seeking to reenter the legislature, told voters: "I am favorable to internal improvements of any kind, that will not cost more than they are worth. I consider it bad economy for an individual, a county, nation, or any other body politic or corporate, to let their expenses exceed their income."[62]

Moving to the next plank of his platform, Lincoln said, "The practice of loaning money at exorbitant rates of interest has already been opened as a field for discussion." Like internal improvement, loan interest was a question relating to economic development. Shortly before the *Sangamo Journal* published Lincoln's platform, the newspaper printed a letter complaining about interest rates and demanding reform from the state legislature. The correspondent said a 60 percent interest rate was typical in Illinois; indeed, we have already seen Denton Offutt paying 60 percent interest to borrow money, and Sangamon County politician Dr. Anson G. Henry also noted that such a rate was common.[63] The newspaper letter writer pointed out that whereas a one-year $1,000 loan in New York would cost $70, in Illinois the cost would be $600. At this time down in Madison County, Illinois, a man wrote: "We could lend out plenty at twenty percent to twenty-five percent. Often forty percent is paid. It cannot be called usury here."[64] Not when the going rate was 60 percent. The *Sangamo Journal* letter writer thought state law should limit interest to 10 percent and asked for legislative candidates' views. The writer declared that people should support no one who failed to pledge for reform.[65]

On this topic, we should consider what officers of the Shawneetown Bank of Illinois said a while later. They noted that its charter capped its loan interest at 6 percent. One result was that "money borrowed from banks by the wealthy might only be used in lending again to another class at an advanced rate."[66] By implication, the bank was operating less as a source of capital for economic development than as a provider of funds to upper-class loan sharks on whom farmers and small businessmen had to depend for loans. The price of loans, like other prices, resisted regulation. When the price of bank loans was limited to 6 percent, all available capital at that rate was snapped up by loan sharks, who in turn would lend it out at whatever rate the market would bear.

Usury also drastically affected homestead farms. Settlers would choose a tract of good-looking unclaimed virgin land and spend years clearing timber, plowing fields, fencing in crops, constructing a residence and outbuildings, and doing everything else involved in establishing a self-sustaining farm. Often, however, the settlers didn't own this acreage. They were squatters because the land was owned by a governmental entity that was not yet offering the area for sale. A newly arrived Illinois resident named Stephen A. Douglas told his brother-in-law, "Do not suppose that all the good land is yet taken up, for not more than two-thirds of the land in this state has yet been brought into market."[67] If settlers couldn't afford to buy land from a real estate operator, or if they preferred the government acreage, they might squat on public land where they could farm for free. A common plan was to raise crops to make enough money to buy the land when it came on the market,[68] thereby allowing penniless but industrious persons a chance to become farm owners through the labor they invested.

There was always a chance that a real estate operator would eventually buy legal title to the property, a risk that was well understood by settlers and created a continual undercurrent of unease in their lives. The risk might be reduced by pre-emption, a privilege occasionally granted by the state or U.S. government entity owning the land, allowing settlers the first chance to buy title to the property when it was offered for sale. When the land came up for sale, however, the government required payment in cash. Squatters with valuable farms might lack enough cash to buy title to the property when the moment for purchase arrived. A similar situation could occur when settlers were already buying title to their farms from the U.S. government on the installment plan and were short on cash when the next payment fell due. To save the farm, a settler often had to borrow money. There being no banks with loans available at legal interest rates, especially considering the kind of security that most settlers could offer, farmers had to pay whatever usury was demanded by loan sharks. The *Sangamo Journal* bemoaned one sale in which "many excellent citizens lost their farms, and others are paying devouring claims of interest for money borrowed to effect their purchase."[69] Said one observer:

> I have witnessed in Illinois acts of open and barefaced rapacity. . . . I have seen large numbers of those to whom, on account of previous occupancy and improvement, the legislature had humanely and wisely granted a right of pre-emption, in the counties of Sangamo[n] and Morgan, not only despoiled of all the benefits conferred by the act, but driven to the oppressive alternative, of surrendering their dwellings and all the improvements of their farms, the fruit of many years labor and privation, or paying the exorbitant interest of seventy-five percent per annum, and then mortgage their farms to secure the payment.
>
> Thousands of dollars have been loaned at this rate in those counties to those who were anxious to save their possessions at the sale of seminary lands [state land sold to raise money for education, supposedly]; and who, at the time of borrowing, fondly but vainly hoped that by the disposal of [live]stock or the . . . growing crop, they should be able, in the progress of six months or at most a year, to discharge the liability. But interest accumulating at this rate doubles the principal every fifteen months; and the two hundred dollars which was borrowed to secure the payment of a quarter section of land becomes, at the expiration of that term, four hundred—a sum which remains to few of our farmers at the end of the year, after providing all the articles of necessity or comfort which a family require; and those who lend at this rate understand arithmetic too well not to renew their notes or enforce the collection of them at the end of the term. I have been told that even ten per cent per month has been given and received for the loan of money in the county of Morgan.[70]

Many voters were settlers threatened by such a situation, and they were extremely concerned about usury laws. Sharks were making a hatful of money by doing nothing, while merchants and farmers slaved to produce enough wealth to repay the loans. "Slaved" is a term used deliberately, as resentment was growing toward loan sharks, who lived a life of ease while their debtors labored to produce wealth for them. So what was to be done?

Some argued that nothing should be done, as regulating interest rates infringed on lenders' rights. Some argued that legal limits on interest rates had the effect of driving them higher.[71] Such unpalatable reasoning was intolerable to voters, however, and Sangamon County candidates had to offer some alternative.

Lincoln declared: "It seems as though we are never to have an end to this baneful and corroding system, acting almost as prejudicial to the general interests of the community as a direct tax of several thousand dollars annually laid on each county, for the benefit of a few individuals only, unless there be a law made setting a limit to the rates of usury. A law for this purpose, I am of opinion, may be made without materially injuring any class of people. In cases of extreme necessity there could always be means found to cheat the law." Likening interest to taxation is an early example of his rhetorical skill in presenting an abstract concept in concrete terms understandable to ordinary voters. His stance could be translated thus: High interest rates benefit a handful of persons while harming the community at large. Such evil should be eliminated by law. Limiting interest rates won't hurt any group of citizens. If loans dry up at the legal rate or a person desperately needing a loan isn't creditworthy enough to obtain one at the legal rate, a way can be found to provide loans at an ostensibly illegal rate.

Lincoln's stance on interest rates seems odd, arguing that legal regulation was needed but could be evaded if necessary. Given the perimeters in which the topic was debated, I believe this is what he meant: A law should be passed to protect common people from being exploited by loan sharks. A possibility existed, however, that such regulation could dry up the supply of capital for loans, thereby preventing squatters from buying their farms or constricting economic development even worse than high interest rates did. Therefore, the law should make high interest rates so inconvenient for lenders that they normally would not charge high rates, but lenders could do so if the economy's or an individual's need for loan capital was dire enough to make the legal inconvenience worth surmounting. What such inconvenience might be is unclear, but convenient ways existed to evade an interest limit. For example, a person needing a one-year loan might receive a one-day loan at the legal rate, with a penalty calculated at 20 percent a year for each day the loan remained unpaid, a clever trick that the Illinois supreme court finally forbade.[72] A variation sustained by the Illinois supreme court was to make the loan payable in a commodity of varying value, such as paper notes issued by banks, as Illinois usury regulation applied only to loans based on articles of supposedly steady value, such as gold or silver. When the state supreme court approved that method of avoiding the limit on loan interest rates, the law partnership of Abraham Lincoln represented the lender.[73] And a loan could always be made at high interest if the lender was unconcerned about enforcing the contract in court, either because of trust between creditor and debtor or because the creditor could rely on intimidation.

Lincoln's competitor Edward Robison took a stronger but somewhat different stance: "I am not an extortioner, neither am I favorable to the practice of principle of extortioning . . .; but I do think that a man has as great a right to loan his money at a high interest, as he has to sell his property at a high price. If such a law was in force, it would not prevent men from loaning above the rate prescribed."[74] In rhetoric, at least, state representative candidate Thomas Neale was stronger yet:

Another subject of absorbing interest is daily presenting itself before us with an appalling aspect. I mean the practice of loaning money at an exorbitant interest . . . from forty to three hundred percent per annum. Burdensome as this must be to any community, it might have been borne with patiently, until it would have regulated itself; but when we see our country flooded with the capital of foreign specula-tors in money, who have no interest in our permanent good, and who may be compelled to call in all their capital with the accumulation of at least fifty percent, from the hard earnings of our citizens, on the event of a failure to re-charter the United States Bank, with proper limitations of her power, and perhaps when it is least expected, we are admonished by every principle of self preservation, and the future welfare of our country, to say to the usurer, "Thus far thou *mayest* go, but *shall* go no farther."[75]

If Neale had stopped at condemning loan sharks, he probably could have been assured of wide agreement from voters. By linking the issue to the Bank of the United States, however, Neale went farther than he needed to. The bank oper-ated under a federal charter coming up for renewal, and President Jackson wanted to prevent renewal. Neale may well have been correct that failing to renew would create financial pressure, causing lenders to demand immediate repayment of Illinois loans, which in turn would cause hardship among Illinois debtors. By making that argument, however, he was defending the bank's useful-ness. That identified him as a Whig and put him at odds with Sangamon County's Democrats. And this was a strong Democratic year in Sangamon County. These national party matters could be touchy. Incumbent representative John Dawson claimed he was a general supporter of Jackson's Administration, though in the legislature, he said, "I felt it my duty to pursue a straightforward course, without regard to party or party feelings, as I thought the better to secure the rights and interests of my immediate constituents—believing that the best interests of my constituents was to be obtained by a union of all political parties."[76] That expla-nation of irregularity on party questions was insufficient in some quarters: "Mr. Dawson, an original Jackson man of our county, now a candidate for the legisla-ture, has been attacked severely" by a supporter of Martin Van Buren (Jackson's choice for Vice President in that 1832 election year).[77] "Original Jackson man" was often a code phrase for Democrat turned Whig; the *Chicago Democrat* aptly analyzed the phrase, noting that Benedict Arnold was an original patriot and Judas Iscariot an original Disciple.[78]

George Forquer, who was running with the Democrats, simply said that usury was a problem, with interest getting so high as to interfere with economic growth. "So long as these exactions were confined to the purchasers of public land, a plausible justification was found for them in the supposed and sometimes real, advantage derived from them by the purchaser." Forquer probably meant that settlers lacking creditworthiness could turn to loan sharks for gold to buy land offered by the government, a title to the family farm perhaps being worth high interest rates. Citizens needing money for other purposes, however, might also have to deal with loan sharks now. "Whenever the hard earnings of the industrious farmer, mechanic, and laborer, become the prey of the ruthless usurer, then the time has come for the law to prohibit the practice."[79]

Usury was only one aspect of a broader exploitation that Illinois residents were beginning to perceive and articulate. "Miners and farmers should have ground to dig upon, and cultivate, and houses to live in, and fuel to burn," said a writer in an Illinois mining district newspaper.

> Can any good reason be shown why all the groves of timber, through-out the mines should be monopolized by a few favored capitalists, to the entire exclusion of diggers [miners] and farmers? In one or two seasons more there will scarcely be a stick of timber left in the interior of the country. . . .
>
> Our government is not unjust, and will not suffer all the valuable parts of our fair country to fall into the hands of a few nabobs, to enable them to tyrannize and lord it over the industrious diggers, the stamina of the country. . . . The digger and farmer, or in other words the laborers who sustain and enrich the country, should receive the fostering protection of government.[80]

Lincoln's election platform next addressed education. Establishing and funding a system of public schools that could be attended by all children free of charge was under consideration. "I view it as the most important subject which we as a people can be engaged in." He wanted "every man" to "receive at least a moderate education, and thereby be enabled to read the histories of his own and other countries, by which he may duly appreciate the value of our free institutions . . . to say nothing of the advantages and satisfaction to be derived from all being to able to read the scriptures and other works." He hoped that "education, and by its means, morality, sobriety, enterprise, and industry, shall become much more general than at present." In *Elements of Political Economy*, a book Lincoln later read and liked,[81] author Francis Wayland took Lincoln's argument to a higher level:

> *Intellectual cultivation excites a people to exertion.* Ignorant men are indolent, because they know not the results that may be accomplished, nor the benefits that may be secured by industry. . . .
>
> Improvement in knowledge, in order to be in any signal degree beneficial, must be universal. A single individual can derive but little advantage from his knowledge and industry, if he be surrounded by a community both ignorant and indolent. . . . This is specially the case,

where a government is, in its character, popular; that is, where laws emanate from the more numerous classes. In such a case, not only is an intelligent man not benefitted, but he is positively injured, by the ignorance and indolence of his neighbors.[82]

As with Sangamon River improvement, candidate Lincoln did not say he would introduce legislation to promote education but did pledge to support effective proposals introduced by others. His avoidance of specifics may best be explained by the stance of state senate candidate George Forquer, who declared himself in favor of education but observed, "until our country becomes more densely populated, and less difference of opinion prevails on this subject, I doubt the practicability of preparing any coercive system of common schools which would be sustained by the people."[83] Sangamon County School Commissioner Erastus Wright was hotter about the failure to establish common schools across the county: "I am persuaded the greater difficulty lies in the selfishness, and want of forbearance and reconciliation on the part of the citizens. As yet we have no practical school system adopted, by which every family may have the privilege of educating their children with little or no inconvenience."[84]

Last, Abe Lincoln acknowledged discontent about several types of laws, including those dealing with estrays, debt executions, and roads. Estray laws governed what had to be done when horses and other animals were found after straying from owners. Execution laws regulated the confiscation and sale of debtors' property to reimburse their creditors. Road laws required male residents to donate labor for road maintenance, a short-term civilian draft by the county government, but discontent also seems to have existed about other road law aspects. Lincoln acknowledged controversy over those matters but avoided taking a stand on any. His competitor Edward Robison did declare himself on two of those laws, wanting roads to be established without surveying by the county surveyor and wanting to permit finders to keep unclaimed stray animals instead of having them sold by the county.[85] State representative candidate Thomas Neale addressed the road labor issue, saying able-bodied persons must be required to work on roads "under the direction of a supervisor in each road district, a sufficient time to put the roads in good repair, and keep them so."[86] State senate candidate George Forquer wanted a new system of road districts providing sufficient manpower that road district supervisors could call upon for repairs.[87]

Lincoln concluded his platform: "Every man is said to have his peculiar ambition. . . . I have no other so great as that of being truly esteemed of my fellow men, by rendering myself worthy of their esteem. How far I shall succeed in gratifying this ambition is yet to be developed." Noting his lack of acquaintance with county residents and his lack of support from little big men, he stated: "I am young and unknown to many of you. I was born and have ever remained in the most humble walks of life. I have no wealthy or popular relations to recommend me. My case is thrown exclusively upon the independent voters." Expressing hope for victory and acknowledging possibility of defeat, he declared, "If the good people in their wisdom shall see fit to keep me in the background, I have been too familiar with disappointments to be very much chagrined."

Someone who participated in the election and was one of the shrewdest Sangamon County politicians noted a key issue that Lincoln's platform ignored: "The New Salem people were already then interested in a project for getting themselves set apart into a new county (afterward Menard County), and Lincoln being their local candidate, they expected to make him instrumental in bringing this about. This helped to give him the solid vote of New Salem."[88] Among other things, a new county would open a complete set of county jobs for little big men.

In considering Lincoln's platform outlining his stance on all these issues, we might to do well to remind ourselves that he was only twenty-three years old.

Such were the issues, but they were not decisive. Political party loyalties also were a factor, and personal loyalties to candidates were just as important. In 1832, deals could cross party lines. Democrat Dr. Jacob Early, described as "a Methodist preacher, and an office hunter,"[89] explained how state legislature candidates of Sangamon County campaigned in private.[90] Dr. Early said that in March 1832, a Springfield Whig lawyer named John T. Stuart, soon enough to be known by the nickname Jerry Sly, "enquired of me if I knew where Peter Cartwright was? I told him I did not know." Stuart and Democrat Reverend Cartwright were two of the more powerful candidates for representative in Sangamon County. This is the same Cartwright who earlier debated Lincoln in a farm field. Stuart explained to Early that he wanted to meet with Cartwright "to effect a reconciliation with him. He [Stuart] told me he would go for Peter Cartwright, if he, Cartwright, would go for him. That he knew what cords and wires to pull for the purpose of defeating Cartwright, and that he would work them should Cartwright go against him. But should Cartwright conclude to go for him, he would elect Cartwright, and Cartwright could elect him; and that he wished me [Early] to inform Cartwright of these proposals." Pretty soon there was a rush to make this arrangement, as John Stuart, Abe Lincoln, and many other men were leaving Sangamon County to fight Indians who had entered the northern end of the state in violation of a treaty.

As voters could select four candidates, aspirants could make deals such as a Peter Cartwright–John Stuart alliance, by which their supporters would vote for both candidates. The opposite could also be done; for example, Stuart could pull wires so his supporters would refuse to vote for Cartwright. And Reverend Cartwright could do substantial damage to Stuart if left free to campaign against him without opposition while Stuart was away in the Indian war. Stuart apparently hoped to make an arrangement through which the two candidates' little big men would cooperate while, more importantly, preventing Cartwright from working against him while he was chasing Indians and unable to defend himself against politicians back home. Early said, "The next time I saw Cartwright I gave him the statements as above, when he declined so doing, and declared that he intended to run without identifying himself with any man, or set of men." That Cartwright intended to disregard the little big men is unlikely, but unquestionably he was known well enough from years of circuit preaching that he could spurn Stuart's combination offer and threat.

Later in 1832, Cartwright recalled a curious discussion with Stuart: "Sometime last spring (either on the day the volunteers started from the town of Springfield, or the day before they started) . . . John T. Stuart, in a conversation with me, admitted he held the conversation with Dr. Early . . . but Mr. Stuart remarked . . . that he was not sincere in those propositions."[91] Why Stuart would say such a thing to Cartwright is bewildering. Assuming Cartwright was truthful, one can only guess it had something to do with Stuart's frantic negotiations with other politicians before he left town.

William H. Herndon's father, Democrat Archie Herndon, who was running for state representative, revealed the following scene from the office of Springfield attorney William L. "Big Red" May. President Andrew Jackson had recently appointed May to the lucrative federal job of U.S. Land Office Register in Springfield, a vacancy that occurred by Jackson's removal of Whig John Todd as Land Office Register, an office which Dr. Todd had received from President John Quincy Adams. This switch caused more turmoil than usual, as Big Red May had changed from Whig to Democrat,[92] and his turncoat behavior had earned him a substantial reward from Jackson to the detriment of a reliable Springfield Whig, Dr. Todd. Or maybe "formerly" reliable would be a better description, as Dr. Todd was publicly supporting Democrat Cartwright for state representative.[93] Until recently, however, Cartwright had been a Whig, and in 1832, realization of his shift may not have sunk in among all Whigs. County political alliances were in considerable flux. Four years earlier, Elijah Iles, possibly Springfield's biggest businessman, was such a strong Whig that he was a John Quincy Adams candidate for the Electoral College.[94] Now Iles was publicly supporting Democrat Cartwright,[95] but again, word about Cartwright's shift may not have reached everyone. John Stuart later recalled the legislature campaign as "a bitter fight between the Jackson and Clay men, and there were a great many Jackson men down there."[96] William H. Herndon's father said at the time:

> Myself and May were conversing. John T. Stuart came in. Said he, "Gentlemen, have you made out your ticket?" [That is, have they determined which candidates for their allies to support and which to oppose?] May observed, "We have no ticket." Stuart then said he understood matters; and if the ticket was made up and he was left out, that he could measure arms with any of us. Some conversation then ensued which I don't recollect. Cartwright's name was mentioned by either Stuart or May. . . . Stuart threatened if Cartwright and his friends did not run him, he, Stuart, would pull the plank from under Cartwright; and further, he could work the wires as well as any

person, and would do it—that he, Stuart, knew where to touch them. Said May to Stuart, "Suppose Cartwright and his friends should run you, what could you do for him?" Said Stuart, "I will not promise any more than my own support." Said May, "You want Cartwright and his friends to go for you, and won't agree to bring him any support!" Said Stuart, "If I go, so my friends will." Said May, "What number of your friends will go with you, do you think, Stuart?" Said Stuart, "I think 200." Said May, "Well Stuart, I have nothing to say in this matter, but I will see Cartwright and his friends, and tell them what you have said." In that conversation I understood Stuart that he would go all the ticket with the exception of [George Forquer's opponent William] Elkin. "Elkin," said he, "I have promised my support to him long since."[97]

Early said that incumbent state representative Col. Dick Taylor vouched for the above. Taylor had been a Whig but was now running as a Jackson supporter and, evidently according to Dr. Anson G. Henry, claimed authority to make deals on Cartwright's behalf.[98] Stuart later explained: "That was a year of the reorganization of parties. Forquer and some of the other prominent old Clay Whigs had gone over to the Jackson party."[99] For quite some time, Illinois politics had been divided into two factions: supporters and opponents of Ninian Edwards, who served as governor and U.S. Senator. In the mid-1820s, a third faction emerged of those who supported Gov. Edward Coles and also opposed efforts to convert Illinois into a slave state. Those alliances, however, were evolving into parties distinguished by their attitude toward President Andrew Jackson—Democrats supporting Jackson, and Whigs opposing him.

Forquer had aligned himself with Edwards, who in 1829 had gotten the legislature to elect Forquer as attorney general with help from state representative John Reynolds, nicknamed "the Old Ranger." That help converted Edwards from a tough opponent of Reynolds into a supporter of the Old Ranger's 1830 gubernatorial campaign, a switch considerably muddying the state's political loyalties. Taylor, Big Red May, Billy Herndon's father Archie Herndon, and a fellow named James Adams were a clique working against Sangamon County followers of Edwards. Forquer had received significant help from Reynolds in the legislature's attorney general election, and when Sangamon's anti-Edwards clique offered to back Forquer for state senate in 1832, he switched sides from Edwards and the Whigs to Reynolds and the Democrats.[100] Evidently Whig leader Dr. Anson G. Henry said Forquer promised to do his best to bring his supporters along with him.[101] "Democrats" must be understood in a loose sense; many were willing to cooperate with Whigs whenever such cooperation portended personal advantage. Participants in this loose Democrat-Whig alliance were called the "coalition." A young Illinois Democratic activist named Stephen A. Douglas thought this kind of deal was madness and would later wage a campaign for party discipline.

Stuart explained: "McConnel, Cavarly, Green, Forquer, May, Ford, Cartwright, and others who had been old Clay men had gone over to the Democrats. In fact they had asked me to go with them, and because I refused to do it they attacked me very bitterly. They looked on me as having views for Congress in this District, and also as having a chance to win; and therefore they were bent on defeating me."[102] As part of the campaign against John Stuart, Early posed a few public questions:

> Did you not propose a union of your friends with the friends of Col. E. D. Taylor, and did you not say to him that an arrangement of that kind could not fail to secure you both—that your friends were his friends, and that he would greatly injure his popularity by giving his influence and support to Forquer, Cartwright, and others? Did you not propose to form a political alliance with A. G. Herndon, and did you not promise to support him if he would support you? Did you not say to Herndon that you believed he possessed more transferable strength than any man in the county, and that by a union of your friends with his, you both could be secured? Did you not authorize Jonathan H. Pugh to make similar proposals to Peter Cartwright, and did not Pugh, in obedience to your wishes, pledge himself for you and your friends, that Cartwright would be supported by you and them, if he would support your election?[103]

Lincoln's name is conspicuously absent from these discussions by the county's political insiders. He wasn't a factor worth their consideration.

As New Salem physician Jason Duncan rode the county, he campaigned for Lincoln. "So little was known of Mr. Lincoln by the inhabitants of Sangamon . . . that when a few miles out of town in my rides [I] would be asked who Abraham was. They had never heard of such a man." Duncan said he "would recommend him to their consideration not as a tried politician but a young man of extraordinary talents."[104]

Lincoln, however, suspended his personal political campaigning almost as soon as it started in order to do military campaigning. He, other candidates, and numerous other men responded to a call for volunteers to repel Indian attacks in northern Illinois.

INDIAN WAR

$\mathbf{A}$s wars go, the Black Hawk War was minor, and indeed accounts sometimes treat it semihumorously. "We had a first rate time on this campaign," John T. Stuart said. "The whole thing was a sort of frolic."[1] For some participants, however, the business was deadly serious.

Actually there were two Black Hawk Wars, one in 1831 and another in 1832. Both had the same cause as every other Indian war: Whites wanted land where Indians roamed or resided, and they were unwilling to seek a way to peacefully share the region. We'll never know if peaceful coexistence was possible, as the concept was alien to most whites' way of thinking. Pioneers did leave behind dim evidence of what might have been. One woman described conditions in the Black Hawk War region a few years before fighting broke out:

> To live among the Indians and not to fear them, would scarcely seem possible to many a reader; yet this was true of the writer, whose childhood was passed among them. . . .
>
> Many of their habits were startling. It was their custom while in towns to saunter about the streets in a very indifferent manner; and if they chose, to take a look at the interior of any house they might be passing. Men, women, or children would spread their blankets to the top of their heads, to exclude the light, and then peer through the windows, to their heart's content. This was done at any home and no one dared resist the intrusion. Indians never herald their approach, either in peace or war. They never knock at a door; but stalk in, and squat themselves on the floor. . . . You always heard a man come in,

as his step was firm, proud, and full of dignity. The women, however, made no sound.[2]

Another account told of a woman's experience in the region a few years after the wars. "Once she was sitting at home, a shadow darkened the room, and on looking up, she saw a tall Indian standing in the door, attracted there by the odor of something which was being cooked. He entered and raised the cover of the kettle, asking many questions about it."[3] Here we glimpse the beginnings of a tantalizing alternative history, colonists and natives learning customs novel to each, merging into a new way of life for both.[4]

But most interactions with Indians involved threats, unspoken or otherwise, from whites who coveted real estate. Black Hawk reportedly was perplexed by land dealings, saying that "land cannot be sold. . . . Nothing can be sold but such things as can be carried away."[5] Such a philosophical stance may be intriguing, but settlers and politicians had little interest in philosophy. Indians understood the threats hovering behind every real estate negotiation, and such understanding colored their attitudes. Some were willing to move west away from the whites; others wanted to make a stand, however hopeless it might be, centuries of experience having demonstrated that whites would follow them wherever they went and evict them again. The latter group of Indians held that though whites would win, at least they would pay a price for their victory. Black Hawk was among them. As he later explained: "I did not expect to conquer the whites, they had too many horses, too many men. I took up the hatchet to revenge injuries which my people could no longer endure. Had I borne them without striking, my braves would have said, 'Black Hawk is a woman—he is too old to be a chief!'"[6] Indian leaders responded to political pressures, just as white leaders did.

A nineteenth-century chronicler described Black Hawk:

> Small of stature, but he was finely formed, and his eyes were bright and intelligent. He had a quick sense of propriety, and his manners were dignified and graceful. He had a lively sense of honor, and was remarkable for his uprightness and fair dealing. . . . Nature made him a nobleman, and gave him that spirit of chivalry, which has been celebrated in poetry and song. He was a kind and affectionate father. . . . Black Hawk was a good deal of a diplomatist, too, he would say the right thing at the right time, and he gained the good will of all with whom he came in contact. . . . Had he been born in happier days and a member of a civilized race, his talents would have made for him a grander name.[7]

An early-twentieth-century chronicler,[8] however, portrayed Black Hawk as not just fierce, but psychopathic, with apparently genuine feelings of friendliness overtaken in a moment by rage or coldly disregarded in premeditated plans to gratify himself with murder.

In 1831, while Lincoln was on his New Orleans flatboat trip, Black Hawk and his entourage, known as the British Band because of their anti-American alliance with the British during the War of 1812, was roaming northern Illinois. Aside from women and children, Black Hawk had a potential fighting force of a few hundred men. Not much in the way of the world, but pretty overwhelming when they encountered an isolated cabin or a small settlement. Settlers instantly understood that their immediate interest was best served by obeying Black Hawk's demand that they get out fast and get out now. The British Band implemented a scorched-earth policy on encountering white farms and villages. The Illinois legislature passed a resolution urging that somebody do something:

> Bands of Indians, and particularly a band of Sacs, commanded by the well known war chief, called the Black Hawk, have been in the habit of hunting upon ceded lands within the limits of this State, committing trespasses upon the lands of individuals, by making sugar and destroying their sugar trees, killing their hogs, stealing horses, and otherwise so demeaning themselves as to keep up a constant state of alarm . . . and whereas, the said Black Hawk . . . has announced his intention to resume the possession of the said lands in the ensuing spring, and to maintain possession thereof by force of arms, if necessary: Therefore,
>
> Resolved by the Senate and House of Representatives of the State of Illinois, That all such transactions on the part of said Indians, are violations of the rights of the citizens of this State, which demand the protecting arm of the Government, and would justify a resort to immediate force. . . .
>
> Resolved, That our Senators in Congress be instructed, and our Representative requested, to unite in bringing this case before the President of the United States, requesting him to have all the Indians that now reside, or hereafter attempt to remain on ceded lands within the limits of this State, removed therefrom.[9]

Upon learning of the situation, Gov. John Reynolds, the Old Ranger, sought help from two U.S. Army generals stationed in St. Louis. One general took several companies of army Regulars into the region and discovered that his force wasn't big enough to shock or awe the British Band. He thereupon sought mounted volunteers from Governor Reynolds. Reynolds called on northern and central counties to send help to the U.S. Army, and about fifteen hundred men responded. One volunteer regiment was commanded by Sangamon County sheriff James D. Henry. Congressman Joseph Duncan, who was seeking reelection, commanded the brigade of regiments. One volunteer noted that in addition to farmers, "our army is swarming with lawyers, doctors, &c."[10] State attorney general George Forquer's half-brother Thomas Ford was a volunteer, and he said the brigade "was the largest military force of Illinoisans which had ever been assembled in the state, and made an imposing appearance as it traversed the then unbroken wilderness of prairie."[11] Perhaps that appearance helped persuade Black Hawk and some other British Band leaders to accept the U.S. Army field general's invitation to parley. A frank exchange of views established the impossibility of amicable agreement. As the Americans prepared to attack the British Band stronghold, the Indians, who had no trouble counting, skulked away across the Mississippi River, territory where they had a legal right to be.

Just before the planned attack, Governor Reynolds, who was on the scene as overall commander of Illinois forces, reported himself sick and retreated to a boat, where he recovered after learning that an attack was unnecessary. A later hostile chronicler noted, "Not only in coarse jest, but in serious earnestness, he was charged with cowardice, and few doubted that his sickness was feigned to evade the expected battle."[12] A disgusted U.S. Army officer noted that Reynolds used health as an excuse to ride overland in a cart, "which, had I met it elsewhere, I should have taken for a Jersey fishcart." The crude vehicle had leather curtains: "With these sable barriers was the stronghold defended on all sides against the weather—and there, *Jupiter tonans!* there lay his linsey-woolsey Excellency, coiled upon a truss of tarnished straw. . . . I had like to have died." The same officer noted that Reynolds was commander in name only and took no active role, rumor attributing his presence to possible political harvest he could later reap by advertising his role as a wartime governor and field commander.[13] The governor's military deputy, militia general Joseph Duncan, asserted privately: "You, and every man on the expedition well know that he did not command. The constitution of the state expressly prohibits him from exercising such a command. . . . As to all the honors of the command he is welcome to that, but he knows that he would not have been permitted to exercise any command if he had have wished to, for I told him so before I entered on my duties. . . . His excellency carried no arms . . . and if he was ever in front, or at the head of the army, I did not see him except once in Bledsoe's wagon." In addition to being a militia general, Duncan was a U.S. Representative in Congress, where he was confronted by a request Reynolds submitted for Congress to pay him for wartime services as the state's commander-in-chief. Duncan moaned, "Now what could be more embarrassing than such an occurrence as that of his claiming pay for services which he did not nor could not render."[14]

Upon entering the British Band's abandoned stronghold, an Indian town that in former times had a population approaching seven thousand, perhaps making it the biggest human habitation in Illinois, the Americans burned it to the ground. Black Hawk grudgingly signed a treaty agreeing that the British Band would stay west of the Mississippi River. Governor Reynolds persuaded the U.S. government to give the Indians enough food to make crop cultivation unnecessary by them, thereby removing any need for them to return to Illinois cropland. Some volunteers then complained, "We give them bread, when we ought to give them lead."[15] The army was demobilized, and the first Black Hawk War ended without "a single person, by disease, accident or otherwise, having lost his life."[16] A war without fatalities.

This cessation of hostilities, however, turned out to be not a peace, but an armistice.

The winter of 1831–32 was tough for the Indians. According to the Edwardsville, Illinois, paper of December 16, 1831: "We learn from travelers who left the mouth of the Ohio on the 7th inst., that snow had fallen at that place to the depth of eight or ten inches; that the Mississippi was frozen over as far down as St. Genevieve, and the Ohio below Shawneetown. . . . The weather has been remarkably severe for the last three weeks, and snow, to the depth of an inch or two, has fallen—indeed more severe weather has not been experienced in the last fifteen years."[17] Two months later, on February 17, 1832, the same paper reported: "Severely cold for the last week; a fall of three or ten inches snow on the 22d, with the most intense cold; the coldest this winter. This morning the thermometer was 20 degrees below zero, at eight o'clock, A.M."[18] In May 1832, one Illinois resident noted, "Last winter was cold here, as any Connecticut winter; generally they have been very mild heretofore."[19] Game was scarce, and harvests had been poor. The Edwardsville paper of May 8, 1832, showed just how bad the weather had been: "The last severe winter nearly destroyed all the wheat in the country."[20] Rations the U.S. government supplied to the Indians evidently were insufficient, and their situation was later described as "abject misery and starvation."[21] Black Hawk decided to take his followers back to the area of Illinois that had been so fertile for their corn crops.

Black Hawk's return to Illinois was greeted with a mix of apprehension and anger. The state was still home to a few Indians, whose nonhostile presence vexed settlers. In January 1831, the state legislature had resolved "that the committee on the Militia be instructed to report a bill providing for the expulsion of strolling bands of Indians in this State, from lands to which the Indian title has been extinguished."[22] A year later, in January 1832, Governor Reynolds heard of "about one hundred Indians in the Illinois River bottom near the mouth of the Spoon River, and that the citizens and they are not on friendly terms. I fear that some mischief may be done. The same letter informs me that the whites had whipped several of them 'in a most inhuman manner.'"[23] Black Hawk's contingent was unlikely to submit to such abuse.

Reynolds may have given thought about how to respond if mischief arose. In a step unusual for that era, he had earlier directed John T. Stuart and a Morgan County attorney-politician named William Thomas to investigate and report about circumstances of the 1831 war. Their report to the governor said that Black Hawk had access to a formidable force of Indian allies and that they were determined to retain their Illinois lands. Newspaper coverage of the report noted that in 1831, the British Band had not been expected simply to abandon their village stronghold and retire peacefully, but instead had been expected to sally from their stronghold and proceed to eradicate white settlements along the Mississippi River. Traveling lightly enough to outdistance pursuers, upon spotting soldiers the British Band could simply hop across the river to the west side's legal sanctuary for Indians, thereby escaping any chastisement. An outpouring of state militia forces was credited with thwarting that scenario, forcing the British Band across the Mississippi before they could ravage the Illinois frontier.[24]

Such was the official "establishment" thinking about Black Hawk's intentions.

Like other able-bodied men of Illinois, Lincoln was a militia member. A well-regulated militia was considered necessary to the security of a free state, and the right of the people to keep and bear arms was not infringed upon. Militia units held occasional drills where members, who furnished their own rifles, received very basic military training. Officers ran through elementary commands, and enlisted men in civilian garb went through the motions of implementing them. Ten and twenty years later, Illinois men attracted to martial exertion would form decent semiprofessional local militia units. In the early 1830s, however, Illinois frontier militia drills were akin to time required for county road repair service, an obligation to be gotten through as easily as possible. Finishing a muster with rounds of liquor was common, enough so that boys playing militia included the custom in their play.[25]

Lincoln was not only a militia member but an officer, a company captain in the 31st Regiment of militia. In that era, militia officers were typically chosen through election by men they led, and Lincoln's election on April 7 portended well for his state legislature campaign, which was then under way.[26]

In mid-April, word arrived in New Salem that the governor had proclaimed that the state was being invaded by Black Hawk's band. Governor Reynolds called for volunteers to repulse the invasion, with a draft if volunteers were insufficient.[27] Local notables quickly volunteered, setting a proper example that encouraged other citizens to step forward. Less publicized was the practice of notables then quietly paying ordinary folk to take their places as substitutes.[28] Reynolds set April 22 as the time and Beardstown as the place for a general rendezvous of militia. Technically, these volunteers were not the Illinois militia, but constituted a special force organized from within the militia for the express purpose of fighting Black Hawk. For convenience, however, I refer to this force as militia, as did many persons of the era. In theory, all special force members were militiamen; the distinction between militia and the special force was strictly bureaucratic.

Reynolds's call met with much approval. "These Indians must be taught to respect their treaties," said the *Sangamo Journal*.[29] A week later, the newspaper reported: "It appears that the governor is determined at once, to drive Black Hawk and his associates, from the limits of our state. There can be no object in parleying any farther with him or his gang. Summary and spirited measures must be used, or our citizens will be subjected yearly to the incursions of this Indian banditti."[30] The same newspaper published intelligence reports warning of danger: "I have been informed by the man I have had wintering with the Indians, that the British band of Sax Indians, is determined to make war upon the frontier settlements."[31] Based on report from friendly Indian chiefs, word arrived that "the British band of Sacs . . . are preparing to lay waste the frontiers."[32] A government Indian agent warned, "Nothing short of arms will deter the British band from their purpose."[33] Such intelligence alerts, combined with news that Black Hawk's entourage had entered Illinois, created high alarm.

People initially accepted the governor's proclamation at face value, having no instant access to alternative reliable sources of information. When he first received word that Black Hawk and his entourage had entered Illinois, Reynolds's main concern was not whether these Indians threatened settlers, but whether taking the field against them would add to his political popularity.[34] He was serving as governor, but that high office hadn't satisfied his ambitions. As the war began, Galena militia officer Henry Dodge scoffed:

> Governor Reynolds was elected simply from the fact of his being an old ranger; Reynolds, like all ordinary men in such cases, will pretend to set an example of militiary spirit; he will do so; the militia will be called out; the Indian affair being so easily quashed last season; a great many cowardly turbulent fellows will get offices; thinking there will be no fighting—that the Indians are afraid of them, and that 'tis only to show themselves and they'll run; his cowardly foresumption will ensure them defeat; the Indians will fight, and the Suckers will run away.
>
> This will be precipitated by the eagerness of Reynolds, and his batch of pseudo military politico statesmen; to reap all the glory. [U.S. Army] Gen. Atkinson will move slowly with his supplies and camp, equipage; the Suckers will advance in front, and some outbreak of that cowardly presumptuous confidence will satisfy the inflated leaders that they can whip the Indians, a disorderly and careless advance will be the consequence; which will eventuate in disaster—mark me! I predict this as a necessary consequence; I know the men.[35]

Events would prove Dodge a keen analyst.

Governor Reynolds issued a proclamation of hostilities at prime crop-planting time. During the war, militiaman William Orr expressed astonishment "that at so important a time of the year, particularly to the farmer, we would have been *prematurely*, if not *unnecessarily* called from our homes." He said that although the governor's call for volunteers implied that forces had been requested from the governor by U.S. Army Gen. Henry Atkinson, in reality the general had simply advised the governor that Black Hawk's Indians "had crossed the Mississippi in a hostile attitude." Actually, Atkinson's language to Governor Reynolds was stronger than that: "I think the frontier is in *great danger*, and I will use all the means at my disposal to cooperate with you in its protection." The skeptical Orr noted: "The Indians crossed at Rock Island, and passed Dixon's Ferry on Rock River without committing one overt act of hostility; persons and property were alike respected by them. From this fact it may be inferred, that it was not their intention to become the aggressors." Orr observed, "Their march was not in the direction of the settlements, but into an interior and inhospitable part of the country." Militiaman Orr bluntly declared that the governor's "*warlike* disposition, (or, rather the *electioneering mania* that seems to have taken possession of him) . . . hastily and prematurely" called for volunteers to repulse Black Hawk. Militia went into the field "without any preparation, without even an inspection of horses, equipment, etc." He continued, "I cannot be persuaded that the Indians crossed our border with any hostile intention beyond that of raising corn for their subsistence; and whilst I freely grant that this was an infraction of the treaty of Rock Island . . . the manner in which we have attempted to repel it was unwise and injudicious."[36] Even a newspaper staunchly supporting the war expressed reservations as the militia left for battle in April:

> What we deem most unfortunate in this affair is, that the government should at this particular period of time, press their demand upon the Indians. The citizens of Illinois are mostly farmers, and now is with them the most busy season of the year. Corn is the crop on which they place the most dependence, and this is the very moment of making preparations for planting.[37] Our citizens cannot leave their farms at this time without a great—a very great sacrifice. The militia of Illinois are not usually backward when their country calls for their services. Yet such was the pressure of the claims of their families upon the militia, that in many cases drafts have been compelled.[38]

Well into the war, while militiamen were still in the field, another newspaper complained, "The cornfields have been a prey to *beast, bird,* and every *creeping thing,* so that, with bad seed and the common enemies to contend with, the farmers have an unpromising prospect before them; to say nothing of the loss of hands to cultivate the fields which are now employed on the frontiers, in defending our inhabitants."[39]

Despite such hesitations, general enthusiasm existed for going after the Indians. A nineteenth-century chronicler said that settlers expected the war to boost economic prosperity via government purchases, which promoted support for the conflict.[40] But that motive lacked universal endorsement. The *Vandalia Illinois Advocate* complained, "There are individuals too, in the country, who have *profited largely* by the late troubles with the Indians, and who, regardless of the general injury which the country might sustain, would gladly see it again involved in savage warfare."[41] Potential for gain ranged beyond government contracts; the *Sangamo Journal*'s copublisher wrote to one of his brothers: "The two last winters together with the Indian disturbances on our frontier has done much towards improving the country . . . driven off the lazy dissipated N. and S. Carolinians, Georgians, Tennesseeans. . . . Consequently great bargains have been and are to be had, by purchasing secondhand, or improved farms."[42] Complaints arose about white men making money by arming the British Band. Said one militiaman:

> It was known that the Indians were unprepared for war the year preceding, but during the season they were indefatigable in procuring arms and ammunition, in which they were kindly assisted by the traders. To these people may be attributed the disorders which followed; as from the quantity of munition furnished the Indians, they must, undoubtedly, have been apprised of their designs—and in administering to which, they rendered themselves equally culpable, showing pretty conclusively, that there is more danger to be apprehended from the cupidity of the trader, than from the savages themselves.[43]

Aside from financial gain, yet another motive for war was observed by a nineteenth-century historian: Combat appealed to "lawless adventurers, destitute alike of principle or property, who infest frontier settlements as tigers do the jungles."[44] "Hatred of the Indian," noted another nineteenth-century chronicler, "was hereditary; there was scarcely a man on the frontier, who had not lost a father, a mother, or a brother, by the tomahawk."[45] Abe Lincoln's uncle Mordecai was a good example. A Kentuckian repeated a story he had heard: "There came a few Indians through there, and old Mordecai heard of them passing through, mounted on his horse, and took his rifle gun on his shoulder and followed on after the Indians and was gone two days. When he returned he said he left one lying in a sink hole, for the Indians had killed his father, and he was determined to have satisfaction."[46] Said a nineteenth-century observer of Western characters:

> [A pioneer's] vengeance was as rapid as it was sometimes cruel. No odds against him could deter him, no time was ever wasted in deliberation. If a depredation was committed in the night, the dawn of morning found the sufferer on the trail of the marauder. He would follow it for days, and even weeks, with the sagacity of the bloodhound, with the patience of the savage: and, perhaps, in the very midst of the Indian country, in some moment of security, the blow descended, and the injury was fearfully avenged! The debt was never suffered to accumulate, when it could be discharged by prompt payment—and it was never forgotten! If the account could not be balanced now, the obligation was treasured up for a time to come—and, when least expected, the debtor came, and paid with usury![47]

Uncle Mord had moved to Illinois and surely would have relished the opportunity to hunt Indians in the Black Hawk War, but he had died two or three winters earlier. While outdoors and drunk, he apparently got off his horse in order to lie down and sleep it off. He froze to death.[48]

Avoiding arcane details of military organization, suffice it to say that Illinois military forces operated in ways that would be intolerable today. Volunteers enlisted for only three or four weeks and were free to go home afterward. One veteran recalled, "The company I went with found the army at Dixon's [Ferry]; remained there about a week, disbanded and returned home."[49] Speaking of militia campaigning against Indians, a nineteenth-century analyst noted, "Every man was fully at liberty to abandon the expedition whenever he became dissatisfied, or thought proper to return home."[50] Thus sustained military operations were impossible; commanders might not know what size force would be available the next week. Some volunteers were so independent that they refused to enlist at all, traveling with organized units and willing to fight but refusing to accept pay or orders.[51] Units elected their officers; as enlistments expired and new units formed from reenlisted or fresh personnel, new elections could change a captain to private and vice versa. Such changes undermined officers' authority and encouraged resistance to unpopular orders; treating orders seriously was difficult anyway when the men were going home in a couple weeks. A lackadaisical approach to discipline prevented elementary and necessary military behavior such as vigilant sentries and coordinated firing in combat.

During the conflict, a disgusted militiaman summed up the situation: Men who died were lost "by the incapacity of those *would-be officers*. . . . They never drilled the men, or made anything like an attempt to practice them in the necessary evolutions. The whole time that I was out I never witnessed a company drill, a battalion drill, or regimental drill, nor a brigade drill." He added, "I never heard a roll call." The men should "have been made skillful in the few manœvres necessary in an engagement with the Indians—such as forming line, dismounting, disposition of horses, etc. . . . There was a total absence of discipline; orders were obeyed or disobeyed as suited the pleasure or convenience of the men."[52] Soldierly discipline was considered undemocratic and therefore intolerable. At about this time, an immigrant to Illinois declared, "No man acknowledges another his superior unless his talents, his principles, and his good conduct entitle him to that distinction."[53] Said one observer of the nineteenth-century militiaman: "He stood up in the native dignity of manhood, and called no mortal his superior. When he joined his neighbors, to avenge a foray of the savages, he joined on the most equal terms—each man was, for the time, his own captain."[54] Encounters between militia and Indians were more like armed street brawls than military engagements. The Illinois militia's ability to prevail over the British Band proves the Indians' weakness. British Regulars probably would have made short work of Illinois volunteers.

New Salem volunteers formed their own hometown company and on April 21 overwhelmingly elected Lincoln as their captain. Men lined up behind the candidate they favored, Abe Lincoln or Bill Kirkpatrick. Lincoln began with about 75

percent of the men, and most who lined up with Kirkpatrick switched sides when they saw the trend. Perhaps the result was unsurprising, as the company was basically made up of the same men who had elected Lincoln captain in the 31st Regiment a couple weeks earlier. Still, the latest militia election victory was a good portent for New Salem's support of Lincoln in the August state legislature election.[55]

William Miller, a Springfield tavern keeper and militia major, recalled, "Upon his being elected he, in a very plain unassuming manner, thanked the company for the confidence they had expressed in electing him to command and promised very plainly that he would do the best he could to prove himself worthy of that confidence."[56] Speaking of himself in the third person, Lincoln said he "to his own surprise, was elected captain. . . . He has not since had any success in life which gave him so much satisfaction."[57] He probably retained civilian attire; officer uniforms were custom tailored, an expense Lincoln is unlikely to have absorbed. Tailor shops were in short supply in the wilderness anyway. We know he even lacked an officer's sword.[58] Officers received funding for a servant, and we do see reference to Lincoln's orderly.[59] Other officers had servants as well. A militiaman recalled that Gen. Henry Dodge brought along "Joe, a negro man of Dodge's who attended him . . . being a kind of baggage and munition wagon for the general and his son. . . . An indubitable proof of negro intelligence and sagacity, and complete overthrow of that doctrine of slaveholders, who propagate the belief of mental torpidity."[60]

Company members included Pvt. John M. Rutledge and Pvt. David Rutledge, brothers of Ann, who would become a love interest of Lincoln; Cpl. William F. Berry, who would later be Lincoln's partner in a New Salem store; Cpl. Alexander Trent, the fellow apparently willing to fight a duel to defend his claim of a deal between John Reynolds and Bowling Green; and Sgt. Jack Armstrong, leader of the Clary's Grove Boys.

Maj. William Miller described Lincoln's company as "the hardest set of men he ever saw."[61] "He had the wildest company in the world," Maj. John T. Stuart said. "It was mainly composed of the Clary Grove boys."[62] Reportedly Lincoln was eager to see how his company of toughs would react when shot at.[63]

"I fell in with Lincoln first when he was captain," John T. Stuart said. "I knew him very well in this expedition. He was then noted mainly for his great strength, and skill in wrestling and athletic sports—in fact he had the reputation of being the best wrestler in the army. He could generally throw down anybody he came across."[64] Maj. William Butler, who owned the farm where Lincoln debated Reverened Cartwright, recalled: "During this campaign the men followed the usual sports of the camp—they were wrestling and horse racing. Lincoln being an excellent wrestler threw down most everybody he came to."[65] Maj. William Miller recalled, "He was with them all the while in jumping or foot racing, and Lincoln done the wrestling for the company against every bully brought up."[66] Slicky Bill Greene felt likewise: "He was the finest wrestler that belonged to that army except a man by the name of Thompson." Lincoln, who lost a wrestling match with Lorenzo Dow Thompson, declared, "That man could throw a grizzly bear," and added, regarding his match with Thompson, "The whole army was out to see it."[67] The official excuse for the match was to decide which company got its choice of camping ground. Slicky Bill recalled:

> The company bet their knives, blankets, tomahawks, etc. on Mr. Lincoln's wrestling. The man Thompson was his opponent. . . . Thompson threw Lincoln fairly the first fall. Lincoln remarked to his friends, "This man is the most powerful man I ever had hold of. He will throw me, and you will lose your all unless I act on the defensive." Mr. Lincoln caught Mr. Thompson and held him off some time. At last the man got the crotch lock on Mr. Lincoln. Lincoln slid off, but the man caught him and partially threw Mr. Lincoln. We were taken by surprise at the result, and being unwilling to give up our property and lose our bets, got up a kind of an excuse as to the result in order to avoid giving up our bets. . . . A fuss was about to be a fight in the companies generally. Lincoln rose up and said, "Boys, the man actually threw me once fair—broadly so—and the second time, this very fall, he threw me fairly, though not apparently so."[68]

In addition to friendly athletic competition, Lincoln's storytelling, both solo and in contests, promoted goodwill among the militiamen.[69] "His men idolized him," Bill Greene said.[70] Jack Armstrong's brother-in-law similarly noted, "All the men in the company, as well as the regiment . . . loved him well, almost worshiped him."[71] A member of another company said of Lincoln's men, "No man but Lincoln could do anything with them . . . Lincoln was their idol, and there was not a man but what was obedient to every word he spoke. . . . When any of his company got into a muss or quarrel Lincoln could stop it at a word, he had such perfect control over them."[72] "Everybody liked him," John T. Stuart stated, adding, "Lincoln had no military qualities whatever except that he was a good clever fellow and kept the esteem and respect of his men."[73] This was crucial for an Illinois militia officer.

One militiaman at the Beardstown rendezvous noted a curiosity: Governor Reynolds seemed to favor St. Louis citizens in appointments. "The commissary is a merchant of the same city and who will not fail to realize a handsome fortune from the place."[74] Courting wealthy businessmen was to the governor's political advantage. Their Missouri residence was less important than their goodwill. Although Reynolds supposedly was commander-in-chief of Illinois forces, he wisely left military matters to his generals and devoted himself to schmoozing among the ranks. As one observer put it, "If he could have done so, every man would have been promoted."[75] Schoolteacher Charles Henderson arrived in Beardstown and presented himself to Reynolds, asking if he could serve. "'Yes,' said the governor, 'I can take you as a volunteer aide, we want a good many of that kind now.' 'Well, governor, that will suit me,' said Charley, 'what are the duties of the position?' 'Well,' said the governor, 'go along, feed your horse from the sub-sistence department, yourself at my quarters, assist me some with my writing, help the quartermaster and commissary when they call on you, and when we get where there is any fighting to be done pitch in and fight like h——l.'"[76] Such was the casual way in which Governor Reynolds passed out appointments for managing the army.

At Beardstown, Lincoln put his company through light drilling. Decades later, he reportedly admitted, "I could not for the life of me remember the proper word of command for getting my company endwise so that it could get through the gate, so as we came near the gate I shouted: 'This company is dismissed for two minutes, when it will fall in again on the other side of the gate!'"[77]

In camp, Lincoln drew supplies for his company, including fifty pounds of lead and five and a half gallons of whiskey. On April 26, Pvt. Orville Browning, in another company, wrote in his diary: "Warm and sultry. Encampment much infested with rattlesnakes. Killed several. At eight o'clock commenced raining and continued without intermission during the night. Had no tents. Could not sleep. Stood in mud ankle deep till day."[78] The next day, he recorded: "Marched through mud knee deep to our horses in Rushville. Stopped and took some refreshments. Got merry and continued our march."[79] Later accounts of this day say that poor discipline, contempt for military appointments, and friendly elec-tioneering by officers running for office back home all combined to produce an atmosphere of holiday-type amusement.[80]

On April 28, Lincoln's company was officially enrolled in state service, enti-tling the unit to draw supplies from the state quartermaster. Lincoln quickly obtained whiskey and weapons for his men. At that time, as later, state armories lacked the most advanced weaponry. When Quartermaster General Cyrus Edwards, brother of Ninian, issued thirty muskets and bayonets to Lincoln, those guns were flintlocks and surely smoothbore. Musketball cartridges were issued later, paper containers that a militiaman ripped open with his teeth, allowing him to pour a premeasured amount of powder and shot down the gun barrel, which he tapped home with a ramrod. That loading technology was familiar in the Ameri-can Revolution. Militiamen in active service got free muskets, but officers were expected to pay for their personal weapons.[81]

From Beardstown, the Illinois force had marched to Rushville. There Lin-coln's company was integrated into a regiment under Col. Samuel M. Thompson. A week earlier, Thompson had been a lieutenant in Lincoln's company; now Thompson outranked Lincoln. Indiscriminate firing of guns at the Rushville encampment, probably for fun, became so prevalent that Brig. Gen. Samuel Whiteside had to issue an order prohibiting the practice.[82] Whiteside was the brigade's ranking militia officer and no shirker, being experienced in hand-to-hand fighting against Indians. As things turned out, however, such experience didn't transfer into strategic skills or control of his forces.[83]

Now the army began marching forty-five miles toward Yellow Banks. On May 2, Private Browning wrote: "Encamped at night, by order of Mr. [Maj.

Nathaniel] Buckmaster, in a large prairie, two miles from timber or water. Night cold and tempestuous—much dissatisfaction and murmuring among the troops. All cursing Buck for keeping them in the prairie."[84] One militiaman recalled that despite belief that hostile forces were near, the camped Americans posted but few sentries.[85] An indignant militiaman complained: "I was on guard several nights and from the number of men we always found *snoring* on their posts we could not but believe that the Indians might on any night have commenced the work of death before we would have been aware of their approach. I *never heard a sentinel instructed in his duty*, and I never knew the officers to go round the guard for the purpose of assuring themselves of the vigilance of the sentinels. Thus we slept every night in a manner unguarded."[86] One night early in the war, John T. Stuart was supposed to be relieved from his sentry post at midnight, but the officer in charge simply forgot about him. Apparently no one remembered until he was elected major the next morning, when someone went out to give him the news.[87]

According to the account of Bill Greene, who was there, it may well have been while troops were in foul temper about camp conditions on May 2 that an old Indian named Jack came into camp.[88] He possessed a safe-conduct letter from Lewis Cass, who had recently become President Jackson's Secretary of War after serving for almost two decades as governor of Michigan Territory under various Presidents. Present-day Wisconsin was part of that territory, and much of the Black Hawk War occurred along the Wisconsin-Illinois borderlands. Members of Lincoln's company not only treated the old man as a prisoner, but also decided to kill him, on the theory that killing Indians was the army's mission. Lincoln quickly appeared and vetoed the plan. He was thereupon accused of cowardice, and Lincoln instantly invited anyone who doubted his courage to step forward and try his mettle, adding that any members of the company planning to kill the Indian would have to kill their captain first. His manner was so firm that the Indian was released. So the story goes.[89] It has been widely questioned, but Lincoln left no objection among marginal notations he wrote in an 1860 biography that mentioned the incident.[90]

Although controversy exists about whether Lincoln interceded for an old Indian, we do know that such situations arose. One militiaman noted: "His company was all young men and full of sport. While at Dixon['s Ferry] some six or eight friendly Indians with white flags hoisted came to us from Paw Paw Grove and urged protection against other Indians. Some of our men suspected them for spies, and they had to be put under guard to keep the soldiers from killing them. . . . They was doubtless what they professed to be, friendly disposed."[91] And although little is said about it, friendly Indians were part of the American entourage. George Harrison recalled "ninety-five Potawatomis, a few Winnebagos and Menominees, which Indians usually accompanied our company, both in camp and on the move."[92] He even spoke of footrace and wrestling competitions between whites and these Indians, along with friendly games of cards, checkers, and chess. He added, "The main object with them in becoming part of the army probably was to get plenty of beef, but the ostensible object was revenge on their enemies, the Sacs and Foxes."[93]

En route to the Yellow Banks settlement, the army found Henderson River ten feet deep, fifty yards wide, and "running like a milltail," in the words of Governor Reynolds.[94] One soldier recalled: "To cross this river we cut down trees, and pack and fill in with brush so as to make a bridge to get over on. Our baggage train was drawn by cattle and horses. We took the wagons across by hand, and the cattle and horses had to swim the stream. We was one entire day and night building and filling in to bridge. . . . In getting down the steep banks to the river the horses was compelled to slide down. In so doing several was killed." Private Browning wrote: "Henderson River; not fordable—no boats or canoes. . . . Army crossed in great disorder by felling trees into the river at different places . . . troops crossed with difficulty and swam their horses—two or three horses drowned. . . . Provision scarce. Hogs shot by soldiers. . . . No guard placed out at night."[95] Reaching Yellow Banks, the army found the settlement unpanicked by the Indian threat—indeed, virtually at ease. Arrival of what one trooper called "a considerable body of Indians of the Cherokee tribe" caused no alarm; the militia even treated the friendly Indians to a hoedown.[96]

Lacking food reserves, the militia couldn't leave Yellow Banks. In fact, the provisions situation was so critical that disintegration of the army was a distinct possibility. Reynolds sent urgent food requests to Fort Armstrong. An irritated volunteer wrote at the time, "Had our army been under anything like military direction and management, some of our numerous baggage wagons instead of being devoted exclusively to the convenience of the officers, would have been made really useful to the army, by carrying provisions."[97] From Fort Armstrong, General Atkinson instantly sent a steamboat down the Mississippi to Yellow Banks. That boat's arrival the day after Governor Reynolds sent out his pleas, along with the nearly simultaneous arrival of another steamer, the *William Wallace* from St. Louis, not only saved the army, but also left it in the unusual position of having extra food.[98] Troops then marched twenty miles to Rock Island, where they were mustered into federal service.

Among other things, "federal service" meant that troops would be paid by the general government rather than by Illinois—someday. Men weren't paid at the time, but instead, after the war, federal agents would travel across Illinois to make lump-sum settlements with veterans. The pay rate shocked some:

> Call our farmers from their ploughs, our mechanics from their benches, our merchants from their stores, in the most busy and important season of the year, and give them twenty-one cents a day as compensation!! . . .
>
> Those men who have gone out this inclement season, have done it at the immense hazard of health and life. Without suitable camp equipage, they have been compelled through all the cold and almost continued heavy rains, to encamp in open fields. And yet members of

Congress, no better than they are, warm in their snug berths, and
contentedly receiving eight dollars a day, give to the volunteer soldier
twenty-one cents a day![99]

"Federal service" also meant that the general government, instead of Illinois,
funded the militia's provisions. Federal and militia forces weren't smoothly integrated, however. Resentment arose when U.S. Army troops received preference
in rations, to which Lincoln objected. He helped U.S. officers understand the
wisdom of treating all soldiers the same, and Lincoln's role in equalizing treatment gained him respect and popularity among militia officers as well as enlisted
men. Bill Greene remembered an incident involving an order from a U.S. Army
officer. "Mr. Lincoln was ordered to do some act, which he decreed unauthorized. He, however, obeyed but went to the officer and said to him, 'Sir, you forget that we are not under the rules and regulations of the War Department at
Washington, are only volunteers under the orders and regulations of Illinois.
Keep in your own sphere, and there will be no difficulty. But resistance will hereafter be made to your unjust orders.'"[100]

A day or two after the militia was mustered into federal service, U.S. Army
Regulars, under command of Col. Zachary Taylor, arrived to augment the force.
This is the same Taylor who later became President of the United States. On U.S.
Army General Atkinson's order, General Whiteside marched fifteen hundred
militiamen along Rock River in pursuit of the British Band of Indians. According
to Pvt. David Pantier, Lincoln's company suffered a delay on beginning its
march. Pantier said that the previous night, a fellow from a Greene County company had approached members of Lincoln's company with a plan to pilfer the
officers' liquor supply. Using a tomahawk and buckets, the men succeeded in
their plan. "In the morning Capt. Lincoln ordered his orderly to form the company for parade. But when the orderly called the men to parade, they called
'parade,' too, but wouldn't fall into line. The most of the men were unmistakably
drunk. The rest of the forces marched off and left Capt. Lincoln's company
behind. The company didn't make a start till about ten o'clock, and then after
marching about two miles, the drunken ones laid down and slept their drunk off.
They overtook the forces that night." Pantier said Lincoln was punished for his
company's conduct, "put under arrest, and was obliged to carry a wooden sword
for two days."[101] While Lincoln's men slept off their drunk, the column marching
ahead of them needed every person's assistance. The men had to help weary
horses drag wagons through muddy trails. After pushing through twenty-six
miles, men and beasts were worn down at day's end.[102]

The next day, American forces reached the old Indian village of Prophet-
stown and paused to burn it. In order to increase speed of travel, General Whiteside then ordered that baggage wagons be left behind. He pushed the militia as
hard as he could toward Dixon's Ferry, which they reached the next day.

Upon arrival at Dixon's Ferry, the militia army had used up its provisions
and now bought flour and whiskey from merchant John Dixon. John T. Stuart

remembered, "The boys had a spree."[103] Much grumbling arose about waiting for U.S. Regulars to arrive, and most of the militia under General Whiteside's command wanted to quit the war and head homeward. The militia force at Dixon's Ferry included Maj. Isaiah Stillman's fresh battalion. For some reason, Whiteside declined to accept that unit into his brigade, thereby leaving it an orphan battalion taking orders directly from Governor Reynolds.[104]

Militia in battalions under Majors Isaiah Stillman and David Bailey were eager to hunt Indians and grew restive while waiting for General Atkinson's U.S. Army reinforcements. Things weren't at the stage of mutiny, but Governor Reynolds found it wise to order the militiamen to do what they wanted to do. A skeptical militia officer took a less charitable view, believing that Reynolds hoped he could make extraordinary political gain if officers under his command defeated Black Hawk before U.S. Army Regulars arrived.[105] An observer at the time asked, "If General Atkinson, with a force of three hundred United States Infantry and one piece of artillery deems it unsafe to march in pursuit of the enemy, why did Gov. Reynolds order . . . two hundred and sixty raw volunteers to pursue the Indians"?[106] John Dixon advised Stillman that a force of that size was insufficient for the job.[107] One militiaman rode up to Dixon and demanded: "Where's y' Injins? If you want y' Injins killed, fetch 'em on!"[108] The two raw battalions headed off, Stillman's toward Old Man's Creek, where some of the British Band were reported to be.[109] A nineteenth-century historian observed: "Their baggage wagon came on slowly, loaded with ammunition and whisky. In order to dispense with the wagon, the whisky barrel was broken open and every man took what he wanted. They filled their canteens and bottles and coffee pots, and men rode up and down the line offering everybody a drink."[110] Two other nineteenth-century chroniclers noted that on reaching the creek, "the volunteers were now strung along a half mile of hill and valley, with no more order or care than if they had been chasing rabbits."[111]

As the Americans approached Black Hawk's camp, three unarmed Indians appeared with a white flag of truce. Rather than treat them as envoys, the militia took them prisoner and killed one. Authorities conflict on whether the militia killed the other two also or managed to let them escape.[112] Many of Stillman's men rushed forward as fast as they could in hopes of finding more Indians. Those militiamen succeeded.

Black Hawk himself was present. "The fight with Black Hawk was about sundown," John Hanks said, "about 700 Indians and about 200 white."[113] The number of Indians was Hanks's estimate, not an official census. One militiaman said the advancing Indians were like the vast flocks of pigeons seen in Indiana.[114] Another said the Indians came on "like swarms of summer insects."[115] Three fine authorities say the Indian force totaled forty.[116] Another fine authority says the main Indian battle force was seven hundred, but only thirty or forty pursued the fleeing Americans.[117] Whatever the number, it was sufficient to defeat the militia. "They fled in all directions," said a member of another unit.[118] "On they went," said a later state attorney general, "until the Indians got tired of chasing."[119] The flight was so precipitous that Black Hawk suspected a trap and ordered a halt. His own men, however, refused to obey and kept pursuing Americans, taking no prisoners.[120]

The governor's judgment of the debacle was harsh. He declared that Stillman's force had showed no discipline and considerable recklessness in the straggling chase, pursuing six Indians seen on the hilltop after the three Indians under flag of truce were seized as prisoners. Stillman himself exhibited carelessness or incompetence in security and discipline at camp. Governor Reynolds stated: "The cause of this disaster was the want of discipline, subordination, and the proper previous arrangements of the officers. . . . This battle, and hasty retreat was much condemned by the army, and the public generally." Reynolds inspected Stillman's abandoned campsite the day after the defeat and saw empty liquor kegs, leading him to conclude that drunkenness among Stillman's volunteers was a factor.[121] John Hanks, who was in Stillman's unit and at the run, confirmed that the action "grew out of the drunkenness."[122] Forty years after the incident, an Illinois historian wrote, "No very accurate account of the famous fight at Stillman's Run has ever been published, because . . . most of the gentlemen who were engaged in it had taken too much spirits from the barrel which was broken open in the afternoon of the last day of the expedition."[123] Sixty years afterward, a historian described the militiamen as "excited and maddened by liquor."[124] Usher Linder, who later served as state attorney general, called the incident "a dishonor to the arms of Illinois."[125]

James Strode was a militia colonel but, because of Illinois's military organization, was serving as a private under Stillman. Strode was also a state senate candidate at the time. He acknowledged that his own conduct on the scene was less than gallant: "I espied the advancing host. When I saw they were gentlemen without hats I knew that they were no friends of mine and I whirled and turned my horse's head to the rear and put my stirrups into his flanks. He stumbled and fell, but I did not wait for him to rise or to secure my saddle bags. I was in great haste, and at once escaped into the thicket."[126] Strode confessed, "I followed the example of my companions in arms and broke for tall timber, and the way I run was not a little."[127] Years later, when Strode and his law partner, Thomas Ford, had each achieved higher political office, Ford rubbed salt into the wound in the genial malicious way that was so natural to him. The two old friends were in Chicago one day, where Strode was U.S. Land Office Register and Ford was a state judge. While Ford stood on the Tremont House stoop, picking his teeth after dinner, a rustic passerby asked if Ford could tell him the location of a place called "Stillman's Run." Ford noticed Strode crossing the street nearby and, with a smile, quickly urged the stranger to get the geographic information from the Land Office Register. When the stranger called out and headed over, Strode saw Ford watching and knew something was up. Strode brusquely told the hapless stranger that he was unaware of a place called "Stillman's Run."[128]

A soldier back at Dixon's Ferry recalled the return of Stillman's militia. "About twelve o'clock that night they commenced coming into our camp, and kept coming in all the remainder of that night and next day."[129] Levi Danley "was acquainted with many of them, and saw them just before they went from McLean County. At that time they . . . were talking of what they were going to do. Some were going to have a feather from old Black Hawk . . . but at midnight, when they came back from Stillman's Run, Mr. Danley says he heard no more talk of capturing Black Hawk's feathers."[130]

Upon receiving word of the defeat of Stillman's battalion, General Whiteside's army headed toward the battle area. A militiaman related, "We took up our line of march," but upon arriving at the scene of defeat, "we were compelled *to march back again*, because we had nothing to eat!" New Salem militiaman Royal Clary also said they "had no provisions, had had no provisions for four days, occasionally an ear of corn."[131] Before the militia left the battleground, "As the sun began to throw his evening rays upon the broad expanse of prairie, we approached the scene of the late conflict and beheld the headless trunks of those who had fallen laying 'stark and stiff' upon its green carpet." Everyone was sobered by the sight.[132] Another militiaman reported: "On the second day after the battle the army under General Whiteside was camped on the battleground, gathering up the dead and wounded. The dead was all scalped, some with the heads cut off, many with their throats cut and otherwise barbarously mutilated. Of the wounded we found few in number, and they hid in the brush as well as they could."[133] About a dozen militiamen died at Stillman's Run. "Their guns were broken into fragments, and the ghastly wounds inflicted by rifle balls, spears, butcher knives and tomahawks were frightful. . . . Some were beheaded, some had their hands and feet cut off, while their hearts and other internal organs, were torn out and scattered over the prairie. The mangled fragments were gathered together, and buried in a common grave."[134] In the delicate phraseology of a later chronicler, "The sight of the mangled remains of their comrades did not inspire the majority of the men with a wish to prolong their service."[135]

The army was now ordered to pursue the Indians. One pursuer recalled, "This was thought to be a dangerous undertaking, as we knew Indians was plenty and close at hand."[136] Scouts proceeded ahead. "To provide as well as might be against danger," said the same militiaman, "one man was started at a time in direction of the point. When he would get a certain distance, keeping in sight a second would start, and so on, until a string of men extending five miles from the main army was made, each to look out for Indians and give the sign to right, left, or front by hanging a hat on the bayonet. . . . To raise men to go ahead was with difficulty done, and some tried hard to drop back."[137] The Americans found plenty of evidence of the Indians who had attacked Stillman's unit but encountered no Indians. Pursuit was called off.

The men then returned to Dixon's Ferry on a rapid march. Tired and hungry, they were ready to abandon the war but stayed on at the governor's urgent request. The next day, U.S. Army General Atkinson, 320 regulars, and a 6-pounder cannon reached Dixon's Ferry. Immediately upon arrival, Atkinson issued Order No. 16: "The frequent unauthorized firing of arms in and about the vicinity of the encampments of the different corps of the army, composed of the U.S. Infantry and the state troops now in the field, compels the Commanding General to forbid a practice so dangerous to the individual members of the different corps and derogatory to the military character of well-organized troops. No officer or private, therefore, will fire again in camp or on the march without permission or an order from the commanding officer of his regiment or company."[138]

Being a champion politician, Governor Reynolds convinced General Atkinson that a few Regular army officers should be on the governor's staff and a few militia officers on Atkinson's staff. They all dined together at the table of John Dixon, for whom the town was named. Improbable as it seems, here in this genial social setting, Lincoln apparently met Colonel Taylor's adjutant, a West Point lieutenant named Jefferson Davis. The possibility of this acquaintanceship has been challenged on the grounds that official records show that Davis was on furlough throughout the war. Official records are sometimes misleading, however, and we have excellent reason to believe that Davis was present in the field and simply didn't bother completing furlough paperwork until mid-August, when he was back at headquarters. Indeed, the longer he stayed on furlough, the more freedom he had to be on the scene of war action without orders to be somewhere else. Davis more than once spoke of that war service, and he mentioned it in writing as well. Militia officer (and state treasurer) Jack Dement talked about knowing Davis in Illinois during the war. Supposedly Lincoln spoke of knowing Davis there as well, and the governor's mess arrangement at John Dixon's table makes such a meeting plausible.[139] Davis considered Dixon a lifelong friend and felt the same toward Lt. Robert Anderson, who was on the scene in Illinois and verified that Davis was there as Colonel Taylor's adjutant, though Anderson was imprecise on dates of service.[140] By 1861, Anderson had risen in rank and commanded a fort named Sumter. During the Civil War, Lincoln's private secretary John Hay publicly mentioned that Davis had served in the Black Hawk War.[141]

Lieutenant Davis probably made an impression on people he met in Illinois. His wife wrote that in those days, he "had no beard, or so little as to be scarcely perceptible, and his smooth face, fresh color, and gay laugh, gave the impression of a boy of nineteen."[142] He had already spent several years on the northwest frontier, essentially present-day Wisconsin. William Selby Harney was then a U.S. Army captain serving with Davis in the Black Hawk War. They amused themselves as best they could in off-duty hours. As Davis's wife described: "Frontiersmen used to bring wolves to the officers for races, as foxes are chased with horse and hound. It was their favorite game. Sometimes they fought their dogs against the wolves, and Mr. Davis and General Harney, four years ago, when the general was our guest, were comparing their recollections of a wolf fight with their dogs, and General Harney seemed very proud of chasing a wolf down on foot, and having what he called a 'fist fight' with it, during which he choked it to death by main force."[143]

Davis was robust at that time in his life and tenacious always. When his steed reared so vigorously in an attempt to throw him from the saddle that the animal fell, he jumped clear before the horse hit the ground and remounted as it began standing up. His wife recalled that on one reconnaissance, Davis and his men "met a party of Indians upon their return and asked the way; a brave stationed himself in the path and indicated the wrong road. Lt. Davis without further parley spurred his high-mettled horse . . . upon the Indian, seized him by the scalp-lock, and dragged him after him some distance. The attack was so quick that it disconcerted the rest, and the soldiers rode by without further molestation." Some gun-toting militiamen may have expected a lark against bow-and-arrow Indians, but Davis respected primitive weaponry, once seeing an Indian shoot an arrow that went into one side of a buffalo and emerged from the other.[144]

A couple days after General Atkinson issued his order against unauthorized firing of guns, the Americans headed up Rock River, making about thirteen miles. The next day, they made four miles. Supposedly the advance was intended to find Indians, but in reality it was make-work to keep the militia busy and deter members from going home.[145]

A week after Stillman's Run, Indians visited a pioneer settlement. Teenager Sylvia Hall reported:

> Pettigrew, with a child in his arms, flew to the door and tried to shut it, but failed to accomplish his object, being shot, and fell in the house. . . . Mrs. Pettigrew had her arms around [Sylvia's sister] Rachel at the time she was shot, and the flash of the burning powder blew in her face. We were trying to hide or get out of the way, while there was no place to get. We were on the bed when the Indians caught us, and took us out into the yard . . . and while going, we saw an Indian take Pettigrew's child by the feet and strike its head against a stump, and Davis's little boy was shot by an Indian, two other Indians holding the boy by each hand.

The body of Mr. Davis, a powerful blacksmith, was found with dozens of wounds, his gun contorted in various directions. The Hall sisters' brother John evaded capture and later described the sight he found upon returning: "What a scene presented itself! Here were some with their hearts cut out, others cut and lacerated in too shocking a manner to mention, or behold without shuddering." A later chronicler said, "The women were butchered, and, after the most revolting mutilations, their bodies were hanged, heads downward, to neighboring trees." According to another account: "The Indians afterwards related with an infernal glee how the women had squeaked like geese when they were run through the body with spears. . . . The little children were chopped to pieces with axes; and the women were tied up by the heels to the walls of the house; their clothes falling over their heads, left their naked persons exposed to the public gaze."[146] Still another chronicler wrote that the Indians "mutilated the bodies terribly, and the inside of the house looked like a slaughter pen."[147] New Salem militiaman Royal Clary wasn't there but heard that the Indians "cut one woman open, hung a child that they had murdered in the woman's belly that they had gutted. Strong men wept at this; hard-hearted men cried."[148] A couple weeks later, captors released the Hall sisters on payment of a substantial ransom.[149]

"TO THE CITIZENS OF ILLINOIS. *TO ARMS!!*" cried a proclamation by Illinois supreme court justice and Adj. Gen. Theophilus W. Smith.

> Seventeen defenseless men, women and children, have recently fallen victims to a barbarity, unparalleled even in the history of savage massacres. . . . The terrific war-whoop and yells of these fiends, echo through your forests and over your plains; and this daring and barbarous foe, flies from point to point, in the work of blood, desolation and death; with the celerity and untiring energy of the Arab of the desert. From the Mississippi to the Wabash, and the lakes, he is in motion, and no doubt now remains that the most extensive and daring combination of a very numerous portion of the savages on our widely extended frontier, has been formed for the work of destruction.[150]

The American army continued heading up Rock River until it reached the vicinity of Old Man's Creek in the area of Stillman's Run. General Atkinson and his Regulars then turned around and returned to Dixon's Ferry, leaving Col. Zachary Taylor as federal officer in charge of the Illinois militia force.

On May 22, when Atkinson and his Regulars arrived at Dixon's Ferry, the general sent Indian Agent Felix St. Vrain and five or six companions to carry dispatches. Accounts conflict over whether the mission was northwest to Galena or southwest to Fort Armstrong at Rock Island. St. Vrain was a sensible choice, known among Indians and on good terms with many, and thus likely to get through hostile territory safely. En route, he encountered a chief who had adopted him as a brother. The chief and his party, however, immediately killed St. Vrain and most of his companions; one escaped. No trace was found of Aaron Hawley, although his coat was acquired by Black Hawk. St. Vrain's body was found by his brother-in-law George Jones, a U.S. Army officer who had been a Transylvania University classmate of Jefferson Davis. Jones said: "It was I who found the mangled body of Mr. St. Vrain. . . . His head, hands and feet were cut off his body, and the most of his flesh, which the famishing Indians ate. His heart was also cut out of his body, and cut up into small pieces and given to their young men and boys to swallow; he to be adjudged to make the best warrior who would swallow the largest piece without chewing. His head, hands and feet were used in their war dances as trophies of war."[151]

The day after Atkinson sent St. Vrain on his fatal mission, the Illinois militiamen were still marching around many miles to the northeast. A small party looking for missing horses stayed out past dark, and in the gloom, they found a big group of Indians quietly moving north and away from the army encampment. Such a discovery spread consternation through militiamen back at camp, many of whom had planned on heading back to home forthwith. U.S. Army officers

Zachary Taylor and William Harney urged chase. Disagreement on whether to follow the Indians was so great that Governor Reynolds convened a brigade officers' meeting and put the proposition to a vote. It ended in a tie, and therefore the proposition to find the Indians lost. General Whiteside was so disgusted by the vote's outcome that he proclaimed he would no longer lead this group of soldiers except to deliver them to a place of mustering out.[152] The next day, Whiteside issued a general order: "The great disorder in the brigade occasioned by the men's quitting their places in the line and scattering over the country, renders it absolutely necessary to inflict punishment on everyone who violates orders in that particular."[153] When soldiers must be ordered to refrain from deserting, a military unit's effectiveness is near its end.

On the day troops were forbidden to desert, the army traveled twenty-five miles toward Fox River and Ottawa in order to be mustered out.

> On our march from Dixon['s Ferry] to Fox River, one night while in camp, which was formed in a square enclosing about forty acres, our horses outside grazing about nine o'clock got scared, and a general stampede took place. They ran right through our lines in spite of us, and ran over many of us. No man knows what noise a thousand horses make running unless he had been there. It beats a young earthquake, especially among scared men. . . . We expected the Indians to be on us that night. Fire was threw. Drums beat. Fifes played. Which added additional fright to the horses. We saw no real enemy that night. A line of battle was formed. There was no eyes for sleep that night. We stood to our post in line, and what frightened the horses is yet unknown. . . . We spent two days in hunting them.[154]

Mustering out of the militia force began when it reached Ottawa. Colonel Taylor recommended that Governor Reynolds try to persuade men to reenlist, in hopes that enough would stay on to form half a dozen companies. Quite a few militiamen had no interest in reenlisting and headed home.[155] Lincoln, however, stayed on. "I was out of work," he later said, "and there being no danger of more fighting, I could do nothing better than enlist again."[156] He joined a company commanded by Alexander White but a day or so later shifted to a company headed by Springfield merchant Elijah Iles. General Whiteside, Maj. John T. Stuart, and Captain Lincoln joined Captain Iles's ranger company as privates.[157] This was a three-week enlistment. U.S. Army Lt. Robert Anderson mustered them into federal service. Anderson later reported that Lincoln's weapons were valued at $40 and his horse and equipment at $120.[158] Lincoln's horse was borrowed.[159]

About this time, Dunkard minister Adam Payne (or Paine) was preaching in the war country. Legislature candidate Peter Cartwright later wrote that Payne had gone north "somewhere this side of Chicago, and wanted to come down the country toward the old mission. He was admonished not to venture, and was assured the Indians would kill him, but he was so visionary that he said he was not afraid to go alone, right in among them, for the Lord would protect him." Three Indians captured, shot, and beheaded him. A later chronicler noted that "a long black beard flowed from the victim's chin, and by this one of the party seized the head, threw it over his shoulder and together the three returned to camp." Reverend Cartwright noted that "after scalping it, they placed it on a pole and stuck the pole erect in the ground. . . . The next day, as a company of men passed, they saw Paine's head sticking on a pole, and his body greatly mangled by the wolves; and this was an end of his commission to convert the world, Indians and all."[160]

General Atkinson ordered a militia company to Dixon's Ferry, where Col. Zachary Taylor commanded a small force guarding supplies. Just as the company reached Dixon's Ferry, the survivor from Indian Agent St. Vrain's party arrived, saying that Indians had attacked and killed everyone but him. Reportedly Taylor immediately ordered the militia company to the scene, but en route, the militiamen panicked and fled back to headquarters. Taylor became skeptical of the Illinois militia's worth, telling General Atkinson, "The more I see of the militia the less confidence I have of their effecting anything of importance."[161]

When Atkinson received word of what had happened, he ordered Captain Iles's ranger company to report to Taylor. "This was at night," Iles recalled. "The next day was a busy day with the boys—cleaning guns, running bullets, picking flints, etc., etc.; (we used the old flintlock at that day). Most of the company had doubled-barreled guns, and the U.S. officers furnished us with holster and belt pistols. We expected to have to fight our way from Dixon to Galena."[162]

From Dixon's Ferry, Captain Iles's ranger company proceeded toward Galena. "I had about fifty men well equipped and eager," Iles said.[163] John T. Stuart remembered, "J. D. Henry was with us, and practically had charge of the company." Sangamon County sheriff Henry was then a militia officer rising in rank; he would soon become a general and have a crucial role in the war. When he learned that Iles's ranger company was heading toward Indian action, he attached himself to the unit for adventure.[164] Now he drilled the company in coordinated firing. "I considered him a host," Iles said.[165] "Henry was a military man," Stuart noted. Major Henry kept close tabs on what the men were doing and forced them to pay attention to their surroundings. "There were Indians all about us," Stuart recalled, "constantly watching our movements."[166] Action appeared imminent on the first day of march. With the rangers was John Dixon, a prominent frontier businessman whose skills kept much of the army provisioned and an expert on Indian ways. He served as the company's guide.[167] Captain Iles reminisced:

> Just at sundown of the first day, while we were at lunch, our advance
> scouts came in under whip and reported Indians. We bounced to our
> feet, and, having a full view of the road for a long distance, could see
> a large body coming toward us. All eyes were turned to John Dixon,

who, as the last one dropped out of sight coming over a ridge, pronounced them Indians. . . . I asked General Henry to take command. He said, "No, stand at your post," and walked along the line, talking to the men in a low, calm voice. Lieutenant Harris, U.S.A., seemed much agitated; he ran up and down the line, and exclaimed, "Captain, we will catch hell!" He had horse-pistols, belt-pistols, and a double-barreled gun. He would pick the flints, reprime, and lay the horse-pistols at his feet. When he got all ready he passed along the line slowly, and seeing the nerves of the men all quiet—after General Henry's talk to them—said, "Captain, we are safe; we can whip five hundred Indians." Instead of Indians, they proved to be the command of General Dodge, from Galena . . . *en route* to find out what had become of General Atkinson's army. . . . My look-out at the top of the hill did not notify us, and we were not undeceived until they got within thirty steps of us. My men then raised a yell and ran to finish their lunch.[168]

Dixon "says that in their marches, when approaching a grove or depression in which an Indian ambush might be concealed, and when scouts were sent forward to examine the cover, Lincoln was often selected for that duty, and he adds that while many, as they approached the place of suspected ambush, found an excuse for dismounting to adjust girths or saddles, Lincoln's saddle was always in order."[169]

When Lincoln and the rest of Iles's company reached Galena, the town was in bad shape. Galena was in deep in the war zone. Local newspaper editor Addison Philleo noted, "By unanimous vote of the citizens, Col. J. M. Strode was requested to proclaim for a day or two, military rule."[170] Col. James Strode, of Stillman's Run humiliation, took command of Galena's four hundred residents, male and female, military and civilian. His law partner, Thomas Ford, later wrote: "Even here in this extremity of danger a number of the inhabitants yielded their assistance unwillingly and grudgingly. There were a number of aspirants for office and command; and quite a number refused obedience to the militia commander of the regiment. . . . He immediately declared martial law; the town was converted into a camp; men were forced into the ranks at the point of the bayonet; and a press warrant from the colonel in the hands of armed men procured all necessary supplies; preparations for defense were kept up night and day."[171] Another contemporary observer noted: "Col. J. M. Strode found it necessary for the protection of Galena and the mining country to declare martial law and to forbid any man from leaving the country without the permission of the commanding officer under the pains and penalties of desertion. This prompt and energetic movement of Col. Strode it is supposed saved Galena from the flames, and the whole mining country from scenes of human massacres."[172] Such was the atmosphere found by Captain Iles's company.

Another part of Galena's atmosphere was indicated in William H. Herndon's telegraphic notes of an interview with John T. Stuart: "Got to Galena—went to the whorehouses—Gen. Henry went—his magnetism drew all the women to himself—All went purely for fun—devilment—nothing else."[173] A little later, another visitor reported: "This town was built more by accident than by design. The site [sight?] of it is the most uncouth for a town that moral eyes ever beheld."[174] Someone else asked: "Will you have the goodness to inform me how many faro and roulette banks your town affords at this time? As I understand the gentlemen of the profession have collected from all parts of the country."[175] Said an observer of Galena's assorted entertainments, "There are many attractions of a vicious kind in this place at the present time so well calculated to lead incautious young men astray, that it needs the utmost fortitude on the part of those who do not countenance them."[176] Three years after the war, people at a meeting in nearby Dubuque, a few miles up the Mississippi River, complained that "honest and upright citizens of a community are annoyed and molested by the continual revelings and midnight plots of outlaws and fornicators" and "we consider the persons who advised those unnatural women to remain in their lodgings contrary to public opinion (with the persons who furnished them with firearms) enemies to the laws of their country."[177]

A visit to a town's whorehouses could be rewarding but always entailed risk. During the Black Hawk War, Illinois residents heard "by gentlemen from St. Louis . . . that a very serious *riot* took place there on Friday last, in which several houses were either pulled down or otherwise injured. The riot is said to have been caused by the murder of a respectable man in one of the Magdalene establishments."[178] "There was a very orderly riot at St. Louis," the *Sangamo Journal* explained. "A young man having been murdered in one of the Magdalene establishments, a great number of citizens collected, and pulled down and otherwise injured several houses occupied by that community. The whole affair was conducted in a . . . civil manner, and the citizens returned to their several employments as if nothing had happened."[179]

After observing the Galena scene, Iles's company returned to Dixon's Ferry, carrying reports and correspondence from Colonel Strode. Back at Dixon's Ferry, Captain Iles warned Col. Zachary Taylor that Galena residents were so discouraged that they would be unable to mount a defense against attack.[180] Taylor sent Iles's company to General Atkinson at Fort Wilbourn on the Illinois River, along with a report to the general.

The three-week militia enlistment having expired, Iles's company dissolved at Fort Wilbourn, and the men were mustered out. Lincoln reenlisted again, this time for four weeks, as a private in the independent spy company of Capt. Jacob M. Early. John T. Stuart and Elijah Iles also enrolled as privates under Early.[181] Captain Early had been a private under both Lincoln and Iles; now the roles and ranks were reversed.[182] "Independent" meant that Early took his orders directly from the commander-in-chief, a title given to both General Atkinson and Governor

Reynolds but probably exercised by Atkinson. Spies were treated as members of an elite group; for example, they could draw unlimited amounts of rations and were relieved from camp duties.[183] Lincoln, his stepbrother John Johnston, George Harrison, and a couple other fellows were company messmates.[184] Food always seemed in short supply; Lincoln once proclaimed, "Although I never fainted from loss of blood, I can truly say I was often very hungry."[185] A spy company served as the army's front guard, traveling in advance of the main body. As the name implies, members of the company were dispatched in small units to locate and spy on Indian forces. Members also acted as express couriers, riding solitary through potential or actual hostile territory. Spies did not have a cushy assignment; they had special privileges in camp but also took special risks.

General Atkinson's June 17 order forbidding liquor sales to Illinois troops implied a continuing problem of drunkenness among the militia.[186] The order also implied that camp followers had been only too glad to make money by keeping the militia unfit for service. Such difficulty was by no means limited to militia. About this time, the U.S. Surgeon General noted that running alcoholics out of the U.S. Army could well disintegrate the corps.[187] In an order for the Black Hawk War theater, Maj. Gen. Winfield Scott commanded "that every soldier or Ranger who shall be found drunk or sensibly intoxicated after the publication of this order, be compelled, as soon as his strength will permit, to dig a grave at a suitable burying place large enough for his own reception, as such grave cannot fail soon to be wanted for the drunken man himself or some drunken companion."[188]

On June 19, a traveler wrote: "Every few miles on our way we fell in with bodies of Illinois militia proceeding to the American camp [at Dixon's Ferry], or saw where they had encamped for the night. They generally stationed themselves near a stream or a spring on the edge of a wood, and turned their horses to graze on the prairie. . . . Some of the settlers complained that they made war upon the pigs and chickens. They were a hard-looking set of men, unkempt and unshaved, wearing shirts of dark calico, and sometimes calico capotes."[189]

On June 20, Captain Early's spy company was mustered into federal service in a brigade commanded by Gen. James D. Henry.[190] Lincoln's weapons now were valued at $15, his borrowed horse and other equipment at $85, a decline in value indicating their hard use.[191] He acknowledged that at some point during the war he accidentally bent his musket.[192] Poor treatment of horses was chronic throughout the Illinois forces. Inadequate or wasted feed and an astonishing lack of animal care converted a large portion of mounted volunteers into foot soldiers.[193] Royal Clary explained:

> The ox teams did more good than a thousand horses; they could go through mud and mire, slosh and rain, and do well. No so with horses. We couldn't follow the Indians for more than three or four days. It was impossible for our horses to carry man, gun and his food, the horse himself and his food, through the muck and mire, swamp and brush. The horses gave out, wore literally out. No grass, no noth-

ing, too early for grass in May. Cold up there. The horses were jaded. The clothes of the men gave out, torn to pieces by briar and brush. We carried our tents on our horse. The poor horse carried everything. The baggage wagons couldn't keep up, no roads and no bridges and no ways to travel. And hence the horses suffered all.[194]

From Fort Wilbourn, Captain Early's company was soon dispatched to Dixon's Ferry. There word arrived of sharp combat about forty-five miles north at Kellogg's Grove. Col. Zachary Taylor had ordered Illinois state treasurer Jack Dement to take a battalion to that vicinity. Lincoln's messmate George Harrison explained that on this assignment, Dement's men "stopped in this grove at noon for refreshment," a turn of phrase suggesting they got liquored up. On receiving a report of Indians in the vicinity, Major Dement and four dozen men decided to see if they could make contact, leaving a token force behind in a log blockhouse. Just as Dement and his private, Zadoc Casey, who was then Illinois's lieutenant governor, were preparing to leave on the mission, a messenger arrived with word that Indian spies were nearby. Disobeying orders, many of the battalion, as explained by George Harrison, "broke after them, some on horseback, some on foot in great disorder and confusion, thinking to have much sport with their prisoners." Dement believed the "spies" were bait to lure the militia into a trap and frantically chased his men in an unsuccessful attempt to halt them.

When they reached a ravine, three hundred warriors—screaming, naked, and carrying spears, tomahawks, and knives—charged toward Dement's men, who instantly panicked. Dement's efforts to call an orderly retreat were unsuccessful as the militia disintegrated, each man fleeing as best he could without regard to his companions' safety. A later state attorney general said: "Dement did all he possibly could to rally his men and make them fight; that he turned more than once in his saddle, and fired his gun at the savages, but to rally his men was utterly impossible. They ran like sheep chased by a gang of wolves. . . . Dement would ride and get in advance of them, and waving his sword, would cry out, 'Halt! halt! halt!' but it was all of no avail."[195] Four or five on foot died as the mob proceeded back to the blockhouse, where, Harrison said, the balance of Dement's force was "terrified by the screams of the whites and the yells of the savages." There the Indians, who turned out to have guns, kept up such intense fire that bullets whizzed through openings between logs. Inside the fort, Dement was grazed by three bullets. After killing fifty horses and capturing the rest, the Indians retreated. Believing renewed attack likely, Dement sent five messengers to Dixon's Ferry the next morning, hoping at least one would get through.

Upon arrival of the news at Dixon's Ferry, reinforcements including Captain Early's spy company were immediately dispatched to Kellogg's Grove. They began arriving about twelve hours after Dement sent out the call—incredible promptness, considering that the request and response involved a ninety-mile round-trip through wilderness. George Harrison recalled: "The dead still lay unburied until after we arrived at sunrise the next day. The forted men, fifty strong, had not ventured to go out until they saw us; when they rejoiced greatly that friends, and not their dreaded enemies, had come. They looked like men just out of cholera, having passed through the cramping stage. The only part we could then act was to seek the lost men, and with hatchets and hands to bury them." "I remember just how those men looked," Lincoln once mused of the dead, "as we rode up the little hill. . . . The red light of the morning sun was streaming upon them as they lay, heads toward us, on the ground. And every man had a round red spot on the top of his head, about as big as a dollar, where the redskins had taken his scalp. It was frightful, but it was grotesque, and the red sunlight seemed to paint everything all over." The person talking with Lincoln remembered that he then "paused, as if recalling the vivid picture." The five corpses, Harrison noted, had been "cut into small pieces" by the Indians. The Americans excavated a crude mass grave and interred the remains. John T. Stuart said, "We passed where Dement had been whipped the day before, saw the traces of the battle, dead horses, etc."

Lincoln and a couple other members of Early's spy company tracked the trail of a young chief and found his body. Some militia trackers determined that the Indian force had broken up and departed, but Lincoln and others urged pursuit. Indeed, said Harrison, "squads of Indians [were] still showing themselves in a menacing manner, one and a half miles distant." A militiaman recalled, "When fighting was expected or danger apprehended Lincoln was first to say, 'Let's go.'"[196] After evaluating the circumstances, however, Brig. Gen. Alexander Posey decided against attempting chase. Lincoln and the other soldiers returned to Dixon's Ferry.[197]

People in Illinois began wondering what was wrong with the militia. "In the two encounters that have taken place our men, as might have been expected, were shamefully whipped, and in the last instance, by an inferior force of Indians," wrote one perplexed observer at the time. "From what he [Black Hawk] saw of us, he must, savage as he is, have acquired additional contempt of us every day."[198] Another observer declared, "It does indeed almost seem as if the hand of God was stretched forth to protect the Indians."[199]

After heading south to Dixon's Ferry, Early's company joined the main army's northward trek into an area that later became part of Wisconsin. Moving ahead of the main force, Early's company discovered fresh tracks of the British Band. Upon the army's arrival at Lake Koshkonong near White Water River, Early reported the find. Officers decided to move in pursuit. First thing the next morning, they dispatched some militia, who returned saying that Early's report had been incorrect. Early's spy company did more scouting but with inconsequential results.[200]

The army proceeded toward White Water River, through unpleasant terrain described as sinkholes and swamp.[201] "I had a good many bloody struggles with the musquetoes," Lincoln said.[202] Marchers went across the so-called "trembling lands, which are immense flats of turf extending for miles in every direction, from six inches to a foot in thickness, resting upon water and beds of quicksand. . . . The horses would sometimes, on the thinner portions, force a foot through and fall to the shoulder or ham."[203] Despite a little hostile gunfire, as the days progressed, scouting by Early's company failed to yield signs of the British Band.[204]

Acting upon report that the British Band was on a large island in Lake Koshkonong, Early's spy company took to rafts and landed on the island, followed by two U.S. Army companies. Although Indians weren't found, Early reported that his men had located evidence of a large Indian group. Further investigation failed to confirm that intelligence finding. Indeed, Col. William S. Hamilton, son of President Washington's Treasury Secretary Alexander Hamilton, delivered a contrary report. Hamilton was a prominent businessman from the mining district, up toward Galena. Among other Black Hawk War services, he commanded a unit of Indians allied with the Americans against the British Band and did spy work with his men.[205] Whether he crossed paths with Lincoln seems unrecorded. On this day, Hamilton said he had found the British Band's trail on the lake's far shore, but those signs were a week and a half old. The Indians seemed so far ahead that General Atkinson suspended the chase.[206]

Food supplies and enlistment times were running out. Captain Early's company was dissolved in Wisconsin, and its men were free to go home. The Black Hawk War continued, but Lincoln's participation was done.

CHAPTER 6

POLITICIAN, MERCHANT, POSTMASTER, SURVEYOR

Back in Sangamon County, the state election was coming on fast in August 1832. New Salem was three hundred miles away, and Lincoln needed to be there to resume local campaigning.

Abraham Lincoln, John T. Stuart, and George Harrison headed back to Sangamon County together, with the whole disbanded company traveling together at first. The night before starting off, Lincoln and Harrison lost their horses to thieves, "probably by soldiers of our own army," Harrison said. "I laughed at our fate, and he joked at it." Stuart still had a mount and shared it with them. Other veterans shared their horses as well, everyone taking turns walking. Some walking was done to spare the animals, which were in bad shape. "Many of their backs were too sore for constant riding," Harrison said. Upon reaching Peoria, the men went their separate ways.[1]

In Peoria, Harrison and Lincoln bought a canoe and headed down the Illinois River. "Lincoln made an oar with which to row our little boat. . . . One of us pulled away with our one oar, while the other sat astern to steer, or prevent circling. The river being very low was without current, so that we had to pull hard to make half the speed of legs and land. In fact we let her float all night, and in the next morning always found the objects still visible that were beside us the previous evening." Paddling along, they encountered a raft whose occupants offered a hearty meal to the canoeists. They welcomed the offer; returning veterans were as short on food as they had been throughout the campaign. One former militiaman recalled that throughout the entire homeward journey, he ate only a mix of meal and water baked in rolled-up bark.

When Harrison and Lincoln reached Havana, Illinois, there was no point in proceeding farther by river, which would angle them farther away from New

Salem. They sold the canoe in Havana and struck off on foot, occasionally crossing sand ridges. "As we drew near home, the impulse became stronger, and urged us on amazingly. The long strides of Lincoln, after slipping back in the burning sand six inches every step, were just right for me; and he was greatly diverted when he noticed me behind him stepping along in his tracks to keep from slipping."[2] A traveler in Sangamon County described the black sand, saying it "seems of a penetrating nature, and adheres to the skin like soot. Before being aware of this circumstance, I marveled at the filthy appearance of some of the inhabitants, who did not wear stockings, and at evening I sometimes found my feet and ankles coated with black dust, after having been washed half a dozen times, in course of the day, in wading streams."[3]

New Salem veterans held a frolic to celebrate their homecoming. "Nearly all of them got drunk," said Daniel Burner. "Some of them came pretty near being hurt. Jack Armstrong was sitting astride his horse, with his gun in his lap, and was fussing and quarreling, when his gun went off and the bullet went through Dave Edgar's hat—I think it was Dave—and grazed his head. This started the melée, and for a while things looked risky. Lincoln had nothing to do with this drunken celebration."[4]

Almost thirty years later, George Harrison reminded Lincoln of "the attachment [that] commenced in the Black Hawk campaign while we messed together . . . when we ground our coffee in the same tin cup with the hatchet handle—baked our bread on our ramrods around the same fire—ate our fried meat off the same piece of elm bark—slept in the same tent every night—traveled together by day and by night in search of the savage foe—and together scoured the tall grass on the battleground . . . in search of the slain." Harrison said their shared experience meant they would always be honest with each other.[5] Bonds formed by men who serve together in military campaigns are so familiar as to need no comment. Such bonds tended to be especially significant in an era when members of a company hailed from the same vicinity and would continue to interact with one another in civilian life. The Black Hawk War had the distinction of including numerous politicians who served among their voters and developed bonds with them. Few of a breed later known as "chickenhawks" were observable; Illinois candidates appear to have supported the war unanimously, and most of them instantly seized the opportunity to march off to combat. Candidates who didn't respond to the call for military volunteers, such as Edward Robison, felt a need to explain: "As my eyesight has somewhat failed, and my constitution more enfeebled than most men of my age, I do not think I could serve my country profitably in the army, although in the last war I became experimentally acquainted with the duties of both soldier and officer. But at this time, and under existing circumstances, I do not think it prudent for me to undertake that kind of service."[6]

Politicians serving in the 1832 Black Hawk War included Gov. John Reynolds; future gubernatorial nominees James W. Stephenson and Cyrus Edwards; future U.S. Senators William L. D. Ewing, Sidney Breese, and Orville Browning; future U.S. Congressmen Adam W. Snyder, Edward "Ned" Baker, William A.

Richardson, Orlando Ficklin, and John J. Hardin; state supreme court justice Theophilus W. Smith; lieutenant governor Zadoc Casey; future lieutenant governor Stinson H. Anderson; future lieutenant governor candidate Alexander Jenkins; state treasurer Jack Dement; future state treasurers John Thomas and William Butler; former state attorney general James Turney; future state auditor Levi Davis; future state senators James Strode, William Thomas, James Ralston, and Joseph Gillespie; future state legislator and public works commissioner Murray McConnel; and multiple office holder David Prickett. Civilian Benjamin Mills delivered dispatches to Washington, D.C., from Galena—a mission that helped him win election to the legislature that year but soon backfired politically and raised questions about his patriotism. From Sangamon County alone, there were sheriff James D. Henry, future sheriff Garret Elkin, future judge Thomas Moffett, Democratic activists John "Candlebox" Calhoun and Jacob M. Early, and legislature incumbents or candidates Elijah Iles, Thomas M. Neale, William Carpenter, William Constant, John Dawson, Achilles Morris, Richard Quinton, John T. Stuart, Abraham Lincoln, and Jonathan H. Pugh, who in 1832 was running for Congress. Bowling Green raised a company around the start of June, awaiting an order from Governor Reynolds to proceed into action.[7] This list has virtually enough names to form a company composed solely of office seekers, and it simply includes those names I've happened to notice without doing any special research on the topic.

I suspect that few candidates failed to take advantage of informal electioneering opportunities presented by close contact with voters among the militia. Moreover, such close contact gave the electorate an unusual perspective on candidates' merits. As one newspaper later put it, self-advertisement of "mock heroics of the late Sauc war, for which there are so many claimants for praise in our state,"[8] might fool some homefolk, but those who served in the war knew which men were brave and true. George Harrison remembered political discussion with Lincoln during the war: "He was acquainted with nearly everybody, and he had determined, as he told me, to become a candidate for the next legislature."[9] Said one militiaman: "Many of the officers were candidates at home for the legislature, and other places of civil trust, and they invariably declared, ere their arrival at the place of rendezvous [Beardstown in April], that they would evince their disinterestedness and patriotism by not accepting any military office. But their patriotism did not prove equal to the task." Another militia volunteer contemptuously spoke of "the little great men, who are as abundant in this happy land of creative attribute, as duck weed in a marsh, and as self-conceited as any lover of perfection of his species could desire; and . . . their speculations into the future were then embodied into petty intrigues, with pay and perquisites of a captain or lieutenant in the prospective."[10] They quickly sought officer appointments and "availed themselves of every privilege their rank could give them," said a disgruntled militiaman. He also declared that "electioneering importunities and solicitations . . . caused many of us to pause for a moment and reflect whether we were not going on some frivolous holiday excursion, and not to encounter hostile Indians."[11]

Another critic complained: "It must be very 'stirring times' indeed, when, with 30,000 military at his command, the governor cannot *control* or *expel* 600 'poor Indians' without taking every civil officer from his post. If it is right for gentlemen who receive 600, 800, and $1000 a year, of the public money, to leave their offices by the month and year together in the hands of *clerks*; let the people know it, that the amount of their salaries may be reduced or the offices abolished."[12]

After mustering out, candidates had to move rapidly to make up for lost time back home. They tried to describe their absence in a way that would yield political advantage. Thomas Neale told Sangamon County voters, "It was my intention at a much earlier period to have submitted my views to you on the subjects proposed, but from my absence on the recent campaign and my ill health since my return, I have been prevented from doing so."[13] John Dawson explained, "I have been absent from home this spring, in the service of my country, which has on my return compelled me to attend closely to my farm, preventing me from mixing with my fellow citizens as much as I would wish to have done, yet I hope my friends will appreciate the motive."[14] Earlier, the *Sangamo Journal* printed a list of candidates who had been away on war duty "periling their lives in the service of their country" but omitted Lincoln's name. We can imagine his consternation upon arriving home and discovering the omission. The July 19 issue acknowledged "omitting, by accident the name of Capt. Lincoln, of New Salem."[15] The timing of this correction actually was better than if he had been included in the original list back in May, as it now brought his name before voters as a war veteran just before the election.

"We got home about ten days before the election," John Stuart recalled. "We had a very exciting contest. I was elected, and Lincoln was defeated. In that canvass they attacked me very fiercely. . . . I used to be out making speeches and electioneering all day, and came home almost every night to issue a new handbill against some new charge or attack on me. I was bold and aggressive and pitched into them on the stump, and charged them with 'combination,' and 'trade' etc."[16] In other words, he attacked them for achieving the kind of little big man deals he himself had been seeking, if we believe men like Dr. Early, Reverend Cartwright, Dick Taylor, and William H. Herndon's father. Dr. Early indignantly protested that John Stuart "has attempted to invalidate the testimony of others, by pleading a bad memory. I would advise this self-styled man of honor, for his own benefit, to write a diary, to aid him in making falsehoods correspond." When Early said he could provide a sworn statement that Stuart had pledged to get two hundred votes for Cartwright, Stuart "positively denied, laying his hand on his heart, and appealing to his God and his conscience for the truth of his assertion." Early continued:

> I am truly sorry that circumstances have rendered it necessary to expose the duplicity and intrigue of this man. . . . Must not that man be far gone in crime, and deeply sunken in infamy, who could lay his hand to his heart, and appeal to his conscience, and the Almighty

Maker of heaven and earth, for the truth of a statement which he knew to be false. . . ?

Let him go to [the state capital of] Vandalia and occupy a seat which he has obtained by violating every principle dear to a man of honor and truth. I envy him not his elevation; for truly, he has paid dear for it; and should the ghost of his murdered conscience rise up and haunt him, I would advise the young man occasionally to refer to the admonitions of his father; for I am told he had one, pious and respectable; and although he may never wipe from his character the foul stain he has fixed upon it, he may yet obtain the forgiveness of that God whom he has made a witness to his infamy and guilt.[17]

In the frantic ten days of campaigning across the county, Stuart and Lincoln worked together, both running as Whigs supporting the policies of U.S. Senator Henry Clay.[18] According to a later account, the Clary's Grove Boys accompanied Lincoln where possible.[19] Stuart recalled: "He was not then known outside of the New Salem precinct. Sangamon County was . . . an immense territory to travel over, and it was utterly impossible to get over every part of it in a ten days' campaign."[20] According to Henry McHenry: "I heard him making his first speech after returning from the Black Hawk War. He brushed up his hair from his tall dark forehead and said: 'Gentlemen, I have just returned from the campaign. My personal appearance is rather shabby and dark. I am almost as red as those men I have been chasing through the prairies and forests on the rivers of Illinois.'"[21] Slicky Bill Greene remembered a speech at Petersburg "on the election and the causes which he advocated. It was what the world would call an awkward speech, but it was a powerful one, cutting the center every shot."[22] Abner Ellis, a business associate of both William H. Herndon's father and Josh Speed (who would become Lincoln's best friend), said:

I accompanied him on one of his electioneering trips to the Island Grove, and he made a speech which pleased his [Whig] party friends very well indeed, though some of the Jackson men tried to make sport of him. He told several anecdotes in his speech and applied them as I thought very well. He also told the boys several stories which drew them after him. I remember them but modesty and my veneration for his memory forbids me to relate.[23]

Treating voters to ribald jokes probably curried as much goodwill as treats of liquor would have. Billy Herndon's cousin James Herndon remembered a speech at Pappsville on a day when a crowd had gathered for a public sale. There Lincoln said he became a candidate at urgings from "many friends." He said something like this: "My politics is short and sweet, like an old woman's dance. I am in favor of a national bank, high and protective tariff, and the internal improvement system."[24] Such advocacy would have firmly identified him as a

Whig. James Herndon recalled "a general fight" at the sale. "Saw Lincoln catch a man by the nape of the neck and ass of the breeches, and toss him ten or twelve feet easily."[25] Row Herndon's recollection of the fight was more explicit: "It was on that day that I whipped Jesse Dodson and his friends. . . . Mr. Lincoln pitched in and threw them about like boys. I think he was about to commence speaking when the fight commenced. I know that it made him many friends. As soon as Dodson hollered Lincoln pulled me away and [said] to them that if any more of them wanted to [be] thrashed, just fetch them on. But they was all satisfied."[26] Such a performance probably made more impact on voters than any speech could. A Springfield resident remembered fracases at the county seat as well: "In addition to the speeches at the courthouse they used to have a good many fights at the groceries [saloons]. Two gangs of country bullies used to meet here and fight one another. One was from Lick Creek, and the other from Spring Creek. I had seen a good deal of that sort of thing in Kentucky, and was somewhat used to it, but a stranger would have considered this a pretty hard country, I suppose."[27] Settlers around Sugar Creek met during the 1832 election and passed this resolution:

> Whereas it is a well known fact that the common plan of election-eering adopted by candidates, [is] of visiting almost every elector throughout the county or district, for the purpose of influencing their votes (a plan which heretofore has been a sure means of preferment to office) and whereas it is an opinion becoming general among the people, that those candidates are most sure of success who resort to the most corrupt means to secure their election; therefore
> Resolved, that it is the opinion of this meeting that the present mode of electioneering, by visiting almost every elector within the county or district, and treating them with ardent spirits, for the purpose of influencing their votes, is in the highest degree fraught with corruption, and dangerous to our liberties, degrading to the candidate and insulting to the elector: and prevents in a great degree our ablest citizens from suffering their names to be entered on the list of competitors for office.[28]

George Forquer's half-brother recalled the previous election's atmosphere:

> The stump speeches being over, then commenced the drinking of liquor, and long before night a large portion of the voters would be drunk and staggering about town, cursing, swearing, hallooing, yelling, huzzaing for their favorite candidates, throwing their arms up and around, threatening to fight, and fighting. . . . I have seen hundreds of such persons in the town of Springfield. . . . Towards evening they would mount their ponies, go reeling from side to side, galloping through town, and throwing up their caps and hats,

screeching like so many infernal spirits broke loose from their nether prison.[29]

Row Herndon said of Lincoln's electioneering:

During the summer campaign for the legislature I heard him speak frequently, and he was a full match for any that was on the track. In one of his speeches he said, "Fellow citizens, I have been told that some of my opponents have said that it was a disgrace to the county of Sangamon to have such a looking man as I am stuck up for the legislature. Now I thought this was a free country. That is the reason that I address you today. Had I have known to the contrary, I should not have consented to run. But I will say one thing. Let the shoe pinch who it may, when I have been a candidate before you some five or six times and have been beaten every time, I will consider it a disgrace and will be sure never to try it again."

Such sentiments are those of a man with strong ambition. Apparently measuring himself against a competitor, Lincoln added, "I am bound to beat that man if I am beat myself."[30] Here we see a professional politician's attitude, taking advantage of a potential loss to evaluate his strength. Lincoln may have been measuring himself against William H. Herndon's father, Archie Herndon, who was running for state representative. Slicky Bill Greene recalled that Lincoln "cut Herndon off at the knees in debate at Petersburg. Herndon called Lincoln an interloper. Lincoln said when he had been a candidate as often as Herndon he would quit."[31] Note political insider Archie's attitude that a political outsider like Lincoln had no business participating as a candidate in elections.

The frantic campaign's speaking climax was a meeting in Springfield on August 4. Around then, word had just arrived in Sangamon County that President Jackson had vetoed rechartering the "Monster of Chestnut Street," also known as Bank of the United States,[32] an institution viewed by the President and his supporters as dangerous to American liberties but by Henry Clay and his supporters as crucial to national prosperity. Clay had timed congressional renewal of the bank's corporate charter in order to provoke a reaction from Jackson that could be used as a political issue in the 1832 elections. U.S. Senator Thomas Hart Benton displayed reactions from *Niles Weekly Register*, considered one of the finest and most reliable newspapers of the era:

"We learn from Cincinnati that, within two days after the veto reached that city, building-bricks fell from five dollars to three dollars per thousand."

"An intelligent friend of General Jackson, at Cincinnati, states, as the opinion of the best informed men there, that the veto has caused a depreciation of the real estate of the city, from twenty-five to thirty-three and one-third percent."

"We are credibly informed that several merchants in this city [Cincinnati], in making contracts for their winter supplies of pork, are offering to contract to pay two dollars fifty cents per hundred, if Clay is elected, and one dollar fifty cents, if Jackson is elected."

"Baltimore. A great many mechanics are thrown out of employment by the stoppage of building. The prospect ahead is, that we shall have a very distressing winter. . . . Many who subsisted upon labor, will lack regular employment, and have to depend upon chance or charity; and many will go supperless to bed who deserve to be filled."

"Brownsville, Pennsylvania. We understand that a large manufacturer has discharged all his hands, and others have given notice to do so. We understand that not a single steamboat will be built this season, at Wheeling, Pittsburgh, or Louisville."[33]

National issues were a major element in Illinois elections, and the bank news hit Sangamon County at a perfect moment to cause maximum consternation and minimal understanding as voters went to the polls two days after the August 4 joint appearance of legislature candidates in Springfield. In the Western style of campaigning, candidates posed questions to one another at such meetings. The chronology of events suggests this meeting may have been the place where an eyewitness saw Lincoln take on his opponent, Reverend Cartwright. Prevailing against Cartwright required formidable talent. Someone who saw the reverend that summer described the reverend's appearance:

His figure was not tall, but burly, massive, and seemed to be even more than gigantic, from its crowning foliage of luxuriant, coal black hair, wreathed into long, but rough and curling ringlets. And a head that looked as large as a half-bushel; beetling brows, rough and craggy of fragmentary granite, irradiated at the base by eyes of dark fire, small and winkling like diamonds in a sea . . . ; a swarthy complexion, as if embrowned by the kisses of sunbeams, rich, rosy lips, always slightly parted, as if wearing a perpetual merry smile.

When before an audience, Cartwright's voice had a "loud, beautifully modulated tone . . . that rolled on the serene night air like successive peals of grand thunder." Someone watching a Cartwright performance remembered that "all of a sudden his face reddened, his eye lightened, his gestures grew animated as the features of a fiery torch, and his whole countenance changed to an expression of inimitable humor; and now his wild, waggish, peculiar eloquence poured forth like a mountain torrent. Glancing arrows of wit, shafts of ridicule, *bon mots*, puns and side-splitting anecdote sparkled, flashed, and flew like hail, till the vast auditory was convulsed with laughter. . . . His every sentence was like a warm finger tickling the ribs of the hearer." Then Cartwright could switch his tone to seriousness and move his audience in that direction.[34] This was the sort of orator that Lincoln now took on at a political meeting.

Lincoln "asked Cartwright if General Jackson did right" with the veto. As Jackson's lengthy veto message had been printed only two days earlier in the *Sangamo Journal*, and it was quite possible that Cartwright had not seen it, let alone digested it, Lincoln's question would have put the reverend in a tight spot. "Cartwright evaded the question and gave a very indefinite answer. Lincoln remarked that Cartwright reminded him of a hunter he once knew who recognized the fact that in summer the deer were red and in winter gray, and at one season therefore a deer might resemble a calf. The hunter had brought down one at long range when it was hard to see the difference, and boasting of his own marksmanship had said: 'I shot at it so as to hit it if it was a deer and miss it if it was a calf.' This convulsed the audience, and carried them with Lincoln."[35] Turning an audience against Cartwright was a masterful feat. Attorney Stephen T. Logan watched the Springfield meeting and said:

> I had very soon got acquainted with Stuart, because we were both Whigs. Stuart and Lincoln were the only two men who attracted my attention in that canvass.
>
> I never saw Lincoln until he came up here [to Springfield] to make a speech. I saw Lincoln before he went up into the stand to make his speech. He was a very tall and gawky and rough looking fellow then—his pantaloons didn't meet his shoes by six inches. But after he began speaking I became very much interested in him. He made a very sensible speech.
>
> It was the time when [U.S. Senator Thomas Hart] Benton was running his [monetary] theory of a gold circulation. Lincoln was attacking Benton's theory and I thought did it very well.
>
> It was a speech of perhaps half an hour long. All the candidates made speeches.[36]

Logan was a man of no small intelligence, and Benton's theory about using a gold-based currency instead of paper money involved sophisticated economic arguments. By refuting Benton's arguments to the satisfaction of Logan, Lincoln demonstrated his appeal among the full range of Sangamon County voters, from the Clary's Grove Boys to attorneys who applied tight logic to intellectually complicated issues. During the campaign, John Stuart, too, was struck by Lincoln's "very sensible and interesting speeches."[37]

Whatever the effect of Lincoln's Whig sentiments might have been elsewhere in the county, they caused him no harm in New Salem. Stephen T. Logan watched the young man campaign and, speaking of another election, noted the spirit of 1832: "The Democrats of New Salem worked for Lincoln out of their personal regard for him. That was the general understanding of the matter here at the time. In this he made no concession of principle whatever. He was as stiff as a man could be in his Whig doctrines. They did this for him simply because he was popular—because he was Lincoln."[38] Jason Duncan recalled, "Though the New Salem precinct was largely for Jackson, such was his [Lincoln's] personal popularity that he obtained a [New Salem precinct] majority, very many Jackson men of the most violent party feelings voting for him, on the grounds they believed him an honest and worthy young man."[39] The hometown majority, however, was not enough to carry Lincoln into the legislature.

When the voters spoke, announcing their choices out loud in public, they elected four state representatives. John Stuart recalled: "Taylor, Morris, and Cartwright were elected as Jackson men. I was elected as a Clay man."[40] Reverend Cartwright ran fourth in the list of winners. After years of preaching and campaigning throughout the county, he got only 815 votes, and that was in a time when voters were permitted to vote for four candidates when there were four vacancies. Voters could name him as a courtesy and still vote for three other candidates. Even under those circumstances, he barely made the list of winners, edging out Archie Herndon by only 9 votes. In New Salem precinct, Cartwright was particularly unpopular, coming in seventh. County voters defeated Rep. John Dawson, whose loyalty to President Jackson was under question. Voters also defeated Thomas Neale, whose comments about usury challenged President Jackson's stance on the Bank of the United States, and Edward Robison, who said lenders should be allowed to charge as much interest as they could get. In the state senate election, Democrat George Forquer barely won, getting 1,086 votes while Whig William F. Elkin got 1,077.[41]

Lincoln's 657 votes put him in the bottom half of the thirteen candidates who ran for representative, with almost half of his total coming from New Salem. Almost everyone there voted for him. (Keep in mind that a voter didn't have to vote for Lincoln exclusively, but could simultaneously vote for three other candidates as well.) Such an outcome suggested that if he had opportunity to become known across the county, as he was known around New Salem, votes for him might increase considerably. He hadn't done anything wrong in the election; he simply had to do more of what he had been doing.

In retrospect, William Butler remembered that during the campaign, Lincoln's replies to questions were "always characteristic, brief, pointed, à propos, out of the common way and manner, and yet exactly suited to the time, place, and thing."[42] "The contest was a spirited one," Jason Duncan said. "Though he was beaten . . . it served to bring his name prominently before the people."[43] Springfield lawyer Stephen T. Logan said: "One thing we very soon learned was that he was immensely popular, though we found that out more at the next election than then. . . . In the election of 1832 he made a very considerable impression upon me as well as upon other people."[44] No Sangamon County politician was more professional than John Stuart, and his testimony shows that Lincoln's friends were right in thinking he could use the 1832 campaign to position himself for a win in 1834:

> Lincoln in this race, although he was defeated, acquired a reputation for candor and honesty, as well as for ability in speech making. He made friends everywhere he went. He ran on the square, and thereby acquired the respect and confidence of everybody.
>
> In this election Lincoln got, I believe, nearly every vote in his own precinct of New Salem. . . . Besides this demonstration of home strength, he made a very great reputation all over the county. . . .
>
> Everybody who became acquainted with him in this campaign of 1832 *learned to rely on him* with the most implicit confidence.[45]

"The result," Robert Rutledge said, "was highly gratifying to him and astonished even his most ardent admirers."[46] His rail-splitting associate George Close summed it up thus: "Lincoln had nothing, only plenty of friends."[47] Lincoln was ready for the 1834 election.

His admirers were ready for celebration, at least if one authority was right in thinking the following incident likely occurred in August 1832,[48] a reasonable though unproven supposition. Abner Ellis saw the incident:

> It was at New Salem. The boys were having a jollification after an election. They had a large fire made of shavings and hemp hurds, and some of the boys made a bet with a fellow that I shall call Ike, that he could not run his little bobtail pony through the fire. Ike took them up, and trotted his pony back about one hundred yards, to give him a good start as he said. The boys all formed a line on either side to make way for Ike and his pony. Presently here he come full tilt with his hat off and, just as he reached the blazing fire, raised in his saddle for the jump straight ahead. But [the] pony was not of the same opinion. So he flew the track and pitched poor Ike into the devouring element. Mr. Lincoln saw, and run to his assistance saying, "You have carried this thing far enough." I could see that he was mad, though he could not help laughing himself. The poor fellow was considerably scorched about the head and face. Jack Armstrong took him to the doctor, who shaved his head to fix him up, and put salve on the burn, etc., etc. I think Mr. Lincoln was a little mad at Armstrong, and Jack himself was very sorry for it. Jack gave Ike next morning a dram, his breakfast, and a sealskin cap, and sent him home.[49]

About the time of the Illinois election, the state militia and U.S. Regulars defeated Black Hawk at the battle of Bad Axe in Wisconsin. Earlier, Sangamon County Sheriff James D. Henry had a key role in the battle of Wisconsin Heights, where, under his generalship, Illinois militia defeated the British Band. That victory was hailed at the time, but later historians regarded it as minor, its outcome due more to Black Hawk's treatment of the encounter as a rear-guard action than to Illinois military prowess. At Bad Axe, the brigade under General Henry's command was the first to make contact with the British Band. He then pressed forward so vigorously that his men engaged in bayonet fighting before the U.S. Army and the rest of the militia units arrived. Considerable numbers of Indian women and children were killed. Someone noted that warriors didn't bring along women and children,[50] a fact raising question about the circumstances of the killing. This action ended the war, and the capture of Black Hawk some days later was an anticlimax. A soldier wrote at the time:

> When a party of emaciated and nearly starved women and children were taken prisoners . . . they all expected, as a matter of course, to be slaughtered. They ran about, in their agony, to every white man present, offering them the hand of friendship. As soon as possible they were informed that the Americans did not war against women and children—and they became more at ease. Their appearance was wretched in the extreme. A great many had starved to death, and their bodies were continually passed over by the troops in pursuit.[51]

A while later, a newspaper item appeared at the state capital: "We have lately received a letter from one of the oldest and most enterprising Indian traders on the northwestern frontier, upon whose word we can place the utmost reliance, who informs us that there is not the least grounds to apprehend any further difficulties with the Indians; that they are a *conquered people*; that they have seen and felt their inability to contend with the whites."[52]

Soon after the August 1832 election, John J. Hardin received a letter about a situation eventually involving several persons who became associated with Lincoln. As John's career will intertwine with Lincoln's, let me introduce Hardin more formally at this point.

John J. Hardin was born in Kentucky about the same time as Abraham Lincoln but in more auspicious circumstances. Hardin's father, Martin, soon became U.S. Senator from Kentucky, and John's close relative Ben Hardin was a U.S. Representative. Ben had a sarcastic oratorical style; a connoisseur of the genre likened it to "a coarse kitchen butcher-knife whetted upon a brick-bat."[53] John acquired that talent as well, being noted for "meat-axe oratory."[54] Pugnaciousness seemed to run in the family. The son of Illinois politician Adam Snyder wrote:

> It was related in "Egypt" [southern Illinois] that when Jeptha Hardin [Ben's brother] was Circuit Judge of the Gallatin district . . . [state senator] Jeff Gatewood, one of the attorneys, became involved in a quarrel with him when arguing a motion, and losing control of his

temper, called His Honor a liar. . . . "Sheriff," said he, "adjourn court for one hour, and bring Mr. Gatewood to the vacant lot behind the court house." That order was at once executed, and the Judge and lawyer immediately "shed" their coats, and proceeded to settle the insult by wage of battle. The conflict was short, sharp and decisive. Though Gatewood was a stout, athletic man, the Judge thrashed him soundly, and in less than half an hour was again on the bench dispensing law and justice.[55]

Like his father, John was educated at Transylvania University. He studied law under Kentucky's chief justice John Boyle, who was a veteran of intense political combat, having served on congressional committees that managed impeachments of U.S. District Judge John Pickering and U.S. Supreme Court Justice Samuel Chase.

John's fellow Morgan County politician Joseph Gillespie described him as of "medium height, erect figure, square build, with a pair of highly-expressive hazel eyes. His step was firm and elastic, with a striking military bearing. His physique was in perfect harmony with his mind."[56] He was attracted to military endeavor throughout his adult life, achieving the rank of Illinois militia general. A chronicler from that era wrote: "He was very fond of hunting and went out one morning to try his luck for deer. At that time there were plenty along the Illinois river. He did not have to travel far until he saw a deer and drew up his gun and fired at it, but instead of killing the deer the breech pin flew out of his gun and struck him in the face making a terrible wound."[57] His legislative colleague Joseph Gillespie described the severity of the injury: "One of his eyes was blown out by the explosion of the gun at the breech. Such, however, was his indomitable will, that he walked home—several miles—suffering the most intense pain and agony, which would have unnerved any other person."[58] Fellow Illinois politician Gustave Koerner said that despite a destroyed eye, "his features were very handsome and his complexion as delicate as a woman's. He was somewhat impulsive, but in the main his character was winning and amiable. No man could have had warmer personal friends."[59]

John Hardin moved to Illinois about the time Lincoln came to the state and set up a law practice in Jacksonville. "I once inquired of Mr. Smith [Hardin's law partner] how Hardin stood as a lawyer. He said when he took a case and studied it thoroughly he was strong."[60] Such faint praise suggests a style of practice all too familiar to many attorneys' clients. His correspondence files contain assorted letters from people complaining of neglect to their law business, and I noticed one complaint of incompetence from a relative needing a power of attorney from Hardin, which document the lawyer botched. His successor as state's attorney privately said, "I have now been once around the circuit and have not lost an indictment, whereas my friend Hardin used to lose from one third to one half."[61] Early in his law practice, Hardin told a cousin: "My prospects are encouraging. Business to be sure, is now much interrupted from the fact that we have but two courts in the year, and only one week to do our business. . . . In addition to which the justices [of the peace] have jurisdiction [in cases up] to $100, and it is not usual to employ lawyers before them except in very difficult cases."[62] A couple years later, a visitor to Jacksonville told the same cousin: "The bar is a very weak one. . . . Their business is done in a very loose irregular manner, and neither the court or bar appear to be versed in rules of equity, law or practice."[63]

The autumn after arriving in Jacksonville, Hardin wrote to a relative back in Kentucky:

> Concerning the great and important matter of girls, it is not in my power to boast much. We have some sprightly ladies in town though they are few. . . . I think it would improve if it were not for one reason, the girls get married so soon there is no time for improvement. Enterprising young men are numerous and when they have entered their land they want wives, and will have them. It has occurred to me that a considerable speculation might be made by a qualified person who would bring out a cargo of the ladies. . . . If they should be landed here shortly they might command in market at least several head of cattle apiece.

Hardin concluded with, "My love to the girls and tell them, bless their hearts, I should like to see a cargo shortly."[64] The letter was enjoyed so heartily that it got passed around to assorted family members. Hardin's third cousin Mary Todd heard her father read it aloud.[65]

Three months after sending that letter, Hardin married Sarah Smith. A well-wisher told him in June 1831: "I am truly gratified that you and Sarah are well pleased with the country. . . . The political contest is waxing warm and Kentucky will give in August a fatal stab to Jackson & Tyranny."[66] From military camp during the first Black Hawk War (the one without fatalities), Hardin wrote to his pregnant wife: "The war appears to [be] over. We have traveled through the most beautiful country I have ever beheld. . . . Indians have frequently been seen and one or two taken, but not one has been fired at or killed, neither have we lost a single man. . . . Expect to see us all return as safely as we started."[67] Sarah once wrote to her husband: "Our little one, O I wish you could see our little playful actions in evenings when we stop on the road she skips and plays like a little kitten. She has got right fat."[68] On a visit to Kentucky, Sarah wrote: "I do not think I would come to Kentucky to live for any consideration. I could not realize what a beautiful country Illinois is and how happily we have lived together until I came here. . . . My dear husband, how my poor heart melts when I think about you, and I cannot express myself more elegantly than by simply saying, I do want to see you so badly."[69]

John Hardin's father died in 1823, leaving about $50,000 in debts. His widow, Elizabeth Logan Hardin, was feisty enough to reject recommendations that she liquidate the estate. Instead, she set to work producing enough income from the estate to pay off its obligations.[70] She remarried, her new husband being Porter Clay, brother to Harry of the West. John Hardin now acted as Henry Clay's business agent in Illinois, handling cattle and land deals there for the U.S. Senator.[71] Making a profit from the Hardin Kentucky plantation proved challenging. Porter complained: "It takes more than the money I received for the hemp to pay our present overseer whose time expires on the first of September. He let the negroes steal nearly half of last year's crop whilst we were absent in the spring. If I stay here seven years I will never have another overseer."[72] Soon after the August 1832 Illinois election, Porter sent Hardin the letter previously referred to, the one about a situation eventually involving several persons who became associated with Lincoln: "You did not say definitively before you left us whether you would consent for the land and negroes to be sold this coming year or not, nor what was your thoughts upon the subject. Your ma wishes you to speak freely your mind. She thinks it would be a ruinous business to rent out the farm and hire out the negroes."[73]

That letter illustrates a point frequently forgotten, that Illinois citizens, such as John Hardin, could own slaves. They couldn't be used in Illinois but could be worked on the master's behalf in some other state. A document dated three months later, that was signed by Mary Todd's uncle and wound up in Hardin's files, perhaps because Hardin had been suing the uncle on behalf of the uncle's sister Maria,[74] illustrates another frequently forgotten point.

> I John Todd of Sangamon County Illinois, in consideration of the sum of four hundred dollars . . . do hereby grant . . . unto Maria L. Todd of Madison County, Kentucky, her heirs and assigns, a colored woman named Phoebe, aged about twenty-two years, also the three children of the said Phoebe, one named Benjamin aged about five years, one named Emily aged about three years, and one named William aged about nine months. And I will warrant and defend the said Phoebe and her children unto the said Maria L. Todd her heirs and assigns, against the claim of all and every person, so long as the said Phoebe is bound to serve by this indenture, recorded in the County Commissioners office of St. Clair County, Illinois; and until the said Emily reaches her eighteenth year and the said Benjamin and William their twenty-first year respectively.[75]

Indentured (sometimes called "indented") service was a type of slavery that was legal in Illinois. The difference between slavery and indentured service was that a slave was bound for life, but a time limit was placed on how long an indentured servant could be held. Within that time limit, however, a master's or mistress's power over that servant was as complete as power held over a slave. The Illinois constitution used the term "owners" to describe masters and mistresses of indentured servants; court cases referred to these servants as "slaves."[76] They could be bought or sold:

"For Sale, a first rate female house servant now in Alton, and two valuable indentured servants (a man and his wife). Enquire of the Editor of the *Alton Spectator*."[77]

Juveniles could make a similar indenture agreement by which they became apprentices, thereby acquiring the status of slave until the apprenticeship ended.[78] That such apprentice servitude wasn't always pleasing, and that adult owners of the child's labor didn't regard such ownership lightly, is implied by a type of newspaper ad seen routinely in Illinois:

"Ranaway, from the subscriber, living in Shelbyville, two apprentices to the tanning business; one of them, Jesse Banta. . . . The other (William Frazer) . . . has lost the little finger of his right hand. . . . I will give $10 to any person who will deliver me those boys, or $5 to have them confined so that I get them again. I will put the law in force against any person for harboring or employing either of them."

> —John D. Bruster, *Vandalia Illinois Intelligencer*,
> May 15, 1830

"Ranaway from the subscriber on the night of the 23d instant, two indentured apprentices to the printing business, viz:—Riley Watson, aged about 16 years; wore away a dark mixed woolen roundabout, and pantaloons and vest of same—and carried off other clothing. Also James A. Glasscock, about the same age and similar clothing. These boys will probably seek to escape by steamboat to the lower country. All persons, steamboat captains and others, are hereby forbidden to carry them off, or in any way to further their escape, or harbor, or employ them, on penalty of the law. . . . The *St. Louis Republican*, *Louisville Journal*, and *Natchez Free Trader*, will please publish the above three times each, weekly."

> —Simeon Francis, Springfield, *Sangamo Journal*,
> October 21, 1837

"Ranaway from the subscriber on Thursday last, an indented apprentice named John Paul, 14 years 6 months old . . . followed by a young black dog."

> —John S. Vredenburgh, Springfield, *Sangamo Journal*, March 11, 1842

Gov. Ninian Edwards complained about indentured servants fleeing Illinois and told the mayor of St. Louis that something should be done about it.[79]

Adult indentured servants signed a contract agreeing to the arrangement, but children born to them could be held for years by the master or mistress without agreement by the juveniles. Moreover, an indenture might be extended past the expiration date if the servant signed a contract agreeing to continue in servitude. William H. Brown, an Illinois politician of the era, noted that slaves were brought into Illinois, whose owners then offered them indentured servant contracts running from seventy to ninety years; other authorities noted contracts running even longer.[80] Ninian Edwards referred to such contracts as "beneficial to the slaves"[81] (note the word he used to describe indentured servants). How much coercion was involved in such contracts is unclear, but I doubt that anyone with viable options would agree to be someone's slave. Brown said "fraud or collusion" were inherent: "Cases were not uncommon where the unfortunate servant before going to the [county] clerk's office was whipped into a proper state of mind, 'freely and voluntarily' to enter into contract with his master. But in all cases it was well understood that if his consent was not given, the slave would be immediately removed to a slave holding state, to remain in bondage in the hands of someone perhaps less kind than his present possessor."[82]

Instances are known in Indiana of slaves signing what they believed to be emancipation papers, only to learn the document indentured them for many years; some such indentured servants were later sold into perpetual slavery before their indentures ran out.[83] Apparently what counted was the signature or mark, not what the signer understood the document to be. An authority noted that Illinois county "records reveal that the practices relating to slavery and Negro servitude in southern Illinois did not conform to the statutes enacted for their regulation. It is also evident that public officials were aware of the inconsistency and even participated in the evasions." The same authority was unable to find proof that indentured servants went free upon expiration of their terms but did find proof that Americans with the legal status of outright slave lived in Illinois from 1809 to 1846.[84]

Illinois statutes had the following provisions:

In all cases of penal laws, where free persons are punishable by fine, servants shall be punished by whipping, after the rate of twenty lashes for every eight dollars.[85]

If any slave or servant shall be found at a distance of ten miles from the tenement of his or her master, or the person with whom he or she lives, without a pass, or some letter, or token, whereby it may appear that he or she is proceeding by authority from his or her master, employer, or overseer, it shall and may be lawful for any person to apprehend and carry him or her before a justice of the peace, to be by his order punished with stripes, not exceeding thirty-five, at his discretion.[86]

If any slave or servant shall presume to come and be upon the plantation, or at the dwelling of any person whatsoever, without leave from his or her owner, not being sent upon lawful business, it shall be lawful for the owner of such plantation, or dwelling house, to give or order such slave or servant ten lashes on his or her bare back.[87]

Also, unauthorized dancing by three or more slaves or indentured servants was punishable by not more than thirty-nine lashes.[88] Indenture agreements could include restrictions beyond statutory ones. For example, Hardin's later law partner, David A. Smith, came to Jacksonville from Alabama. Although new Illinois citizen Smith emancipated his Alabama slaves in 1837, he didn't want to go without comforts that slavery could provide. An 1839 indenture agreement said:

A mulatto boy named Nathan about eighteen years old . . . has signified his willingness . . . to be bound as aforesaid to David A. Smith . . . until he the said Nathan shall arrive at the age of twenty-one years, during all of which time the said servant his said master shall faithfully serve. His secrets to keep and his lawful commands everywhere and at all times readily obey. He shall do no damage to his said master nor knowingly suffer the same to be done by others. He shall not waste the goods of his said master nor lend them unlawfully to any. At cards or dice or any other unlawful game he shall not play. Matrimony he shall not contract during the said term of his servitude. Taverns and houses or places of gaming he shall not resort. From the service of his said master he shall not absent himself.[89]

Newspapers routinely carried ads seeking Illinois slaves who had absented themselves:

"$30 REWARD. Ranaway from the subscriber at his camp, two miles east of Alton, a negro man named Patrick . . . has a particular mark on his right hand, having had two fingers cut off close to the hand, the little finger & the one next to it. . . . I think it probable that he will continue to skulk about in this neighborhood until I cross the river, when he will show himself."

—Snowdon Maddux, *Edwardsville Illinois Advocate*, November 13, 1832

"EIGHT DOLLARS REWARD. Ran away from the subscriber, on Wednesday, the 12th inst., a negro man named Stephen . . . shows his teeth when he laughs, speaks English and French, stammers when questioned, and is rather simple, is a little hard of hearing, has had a sore on his left eye. . . . I will give the above reward for apprehending the said negro, securing him in the jail at Belleville; fifteen dollars, if taken out of St. Clair County and secured in any jail; and twenty dollars if taken out of the state and secured in any jail so that I get him again."

> —John Hays, St. Clair County, Illinois, *Sangamo Journal*, February 9, 1833

"$10 REWARD.—Ranaway from the subscriber . . . a negro woman named Nancy, from 40 to 50 years of age . . . her hair turning gray. She has weak watery eyes, and is very fond of whiskey. . . . She is very fond of smoking. . . . All persons are forbid harboring said negro on penalty of the law, as she is a thief."

> —H. L. Camp, Kaskaskia, *Vandalia Illinois Advocate and State Register*, May 3, 1834

Illinois governor Thomas Ford said the Black Code's harsher elements became unused by the 1840s,[90] but nonetheless those laws stayed on the statute books. Their threats remained, and a credible threat can control behavior. Black slaves were considered numerous enough to be a government revenue source, annually taxed by Illinois at a rate of one-half of one percent of their value as property, with proceeds turned over to Illinois counties to help fund county government needs.[91] Slavery was considered real enough in Illinois that in January 1835, Rep. Christian Blockburger introduced a resolution stating, "It has become necessary to amend the present Constitution of this State so as (among other things) to prohibit slavery within her limits."[92] The resolution was tabled.

The question of what to do about the Hardin family's blacks apparently simmered. John Stuart got involved. In August 1833, he told John Hardin:

> Yours by Charles has been received. Uncle [probably Dr. John Todd] is confined to his bed with the bilious fever. It is at all times unpleasant for me to converse with him in relation to such matters. In his present situation I concluded [?] but I would not do so until you come up to court. I think too the boy is too small to ride so far on horseback. I think too when you remove one of the negroes, you should take them all. The mother is of a violent temper, and when there is a removal take them all together, and I think also the sooner you do this the better.[93]

Translation: Stuart didn't like to talk about breaking up a slave (or indentured) family, and in this case there might be slave resistance, so a sale encompassing the entire slave family was prudent; fast action was necessary. Whatever was going on was getting tense. A few weeks later, Maria Todd sent John Hardin a warning: "I conceive it proper to put you upon your guard. . . . You know, John, that lawyers are tricky persons generally. After you left us I discovered that D[r]. Todd had authorized Joh[n] Stuart to try to compromise this unpleasant business between us."[94] So Stuart's advice wasn't necessarily from a disinterested relative, but from an attorney looking out for a client's interests. John Hardin sent some sort of response to Maria in Kentucky, and she then told him:

> Owing to the absence of R. S. Todd [father of Mary] from Lexington, I could not give you an answer. I learned two days since that the hundred and fifty dollars forwarded by yourself had been left in the care of R. S. Todd. . . . I have not heard from Mr. Clay. I saw John T. Stuart while in Kentucky. He did not name the seventy dollars you allude to. . . . I took it for granted you had made the best sale of those slaves you could. The boy you have I expected you to take and give me a fair price, for I had confidence to believe you would not offer me less than his value. Therefore you can consider him yours.[95]

A letter Maria sent to John Hardin a couple weeks later indicated the convoluted nature of that transaction. "You wished to know if I had received seventy dollars by Mr. Forquer. I learned from Robert Stuart by last evening's mail that a check on the Louisville Bank for sixty dollars had been forwarded to him from that gentleman for myself." Maria Todd thereupon issued the following document: "I hereby convey all my interest in a black boy by the name of Benjamin to John J. Hardin of Illinois."[96]

The sequence of correspondence has many gaps, but it supports the following scenario. Mary Todd's uncle in Springfield sold a black family to Maria L. Todd in Kentucky. Although the uncle may have been a slaveowner,[97] because the adult woman was referred to as an indentured servant,[98] that suggests the black family resided in Illinois. Under state law, sending a black indentured servant out of Illinois invalidated the indenture,[99] so the indentured servants being sold on Maria L. Todd's behalf had to remain in Illinois; they couldn't *legally* be sent into perpetual slavery in a slave state, and a transaction handled by Illinois lawyers likely would have observed that restriction.[100] John Hardin wanted the child Benjamin from that family but had no use for the other three family members. In advising how to sell them for Maria L. Todd's financial benefit, Stuart recommended against breaking up the family because resistance could be expected from the mother. John Hardin nonetheless broke up the family, sending Maria L. Todd the sale proceeds (a transaction involving Mary Todd's father) while taking Benjamin as a personal servant. I acknowledge the possibility that events transpired otherwise, but the foregoing scenario is a reasonable interpretation of the records. A couple years later, someone offered Hardin and his wife, Sarah, "a first rate little girl," saying, "I have no doubt but that she would be a great assistance to Sarah. I can bring her out with me if you wish it."[101] And indeed at the age of eight and a half, Dolly, a propertyless minor, made her mark on an indenture agreement in which she agreed to serve John and Sarah until the age of eighteen, her master and mistress promising to teach her "sewing, knitting and cooking."[102]

We see Lincoln's eventual associates having routine involvement in slave commerce. His first law partner, John Stuart, acknowledged that such transactions were by no means new to him, and he at least handled indenture paperwork afterward.[103] Mary Todd's uncle was a seller, and her father handled part of a subsequent purchase made by her cousin John Hardin. For these intelligent and genteel persons, slavery wasn't a horror, but simply an element of their financial well-being and personal comfort. Such was the circle that Lincoln would inhabit after the 1830s, whose lifestyle he would more and more openly question. Many in that social set would consider his defiance as betrayal and would react not only with opposition, but also with rage.

Back in New Salem, with Denton Offutt's enterprises gone, Lincoln had to find another way to earn income. He wrote in the third person: "He was now without means and out of business, but was anxious to remain with his friends who had treated him with so much generosity, especially as he had nothing elsewhere to go to. He studied what he should do—thought of learning the blacksmith trade."[104]

Instead, he decided to try storekeeping, this time as a proprietor rather than an employee. Good authorities conflict so much in their explanations of Lincoln's storekeeping that some have to be wrong. Part of the trouble comes from conflicts in statements by people who interacted with the store; part comes from scanty documentation; part comes from miserable handwriting in documents. I think my version is close to being correct.

When Lincoln began storekeeping, he was boarding with William H. Herndon's cousin Row Herndon.[105] Row and his brother Jim had opened a New Salem store a couple years earlier.[106] Henry Clark called it "a kind of grocery," in other words, a saloon.[107] Bill Greene and Row said it sold other goods besides liquor.[108] Jim Herndon had recently sold out his share to William Berry. "I didn't like the place," Jim said of New Salem,[109] and now Row offered his own interest in the store to Lincoln. Good authorities say the transaction was in August after the election;[110] Row's memory of the date was less certain, but he said it could have been autumn of that year.[111] This wasn't a cash deal; Lincoln simply gave a note promising later payment.[112] Because such notes were often for six months, and an April 1833 transaction seemed to renew the inventory purchase note, that renewal implies Lincoln bought the inventory in October 1832.

Lincoln was now the business partner of William Berry, the son of Old John Berry, a Presbyterian farmer-minister who, according to one local resident, "did as much to civilize and christianize the central part of Illinois as any other living man."[113] William had been a corporal in Lincoln's Black Hawk War company, so the two young men were well acquainted. A local resident described young Berry as "a wild fellow—a gambler."[114] One Lincoln biographer called Berry a fighter.[115] "Idle, shiftless," another described him.[116] A Clary's Grove settler said, "It always was a mystery to me why a man of Mr. Lincoln's integrity would enter into partnership with such a character."[117] One story says Lincoln did it at the request of Berry's father, who thought Lincoln would be a steadying influence on Berry.[118] I think it more likely that the arrangement was a product of chance; two young acquaintances who wanted to go into business were acquiring inventory at the same time, and thought it made more sense to collaborate than compete. William Berry sounds no different from many of the New Salem crowd with whom Lincoln got along well.

"A store," said an Illinois visitor around 1840, "is a grand melange of things of the most different qualities and it proposes to supply the inhabitants with all the necessities and luxuries they may require. They are sources of great profit; and a person with a little capital and some knowledge of the business, can scarcely fail, with ordinary prudence, to realize an independence. The prices charged for goods of the most ordinary quality, are truly exorbitant."[119] An earlier Illinois visitor said, "Trade . . . is exceedingly profitable. 75 to 100 percent is reckoned a good profit; 50 percent is a living profit; 25 percent, will not keep a man to his business, he will look out for something else."[120] George Forquer's half-brother Thomas Ford declared, "The great majority, in fact nearly all the merchants, were mere blood-suckers, men who with a very little capital, a small stock of goods, and with ideas of business not broader than their ribbands nor deeper than their colors sold for money down, or on a credit for cash, which when received they sent out of the country [they drained specie from Illinois and thereby hindered economic development]."[121] In 1835, Stephen Douglas wrote to a relative: "Merchandising is a tolerably good business, for those who understand it well, and have a sufficient capital to meet all of their engagements. We have but a few such merchants here however, and consequently merchandising among the Suckers is considered rather a dangerous business."[122] Such were typical opinions of the trade Lincoln was taking up.

The nature of the Berry & Lincoln store, whether it was a general merchandise operation or a saloon or something in between, has been long debated. Given that the business was public and patronized by numerous people, disagreement about its nature is puzzling. "I had occasion to be in the store very often while I was carrying the mail," Harvey Ross said. "The stock consisted chiefly of groceries, but they also had many notions, hats, mittens, etc."[123] James Davis left a good description: "The store was a mixed one—dry goods, a few, groceries such as sugar, salt, &c., and whiskey—solely kept for their customers, or to sell by the gallon, quart, or pint—not otherwise."[124] McGrady Rutledge said: "I have been in Berry and Lincoln's store many a time. The building was a frame—one of the few frame buildings in New Salem. There were two rooms, and in the small back room they kept their whiskey. They had pretty much everything . . . sugar, coffee, some crockery, a few pairs of shoes (not many), some farming implements, and the like. Whiskey, of course, was a necessary part of their stock."[125] By such testimony, customers who purchased goods might be entitled to a free drink but otherwise could obtain liquor only by bulk purchase for carry-out. That mode of operation was typical for frontier stores.[126] Lincoln later declared he "never kept a grocery anywhere in the world" but said on the same occasion, "I don't know as it would be a great sin, if I had been" a grocery keeper.[127]

Documentary evidence exists that the Berry & Lincoln store sold more than liquor. At the end of October 1832, Lincoln and Nelson Alley, who was buying the tavern owned by Ann Rutledge's father, gave a $104 promissory note to Sheriff James D. Henry for "value received." Henry was acting on behalf of Vincent Bogue's creditors. Bogue had left town after his *Talisman* steamboat enterprise went bad. He had obtained the *Talisman*'s cargo through credit rather than cash. Creditors attached some of his property, and reportedly Bogue assigned his Sangamon County property to them. Supposedly he also assigned debts due to him. State representative-elect John Stuart represented Bogue's debtors. State senator-elect George Forquer and lawyer Stephen T. Logan represented creditors. The three attorneys worked out a settlement. A reasonable guess is that Lincoln and Alley were purchasing some of Bogue's old goods and intended to sell them at a profit in New Salem. The note was dated three days after the sheriff's sale of Bogue's goods and was for the six-month term specified at the auction. As we shall see later, the transaction would become a problem.[128]

In the presidential election a few days after the purchase of Bogue's goods, Lincoln's vote for electors pledged to Henry Clay put him in a distinct minority, New Salem giving General Jackson's electors a majority of well over a hundred votes. (Then, as later, people didn't vote for presidential candidates directly, but instead voted for candidates to the Electoral College, which chose the President.) Lincoln served as a New Salem polling-place clerk and was the final voter of the day, thereby well aware of the trend when he declared his vote out loud for Henry Clay. Lincoln received $3.50 for his election services.[129]

As noted earlier, Illinois militia who fought in the Black Hawk War didn't receive pay at time of service. Instead, federal paymasters toured Illinois months later to settle up. Although paymasters referred to muster rolls, veterans typically presented certificates attesting to length of service and rank and would then be paid accordingly. Such a system exploited ordinary people for the benefit of wealthier citizens. Veterans who were pressed for cash would sell their pay claims to speculators. One such speculator was Sangamon County legislature candidate Thomas Neale[130]; another appears to have been U.S. Land Office Receiver and former Sangamon County sheriff John Taylor.[131]

"Speculator" is a misleading term, as profit was guaranteed. For example, using made-up figures to illustrate the principle, a veteran entitled to $40 might sell that pay claim to a speculator for $30 in immediate cash. The speculator could afford to wait a few months for the paymaster's visit and then receive $40, a clear and risk-free profit of $10; figured on an annual basis of capital turnover, this is even better than it looks, perhaps yielding an annual profit of 50 percent or more.

Pressure tactics might encourage veterans to sell their claims. For example, rumors might be circulated that Congress was going to fund only a portion of veterans' pay claims, giving veterans $15 for a $40 claim. A friendly speculator might then offer a veteran the "favor" of buying his $40 pay claim right now for $20, or the veteran could take his chances and hope that Congress would eventually provide the $40. Aside from being sold for cash, pay claims might be bartered. An additional element of awkwardness for veterans of the 1831 campaign against Black Hawk was that notices of the paymaster's travels to Illinois towns began appearing while the 1832 war was under way. Thus militiamen on active duty in 1832 might be unable to be present and get paid for their 1831 service, a situation providing more motivation to sell their claims.[132]

The date when Lincoln received full settlement for Black Hawk War service is unclear. We do know he was paid $26 in January 1833 for twenty-one days spent in Captain Iles's company, a total reflecting a deduction of $2.62 for rations. Lincoln apparently received about $125 for his services in the Black Hawk War, perhaps $32 for use of his borrowed horse, and another $20 for horse feed. Authorities presume he turned the horse rent over to the animal's owner, especially since the horse was stolen from him and therefore not returned to the owner.[133] Veterans were legally entitled to compensation for loss of horses and other property in federal service, but collecting was difficult.[134] Financial treatment of veterans was a matter of public complaint in Springfield:

> On Tuesday a portion of the volunteer troops, who served in the late Indian war, were paid off in this town. The occasion brought together a considerable number of the officers and soldiers who were engaged in the last arduous campaign. The amount paid here was about fourteen thousand dollars—a sum which is hardly a tithe of the loss suffered by this country, in various ways, from the Indian war. Whatever it be, however, it is more than probable that it is the last pittance our citizens will ever receive for defending their frontiers against the incursions of savages. If there should be Indian disturbances hereafter, the mischief will be confined to the country west of the Mississippi.[135]

In January 1833, a few days after Lincoln received some cash for his Black Hawk War service, he and Berry unexpectedly had an opportunity to strengthen their store's position in New Salem commerce. They had two competitors in town, one store run by Sam Hill and one run by Reuben Radford. Slicky Bill Greene told Radford's fate this way:

> Radford had a store. . . . A friend told him to look out for the Clary Grove boys or they would smash him up. He said he was not afraid. He was a great big fellow. But his friend said, "They don't come alone. If one can't whip you two or three can; and they will do it." One day he left the store in charge of his brother with the injunctions

that if the Clary Grove boys came not to let them have more than two drinks. All the stores in those days kept liquors to sell, and had a corner for drinking. The store was nicely fitted up and had many things in glass jars nicely labeled. The Clary Grove boys came in and took two drinks. The clerk refused them any more as politely as he could. Then they went behind the counter and helped themselves. They got roaring drunk and went to work to smash everything in the store. The fragments on the floor were an inch deep. They left and went off on their horses whooping and yelling. Coming across a herd of cattle they took the bells from their necks and fastened them to the tails of the leaders and chased them over the country, yelling like mad. Radford heard them, and mounting, rode in hot haste to the store.

William H. Herndon thought the chastisement wasn't necessarily unjust, saying Radford "was a vile slanderer, and I suppose he slandered the men or women. Radford was a vile, blustering, crazy fool. I knew Radford and his wife, and good Lord deliver me from such a couple. If we could get at the bottom of the story, I guess that the people were more than half right." Because Radford apparently assumed the drunken Clary's Grove Boys had tanked up at his store, this implies that the Berry & Lincoln enterprise didn't sell liquor by the drink at that time. Given Lincoln's high standing among the Clary's Grove Boys, they surely would have done their drinking business with him if the Berry & Lincoln store were a grocery, and such may have been assumed by anyone observing drunken Boys heading away from New Salem. Radford's contrary assumption thus suggests that Berry & Lincoln wasn't a grocery.

"I saw Radford ride up," Bill Greene said. "His horse was in a lather of foam. He dismounted and looked in on the wreck through the open doors. He was aghast at the spectacle and said, 'I'll sell out this thing to the next man that comes along.'" Bill offered $400 on the spot. Radford agreed to take $23 in cash then and two notes of $188.50 each in which Greene promised to pay the $377 in six months. Greene, who was Radford's commercial landlord, put up the store building and town lot as collateral. Lincoln was present at the scene and handled the paperwork, the kind of paralegal work he had been doing routinely.[136]

We need have little doubt about Lincoln's distress while attending to the legalities, because Bill had just beat him out on a great bargain for merchandise. Bill, however, was experiencing buyer's remorse—not only because he apparently had insufficient merchandising experience and no idea on how to raise the $377, but also because of what his father was likely to do to him for incurring such a debt. (Bill was just turning twenty-one and still lived with his parents.) Lincoln suggested giving the store stock what he called an "inventory." Bill replied, "Abe, I don't believe this store will stand another one just at this time." After clearing up the misunderstanding about the term "inventory," they proceeded to take one.[137] They figured the store's value at $1,200. Neither the store nor Bill were in a good position to proceed with mercantile business, and Lincoln saw the opportunity to eliminate one of the two stores competing against the Berry & Lincoln enterprise.

After discussion, Berry and Lincoln offered $750 if Bill would sell out to them, and he agreed. First Berry and Lincoln paid around $250 in silver coin. Berry threw in an excellent horse with good saddle and bridle. In addition, Berry and Lincoln assumed responsibility for paying off the two $188.50 notes Bill had just given to Radford. Slicky Bill Greene still owed $377 to Radford, secured by a mortgage on the building and town lot, but Berry and Lincoln now owed $377 to Greene. By putting $23 to work for a few hours, Bill had offset $377 in debt paper while acquiring around $250 in cash plus a good horse with gear.[138]

Berry and Lincoln moved their operation into the store building owned by Bill, formerly occupied by Radford. At some point, they also obtained the inventory of James Rutledge, who had either acquired it in payment of a debt or briefly tried running a store, or possibly both. The Rutledge store has been described as a grocery. I doubt it sold liquor by the drink if Rutledge also had a tavern, but I'm unsure whether those two businesses overlapped. A promissory note was Berry's payment to Rutledge for the inventory. Berry and Lincoln had now bought out every competitor in town except Sam Hill. In the words of one distinguished student, "Within a few weeks two penniless men had become the proprietors of three stores, and had stopped buying only because there were no more to purchase."[139] Sam Hill's wasn't for sale.

In addition to convivial conversation with store visitors, Lincoln gained popularity through scrupulous honesty in commercial dealings. "Mr. Lincoln, I observed, was always very attentive to business, and was kind and obliging to the customers of the store, always having pleasant things to say to them; and they had so much confidence in his honesty that they preferred to trade with him. . . . I noticed that this was particularly true of the women customers; they would often say that they liked to trade with Mr. Lincoln, for they believed that he was honest and would tell them the truth about the goods."[140] Another New Salem merchant, however, said the feeling wasn't mutual; Lincoln "always disliked to wait on the ladies; he preferred trading with the men and boys, as he used to say."[141]

Toward the beginning of February 1833, Lincoln prepared a petition to the Sangamon County commissioners asking that they provide sufficient subsistence for Benjamin Elmore. Unemployed persons with income insufficient to meet basic needs were routinely auctioned off to masters as indentured servants,[142] but the petitioners believed Elmore was too mentally deranged to support himself. Lincoln, Bowling Green, Row Herndon, and others signed it themselves, and Lincoln signed the names of nineteen more New Salem residents. The prayer was granted, and a few years later Lincoln worked to increase the amount of support Elmore received.[143] I mention the matter simply to document that an element of compassion did exist among town residents, and that in the 1830s, government was already considered to have a role in helping the helpless.

When Lincoln had power to do a small kindness to help someone, he didn't wait for a group, let alone the government, to act. Ann Rutledge's brother Robert recalled:

> "Ab Trout," a poor barefooted boy, was engaged one cold winter day in chopping a pile of logs from an old house or stable which had been pulled down. The wood was dry and hard, and the boy was hard at work, when Lincoln came up and asked what he got for the job and what he would do with the money. "Ab" said $1.00 and pointing to his naked feet said, "A pair of shoes." Abe told him to go in and warm, and he would chop awhile for him. The boy delayed a little, but Lincoln finished the work, threw down his axe, and told him to go and buy the shoes.[144]

In March 1833, storekeepers Berry and Lincoln received a permit, the meaning of which has been hotly contested in some circles over the years. The Sangamon County commissioners granted them a license to sell liquor by the drink. Signing his own name and Lincoln's as well, Berry gave a $300 bond pledging their obedience to state tavern-keeping laws. Such obedience was with a wink and a nod, as part of the requirement in such a license was to provide lodging to travelers. The Berry & Lincoln operation didn't do that, but neither did three New Salem groceries having tavern-keeping licenses. Because Lincoln didn't personally sign the bond, argument has been made that he either didn't know about it or else disapproved of obtaining a tavern license. We could just as easily argue that because both men didn't need to make the trip to the county seat of Springfield, Lincoln stayed home and minded the store. Bowling Green signed as surety, and given the close relationship between him and Lincoln, I doubt that Green would have participated in the transaction without Lincoln's approval.[145]

Such a license is evidence of financial strain in the store. Treating customers to a drink when they bought merchandise is one thing. Selling drinks to one and all, however, is likely to change a store's clientele and character. Given Lincoln's temperance leanings, a decision to sell drinks was surely reluctant on his part. Such a move made sense, however, if cash flow needed to be improved. A typical frontier store sold most goods on credit. Whiskey, however, went for cash.[146]

A general store that retailed liquor by the drink wasn't a grocery, so it is possible to deny that the Berry & Lincoln enterprise was a grocery. If, however, the denial is meant to imply that people couldn't buy drinks of beverage alcohol, such implication would be misleading. We have the testimony of clerk Daniel Burner: "We sold whisky. There was nothing in it [the store] so far as I could see but liquid goods. In short, I never saw anything else there. . . . I used to deal out forty-rod [whiskey] at six and one quarter cents a big glassful."[147] Burner's description of one-item store merchandise is exaggerated, but his recollection of drink pricing seems precisely in keeping with price regulation imposed by the county license.[148] Other old residents, too, spoke of the operation as a grocery.[149] There is, however, also adamant testimony to the contrary. Said James Davis, "Am a Democrat. Never agreed in politics with Abe. . . . Give the devil his due: He never sold whiskey by the dram in New Salem. I was in town every week for years. Know, I think, all about it."[150] Others said the same.[151] If indeed the business had shifted to selling "liquid goods" exclusively, that would be a substantial change from what it once was. Royal Clary remembered a dual business in the building: Berry and Lincoln retailing goods while Slicky Bill Greene ran a grocery at one end of the structure.[152] At any rate, apparently the saloon trade became big enough to crowd out memories of the merchandise and dry-goods operation.

Although groceries were common enough and well patronized, growing numbers of citizens regarded the business as harmful. In an 1833 address to the Tazewell County Temperance Society, Jones A. Mendall, Esq., declared:

Last summer, when your frontier was threatened by an invasion of Indians, I saw you spurning all minor considerations, flock to the standard of your country, with a manifestation of feeling truly American. You showed a nobleness of principle and conduct, that would have done honor to the age of Leonidas, of '76, or any other. There was then no cowardice; no flagging; no recoil of principle or conduct. And now, when an enemy more ruthless than all the savages of this continent combined, invades your land—when a pestilence more terrific than cholera has covered the land with the leprosy of disease and death—when a destroyer of morals and religion more fell than a legion of devils incarnate, threatens to prostrate everything valuable—can you be backward in the great work of reformation so necessary?[153]

The temperance movement was concerned with more than alcohol. In 1834, the *St. Louis Observer* reprinted an article on "Evils of Opium in South-Eastern Asia."[154] In 1833, a Vandalia newspaper noted, "An Anti-Tobacco Society has recently been formed in Ulster County, N.Y. About fifty persons have pledged themselves to discountenance the use of the narcotic."[155] In 1831, the *Illinois Monthly Magazine* had noted, "Such is the nature of tobacco . . . that it must be one of the most powerful substances of which we have any knowledge. . . . Tobacco, having powerful and fatal properties, must, or at least may be, a dangerous thing to tamper with. . . . It is impossible for those who have never used tobacco, even to imagine the strength of the appetite for it, when once fully formed. I cannot suppose that the thirst for ardent spirits exceeds it in strength."[156] In 1833, even caffeine was a concern in some circles: "A New York temperance paper says that there has been an increased consumption of coffee in the United States during the last year."[157] Anyone who retailed liquor by the drink in the 1830s risked losing as much goodwill as was gained by such trade. In 1835, Stephen Douglas privately, and correctly, said, "Distilling and retailing liquors is very profitable, but in these days of temperance not very honorable."[158]

In addition to the store, Lincoln picked up odds and ends of income in other ways. Probably toward early 1833, he earned money by piloting to Beardstown a flatboat of family belongings for New Salem residents who were moving to Texas. The experience demonstrated the hazard of such enterprise even when conducted by an experienced riverman. Lincoln once commented that in the last fifteen or so miles above Beardstown, "this route is upon such low ground as to retain water in many places during the season, and in all parts such as to draw two-thirds or three-fourths of the river water at all high stages."[159] You had to know the river channel and stay in it, lest flood waters carry you into some field. While Lincoln piloted the migration family's flatboat, the Sangamon River "was very full, overflowing its banks," said John McNeil. "They lost the river as I heard Mr. Lincoln relate, and ran about three miles out in the prairie." How they got the flatboat back into the river and its current is unrecorded.[160]

During April 1833, Lincoln served as witness or juror in several Sangamon County circuit court cases, picking up $1.75 for his services.[161] Most were routine debt litigation, but one case had a different nature. A couple years earlier, while Lincoln was building the flatboat he took to New Orleans, John Marshall threw a robust party somewhere around New Salem. Thomas Edwards swore it was "a mere frolic, which was got up and conducted for amusement, and which was commenced by Marshall. . . . There was no ill feeling manifested towards the person or property of said Marshall or his wife, and . . . all that was done at that time was innocent in design, and until near the close of the transaction, it was neither known or thought to be disagreeable either to said Marshall or his wife." Sally Marshall explained what bothered her: "Thomas Edwards did on the night of the second instant enter the dwelling of John Marshal[l] and commence a conversation with his wife in substance this, that he would do as he pleased with her, and Edwards did throw his cloak down on the floor and said he would throw her down there and would fuck her (that is, would have carnal knowledge of her), and her husband should stand and see it." Edwards replied, "All that was done by this deponent [was] conversation in words alone, without any act that could amount to an assault." He said when he arrived at the Marshall house, John told him to halt, and Edwards did so. Any noise and fuss was then created by Marshall. Edwards offered a string of witnesses to back him up, including Slicky Bill Greene and William Clary of Clary's Grove. He was indicted for riot and attempted rape.

Jack Armstrong, leader of the Clary's Grove Boys, stood as surety guaranteeing a bond that Edwards would show up for trial. Other sureties as the case moved along included Armstrong's half-brother Bowling Green, Bill Greene, William Carpenter, John C. Vance (the farmer from whom Lincoln had borrowed a grammar book), Lincoln's store partner William Berry, and Lincoln himself. In a case that had to have caused juicy local conversation, that string of sureties had political importance. They included not only members of Captain Lincoln's Black Hawk War company, but also two hopefuls for the state legislature, Carpenter and Lincoln. In the early twenty-first century, not many state legislature aspirants would be willing to sign a bond for someone accused of attempted rape, but then, neither Carpenter nor Lincoln had to worry about women's votes. Given its local notoriety, the Edwards trial was moved to another county. George Forquer began the prosecution, but eventually state's attorney John J. Hardin dropped both the riot and rape cases.[162] I'm inclined to think Edwards was innocent, given Lincoln's known attitude about rape. "In every case he [President Lincoln] always leaned to the side of mercy. His constant desire was to save life. There was only one class of crimes I always found him prompt to punish—a crime which occurs more or less frequently about all armies—namely, outrages upon women. He never hesitated to approve the [death] sentences in these cases. This was the only class of cases I can now recall in which he was unhesitating in his action."[163]

Soon after the April court services, Lincoln got a good break. The New Salem post office was run by his merchant competitor Sam Hill. Postmasters got a percentage of receipts, but the New Salem postal trade brought little income. Having the post office in Hill's store, however, was commercially advantageous for him, bringing in all sorts of people who might be tempted to make store purchases while doing post office business. Such a store–post office combination was by no means unique to New Salem. Supposedly, however, Hill gave store customers preference over postal patrons, making ladies wait for their mail while he measured out bulk quantities of liquor for male customers. The story goes that the women inspired a petition asking for a new postmaster. In the words of town physician Jason Duncan, "Considerations connected with the public good prompted me with others to prefer charges at the department against Hill." Reportedly the petition was signed by most users of the New Salem post office and recommended Lincoln as a replacement postmaster. Duncan said Lincoln opposed the effort on his behalf, not wanting to cost Hill his office. If those hesitations existed, they didn't deter the effort, and if Lincoln had been all that hesitant, he could have squelched it.

Protocol required some postmaster to send the petition to Washington; Havana postmaster Ossian M. Ross did the honors and sent along his own endorsement of Lincoln. According to Duncan, postal authorities demanded an explanation from Hill, but instead of mounting a defense, he gave up the duties. President Andrew Jackson appointed Lincoln postmaster in May. They were of different political parties, but speaking in the third person, Lincoln later explained the appointment was "too insignificant to make his politics an objection." About this time, a commentator noted, "The business of the General Post Office, unlike the other operations of the government, has a constant and intimate relation to individuals and the private intercourse of society. To admit into such an office a purely party offices [sic], and to establish over it a supervision designed to accommodate and sustain a party, would be abhorrent and dreadful. Society would be unhinged, confidence destroyed, and all the utility of the establishment annihilated." Rural postmasterships took up little of a President's thought; during the Civil War, Lincoln spent seconds scanning an application for one such post, endorsed by a Democrat, and approved it.[164]

Postmasters held customer fees for quite some time and had to guarantee eventual payment to the federal government. One of the two persons who stood surety for postmaster Lincoln's $500 bond was Nelson Alley, Lincoln's partner in the purchase of Bogue's store goods the previous autumn. The other surety was Alexander Trent, corporal in Captain Lincoln's Black Hawk War company, with whom Lincoln had prior and later financial dealings.[165]

A rural post office of that day wasn't a building. A postmaster operated in a structure mainly used for some other purpose; perhaps he even did business from a private residence. There might be a pigeonhole box for sorting, or there might not. The Berry & Lincoln store's door had a slot for depositing letters.[166] Generally persons came to the postmaster to collect their mail, but Lincoln would deliver in New Salem or even walk into the countryside if he knew someone was impatiently awaiting a letter.[167] Urgency wasn't necessarily the only reason for such an excursion. Postmaster Lincoln once received five letters addressed to Jonathan Colby and decided to deliver them. Finding the farmer at his plow, the postmaster announced simply: "There was a pretty heavy mail for you this morning, Colby. I thought I'd bring it out."[168] Lincoln provided such extra services merely because he wanted to, and those extras must have increased good feeling toward an already well-liked young man. The job was a significant boost to his political ambition. Now voters from all over this part of the county were coming to him in New Salem, allowing him to get acquainted without extensive travel taking him away from his work.

Many federal offices were subject to vigorous competition because they were so lucrative, but rural postmasterships were a glaring exception. They entailed copious record keeping to prove the postmaster's financial obligations to the postal service, and pay was meager. The pathetic income was so notorious as to be recognized by the Illinois state constitution, which forbade state legislators to hold "lucrative office under the United States" but explicitly exempted postmasters from that prohibition, declaring that postmasterships "shall not be considered lucrative offices."[169] Lincoln apparently received a bit over $50 a year.[170] At that time, Illinois farmhands were making about twice that amount in labor involving considerably more perspiration,[171] so despite the modest raw amount of income, Lincoln wasn't doing badly in comparison with alternatives open to him. He also got a few official perquisites: being able to receive his personal letters free (in that era, recipients instead of senders paid the postage), to send them free as well (relieving recipients from postage obligation), and to receive each day one newspaper postage free.[172] An unofficial perquisite was every newspaper passing through his post office. "Never saw a man better pleased," physician John Allen said. "Was because, as he said, he would then have access to all the newspapers—never yet being able to get the half that he wanted before."[173] Days and even weeks might pass before people in outlying areas called for their mail, and all that time he could read their newspapers without having to subscribe. For a man of Lincoln's interests and income, that was a major benefit to the job.

Mail carrier Harvey Ross left an anecdote of an unusual event—a circus in Springfield—that may illustrate typical conditions at the New Salem post office. In the summer of 1833, Ross arrived at the Berry & Lincoln store to deliver incoming mail and pick up outgoing. He learned that postmaster Lincoln was in the countryside. Ross pounded and shouted at the store door, trying to rouse Berry, who was sleeping off a drunk from a dance he attended the night before. Figuring half an hour was a decent amount of time to act as an alarm clock, Ross headed off to his next stop of Sangamo Town, where he left the New Salem mail with the postmaster, surely Lincoln's political ally Dr. Anson Henry, and headed to Springfield. There he saw the circus parade and the show itself. Two elements of the show earned special comment. One was exhibition of a giant snake. Pioneers feared the reptiles, and when its handler took the huge anaconda from its cage and carried it toward the audience, a near panic threatened until the handler relented to cries imploring him to recage the creature. The other remarkable event was a female performer standing on a running horse, a feat not even the most expert local rider thought possible. After the show, Ross crossed paths in Springfield with Lincoln, who was miffed about the mail not being changed back in New Salem, as the failure reflected badly on him and could get him in trouble. He became less concerned when Ross explained that the undelivered New Salem mail was back in Sangamo Town instead of with the Springfield postmaster. Lincoln then headed back to New Salem via Sangamo Town, where he picked up the mail intended for New Salem delivery.[174] In addition to official duties, Ross would deliver Berry & Lincoln store parcels to customers,[175] apparently an informal merchant delivery service, illustrating Lincoln's interest in accommodating people.

Lincoln's store's income was becoming problematic.[176] In frontier stores, customers typically ran a tab for most items, settling up around Christmastime,[177] and settlements might be in kind instead of in cash. Some merchants secured mortgages on customers' crops in order to guarantee payment of accounts, a legitimate business practice, to be sure, but one that nurtured resentment in the countryside against capitalists in town.[178] There being no comments about "meanness" in the Berry & Lincoln store's dealings, I'm inclined to think they didn't take mortgages on crops. "I remember one transaction in particular which I had with them," McGrady Rutledge said of Berry & Lincoln. "I sold the firm a load of wheat, which they turned over to the mill."[179] Given the poor state of navigation on the Sangamon River, the firm was quite limited in its ability to transform country produce into cash. An observer in the era described another method of paying in kind: "Some farmers, for instance, make use of the bad weather, to make shoes, barrels or other things. All these things they take to the merchant to sell. This seems to be the most advantageous as also the most respectable way. It is but natural that such a method should lead to barter, with which the merchant usually makes a double profit."[180] Stores thereby acquired inventory with no cash outlay while serving as a vicinity's central marketplace. An anecdote illustrates that the Berry & Lincoln store operated that way:

> I went into the store one day to buy a pair of buckskin gloves and asked him if he had a pair that would fit me. He threw a pair on the counter. "There is a pair of dogskin gloves that I think will fit you, and you can have them for seventy-five cents." When he called them dogskin gloves I was surprised, as I had never heard of such a thing before. . . . So I said to Mr Lincoln, "How do you know they are dogskin gloves?" I believe that he thought my question was a little impudent, and it rasped him somewhat that I had the audacity to question his word. "Well, sir," said he, "I will tell you how I know they are dogskin gloves. Jack Clary's dog killed Tom Watkins' sheep, and Tom Watkins' boy killed the dog, and old John Mounts tanned the dogskin, and Sally Spears made the gloves, and that is how I know they are dogskin gloves." So I asked no more questions about the gloves, but paid the six bits and took them.[181]

"Book assets" and barter, however, didn't pay wholesale suppliers for replenishment of goods. Clerk Daniel Burner said Lincoln suggested that Berry ask his father, Reverend John, for a loan to replenish the store's liquor supply. Asking a minister to fund a whiskey operation was so preposterous as to either damage Burner's credibility or demonstrate Lincoln's desperation. Burner said William Berry declined to approach his father.[182] Since whiskey was a cash sale item, sales should have funded new stock and left a profit besides. Failure to do so indicated a problem. Burner's description of the problem is supported by other sources as well: "Lincoln did not drink much himself. Only once in a while did I see him take anything. His partner, William Berry . . . was a hard drinker, but the liquor appeared to have little effect on him. Finally, when the stock got low, Lincoln remarked dryly: 'Berry, if we had not been such good customers ourselves our stock would have lasted longer.'"[183] If Berry was using up the inventory, Lincoln may well have felt it simple justice for Berry to finance replenishment by getting a loan. Burner is also quoted, however, as saying Lincoln suggested the loan so the partners could buy out a new store being opened by Nicholas Garland.[184] Such a purpose would be in keeping with the Berry & Lincoln mode of operation, buying out competitors.

The store's finances involved some complexity. About the time Lincoln became postmaster, his storekeeper partner, Berry, gave Springfield merchant Eli Blankenship a "conditional deed"—basically a mortgage—on a New Salem town lot where the Berry & Lincoln store had been located before they moved to the building used by Radford. This mortgage backed an April 1833 promissory note that Lincoln had just given Row Herndon and that Row instantly assigned to

Blankenship.[185] Blankenship was involved because Jim and Row Herndon had bought their old store's inventory from him. When, in 1832, Berry and Lincoln had bought that inventory from the Herndon brothers via promissory notes, one from Berry and one from Lincoln, the Herndon brothers assigned those notes to Blankenship to extinguish the brothers' debt to him.[186] So the money the Herndon brothers had owed to Blankenship was now owed by Berry and Lincoln. The April 1833 transaction indicates that the 1832 Berry and Lincoln promissory notes had come due and the two men were unable to pay Blankenship. Rather than insist on payment, Blankenship now accepted a conditional title to New Salem real estate owned by Berry. If Lincoln paid off the new promissory note in cash, however, the town lot would revert to Berry. As the conditional deed valued the real estate at $250, that amount implies that Lincoln's new note was for $250 and that Blankenship would simply cancel the note if Lincoln couldn't pay off, Blankenship taking Berry's real estate instead of suing Berry and Lincoln for the money. This April 1833 arrangement combining the financial responsibility of Berry and Lincoln to Blankenship seems to have substituted for the individual responsibility each had taken on in 1832 via Berry's note to Jim Herndon and Lincoln's to Row Herndon (which individual notes the Herndon brothers had assigned to Blankenship).

The April 1833 arrangement implies a close and trusting financial relationship between Berry and Lincoln. It also demonstrates that Berry was a man of some property and that New Salem appeared to be moving toward a thriving future—or else a Springfield merchant would have no interest in a New Salem lot, especially at that price. Suggestion has been made that the conditional deed shows an end to the Berry-Lincoln partnership, but I am unpersuaded. One partner pledged his honor to Blankenship; the other pledged real estate. That doesn't sound like an end to mutual involvement, particularly since neither partner was paying the other anything in the transaction; the debt was to a third party and assumed by both partners.

In autumn 1833, financial pressure increased on Lincoln. In September, Nelson Alley defaulted on the $104 promissory note they had given the creditors of Vincent Bogue a year earlier when purchasing Bogue's store goods. Democratic state senator George Forquer now sued Lincoln on the creditors' behalf, and a court found him liable for the full amount. He paid in six installments over the next few weeks, completing the process in March.[187] Even at this distance, we can almost feel the strain as he scrambled to furnish a little more money every month or so.

In October, the $377 of notes due to Radford for his store goods came due. The notes were owed by Slicky Bill Greene, but he was unable to pay because Lincoln and Berry were unable to pay the $377 note they had given to Bill when buying Radford's inventory from Bill. Radford allowed Bill Greene to renew the obligation rather than pay it off, but this time Berry and Lincoln had to sign as well. (Perhaps Greene gave up their note to him, in exchange for their participating in his obligation to Radford.) Greene, Berry, and Lincoln each pledged liability to Radford for the full amount; if anyone defaulted, the remaining note givers had to make up the difference. The full amount was now given as $379.82, but a credit of $125 was applied, making the net obligation $254.82. Another important aspect to this renewed note was that it was renewed for one day. Instead of the sum being carried another six months, it was now payable on demand. This was an invitation for Radford to sell the note to someone who would then proceed to sue for immediate collection.[188] And Radford wasn't the sort of person to let a debt ride longer than necessary: "The subscriber being determined to collect the debts due him at and near New Salem, gives notice that he will attend in New Salem on Saturday the 20th, and on Saturday the 27th of April, instant, for the purpose of receiving his dues. All those debtors who neglect to come forward on one of those days and pay him his demands, will find their accounts in the hands of a magistrate in Springfield, who will be instructed to enforce their immediate payment. Reuben Radford. April 11, 1833."[189]

About his partnership with Berry, Lincoln later wrote, speaking of himself in the third person: "They opened as merchants; and he says that was *the* store. Of course they did nothing but get deeper and deeper in debt." Using the metaphor of a candle that is almost used up, he declared, "The store winked out."[190] Other accounts say Lincoln was so irked about Berry's getting a tavern license that the partnership dissolved[191]; that Berry's recklessness caused the business to fail[192]; that Lincoln sold out his interest to Berry[193]; or that Berry sold out his interest to Lincoln.[194] If, however, we take Lincoln's statement at face value, the two men remained partners throughout the store's life, and Lincoln blamed nobody for the store's failure.

Berry and Lincoln sold what remained of their business to the Trent brothers, Alexander, who had stood surety for Lincoln's postmaster appointment, and Martin. Earlier, Lincoln and Alexander had an awkward business interaction. A few days after Lincoln bought the Radford store inventory from Slicky Bill Greene, Ann Rutledge's brother David conveyed part of a New Salem town lot to Alexander and Martin Trent, with Lincoln handling the paralegal paperwork. Greene and Lincoln stood sureties for a $150 bond that David gave to guarantee performance. Rutledge failed to perform, and in August, the Trents sued him and his sureties. They settled out of court the next month.[195] Apparently the settlement was amicable; toward the end of December 1833, Alexander stood surety on a $100 appeal bond posted by Berry and Lincoln, who were appealing a verdict against them on one of their store-related promissory notes.[196] The transaction conveying the Berry & Lincoln enterprise to the Trents was by promissory note, New Salem's standard mode of commercial operation. Lincoln and Alexander Trent had had continual business relations, plus an emotional bond of service together in New Salem's hometown company during the Black Hawk War. Just before payment to Berry and Lincoln came due, however, the brothers Trent escaped payment by fleeing town, restoring the load of debt to Berry and Lincoln after the Trents had sold as much of the merchandise as they could. Creditors seized the remaining inventory. Then Berry died. As notes relating to the store came due, Lincoln had no one who could take over responsibility from the Trent brothers and no money to pay.[197] But in 1833, all those consequences were still in the future.

The *Sangamo Journal* printed a general commentary that aptly summarized Lincoln's storekeeping experience:

> The life of a merchant is, necessarily, a life of peril. He can scarcely move without danger. He is beset on all sides with disappointments, with fluctuations in the current of business, which sometimes leave him stranded on an unknown bar, and sometimes sweep him helpless into an unknown ocean.—These vicissitudes depend on causes which no man can control; and are often so sudden, that no calculation could anticipate, or skill avoid them. To risk much, to be exposed to hazards, belongs to the vocation of a merchant; his usefulness and success depend, in many cases, on his enterprise. He must have courage to explore new regions of commerce, and encounter the difficulties of untried experiments. To be unfortunate in such pursuits is no more disgraceful to an upright trader, than to fall in the field of battle is dishonorable to the soldier, or defeat to a general who had done all that valor and skill could achieve to obtain the victory.[198]

In his White House years, Lincoln reportedly said someone woke him in the wee hours of Tuesday, November 12, 1833, with the exclamation, "'Arise, Abraham, the day of judgment has come!' I sprang from my bed and rushed to the window, and saw the stars falling in great showers!"[199] Many people panicked. A preacher over toward Shelbyville was traveling before dawn, and "as he went along the way, at every settler's house, the people seemed crazed with fright and were on their knees imploring mercy."[200] Lincoln wasn't among the panickers and used his knowledge of astronomy to analyze the streaks of light: "Looking back of them in the heavens I saw all the grand old constellations with which I was so well acquainted, fixed and true in their places."[201] As a Galena newspaper said soon after, "There is no occasion to recur to supernatural causes to account for what may be easily accounted for by our ignorance of natural ones."[202] A correspondent in the Beardstown newspaper reported: "The whole firmament was lit up with fiery particles of liquid fluidity, which descended in copious showers. The brilliancy of the scene was very dazzling and painful to the nerve of the strongest eye. The translucid beauty which some of these twinkling luminaries seemed to present was beyond description. Others, more fiery in appearance, seemed to dart from the farthermost verge of heaven, presenting in their downward course, one entire vivid sheet."[203] A Springfield witness reported the "falling of a shower of fire. . . . The air was entirely calm, and the atmosphere was free from clouds. The scene presented was one of extraordinary sublimity."[204]

As days passed, reports arrived from more distant places. In Cincinnati, "the whole firmament was incessantly traversed, in all directions, by luminous streams of electric light. . . . The streaks of light were of inherent intensity, sometimes contracting in a slender line, at others presenting the appearance of a broad rectineal flash. Frequently, when approaching the horizon, they exhibited at their termination, an appearance somewhat similar to an explosion, lasting for some seconds, a rich mellow light blended with all the hues of the rainbow."[205] "Imagine," said a Kentucky observer, "large flakes of snow, and that each flake . . . to take fire in its passage and fuse like a bombshell before bursting, leaving a long train of lurid fire attached to its train, and thousands of these or as many as the eye could comprehend by its glance, descending continually . . . for several hours."[206] A New Yorker reported thousands in every ten-minute span: "It was as difficult to count them as to number the raindrops."[207] Connecticut reported, "The streets were occasionally as light as noonday."[208] In New England, "an old sailor said he had been all over the world—he had been on deck at all hours of night, and in every sea and in all weathers, and he had never seen such a sight as this."[209] The *Sangamo Journal* reported, "We learn from the *Columbian Spy* that, at a public place where it was usual to dispose of a good many drinks on market mornings, but one was sold on the morning of their [the meteors'] occurrence, and no charge was made for that!"[210]

"The stars did indeed seem to be falling," said one witness, "as a fig tree when casting its untimely leaves. It reminded the wicked of that dreadful catastrophe when God rained fire and brimstone upon the wicked inhabitants of Sodom and Gomorrah."[211] The heavenly display converted many to Christianity and was a godsend to preachers at camp meetings. Thereafter, 1833 was called "the year the stars fell."[212] Hope was expressed that the phenomenon had cleansed the atmosphere, resulting in the "destruction of the main cause of cholera, which poisoned the air, calling for the thankfulness of all in a beneficent creator, who in the midst of deserved judgment remembers mercy."[213]

Not all received mercy.

On the night of the great meteoric shower in Nov. 1833, I was at Remley's tavern, twelve miles west of Lewisburg, Greenbrier Co., Virginia. A drove of fifty or sixty negroes stopped at the same place that night. They usually "camp out," but as it was excessively muddy, they were permitted to come into the house. . . . Their supper was a compound of "potatoes and meal," and was, without exception, *the dirtiest, blackest looking mess I ever saw.* I remarked at the time that the food was not as clean, in appearance, as that which was given to a *drove of hogs,* at the same place the night previous. Such as it was, however, a black woman brought it on her head, in a tray or trough two and a half feet long, where the men and women were promiscuously herded. The slaves rushed up and seized it from the trough in handfuls, before the woman could take it off her head. They jumped at it as if half-famished.[214]

After the store folded, Lincoln still had his postmastership for income, and Sam Hill let him relocate the post office to Hill's store. Given the circumstances under which the post office moved away from Hill's store in the first place, his offer was generous. It was also beneficial to Hill, increasing traffic in his store. In addition, Lincoln performed store clerk duties for Hill.[215]

Lincoln picked up odds and ends of income, perhaps in the form of board rather than cash, by helping in a store started by Abner Ellis and doing farmhand work and paralegal tasks.[216] Then, sometime in the autumn of 1833, a good break came: Lincoln was hired to survey land for the county. This job would pay him to circulate among voters throughout the county while bringing him into close contact with capitalist land speculators. He got the job through Pollard Simmons.

Simmons was one of the New Salem–area Democrats with kindly feelings toward the Whig politician Lincoln. Simmons had a talk with John "Candlebox" Calhoun, the Sangamon County surveyor and a prominent Democrat. The infamy through which he earned his nickname was still some years in the future. Candlebox was one of several children born to an Irish Protestant immigrant reportedly named Cahoun, who married an American woman. After studying law, Candlebox moved from Boston to Illinois, where he worked a stint as a schoolteacher, one of his pupils being William H. Herndon.[217] If a name change occurred, it may have been done at an early date by his father, as Candlebox had brothers named Calhoun. Another Illinois emigrant from the East named John Calhoun, with the same birth and death years as Candlebox, founded the *Chicago Democrat* newspaper. These are two different persons. Occasionally, still another John Calhoun, statesman of South Carolina, will enter our story. Because three John Calhouns may be confusing, I generally refer to the Illinois politician by his nickname, Candlebox.

Like Lincoln, in 1832 Candlebox voted for Henry Clay for President, but that required crossing party lines and repudiating his party's hero, Jackson. Calhoun explained: "I then thought the United States Bank could be so modified as to secure all its benefits. Without continuing any of its evils. Upon this ground alone my vote was governed."[218] Such explanation was a little thin, and he had to do a lot more explaining, but that will suffice for now. Candlebox was playing both sides of the game.

Candlebox thirsted for public office and developed a mutual aid network among the like-minded. "John discovered that he had a marvelous fitness for office from the time he arrived in this county," noted one hostile onlooker, "and he has been familiarly used since, as occasion required, by certain individuals, with the hope of securing office."[219] By December 1832, he had enough pull statewide to last six ballots when running unsuccessfully to be secretary of the state senate.[220]

A sarcastic observer commented, "Everyone recollects his *gentlemanly* conduct towards Mr. Stuart . . . for which the exertions of his then new associates (after they had in vain attempted to make him secretary of the state senate) he was appointed county surveyor, over the heads of several of our old and better qualified citizens."[221] That appointment came soon after the senate secretary contest.[222]

Records of how the appointment process worked are hardly meticulous, but a reasonable supposition is that William L. "Big Red" May was involved. May, Candlebox, and newly elected state senator George Forquer were publicly described as general allies.[223] Big Red May was Register of the U.S. Land Office in Springfield.[224] Land Office appointments were one of the President's juiciest patronage plums, with officers making big money from fees paid by individuals buying public land from the U.S. government. Moreover, incautious officers dipped into land office revenue for personal gain until they had to hand over the funds—a common but risky practice.[225] And the Springfield district's sales volume was one of the system's biggest. Another not quite legal practice involved congressionally issued land scrip, a term sometimes used synonymously with land warrant, which could be traded for public land. Persons uninterested in land could sell their scrip at a discount. A land officer could acquire scrip in that way, perhaps paying $70 for $100 worth of scrip, pocketing $100 cash that a settler paid for land, sending $100 of scrip to Washington instead of money, and clearing an automatic profit of $30 on the transaction.[226]

An apparently legal practice was for land officers to operate as private money changers, buying at a discount a settler's paper bank notes that had less than face value, and furnishing the settler with full-value paper bank notes that the federal government would accept.[227] Alternatively, land officers might loan the purchase price outright to settlers at a hefty interest rate.[228] In addition, some officers involved themselves in land speculation; apparently Big Red ran deals with Springfield land operator Philip Clayton Latham.[229] And Springfield Land Office officialdom was known to promote formation of new counties to help insiders seeking to establish new town sites.[230]

To maximize income from all these angles, officers needed help from someone who understood the importance of surveying land expeditiously, a process that also provided detailed information on the land's resale value, allowing speculators to choose the best parcels for purchase from the U.S. government. We can comfortably infer that Candlebox Calhoun understood Big Red's needs. Whether Calhoun understood anything about surveying is unclear, but he could hire deputies to perform fieldwork and still make good income from survey fees. Statute language said merely, "It shall be the duty of the said county surveyor to make all surveys within the bounds of his county, that he may be called upon to make."[231] Under standard division of authority, surveyors for the U.S. Land Office would examine land owned by the United States in order to help prepare it for sale to private buyers. County surveyors apparently did similar work on public land owned by counties and also did tasks such as measuring out town sites and mapping new roads or rerouting old ones. In their spare time, not as government employees, county surveyors or their deputies would moonlight on tasks such as establishing bound-aries on acreage already owned by someone or measuring a horse-race track.[232] Although no direct connection existed between the U.S. Land Office and the Sang-amon County Surveyor, given our knowledge of the personalities involved and how the world turns, we may be confident that any membrane separating the two insti-tutions in Springfield was permeable. That's not to say anything illegal or even unethical was going on. We can, however, be confident that political allies May and Calhoun were doing whatever favors they could for each other.

Candlebox, however, was in a jam—at least, according to two superb stu-dents of Lincoln's life.[233] They portray Candlebox as vexed by demands from farmers needing their farms surveyed and real estate developers needing the same service for town lots, along with official location certified for a town. Our distance from that scene makes viewing difficult. Land business was so brisk and surveying so complicated that apparently a backlog of unperformed surveys was blocking transfers of land titles. Less apparent is how much work had to be done by the county surveyor, how much by the U.S. Land Office, and how much by private surveyors. People not only were confounded about using unsurveyed land, but also were likely experiencing delays in getting money owed on land transfers that were awaiting survey records that could be entered in county deed books. Among them were wealthy individuals who could have major influence on local and statewide elections. Aware of those individuals' needs, Calhoun had to find survey crews who could be depended on to work hard and accurately (inaccurate surveys were a common complaint throughout the West). Candlebox would, therefore, be open to suggestion from a local Democratic leader recommending someone who would make a good deputy surveyor.

A deputy surveyor job involved hard work but also brought in a decent income through fees plus a per diem expense allowance.[234] Therefore, the job was a valuable local political patronage appointment. From what we know, Candlebox Calhoun owed Lincoln nothing in the way of favors. A reasonable sup-position is that Pollard Simmons was a little big man, and Calhoun thus had rea-son to accommodate Simmons where feasible, in order to increase his own political strength in the county. That scenario would lead us to believe that Sim-mons urged Calhoun to appoint Lincoln and that Calhoun did it as a favor to Sim-mons. Accounts of Calhoun's conversation with Simmons differ in detail, but the result was that Candlebox decided to hire Lincoln as a deputy county surveyor. Simmons rode around looking for Lincoln and found him splitting rails. The stan-dard version is that Lincoln asked whether he would be expected to change his politics in order to get the job—an important question for someone who was plan-ning to run again as a Whig candidate for the legislature. Upon being reassured he could remain an active Whig, Lincoln accepted the job.[235] Someone who heard a garbled version of the story from Simmons asked President Lincoln if it were true. He replied: "The old man must have stretched the facts somewhat. . . . I think I should have been very glad of the job at that time, no matter what administration was in power."[236] The fellow who married Calhoun's sister-in-law said:

[Lincoln] called on Calhoun, then living with his father-in-law, Seth R. Cutter, on Upper Lick Creek. After the interview was concluded, Mr. Lincoln, about to depart, remarked: "Calhoun, I am entirely unable to repay you for your generosity at present. All that I have you see on me, except a quarter of a dollar in my pocket.". . . My wife, then a miss of sixteen, says . . . that she distinctly remembers this interview. After Lincoln was gone she says she and her sister, Mrs. Calhoun, commenced making jocular remarks about his uncanny appearance, in the presence of Calhoun, to which in substance he made this rejoinder: "For all that, he is no common man."[237]

Back in Indiana, Lincoln had supposedly studied surveying, borrowing books from Reuben Grigsby and getting advice on the topic from James Blair, and Slicky Bill Greene indicated that Lincoln in Illinois had examined a surveying book owned by Greene.[238] Whether or not the new deputy surveyor had prior knowledge of the topic, he embarked on an intense program of study, using books loaned by Candlebox.[239] Surveying is not a simple topic; it involves meticulous manipulation of instruments, such as comparing nighttime astronomical observations of true north with daytime compass readings, along with understanding of geometry and trigonometry and factoring in the earth's curvature. For several weeks, Lincoln applied himself so severely to study that he neglected meals and stayed awake deep into the night. Neighbors began to notice untoward changes in his face and physique.[240] Town schoolmaster Mentor Graham tried to help[241]; some others just urged him to back off from the punishing pace.[242] Jack Armstrong's brother-in-law said Lincoln looked like a man coming off a two-week whiskey spree.[243] Lincoln said simply that he "procured a compass and chain, studied [textbooks by] Flint and Gibson a little, and went at it. This procured bread, and kept soul and body together."[244]

Such work could be brutal. Some years earlier, a federal official observed regarding surveyors and their crews, "None but men as hard as a savage, who is always at home in woods and swamps, can live upon what they afford." He said a surveyor had to be someone "who can travel for days up to the knees in mud and mire, can drink any fluid he finds while he is drenched with water also—and has a knowledge of the lands . . . equally patient and persevering."[245] Up toward Chicago, north of Lincoln's survey territory, in 1833, John D. Caton helped survey through timber and alder swamp. "Every foot of the way had to be cleared by the ax-men, so it was very slow work," Caton said. "Very slow progress in the dense thicket, all being idle most of the time except the ax-men, whose constant blows could be heard at a considerable distance."[246] Of Lincoln, one nineteenth-century chronicler wrote, "When Mr. [Abner] Hall and Benjamin and John Wiseman were laying off the . . . section into small lots for sale, Mr. Lincoln was their surveyor, . . . passing silently through the deep ponds which the others were glad to avoid."[247] Such ponds didn't stop a geometrical line, nor did they stop Lincoln's pursuit of that line.

When he started surveying, Lincoln boarded with Bennett and Elizabeth Abell. Elizabeth recalled: "Lincoln would come in at night all ragged and scratched up with the briars. He would laugh over it and say that was a poor man's lot. I told him to get me a buckskin, and I would fix him so the briars would not scratch him. He done so, and I foxed his pants for him."[248] Surely his finances had been what prevented him from using such protection, as that kind of armament was routine: "Many of the frontier people dress deerskins, and make them into pantaloons and hunting shirts. These articles are indispensable to all who have occasion to travel in viewing land, or for any other purpose, beyond the settlements, as cloth garments, in the shrubs and vines, would soon be in strings."[249]

Lincoln took a small crew with him, either paid assistants or local volunteers, to help manipulate equipment.[250] They lugged along axes, stakes, poles, flags, a plumb bob or two, large pins, and a chain, which was a robust version of a tape measure. Lincoln carried a compass—not just any old compass, but a Rittenhouse vernier compass, described by an expert who used it in a historical demonstration of Lincoln's instruments as "one of the best instruments that could be procured then." The expert admired its "beautiful brass," saying, "The compass glass would need only the touch of a wet finger to dampen off any static electricity."[251] This was not a pocket compass, but a large instrument supported by a pole, with slits and peepholes used for sighting markers. A vernier compass allows measurements more precise than a plain compass will allow, as fine as a minute of arc, and is especially suited to finding lines from prior surveys. Before doing fieldwork, Lincoln did homework, studying records in Springfield's U.S. Land Office in order to get a good idea of what he needed to determine. He planned out surveys in advance rather than improvising on the spot.[252]

Faulty surveys were a bane of the West and created consternation, but accuracy in Lincoln's work is well attested, not only his field measurements, but also notes and maps he produced.[253] Jack Armstrong's brother-in-law gave an example:

> The neighbors had a disputed corner in Township 18 North of Range 8 West. We agreed to send for Lincoln and to abide by his decision as surveyor and judge. He . . . stopped with me three or four days and surveyed the whole section. When the disputed corner [was] arrived at by actual survey, Lincoln then stuck down his staff and said, "Gentlemen, here *is* the corner." We then went to work and dug down in the ground—and found about six or eight inches of the original stake, sharpened and cut with an axe and at the bottom a piece of charcoal, put there by Rector, who [about a dozen years earlier] surveyed the whole county.[254]

In later years, another test proved Lincoln's accuracy when surveyors working from his notes found a broken pot with a bottle in it, where Lincoln said he had buried them to mark a survey corner.[255]

Some fieldwork took more than a day. "I have often seen him shoulder his compass and start out and be gone for two weeks. He would stay at Jack Armstrong's sometimes for a week or so."[256] John Weber said Lincoln told him about staying with an emigrant from Pennsylvania who was reputedly wealthy, a supposition that had been accepted as fact:

That he had plenty money induced the people at Salem to believe him to be an old Pennsylvania miser, and under such impression very little respect was entertained for him. . . . Mr. Lincoln was called upon . . . to survey some land in which this Pennsylvanian was interested. The day was agreed upon, and at the fixed time the interested parties were all on hand, and the work was pushed forward with energy. The evening was cold, and most of the persons engaged in the work went to the Pennsylvanian's house to supper, and after an excellent supper was disposed of, the company seated themselves around a big log fire in a big fireplace, such as the people had in those days. All were in fine humor for amusement. Mr. Lincoln told them an anecdote which was received with applause. The Pennsylvanian then told one in reply, which was approved by an uproar of laughter. One anecdote was told after another until midnight, at which time the Pennsylvanian said it was now time to retire. Mr. Lincoln replied by saying in a moment, "Sir, before retiring I wish to show how easy persons may be deluded by forming conclusions upon ideas not based upon facts." He then addressed himself to the Pennsylvanian, saying that "when we folks up in Salem first heard of you, we heard you were a Pennsylvanian and had considerable money, from which we concluded you were an old miserly Dutchman, but the facts show that we were very much mistaken, and I am happy to acknowledge that I have been very agreeably disappointed." "Well," said the Pennsylvanian, "as you have done me the honor to give me an account of the first opinion formed by you of me, it is no more than right that I should now report my first opinion of you," and then said, "When I first heard of you, I heard that you had been a candidate for the legislature, consequently I had come to the conclusion that on your arrival here I would see a smart looking man." At the close of this statement Mr. Lincoln laughed heartily.[257]

Lincoln's survey work gave him expert knowledge of land in Sangamon County and put him in an excellent position to make money through real estate speculation. Even if he lacked funds to speculate, he could have earned commissions from men engaged in that trade, with whom he interacted while pursuing his profession. Apparently he never attempted to capitalize on his firsthand knowledge about lands being sold and resold.[258]

Fieldwork also may have reduced his postmaster income, perhaps forcing him to pay someone, via a share of the proceeds, to act as his deputy while he was out of town. Although volumes of his field notes have disappeared,[259] judging from what remains, he must have been intensely busy with surveying. For instance, we know he devoted much of January and February 1834 to that task, hardly the most pleasant time for extended outdoor excursion.

> "The thermometer on Friday morning stood at 8 degrees below zero. We have sufficient snow to make *in*-tolerable sleighing. This is no time to concoct editorials. Ye that have wood to spare, remember the printers now."
>
> —*Sangamo Journal*,
> January 4, 1834

> "At this place the thermometer was as low as 18° below zero for several mornings. At Jacksonville, according to the *Patriot*, the cold was, on the 4th at 26°, and on the 5th at 28° below zero."
>
> —*Vandalia Illinois Advocate and State Register*,
> January 18, 1834

> "A man was found frozen to death, during the intense cold weather of last week, on the prairie between this place and Blue Island. He was in all probability devoured by wolves, as a few mangled remains of the body and some remnants of clothing was found at the place where he is supposed to have fallen."
>
> —*Chicago Democrat*,
> January 14, 1834

CHAPTER 7

POLITICS OF 1834:
GOVERNOR AND
LEGISLATORS

Politics never stops, and in January 1834, Springfield politicos were laying plans to win one of the state's greatest battles—relocation of the seat of government. The state capital had been moved once before, from Kaskaskia to Vandalia. Now an effort was proceeding to move it from Vandalia. The project had already been under way two years and more. In July 1832, state senate candidate George Forquer had declared, "It is a fact too notorious both at home and abroad, to attempt to conceal it, that Sangamo aspires, at some future time, to have the seat of government removed hither, and it is perhaps only necessary for me to say that, could I ever have any agency in producing this result, it would be done."[1] A candidate's stance on the issue had immediate political consquences. "I supported you in 1832 for the [state] senate," William L. "Big Red" May publicly declared to Forquer. "It is my belief that a desire to effect some local measure, and among them the removal of the seat of government from Vandalia to Springfield, induced that portion of the Jackson party with whom I acted to prefer you to Col. Elkin, your competitor."[2] In 1833, a northwest Illinois newspaper proclaimed, "It is time the people should begin to examine this subject,"[3] but public arguments for relocation were all a smokescreen for the real reason, which few dared to utter aloud: Businessmen, especially real estate speculators, would make money if the state capital were located in their town. But what town?

To that question, no answer yet existed. Advocates spoke on behalf of various burgs, indeed even for a particular stretch of land where no town yet existed. And Vandalia's business establishment had by no means conceded to losing the seat of government. The issue would be decided by the legislature, whose solons likely were perplexed because disagreement existed among powerful persons who stood to gain or lose from the decision. No matter how a legislator voted, weighty enemies would inflict punishment for that vote. I suspect the solons were therefore attempting to sidestep accountability by putting the matter to a vote of the people at the August 1834 state general election. Voters could choose among Jacksonville, Springfield, Alton, Vandalia, Peoria, or the state's geographic center: "The place or point receiving the highest number of votes shall forever hereafter remain the seat of government for the state of Illinois."[4] Despite firm-sounding language, that vote might be nonbinding on the legislature,[5] but a consensus in favor of a one locale or another still could have powerful influence.

Sangamon County politicians favored moving the capital to Springfield. This county, however, was the target of resentment from counties with smaller populations, and therefore fewer legislators. Feeling existed that Sangamon routinely sought to force its way on the state, earning it the nickname "Empire County."[6] If united, smaller counties could thwart Sangamon's effort to gain the seat of government—the greatest patronage plum the legislature might ever command. Sangamon's political leaders responded with a plan.

The campaign opened with a call for a January 4, 1834, meeting at the Sangamon County courthouse in Springfield, with a simultaneous call for a statewide convention to meet in the same town a month later.[7] The January 4 meeting was bipartisan, with Sangamon politicians of all political stripe uniting in common cause. Whig Dan Stone was chairman. A committee composed of his fellow Whig John T. Stuart ("Jerry Sly") along with Democrats Peter Cartwright and Stephen Logan (Big Red May's law partner) produced resolutions expressing concern that in the August election, a small minority could decide the issue through a plurality. Instead of the original plan for a statewide convention in February, the courthouse meeting called for an April convention of northerly counties to concentrate the north's efforts on one locale. The meeting also declared the importance of physically linking Lake Michigan with the Illinois River.

Here we see a strategy emerging. First a statewide convention was abandoned as too unreliable for Springfield's benefit. Next, Sangamon's politicians implied their support for an enterprise dear to politicians and businessmen of northern Illinois: a long-discussed huge public works project connecting Lake Michigan with the Illinois River. A Chicago writer had publicly declared: "It would be well enough to remind our neighbors of Sangamon County that Springfield is a candidate for the seat of government of this state, and it would not be amiss to apprize them of the fact that the County of Cook will be enabled to give about six or seven hundred votes at the next election. Now, Mr. Editor, who knows but what we might be induced to go for Springfield if the citizens of that place would show a disposition to aid us in forwarding the commencement of the canal or railroad between this place and the Illinois River."[8] Simultaneously, Sangamon called for northern Illinois counties, which would reap the largest and most immediate benefit from the public works project, to send delegates to an April meeting in Rushville to choose one town for the new seat of government and unite northern support for it.

Clearly Sangamon's hope was to pledge its legislators to act in concert with legislators of all northern counties in order to outvote southern legislators who didn't want to spend public money for the Lake Michigan–Illinois River project. In return for that help from Sangamon, the plan was for politicians of northern counties to unite with Sangamon to get out the vote in favor of whatever town the April convention agreed upon, combining northern voters as a juggernaut instead of splitting their choices ineffectually among several town choices. By linking the state capital question to the Lake Michigan–Illinois River internal improvement, Sangamon County's politicians recast the seat of government issue as northern Illinois interests versus southern Illinois, hoping to have a united north prevail over a fragmented south.

Sangamon County delegates to the April convention in Rushville were selected: John Stuart, Logan, Cartwright, Forquer, Dick Taylor, and Samuel Morris. Four of those individuals were state legislators. A Committee of Correspondence was assigned to crank up the Rushville convention: Simeon "White Bear" Francis, Dan Stone, Forquer, John Stuart, Logan, and C. R. Matheny. Immediate praise came from the *Chicago Democrat* newspaper about the Springfield courthouse meeting's support for the Lake Michigan–Illinois River project, boding well for Sangamon's strategy.[9] Over the next couple months, Sim Francis made liberal use of the *Sangamo Journal*'s columns to promote the Rushville convention,[10] and support for the convention began to build.[11] Thomas Ford's law partner, James Strode, led a Galena meeting supporting both the convention and connection of Lake Michigan to the Illinois River[12]; Knoxville held a similar meeting.[13] Chicago politicians were somewhat leery, favoring the Rushville convention but hesitant to link the public works project to changing the seat of government.[14] Their hesitation probably came from having more at stake in the public works project than other northern counties or Sangamon did, with Chicago politicians fearing that Sangamon couldn't put together a big enough coalition to defeat southern legislators, who might want to hold the public works project hostage to the seat of government issue.

Vandalia's supporters instantly saw the threat to them but could offer nothing to unite the south. A Vandalia newspaper declared, "The manner in which they speak of the growing little town of Alton, certainly comes with very ill grace from such a place as Springfield; and at a time too, when they are themselves endeavoring, by at least every honest means, to remove from this place the seat of government, in order to increase the already towering pride and wealth of the empire county."[15] But such a declaration, even with its veiled accusation that Sangamon's wire-pullers were being dishonest, could scarcely pull Alton's politicians behind Vandalia, as Alton was seeking the seat of government for itself; indeed, Sangamon politicians thought the choices in August's plebiscite were designed to divide the northern vote in order to benefit Alton.[16] So the south remained fragmented while the north began to coalesce into a united front.

In other news from this period:

"We learn from Madison County that a few weeks since a small party of men went into the African settlement in that county, in order to arrest a black by the name of Peter, whose case was decided at the late sitting of our supreme court. The negro made fight, and fired his rifle, which being struck by one of the party at the instant, the ball passed through the roof of the house. A pistol was then fired at the breast of the negro, who fell, but immediately arose, and made his escape. The party being too weak to capture the runaway, left a man by the name of Adams to keep watch, while they went for assistance. During their absence, Adams was set upon by two or three female negresses, who assailed him with an axe and clubs, cutting and mauling him in a shocking manner. The next day or night the examination and search was renewed; the females defended themselves by throwing scalding water upon the whites, by which several were scalded severely. During the fracas, a gun went off at half-cock, as is said, lodging the ball in the groin of one of the females, whose life, it is said, is despaired of. The negroes were subdued, and one or two lodged in jail (females)—they have since been bailed out, as we understand. The negro whose case was decided by the court has, we understand, made his escape.

"The above may not be a very correct account of the affair, but we believe the outlines are correct. So much for free negroes, and the benefits of a 'Colonization Society' in Illinois."

—*Vandalia Illinois Advocate and Register*,
January 18, 1834

"*RUNAWAY NEGRO.* I HAVE confined in the jail of Clinton County, a *Negro man*, supposed to be a runaway. . . . Scars on the back of each shoulder, about the same place, appearance of four shot in the right arm, below the elbow—some scars on the back and legs supposed to be from the whip. . . . The said negro calls his name Stephen Long. . . . The owner, if any, is requested to apply for said Negro."

—Joseph Huey, Sheriff, *Vandalia Illinois Advocate and State Register*, September 3, 1834

"Notice. There was committed to Jail a Runaway Negro man . . . who says . . . that his name is Henry Mead."

—John Harris, Sheriff, Macoupin County, Illinois,
Vandalia Illinois Advocate and State Register,
September 3, 1834

"*BROKE JAIL.* ESCAPED from the jail of Macoupin County, state
of Illinois, on the 9th of September, 1834, a runaway negro man. . . .
He calls his name Henry Mead."

—*Vandalia Illinois Advocate and State Register,*
September 17, 1834

+≻═ ═≺+

At the end of February, Abe Lincoln prepared a petition to the Sangamon County
commissioners, asking them to appoint persons to plan out a road starting at
Musick's Ferry, on a tributary of the Sangamon River known as Salt Creek. The
road would pass through New Salem and head toward the county line in the
direction of Jacksonville. Lincoln and eighty-seven others ostensibly signed the
petition. I say "ostensibly" because the final dozen signatures were all in Lincoln's handwriting.[17] Normally such petitions would simply ask that the best
route be determined; this document was unusual in that it specified that the route
had to be through New Salem. An older, more circuitous road connected Jacksonville to Sangamo Town, where Abe had helped build the flatboat he took to
New Orleans. The new route's directness would divert traffic from the old road
and from Sangamo Town.[18] The proposed road certainly had political implications for Lincoln, demonstrating that he wanted to boost the economy of New
Salem at the expense of Sangamo Town. The road would also help Petersburg, a
settlement along the Sangamon River a few miles from New Salem, a settlement
being promoted by real estate developers for whom Lincoln would later do survey work.[19]

On March 1, "a respectable meeting of the citizens of New Salem"[20] convened to nominate a candidate for governor. The custom was for such meetings to
endorse candidates for various offices, who would eventually announce whether
they would yield to public clamor and run for office. Such meetings might be
called for a precinct or an entire county. Anyone could participate by showing up,
though proceedings tended to be orchestrated by meeting organizers. Party con-
ventions were just starting to make a tentative appearance in Illinois, and voters
still zealously engaged in the right to decide not only who would be elected, but
also who would run. Such meetings were always described as "respectable," an
adjective applying both to decorum and the number of participants. A skeptic
once asked how many had to attend a meeting to make it respectable but received
no answer.[21] Someone might run for a local office without endorsement of such
meetings and have excellent prospects of getting elected, but the higher the
office, the more important were calls from such gatherings.

Bowling Green acted as chairman of the New Salem meeting and appointed
Abe Lincoln as secretary. According to Lincoln's record of proceedings, John
Allen, a town physician; Nelson Alley, Lincoln's business associate; and Sam
Hill, Lincoln's business competitor quickly formed a committee to write resolu-
tions. After a few minutes, they submitted resolutions, adopted unanimously. Via

that action, the meeting said Illinois needed a governor "free from and above party and sectarian influence"; a governor willing to enforce laws and promote development of Illinois resources was crucial; and Gen. James Dougherty Henry was the man.[22]

The meeting thereby proclaimed that ministers and Democratic wheelhorses need not apply. Opposition to Democrats was one thing, but public declaration of hostility toward politically active ministers was bound to draw attention and was the sort of thing that could easily be twisted to become alleged evidence of hostility toward religion. We may infer from newspaper commentary[23] that the meeting had a particular Democrat and a particular minister in mind for disapproval: Democrat Joseph Duncan and Rev. William C. Kinney.

U.S. Rep. Joseph Duncan's heroic physical frame was a political asset in the West, reinforced by brown eyes described as "piercing," dark curly hair, and a smooth-shaven face.[24] He had arrived in Illinois from Kentucky about fifteen years earlier, "in easy, gentlemanly circumstances," his brother-in-law William Linn said.[25] A later observer said of Duncan: "His house is the rendezvous of all friendly and social circles of his numerous friends and acquaintances. His fund of anecdote and happy temper is the delight of every party."[26] Duncan established a farm and mills that increased his wealth. Fire destroyed his mills. Nothing is said about the cause, but notices like these appeared in Illinois newspapers:

> "The sawmill, on Indian Creek, Morgan County, belonging to [Whig activist] Francis Arenz, Esq. was consumed by fire on the night of the 31st of December—the work of an incendiary. Mr. Arenz offers 200 dollars reward to anyone who may find out the villain or villains, and adduce such proof as to have him or them convicted."
>
> —*Vandalia Illinois Advocate and State Register*,
> January 25, 1834

> "The steam grist and sawmill of J. H. Randle & Co. of Edwardsville, together with a large quantity of grain and flour, was burnt on the morning of the 16th inst. supposed to be the work of an incendiary. Loss estimated at 5,000 dollars."
>
> —*Illinois Adv.*, clipped in *Chicago Democrat*,
> May 14, 1834

> "The dwelling house of James Pierce, Esq. (the halfway house between this and St. Louis) was burnt down on Saturday night last, together with a large proportion of his household and other furniture. It is believed to have been the work of an incendiary."
>
> —*Vandalia Illinois Advocate and State Register*,
> November 19, 1834

Whatever their cause, the fires left Duncan in substantial debt, but he rebuilt the mills and clawed his way back to prosperity. Soon after rebuilding, he won election to the state legislature, and two years later, he was elected to the U.S. Congress, a position to which he was reelected again and again and that he still held when he was running for governor.

During his congressional years, he became a real estate operator with holdings across the state. About the time of Lincoln's Henry-for-Governor meeting in New Salem, another Sangamon County meeting promoting General Henry declared, "We believe Gen. Duncan has had his mind more occupied with his own pecuniary interests, since his election to Congress, than the interests of his constituents."[27] He was considered the wealthiest man of Illinois.[28] For weeks, Illinois Whig newspapers had been defending Duncan against charges of financial corruption,[29] a rather unusual stance for Whig papers to take in coverage of a Democratic officeholder, but as we shall shortly see, there was good reason for those newspapers' friendliness.

In Congress, Duncan spoke of his attachment to Jackson and Democrats, but his actions tended to promote Whig policies of Harry of the West, U.S. Senator Henry Clay. Private evidence of Duncan's friendliness to Whiggery is presented by his extensive correspondence with John J. Hardin, a Whig leader of Morgan County, Illinois, who would eventually become the state's most prominent Whig. Admittedly the two men had personal reasons to stay in touch—both were Kentucky aristocrats, Hardin's widowed mother was married to Harry of the West's brother, and Harry had advised Duncan's wealthy wife to marry Duncan[30]—but I'm sure the basis of cordiality was more than personal.

The clash between Duncan's Democratic rhetoric and Whig reality confused Illinois voters. Some were beginning to wonder what was going on. In February 1834, one Democratic newspaper reported his voting "against the friends of General Jackson."[31] A month later, another said Duncan had "failed to sustain the administration of Jackson."[32] Earlier, the state's preeminent Whig paper, the *Sangamo Journal*, editorialized approval of Duncan's stance on the "Bank of the U. States, the Tariff of Protection, and the system of Internal Improvements." In all these, Duncan had supported Harry of the West instead of Jackson. "In respect to these great measures," the *Journal* said, "he has been steadfast [in support for Whig positions]. But like many other men of the day, while he has opposed the principal measures of Gen. Jackson's administration, he is still a Jackson man."[33] Duncan worked against Jackson but still supported him? Nonetheless, despite growing doubts about Duncan among Illinois Democrats, he said he was one of them, so they gave him substantial backing in the governorship election. As things turned out, in the gubernatorial election, Duncan would also receive heavy support from Whigs.

Duncan's plans for gubernatorial candidacy caused a stir in Washington, where Jackson Administration officials had a much better understanding of Duncan's political orientation than Illinois voters did. Duncan later said that the administration dispatched agents to Illinois to work against him, though the Jackson regime drew back after he complained.[34]

A Sangamon County handbill attempted to hurt Duncan with the statewide nonpartisan issue about moving the state capital:

> If Gen. Duncan is elected the whole north will be divided and distracted; Springfield will lose all possible chance of becoming the seat of government. . . . He is for Jacksonville and he dare not desert it. His own personal [real estate] interests, to the probable amount of fifty thousand dollars, would secure his support to that place. . . . If Duncan is elected the hopes of Springfield will be destroyed. . . . Let us then as citizens of Sangamon, give our votes in such a manner as to promote our own interests. Let us think it more important to secure the seat of government than to elect any man; and let us give our votes to the man, most likely to advance our own interests, by the defeat of Duncan.

The handbill, however, was unclear about who that man should be.[35] And although the handbill implied Duncan had staked his personal fortune on moving the capital to Jacksonville, in 1834 Duncan and two other men were investing in a projected townsite called Illiopolis, supposedly at the geographic center of the state, one of the plebiscite choices for a new capital, an investment worth nothing unless the seat of government moved there. Duncan's two Illiopolis associates were land speculator and Springfield U.S. Land Office Receiver John Taylor (Dick Taylor's father-in-law) and Springfield merchant Eli Blankenship, to whom Lincoln had become indebted through transfers of Berry & Lincoln store obligations.[36] Taylor and Blankenship, however, were in a distinct minority on this question among Springfield's political and business elite.

Soon after Duncan's candidacy announcement, one of the state's strongest and most prominent supporters of Jackson, the Rev. William C. Kinney, was brought forward to compete. A contemporary evaluation of this "Great Political Horse Race" named Kinney as the steed *Preacher,*

> a horse of considerable strength, long winded, and just fast enough to lose money on. . . . His temper is so extremely uncontrollable, that it requires a *committee* of grooms to govern him. . . . On his left hind foot, will be found a considerable tumor, which occasions a perceptible lameness, incurred in a rencounter at Edwardsville with a certain bank. He was rendered weak in the back by opposing the Canal, and whickered out that "the blue-bellies" would take the state,—and his hamstrings were much cut by Jackson, when the President told him he was a preacher and had a higher office than he [Jackson] could bestow on him.

Preacher has suffered from "too free use of the *Kane*. . . . His neigh is not of that lively and sonorous character which once reverberated through the beech woods of Illinois."[37]

More knowledge of Kinney might enhance appreciation of that satire's zing and succinctness. Before Illinois became a state, Kinney had achieved business prosperity there, operating both a farm and store. Said one chronicler, "He bought and sold anything offered or demanded, from whiskey, pigs and chickens, to negro slaves and farms, and amassed a large and valuable estate."[38] Poor education didn't prevent Kinney from becoming a wealthy merchant, but he remained illiterate until he married. Even after his wife taught him to read and write, Kinney felt uncertain enough of those skills that he depended on others to prepare written versions of his speeches for him.[39] His wife's father, Elias Kent Kane, was an indentured slave-owning[40] U.S. Senator from Illinois while Kinney was lieutenant governor in the 1820s and while Kinney was running for governor in 1834.

Soon after Abe Lincoln was born, Kinney became a licensed Baptist minister while continuing his business activities. George Forquer's half-brother Thomas Ford recalled: "Mr. Kinney was one of the old sort of Baptist preachers; his morality was not of that pinched up kind. . . . It was said that he went forth electioneering with a Bible in one pocket and a bottle of whiskey in the other; and thus armed with 'the sword of the Lord and the spirit,' he could preach to one set of men and drink with another, and thus make himself agreeable to all."[41] Not quite to all. When he ran for governor in 1830 a critic asked:

> [Could] a preacher . . . be found so callous in his feelings, and lost to every sense of moral obligation as to prefer the transient glory of men to the more exalted and honorable pursuit of expounding the sacred mysteries of the Scriptures. . . . A preacher who could forego the soul-cheering and pious gratification of redeeming one wayward soul from ruin's brink, or of turning one from the error of his way, for the ephemeral pageantry and vain pomp of official dignity in a human government, and neglect the more important duties of the ministry; to spend his time, his talents, and his money, in the groveling pursuit of temporary triumph or political victory, is wholly unworthy the people's confidence. A hypocrite in religion, a demagogue in politics . . . William Kinney, a political, farming, mercantile, stock-jobbing preacher.[42]

Future lieutenant governor Gustave Koerner, who was a German immigrant, remembered the portly Kinney as "hospitable to a fault, almost, he was fond of good living, of fine horses and of good company. He soon associated with the Germans, and became remarkably fond of Rhine wine, perhaps too much so."[43] Indeed, a correspondent told Koerner, "Our friend Gov. Kinney is very unwell. Drink will kill him."[44] Koerner called Kinney "a bright man, a very fine and witty conversationalist."[45] John Reynolds, the Old Ranger, referred to Reverend Kinney's "inexhaustible store of pithy and pointed anecdotes, which he used to effect, on many occasions." Reynolds, who knew something about successful electioneering, recognized Kinney as "one of the most efficient canvassers with the people."[46] Koerner reported, however, that despite the preacher's conviviality, Kinney had "frequent fits of despondency" and "was inclined to look generally on the dark side of things."[47]

Soon after achieving political fame through his prominence in the unsuccessful attempt to convert Illinois into a slave state in the 1820s, Kinney was elected lieutenant governor and served from 1826 to 1830, which service earned him the lifelong honorary title "Governor." Gov. Ninian Edwards, one of the state's largest owners of indentured slaves,[48] charged that while Kinney was president of the state bank's Edwardsville branch, the reverend used that position to swing a loan for establishing a proslavery newspaper during the free state-slave state controversy. The loan was on insufficient collateral; when the sum wasn't repaid, the state government wound up not only as the proslavery newspaper's financier, but also as an important donor to the slavery campaign.[49] Some might call the transaction incompetent; some might call it corrupt. Kinney's stance on slavery wasn't forgotten. When he ran for governor in 1834, someone noted that he was "opposed by the old [anti-Democrat] Federal Party [an epithet for Whigs] in this state, as well as by many who cry PREACHER. . . . Mr. Kinney is also opposed by another class of citizens, who are known in this state as the almost exclusive enemies of *negro slavery*, and who, from daily practice, know the extent of its evils."[50] Long after the election, an indignant Kinney finally sputtered:

> As to the charge, if such a one there be against me, relative to my conduct as a director, or my transactions in any manner in the state bank, or any other public institution whatever, I pronounce the author a bare calumniator and liar, and that such men are unworthy of my notice, or any other man who has a standing knee-high to a mouse, and I now say at once for always, let anyone and everyone say what they please relative to my religious principles or sentiments, or that I am Jackson, Van Buren, or the Devil in politics; yet I challenge the world, after a residence of forty-two years in this country, to say that I have ever stooped to any low and dishonorable act to gain a pecuniary advantage over any man, or institution whatever.[51]

But no one seemed to be saying that Kinney personally profited from the sweet bank loan financing the proslavery newspaper; here he denied what no one had alleged.

Thomas Ford noted, "Mr. Kinney had the name of being a whole hog, thorough-going original Jackson man."[52] John Reynolds called him "simon-pure of the Jackson party."[53] Another observer described Kinney as "Jackson up to the hub."[54] A respectable meeting in Belleville endorsed Kinney for governor this way: "Permit us to urge on the voters of Illinois this one fact, and rest upon it as the sheet anchor of our hopes in the approaching canvass:—it is this ☞ *in his whole political life he has been found upon the side of the democracy of the American people*—and his views and sentiments energetically opposed to ARISTOCRACY."[55]

In 1830, he ran for governor unsuccessfully against the Old Ranger, John Reynolds, who later characterized Kinney as "candidate of the furious *ultra* Jackson party, that would govern the state with a rod of iron, as to party rage and proscription. Proscription for opinion's sake had just commenced, and was only popular with the extreme *ultra* politicians."[56] Up to now, federal officeholders who opposed a new President's policies had been suffered to remain in office, but Jackson saw the inutility of depending on men who opposed him and started replacing them with men who supported his policies. Such a management principle has enough common sense as to be unremarkable now, but when Jackson implemented the practice, it was an innovation and was loudly condemned by his opponents as violating federal officials' freedom of conscience and as a step toward dictatorship. Indeed, Reynolds's disapproval revealed that his own support for Jackson was lukewarm. When someone asked, "Does Mr. Kinney consider the turning of a man out of office, because he did not vote with the majority, *reform*?" a defender of the minister replied, "He understands that to be the meaning of the *people* when they turned Adams, Clay, & Co. out of office, and presumes Gen. Jackson is just finishing the work they began."[57]

Kinney supported Jackson so strongly that he traveled to Washington in 1829 to attend the general's inauguration. Reportedly the preacher sought a patronage appointment from the President, who allegedly responded that the pulpit already provided Kinney with a higher position than Jackson could ever give. If that scene occurred—and Kinney denied that it did—it failed to dim his enthusiasm for the Jackson Administration.[58] Reynolds recalled that Kinney "had considerable agency at the federal city [Washington, D.C.], in the proscription visited on the Whigs of Illinois. It was said he remarked, that the Whigs should be whipped out of office 'like dogs out of a meat house.'"[59] Under the pseudonym "Fayette, Junior," one of Kinney's defenders, perhaps the minister himself, explained the "meat house" remark: "If you mean such men as circulated coffin handbills [in the 1828 election campaign, portraying Jackson as having unjustly executed six militiamen in 1815], slandered Gen. Jackson, and his now deceased wife, or who used the patronage of the government to control elections, or public defaulters— we say if he did give such advice, he performed but an act of duty."[60]

In addition to political partisanship that was a little too advanced for Illinois voters when he ran for governor, Reverend Kinney was just as partisan in sectarian matters. Old Ranger Reynolds noted, "He was represented to have said that the Methodists were like the blacksmith's dogs, being used to the sparks of fire in the smith shop, they could stand the brimstone fire below."[61] Such remarks didn't go down well with Methodist preacher Peter Cartwright and his contingent. They also didn't go down well among skeptics of religion and defenders of separation between church and state, as illustrated by this letter to the editor from "Miner" in the July 24, 1830, *Galena Miners' Journal*:

> Mr. Candor says, "that the Holy Writ tells us that he who does not provide for his household is worse than an infidel." Now, sir, if that text of Scripture is intended to prove that after the unity of church and state, the ministers of the sacred gospels are authorized and *required* to hunt out, search for, through storms and slander, for offices, whether executive or ministerial, in order to provide "for his household," then indeed will our churches be closed, our sanctuaries of justice disregarded and condemned, and the tocsin will be sounded for that priest, who with his altars and his gods blended, can muster the greatest force of enthusiasts and carry their point by delusion and by storm.

When Kinney ran for governor in 1834, a critic shouted:

> Your final Judge will require of you a faithful account of your stewardship here, before that tribunal no empty plea will avail. Consider then your awful responsibility, your duty to your country, and as you have to escape condemnation yourselves, let this Preacher Candidate [Kinney] know that he cannot, nay he shall not get into an office for which he is wholly unfit and incompetent.
>
> Then let us all, with steady step, and eye unmoved, approach the polls . . . and by the decisive and potent voice of our free suffrages, proclaim *down with the Preacher Candidate, his understrappers, and machines.* Long live liberty—Long live our free institutions—Long live our Constitution.[62]

Article 6, section 3, of the Constitution was taken seriously: "No religious test shall ever be required as a qualification to any office or public trust under the United States." The Illinois constitution had the same sort of provision. Reverend Kinney's religious conduct became a hot enough issue that he finally addressed it shortly before election day: "The apprehended evil of a union of church and state, by admitting preachers into civil office, can have no application to my particular case. . . . There is not a republican among us more zealously opposed to church and state principles than myself."[63] Read a second time, Kinney's explanation becomes a little obscure (his friend Koerner called him "a very poor writer"[64]), but his tone seems to be defensive of secular government, and that stance is confirmed later when allies of Peter Cartwright attack him.

Kinney already had a run-in with Cartwright's contingent and others in the 1830 governorship race. An eyewitness reported what happened when Kinney made a speech in Springfield:

A few of the partisans of Judge Reynolds [the Old Ranger] treated him in a manner the most shameful that was ever witnessed in an enlightened society. It is due, however, to our citizens, to say that the greatest species of indignity offered to Gov. Kinney, was from a Mr. William S. Hamilton, who is not an inhabitant of this state, and who, after having abused Gov. Kinney in a public speech, had the effrontery to call him a damned liar. The Rev. Peter Cartwright, grown bold from the calm and dignified manner in which Gov. Kinney deported himself, attacked him in a very violent and abusive manner; but his attack reminded me of the boy, who, having caught a buffalo calf in the prairie, found it a very difficult matter to effect a safe retreat. Mr. Cartwright fared rather worse than the boy—having been twice proved and convicted of lying. The redoubtable George Forquer repaired to the ground, armed with a large horseman's pistol belted around him. . . . I have no doubt but that the plan of attack was arranged beforehand.[65]

Forquer and his half-brother Thomas Ford had been writing campaign material for Reynolds.[66] Another commentator noted, "It seems that when Mr. Kinney made his speech at Springfield, George Forquer appeared on the ground, belted to a large horseman's pistol! What an '*impulsive* man!' Has he no friends to take care of him? If that terrible pistol had gone off, it might have kicked him over, and perhaps have scared him out of his wits."[67]

Still more controversy swirled around Kinney regarding his attitude toward the Illinois & Michigan Canal, intended to link Lake Michigan with the Illinois River, thereby providing an uninterrupted inland water route from New York State to New Orleans. In addition to economic impact, the project had geopolitical significance. Without the Canal, commerce using the Mississippi River would encourage Illinois to have its primary loyalties to the West and South. A canal linking Illinois commerce to the Great Lakes, however, would counterbalance those loyalties and give the state a balancing allegiance to the East, supplementing linkage that the Ohio River already encouraged via Philadelphia and Baltimore commerce. Thereby the Canal would reduce Western and Southern sectional proclivities of Illinois and promote instead a broader national loyalty.[68] This Illinois & Michigan Canal was the internal improvement project that Sangamo politicians were using as bait to get votes for Springfield in the August seat-of-government plebiscite.

In addition to obvious potential economic benefit to the nation, the Canal offered potential local economic benefit for Illinois real estate promoters, depending on its exact route and terminal points. The prospect had much to do with boom times being experienced in Chicago. And, oh yes, there were the hopes articulated by William Elliott, candidate for state representative from the Knox County area, the sort of hopes nurtured elsewhere by busted New Salem merchants Denton Offutt and Vincent Bogue: "The farmer will then have something to labor for: and for one bushel of grain now grown, five hundred will be produced: money instead of being as now scarce, will be abundant and the merchant receiving his pay in that article, and getting his goods by a cheap method of transportation, would realize more profit and still be able to sell to the consumers fifty percent cheaper than at present. These are truths, that cannot be controverted."[69] Strong public support existed for the project, although southern Illinois river counties were hostile, fearing the Canal would cut their river transport business. Still, hesitations mainly related to who would pay for construction and who would benefit most from completion.

Although he was on record as favoring the Canal,[70] in one of Kinney's indiscreet moments he reportedly portrayed it as a type of flood hazard, threatening to flood Illinois with blue-bellied Yankees, a sentiment linked by some to his resentment about the failure to convert Illinois into a slave state.[71] Unfavorable reaction to that report became strong enough that Kinney finally denied the "stale and nonsensical charge of being inimical to the immigration to our state of the valuable and industrious population of New England, whom I have been made to designate as 'blue-bellied Yankees,' [which] I pronounced to be a gross misstatement or perversion of fact. It may be true that I have made use of the words 'blue *light* Yankees.'"[72]

Such a denial reopened lingering hard feelings in Illinois about the War of 1812, in which British-allied Indians threatened settlers, memories rekindled in the recent Black Hawk War struggle against the British Band. For decades, Democrats railed against Blue Light Federalists of New England, who opposed the war and allegedly used blue lights for sending secret signals to help British military operations, as reported in the April 16, 1814, *Vincennes Western Sun*:

> Blue lights again. On Thursday the 10th instant at New London, the weather being thick and snowy, and favorable for the departure of our squadron, Com. Decatur called all hands on board, it is thought with an intention of putting to sea. Blue lights were immediately put up at Long Point, and distinctly seen from Fort Trumbull, and signal guns were discharged at intervals from the enemy's squadron. The lights were seen at intervals throughout the whole night, and the intentions of the commodore are thus again completely frustrated.

Illinois Democrats published a speech by Jackson adviser Felix Grundy, who asked:

> Where are those men who, during the last war, discouraged the enlistment of soldiers? Where are those who used their influence to prevent loans of money to the government in its utmost need? Where are all the moral traitors of that gloomy period? Where are those who

thought it immoral and irreligious to rejoice at our victories and mourned at the defeat of our enemy? Where are those who denominated James Madison as a tyrant, usurper and despot; and proclaimed that the country would never prosper until he was sent to Elba? Where are the "blue light" gentry, who gave private signals to the enemy to enable them to murder our citizens? These men are not found in the ranks of [Jackson's] Administration; they will pursue the present Chief Magistrate with their hatred to his grave, and when dead their enmity will not cease.[73]

That kind of rhetoric fired up Illinois Democrats, but the problem with Kinney making the War of 1812 a campaign issue was that his own record in that war was controversial. Kinney hadn't served in the military during that war, "a small matter," John Reynolds acknowledged, "yet it had an effect in the election."[74] A larger political problem came from accusations that Kinney was a war profiteer, skinning volunteers who bought needed supplies from him. Reverend Kinney responded by saying a now-deceased veteran had urged him to run for governor and produced a statement from one veteran saying that Kinney had been fair when selling supplies to soldiers.[75]

A Sangamon County meeting favoring General Henry for governor dismissed Robert K. McLaughlin's candidacy by saying, "We are not aware of his having anything to recommend him to the confidence of the people, independent of having served them in the capacity of state treasurer without proving a defaulter."[76] Actually, that was no mean recommendation, given the frequency with which newspapers of that era announced that public moneys had disappeared while under custody of various officials. McLaughlin's accomplishment along that line was commented about at the time: "As former treasurer of the state, he is able to prove his *honesty*, which is *nine points* in an election."[77] A satirical evaluation likening gubernatorial candidates to racehorses had an uncomplimentary evaluation of McLaughlin, who, in addition to having controlled the state's purse, was Joseph Duncan's uncle:

[*Uncle Pursey*] is a fine fat-looking old stud, but rather clumsily limbed for the turf . . . , and it is thought will be run bare-backed, as his life has been one of ease and retirement, and no galls or saddle marks perceptible. His wind is quite short . . . ; it is quite evident that he never was intended for the turf, and would never have been entered but for some accidental circumstance. . . . He has been eating nothing but *parched* corn and sucking eggs for four months. . . . He is greedy for *corn* in any sense and at all times.[78]

The last sentence may have alluded to hard drinking. Besides being a relative of Joseph Duncan's, McLaughlin had another family connection to Illinois politics, being married to a niece of the state's first governor, Shadrach Bond. Bond was a genial duelist, a six-footer, dark in eye, hair, and complexion. He had one of the larger holdings of indentured slave servants in the state.[79] In the 1820s, Bond helped lead the effort to convert Illinois into a slave state. With the failure of that scheme, he pretty much disappeared from public notice.

> Miss Emily Catharine Bond, the eldest daughter, of Governor Bond, aged 14 years, 9 months and 19 days . . . retired to bed on Monday evening at the usual hour, with every appearance of health. On the following morning, about daybreak, her father, hearing a groan, hastened to her apartment, and found her speechless, insensible, and nearly lifeless. She expired in about forty minutes. The cause of her death is unknown; its suddenness fills society with awe.[80]

Like Bond, McLaughlin owned indentured slaves.[81] Pioneer Christiana Tillson wrote:

> Caleb and Lucy were the indentured slaves of Robert McLaughlin. . . .
> Your father came home from Vandalia at one time and told me that Mr. McLaughlin asked him to buy out their indentures; said that Lucy was valuable to them, but Caleb was getting old, and quarreled with the other negroes, and unless he could find someone to take them he had made up his mind to send them to New Orleans and sell them. Caleb was sixty years of age and Lucy thirty, and they had about twenty-five years to serve.

Caleb and Lucy ran away from McLaughlin, seeking shelter at the Tillson household. "As there was a penalty attached to those who harbored runaway slaves, your father wrote immediately to Mr. McLaughlin, informing him of our morning surprise and asking him what to do with them." McLaughlin journeyed to the Tillson residence, where, it was reported:

> [He said he] had made up his mind that if your father would give him five hundred dollars for the time Lucy was to serve, thirty years, and fifty feet of plank from his mill for Caleb's indentures, which were not for as long a time as Lucy's, he would give him a quit-claim to their future services. If not, he should take them to New Orleans, where he could get a higher price, but, professing a kind sympathy for their welfare, would prefer to make the sacrifice. . . . Your father's wish was to retain them, and as my kitchen labors were to be abated, and feeling, too, as he did, that I could not think of having them sent off to the slave pens of New Orleans, we both concluded to keep them. Work was made lighter, but conscience not quite easy.[82]

238 • THE EARLY YEARS

Lincoln and many other Illinois residents credited James Henry as the architect of victory against Black Hawk.[83] In choosing a war hero general without partisan background as a candidate for chief executive, Lincoln and his associates were following a strategy that Whigs would later use repeatedly on a national scale, nominating Generals Harrison, Taylor, and Scott for President. General Henry also was the Sangamon County sheriff, so he could be assured of substantial support from one of the state's most populous counties—an excellent voter base to build on. His candidacy would promote the fortunes of Sangamon County politicos who took passage on his ship. Although initial support was coming from his old home county of Madison and his current one of Sangamon, this was no favorite-son candidacy designed to preserve options while other candidates sorted out their strengths.

Another Sangamon County meeting besides the New Salem one had already brought out Henry, and the *Alton Spectator* declared back in February: "He has executed the trusts reposed in him with ability and zeal. It will be long before the people of this state forget his valuable services in the field during the late Indian disturbances; or cease to ascribe to him the principal credit of the happy termination of that protracted war."[84] A meeting down in Madison County described him as "neither a lawyer, a physician, nor a clergyman. He is emphatically a workingman—a mechanic. This is a sufficient warrant for the belief that he will continue a firm friend to the industrious and laboring classes."[85] A Sangamon County meeting issued an "Address to the People of Illinois," noting that "after having served four years [as sheriff], he was almost unanimously reelected over his opponent (who would probably have beaten any other man in the county). Only losing about eighty votes out of upwards of two thousand."[86] That kind of vote ratio was likely to impress professional politicians unmoved by friendship for the workingman.

One of the four authors of the glowing address to the people was Dr. Anson G. Henry,[87] who was promoting General Henry's candidacy around Sangamo Town.[88] Physician Henry at one time ran his practice from General Henry's Springfield office,[89] a measure of their close association. Lincoln's association with Dr. Anson Henry would become even closer than the general's. Another of the four authors was Sangamon County Coroner James Shepherd, who was running for state legislature—exemplifying an office seeker who saw strength through association with General Henry.[90] State senator George Forquer's half-brother Thomas Ford, who was shifting his allegiance to the Democrats and would one day be elected governor, figured that in the August election, Henry would win with more than twenty thousand votes,[91] a majority so crushing that opponents hardly needed to bother campaigning.

General Henry's birth date was obscure.[92] After a childhood spent in poverty, Henry became a shoemaker in Edwardsville. An acquaintance named Joseph Gillespie remembered, "He felt that he possessed the highest qualities of manhood and greatness, and yet was doomed, by the accident of birth, to ignominy."[93] The "accident" was illegitimacy. "The paternity of General Henry was not known to many besides himself," said Gov. John Reynolds, who knew Henry well. "It was, no doubt, this subject that his sensitive soul could neither *forget or forgive.* . . . His father called to see him at Edwardsville; but his son refused to see the father."[94] Gillespie noted: "He was extremely unhappy, and yet he was extremely ambitious. He knew that he was greatly admired; still, he would never go into society. He found himself, at maturity, illiterate, and he . . . became almost frantic at the thought of his deficiency in this respect. . . . Attended a 'night-school'. . . . I attended along with him. He was the most earnest student I ever knew. He would beg me to come to his shop and read to him, while he was at work, which I often did. . . . He was a thorough fatalist."[95] John Reynolds described him thus:

> Large, six feet high, proportionably formed, and possessed a manly and dignified bearing. He was exceedingly modest and retiring, until his passions were aroused, and then he showed an intensity of feeling, and an iron will, which was irresistible so far as he had the power to act. In company he was generally taciturn, and mostly appeared to disregard the charms of society, but seemed to be moody and melancholy. . . . At long intervals he indulged in frolics [drunken binges]; and then, if his anger was excited, he was reckless and desperate. He knew and cared as little of danger and death as a marble statue. . . . It appeared that he cared not much for life, but all for honor.[96]

Henry became more and more attracted to military endeavor. Gillespie noted, "He studied everything pertaining to military life with the most intense application and idolized Alexander the Great, Hannibal, Caesar and Napoleon."[97] In Edwardsville, Henry formed and drilled a company. About 1826, he moved to Springfield and became a merchant. He interrupted his mercantile pursuit twice to fight wars against Indians, but each time the Indians backed off before he had a chance to prove his military ability, luck that he cursed. Finally, in the Black Hawk War, he demonstrated what he could do, to the rejoicing of Illinois and the consternation of superiors whose orders he repeatedly violated.

Upon his return home, Springfield put on that era's equivalent to a tickertape parade and television interviews. A newspaper poem declared in part:

> At length a warrior rose,
> Like lightning on our foe,
> Who sought the savage in his den—
> . . . .
> Brave Henry, foremost in the fight,
> To him we owe the meed of might.
> The Bard his deeds should tell,
> And proud our Sangamo should be
> That boasts a warrior such as he![98]

Miller's Hotel hosted a ball honoring not only the returned Henry, but, in a classy touch, all the men he had commanded as well. A happy crowd carried on pleasantly.[99] John Reynolds noted an oddity, however: "He possessed a diffidence, or extreme sensibility, that prevented him from ever appearing in the society of ladies. At the close of the Black Hawk war, the citizens of Springfield, his residence, gave him a splendid party, in honor of his services in that war; and at it, he never once appeared in the apartments where the ladies presided."[100] During the war, he had exhibited no such reticence at the whorehouses of Galena, but those residents didn't possess the social status of "lady."

Said Gillespie: "He was as ambitious in his aspirations as Lucifer; and as humble in his pretensions as Lazarus. He was wonderfully reticent as to what he was, but extremely communicative as to what he would like to be."[101]

Two days after New Salem's Henry for Governor event, the Sangamon County commissioners gave Lincoln a contract to survey the new road from Musick's Ferry through New Salem and toward Jacksonville, called for in the petition he had prepared a few days earlier. As both Whig politician and deputy county surveyor, he would have been well known to the commissioners by now. One helper on the survey crew was Hugh Armstrong, Jack's brother, who had served in Captain Lincoln's Black Hawk War company. Another helper was Jack Kelso, who somewhat mystified townsmen. "Uncle" Jimmy Short called him "very lazy,"[102] a description that some had also applied to Abe and perhaps had the same origin: Kelso read a lot. Billy Herndon called Kelso an educated man, "deeply and thoroughly read in Burns and Shakespeare."[103] Abner Ellis recalled: "When other people got drunk at New Salem, it was the usual custom to tussle and fight . . . but when Kelso got drunk he astonished the rustic community with copious quotations from Robert Burns and William Shakespeare."[104] According to Hardin Bale, "Kelso and Lincoln were great friends."[105] Jimmy Short remarked, "Kelso was a great fisherman."[106] Royal Clary noted, "He could catch fish when no man could get a bite."[107] "Abe loved Shakespeare but not fishing," Caleb Carman said. "Still, Kelso would draw Abe. They used to sit on the bank of the river and quote Shakespeare, criticize one another."[108] A local historian wrote, "Jack would fill his basket with black perch, weighing from two to six pounds, and then with twenty-five pounds of fine fish would walk down to Petersburg and sell them." The same authority said, "Jack Kelso was a boss hunter and not only supplied his own family, but always kept venison hams for sale," and "in the fall he would find enough bee trees to furnish him with honey." More could be said of him, but I am content with how the local historian summed up Kelso's situation: "He always lived well and was a happy man."[109] Although Kelso didn't pursue a particular trade, his presence on Lincoln's survey crew demonstrates that he was willing to take on hard physical labor.

For five days, the crew hacked through a couple dozen miles to establish the Musick's Ferry road route. The selected route ran by Clary's Grove and the farm of Russell Godbey, the fellow from whom Denton Offutt had bought the hogs whose eyes they sewed shut to load them on the flatboat bound for New Orleans.

Godbey was also the one from whom Abe had gotten the buckskin used to fox onto his pants after they were damaged while surveying Godbey's property. The road also went by section 16, land owned by the county that Abe would survey for sale.[110] A road raised the dollar value of any nearby property. About the same time he was surveying the Musick's Ferry road, Abe also surveyed the Jesse Gum farm near the route.[111]

On April 5, 1834, a standard respectable meeting of citizens convened at the Richland School House, in Peter Cartwright country a few miles southwest of New Salem, declaring, "We wish to put down party spirit, and elect men on their merits—Farmers would prefer being the bone and sinew of our country." The meeting's candidate endorsements spanned a mix of party affiliation: Peter Cartwright, John Dawson, Job Fletcher, and Samuel Morris for state representatives; William F. Elkin for state senator; Big Red May for Congress; and General Henry for governor.[112]

On the very day of that meeting, however, the *Sangamo Journal* announced General Henry's death at about thirty-five years old. For some time, he had been suffering from consumption, ascribed to hardships in the war. He died in New Orleans, where he had gone in hopes of recovering his health. Springfield memorial services were handled by politicos of a distinctly anti-Jackson hue, such as Simeon "White Bear" Francis, Thomas M. Neale, Dan Stone, John Williams, and Garret Elkin. Elkin would be elected to fill the now-vacant office of sheriff. Over in Jacksonville, memorial observances were run by John J. Hardin.[113] Regrets among Henry's admirers were unquestionably sincere and had to have included consternation at the foiling of the closest thing politics has to a guaranteed election victory. Henry's demise dealt a blow to anti-Jackson politicians such as Lincoln.

Two days after Henry's death was announced in early April, Lincoln found himself being sued by John Stuart's law partner, Henry Dummer, on behalf of Peter Van Bergen.[114] Dummer, who trained at Bowdoin and Harvard, had come to Sangamon County from Cincinnati a couple years earlier on the *Talisman*.[115] This lawsuit developed from the $379 promissory note owed to Reuben Radford by Lincoln, William Berry, and Slicky Bill Greene. At some point after the note had been renewed back in October and made payable on demand, Van Bergen had acquired it. Circumstances of the transfer are unclear. Perhaps Radford gave the note in payment of a debt he owed Van Bergen; perhaps the note was security for a loan that Radford couldn't pay; or perhaps Radford simply sold it outright. In the third scenario, Van Bergen's acquisition of the Lincoln-Berry-Greene note from Radford wasn't necessarily a purchase of that individual note. Like many merchants, Radford may well have had a stack of old and slow notes that had remained uncollected so long that he was willing to sell them in bulk and at a discount to someone who made a living by collecting debts. Reality seems to have been a combination of those possibilities.

In a document prepared by John Stuart, Van Bergen said that Radford had assigned the Lincoln-Berry-Greene $379.82 note to him. The note showed a $125 credit, giving it a net value of $254.82. Van Bergen promised to collect the note and apply proceeds to a $154 debt owed to him by John Hackett. John Stuart's penmanship obscures understanding of exactly what happened, but Radford was intertwined with Hackett's obligation to Van Bergen, and Van Bergen's collection of the Lincoln-Berry-Greene note was intended to extricate Radford from that entanglement. In his lawsuit, Van Bergen turned the screw tighter on Lincoln, Berry, and Greene by adding damages for nonpayment and demanding a total of $550, claiming $500 of that was the debt. How he could claim that is unclear, as case records made the $254 figure plain, and a year's interest wasn't 100 percent.[116]

Van Bergen was remembered as a man who believed in direct, forceful action. A Springfield resident recalled "the pleasure we boys had with our little hand sleds, sliding down the hills and hitching on to the sleighs and sleds going along the streets. Sometimes there would be as many as a dozen strung after one sleigh. . . . This was great fun for us boys, but a great annoyance to the young men and women in their sleigh riding and to lovers of fast trotting and pacing horses." He went on:

> Dr. Gershom Jayne, Peter Van Bergen and Gordon Abrams, the three most noted horsemen of the day . . . were annoyed by the boys. . . . After a six or eight inch fall of light snow in the night, they invited the boys to fasten onto their three sleighs for a ride. We were delighted . . . and they started north on Second Street at a slow jog and all went merry as a marriage bell until we got to Madison Street, when they turned east on it and put whips to their horses. There having been no travel on this street, our little sleds plowed into this snow, covering us completely with snow, so we could hardly see or breathe. All the boys but two dropped out by the time they got to Third Street. Of the two that remained, one stuck as far as Fourth Street, when he had to give in. William Herndon was the only one that went through to the starting place.[117]

As Van Bergen's lawsuit against Lincoln began, a northwest Illinois newspaper printed this general commentary from a New York periodical:

> Does the Farmer, who produces the very necessaries of life, get anything like as well paid for his labor as the Merchant, who merely distributes them?
>
> Does the Mechanic, who produces so many things which add to the comforts of life, get one-fourth as much for his own use as the privileged Banker?
>
> Does the useful Laborer, the man who digs into the bowels of the earth, or fells the trees, or carries the hod, receive for his labor a tithe

of what is obtained by the Lawyer, whose principal study is to acquire the knack of deceiving and perplexing a jury . . . ?

The farmer, the mechanic, the useful laborer in any occupation, should get at least as much for their labor as the men employed to distribute it; no man should be privileged as the banker is, to take a mite out of the general stock without rendering an equivalent. . . .

Now is the time to decide whether we shall have a Republic in fact, or only a Republic in name.[118]

The Rushville convention on moving the state capital convened April 7. Stephen Logan (Big Red May's law partner) and Dick Taylor had dropped out of the Sangamo delegation, replaced by Forquer's law partner, Samuel H. Treat, and legislative candidate William Carpenter. When a couple dozen delegates had assembled, they began the proceedings. One-fourth of those present were Sangamon County delegates. John Stuart, whose law partner was suing Lincoln that day, immediately introduced a resolution appointing a committee to recommend action to the convention. In the midst of this action, more delegates arrived, indignant that proceedings had started without them. Stuart and his allies used parliamentary maneuvers to prevent debate, carried the vote to have a committee do the convention's work, and left the minority unable to express the views of their constituents. "The majority," fumed one observer, "knowing their power, have used it improperly, wantonly and despotically." The next day, the committee urged citizens to vote for Springfield at the August plebiscite. Despite some support for Alton, Peoria, and the state's "geographical center," the convention agreed to recommend Springfield. Stuart and Forquer got appointed to a committee directed to bring the convention's decision to the people in an address. That address gave various reasons for Springfield's selection, claiming much popular support for the town, noting that it was the closest to the state's center, in a rich and healthy setting with "growing prospects." Much else was said about Springfield's superbness.

A minority report of delegates complained that Springfield advocates had rigged the proceedings. The *Chicago Democrat* grumbled that rather than promote cooperation among northern counties, "those most influential in 'getting up' the convention . . . came, apparently determined and prepared to carry a particular and favorite measure '*nolens voleris*'; and did ultimately succeed in carrying the measure by means the most unwarrantable and unjust." In other words, Springfield's advocates came for the purpose of winning rather than to discuss what should be done. The *Beardstown Chronicle* was unperturbed, declaring "no better selection could have been made than Springfield." The paper added, "One of the reasons why we think the people should at the next August election decide the important question of the future seat of government is to remove at once this subject from the action of our next legislature, and thereby prevent some thousands of dollars to be expended in time that otherwise would be spent in debating that question." A Rushville convention minority declared the plebiscite "unconstitutional, corrupt, impolitic, and absurd." The Peoria delegation and a few other members thought the convention shouldn't have recommended a locale to voters but instead should have just called for repeal of the law setting the plebiscite. A public meeting in Jacksonville had taken the same stance. That approach, however, would have been a call for inaction, as the legislature would not meet again until months after that plebiscite election.[119] Somewhat ominously, a Vandalia newspaper said of the convention, "We had fondly hoped that good people of the *north* would have suffered the seat of government to have remained at Vandalia, until the canal or railroad connecting the waters of the Lakes with the Illinois [River], should have been commenced."[120] The implication here was that southern Illinois legislators would now seek to thwart that internal improvement project, just as Chicago politicians had apparently feared when Sangamon's politicians decided to link that project's fate to Vandalia's.

The Rushville convention was but the opening skirmish in the battle for moving the state capital, a battle in which Lincoln would become the key leader while using tactics that opponents would characterize as unstatesmanlike.

While the Van Bergen lawsuit against Lincoln got under way, on April 19, 1834, the *Sangamo Journal* announced Lincoln's candidacy for the state house of representatives. As in the previous election, about a dozen candidates vied for four representative slots. Some candidates had run in 1832: Abraham Lincoln, William Carpenter, Richard Quinton, John Dawson, Thomas Neale, and incumbents John Stuart and Rev. Peter Cartwright. Rep. Edmund D. "Dick" Taylor was seeking the state senate this time. Springfield businessmen noted the campaign's progress. Fleming & Saum, tailors, advertised, "Candidates can be furnished with coats which can be easily turned."[121] Barber and free black William Fluerville declared:

> Times are pregnant with important events. Among them, and not the least, is the approaching election. I am personally friendly to all the candidates. No one of them has any reason to fear my opposition. I shall exert myself to secure the election of them all. To effect this object I would say to them that nothing is so necessary as to have "a smooth face." I am an adept in making smooth faces. My terms are very moderate. I shall rise in price on some after the election.[122]

About a week after Abe Lincoln's candidacy for the legislature was announced, the Sangamon County circuit court handling the Peter Van Bergen lawsuit against Lincoln, Berry, and Greene announced that Slicky Bill Greene owed $223 on the old Reuben Radford note. The court warned that at the autumn court term, Lincoln and William Berry would be made liable as well unless they could convince the judge otherwise. That they weren't included immediately was sheer chance; the court official who had subpoenaed Slicky Bill had failed to find Berry and Lincoln.[123]

At the end of April, the financial vise squeezing Lincoln got cranked tighter by his creditors. Tom Watkins had brought suit against him. Watkins was the livestock raiser whose sheep had been killed by the dog that was turned into the pair of dogskin gloves Abe sold. He also owned the horse-race track that Lincoln had surveyed. In order to do surveying around the countryside, Lincoln needed a horse. Back in January, Lincoln had bought one from Watkins. Tom's son explained, "Lincoln was a little slow in making the payments, and after he had paid all but ten dollars, my father, who was a high-strung man, became impatient, and sued him for the balance." Lincoln paid, as he would have done without a lawsuit.

That lawsuit has been confused with another one run against Lincoln by William Watkins. In December 1833, that action started in Bowling Green's justice of the peace court. Storekeepers Berry and Lincoln had given a $52.36 promissory note to Augustus Knapp and Thomas Pogue, who engaged in storekeeping and other mercantile enterprises at Beardstown and Pappsville. The Beardstown operation was called "the largest distributing store in that part of Illinois," a wholesale supplier to retail stores across several counties. The street outside their Pappsville store is where Lincoln interrupted an 1832 campaign speech in order to help James and Row Herndon in a fight. Knapp and Pogue assigned the Berry & Lincoln promissory note to William Watkins, who sued for collection in Bowling Green's court. Green ruled against Lincoln and Berry on December 24. Merry Christmas. Berry didn't resist judgment against him, but Lincoln appealed to the Sangamon County circuit court. Alexander Trent, one of the brothers who had bought out Berry & Lincoln, stood surety on Abe's $100 appeal bond, a bond given to assure that Lincoln could pay the judgment if he lost the appeal. At the end of April 1834, the circuit court awarded Watkins $58 and ordered Berry and Lincoln to pay.[124]

A few days later, on May 5, Sangamon County elected Garret Elkin to complete James Henry's term as sheriff. Garret was brother to William F. Elkin, the Whig state senate candidate who had been defeated by George Forquer two years earlier and was running again for senator this year. New Salem men voted for sheriff at the house of Lincoln's former store partner, William F. Berry. State representative candidate Lincoln was an election clerk, gaining an opportunity to renew acquaintance with voters and be paid a couple dollars for doing so.[125]

On June 2, the Sangamon County circuit court ordered the sheriff to seize enough property from Slicky Bill Greene to yield $223.24 plus costs plus $7.6375 interest for the debt owed to Peter Van Bergen. The sheriff, however, was unable to find that Slicky Bill had any property of financial value.[126] Therefore, Van Bergen would have to get his money from Berry and Lincoln.[127]

A couple days after the June 2 court order, Dr. Charles Chandler overtook Lincoln and another man as all three were headed toward Springfield. Chandler was using whip and spur, and his winded horse was "covered with lather, foam from head to foot." Abe asked what was happening. Chandler had a modest farm and planned to acquire eighty unclaimed acres of public land adjoining it. By tradition of the West, such was his right. Another resident in the region, however, decided he wanted the same tract and headed for the Springfield U.S. Land

Office to acquire the property. He made the mistake of blabbing his plan. As he headed off, friends of Chandler's rushed to his farm with the news. Initially he despaired. The reason he hadn't acquired title to the land already was that he lacked sufficient specie or equally good money for purchase, a problem partly of modest personal wealth and partly of currency scarcity on the frontier. His friends combined their resources and handed Chandler enough money to thwart the land grabber, his attack on Chandler being regarded as an attack on all. Chandler's competitor had a head start but was proceeding at a less urgent pace, believing success was guaranteed. Dr. Chandler knew shortcuts across the countryside and pressed his horse as hard as possible, encountering Lincoln about fourteen miles out of Springfield. Abe instantly swapped mounts and told Chandler to fly. Chandler rushed into the Land Office, counted out his money, told Big Red May (the Register) to serve up the acres, waited for his competitor, and administered to him a vigorous verbal lashing. The blackguard was lucky that's all he got. "Sometimes a stranger 'entered out the settler.' . . . This was one of the meanest things, in the estimate of a pioneer, that a white man could be guilty of, and always demanded the attention of the Regulators. In this manner, a man by the name of Alexander Wheeler entered out Tolbert Hite. Wheeler was called upon by the Regulators, and after a speedy examination, they decided to give him one hundred lashes, which they did."[128]

A chronicler wrote:

> The story is told of one "jumper" who resisted. . . . The committee exhausted their verbal arguments in vain; then, putting a rope around the waist of the culprit, led him to a pond, cut a hole in the ice, and immersed him. He was soon drawn out, but, being still in a combative and profane frame of mind, was treated to another ducking, and on his second coming out was unable to continue his side of the debate; so the negative was declared, closed, and, after returning to the house, the dripping defender of that side set his signature to the papers and with uplifted right hand swore that it was his "voluntary act and deed."[129]

Emotional public support existed for farmers organizing to defend their homes.[130] In 1835, an Illinois settler whose homestead was threatened by a jumper told another pioneer, "I'll kill him; and, by agreement of the settlers, I am to be protected, and if tried, no settler dare, if on the jury, find a verdict against me."[131] In autumn 1834, an Illinois settlers meeting declared, "'Where there is *union* there is *strength*.' Let us be united as one man, and be determined to defend each other's rights."[132]

After Abe arrived in town, he looked up Chandler and learned all was well. The two men became personal and political friends ever after.[133] Any talk about the incident must have been powerful advertising of state representative candidate Lincoln's determination to give settlers fair treatment. And though neither Chandler nor the New Salem candidate knew it then, the incident would someday help Lincoln's political efforts in Eastern states.

About a month after thwarting that land grab, an incident occurred that was of no great moment but illustrates small kindnesses and minor frustrations in Lincoln's daily life. George Spears was a Clary's Grove Boy who subscribed to the *Sangamo Journal*, with delivery by U.S. mail. As postage then was paid by mail recipients, not by senders, Spears was supposed to pay the postage before picking up his newspaper. As a favor, Abe allowed Spears to run a tab rather than pay each time. This was contrary to law, but the chance of any untoward consequence was near zero. One day Spears handed money to a friend going into town and asked the fellow to apply the sum to the post office account. Knowing the friend was likely to get drunk in town, a condition in which he was apt to forget the post office business, Spears asked him to get a receipt from Lincoln so that Spears could know all was well. Apparently, and understandably, the friend didn't explain the reason when asking Abe for a receipt. Lincoln wrote out the receipt and added a note: "I am somewhat surprised at your request. . . . The law requires newspaper postage to be paid in advance, and now that I have waited a full year, you choose to wound my feelings by insinuating that unless you get a receipt I will probably make you pay it again." According to family tradition, upon getting the note, Spears immediately rode into town to clear up the situation.[134]

In addition to being literate, Spears apparently owned an indentured black,[135] a fact worth noting not only as an example of slavery around New Salem, but also to illustrate how a shortage of specie inconvenienced even individuals of ample means. "One pioneer, Gardiner, by name, used in old age to relate that, despite the fact that he owned a well-stocked farm of six hundred acres, he was unable on occasion to pay postage on the letters that came to him [due to lack of coins], and they would lie for weeks in the post office before he could claim them."[136] This problem was nothing unusual,[137] but Lincoln's accommodation to a postal customer was.

Lincoln wasn't well known in the county seat of Springfield in 1834, and Abner Ellis, with whom he stayed when overnighting there, took him around to Springfield's leading Whigs in order to get acquainted.[138] At various times, Ellis was a business associate of Archie Herndon and Josh Speed. Lincoln seems to have needed some introducing. A fine student of Lincoln's life recorded that Peter Wallace "told me once that in Springfield, where he was living in 1834, there was much hooting at Lincoln's ambitions."[139]

How much electioneering Abe did around the county is unclear. Jesse Weik's ghostwriting had Billy Herndon say, "I have Lincoln's word for it that it was more of a hand-shaking campaign than anything else."[140] I'm inclined to think that any personal one-on-one campaign travels had to be combined with surveying work. His old business associate Charles Maltby said Lincoln was a master when he did stop at residences, discussing farm prospects with farmers, talking about family topics with their wives, telling children pleasant stories from his own childhood, and radiating a warm friendliness that was infectious.[141]

Although a campaign for elective office never stops until polls close on election day, the pace of a campaign changes. In July, the pace picked up as the August 4 election day approached.

One authority says that Clary's Grove Boys accompanied Lincoln during campaign events, enforcing rude discipline on onlookers who might be inclined to disrupt the candidate's speeches or crowd-working.[142] Russell Godbey remembered, "When a fight was on hand Abe would say to me, 'Let's go and break up the row' with a laugh, and we generally did." Although Lincoln had the brawn for pitching into a fight, Godbey remembered that Lincoln preferred to use charm, wading in with jokes and stories that converted the crowd atmosphere from hostility to geniality.[143] Being able to stop a frontier fight with words demonstrated awesome power over fellow men. Such skill must have boosted respect and admiration from fellow citizens. Row Herndon recalled:

> He came to my house near Island Grove during harvest. There was some thirty men in the field. He got his dinner and went out to the field where the men were at work. I gave him an introduction, and the boys said that they could not vote for a man unless he could make a hand. "Well," said he, "boys, if that is all, I am sure of your votes." He took hold of the cradle, led the way all the round with perfect ease. The boys was satisfied, and I don't think he lost a vote in the crowd. The next day was [a public] speaking at Berlin. He went from my house with Dr. Barrett [a prominent Whig activist], the man that had asked me who this man Lincoln was. I told him that he was a candidate for the legislature. He laughed and said, "Can't the party raise no better materials than that?" I said, "Go tomorrow and hear all before you pronounce judgment." When he come back I said, "Doc, what say you now?" "Why, sir, he is a perfect take, in he knows more than all of them put together."[144]

Lincoln did not publish a platform as he did in 1832, but we know he declared his support for internal improvements in Illinois and talked about how they would promote exploitation of the state's natural wealth, thereby helping citizens.[145] Denny Hanks claimed that "in all the rough-and-ready debates and arguin's and talks about improvements and navigatin' he could beat any man in the whole country up and down the Sangamon River."[146] One of Lincoln's big crowd pleasers was his call for constructing a canal from Beardstown, the region's big port on the Illinois River, to a point on the Sangamon River a few miles downstream from Petersburg.[147] An internal improvement like this would certainly boost prosperity in Petersburg and New Salem, but calls for such a project were unspoken acknowledgment that commercial navigation on the Sangamon River was impractical. The three towns were already linked by the Sangamon River's natural water route, and abandoning it in favor of a canal shows that promoters' schemes for the river just two years earlier had been no more than that.

John Hill, who was in a position to know but whose veracity is questionable, said Lincoln was the candidate of those who favored breaking up Sangamon County.[148] Hill's story is supported by John Potter.[149] Whether to create a new county was a question crossing party lines, affecting real estate developers, and if enacted, creating an entire set of large and small county offices for politicians unable to find positions in the Sangamon County government. Two leaders in that division effort were Jack Armstrong's brother Hugh and Jack's brother-in-law Ned Potter. Their allies included Jack Armstrong, William Berry, Mentor Graham, Jack Kelso, Charles Maltby, and James Rutledge.[150] Lincoln pledged to work for dividing the county; indeed, he had already made such pledge in the 1832 election.[151]

Apparently an undercurrent flowed through the campaign regarding Lincoln's skepticism about Christianity. It's hard to say whether these murmurings helped him, hurt him, or made little difference. James Matheny recalled, "In 1834 and 5, my father being a strong Methodist—a kind of minister and loving Lincoln with all his soul, hated to vote for him because he heard that Lincoln was an infidel."[152] "Infidelity" was a large house with room for a variety of inhabitants. One pioneer noted, "In them days, if a man doubted the Bible being exactly true in everything, and if he did not believe in fire and brimstone, he was called an infidel."[153] A twentieth-century scholar explained: "The word 'infidel' was freely and loosely used. A person who held that the earth traveled around the sun would be an 'infidel.' Anyone who had doubts about the Bible would be an 'infidel.' A Christian of another denomination was occasionally labeled an 'infidel.'"[154] Russell Godbey said that his brother-in-law Isaac Snodgrass "told me not to vote for him because Abe was a deist. I did it. . . . Voted for him in 1834."[155] So much for the electoral downside.

As we have seen, however, Lincoln helped lead the New Salem meeting that nominated James Henry for governor and that concluded that ministers should stay out of politics. Adoption of such a resolution by a public meeting shows some opposition to political ministers around New Salem. Of course, that isn't the same as opposition to Christianity, but it could easily be twisted as such, a flexibility enhanced by Lincoln's known skepticism about Christianity during his New Salem years. Billy Herndon declared, "When Mr. Lincoln was a candidate for our legislature he was accused of being an infidel, and of having said that Jesus Christ was an illegitimate child."[156] Once started, rumors take off with a success seldom known to human endeavor. In politics, however, rumors tend to get prodded along. I suspect Rev. Peter Cartwright contributed to those whispers about Lincoln, and evidence that Lincoln possessed similar suspicions exists in the form of robust verbal attacks he made on Cartwright after the election was over, in which Lincoln hid behind false names. Cartwright was known to question his opponents' religious faith. In 1829, he openly proclaimed Lieutenant Governor Kinney to be one of the "great and mighty priests among the sons of Beliel [Satan]."[157] Cartwright proclaimed:

> And it came to pass, that when William [Kinney] the high priest, and little governor of the realm, heard what was done, that he laughed and rejoiced greatly, saying, "Blessed be the god of Baal, for he hath delivered us from the power of Moses [Lemen] and Peter [Cartwright] the priests, and Elijah [Iles] the prophet, and [Archibald] Job, the man of God."
>
> Moreover it came to pass in those days, that William [Kinney] and Zadock [Casey], the high priests of Baal, said, "Assemble the people together, and let us rejoice, for now we can eat, and get drunk, and swear, and hunt, and shoot on the Sabbath, and buy votes with strong drink, and we shall be elected governor and lieutenant governor over this realm."[158]

Reverend Cartwright made those remarks regarding the failure of his bill for "prevention of vice and immorality," which said in part:

> If any person shall be found reveling, fighting, or quarreling, doing or performing any worldly employment or business whatever, on the first day of the week commonly called Sunday, (works of necessity and charity only excepted) or shall use or practice any game, sport, or diversion whatever, or shall be found hunting or shooting on the said day . . . [he] shall be fined not less than three dollars nor more than ten dollars.[159]

The next year, Kinney complained:

> I have been accused of being an encourager of vice and immorality, on account of my opposition to the bill introduced into the legislature by Peter Cartwright, entitled "an act for the suppression of vice and immorality." This bill passed the house of representatives last session and met its final doom in the senate, over which I had the honor to preside. And although I gave no vote on this bill, I believed . . . it contained features inconsistent, unconstitutional and improper to become a law of this state, for every constitutional feature in it was already provided for in the criminal code, and that it was calculated to produce an endless and unwarrantable litigation, disturb the peace of civil society, and effect no other purpose than to gratify the ambition of ecclesiastical tyrants, and fill the pockets of a few pettifogging lawyers, most of whom are now clamorous against me. I am

accused of being hostile to religion, for opposing the bill to incorporate religious societies. . . . I considered it also to be unconstitutional.

I hope I shall ever be found opposing every measure that has the most distant tendency to connect church and state, and that I shall never be found acting in concert with that class of preachers who ought to be considered dangerous to the civil rights and religious liberties of the community.[160]

A defender of Kinney explained the religious society incorporation bill:

There was a bill before the senate for the incorporation of all religious, tract, and Bible societies in this state, the object of which . . . was not more nor less than to combine all religious denominations, tract and Bible societies into one body politic, to be unified by the coaction of legislative enactment. Had this bill passed, we might date the period of destruction to all our liberties from that time; but thanks be given to God that at the time when there could be no one found in the legislature who possessed independence enough to rise to oppose a bill which had so strong a force not only in the members of the legislature, for the lobby was crowded with its advocates, freedom found its advocate, and we found our liberties protected by William Kinney. He rose amidst the hisses of his opponents and defended the rights of a free people. He addressed the senate at length in opposition to the passage of the bill, and soon changed the minds of the members, the vote was taken and the bill did not pass. And since he has become a candidate for governor, his enemies have deigned to search the journals of the senate to find the record of that vote and publish it . . . in order to drag into use against him the prejudices of the religious societies.[161]

As the years went by, Lincoln's religious thinking seems to have changed, but around New Salem he apparently had a reputation as a skeptic about religion. Much, but not all, we know of his thinking in those years comes from interviews and correspondence collected by Billy Herndon. Some who furnished information to Herndon subsequently expanded on what they had communicated, particularly regarding changes in Lincoln's thinking after he left New Salem. His lawyer colleague Henry C. Whitney put it this way: "Proof that he was a sincere Christian in 1862, '63, and '64, is quite as convincing as the proof that he was an infidel in 1832, '33, and '34."[162] I believe Billy Herndon's data, as far as it goes, is authentic.

Supposedly in Lincoln's New Salem years, he wrote an essay advocating skepticism about religion. Some persons argue that such a composition is inherently unlikely, as Lincoln shunned avoidable offense to voters. Nonetheless, village resident Hardin Bale said, "About the year 1834 A. Lincoln wrote a work on infidelity, denying the divinity of the Scriptures and was persuaded by his friends—particularly Samuel [Hill]—to burn it."[163] I find Bale's testimony strong, as he offered it scarcely a month after Lincoln's death, long before any national controversy had arisen about Lincoln's religious beliefs. Isaac Cogdal said, "I have talked this often and often with him commencing as early as 1834. . . . I do know that Mr. Lincoln did write a letter, pamphlet, book, or what-not on the faith as I understand he held—denying special and miraculous revelation, inspiration, and conception."[164] By using comments from Abe Lincoln and friends, James Matheny dated the production around 1834–35. He declared forthrightly: "Lincoln did write a pamphlet attacking the divinity of Christ, special inspiration [of the Bible], revelation, etc. All these things were talked about in 1835–6 and 7." Matheny repeated explicitly, "Mr. Lincoln did tell me that he did write a little book on infidelity."[165]

New Salem merchant Samuel Hill's son John earned a reputation for unreliable reporting, but nonetheless, comparing John's statements with those from others is worthwhile. While Lincoln still lived, John said, "He employed his intellectual faculties in writing a dissertation against the doctrine of the divinity of the scriptures. Of this he soon repented, and consigned his production to the flames. He had designed it for publication, but his senior friends, pointing him to Paine and Voltaire, wrought a change in his intentions."[166] Regarding Lincoln's little book, John added in June 1865:

Since my early childhood I remember to have heard it alluded to, hundreds of times by different old settlers. . . . I have a better remembrance of it by my father's connection with it. You know that there are always some few things that strike into the mind of a child at early age which time will never eradicate. . . . When I heard of my father having morally compelled Mr. Lincoln to burn the book on account of its infamy &c., pointing to Voltaire, Paine &c., the circumstance struck me so forcibly that I have never heard the word infidelity, Paine or Voltaire since, without thinking of it. . . . I had always thought my father to be averse to religion. . . . It was in the wintertime, as tradition says it was done in father's store, while there was fire in the stove.[167]

According to Billy Herndon:

In 1835, he wrote a small work on "Infidelity," and intended to have it published. The book was an attack upon the whole grounds of Christianity, and especially was it an attack upon the idea that Jesus was the Christ, the true and only Son of God. . . . Lincoln and [New Salem merchant Samuel] Hill were very friendly. Hill, I think, was a skeptic at that time. Lincoln, one day after the book was finished, read it to Mr. Hill. . . . He [Hill] tried to persuade him not to make it public—not to publish it. . . . Lincoln refused to destroy it—said it should be published. Hill swore it should never see the light of day. He had an eye to Lincoln's popularity—his present and future success, and believing that if the book were published, it would kill Lincoln forever, he snatched it from Lincoln's hand when Lincoln was not expecting it, and ran it into an old-fashioned tin-plate stove, heated as hot as a furnace; and so Lincoln's book went up to the clouds in smoke. It is confessed by all who heard parts of it that it was at once able and eloquent. . . . His argument was grounded on the internal mistakes of the Old and New Testaments, and on reason, and on the experiences and observations of men. The criticisms from internal defects were sharp, strong, and manly.[168]

Not all New Salem settlers remembered Abe's manuscript in the same way. Jack Armstrong's brother-in-law Henry McHenry recalled: "As to the book or pamphlet, I do not recollect about what it 'did say' or 'tried to say,' but it was I am sure written after the death of Miss Rutledge. And I never heard any scoundrel, '*orthodox*' or heterodox, or anybody else bring the charge of infidelity against his production until they found that they might make political capital."[169] Here we see doubt about what the book said, which was exploited by opponents of Lincoln. New Salem resident Mentor Graham went further, describing a conversation with Lincoln in 1833:

One morning he said to me, "Graham, what do you think about the anger of the Lord?" I replied, "I believe the Lord never was angry or mad and never would be; that His loving kindness endureth forever; that He never changes." Said Lincoln, "I have a little manuscript written, which I will show you"; and stated he thought of having it published. Offering it to me, he said he had never showed it to anyone, and still thought of having it published. The size of the manuscript was about one-half quire of foolscap, written in a very plain hand, on the subject of Christianity and a defense of universal salvation. The commencement of it was something respecting the God of the universe never being excited, mad, or angry. I had the manuscript in my possession some week or ten days. . . . I remember well his argument. He took the passage, "As in Adam all die, even so in Christ shall all be made alive," and followed up with the proposition that whatever the breach or injury of Adam's transgressions to the human race was, which no doubt was very great, was made just and right by the atonement of Christ.[170]

Although Graham was on the scene, his testimony is sometimes questionable. Perhaps Abe Lincoln wrote more than one manuscript, but Graham's claim that Lincoln accepted "the atonement of Christ" is so contrary to what we know of Lincoln in New Salem as to throw Graham's entire statement into doubt.[171]

Although what Abe *wrote* in New Salem is controverted, we have adamant testimony about what he *said* in the late 1830s. Ann Rutledge's brother Robert remembered Lincoln singing a humorous parody of the hymn "Legacy."[172] Abe's New Salem business partner Charles Maltby declared, "Lincoln, at this period of his life, was not a religious man." Maltby added, "Nor did he subscribe to any religious creed."[173] Samuel Hill's wife, Parthena, asked Abe, "Do you really believe there isn't any future state?" She said he answered, "Mrs. Hill, I'm afraid there isn't. It isn't a pleasant thing to think that when we die that is the last of us."[174] Billy Herndon didn't live in New Salem with Lincoln but talked with persons who did. At New Salem, according to Billy Herndon:

> Mr. Lincoln became acquainted with a class of men the world never saw the like of before or since. They were large men—large in body and large in mind, hard to whip, and never to be fooled. . . . They were men of their own minds—believed what was demonstrable—were men of great common sense. . . . They were skeptics all—scoffers some. These scoffers were good men, and their scoffs were protests against theology—loud protests against the follies of Christianity. They had never heard of Theism and the newer and better religious thoughts of this age. Hence, being natural skeptics, and being bold, brave men, they uttered their thoughts freely. They declared that Jesus was an illegitimate child. I knew these men well, and have felt for them. . . . These men could not conceive it possible that three could be in one, nor one in three Gods; they could not believe that the Father ruined one of his own lovely children. This was monstrous to them. They were on all occasions, when opportunity offered, debating the various questions of Christianity among themselves; they took their stand on common sense and on their own souls; and though their arguments were rude and rough, no man could overthrow their homely logic. They riddled all divines. . . .
>
> It was here, and among these people, that Mr. Lincoln was thrown. About the year 1834, he chanced to come across Volney's *Ruins*, and some of Paine's theological works. He at once seized hold of them, and assimilated them into his own being. Volney and Paine became a part of Mr. Lincoln from 1834 to the end of his life.[175]

Jesse Weik's ghostwriting has Billy Herndon say explicitly: "Volney's *Ruins* and *Payne's* [sic] *Age of Reason* passed from hand to hand, and furnished food for the evening's discussion in the tavern and village store. Lincoln read both these books and thus assimilated them into his own being."[176] Abner Ellis, business associate of Josh Speed and Billy Herndon's father, indicated that Abe said he read Volney's *Ruins* and Paine. Apparently Lincoln didn't specify which of Paine's works, but the context of Ellis's testimony points to *The Age of Reason*.[177]

After serving as a firebrand of the American Revolution, Thomas Paine went on to fight other battles. The basic content of Paine's *Age of Reason* is familiar to Bible scholars and even to many laypersons of the twenty-first century, but it must have been astonishing, disquieting, and exciting to backwoods intellectuals of the early nineteenth century. Part of Paine's analysis was historical, questioning the reputed authorship of various books in the Bible. His historical examination noted miraculous stories of ancient times outside a biblical context, ones that no one believed anymore. Another part of Paine's analysis was based on logic, demonstrating that contradictions in Bible passages meant that some had to be false. Using logic to examine evidence must have had particular appeal to Lincoln. Still another part of Paine's argument was based on morality, not only criticizing horrific deeds glorified in the Bible, but also noting later horrors committed in the name of Christ. Paine was particularly blunt about the avarice of clergy.

Paine wrote: "But some, perhaps, will say: Are we to have no word of God— no revelation? I answer, Yes; there is a word of God; there is a revelation. THE WORD OF GOD IS THE CREATION WE BEHOLD and it is in *this word*, which no human invention can counterfeit or alter, that God speaketh universally to man." "Do we want to contemplate his power?" Paine asked. "We see it in the immensity of the Creation. Do we want to contemplate his wisdom? We see it in the unchangeable order by which the incomprehensible whole is governed. Do we want to contemplate his munificence? We see it in the abundance with which he fills the earth. Do we want to contemplate his mercy? We see it in his not withholding that abundance even from the unthankful." Paine declared, "The only idea we can have of serving God, is that of contributing to the happiness of the living creation that God has made."[178]

Paine was a deist who accepted the existence of God but rejected the Bible as a record of God's activities and wishes, yet Paine's book earned him the label of "atheist." In a public debate on a steamboat regarding Christianity, Peter Cartwright protested to an opponent who cited Paine, "Such a degraded witness as Tom Paine can't be admitted as testimony in this debate." Cartwright said when the debater refused to desist in that tactic, "I took him by the chin with my hand, and moved his jaws together, and made his teeth rattle at a mighty rate."[179]

In *The Ruins; or, Meditation on the Revolutions of Empires: And the Law of Nature*, Constantine Francis Volney presents learned research in a fantasy setting, where a great spirit preaches to multitudes of persons gathered from around the world. Among other things, the book critiques Christianity, Islam, and many other religions. Volney examines their origins and inconsistencies, their commonalities and borrowings from one another. He examines mythological links among them, foreshadowing Freud's *Moses and Monotheism*, James Henry Breasted's *The Dawn of Conscience*, and Campbell's *The Hero with a Thousand*

Faces. Such information was surely startling to a reader whose acquaintance with religion came from itinerant preachers and pioneer neighbors. Volney put that kind of religion in a context questioning what it was all about. He concluded, "To any man whatever, who observes with reflection the astonishing spectacle of the universe, the more he meditates on the properties and attributes of each being, on the admirable order and harmony of their motions, the more it is demonstrated that there exists a supreme agent, a universal and identic mover, designated by the appellation of God; and so true it is that the law of nature suffices to elevate him to the knowledge of God." Such understanding results in "a worship wholly of action; the practice and observance of all the rules which the supreme wisdom has imposed on the motion of each being; eternal and unalterable rules, by which it maintains the order and harmony of the universe."[180] The notion of a universe governed by law had great appeal to Lincoln.

From Volney's *Ruins*:

> Then turning towards the west [toward the United States]: Yes, continued he, a hollow sound already strikes my ear; a cry of liberty, proceeding from far distant shores, resounds on the ancient continent. At this cry, a secret murmur against oppression is raised in a powerful nation; a salutary inquietude alarms her respecting her situation; she enquires what she is, and what she ought to be; while, surprised at her own weakness, she interrogates her rights, her resources, and what has been the conduct of her chiefs.
>
> Yet another day—a little more reflection—and an immense agitation will begin; a new-born age will open! an age of astonishment to vulgar minds, of terror to tyrants, of freedom to a great nation, and of hope to the human race![181]

For a thoughtful and inquiring person previously exposed only to frontier divines, the impact of such books surely must be hard to exaggerate. Some readers of Paine and Volney might react by concluding Christianity is invalid, but other readers might be unsatisfied and probe deeper, realizing that just because claims by particular salesmen of religion are wrong, that doesn't mean the product is worthless. Later we shall see indications that Abraham Lincoln was such a prober, but not until he encountered the written work of a learned minister who confronted types of evidence considered by Paine and Volney. In New Salem and in Lincoln's early Springfield years, he seems to have rejected the church of his family and neighbors.

Of Abe's early Springfield days, Billy Herndon said: "Mr. Lincoln moved to this city in 1837, and here he became acquainted with various men of his own way of thinking. At that time they called themselves free thinkers or free thinking men. I remember all these things distinctly, for I was with them, heard them, and was one of them. Mr. Lincoln here found other works, Hume, Gibbon and others, and drank them in."[182]

Some prominent spokespersons of religion denied that freethinkers could possess morals and ethics. Unitarian leader Dr. William Ellery Channing asked:

What is there in human nature to awaken respect and tenderness, if man is the unprotected insect of a day? And what is he more, if atheism be true? Erase all thought and fear of God from a community, and selfishness and sensuality would absolve the whole man. . . . Virtue, duty, principle, would be mocked and spurned as unmeaning sounds. A sordid self-interest would supplant every other feeling, and man would become in fact, what the theory of atheism declares him to be, a companion for brutes![183]

Some religious persons viewed freethinkers as not only immoral, but also a threat. The *Christian Advocate and Journal* warned in 1834:

The Christian community seems not to be sensible of the extent to which the principles and power of infidelity have already arrived in this country, nor of the danger to which we are exposed. Infidelity is at war with all our institutions, civil as well as religious. Every thing withers at its touch. Though the land be as the garden of Eden before it, yet after it it shall be most desolate. Such has been the effect wherever infidelity and atheism have had the ascendancy. Within a half century past the world has seen sad proof of the truth of this remark, even in France. . . .
There is more infidelity and atheism among us than most people are aware of. Infidelity exists in organized societies, or rather clubs, in different parts of the country. There is much of it in our national and state legislatures. It is aiming at the possession and control of the literary institutions of the land. The Girard school, with its immense funds, is designed to be a purely atheistical institution. It has also the entire control of the press in several instances. These things indicate that a time of darkness and distress is approaching unless it be checked.[184]

Freethinkers gloried in the unease they caused among the religious. A northwest Illinois newspaper printed an East Coast item saying:

The great battle between religious superstition and enlightened reason, which will decide the destiny of our country, at least, for the present century, is soon to be fought! Powerful efforts are being made on the side of priestcraft to put down everything that is liberal. . . . Friends of humanity, of civil and religous liberty! It is your duty to be active, to exert yourselves unremittingly to advance the glorious cause you love.[185]

A few years later, the *Quincy Whig* said, "The argument . . . that religious people should select and support religious candidates for office—that religion should be a paramount qualification for office—is a system of exclusivism which we desire never to see adopted in a community. The evils which would result from such a system are so manifest that it will be unnecessary to repeat them here."[186]

James Matheny was in the first tier of Lincoln's early Springfield friends. Matheny recalled Bible discussions among members of a Springfield poetry club consisting of a few young men, including Matheny, Evan Butler, Newton Francis (brother of Simeon), and Lincoln. Lincoln "would bring the Bible with him, read a chapter, argue against it. . . . Lincoln was enthusiastic in his infidelity. As he grew older he grew more discreet, didn't talk much before strangers about religion. But to friends—close and bosom ones—he was always open and avowed. . . . Lincoln used to quote Burns. Burns helped Lincoln to be an infidel as I think—at least he found in Burns a like thinker and feeler."[187] A fine student of Lincoln's life wrote: "He constantly recited Burns's immortal satire on unction and hypocrisy, 'Holy Willie's Prayer.' That attack of the Scottish poet on religious conceit, together with his 'Address to the Unco Guid, or Rigidly Righteous,' may almost be said to have stated Lincoln's views on the religion of the times, at this period of his development."[188] Matheny said he "heard Lincoln call Christ a bastard. He [Lincoln] and William D. Herndon [relative of Billy Herndon] used to talk infidelity in the clerk's office in this city about the years 1837–40."[189] Many years later, speaking of the time around 1839, Lincoln's colleague Milton Hay declared to his nephew John, "Candor compels me to say that at this period Mr. Lincoln could hardly be termed a devout believer in the authenticity of the Bible (but this is for your ear only)."[190]

Matheny also recalled: "Lincoln attacked the Bible and New Testament on two grounds. First from the inherent or apparent contradiction under its lids, and secondly from the grounds of reason. Sometimes he ridiculed the Bible and New Testament—sometimes seemed to scoff it, though I shall not use that word in its full and literal sense. Never heard that Lincoln changed his views though [I was] his personal and political friend from 1834 to 1860. Sometimes Lincoln bordered on absolute atheism: He went far that way."[191] Billy Herndon said, "Lincoln told me a thousand times that he did not believe that the Bible, etc., were revelations of God, as the Christian world contends."[192] Such frank expression of views by Lincoln was only among trusted friends. Otherwise, in the words of his best-ever friend, Josh Speed, "He was very cautious never to give expression to any thought or sentiment that would grate harshly upon a Christian's ear."[193]

Lincoln's first law partner, John T. Stuart, said:

He was an avowed and open infidel. Sometimes bordered on atheism.
I have often and often heard Lincoln and one W. D. Herndon [relative of Billy Herndon], who was a freethinker, talk over this subject. Lincoln went further against Christian beliefs and doctrines and prin-

ciples than any man I ever heard. He shocked me. Don't remember
the exact line of his argument. Suppose it was against the inherent
defects so-called of the Bible and on grounds of reason. Lincoln
always denied that Jesus was the Christ of God, denied that Jesus
was the son of God as understood and maintained by the Christian
world.

John Stuart said those feelings dated "say from 1834 to 1840."[194] Josh Speed,
who was the closest friend Abraham Lincoln ever had and became his roommate
as soon as Lincoln moved from New Salem to Springfield, said: "When I knew
him, in early life, he was a skeptic. He had tried hard to be a believer, but his reason could not grasp and solve the great problem of redemption as taught."[195]

David Davis knew Lincoln after the New Salem years but was in the first tier
of Lincoln's friends. Davis claimed no special knowledge but said that Lincoln
"had no faith in the Christian sense of that term. Had faith in laws, principles,
causes and effects, philosophy. He had self-relying power."[196] Lincoln's last law
partner, Billy Herndon, put it this way: "Mr. Lincoln believed in laws that impe-
riously ruled both matter and mind. With him there could be no miracles outside
of law; he held that the universe was a grand mystery and a miracle. Nothing to
him was lawless, everything being governed by law." Billy added: "If it is true
that Lincoln believed that laws existed and ruled matter and mind, then there
could be no such thing as a miraculous conception and it follows that Lincoln did
not believe that Jesus was God, nor a special child of Him. If it is true that Lincoln believed in law, then there could be no special inspiration, no special revelations, no miracles in his mind; he demanded facts, well-authenticated facts, as
foundations of his belief; he had no faith in 'say soes,' no respect for that kind of
authority in the religious world."[197] Such sounds much like deism.

In the apt language of Billy Herndon: "All this is no evidence of a want of
religion in Mr. Lincoln. It is rather an evidence that he had his own religion."[198]
Abe's good friend from New Salem Elizabeth Abell put it this way: "He was
truly a Christian, not in the common term of Christianity nowadays, long face on
Sunday and grind the poor on Monday, but he was always doing good the same
today and tomorrow."[199] A person such as Lincoln might speak sincerely of belief
in God but would probably be rejected as an infidel or even atheist by such as
Peter Cartwright—and plenty of men such as Cartwright resided around Sangamon County. Indeed, Billy Herndon said of the Clary's Grove Boys, "If the good
minister preached Jesus, and him crucified, with his precious blood trinkling
down the spear and cross, they would melt down into honest prayer, praying honestly, and with deep feeling and humility, saying aloud, 'would to God we had
been there with our trusty rifles, amid those murderous Jews.'"[200]

+≡= =≡+

Abe Lincoln wasn't the only candidate in the Sangamon County state legislature
election. County Coroner James Shepherd of Sangamo Town was running for the

state house of representatives. He said that because of state debt, expenditures must be reduced; a good start would be to lower legislators' pay. Despite a lack of adequate state funding, the Illinois & Michigan Canal should at least be started, along with other internal improvement projects. He favored the common school system. He called for moving the state capital from Vandalia to Springfield. He favored limiting the jurisdiction of constables and justices of the peace to their own precincts. Shepherd ran as an independent and was soundly defeated, pulling barely 150 votes even though he was already a county official.[201]

Democrat William Alvey of Springfield said that reducing the state debt was the number-one issue demanding attention, and the debt had to be reduced without raising taxes. To diminish the state government's debt, he suggested siphoning county revenue to the state government but was open to a better idea. He favored beginning construction of the Canal now if a private corporation built it but felt the work should be delayed if the state financed the project. Alvey believed economic benefits from the Canal would spread across the entire state. "Navigation of the Sangamon River has been heretofore, and is now, a theme of deep interest to the citizens of this county; and as yet nothing has been done to improve its channel for safe and expeditious transportation; yet it is to be earnestly desired that the very first available funds may be appropriated to that object, to ensure a cheap and safe conveyance of our surplus products to market. . . . On this measure, all depends upon the representation from this county." Alvey favored the common school system and said the state capital should be moved from Vandalia to Springfield. He was another losing candidate, getting just over 600 votes.[202]

Democrat Richard Quinton claimed he wasn't a party candidate but was instead an independent. He favored internal improvements, particularly those designed to make the Sangamon River navigable, a project that he thought merited appeal to the U.S. Congress for aid. He favored the Canal, supporting construction by either the state or a private company, and thought the state capital should be moved to Sangamon County. He almost won, John Stuart edging him out by only 125 votes.[203]

In his campaign for state representative, Jehu Durley favored immediate commencement of the Canal, either by a private company or by the government of some state other than Illinois. He wanted the Sangamon River improved for navigation, the state capital moved to Springfield, and the Bank of the United States rechartered. On election day, he came in second from last.[204]

Stances of these losing candidates seem generally in keeping with what most citizens of Sangamon County wanted. Defeats had less to do with platforms than with how much organized support the candidates had. Illinois Whig leader Francis Arenz mused to fellow Whig leader John J. Hardin: "The struggle is over and many a one's fond hopes are blasted. . . . However, conscious of having done my duty towards my adopted country and my friends I submit to the will of the people right or wrong as in duty bound."[205] Perhaps Arenz would have been more consoled if he had known the private comment of Democratic champion Sidney

Breese: "A seat in the next legislature is by no means desirable, as all our state affairs are in a great confusion and embarrassment."[206]

As in the previous election, despite Lincoln's firm public allegiance to the Whigs, local Democrats supported him in 1834. Russell Godbey was an example: "I voted for Lincoln in opposition to my own creed and faith in politics."[207] Springfield attorney Stephen T. Logan expressed a general feeling:

> In 1832 while he got a very large vote in his own precinct of New Salem, they hadn't voted for him very well in other parts of the county. This made his friends down there very mad, and as they were mostly Democratic but were for Lincoln on personal grounds, in the next race (1834) they told their Democratic brethren in the other parts of the county that they must help elect Lincoln, or else they wouldn't support the other Democratic candidates. This they did purely out of their personal regard for him.[208]

In politics, few things happen of their own volition, and Democratic support for Lincoln was well organized. John Stuart explained:

> In 1834 we were candidates again for the legislature. This time he was better known. All the prominent Clay men here [in Springfield] and in other parts of the county were for him. He ran this time by general consent and wish.
>
> Of course there was a strong fight on me again as the Jackson men supposed I was figuring [to run] for Congress.
>
> I remember we were out at Danley's on Clear Lake. They had a shooting match there. The country people met to shoot for a beef (the candidates, as was the custom, were expected to pay for the beefs) and we were there electioneering.
>
> Lincoln came to me and told me that the Jackson men had been to him and proposed to him that they would drop two of their men and take him up and vote for him for the purpose of beating me. Lincoln acted fairly and honorably about it by coming and submitting the proposition to me.
>
> From my experience in the former race in 1832 I had great confidence in my strength—perhaps too much as I was a young man—but I told Lincoln to go and tell them he would take their votes—that I would risk it. . . .
>
> I and my friends knowing their tactics, then concentrated our fight against one of their men—it was Quinton—and in this way we beat Quinton and elected Lincoln and myself.[209]

John Stuart wasn't exaggerating about his enemies' ferocity. What happened to him in the campaign's last week illustrates politics as she was really fought, and by someone with whom Abe Lincoln was closely allied in this election effort. Claiming to have supported Stuart in 1832, "A Citizen of Sangamon" issued a handbill with charges designed to disturb a wide variety of specific voter blocs.[210] This was no amateur production. The "Citizen" noted that although John Stuart said he had voted for a measure easing payment terms for settlers buying state-owned public land, in reality he was one of only eight representatives out of fifty to vote against the law. If the law had been defeated, "would not these lands have been thrown either into the hands of speculators, or the poor purchasers forced into the hands of the usurer to borrow money to pay for them?" The rhetoric was brilliant, implying that a no vote would show that John Stuart was the friend of aristocrats and loan sharks, helping them at the expense of ordinary voters; thereby, Stuart's perfidy could be proved simply by examining the house of representatives journal.

The "Citizen" then asked: "Have you ever disproved J. M. Early's certificate of April 10, 1832, as you said you would when you declared it false? Is not that failure proof of moral perjury?" In this context, a "certificate" was simply a statement signed by someone, not a document lending any special air of credibility. This question seems related to Early's claim in the previous election that John Stuart had tried to make an alliance with Reverend Cartwright. The rhetoric slips around the issue of what constitutes proof while again raising the question of John Stuart's veracity.

The "Citizen" said further:

> You boast much of your *chivalry* in going with the brave volunteers of this county, to defend a *'bleeding frontier from the merciless scalping knife of the Indian.'* Now, on the morning after the defeat of Posey's brigade, when all was alarm and consternation, when your captain (Early [the same Early who claimed John Stuart had attempted an election alliance with Cartwright]) ordered his men to get in readiness to pursue the Indians, did you not report yourself sick and get permission from him to remain behind? Was you *actually* sick? Another reason for remaining behind, suggests itself. Can you procure the certificate of your physician, showing your physical debility on that occasion?

The prudence of making such a public charge against a Kentucky aristocrat was questionable, but again the rhetoric was superb—putting proof in terms of whether John Stuart could produce a written document prepared by a doctor who examined him in the midst of a panicked response to Indian attack.

"Have you not told divers persons that E. D. [Dick] Taylor was the preferable candidate for the senate of this state, that his weight and influence in the legislature was far superior to his competitor, and that he had especially an influence with the southern members which gave him a decided preference, and, sir, have you not denied the above statements in public company, or given counter statements relative to E. D. Taylor's influence and capacity to represent their interests?" Here the rhetoric allows John Stuart to admit support for Democrat Dick Taylor but portrays denial as a lie. Moreover, the accusation drives a wedge between Whig John Stuart and fellow Whigs supporting William F. Elkin, who was again running for the state senate—Elkin supporters who would also be voting for or against John Stuart.

The "Citizen" lays out still more charges, but this is enough to get the drift. The "citizen" soon discovered a reason why his target was called Jerry Sly. An observer relished what was to come:

> *The election* is waxing warm, excitement increasing. The principal batteries have been playing on Mills and May. On Saturday, they were opened upon Stuart—and the fire will be returned this day (so it is said) with fifty or one hundred per cent advance.
>
> Every twenty-four hours (on the average) a new battleline is proclaimed—two fights on Saturday unconnected, with one man being very dangerously dirked. Good lord, deliver us from blood and slaughter.[211]

John Stuart began his response[212] with an appeal to fair play, a tactic always influential with Western voters:

> Why is it that this handbill is issued under a feigned name? . . . The author desires to stab his neighbor's reputation, to wound his feelings, to blight his hopes, and, protected by a feigned name, screen himself from private indignation, and from public scorn.
>
> . . . Why were not these charges made long since? I have been a candidate for five months. . . . Why are they held back until the last week before the election? I appeal . . . whether this fact is not evidence that the author knew that the charges would be refuted. . . . They are the same which A. G. Herndon has been sending secretly to the different neighborhoods of this county for the last four weeks, but never putting them forth in a tangible shape until now.

Stuart thundered, "The [handbill] author sets out with the hypocritical assertion that he was among the number who sustained me at the last election. . . . It is fair to presume that the author is none other than the man who has been secretly circulating these charges for the last four weeks—the man with whom the handbills were deposited—the man who has been the active agent in circulating them, and that man is A. G. Herndon. . . . If he is in fact the author, he has ever been my political enemy, and is now both my personal and political enemy." A. G. Herndon was Billy Herndon's father, Archie Herndon, who had barely been edged out of a seat in the Illinois house of representatives in the previous election, losing by nine votes to Rev. Peter Cartwright. Archie had long alleged that

Stuart had sought a secret alliance with Cartwright to combine their strength during that campaign.

Having begun a counterattack by questioning Archie's honesty, Stuart now proceeded to shift the terms of the debate. Regarding his vote against easy credit for purchasers of Illinois public land, he noted that proceeds from those sales were earmarked for funding a public school system to provide education for children throughout the state at no charge to parents, unlike the subscription schools that Lincoln's parents had to pay for. Were such land sales for "*the poor child*, or *the poor man*? I voted in favor of the *poor child*." That explanation sounds noble but disregards that the legislature was continually borrowing from the public school fund in order to finance ordinary government operations, and those "loans" were not being repaid. As Democratic gubernatorial candidate Kinney stated: "I cannot say that I approve of the present application of the school fund, loaned out as it is to the state, it is increasing it is true [via interest on the loan], but the PRESENT CHILDREN are deriving no benefit from it. . . . What matters it to those *now in need of education* if this fund should hereafter be doubled fourfold or ten-fold. The children would increase in proportion. It is certainly the common school that is now most wanted."[213]

John Stuart said discussion of charges made by J. M. Early in the last election was pointless (a stance that is not the same as disproving them): "If any ask why I did not, after the last election, revive the paper warfare, waged by Dr. Early and myself, I reply, the charge had been made, the issue joined, and referred to the electors of this county to pass upon it. Their verdict, *by my election* as representative, I did understand to be in my favor." But of course, winning an election doesn't mean that voters disbelieve charges made against a candidate; voters may simply decide that the charges are outweighed by other considerations.

Regarding Black Hawk War service, Stuart argued: "In this, I did but do my duty. . . . Can those [such as Archie Herndon] who stayed at home during that campaign, and during the last election, to slander myself and the lamented Henry, say as much? The author of the handbill, not in direct terms . . . implies cowardice to me on one occasion." Stuart explained that his horse and those of two other men had strayed from camp, and the three men spent a day retrieving the animals and riding about forty-five miles to catch up with their company, which was marching toward Posey's brigade. "The next morning . . . our captain marched his company about a mile from Posey's Brigade, and in a few hours returned." Stuart had told his captain that he and his horse were too exhausted to go on that reconnoiter, and the captain made no complaint about Stuart staying behind. "If the skulking author of the handbill, will throw off his mask, and he should prove a man of honor, which I very much doubt, or if any of my enemies who doubt my courage, will name the time and spot; I *pledge* myself to give them evidence on that subject which will remove their doubts." Here was a scantily veiled offer to fight a duel. Dueling was illegal in Illinois, and participants were barred from holding public office. John Stuart's comment was legal, however, as it accepted no specific challenge and could be explained away as referring to fisticuffs or verbal discussion. Stuart was, however, saying he was available for dueling if anyone wanted to take him on.

Regarding the charge that John Stuart had been promoting the candidacy of Democrat Dick Taylor, Stuart said he and Taylor had discussed the topic, and Taylor was satisfied about Stuart's behavior. Stuart said the matter was between him and Taylor, and it was no one else's business. "Col. Taylor and myself, have up to this time, been personal friends." Casting the controversy in terms of private feelings between personal friends evaded the issue of whether John Stuart had been backstabbing the Whig state senate candidate William Elkin. Here I'm inclined to think Archie was on to something; otherwise, Stuart would have met the issue directly.

John Stuart concluded his reply, saying, "My friends will please circulate this among their neighbors, and have them read in their precincts, at the election."

Archie Herndon was never known for backing off and quickly issued a handbill over his own name going over the same ground, denying that he had been working in the shadows, and concluding, "With your usual disposition for gasconading, you remark, 'that if the skulking author of the handbill will throw off the mask, and he should prove to be a man of honor,' you pledge yourself to give him satisfactory evidence of your courage, &c. It is difficult, sir, for me to conceive how a man can be degraded to a proper level with yourself."[214] John Stuart quickly announced:

> The assailant of my reputation is again before the public. But he is now in the proper shape of A. G. Herndon. The application of fire has at last driven this reptile from his shell. . . . The opposition, to me, proceeds . . . from a determination to remove every obstacle to the absolute dominion and control of A. G. Herndon, and a few other persons, over the people of Sangamon County. . . . I had no sooner become a candidate before the last election, than the press opened its batteries against me on general charges, not affecting my private character, of having Presbyterian connections—that my father was a Presbyterian; it was attempted to be shown that I was under the influence of the Presbyterians of the Jacksonville college. I was called a Jerry Sly, and the attempt was made to create a prejudice against me, because I was not a Jacksonian. This mode of attack I met before the people, and they sustained me.[215]

Rather than making much response to Archie's charges, the bulk of this handbill consisted of vituperation against Herndon. But John Stuart was probably entitled to vent anger and frustration. Attack on his alleged work on behalf of Presbyterians might be construed as further evidence of hostility against mixing religion and politics. Or such attack could have been promoted by Methodist preacher-politician Peter Cartwright and his allies, an opponent who never shrank from sectarian battle and may have seen a chance to portray Stuart as connected with Illinois College, a school having Eastern antecedents and abolitionist sympathies. Archie Herndon was known to be quite hostile against the college's abolitionist proclivities, and his attitude was hardly unique among Sangamon County voters.

Cartwright dropped out of the election shortly before polling day, declaring, "There is a part of this community that have stronger claims on me, at present, than those that arise from political considerations."[216] Given his incumbency, prior service in the legislature, continuing prominence in state Democratic politics, and general pugnaciousness, his abandoning the contest at the campaign's peak is curious. His earlier and subsequent behavior showed no reluctance to combine pulpit and politics. Some people felt that Methodists exerted too much power in Illinois. Apparently just after election day, a Kentucky correspondent told John Stuart, "Could you be instrumental in breaking down the Methodistical aristocracy and Jackson misrule in your state, I should think you had accomplished an object worthy of almost any sacrifice."[217] Years later, Cartwright thinly said, "The great national parties were now organized, and, as my honest sentiments placed me in the minority in my county, of course I retired from politics. But . . . I can not see the impropriety of canvassing for office on Christian principles."[218] That excuse for giving up an electoral battle is unbelievable. A zealot fights the good fight regardless of odds and may evaluate victory in terms other than ballots. Admittedly, as we shall see, his scheme to have the Methodists control the state common school system generated controversy during this campaign, but he never shrank from controversy.

Strong pressure indeed must have forced Cartwright to give up in 1834. One of his defenders said: "By declining any longer to be a candidate, he has set an example of moderation and humility, totally at variance with the character attempted to be fixed upon him by his political opponents. . . . The zeal, the energy, the indefatigable industry, and entire devotion with which he advocated and sustained the interests of his constituents, commanded the admiration and endeared him in the affections of his fellow citizens. . . . Ability like his, is needful in the councils of his country."[219]

A Springfield newspaper announced, "On the Saturday immediately preceding the election, a barbecue will be furnished at Hill's Mills, on Sugar Creek, at which all the candidates of every grade, and all the voters of every denomination, are respectfully invited to attend."[220] A New Salem resident wrote of the event: "All I have heard talked of for the last month is politics. Our election takes place the first Monday in August. . . . I attended an old fashioned *Kentucky barbecue* last week for the benefit of candidates where they had feasting and drinking in the woods, the people behaved very well. There were many candidates present and each one made a stump speech."[221] At the campaign's climax, a Springfield newspaper observed: "For nearly the whole of last week, the weather has been excessively warm. On Monday the thermometer rose to 98 degrees—a degree of heat uncommon in this country. The political thermometer has indicated a still higher degree of heat, and has occasioned many '*bill*-ious eructations.'"[222]

Election day was August 4. Hawkins Taylor claimed a role illustrative of the kind of practical support that elected Abe:

> I lived near Salem where Mr. Lincoln lived and was greatly attached to him, and on the morning of the election I started at sunrise for the election precinct on Lake Fork, eighteen miles distant. . . . The prairie grass was higher than I was on my pony, and the result was that I was wet to the skin most of the way. The whole people in that part of Illinois were for Jackson. . . . There was a little junta in Springfield that assumed to run the Jackson party in the county.
> The junta had sent out to every precinct in the county, tickets having four names on them as the true representatives of Jacksonism.

Such printed slips would guide Democratic voters when they announced their votes out loud at the election table. Taylor noted, however, "These tickets were sent to Lake Fork precinct, but they disappeared before the polls were opened." He did not say how the tickets disappeared, but I suspect the occurrence wasn't a mishap. Taylor continued:

> While all the voters were strangers to me, I soon made myself known and useful. There was a supply of blank tickets, and I filled up one hundred and eight of the one hundred and eleven votes polled, and I got Mr. Lincoln's name on each ticket that I filled up. Not one of the voters had ever seen Mr. Lincoln, and few of them had ever heard of him. I let each man name whom he pleased for governor and the other state officers, but not one of them could name four members of the legislature [voters could choose four candidates for state representative], and then I would get in Mr. Lincoln's name. Mr. Lincoln . . . had in almost all the precincts of the county, friends . . . who took an interest in him at the polls.[223]

That kind of energetic support from even a relative handful of activists could allow a candidate to triumph regardless of how well or poorly he was known.

On election day, Lincoln came in second, with 1,376 votes, but that was good enough when four candidates were being elected to the Illinois house of representatives. The other victors were John Dawson, with 1,390 votes; William Carpenter, with 1,190; and incumbent John Stuart, with 1,164. Carpenter was the only Democrat; the other victors were Whigs.

The seat of government plebiscite on the same day produced no consensus, but Alton won a plurality. The vote reported to newspaper readers at the time was Alton, 7,511; Vandalia, 7,148; Springfield, 7,044; geographic center (Illiopolis), 774; Peoria, 486; and Jacksonville, 272. The plebiscite total was about 10,000 less than the 33,239 total votes for governor. The *Sangamo Journal* attributed the drastic difference in plebiscite and governorship vote totals to a belief that the next legislature would repeal the law that had said the plebiscite would decide the issue.[224] I'm inclined to think many voters were simply indifferent about the seat of government.

Joseph Duncan won the governor's election handsomely, his approximately 17,500 votes totaling more than the combined grand total of votes received by all his opponents. The state's most prominent Whig newspaper analyzed the outcome: "General Duncan, a Bank [of the United States], internal improvement and tariff man, is elected governor. For several years his course has been against most of the prominent measures of the administration—having been a Jackson man only in name. He received nearly the entire vote of the opposition [that is, most votes of Whigs], which added to his Jackson votes."[225] Duncan's triumph caused consternation among Jackson loyalists. One asked, "Has he not, from first to last, rode into office upon the wings of Jackson's popularity, and then opposed some of his most salutary measures, and boasted that he differed with the President honestly in opinion?"[226] Another declared Duncan "has by his inconsistency, treachery, deception, and abuses, forfeited all claims to the suffrages of those who have formerly supported him."[227] Still another confronted Duncan directly, telling him:

> No, Jo, we Jackson men took you up when you was young, poor and friendless; we put you in high office and enabled you to make a fortune; and for all this you have joined the [John Quincy] Adams men and become our enemy. You was like a poor colt. We caught you up out of a thicket, fed you on the best, combed the burs out of your mane and tail, and made a fine horse of you, and now you've broke away from us, and are trying to kick us to death for our pains.[228]

In addition to the above gubernatorial candidates, another fellow straggled in dead last, pulling about 880 votes. Ordinarily a candidate with so little statewide support wouldn't be worth a mention, but this particular candidate had influence around Sangamon County. Moreover, James Adams would later be targeted in one of the toughest political attacks Lincoln ever made on anybody.

In the 1820s, James Adams came to Sangamon County from New York State, where he had been a brigadier general, and became a big Illinois real estate speculator. State attorney general Usher Linder described Adams as "a pompous fellow, who dressed in magnificent style, and wore ruffled shirts."[229] Someone else commented that Adams signed his name with a "needless frame of flourishes."[230]

In his law practice at Springfield, however, he became known for painstaking attention to details of clients' cases—a trait as uncommon in lawyers then as now.

He received particular notoriety defending Nathaniel VanNoy in a murder case in 1826.[231] A nineteenth-century chronicler began the story this way: "There lived in the bottoms of the Sangamon River a middle-aged, rough and savage man, whose disposition was quarrelsome, whose habits were intemperate, and whose means of livelihood were suspicious. In fact, his reputation was bad."[232] In a drunken fit, he killed his wife. General Adams spoke for the defense. The same nineteenth-century account said VanNoy "had an old wagon, a plow, one cow and several young cattle growing up, and a small drove of hogs which ran in the bottoms and lived on mast. A few chickens scratched around the old log stable and a couple of hounds completed the inventory of the effects owned by the settler." In payment for his services, Adams "drew up a bill of sale covering every possible thing about the prisoner's place . . . and a few days before the trial he sent some men up, who brought away every movable thing which they could find."[233] Bowling Green was jury foreman. Juror Erastus Wright, who would later watch Lincoln build the New Orleans flatboat in Sangamo Town, wrote, "Our verdict was 'murder in the first degree.' Altho the case was clear, it was a very serious, important, and unpleasant duty to perform."[234]

Several people have documented the unusual circumstances surrouding VanNoy's execution. Wright reported, "It was generally supposed that between three and four thousand assembled at this place to witness the execution."[235] A town resident later said: "I remember about the VanNoy hanging in 1826 and seeing him in the old log jail which stood on the northeast corner of the present courthouse square, with the whipping post about eighty feet west. . . . When the day for the hanging arrived there was a large crowd assembled to witness it. . . . The procession formed at the jail and consisted of wagons filled with men, women and children, men on horseback and men and boys on foot. . . . I thought it was a big muster and wanted to go and see it but my mother would not let me."[236] VanNoy had consulted with a Dr. Philleo (perhaps Dr. Addison Philleo) about resuscitation after the hanging. The doctor advised him to lean forward as the wagon pulled away from his feet, to reduce the likelihood of a broken neck. Dr. Philleo said if that maneuver succeeded, application of electric current might restore life. VanNoy agreed to pay a "reasonable" fee upon success; if the method failed, Dr. Philleo could use the body for dissection. VanNoy followed his physician's advice, and choked to death rather than dying of a broken neck. So far, so good. The sheriff, however, was hostile to reanimating VanNoy and kept the body suspended for the better part of an hour to make sure VanNoy was good and dead. The lifeless form of VanNoy was then delivered to Dr. Philleo and colleagues, who attached battery cables and threw him the juice.[237] "The physicians tried to reanimate by electrical application but failed," wrote juror Erastus Wright at the time. "They are now dissecting him a few doors from mine. Physicians are all getting rich and the lawyers fleece the people."[238]

Onlookers included attorneys James Adams and Benjamin Mills. Watching the medicos peel away flesh from the corpse, Adams commented that the sight was affecting indeed. Mills, aware of the terms Adams had demanded to defend VanNoy, responded, "It is very seldom that a lawyer has the pleasure of seeing his client twice skinned."[239] Years later, Lincoln, too, held Adams's performance in contempt: Adams "induce[d] a man who was under a charge of murder to intrust the defense of his life in his hands, and finally took his money and got him hanged . . . got a man hanged by depending on him."[240] A Springfield resident recalled: "The door and window were wide open and a crowd of men and boys in the street looking on. The citizens became so outraged at this disgusting exhibition, that finally the dissection was removed to the back room."[241]

In the 1820s, Adams won appointment as probate justice of the peace in Springfield, and after the position became elective, he retained that job for the rest of his life, a continuing vote of confidence by the people. When he ran for governor, he was Springfield agent for Hartford Protection Insurance Company of Connecticut, a fire insurance provider. In that capacity, he was a substantial advertiser in the *Sangamo Journal*, a publication glad to get that revenue while criticizing him politically.[242]

Why Adams ran for governor in 1834 is a head-scratcher. Admittedly, he had run for lieutenant governor four years earlier,[243] but that contest's failure cannot have provided much encouragement to seek even higher office. In March 1834, newspapers reported some Peoria County sentiment for his gubernatorial candidacy, and in June, the Whig *Sangamo Journal* printed a letter signed by "Many Voters" of Sangamon County, calling on Adams to say whether he would run for governor and telling him he would have great support in Illinois from Sangamon and counties northward. In a public statement, Adams thereupon declared he was yielding to popular sentiment and agreed to become a candidate at the people's insistence.[244] Given the votes he received on election day—six in Peoria County; eleven in Morgan County, next door to Sangamon; and from northward counties, six in Jo Daviess, five in LaSalle, and four in Rock Island—it is clear no one took his candidacy seriously. And these counties typically covered a much larger geographic region than modern counties of the same name. Such dismal support was obvious from the start.

My guess is that maybe he was running for a local Sangamon County politics reason. There he was known as part of a group working against ex-governor Ninian Edwards, a group whose leaders included Big Red May, Col. Dick Taylor, and Billy Herndon's father, Archie. Two years before the 1834 gubernatorial election, this group had helped persuade state attorney general George Forquer to turn traitor against Edwards, and the group then squeaked Forquer into the state senate.[245] We know that Forquer and his half-brother Thomas Ford had been working in the shadows against Joseph Duncan in 1828,[246] so they may well have been unfriendly toward Duncan's governorship bid in 1834.

The gubernatorial platform of General Adams measures the man who would later come under attack from Lincoln. "Finances, internal improvements, and education," he said, "form the paramount duties of legislation." Noting the state government's inability to meet current expenses, he declared, "A system, calculated as heretofore, to draw from the treasury from two to three dollars for the discharge of one, presents a hopeless future." He called the Illinois & Michigan Canal vital but warned that state finances might require the project to be reduced in scale, thereby limiting the size of ships that could use it. Adams also called for a canal or railroad linking the Wabash and Mississippi Rivers, thereby creating an east-west transit line across the state. He argued that canals were better for the state than railroads, because all money spent on canal construction stayed in the state, whereas substantial amounts spent on railroads went to iron manufacturers out of state. He said the common school system needed to be set up. He said other things as well, but nothing in his platform identified him with any fringe group; General Adams appeared to be mainstream.

He did, however, seem to be of uncertain political loyalties. When he ran for lieutenant governor in 1830, he refused to express a choice between Preacher Kinney and the Old Ranger, John Reynolds, for governor.[247] In 1834, Adams favored rechartering the Bank of the United States and said a secure paper currency provided by the bank was crucial for national prosperity; these were not stances of a Jackson man. He suggested that private enterprise might construct the Canal, a position distinctly Whig and anti-Democratic. He also acknowledged what was a matter of public record: "In the heated contest between [John Quincy] Adams and Jackson, I was found on the side of Adams. But during that campaign and subsequent in the state and county elections, Sangamon poll books will attest my discriminitive votes." Over the years, he voted back and forth among candidates in apparent disregard of party affiliation and pledged that as governor he wouldn't be a party man.[248] In important ways, James Adams ostensibly met the criteria for governor announced by Abe Lincoln's New Salem meeting that had endorsed James Henry. But while General Henry was dead in the grave, General Adams was dead in the water.

> "The emoluments of office in this state are not such as to make it over desirable to a prudent man to be elected. . . . Nothing but impure ambition to be elevated for a time, or the design of unlawfully appropriating to themselves when in office, a share of the people's property, can be their motive. . . .
>
> "Ask an honest man, calculated to fill an office: 'Well, and why are you not a candidate?' his answer is, 'because I do not desire to enter the field with those ambitious office hunters. I do not wish to have my name slandered, my motives and actions misrepresented. I do not wish to spend my time in travelling over the country, making stump speeches, and giving pledges which I cannot, and do not intend to fulfil. If I can serve my fellow men and my country, I will cheerfully do it: but I cannot consent to pursue the present practice of hunting office.' Thus our best men will continue to remain at their

farms and workshops, while those popularity hunters, get by hook or crook to rule over us, and make such laws as suit their selfish interest."

—Letter from "An Illinois Farmer" in *Beardstown Chronicle*, clipped in *Sangamo Journal*, February 22, 1834

CHAPTER 8

POLITICS OF 1834:
CONGRESSIONAL

The other big election, one involving associates of Lincoln, was for U.S. Congress. Illinois had three Congressional Districts, and two of those are of particular interest to our story.

In the First District, the Old Ranger, John Reynolds, was running.[1] His technique was similar to Duncan's: "Talk Jackson and act Whig." Even in his time, observers were fascinated by the hold he had on so much of the Illinois electorate, particularly considering he lacked both charisma and personal integrity. A gossiper reported that William L. May, who would serve in Congress with Reynolds, "says Reynolds is the damndest deceitful man he ever knew."[2] A newspaper letter writer declared, "If his excellency ever entertained any opinion upon the point, it is not probable that he expressed it in the same manner to any two persons."[3] Another critic called him "a slippery article in political trade, and at all times convertible to the highest bidder."[4] Gov. Ninian Edwards was quoted as saying, "Reynolds could be bought and sold,"[5] and, "I am perfectly apprised of his overtures to join the [John Quincy] Adams men . . . while he insists upon others to vote for himself merely because he professes to be a Jackson man . . . of the facility with which he shifts from side to side to suit his own interest, and with what good grace and pleasant countenance he can, on any occasion, make promises that he never intends to fulfill."[6] A writer in the late nineteenth century said that Reynolds's demagoguery "had a charm that made it a splendid agency in the aid of his political aspirations. It had such a fascination when employed by him, it became respectable in the eyes of many who held it in detestation when attempted to be practiced by others."[7]

His achievement of popularity on the frontier was all the more remarkable because he was a teetotaler who also avoided gambling. "I had reached my fifteenth or sixteenth year," Reynolds said, "and had seen in the villages and other places much intemperance and immorality arising out of drunkenness. I deliberately reflected on the subject, and without consulting anyone, or anyone knowing it, I took a solemn resolution never to drink any distilled spirits whatever."[8] Contemporaries vouched for this: "Thousands of people in this state have known that gentleman for many years, and can prove, that he not only does *not* gamble, but that he does not drink; hence it has been often said, that it was [a] matter of surprise that Judge Reynolds, having resided thirty years in this new country, mingled much among the people in private and public life, where drinking and gambling has received a sort of sanction, even among men who hold themselves high, that he should neither drink nor gamble."[9]

His six-foot, big-boned frame was muscular. Lopsided shoulders perhaps encouraged his scuffling walk, and despite easy glad-handing of people he met, his "large and liquid" blue-gray eyes were gloomy as he strolled. His oratorical gestures seemed unnatural, nodding his head and pumping his arm up and down. A politician of the era recounted that Reynolds had "a peculiar way when he wanted to make his remarks impressive, of laying the open palm of his hand on his forehead and drawing it down slowly over his face." Said an acquaintance, "His speeches were in part grotesquely pathetic, in part ludicrously comical, always attracting great crowds." Although he successfully cultivated an impression that he was "one of the people," he did this by air and attitude. In public, he was well groomed, dressed in a fine outfit with shined shoes and tall silk hat, routinely accompanied, at least in his later years, by a slave or servant. Reynolds had one of the state's larger holdings of indentured slaves. His pretensions of having a classical college education convinced most acquaintants but was based on instruction that he and some other young men had received from a minister in Tennessee. (One classmate was Sam Houston, who would go on to glory in Texas and Congress.) Reynolds's modest formal education was nothing shameful, but he portrayed his learning as more advanced than it was, a sham strengthened by a fine memory for a grab bag of trivia and his care to read enough English translations of ancient authors to throw in quotations casually when speaking.[10]

He served as a frontier ranger in the War of 1812, earning him the nickname "Old Ranger," by which he was so well known. He saw little or no combat then and said he didn't expect to because his military unit was large enough to scare away any British-allied Indians without a fight. As governor, he had opportunity to see combat while in the field during the Black Hawk War, but fellow veterans were uncertain that he was able to see any from his hiding places when trouble arose. One contemporary called him "a complete granny."[11]

Reynolds made friends through his law practice, representing acquaintances and poor citizens free of charge. "He was no lawyer when I knew him, nor did he pretend to be; yet in certain cases, as in minor criminal offenses, slander and assault and battery cases, he was a very successful advocate." Such lawyering brought little income, and instead of making money through law, he engaged in real estate speculation. Help from his cousin Joseph A. Beaird, a "shrewd, competent businessman," aided Reynolds in acquisition of wealth. His knowledge of jurisprudence was barely adequate for the modest type of practice he pursued, let alone the supreme court judgeship he attained through political maneuvering. In that post, however, he was wise enough to seek informal advice from attorneys better than him, so he avoided embarrassing himself or the court in his decisions. When John Reynolds was governor, someone was sentenced to thirty-nine lashes for larceny. "I witnessed the punishment, and the governor did also, and said he 'had come over to see the whipping.' He stood by, and witnessed the whipping, and after thirty-eight lashes had been administered said, 'I forgive him one; that's enough.'"[12] In that regard, a successor to Reynolds, Gov. Thomas Ford, reflected about the legislature of 1830–31 during Reynolds's gubernatorial term, when "the criminal code was first adapted to penitentiary punishment, and ever after the old system of whipping and pillory for the punishment of crimes has been disused. In the course of fifteen years' experience under the new system I am compelled to say that crime has increased out of all proportion to the increase of inhabitants."[13]

Reynolds's home life provided ample ammunition for political opponents, but they seemed to steer clear of the topic. His wife was the lovely Catherine Dubuque, daughter of an Indian trader for whom the Iowa town was named. Earlier she had married Michael La Croix, a Canadian citizen who returned to Canada in 1812, supposedly to buy land, and then disappeared. Word arriving that he had died, she married the French Canadian Joseph Manegle in 1815. After the War of 1812 ended, La Croix reappeared. About this time, Manegle died, eliminating the bigamy issue, but Catherine wouldn't go back to La Croix. Instead she married John Reynolds in 1817, reestablishing bigamy. The couple and La Croix lived in vicinity of the small town of Cahokia. La Croix died in 1821, while the Old Ranger Reynolds was on the Illinois supreme court. Catherine was Roman Catholic, but authorities don't indicate what the Church said about her situation. Reynolds was an atheist who admired the works of Tom Paine. An acquaintance said that as Reynolds was dying in the 1860s, a preacher visited and told him of the bliss that awaited him if he would become a Christian. Reynolds "turned, with a look of withering contempt, and gasped, 'The hell you say.'"[14]

He campaigned hard for governor in 1830; "I used up several horses," he said. He electioneered so hard that the story is told of him approaching a human form in a field at dusk to seek support, only to discover he was addressing a scarecrow.[15] "The ladies were also enlisted in the contest," Reynolds said, "and many of them electioneered with great force and effort."[16] Someone else reported that the Reynolds campaign "employed a number of pedlars, who, under the pretense of selling a few notions, enter the cabins of the inhabitants, and after some time spent in rocking a cradle, or perhaps a couple hours wasted in nursing a dirty child, commence operations on the good woman by requesting of her to use her influence with the old man in behalf of this mighty ranger."[17] After winning election as governor in 1830 as a Jackson Democrat, Reynolds announced his support of Whig policies such as a protective tariff and federal financing of internal improvements.[18] A story during that 1830 campaign said that Capt. William

Cantrill "met John Reynolds . . . in St. Louis, last fall, and who commenced a conversation with Captain Cantrill about the election for governor. Reynolds said he understood that a number of citizens of Sangamon [County] went against him. Mr. Cantrill replied, there were, and stated to him some of the reasons. Mr. Reynolds then went on to say, that if it comes to Jacksonism, he was as much Jackson as any man ought to be, and a little more than any decent man ought to be; but he added, we Adams men must keep dark, and he would manage the thing."[19] So his political unreliability was well known when he ran for Congress in 1834. He later defiantly declared, however, "I had the people with me, and I feared nothing."[20]

Reynolds's enemies were as dedicated as his friends. After serving with him in the U.S. House of Representatives, John Quincy Adams stated, "He is untruthful, vulgar and knavish."[21] Another observer called him "the meanest white man in and about Congress."[22] Adam Snyder once snarled: "Why, d———n him, *he* will *never* die. I have been waiting for him to 'kick the bucket' for more than a quarter of a century, and his hold on life seems now to be stronger than it was when I first knew him; he will live forever, sir."[23]

Reynolds's main opponent in the 1834 congressional race was Adam Snyder, whose uncle Simon Snyder served as governor of Pennsylvania,[24] the first German farmer to achieve that post. In 1817, while Adam Snyder was a teenage store clerk in Ohio, he crossed paths with Jesse Thomas the Elder (uncle of Jesse Thomas the Younger), a physically massive and politically prominent fellow from Illinois and Indiana country. "Jesse B. Thomas the late representative from this county, and since delegate to the Congress from this Territory, having succeeded so well in his schemes of villainy and deception, has emboldened him, tho' no longer a citizen of our Territory, to push his illiterate and leather-headed brother . . . on us as a delegate to Congress."[25] The same critic said, "As soon as leisure serves, I shall prepare a complete history of the judge from the time of his *mercantile infamy* until the period of his appointment on the bench of the Illinois Territory."[26] Thomas the Elder owned indentured slaves[27] but hired Adam Snyder to come to Illinois and do wool carding there. Family tradition says Snyder was quite possibly a fugitive apprentice wool carder, thus he may well have been glad for the opportunity to put a few hundred miles more between him and his master. Then and ever afterward, Snyder was prone to bouts of ill health as a result of consumption, but wool carding was a task within his physical capability.[28]

Thomas and Snyder soon learned that they shared the same views in politics, and when the first wool-carding season ended, Judge Thomas suggested that the young man study law with him. When the judge sought a seat in the convention preparing a state constitution for Illinois, young Snyder naturally enough assisted Thomas's effort. That successful effort thwarted desires of John Reynolds, who preferred that Thomas lose, and was the start of a lifelong political rivalry between Reynolds and Snyder. In 1818, the state legislature sent Thomas and Ninian Edwards to the U.S. Senate, with the result that law student Snyder took over Thomas's law office in Cahokia, Illinois. A few weeks later, the legislature made

Cahokia lawyer John Reynolds a justice of the state supreme court. That development left Snyder as the sole law practitioner in town, a distinct advantage in gaining clients. A disadvantage was that he wasn't yet admitted to the bar, but he was able to appear in justice of the peace and probate courts. He was admitted to the bar in 1820, the same year he married a wealthy seventeen-year-old widow. He was twenty-one.[29]

A couple years later, the legislature elected him as a prosecuting attorney, but he soon resigned, having seen there was more money on the defense side of criminal litigation.[30]

In his law practice, he was a litigator, shriveling in office work but blossoming before a jury.[31] His political opponent John Reynolds generously acknowledged: "He always possessed the happy faculty of making the jurors believe he had the right side of the cause. Scarcely any person had superior talent of making a bad case in court look well."[32] In a world where oratorical skill was measured by the hour, Snyder preferred to address a jury for minutes.[33] He followed the same practice in other speeches.[34]

Adam Snyder enjoyed fluency in German and French,[35] a great asset when speaking to crowds in a part of Illinois rich with people of those heritages. It was also a commercial advantage and a reason why he encouraged Gustave Koerner to become his law partner, predicting that Koerner's fluency in German and French would help draw clients from nearby St. Louis.[36]

Snyder farmed along the Mississippi River in the highly fertile American Bottom, a region so named because it was once the far western boundary of the United States. His farm was crossed by the main road to St. Louis, and he gladly provided free accommodations to strangers and friends. His law partner, Gustave Koerner, recalled: "In one respect his German descent showed itself most plainly—he was 'gemuetlich.' His letters to me are full of warmth and in conversation he was full of good-natured humor."[37] As demands on his time called him away more and more routinely, however, chores of hospitality fell ever more on his wife, who found the task horrid.[38]

In 1830, he won election to fill a vacancy in the state senate as an "independent Jackson Democrat,"[39] a characterization generally meaning a person who talked Democratic but aided Whigs. After winning reelection in 1832, he moved to Belleville. The next year, he helped lead the Kinney-for-governor movement,[40] Kinney being an ultra-Jackson man. Snyder once wrote to his friend James Semple, "I am very careful and generally burn political letters, not trusting my best friends with those matters."[41] Obviously Semple couldn't be trusted in that department. As both a historian and a retired politician, I can testify that most officeholders have enough self-admiration that they strive to preserve every scrap of paper documenting their statesmanship. Some are more efficient at that task than others, but any politician who makes a point of erasing his tracks doesn't do so out of humility. After Snyder's death, his family destroyed every piece of his writing that they could find, ostensibly because seeing the material renewed their grief about his demise.[42] The ostensible reason may have been the real one, as they burned his clothing as well. Still, I suspect he would have heartily and gratefully approved.

In the 1834 congressional race against Reynolds, Snyder called for lowering the price of public land, contending that the federal government no longer needed the income, so the land should be distributed to buyers more quickly. Such a policy would probably help his own real estate speculations as well. Snyder and his friend James Semple cooperated closely not only in politics, but also in big real estate operations.[43] In politics, Semple succeeded George Forquer as state attorney general and held that office when Snyder was running for Congress in 1834. Snyder said he hoped Congress would donate to the state more public land along the Canal route, which the state could sell to finance the project. He claimed the project would aid national prosperity while also aiding the Illinois government's prosperity through Canal tolls. Regarding the Bank of the United States, he said: "A well regulated National Bank is not only necessary, but indispensable. . . . The present charter of the United States Bank, should not be permitted to expire, without first chartering a new one, or altering and amending the present one." Such stances were decidedly Whig, but Snyder took a more Jacksonian approach to the tariff, arguing against Henry Clay's protective tariff policy and instead advocating a tariff for revenue only. Snyder argued import duties should be lower for necessities and higher for luxuries, "thereby placing the burthen of government more particularly upon the shoulders of the rich and opulent. No mode of raising a revenue can be more equitable; the consumer pays the duty in proportion to the consumption he makes of the imported article." Through that proposal, Snyder advocated sort of a cross between a sales tax and a graduated income tax. On a local matter, he asserted that adequate compensation was needed for property losses suffered by Illinois militiamen in the Black Hawk War. And he said the West Point Military Academy was currently a bastion of aristocracy and should be more accessible to the poor.[44] Said one Illinois newspaper item:

> This academy was established for the benefit of the orphan boys of the officers and soldiers of the United States Army. Poorly it has answered its end. Few orphans enter the West Point Military Academy. Go there, and you will find it filled with the sons, not of the poor and humble, but with sons of judges, the sons of governors, the sons of Representatives and Senators to Congress, the sons of the most influential. If a wealthy man or a man high in office has a good-for-nothing, worthless, prodigal son, whom he cannot manage, the first thing to be done is to apply for a place for him in this *anti*-republican academy. He will be a fine fellow to lord it over the common soldier.[45]

Another Illinois newspaper item complained:

> Does Congress pass a law, and make an appropriation for opening or repairing a road, building, or repairing a harbor, a pier, or an

aqueduct—a *young cadet* (generally a son of a member of Congress, or Secretary of a Department, or Head of a Bureau) is employed for this service; sometimes a dozen of them at wages varying from two to six dollars per day, exclusive of their army pay and rations! Is a canal or road to be surveyed, none but a *West Point cadet* can do it. Are the Indians about to emigrate west to be settled, or payments to be made to them on this side of the great river—none but a *"dandy officer"* from West Point can be employed, who probably never saw an Indian in his life!![46]

Snyder wasn't the only politician to take on the academy: "The Hon. David Crockett has introduced a resolution into Congress to abolish the military academy at West Point."[47]

According to Reynolds, Snyder acted as if he enjoyed electioneering.[48] Yet he also showed hesitations strange in a vigorous candidate. For example, in the 1834 campaign, Snyder arrived at an influential settler's farm at dusk, hoping to spend the night there and learn whom the farmer supported for Congress. As Snyder came around the corner of a farm building, he saw Reynolds helping the farmer and wife with chores. Snyder quietly turned around without making his presence known and headed away.[49] A bolder campaigner would have strided forward with a hearty hello for everyone and pitched in as well, joking about which candidate could provide the best help. Indeed, John Palmer recalled Reynolds doing something much like that:

> At the spring term of the Madison county Circuit court in 1834, I was present when Hon. Adam W. Snyder, candidate for Congress, had, as he supposed, a meeting of his own. He was addressing the people, when, to his surprise and consternation, Governor Reynolds walked in, and, in his usual affable way, said, "How are you all, fellow citizens?" Then recognizing some persons in the audience, shook hands with them, and enquired about the health of their families. Mr. Snyder paused, and, raising his hands, exclaimed, "My God! will I ever get rid of him this side of Heaven?" And then added sententiously, "When there, I am quite sure I will be rid of him forever."[50]

Snyder was speaking metaphorically here. His son called him "agnostic," being "without a trace of superstition, and wholly unable to believe the miraculous and supernatural."[51] Apparently Snyder wasn't an atheist, however, as he secretly belonged to the Freemasons.[52]

The spoiler candidate in the First Congressional District was Edward Humphreys, jocularly called "Snuff Box." His reputation of strong support for Van Buren apparently made him a favorite of ultra-Jackson men, peeling away votes from Snyder. "Had that damned old fool Humphreys not have run I should have laid out old Reynolds forever," Snyder fumed. "Is it not extraordinary that there is always some creature like that in the way, never strong enough to be elected, but troublesome enough to keep others out."[53]

Because of some Jackson voters going to Humphreys instead of Snyder, and Reynolds gaining what one observer acknowledged to be "nearly the entire Whig party" vote,[54] Reynolds won. "I am *hot* to pay my friends and enemies," Reynolds privately said. "One I will do all for, the other I will add my might to their destruction."[55]

We shall hear more of John Reynolds, the Old Ranger, and Adam Snyder, so their relatively civilized First Congressional District race is worth knowing about, but we also need to know about the nasty Third District race between bald-headed Benjamin Mills and slaveowning[56] William L. "Big Red" May. Incumbent Congressman Joseph Duncan was running for governor, leaving Mills and May to contend for an open seat. This was the district where Lincoln lived and the congressional seat that Democrats correctly expected John Stuart to seek later. Stuart would eventually be successful, and subsequently Lincoln would seek a redistricted version of that seat, as would Big Red's law partner Stephen T. Logan. But for now, we need only view what was happening between Mills and May in 1834.

"A Jackson man—of this there can be no dispute," the *Sangamo Journal* said of Big Red May in 1834.[57] "A violent Van Buren man," said a critic that same year,[58] and Van Burenites were the most extreme Jackson advocates. A correspondent of the *Sangamo Journal* once described May as a "dog of the Jackson party,"[59] but we need not quibble about proper genus designation. Because of Big Red's easy transfer of party affiliation, however, specifying the year is important in specifying his politics. As a nineteenth-century gentleman noted: "He left Kentucky a Whig, but going to Democratic Illinois had turned his political coat. During the Harrison tornado of 1840, he again joined the Whigs and was eloquent against Van Buren and his gold spoons [alleged White House luxuries paid for by taxpayers]. In the succeeding campaign [1844] he once more joined the Democracy."[60] That recounting left out a few flip-flops,[61] but it gives the idea. In 1834, one observer said of him, "A greater compound of meanness and stupidity was never mingled."[62]

During the 1834 congressional campaign, Big Red was Register of the Springfield U.S. Land Office, a lucrative post demonstrating President Jackson's appreciation of his services, and was also law partner of John Stuart's kinsman Stephen T. Logan.[63]

One nineteenth-century observer called Big Red "a man of good address and a capital stump-speaker."[64] Another said: "As an electioneer he was unrivaled—had been a preacher, was a capital story-teller and could play the Arkansas Traveler all through on the violin. . . . When excited his profanity was fearful to listen to."[65]

Big Red was running against state representative Benjamin Mills. Ben was law partner of Jesse Thomas the Younger up Galena way.[66] Thomas the Younger was a nephew of Adam Snyder's patron Jesse Thomas the Elder. As a prosecutor,

Mills earned a fearsome reputation. A spectator who attended a trial where Felix Grundy spoke for the defense, the same Grundy who earlier was Mordecai Lincoln's lawyer and later would be President Van Buren's Attorney General, remembered Grundy commenting that "he had never encountered such a competitor as Mills, and that he considered it inhuman to employ a man of such ability in the prosecution; that it was not giving the accused a fair chance."[67] Ben was a master at fast repartee: "It was told of him that having joined a temperance society and being found soon after in a grocery drinking out of a wine glass, instead of a tumbler, a friend said to him, 'Mills, I thought you had quit drinking?' 'So I have,' said he, holding up the wineglass, *'in a great measure.'*"[68] Some claimed Mills to be a Jackson man; some claimed him to be Whig.[69] The lukewarm support Ben Mills gave to Democratic views implied he was another of the "talk Jackson, act Whig" coalition men. Further support for that supposition is found in favorable treatment he received from the Whig newspaper *Jacksonville Illinois Patriot*. Indeed, Mills was publicly accused of supporting Henry Clay.[70] Andrew Jackson's opinion on the question was public. Soon after taking office, the President fired Mills from his post as Register of the Vandalia U.S. Land Office.[71]

In the Illinois house of representatives, Ben achieved notoriety as an impeachment manager against state supreme court justice Theophilus Smith in 1833. Smith was the father-in-law of Ben's law partner, Jesse Thomas the Younger.[72] He was an emigrant from New York, where he had studied law in the office of Aaron Burr, and was called "Tammany" Smith. He had been a leader in the effort to convert Illinois into a slave state in the 1820s, a struggle in which Mills had been on the opposite side as an antislavery leader.[73] Where Smith garnered ill favor with the legislature, however, was in his continuing Democratic partisanship while a supreme court justice. He was considered a bully acting on behalf of John Reynolds.[74] Complaints against Justice Smith included nepotism, failure to hold circuit court, and being a duelist.[75]

One example will suffice to show the kind of conduct by Smith that disturbed people. In November 1832, former governor Ninian Edwards wrote a detailed account of "a rencounter which I unfortunately had with Judge Smith in the streets of Edwardsville on last Friday night. . . . A little after dark, as I was walking from the upper to the lower town, Judge Smith and another gentleman . . . passed me on horseback, the judge swearing vengeance against someone, and his companion swearing that he should back him in it." It was unclear who was meant for vengeance.

> From a statement subsequently made by the judge's own son . . . the judge went home, deliberately loaded his pistols, and returned to town with the avowed determination of shooting or chastising Mr. William P. McKee and Mr. Cyrus Edwards [brother of Ninian]. . . . He suddenly returned into the street, calling out, "Gov. Edwards, I would be glad to have a word with you." I stopped, he approached me and observed that he should be glad to see me at the tavern in half an hour.

I readily promised to meet him there. . . . He rapidly remarked . . . that he was determined to make every damned rascal *toe the mark.* Being thus accosted, and recollecting the backing I had heard promised him, it occurred to me as not impossible that his object in requesting an interview with me at the tavern and postponing it for half an hour might be to collect some bullies round him with a view to abuse, or at least, to insult me with impunity. As it was then in the night, we entirely alone and the opportunity as favorable as he could desire for saying anything he pleased to me, I could think of no motive he could have for postponement, and the assignment of a different place of meeting, than some such strategy, and hence I demanded to know what his object was. He declined telling me, but said he would explain himself at the requested interview. I replied that, if he did not choose to tell what he wanted with me, I might not be disposed to meet him at all. He then observed that he had observed certain caucusing [regarding impeachment] against him for two or three days past; and that he had too much penetration in such matters not to know whence it proceeded. I assured him, as was truly the case, that if there had been any such caucus as he described, I had had not only no participation in it, but, was utterly ignorant of it. To which he replied that my damned dogs were concerned in it, and made some other remarks personally offensive to myself. These, I bore as well as I could, for feeling that a crippled right hand, which, for nine years past, has disabled me from carving my own victuals, and an affliction in my back which has confined me for a great part of the present year, and still disqualifies me for any active operations, added to the infirmities of age [fifty-seven years old], rendered me unequal to a personal conflict with a strong athletic man, in the prime of life [forty-eight years old], like Judge Smith, I sincerely wished to avoid any rencounter with him; and with that view, repeated my assurance that I had done nothing to which he had any right to take exception, and demanded of him why it was that he thus attacked me in the public streets. . . . Instantly drawing out two loaded horseman's pistols, and presenting the muzzles of both to me, he offered me a choice, and called me a *damned dog.* . . . I did not choose to take either in the position in which they were presented to me, well knowing that before I could turn and present either, he might, and doubtless would, have shot me with the other. . . . My first thought was to knock the pistols out of his hands with my stick, but, it being nothing but a light bamboo walking cane, it was not to be relied upon, and as the only alternative, I knocked him down with my fist, and caned him in necessary self defense till we were separated. . . .

He still continues his threats against Mr. McKee and Mr. Cyrus Edwards, as well as myself, and thus is exhibited, *in a civilized country*, the extraordinary spectacle of a crippled infirm old man, and two of the most peaceable citizens of the state, reduced to the necessity of arming to defend themselves against the ruffian violence or murderous assaults of a judge of the supreme court.[76]

Tammany Smith offered his own version of what happened, saying that Edwards had "publicly declared in the streets of Belleville [sic], that he would chastise me; and arming himself with a large club, he proceed[ed] to accost me in the public square of that town. . . . Aware of his purposes, I invited him to my room at the tavern . . . upon which [invitation] he went off pouring out a torrent of vulgar abuse, threatening me with prostration, and impeachment." Smith said that he had made a casual comment that he saw that a caucus had ended and Edwards was present when Smith made his comment.

> Edwards said, "What do you mean by attacking me." I replied, that I had said nothing to him—and so far from attacking him, that I desired to have nothing to do with or say to him. . . . He instantly replied, "You, sir, are a damned scoundrel," upon which I retorted the epithet, and passed my left hand into my coat pocket behind, observing, that I had a pair of *fixings*, to one of which he was welcome;—he has it, that I presented two pistols and offered him one.
>
> At this moment my left hand was seized by some person behind me, and a most violent blow given, on the under part of the right jaw, from behind, about one inch and a half from the angle of the jaw, which produced an extensive compound fracture, and the dislocation of the jaw bone. The blow was evidently from its power, and effect, given with a heavy weapon, and I believe from the character and position of the fracture, that it was done with the butt end of the pistol wrenched from my hand. Edwards standing directly in front of me, at the same moment of time, gave me a blow over the left eye with a club, or heavy stick . . . under the joint effect of both blows, I was brought to the ground.
>
> In a few seconds, however, I gained my feet, and found I had been deprived of the other pistol and left defenseless, and exposed to the assaults and violence of two persons. I recollected a small pen knife in my pocket, and turning on Edwards with it, he fled into, and shut himself up in the Land Office. . . .
>
> I remained on the ground for more than one hour, disabled and unarmed.

Smith said he routinely went about armed because of threats from assorted persons who were disgruntled by his judicial decisions.[77] Said one of his critics, "I shall as soon expect to see a water snake climb a tree tail foremost as to hear the truth from the Hon. Judge Smith, when *avarice*, *ambition*, or *revenge* shall prompt him to act otherwise."[78]

At the climax of house impeachment proceedings against Justice Smith, Ben Mills spoke for three days.[79] An observer from the time said Ben Mills's "effort was looked upon as transcendently great. I have heard the Hon. Cyrus Edwards [whom Smith had been threatening to kill] . . . declare that he never heard a more finished, scholarly, or eloquent oration, and that it could not be surpassed. Brilliant passages from his address were quoted on the streets at Vandalia [the state capital] for a long time afterwards."[80] A majority of the senate voted to convict but failed to achieve a two-thirds majority, so Smith remained in office.[81] Smith's conduct had been offensive enough to produce a set of impeachment managers spanning the state's political spectrum, from John Stuart to Adam Snyder's friend James Semple, so Ben Mills's leadership role in the impeachment tells us nothing about his own political orientation. But the business does tell us something about the atmosphere of Illinois politics.

During the 1834 congressional campaign, Ben Mills and Big Red traveled together around the district.[82] In a joint appearance at Springfield, Big Red May said he would support Vice President Martin Van Buren, U.S. Rep. Richard M. Johnson, U.S. Supreme Court Justice John McLean, or anyone else the Democrats nominated for President. Big Red was "opposed to the present United States Bank, but was in favor of a National Bank which should not possess what he deemed the objectionable powers held by the present Bank." He also said he favored a permanent preemption law "of the character proposed by Mr. Mills," giving squatters a right to buy U.S. government land on which they had settled.[83]

A few weeks later, another joint appearance in Carrollton went over the same ground but brought out a few more points. According to an eyewitness, Mills said he would support Johnson for President if Johnson were nominated, a promise that Big Red challenged, but Mills reiterated it. Mills praised Representative Johnson's report "to Congress on the Sunday mail question; and concluded by congratulating the country that the report had annihilated the designs of *a certain religious sect, whose object was to connect church and state.*" The eyewitness noted that the Presbyterians, of which Ben was one, had cranked up the issue of whether mail should be handled on Sunday and were suspected of wanting to link church and state. Thus, given Mills's Presybterian affiliation, the eyewitness was taken aback by his statement. (Illinois controversy about Presbyterians can be attributed partly to fussing about Illinois College, a Jacksonville school affiliated with the denomination and notorious as a center of abolitionism.) Equally surprising to the witness was Mills's claim to have no opinion about Jackson's withdrawal of federal deposits from the Bank of the United States. In contrast, Big Red forthrightly endorsed the withdrawal. Overall the witness characterized Ben as evasive: "When a man is elected who is neither one thing nor the other, he is afraid to take a decided course in Congress lest his popularity at home should be impaired. . . . By such conduct he loses the power to serve us, or to promote in any degree our interests."[84]

After Ben made a campaign speech in Jacksonville, members of the crowd pushed forward an enthusiastic Democrat to make a reply. Response from someone in the audience was a Western custom, and this particular replier didn't act reluctant. He was a young attorney named Stephen A. Douglas. An eyewitness said: "His attempted reply and counterattack were so spirited as greatly to arouse the enthusiasm of his party friends, and to inspire a stout Kentuckian standing near me to cry out, 'Hit him again, little fellow! Give him a pair of gaffs.' It was a match of gamecocks with my Kentucky friend."[85] About the time the congressional campaign started, a Winchester meeting discussed President Jackson's policies. Josiah Lamborn led the Whig attack. Lamborn was "known throughout Illinois as its most vituperative orator, and greatest master of invective, whose vitriolic utterances had struck terror to the hearts of those whom he opposed in court and forum."[86] A later governor of Illinois described Lamborn as "inclined to be vindictive, and very resentful of any slight offered him by an opposing attorney."[87] Douglas relished such an opportunity to take on Lamborn, saying, "I could not remain silent." He continued:

> I was then familiar with all the principles, measures and facts involved in the controversy, having been an attentive reader of the debates in Congress and the principal newspapers of the day, and having read also with great interest, the principal works in this country; such as the debates in the convention that formed the Constitution of the United States, and the convention of the several states on the adoption of the Constitution, the *Federalist*, John Adams's work denominated a defense of the American Constitution, the opinions of Randolph, Hamilton, and Jefferson on the constitutionality of the Bank [of the United States], and the history of the Bank as published by Gales & Seaton, Jefferson's *Works*, &c. I had read all of them and many other political works with great care and interest, and . . . I engaged in the debate with a good deal of zeal and warmth.[88]

There may also have been a personal grudge; Lamborn had refused to take on Douglas as a law student, almost ridiculing the young man's abilities.[89] Douglas was twenty years old, practicing law in justice of the peace courts, where he did not need a lawyer's license—the same sort of thing Lincoln had been doing. Soon after getting a law license, in March 1834 he and the editor of the Democrat *Jacksonville News* announced a mass meeting of Democrats. In the words of one of Douglas's friends, "When the day of the meeting arrived, the courthouse was thronged; people poured into town in wagons, on horseback, and on foot. At twelve o'clock a larger concourse of people had assembled in Jacksonville than had ever met there before."[90] Resolutions supporting Jackson and calling for similar meetings across the state had been prepared in advance. Douglas had not intended to present them to the meeting, but with the moment for action at hand, the person chosen for that task insisted that Douglas do it, saying he owed it to himself to make himself known to such a throng. Douglas seized the moment and the resolutions.

Josiah Lamborn replied for the Whigs, "severe and caustic in reference to Mr. Douglas, and flatly contradicted a statement of fact made by him." Upon completion of Lamborn's address, Douglas's friend said: "Douglas immediately arose, and at once applied himself to a reply to Lamborn. The question of fact he soon disposed of by calling up several Whigs, who declared Lamborn to be wrong." An hour passed, maybe more, as Douglas continued. Lamborn walked out while Douglas was speaking. Douglas's friend stated, "When Douglas concluded his speech, the excitement of the meeting had reached the highest point of endurance; cheer upon cheer was given with hearty vigor; the crowd swayed to and fro to get near the orator, and at length he was seized by them, and, borne on the shoulders and upheld by the arms of a dozen of his stalwart admirers, was carried out of the courthouse and through and around the public square with the most unbounded manifestations of gratitude and admiration." Among other calls of praise, someone referred to him as "the Little Giant."[91] Douglas's adult physical stature was that of a boy, about five feet, two or three inches in height, with the size of his head typical of a larger person but out of proportion to his torso and legs.

The *Jacksonville Illinois Patriot* Whig newspaper was so irked by Douglas's performance that it gave heavy and unfavorable coverage to him for weeks. As Douglas was the first Democratic lawyer in the Jacksonville bar, Democratic litigants in the region began flocking to him. Douglas reflected, "I have sometimes doubted whether I was not morally bound to pay the editor for his abuse according to the usual prices of advertisements."[92]

Regarding the congressional and other races in 1834, Stephen Douglas said: "I felt no ordinary interest and took an active part. I supported the Democratic . . . William L. May for Congress against Benjamin Mills."[93]

In June, Ben Mills and Big Red May decided they had nothing more to say and would cease campaigning. "I have entered into an agreement with my opponent," Big Red announced, "that we should each rest our own prospects on the efforts already made."[94] Their supporters, however, continued campaigning and switched to a style far different from the civility and high tone that had characterized the candidates' joint appearances.

The *Jacksonville Illinois Patriot* Whig newspaper soon printed a pseudonymous letter that attracted attention. The letter charged:

1. Big Red May was indicted for burglary while living in Edwardsville but convinced the witness to leave Illinois, resulting in dismissal of charges.
2. Big Red seduced a woman under promise of marriage around 1825, and she sued him for breach of promise. She agree to drop the lawsuit in return for $200, and after she dropped it May refused to pay cash. He said she could have a horse and saddle or nothing, and she accepted the barter.
3. After Big Red married, "he visited a house in the county of Greene, and remained there some days, representing himself as a single and unmarried man, and courting a young woman who resided in the family."[95]

Here was information that voters could comprehend more readily than disputes about the proper tariff schedule for salt.[96] The information's credibility was enhanced by timing. Rather than make these charges in the campaign's last hours, leaving Big Red no opportunity to reply, a trick old even in that era, his accuser was manly and allowed May plenty of time to respond. That in itself bespoke of the accuser's calm confidence that investigation would verify what he said, a certitude that had to impress the public.

Big Red instantly saw that he had to distribute a defense as widely as possible, so he approached one of the most widely read newspapers in the state, Springfield's *Sangamo Journal*. The *Journal*'s editor, Simeon Francis, had room in his columns for many lengthy political items but could find no room for Big Red's defense.[97] Like the *Illinois Patriot*, the *Sangamo Journal* was a Whig paper. Big Red then said he'd pay regular advertising rates to have his defense published. Politics is politics, but business is business, and Sim Francis was willing to distribute Big Red's explanations around the state on a cash basis.[98] Regarding the charges, May's defense went as follows:

1. "The common opinion is that burglary is the breaking into a house with intent to steal," Big Red explained. "I was there at that time by invitation from a female member of the family." Alfred V. Cavalry (later a state representative) affirmed, "Your entry into the dwelling house was not to commit murder, but to have illicit intercourse with a female then residing there." Regarding failure to bring the case to trial, the judge handling the case recalled, "No arrangement ever took place before me between William L. May and the witness or witnesses to prevent their appearance against him" (which wasn't the same as saying the witness appeared). In those days private citizens could help prosecute criminal cases; such a task wasn't monopolized by state's attorneys. In this case the prosecutor was the woman's husband. May said "the prosecutor was anxious to hush it up, lest it should recoil with disgrace on himself."

2. "I have often freely acknowledged, that in youth, and in early manhood I have committed many follies and indiscretions" and "for which I trusted I had long since made some atonement by an upright moral deportment." "Isabel Rainer, whose name is thus dragged before the public, is now a respectable member of the Baptist Church, the mother of a family of children, the wife of one of our fellow citizens. . . . If I must be crushed, was there no respect due to her feelings, to those of her husband, her innocent children or her relations?

   "If she has erred, the station she now occupies is evidence that she has been sincerely penitent."

   "Out of respect to public sentiment and her feelings, and those of her family, I did compromise the suit, I must acknowledge; but all that part which is intended to shew, an attempt on my part to take advantage of her distress, is false and slanderous." Her brother Joseph Wise now said the suit was settled to satisfaction of all parties.

3. The *Illinois Patriot* letter said Lewis W. Link could verify May's visit to the house where he courted a woman while he was married. Link now denied any knowledge of such event.

Big Red concluded by noting that "the worst of these charges" was made four years earlier, when he ran for the state legislature, and voters back then elected him nonetheless.[99]

These explanations failed to quiet public interest.

The *Patriot* responded with more pen name letters, further distributed as handbills, reviewing the specifics:

1. "You should have answered . . . 'I did break into the dwelling house of my friend in the nighttime, not to commit a felony, to steal ten pounds of bacon, or murder anyone, as the young man supposed who awoke and found my fingers on his throat, but only, my dear constituents, *only* to commit adultery [with] my friend's wife.'"

   "Dr. Tiffin and yourself were acquaintances abroad—you had known his wife previous to her marriage—and for the sake of former years, you were admitted to his home and treated with all the kindness of friendship. He upheld and sustained you when the world had cast you off as a vagabond." "You seduced the affections of his wife and vilely dishonored his bed."

   "You were suspected and were driven from the house. It was then, that taking advantage of the hold you had gained on that unfortunate woman's affections, you seduced her to consent to clandestine meetings with you, and you did meet her once and often. It was with this intent, as you say, that you broke into the house of Dr. Tiffin that eventful night." Indictment was "warranted by the circumstances:—your feeling about the throat of the sleeper, your fleeing on detection, all conspired to show a felonious intent of the blackest character." Tiffin refused to proceed further, abandoning prosecution. "Is it a wonder that he was unwilling, on the discovery of his disgrace to meet the brazen face of the despoiler of his peace, to bear your bitter jibes, and proclaim his infamy in the ears of the world? He did shrink from the prosecution, and from the scene of his disgrace, and, with the little peace that God had left him retired among other scenes with a decayed frame and broken heart to board it there."

2. "Why this stuff about disturbing Elizabeth Rainer's peace. . .? God forbid that I should impute your guilt to that woman—God forbid that I should, as you have done, croak about '*her* errors,' and '*her* reputation,' and excuse your villainy on the score of her frailty."

   "These things you say occurred in your young days. . . . Yes, you were a boy—a hot-blood mettlesome boy, just about arrived at the tender and interesting age of THIRTY" and "a widower with two children."[100]

There was more, but this is enough to get the drift.

Big Red responded by saying all the anonymous *Patriot* letters were the work of one man:

> Like a snake he slips off his old skin, and comes out with a new covering, glistening with added venom, in turn to be discarded and cast off. Like the prowling Indian, sparing neither age nor sex, when he has fired from one cover and his concealment is exposed, he flies to another, where he may lie hid, and assault you when unprepared and unsuspected. . . .
>
> Who is this "Agricola?" Some *puling*, sentimental, *he* old maid! whose cold liver and pulseless heart never felt a desire which could be tempted, except for getting money, for fawning on the great and feasting his malice on slander and detraction. . . . Some spindle-shanked toad-eating, man-granny, who feeds the depraved appetites of his patrons with gossip and slander. We read of a certain sort of men about the Turkish seraglios, who being deprived of their virility endeavor to compensate themselves by the enjoyments of mischief-making. . . . From the spirit in which "Agricola" writes, it might seem he was either born one of this kind of being, or had made himself so, not for the sake of the kingdom of heaven, but for the purpose of increasing his ability and appetite for scandal.

Big Red then uttered an interesting name:

> Those who are seen in this "Agricola" affair are hangers on, the tools and lickspittles of the would-be aristocracy, who are attempting to establish their dominion over the freemen of this country. Peter Van Bergen seems to be the active agent here in Springfield: Many of my fellow citizens have known this man as the agent of Mr. Ware, the great land speculator, moneylender and usurer, who not long since began his operations in this country; and I presume Van Bergen is now endeavoring to regain favor with the wealthy and aristocratic of the country, by a double measure of servility and activity.[101]

This is the same Peter Van Bergen who was suing Lincoln, trying to collect an inflated amount on the old note that Van Bergen had acquired from Reuben Radford. So Van Bergen was considered not only a businessman, but also a politician.

Big Red's complaints drew a pseudonymous response from "Philo-Agricola": "To the fires of the monkey you have superadded, the vigor of the horse. Sir, *such* boasts might have done for the brothel; for the grog shop they were too low; but in a public print, over your own signature and you a candidate for a seat in Congress, what term in language is sufficiently strong to express our deep and abiding abhorrence of such a self-glorious Priapus. Would you vie with the god Hercules in his thirteenth labor?—what, fifty daughters of King Thespeus in a single night?"[102] Such commentary was pretty raw for publicly distributed printed documents in 1834. If such was the content of public discourse about Big Red May, I wonder about private discourse.

About the same time that some character assassins started attacking Big Red May, others were plying the same craft against his opponent Ben Mills.

When northwest Illinois feared the approach of Black Hawk two years earlier, three citizens sent warning to the governor and appealed for help. Those three were Richard Young, later to become a U.S. Senator; James Strode, law partner of Thomas Ford and soon to become Galena's military commander; and Ben Mills.[103] By implication of his role in summoning aid, Mills was a leader in the defense effort. That isn't the way things were portrayed, however, in a pseudonymous letter making the rounds of Democratic newspapers in June 1834 (indicating the papers didn't consider Mills a Jackson man).

Colonel Strode took military command of Galena at the request of its citizens and declared martial law, forbidding able-bodied men to leave. A newspaper letter signed "Henry" said:

> At this trying time it is said Mr. Mills evinced great anxiety to leave Galena for Boston, and intimated that he should do so in defiance of the colonel's order, the legality of which he stood ready to contest; but finding that the colonel had the power and intended to enforce his order, legal or illegal, he then supplicated the colonel for permission to leave, at the same time intimating to the colonel that if permission was refused, he would procure a certificate of physical disability from his physician which would protect him from the hardships and dangers of the service, or to authorize him to leave the country, saying at the same time that he did not wish to be driven to this necessity. The colonel told Mr. Mills that he could not make a distinction between him and other men. Mr. Mills then made application to the surgeon at Galena, who gave him such a certificate as he desired, and upon which he obtained permission from Colonel Strode to leave the country for Boston, and accordingly put out.[104]

That letter was followed by a handbill reprinted in newspapers, signed "A Volunteer of 1832." It said Mills "was among the first to desert the cause, and abandon his property. He applied to the commanding officer for permission to leave the country, which was promptly denied him. He then as the last resort, applied to the surgeon of the regiment . . . [who] gave him a certificate *of physical debility*, which secured his passage *to the abodes of peace*." From Galena, said "Volunteer," Mills took "a letter from the commanding officer to the Secretary of War, communicating to the War Department the state and progress of hostilities in that quarter." His travel was unhurried enough that Washington officials learned of his approach six days before he arrived, word traveling because he announced to persons he met that he was bearing a war dispatch. "On his arrival . . . he handed over his letter, for which as an express bearer, he demanded and received upwards of THREE HUNDRED DOLLARS OF THE PEOPLE'S MONEY!!" Mills "abandoned his home, his friends, the wives and little ones of his neighbors (his own being in a place of safety) to the mercy of the tomahawk and scalping knife" and "took more of the people's money, for running away from and deserting his home, than hundreds of you received for months of toil, privation and danger." The letter declared, "The blood of the helpless women and innocent children, shed by savage monsters on this frontier" and "the spirit you have inherited from your fathers, never will permit you to confer honors and emolument on cowardice and desertion."[105]

Regarding the "Volunteer of 1832" handbill, Ben proclaimed, "ALL the charges, in that handbill contained, *in the manner in which they are expressed, are utterly false.*" (So would some other manner of expressing them make them less than false?) He added: "Such bilious eructations are well suited to the season of the year, the proximity of the crisis, and the dangerous symptoms of the malady. To attack a man, in this manner, behind his back, when fair and open opportunities have been afforded [in joint appearances], is no better than to sneak into his meat house and rob it, when there is no one at home to defend it."[106] A handbill reprinted in the *Sangamo Journal* responded, "You now deny these charges and pretend they were kept back until it was too late for you to circulate your denial over the District. How can you say this when they were made near two months before the election. At the Rushville court which was the 9th of June, you said [you] had seen the piece signed Henry, and that you should take no notice of these charges."[107]

Mills said that a Springfield U.S. Land Office clerk had furnished payment to the handbill's printer and an unspecified "Land officer" had furnished the text.[108] As Big Red May ran that Land Office, Ben was clearly attributing the handbill to May. Big Red denied that he had written the text or that the clerk had paid for printing. Editorial comment in the *Sangamo Journal*, presumably by Sim Francis, affirmed May's denial.[109] A handbill defending Ben disputed the denials from Big Red May and Sim Francis, noting that Land Office Receiver John Taylor, a former Sangamon County sheriff and current business associate of gubernatorial candidate Joseph Duncan, had arranged for publication of "Volunteer of 1832" handbills at the *Sangamo Journal* office and paid for them, and they were stored at the Land Office and distributed by office clerks.[110] A "very large and respectable meeting of the friends of Benjamin Mills" unanimously declared that Big Red had asked some Galena residents to write the "Volunteer" handbill.[111] The same meeting asserted that rather than trying to escape danger, Mills had taken a report to Washington by the request of Colonel Strode, who also asked him to lobby for more federal help against Black Hawk. The meeting unanimously said, "We well recollect the joy that pervaded all classes of the community, on learning that we were to have so able an advocate at the city of

Washington." Ben Mills must have been particularly irked at being attacked on his Black Hawk War record, given that Big Red May never volunteered for service either.[112]

Big Red proclaimed, "The charges . . . made in that handbill, and denied by my opponent, have since been proven to be true by the certificates of Dr. Addison Philleo, and Col. J. M. Strode, of Galena,"[113] certificates simply being signed statements, not special documents. Strode said, "Our citizens had seen many able-bodied militiamen leaving the country in every steamboat, thereby not only weakening the country in its numerical strength, but depriving us also of the most essential elements for our defense, by taking off with them muskets, ammunition, kettles, blankets, &c." He explained, "Positive orders had been published that no able-bodied militiaman should leave the place without permission from the commanding officer, or a certificate from the surgeon or assistant surgeon of physical inability, under the pain of being treated as a deserter."[114] In addition to being regimental surgeon, Dr. Philleo was editor of the strongly Democratic *Galenian* newspaper. He stated: "Benjamin Mills, Esq. applied to me, as the surgeon of the regiment, for a certificate of inability to bear arms, and said he wished to go to Massachusetts, where his family had previously gone. I gave him the necessary certificates, and he embarked on board the boat."[115]

Strode had earlier offered to write Mills a pass to leave town, but Ben preferred a document saying he was physically incapable of fighting. His political defenders said those events proved Strode didn't regard Mills as a deserter, but the question was cowardice, not desertion. Mills was running for state representative at the time (an election he would win), and he was well aware that he needed some plausible excuse for voters who asked why he hadn't served in military forces defending the region. Indeed, he told Strode that a pass to leave town would be "too humiliating."[116] A medical excuse saying he was unfit to fight would avoid the cowardice issue, or so Ben probably hoped. I'm not saying here that Mills was a coward; I'm simply explaining political angles regarding his efforts to leave the war zone. Because Mills was heading for Massachusetts, Strode asked if he could pass through Washington, D.C., and deliver a war progress report to the Secretary of War. Ben agreed. This seemed to be a perfect way to explain why he was leaving town; he wasn't trying to avoid fighting, but instead was delivering a military dispatch by request of the Galena commander, doing the best that a medically unfit man could do in the war. Strode, however, said in his 1834 election certificate that he intended to vote for Big Red.[117]

A handbill reprinted in the *Sangamo Journal* summarized charges against Ben: "You contrived to make your escape from danger, and at the same time to make money by deserting your own home, your neighbors, and friends, and the women and children of your own town."[118]

Although attackers concentrated on Mills's conduct in the Black Hawk War, they didn't neglect other openings. For example, though Ben may have recently joined the Presbyterian Church and been chairman of the Galena Bible Society's annual meeting:[119]

All those who have had an acquaintance with him for the last several years, know that he has been exceedingly intemperate and dissipated, wasting his means or rather other peoples' in the most extravagant and expensive frolics of drunkenness. Many have heard him relate, that when on his way to this state, how he imposed himself upon the people of a town in Virginia, for a minister of the gospel, and that in derision of the holy religion of which he is now a professor, he did actually attempt to preach to the people. He has often, over a glass of wine, acted the part he then played, and related for the amusement of the company, what difficulties he encountered in "rounding off," as he called it, the prayer.[120]

The Virginia congregation was so pleased with his preaching that they gave him substantial funds, under the impression he would expend them to convert heathens when he reached the West.[121]

More substantive charges existed about Ben's Presbyterian connections. He was friendly toward the denomination's Illinois College.[122] A handbill signed "Sangamon" claimed that Mills in the last session of the legislature conspired with Illinois College at Jacksonville to tap the state seminary (college) fund, which the state received from the federal government through a percentage of sales from public lands. Four years earlier, an observer noted the fund had built up to $60,000 and would soon reach $100,000.[123] "Sangamon" accused Mills and Illinois College of wanting to divert the seminary fund and use it to finance a common school system, providing free elementary education to children, instead of to establish a state college in Springfield. "I want him beaten," the handbill author said, "and I want him beaten because he has been, and is now opposed to the best interests of the county [Sangamon], and because he has been, and I believe will continue to be, a mere political tool of that designing and intriguing set of [Presbyterian] priests, who manage the Jacksonville college." The handbill added that the *Jacksonville Illinois Patriot* was the "political organ of the college, [which] came out this spring in favor of Mr. Mills' project to destroy the state seminary fund, and boldly declared that it should be made a question at the election for members to the legislature; and the candidates which the college party support in Morgan [County], have been required to pledge their opposition to a state seminary [college]." The handbill said Mills would work in Congress to get authorization to tap the fund rather than just borrow from it.[124]

Those charges were a nice little roundup appealing to a wide swath of voters. Lurking in the background were questions about separation of church of state and abolitionism, Illinois College being known for friendliness toward abolition, implying Ben's guilt by associating him with Presbyterian ministers and the college. A few months later, Mills himself contributed to suspicions about his possible friendliness toward abolitionism when he publicly defended Lane Seminary students who had organized a nationally publicized "teach in" portraying slavery as a sin and therefore worthy of destruction. After school trustees suppressed the debate, Mills proclaimed that Lane Seminary "stood forth to our admiration like the smitten rock in the wilderness, sending forth its pure waters for the refreshing of a thirsty land; and they have suddenly become turbid and unpalatable. . . . The hopes of the West are deferred. It is the natural result of any attempt to limit the walks of truth. . . . We pretend not here to express any opinion upon abolition or colonization."[125] But Mills thereby said enough to imply where he would stand in a showdown.

Setting up a common school system was a growing issue, with more and more people thinking Illinois had reached a level where the state government was obligated to ensure tuition-free elementary school education for children. In the words of state senator William Archer, a Whig who was running for lieutenant governor that year: "Universities, colleges and seminaries, are for the benefit of the wealthy. Common schools are for the benefit of the poor. In the first, a few only are concerned; in the latter the whole people have a deep interest."[126] The legislature routinely borrowed from funds dedicated for a particular purpose and used the money for other ends. In its previous session, the legislature did exactly that with the common school fund.[127] The controversy regarding Ben Mills was less the borrowing from the seminary fund than the transaction's effect of stymieing establishment of a new college in Springfield, with persons interested in one college lunging for the throats of persons interested in the other. A Morgan County handbill spoke of "the natural jealousy which some narrow minded politicians in Sangamo entertain of Morgan and of her influence, and dictated by some narrow and concentrated prejudice which seeks to put down our college [at Jacksonville], merely because it was not located at Springfield."[128] Rep. Peter Cartwright, a Methodist reverend, opposed diverting the seminary fund to common schools,[129] presumably because such diversion would prevent establishment of a state Springfield college to compete with Jacksonville's Presbyterian institution. The *Sangamo Journal* declared:

> It is well known that a great jealousy exists among many denominations of Christians in this state, and among citizens not connected with any religious denomination, in regard to the objects and designs of the Jacksonville College and its friends. Whether there is an adequate cause for this jealousy is a question not now necessary to be enquired into. . . . What then can be more calculated to inflame and excite this feeling than an effort by the known and intimate and confidential friends of the college, to destroy the seminary fund of this state with the view to preventing this state from ever establishing a university—and with the ultimate design of securing to Illinois College the power of instilling into the minds of our sons its religious and political principles. These are the remarks we hear made every day upon this subject.[130]

This college competition was a big enough issue that gubernatorial candidate Duncan felt a need to deny reports that he was connected with Illinois

College.[131] The issue was of high interest within the Third Congressional District, especially in the populous counties of Morgan and Sangamon. For example, Representative Cartwright privately wrote that he had prepared legislation "to carry the state seminary to Springfield," and "It shall be my ambition to show my constituents that they have not misplaced their confidence."[132] Richard Quinton addressed the issue in his campaign for state representative in Sangamon County, opining that funds coming in for establishment of a state college should be used for that purpose and the institution should be established in Sangamon County, noting that adequate money was available to establish a common school system.[133] There was also the matter of who would control the common schools' teachers; Cartwright was promoting a plan for Methodists to train the teachers, while the Presbyterian Canton Classic School was advertising to specialize in training teachers for common schools.[134] This struggle for control between Methodists and Presbyterians had to create unease among those who supported separation of church and state, so a handbill portraying Ben as a Presbyterian tool monkeying with common school funding surely promoted disquiet. In politics, getting people convinced may be unnecessary; getting them suspicious can be good enough to peel away votes from a candidate.

The "Sangamon" handbill also raised the issue of relocating the state capital. Politicians across the state were scheming to shift the seat of government away from Vandalia, but no agreement existed about where the new location would be. Lincoln would later have no small part in what happened. The handbill said that Ben and others had invested in Peoria land and were opposing Big Red because he would help put the capital in Springfield. "Sangamon" also noted another real estate question agitating the state, an effort to transfer northern counties of Illinois into Wisconsin. This had substantial support in Galena, according to the handbill, which said that people from the Galena area favored the shift and Ben would have "strong temptation" to work for it in Congress.[135]

On election day in August, the same day on which Abe Lincoln won election to the state house of representatives, Big Red won election to the U.S. House. He got about 6,750 votes, Mills about 6,125.

Stephen Douglas crowed: "In this state the election resulted favorable to the cause of Democracy Liberty—our three Congressmen all being friendly to the [Jackson] Administration and opposed to *the* Bank [of the United States], although one of them may be in favor of *a* Bank, unless Gen. Jackson tells him better. In the legislature we have a decided majority, and therefore feel sure of electing a Jackson [U.S.] Senator."[136]

CHAPTER 9

LAW STUDIES, REVENGE, ROMANCE

During the election campaign, John T. Stuart had grown fond of Abe Lincoln and recommended that he study law and become an attorney. Lincoln needed no encouragement, wanting only an opportunity, one now provided by Stuart, who opened his law library to Representative-Elect Lincoln.[1] Slicky Bill Greene said Lincoln "*devoured* all the law books he could get hold of" from any source.[2] The Western frontier had few opportunities to make a living through intellectual work. Schoolteachers, ministers, newspaper editors, politicians, and lawyers were the main choices for intellectual labor. Lincoln had long been drawn toward law, and now he had a good connection with a locally prominent attorney who was willing to help broaden his knowledge of the craft.

This kind of study was unusual enough in New Salem that people remembered it in later years. Jack Armstrong's brother-in-law Henry McHenry recalled that Abe "walked to Springfield for books, borrowed them of John T. Stuart. This is true. First Lincoln said so; others who saw him do it said so." New Salem neighbor Daniel Burner said likewise, "He borrowed books from a man by the name, I think, of John T. Stuart, living in Springfield, and he used to walk over there after the books and bring them back."[3] John Roll similarly noted, "He would walk up here to Springfield, twenty miles, and borrow books from Major Stuart and read them, and bring them back."[4] Other testimony affirms this as well.[5] Reportedly Lincoln said that he read while making the trip.[6] Whether he hiked or rode, there's no question he made the trips. Stuart's law partner, Henry Dummer, was suing Lincoln at this time on behalf of Peter Van Bergen. Dummer, who trained at Bowdoin and Harvard, noted: "Lincoln used to come to our office in Springfield and borrow books. . . . He was an uncouth-looking lad. Did not say much. What he did say, he said it strongly, sharply."[7] Dummer added,

"He surprised us more and more at every visit."[8] Dummer may have been less gruff than those comments imply; Lincoln later told a law student that Dummer was "a very clever man . . . and I have no doubt he will cheerfully tell you what books to read, and also loan you the books."[9]

Lincoln's law studying, which went on month after month, bewildered some folks around New Salem—he was a man clearly capable of earning money through hard physical labor. Russell Godbey recalled: "The first time I ever saw Abe with a law book in his hands he was sitting astride of Jacob Bale's woodpile in New Salem. Says I, 'Abe, what are you studying?' 'Law,' replied Abe." Godbey exclaimed, "Great God Almighty."[10] Of the law study, Jack Armstrong's brother-in-law McHenry commented, "We plagued Lincoln for it."[11] Abe retreated to where he could read in peace. Ann Rutledge's brother said: "I think he never avoided men until he commenced the study of law. . . . In the summer season he frequently retired to the woods to read and study."[12] McHenry described how Abe "used to read law . . . barefooted, seated in the shade of a tree—would grind around with the shade."[13] He added, "Lincoln would come out and stay with me a week or two at a time, reading law."[14] McHenry said Lincoln "was so absorbed that people said he was crazy. Sometimes did not notice people when he met them."[15]

We may imagine reactions from New Salem residents by extrapolating from what was said by a shrewd observer of Western characters in Lincoln's time: "The pioneer was not indolent, in any sense. He had no dreaminess—meditation was no part of his mental habit—a poetical fancy would, in him, have been an indication of insanity. If he reclined at the foot of a tree, on a still summer day, it was to sleep."[16] The typical pioneer had no intellectual interests, cared nothing for poetry, and stretched out beneath a tree for shut-eye instead of study. What's amazing isn't that Lincoln's values differed so profoundly from those of most folks around New Salem, but that typical pioneers did not simply tolerate Lincoln but liked and admired him. His ability to charm them is evident, but explaining such power is harder than acknowledging it.

Although John Stuart loaned books, he doesn't seem to have given Lincoln any particular assistance in mastering them. Lincoln's best friend, Josh Speed, recalled, "He studied them at his humble home on the banks of the Sangamon, without a preceptor or fellow student."[17] "I did not read with anyone," Lincoln later told a potential law student. "It is of no consequence to be in a large town while you are reading. I read at New Salem, which never had three hundred people living in it. The *books*, and your *capacity* for understanding them, are just the same in all places."[18] He told another potential law student: "Get books, sit down anywhere, and go to reading for yourself. That will make a lawyer of you quicker than any other way."[19] "Get the books, and read, and study them carefully," he told still another potential law student. "Work, work, work, is the main thing."[20] Ann Rutledge's brother Robert said, "He seemed to master his studies with little effort, until he commenced the study of law, in that he became wholly engrossed."[21] Supposedly he even studied law during surveying expeditions.[22] "I know he sat up late at night and studied hard," Caleb Carman said. "He used to worry, tire himself down at study and work at Salem—would retire to [Jack] Armstrong's, [Jimmy] Short's, [Mentor] Graham's, and other places to get recruited [refreshed]."[23]

Lincoln's study of jurisprudence covered the basics needed in frontier litigation but didn't approach the kind of training necessary for success in Eastern courts, where issues might be more complex and counsel may have had formal law school education in addition to training with senior attorneys. Indeed, years later, when he was one of the West's finest lawyers, he would have a shocking litigation experience with Eastern attorney Edwin Stanton. To say that Lincoln's self-education in jurisprudence wasn't equivalent to college training simply states a fact easy to forget, given his intelligence and eventual achievements.

At the end of 1834, the abbreviation "Esq." appeared after Lincoln's name in the public prints.[24] That may have been a premature award of lawyer rank but more likely was timely recognition of his status as a state legislator.

At the end of August, the Sangamon County sheriff was ordered to seize $58 of property from Representative-Elect Lincoln and William Berry to satisfy the April judgment won against them by William Watkins. Before the seizure, Berry was able to pay off $42 of the debt. An additional notation by the sheriff indicates that all but $6 may have been paid in cash. Whether Watkins decided that was good enough or to proceed with a seizure and public auction of $6 worth of property is unclear.[25] Also at the end of August, Abe was again warned to appear at the upcoming September term of the Sangamon County circuit court to show why he shouldn't be included in the April judgment against Slicky Bill Greene in the Van Bergen lawsuit.[26]

In September and early October, while the Van Bergen suit against Lincoln was pending, Abe did survey work at New Boston for Van Bergen and other real estate developers promoting that town site, located many miles northwest of Sangamon County, up in Warren County near the Mississippi River. Van Bergen in turn was working on behalf of state senator Elijah Iles, who at one point had been Lincoln's captain in the Black Hawk War. Van Bergen explained: "Iles had loaned some people some money, and they couldn't pay it; and he took on eighty acres of land. And Iles thought it might be a good thing to lay out a town on it, and said he would give me a share in it if I would attend to having it surveyed etc." Laying out towns was a growth industry in Illinois. Said a Chicago newspaper, "If our land speculators have not the facilities of the genii of the Arabian Nights entertainment for bringing flourishing towns and villages into existence at a word, they certainly possess an art unknown, even in fairy tales, of spreading them out on paper."[27] A disgusted observer said that such operators "produce more poverty than potatoes and consume more midnight oil in playing poker than of God's sunshine in the game of raising wheat and corn."[28] Real estate promoters assured the public otherwise:

"[Middletown] twenty-two miles north of Springfield. . . . This situation is greatly admired by travellers and needs not the eye of the scrutinizing philosopher to foresee that it will become a place of importance. . . . Timber is plenty and good; water is convenient and excellent, and never fails. It is surrounded by a moral, healthy, and industrious population, which will patronize mechanics, merchants, and manufacturers."

—*Sangamo Journal*,
October 20, 1832

"A New Town. There will be sold in the town of Centerville . . . a number of lots. . . . This town is laid out in Macon County, Illinois, near the center of said county . . . on the road from Springfield to Danville; it is a beautiful situation of high rolling prairie on the west in full view of the town, and Sangamon River in sight in the east; the situation is high, and has every appearance of health; the surrounding country is equal in soil, timber, and water, to any in the state; the country is in a high state of cultivation. Enterprising merchants and mechanics, will find it to their interest to settle here."

—*Sangamo Journal*,
July 19, 1834

"A New Town. There will be sold in the town of Berlin . . . a number of lots. . . . This town is laid out in Sangamo County . . . on the road leading from Springfield to Jacksonville and about halfway between the two places. The surrounding country is equal in soil, timber, and water, to any in the state. The country is in a high state of cultivation. . . . Enterprising mechanics and merchants will find it [in] their interest to settle here."

—*Sangamo Journal*,
August 24, 1833

Jacksonville attorney Stephen Douglas had already begun a parallel career in real estate, which would make him rich. In 1834, he told his brother-in-law: "Land within two miles of this place which was entered four years ago at $1.25 per acre is now worth from $15 to $30 per acre. Town lots which sold for $10 and $15 eight years ago are now selling at $1,500. . . . Towns are being laid out every few days, and lots sold for a mere trifle which soon become valuable. Money makes the more go. . . . Fortunes can be made easily."[29]

New Boston became more than a paper town but never became a great commercial center. Van Bergen remembered the expedition with Abe to the wilderness where New Boston town lots would be located: "We started from here [Spring-field] when they had the cholera. I had some good brandy with me and used to take it as a preventative of cholera, but Lincoln always refused to take any even for that purpose. People sometimes refused to let us stay all night when they found we were from Springfield where the cholera was." He noted, "We traveled over there [to the New Boston site] on horseback . . . stayed there about a week." After Lincoln finished the survey, he and Van Bergen apparently went together to file legal documents in Monmouth, seat of Warren County, then back to Sangamon County.[30] The two men had plenty of time to discuss Van Bergen's lawsuit, if they chose to.

Not long after they got back to Sangamon County, William Berry may have reduced his debt to Reuben Radford. Indeed, reliable authorities report that Berry paid off everything he owed Radford, turning over cash plus a $35 horse. One authority notes an additional payment of $50 by Berry to Radford at this time. Supposedly the remainder owed in the spring judgment against Slicky Bill was now owed entirely to Peter Van Bergen, and that is whom Lincoln and William Berry would have to pay if the Sangamon County circuit court found them liable in the autumn court term that would soon open. I am unconvinced that the authorities are correct. The October 1833 note made all three signers liable for 100 percent of the amount; the only way for Berry to drop out was for him to pay 100 percent of the debt and thereby simultaneously relieve Greene and Lincoln of any responsibility. Some other reasons for doubting the authorities are technical enough to be banished to a footnote.[31] Regardless of exactly what was happening, clearly Van Bergen's lawsuit was moving forward.

After winning the governorship race, U.S. Rep. Joseph Duncan resigned from Congress and prepared to assume his new office. Rather than leave the seat vacant for a few months before the new Congress convened and Big Red May took office, a special election was called to fill the short-term vacancy. The candidates were Big Red and Ben Mills.

Yes, Ben was unwilling to take no for an answer and sought vindication from voters.[32] Big Red also sought vindication, declaring:

> Assailed as I have been by the basest scandal and the vilest and
> blackest slander that malice and corruption could suggest, I yet find a
> comfort and a consolation inexpressible in the knowledge that you
> knew them not—that you supported me under the conviction that
> malice alone had dictated their publication. And should malice again
> direct at my character the shafts of scandal and detraction, again I
> throw myself upon your confidence, and shall rest assured that how-
> ever severe may be the trial, I shall yet come forth from the fiery fur-
> nace of persecution unscorched, unscathed, and uncontaminated.[33]

Ben Mills changed his mind about running and withdrew, saying his previous acceptance of a Galena meeting's call to candidacy had been "conditional, and subsequent events have determined me positively to decline."[34] Those events are obscured by our distance from the scene. A supporter of Big Red proclaimed, "Let every Democrat who prefers liberty, rather than a moneyed despotism, in this Congressional District, come to the polls and boldly speak out 'Wm. L. May': He is a tried and well known Democrat, and one who is not afraid to avow his principles."[35] Running unopposed by any serious candidate, Big Red had considerable advantage in the election. On election day in New Salem, the Whig state Representative-Elect Lincoln served as an election clerk[36] and voted for Big Red May,[37] who won. According to the diary of a traveler who arrived in New Salem on election day, he and his traveling companion were invited to vote. The diarist protested that he had hardly been in town long enough to qualify as a voter, but locals told him not to worry about that. So the two travelers voted.[38] Such was the loose atmosphere of elections in New Salem.

That autumn, Lincoln took on Rev. Peter Cartwright. In addition to the assault being politically unnecessary, the election having been settled, Lincoln hid his identity while doing it. Why Representative-Elect Lincoln would choose to attack Cartwright after the election is unclear. Lincoln had faced many vigorous political opponents without exhibiting a need to strike any of them outside the campaign, and even during campaigns, he concentrated on candidates' political positions. My educated guess is that during the 1834 campaign, the reverend may have promoted doubts about Lincoln's religious orthodoxy in hopes that such doubts would hurt Abe on election day. Thomas Ford cited the credo of another politician: "No man could be talked down with loud and bold words, 'but any one might be whispered to death.'"[39] If whispers had been directed against Abe, he surely found such a tactic bothersome—Lincoln's religious beliefs had nothing to do with his public policies or ability to perform as a legislator, but they nonetheless might cost him votes. If so, he probably felt trapped because he couldn't refute a charge of religious unorthodoxy. I also suspect that Cartwright exuded a sanctimonious moral superiority offensive to Lincoln, and Abe felt the preacher was hypocritical. Debating Cartwright on Christianity would be futile, but Abe discovered a way to attack his religious stance in the context of debate on the common school system.

Lincoln received his opening from a letter Cartwright got published in the *Christian Advocate and Journal* in the spring of 1834. The reverend asked:

> Could we not, who live in the "far off West," obtain some pious young men and young women from the older states and conferences, under the influence of our own church, with good literary qualifications, to teach common schools in this state [Illinois]. There is a vast opening here for school teachers. We greatly need them. I am confident that I could give employment to more than 100 immediately in my district, and perhaps 500 in the state. . . .

We expect our conference to form itself into a common school education society. All we lack is the right sort of teachers. These teachers would greatly aid our missionary efforts, train the rising generation, and do a good part for themselves in a pecuniary point of view.[40]

The Methodist church at this time had a "Society for the Promotion of Common and Liberal Education," and Cartwright wasn't alone in suggesting more activism. A few days before he wrote his letter, the *Christian Advocate and Journal* published one from W. Fisk, datelined Wesleyan University, about the need "of supplying the western and southern parts of our country with competent teachers" for common schools, not only to instruct Methodists, but for "the community generally." Fisk thought assurance of employment would encourage more New Englanders to train as teachers, thereby supplying the South and West.[41] Cartwright went further, however, apparently stating that the Illinois Methodist church under his leadership intended to seize the state common school system as it started up, making it an adjunct of missionary endeavor with a goal of capturing students' young minds. "This letter," Lincoln would note, "was published in handbill form and circulated in great numbers throughout Sangamon County [in summer 1834], was posted up on the doors of stores and groceries, and even read in public companies of which he [Cartwright] formed a part, and, so far as I can learn, the authorship was never disavowed by him."[42] A preserved handbill may be a sample of the one mentioned by Lincoln. The item's unsigned commentary has literary characteristics found in a much longer pseudonymous attack dating from autumn 1834, which we know to have been written by Lincoln. The preserved flyer has Lincolnian clarity and even includes phraseology ("Mark the . . .") found in the other. The handbill's commentary said:

Remarks. Our friend Cartwright, in this letter, hopes for success, though he has great sectarian prejudices to contend with. We would here ask our zealous friend, who are those sectarians? We hear him reply they are the Presbyterians; and to counteract them, he would have 500 school masters and school mistresses from the older States and Conferences, under the influence of their own churches. Mark the honesty of our sectarian friend: We expect, says he, our Conference to form itself into a common school education society—all we lack is the right sort of teachers. What are these teachers to effect? They are to train the rising generation—advance the missionary efforts, and the support of a speculative clergy? Is not this enough to make the parson hang his sham'd face, decline as a candidate for office, and hunt a place to hide himself from the free people of Sangamon County?[43]

As we've seen, Cartwright did drop out at the peak of his campaign for state representative. Controversy about his plans for the common school system may have contributed to his decision to give up, but at our distance from the scene, the full story is unclear.

Caleb Carman, who boarded Abe in New Salem, recalled: "Lincoln once wrote an article against Peter Cartwright which was a good one. The name signed to it was Diotrephus. You may bet it used the old man very rough. It was a hard one. It was published in the *Beardstown Chronicle*. . . . Simeon Francis would not publish [it] in the *Sangamo Journal*."[44] Sim Francis was known for giving Lincoln liberal access to the *Journal*'s columns; if a Whig partisan as harsh as Sim chickened, the item must have been tough indeed. We don't know what Lincoln said, but we do know Cartwright was stung. "I hope," he told someone in 1834, "that you will never condescend to tarnish your own reputation by vile and slanderous productions, such as emanated from the pen of Diotrephus of New Salem."[45] In the time of John's Third Epistle, Diotrephus passed judgment on persons who felt called to witness for Christ and expelled them from Christian fellowship if he rejected their claim. The choice of such a pen name demonstrates Lincoln was knowledgeable indeed about church history.

Although Cartwright was friendly toward higher training for the common schools' teachers, he saw college training for ministers as pointless. In a public letter of August 24, 1834, from Pleasant Plains, entitled "Valley of the Mississippi, or the Moral Waste, No. 1," Cartwright complained that older states were sending fancy seminary-trained ministers to the Mississippi Valley on the theory that local talent was unqualified to attend properly to the population's religious needs. He said homegrown and self-taught ministers of the Mississippi Valley region were at least as good as, if not better than, the emigrant ones who, moreover, siphoned off money to national organizations. Each individual church could tend to itself and to local needs without help from any organization of churches. Cartwright said, however, it would be proper for Christian teachers from older states to come to Illinois and teach in common schools. They need not be Methodist but did need to have their primary loyalty to a local church rather than a national religious organization. At the letter's end, he said, "If any editor or individual thinks proper to reply to these hasty remarks, I wish to come out in a tangible form, and with a proper name."[46] That declaration suggests a possibility that the letter was written in response to "Diotrephus." Soon thereafter, Cartwright announced the establishment of Pleasant Plains Academy, providing the kind of education suitable for the common schools' teachers, although not explicitly serving such students.[47]

A letter writer quickly produced a public reply to "Moral Waste," expressing shock and disappointment that Cartwright wanted teachers who were opposed to the American Bible Society, American Tract Society, American Sunday School Union, "&c." All those agencies were described as doing fine work supported by Methodists.[48] Despite the letter's civil tone, Sim Francis had hesitated to publish it, not recognizing the name "Joseph Rogers" signed to the missive.[49] Such hesitation suggests that he had already received an objectionable pseudonymous production (perhaps "Diotrephus") and wanted to be sure the Rogers letter was appearing over a real name.

In a public response to Rogers, the reverend explained his views more thoroughly: "I object to national societies, because the new school Presbyterians are in general at the head of all those institutions. . . . I object to them, because I do most religiously believe that it is wrong to carry them on by a *monied salaried agency*—thereby applying the benevolent contributions of many pious individuals to the support of agents instead of giving to it [it to?] the various objects of benevolence." Regarding agents of these national institutions, "Now let them turn their attention to the riots and mobs that have been raised in Baltimore, New York, Philadelphia, Boston, and many other places, where those very agents, many of them, have come from." Illinois newspaper readers knew exactly what Cartwright was talking about:

"RIOTS. . . . New York, where the mob lately demolished the furniture and windows of sixteen churches, and several other buildings— in Boston where . . . they have lately torn down and burned the buildings of the academy and convent of the Ursuline nuns."

—*Vandalia Illinois Advocate and State Register*,
September 3, 1834

"Further riots in Philadelphia. . . . The first African Presbyterian Church in Seventh Street exhibits serious marks of the fray. . . .

"Not a house, in the dwelling of colored people, was spared. The poor blacks affrighted at the approaching storm had fled houses and even the city and took repose by thousands in the fields and in the neighborhood of the city.

"The mob entered one house where a man . . . was found in his bed asleep. The rioters in despite of his piteous entreaties for mercy, seized the poor fellow and hurled him out of the window. . . .

"Several blacks were inhumanly beaten and dreadfully lacerated. In one house there was a corpse, which was thrown out of the coffin; and another, a dead infant, was taken out of the bed and cast on the floor, the mother being at the same time barbarously treated."

—*Pennsylvanian*, August 15, 1834, clipped in
Galenian, September 15, 1834

"The *Woodbury Herald* of yesterday says that the upper part of Gloucester, New Jersey, 'is literally overrun with blacks, driven by the violence of an infuriated mob from their homes and property in Philadelphia, to seek shelter and protection among the farmers of our country. . . . A temporary sojourn among us, considering the circumstances of the case, may be borne with—but the first indication of a permanent residence should and we feel confident will, call forth a rigid enforcement of the statute against the admission of blacks into our boundaries.'"

—*American Sentinel*, clipped in *Galenian*,
September 22, 1834

"Where, and when," Cartwright asked, "did a mob, or any lawless banditti of heathen, in the West, ever demolish a meetinghouse, or the humble and private dwellings of individuals, or anything of the kind?"[50] That was a theme Cartwright had earlier raised with a national audience, saying, "We in the 'far off west' begin seriously to think that we shall have to extend our missionary labors to the eastern cities to evangelize the heathen of the old country, and thereby put an end, if possible, to those mobs and riots that are becoming so common there."[51] In conclusion, Cartwright told his local critic, "I feel great pleasure in communicating with a gentleman of your mild and manly disposition, and anything you write in this way, will be taken kindly by me"—as opposed to his reaction to "Diotrephus."

John McNamar told Billy Herndon about another attack that Abe penned against Cartwright. "The article alluding to Mr. Cartwright obtained a good deal of notoriety from the fact that Mr. Hill, rather innocently I should think, signed the article with his own name and published it."[52] McNamar had left town long before the article was published and didn't return until long after it appeared, but indeed, just such an article appeared in the *Beardstown Chronicle*. The item must have made a big splash for McNamar to have heard about it.

Samuel Hill's willingness to sign Abe's letter was less innocent than McNamar said. Hill wasn't a churchgoer, and he owned New Salem's biggest store. A town pioneer recalled: "Cartwright appeared to take great pleasure in coming and sitting under Hill's porch and annoying him. He would come and sit for hours and laugh and talk about Hill, while Hill stayed indoors. He was describing one day to a crowd how he viewed Hill's soul. He said he had some doubts whether he had a soul till one day he put a quarter of a dollar on Hill's lips, when his soul came guggling up to get the piece of silver."[53] Getting back at Cartwright was a tough proposition. Hill lacked necessary debate skills, and physical chastisement was problematic: Hill was a small man anyway, and the reverend was famed for his ability to preach a "sermon of strength"[54] with his fists. In old age, Cartwright reminisced, "It was part of my creed to love everybody, but to fear no one; and I did not permit myself to believe any man could whip me till it was tried."[55] He was willing to take on all comers, male or female.[56] Hill was known to hire out his fighting,[57] but no record exists of anyone doing Cartwright for Hill.[58] For Hill, signing Abe's letter was the next best thing to hiring Lincoln's fists. And for Lincoln, the arrangement allowed him to bruise Cartwright without the reverend knowing where the hits came from. One other aspect of the letter was interesting: According to a notice in the same newspaper where the missive appeared, it was printed as a paid advertisement. So the editor didn't welcome the piece. Who paid to run it? Did Lincoln have the funds? Who else would feel strongly enough about Cartwright to pay for the privilege of attacking him? Perhaps Hill himself?

Although not published until November,[59] Lincoln's "Samuel Hill" letter was dated September 7, and Lincoln said he was replying to Cartwright's August 24 "Moral Waste" article:

> Now, if I could possibly conceive that this article was written with a view to aid the true religion in any shape, I should not meddle with it; or, if I could conceive that it was intended to vindicate the character of the "West," I should be the last to censure it. But being thoroughly satisfied that it is wholly a political manoeuvre, and being equally well satisfied that the author is a most abandoned hypocrite (I will not say in religion—for of this I pretend to know nothing—but) in politics, I venture to handle it without restraint.

Note the comment "I pretend to know nothing" about religion; in reality, Lincoln knew plenty. He then proceeded to quote and comment on a sentence from Cartwright's "Moral Waste":

> "For a number of years past, the character of the citizens of the Valley of the Mississippi, has been assailed and slandered to an extent never surpassed in any civilized country." Now, as to the truth of this charge of slander, I know but little. This much, however, I do know—that whenever an Eastern man becomes a candidate for office in this country, this general charge of slander is resorted to, with a view to prejudice men against him. But I must confess that I have never known but one man fairly proved guilty of the charge; and that man was a Western man—and no other than Peter Cartwright. He was proved guilty in the following manner:—
>
> Some time last summer the letter to which he alludes in his "Moral Waste," was discovered in the *Christian Advocate and Journal*, bearing his signature. In this letter, speaking of this country, he says:—"This land of moral desolation." . . . I have not the letter before me, and therefore cannot make many or long quotations from it; but the short one I have made I know is correct, and I well recollect that the whole tenor of the letter was in perfect unison with it.

Lincoln then dissects the August 24 "Moral Waste" letter:

> The next sentence that I shall notice is in these words: "Who are these mighty men that write about the poor heathens in this Valley?" To this I answer that I cannot say who they all are; but that the world has positive evidence that Peter Cartwright is one of them.

Again he says, "Are they not generally found in the ranks of the political and religious aristocrats of the day."

To this I cannot give a direct answer. However, if Uncle Peter be a fair sample of the clan, I should any [say?] they are.

... I believe the people in this country are in some degree priest ridden. . . . Peter Cartwright bestrides, more than any four men in the northwestern part of the state.

He has one of the largest and best improved farms in Sangamon County, with other property in proportion. And how has he got it? Only by the contributions he has been able to levy upon and collect from a priest ridden church.

Referring indirectly to Genesis 3:19, Lincoln declared:

It will not do to say he has earned it "by the sweat of his brow"; for although he may sometimes labor, all know that he spends the greater part of his time in preaching and electioneering.

And then to hear him in electioneering times publicly boasting of mustering his militia, (alluding to the Methodist Church) and marching and countermarching them in favor of or against this or that candidate—why, this is not only hard riding, but it is riding clear off the track, stumps, logs and blackjack brush, notwithstanding.

Cartwright reportedly bragged he could swing four hundred voters any direction he wanted.[60]

For a church or community to be priest ridden by a man who will take their money and treat them kindly in return is bad enough in all conscience; but to be ridden by one who is continually exposing them to ridicule by making a public boast of his power to hoodwink them, is insufferable.

... Such punishments as rebuke will be forever lost upon one of such superlative hardihood and [sic] as he possesses—he has been more than rebuked these twenty years.

... What, in the name of common sense, is it of which Uncle Peter is complaining? He has been quarreling with—nobody knows whom—half down the column of a newspaper, because, as he says, somebody has misrepresented this community by calling it ignorant, &c.; when, suddenly forgetting himself, he calls this same community an "uninformed and abused community".—That he should be heard saying things that he does not believe himself, I do not wonder at; but that after his long dealing in duplicity, he should be found unable to travel halfway down the column of a newspaper without crossing his own trail is passing strange. Speaking of his *Advocate* letter in his "Moral Waste," Cartwright says, "I did not ask for Methodist teachers, and when I asked for those under the influence of our own church, I only meant those that were opposed to American or national societies, &c." Now this is worst of all.

If any of Cartwright's real friends have a blush left, now is the time to use it. He did not ask for Methodist teachers! Will any man risk his reputation for common sense by pretending to believe this? Mark the circumstances. He was writing to the editor of the only Methodist periodical published in the nation—a paper seldomly opened by any but Methodists—so much so that although the letter had been published some considerable time, and the paper had many subscribers in Sangamon County, so far as I can learn, no eye, save that of a Methodist ever beheld it till the editor of the *Pioneer*, through the medium of his exchange list, I suppose, discovered it and republished a part of it.

Does this look like a general invitation to all who were opposed to American or national societies?—To me it appears a general invitation to particular individuals—something of a public call made in a private way.

In other words, a general invitation to insiders. Lincoln goes on with commentary that once again illustrates his close knowledge of church affairs:

But this is not all—"These teachers were asked of the older states and conferences"—mark the word *conferences*. Now I may be mistaken, but if I am not, no church except the Methodist has the word conference in its whole technical vocabulary. I will here venture a legal opinion: If asking for Methodist teachers were a crime of the magnitude of homicide, none of Cartwright's gentlemen of the bar could be found able, intelligent and learned enough to save *his* neck from the halter. . . .

None has a greater thirst for political distinction than Peter Cartwright. When he wrote his *Advocate* letter he had no intention that any Western man, save probably a few of his militia should see it: But, unfortunately, it was discovered. This was a trying time with Peter. He saw, as any man might have seen, that the effect of this letter was fastening itself upon his political prospects with the benumbing embrace of an incubus, and weighing them down with the weight of a mountain. Then came his "Moral Waste," which is nothing more nor less than an effort to shake off the effect of the *Advocate* letter. . . .

Poor ghost of ambition! He must have two sets of opinions, one for his religious, and one for his political friends; and to plat them together smoothly, presents a task to which his feverish brain is incompetent.—Let the *Advocate* letter and the "Moral Waste, No. 1" be presented to an intelligent stranger, and be told that they are the productions of the same man, and he will be much puzzled to decide whether the author is greater fool or knave; although he may readily see that he has but few rivals in either capacity.

Note the occasional reference to law and surveying in the above. John McNamar said Sam Hill "consequently received the skinning that old Peter administered in a public speech at Salem shortly after."[61] Such targeting of Hill indicates Lincoln's authorship remained secret. Cartwright was firing in the wrong direction.

Abe's little war against Peter Cartwright reveals several things. Lincoln was angry at Cartwright, and Lincoln didn't get angry because a person differed with him on a public policy question. Cartwright had done something else to irk Lincoln, something beyond normal politics. We see that Lincoln thought the people of Illinois were oppressed by preachers, and he wanted people to see Cartwright's common school scheme as threatening the separation of church and state. Some persons, at least, agreed with Lincoln. Three weeks after his article appeared, up in Jo Daviess County, a public meeting choosing delegates for a state education convention considered the following resolution: "Resolved that the delegates from this county be instructed to oppose all plans or systems of education which are based upon, or have for their object, the promotion of sectarian doctrines or principles of religious instruction in common schools."[62] The meeting voted down the resolution, but its consideration demonstrated controversy over the topic. About this time, a Quincy newspaper supplied the controversy's broader context:

An established church is incompatible with institutions of a real free country. The tyranny over the conscience is the worst kind of tyranny; darken and fetter it, and send its owner abroad to roam the wide world—he is everywhere a slave—his chains are forged and riveted by the eternal constitution of things, and his mind, giving its own coloring to things round it, throws the blackness of darkness upon the fair face of nature: The walls of his prison-house are limitless and insurmountable. . . . The advance of civil and religious liberty has always been coextensive and together. Bigotry and intolerance have always endeavored to keep the mind dark.[63]

Given all we know, I suspect Cartwright had been encouraging reports that Lincoln wasn't Christian enough and people should withhold their votes from him for that reason. Such a scenario would suggest Lincoln had expressed enough religious skepticism to become publicly known as an infidel. After this flurry, both men would bide their time for years, but they eventually had at it again.

+==+ +==+

Early in November, Representative-Elect Lincoln submitted a survey for adjusting the road connecting Sangamo Town with Athens.[64] Sometime in the first half of November, Abe must have done surveying for David Hart in connection with Hart's plans to sell a small parcel to Elijah Houghton. Both buyer and seller assisted Lincoln in the survey.[65] The job is worth noting mostly as evidence that Abe continued to engage in his occupation despite his need to prepare for the upcoming legislature session. This survey job also later illustrated his effort to provide customer satisfaction, as he not only handled litigation resulting from problems with the sale, but also introduced a relief bill in the legislature to deal with the sale's problems. The customer satisfaction element, however, was some years in the future.

Perhaps in 1834, and perhaps even that autumn, Abe reportedly took on a law case while doing a survey job. Accounts conflict over important details, affecting the date among other things, but they agree that he and one of Ann Rutledge's male kin attended a justice of the peace trial. A fellow young enough to be a minor but old enough to impregnate a girl was being sued on behalf of the pregnant young woman. The youthful man had legal representation, but the girl was unrepresented until Lincoln volunteered when he discovered the situation while on a survey job. The girl was an object of community scorn, but Lincoln turned the trial around as he argued that the male generally possessed more blame in such a situation. Lincoln argued by simile, saying the man's reputation was like a sullied cloth that could be laundered and restored to its former state, whereas the woman's reputation was like a shattered bottle or vase that could never be mended. The argument's implication was that the girl had suffered substantial harm, and the verdict awarded her damages.[66] The anecdote illustrates not only Lincoln's ability to pursue two occupations simultaneously, but also his sense of honor in sexual conduct. His enjoyment of ribald jokes didn't carry over into acceptance of real-life irresponsibility.

In mid-November, the Sangamon County circuit court held a hearing to determine the liability of Abe Lincoln and William Berry in the previous spring's judgment against Slicky Bill Greene for the promissory note that they had given Reuben Radford and he had assigned in whole or in part to Peter Van Bergen. Unnamed attorneys appeared on behalf of Lincoln and William Berry, and the court ordered the two ex-storekeepers to be included in the judgment against Slicky Bill. The total outstanding amount on the judgment was $154 plus costs.[67] Was this a lawyer deal, or had Berry, Lincoln, and Greene paid a sum reducing the note to that amount? This $154 exactly matches the amount discussed in the document Van Bergen signed when he received assignment of the October 19, 1833, note. On the day of the November 1834 court order, Radford wrote on the back of the document in which Van Bergen had agreed to collect the note, "I assign the within obligation to Wm. F. Berry for value received of him this 19th day of Nov [?] 1834. R. Radford."[68] My hesitant reading of "Nov" is rejected by some authorities, who read the abbreviation as "Oct,"[69] seeing the notation as being given on the year's anniversary of the note, rather than on the day of the court order. The date is less important than the notation's apparent meaning that Radford had turned the October 19, 1833, note back to Berry, equivalent to canceling the debt. Yet as we shall see, Van Bergen continued to press the collection suit in a manner devastating to Lincoln, action indicating that Van Bergen owned the note and was not merely a collection agent for Radford.

James Rutledge, father of Ann, was also owed money in connection with the Berry & Lincoln store. Rutledge had accepted a promissory note from Berry in full payment, but when Berry was unable to pay, Lincoln offered to pay half. Rutledge declined the offer, saying the matter was between him and Berry alone.[70] Again we see Abe's acting out a notion of equitable obligation to someone despite a lack of legal obligation. Rutledge may well have been kindly disposed anyway, but I'm inclined to wonder whether his generosity toward Abe had something to do with Ann's feelings.

Ah yes, Ann Rutledge. In a town the size of New Salem, everyone knew everyone else and knew much of their business besides. Ann had substantial business with John McNeil and Abe Lincoln, and New Salem's people-watchers left plenty of reports.

Descriptions of Ann generally concur. Billy Herndon's notes from a conversation with Mentor Graham are as good as any: "Eyes blue, large, and expressive. Fair complexion. Sandy or light auburn hair. . . . About five [feet] four inches. Face rather round. Outlines beautiful. . . . Weigh about 120–130."[71] Long afterward, her apparent fiancé John McNeil wrote this description: "Miss Ann was a gentle amiable maiden without any of the airs of your city belles, but winsome and comely withal, a blond in complection with golden hair, 'cherry red lips and a bonny blue eye.'"[72] By chance occurrence, we have an excellent idea of exactly what Ann looked like; many years after the 1830s, her cousin McGrady Rutledge glanced through an office window, and seeing a young lady, he stopped in astonishment. He asked who the young lady was, saying, "She is the very picture of Ann Rutledge." A photo portrait of the office woman exists.[73] To say someone reminds you of somebody is one thing; it is something else entirely to momentarily think you see a person from long ago.

Mentor Graham spoke of Ann's sociable personality: "Nervous vital element predominated. . . . Hearty and vigorous. Amiable. Kind. . . . She was beloved by everybody. She loved everybody."[74] "Beloved by all who knew her," Esther Summers Bale recalled.[75] "Always gentle and cheerful," her cousin McGrady Rutledge said.[76] "Straight as an arrow, and as quick as a flash," Jack Armstrong's brother-in-law noted.[77] Looking back across the years, her sister Sally said: "I can see sister Ann as she sat sewing from day to day, for she was the seamstress of the family, while the other girls, Nancy and Margaret, aided mother in the general housework and care of the tavern. She taught me how to sew, and I remember her patience with me, as well as her industry and kindness."[78]

Ann's father, James, and his nephew John M. Cameron founded New Salem. Among other things, they built the milldam that grabbed Lincoln's New Orleans flatboat. James was prospering from several mercantile interests when John

McNeil arrived in town from New York State. In 1829, McNeil and partner Sam Hill established New Salem's biggest store, and the thirty-year-old McNeil soon hooked up with teenager Ann Rutledge. His interest in her is easy to understand, given the universal acclamation that acquaintances left about her qualities. On his part, McNeil's preserved correspondence comes from a highly literate, entertaining, and witty conversationalist. Literary allusions in his letters add credence to his claim that in New Salem, he owned copies of works by Shakespeare, Cervantes, and Alexander Pope.[79] McNeil had by his own efforts become one of the wealthiest men in the county, his worth considered about $12,000.[80] To give perspective on what such money could buy, at that time monthly board (a month's worth of prepared meals) in New Salem ranged from $1.00 to $1.25.[81] Then, as now, net worth wasn't net income, but McNeil was prosperous indeed. His attractiveness on more than one level can be understood. Moreover, Ann doesn't sound like the sort of person who would hook up with a dud, let alone a jerk.

We also know that Abe and McNeil became good friends; for McNeil, the fondness lasted beyond Lincoln's death.[82] I cannot imagine Lincoln staying on warm terms with someone he considered dishonest, let alone someone who harmed Ann Rutledge. I suspect, therefore, that the historical record showing McNeil to be a heartless cad omits crucial information. I have no idea what that information would be, but we should remember that what we can see of McNeil must lack an important part of the man he was.

According to Ann's brother Robert, William Berry paid romantic addresses to her but was turned down.[83] This would have been before Berry and Lincoln became store partners. Talk around town was that McNeil's business partner, Sam Hill, was romantically attracted to Ann.[84] Her brother Robert flatly stated that she declined Hill's marriage proposal, and thereupon McNeil began courting her.[85]

In 1832, Ann and McNeil became affianced,[86] at least such was the impression of Ann and those close to her.[87] Folks around town had the same impression.[88] Bowling Green's wife, Nancy, and Ann's aunt Elizabeth Rutledge both commented that Ann acted quite in love with McNeil.[89] He later implied, however, that no engagement had existed, saying he wasn't "in a situation to enter into what Mr. [Secretary of State] Seward would call 'entangling alliances.'"[90]

In some manner, Ann learned that the name "McNeil" was an alias; her fiancé was really named John McNamar. Her younger cousin Jasper, born after her death, said his understanding was that McNeil had signed one or more land deeds as McNamar, and word of this got back to Ann.[91] Because Jasper was wrong in some other things he said about Ann and McNamar, I am uncertain about his version of how Ann learned McNamar's true identity. It is a fact, however, that in December 1831, McNamar bought acreage from James Cameron, a cofounder of New Salem. In that transaction, McNamar signed his real name to the deed, and Lincoln saw him do it.[92]

Regardless of how Ann found out, according to Jesse Weik, McNamar gave her the following explanation:

"I left behind me in New York," he said, "my parents and brothers and sisters. They are poor, and were in more or less need when I left them in 1829. I vowed that I would come West, make a fortune, and go back to help them. I am going to start now and intend, if I can, to bring them with me on my return to Illinois and place them on my farm." . . . The change of his name was occasioned by the fear that if the family in New York had known where he was they would have settled down on him, and before he could have accumulated any property would have sunk him beyond recovery.[93]

Decades later, McNamar still stuck to that explanation.[94] Ann's brother Robert seems to have accepted it, saying: "It seems that his father had failed in business and his son, a very young man, had determined to make a fortune, pay off his father's debts, and restore him to his former social and financial standing. With this view he left his home clandestinely, and in order to avoid pursuit by his parents, changed his name. His conduct was strictly high-toned, honest, and moral; and his object, whatever any may think of the deception which he practiced in changing his name, entirely praiseworthy."[95] The "very young man" described by Robert Rutledge was apparently about twenty-seven years of age when he headed west, hardly a child who would be tracked by frantic parents. Does McNamar's story indicate deceit? Or does it indicate his New York relatives were weird? Historians have treated McNamar himself as weird. Illinois newspapers did carry occasional advertising seeking the whereabouts of someone who headed toward that country and disappeared.[96]

"William E. Kurts, living on Richland Creek, in this county [Sangamon], left Springfield on the 20th day of February last for Xenia, Ohio. He calculated to cross this state to Clinton, Indiana, and from thence proceed by Indianapolis and Dayton to Xenia, Ohio. Nothing has been heard from him since he left; and it is presumed he must have died in some manner on the way."

—*Sangamo Journal*,
July 19, 1832

"Information Wanted. Some six or eight years since, Michael Smith removed from Alabama to the western district of Tennessee, where he shortly afterwards died. His widow and children in very destitute circumstances, went to Illinois; but to what part of that state I do not know. I have information of great value to them; and should be happy to hear from them. David A. Smith. Courland, Alabama."

—*Sangamo Journal*,
July 13, 1833

"Elizabeth McGuire takes this method of informing her father, Mr. John Williams—of whom she has heard nothing for more than seven years, and of whose present residence she is wholly ignorant, that she resides in Nashville, Davidson County, Tennessee and that she is in necessitous circumstances; having been abandoned by her husband for more than four years and taking with him all her three children. . . . She is anxious that her father should see this advertisement, and that he should come and take her to his home."

—*Sangamo Journal*,
October 27, 1832

Missing-person ads appeared elsewhere as well. They were a regular feature in the nationally distributed *Christian Advocate and Journal* of New York.[97] So if McNamar needed to lie low from relatives he was trying to help, an alias wasn't inappropriate. I have known persons whose greed was exceeded only by their selfishness and stupidity, so I think it's possible that McNamar feared his relatives might have taken premature action that would have thwarted his plans to set them up comfortably in Illinois. McNamar may have had his problems, but my impression is that he was juggling them to the best of his ability. Still, I can readily understand why people would assume the worst on learning that a man of mysterious origins was living among them under an alias. According to Ann's sister Sarah, after the alias situation became known, their father ever afterward considered McNamar untrustworthy.[98]

McNamar left New Salem just before Abe returned from the Black Hawk War.[99] Jason Duncan said of McNamar, "Most of the inhabitants supposed he never would return."[100] He had, after all, sold out his store interest to partner Sam Hill.[101] But McNamar had retained the farm, as if he really did intend to return and settle his relatives on it. McNamar jovially described his journey to the East: "I did not go by steamboat nor stage, if that has anything to do with the matter, but rode old Charley, a hero of the Black Hawk War, who had one grievous fault. He would go to sleep occasionally, fall on his nose, and pitch me over his head, which occasioned some profanity, no doubt about it."[102]

"Circumstances beyond my control detained me much longer away than I intended," McNamar said.[103] He explained, "One of those long interminable fevers that sometimes occur in the East came into my father's family and prostrated every member thereof except myself, and continued for months making victims of three of them, one of whom was my father [who died]. So there, you see, 'There is a Providence that shapes our ends and aims, rough hew them how we will.'"[104] The "months" of illness here would seem to total twenty-four, perhaps more. One bout of illness after another through every season of two years is hard to believe. A physician's records show that four members of McNamar's family were ill in the first four months of 1833,[105] but that doesn't explain his continued absence from New Salem in 1834 and 1835. One explanation might be

that McNamar's plan to move his relatives to Illinois had been made without consulting them. Evidently he just showed up one day after having had no contact
with any of them for years and said he wanted all of them to leave the civilized
East to join him on a frontier that had just experienced the nationally publicized
Black Hawk Indian war. A superb student has aptly pointed out that a lengthy
period of persuasion may have been necessary.[106]

Delays holding McNamar back East can be understood, but months and then
years of silence from him are incomprehensible. Mrs. William Rutledge and
apparently Parthena Hill recalled that McNamar and Ann maintained some communication by mail,[107] at least at first. Of the letters from McNamar, Jesse Weik
said, "each succeeding one [was] growing less ardent in tone, and more formal in
phraseology than its predecessor."[108] Berry & Lincoln store clerk Daniel Burner
reported, "He wrote a few letters back to her and then there came no further
word."[109] Sam Hill's wife, Parthena, said, "Ann did not hear of McNamar for a
year or more" and "Ann well thought that McNamar was playing off on her," that
is, had acted in bad faith.[110] As postmaster, Lincoln would have been well aware
of how much mail passed between the two. Ann's sister Sarah described McNamar as "not a sentimental man,"[111] an evaluation with which his second wife
reportedly agreed.[112] Disappearing on one's betrothed goes beyond lack of sentiment. McNamar's treatment of Ann, however, was no different from the treatment he meted out to his parents, whom he claimed to love and be striving for in
New Salem, while for years he left them in ignorance about where he was or
even whether he was alive.

Lincoln treated women differently. Some folks remembered him as awkward
around females, but deficiency in suave drawing-room chitchat doesn't mean that
he lacked interest in women or they found him unappealing. Row Herndon said
Lincoln "was fond of company of both sexes."[113] Jason Duncan put it this way:
"There was a good deal of humor in his composition, sometimes bordering on
innocent mischief, especially among his lady acquaintances, though only with
those he was well acquainted. He would prove to them a complete hectorer. He
was very reserved toward the opposite sex."[114] I'd say that testimony means Lincoln wasn't a womanizer, an evaluation confirmed by other New Salemites,[115] but
though he was politely correct to women he knew casually, he warmed up if they
got to know each other better, and then engaged in a lot of kidding. "He didn't
appear bashful, but it seemed as if he cared but little for them. Wasn't apt to take
liberties with them, but would sometimes," said the son-in-law of New Salem's
Dr. Francis Regnier. The son-in-law got the following example from "Uncle
Jimmy" Short:

> Mr. Lincoln used to tell Mr. Short the following anecdote of himself.
> Once, when Mr. Lincoln was surveying, he was put to bed in the
> same room with two girls, the head of his bed being next to the foot
> of the girls' bed. In the night he commenced tickling the feet of one
> of the girls with his fingers. As she seemed to enjoy it as much as he

did, he then tickled a little higher up; and as he would tickle higher the girl would shove down lower; and the higher he tickled the lower she moved. Mr. Lincoln would tell the story with evident enjoyment. He never told how the thing ended.[116]

Sam Hill's son said Slicky Bill and others spoke of Lincoln showing rawer interest in sex. "Old Joe Watkins (now dead) kept a horse at Salem, and Lincoln requested him that whenever a mare come he would be sure to let him know it, as he wanted to *see it*. Watkins did so, and Lincoln always attended."[117]

Town gossip speculated about whether Lincoln fathered the child of Nancy Burner, sister of his store clerk. "Lincoln never touched her in his life," Slicky Bill Greene said. On this topic, Bill's brother Johnson Greene reported: "Bill Greene and Lincoln used to run the machine [take charge]. They have said in my presence that she was a handsome woman, had not much sense, had strong passions, weak will, strong desire to please and gratify friends." Slicky Bill said, "Lincoln knew the girl, knew me, used to laugh at me and at her." Seemingly referring to Dr. Jason Duncan and Nancy, a townsman mentioned:

> There was a little incident occurred of which Bill Greene was the hero, which may be worth relating as Lincoln enjoyed it hugely. We the youngsters had attended a night [Methodist] meeting en masse at [Ezekiel] Harrison's. On starting home a young doctor who had set up a shop in old Salem not unlike perhaps "Romeo's Apothecary" . . . cut out Bill, that is took his gal from him. Bill trudged along in silence some time. Either meditating on his sins or "nursing his wrath to keep it warm" at length he came alongside of his "bright particular," who with the doctor was leading the column, and began to plead his lost cause with the fair one. The girls in the rear began to hurry up to hear. After many arguments that seemed unavailing Bill finally put in a clincher, saying, "You know we have done things that we ought not if we are going to separate." The girls wilted and fell back in the rear.

Slicky Bill and Lincoln urged Duncan to marry Nancy Burner and leave town, and the doctor did as advised.[118] The reason for such advice is unstated; perhaps the persons who recalled it felt specificity was superfluous.

Ann Rutledge's brother Robert remembered Lincoln's easy interactions with New Salem's females: "When passing from business to boarding house for meals, he could usually be seen with his book under his arm, or open in his hand, reading as he walked. He frequently would seek young female company for entertainment and amusement. On such occasions he uniformly carried his book. Would alternately entertain and amuse the company by witticisms, jokes, &c., and study his lesson."[119] I doubt Lincoln was studying anything hard in such circumstances, but they illustrate his ability to exploit his reading as a way of attracting women. "They all liked him, and [he] liked them as well," Row Herndon said.[120] I suspect Lincoln's known physical prowess combined with conversation on subjects more stimulating than weather and farm business made him a desirable companion for New Salem's female element. Billy Herndon's brother-in-law James Miles recalled: "He and I went to the same house a sparking. He went to see the aunt and I to see the niece."[121] Mentor Graham recalled Lincoln "not unfrequently, as we say in the West, setting up to the fine girls of Illinois."[122] Caleb Carman said, "He frequently visited from 1833 to 1837 young ladies."[123]

Lincoln was no feminist, but at least in his New Salem years, he tended to treat women as equals. Riley Potter gave an example:

> Abe was mighty handy at frolics and parties. Most of the young people would sorter hang back, but Abe had a word for everybody, and especially for the smart girls. There couldn't any of them get the best of him. He was generally asked to help wait on the table and make folks feel sociable. One night Abe was helping the visitors and there was a girl there who thought herself pretty smart. When Abe got to her he asked her if he should help her. She said she'd take something. Abe, he filled up her plate pretty well, and when he passed it to her she says, quite pert and sharp, "Well, Mr. Lincoln, I didn't want a cart-load." Abe never let on that he heard her, but went on helping the others. By and by Liddy got through, and when Abe came around her way again she said she believed she'd take a little more. "All right, Miss Liddy," says Abe loud enough for the whole room to hear, "back up your cart and I'll fill it again." Of course there was a big laugh. Liddy felt awful bad about it. She went off by herself and cried the whole evening.[124]

Abner Ellis reflected, "I think he himself finally made that discovery in a few years, refined ladies could never see much of his humor."[125] Ellis recalled Lincoln's awkwardness around "stylish daughters from the state of Virginia" who visited town with their brother and mother.[126]

Plentiful reports exist of genial friendship between Abe and women of the New Salem vicinity, particularly married women. There seemed nothing salacious in his friendships with married women; perhaps he found this kind of relationship nonthreatening and the ladies were charmed by his genial nature and willingness to do chores while visiting. "When I first saw Lincoln," Mentor Graham said, "he was lying on a trundle bed rocking a cradle with his foot."[127] In a different context, but still to the point, Caleb Carman said:

> While he boarded with me he made himself useful in every way that he could. If the water bucket was empty he filled it; if wood was needed he chopped it; and was always cheerful and in a good humor. He started out one morning with the axe on his shoulder, and I asked him what he was going to do. His answer was: "I am going to try a

318 • THE EARLY YEARS

project." When he returned he had two hickory poles on his shoulders, and in a very short time two of my chairs had new bottoms.

"Abe was very good, kind, and courteous to children and women," Carman added.[128] Said an excellent student of Lincoln's life: "In the home of Rowan Herndon, where he had boarded when he first came to town, he had made himself loved by his care of the children. . . . The widows praised him because he 'chopped their wood.'" Regarding farmers' wives "there was not one of them who did not gladly 'put on a plate' for Abe Lincoln when he appeared, or did not darn or mend for him when she knew he needed it." In a word, he was "obliging."[129] No jealousy among husbands is recorded; on the contrary, they seemed to enjoy his company as much as their wives did. While surveying, Lincoln often stayed at the home of Sam and Parthena Hill.[130] In the John and Polly Cameron home, Lincoln received "motherly kindness and counsels" from Mrs. Cameron.[131] Travis Elmore remembered Lincoln dropping by Rhoda Clary's place, where he "had her to mend his breeches while he sat in bed."[132] William Butler recalled that at the Bennett and Elizabeth Abell place, "she washed for him and he generally lived there in a sort of home intimacy."[133] He was welcome there apparently even after gossip started saying that Elizabeth and Lincoln had begun a sexual relationship.[134] Jack Armstrong's wife, Hannah, reminisced: "Abe would come out to our house, drink milk and mush, cornbread, butter, bring the children candy. Would rock the cradle of my baby. . . . He would nurse babies, do anything to accommodate anybody. . . . A few days before Mr. Lincoln left for Washington I went to see him. . . . The boys got up a story on me that I went to get to sleep with Abe, &c. I replied to the joke that it was not every woman who had the good fortune and high honor of sleeping with a President. This stopped the sport—cut it short."[135] This was a long-standing joke; James Taylor remembered that "Jack Armstrong used to plague Abe a great deal about his—Abe's—son, which he had by Mrs. Armstrong; it was a joke—plagued Abe terribly."[136]

I mention Abe's easy friendships with women who were "spoken for" because the beginnings of his relationship with the engaged-to-be-married Ann Rutledge surely fit into that pattern. Over the years, Lincoln took his meals at several places in New Salem. Authorities conflict over when he began boarding at the Rutledge tavern, but opportunities were plentiful to interact with that household regardless. Mrs. Bowling Green said Lincoln began courting Ann in 1832 or 1833.[137] We know that by January 22, 1833, he was finding excuses to spend time with her. He was probably in a good mood that day; he and William Berry had bought the Radford store inventory just a week earlier, and Lincoln was probably excited about the store expansion. On January 22, he and Ann's brother John were horsing around inside the Rutledge home and accidentally damaged a bed. Lincoln promised to help Ann fix it the following morning; he could easily have found someone else to assist. During the repair job, Lincoln sent Ann's sister Nancy over to Row Herndon's nearby cabin for a tool. Row's wife was a sister of Ann's teacher Mentor Graham. Nancy related:

When I arrived there Mr. Herndon was loading his gun to go hunting, and in getting ready to go out his gun was accidentally discharged, and his wife, who was sitting near, talking to me, was shot right through the neck. I saw blood spurt out of each side of her neck, her hands flutter for a moment; then I flew out of the house and hurried home and told Annie and Mr. Lincoln what had happened. I can never forget how sad and shocked they looked, after having been so merry over their work just a moment before.[138]

"TERRIBLE ACCIDENT. We learn that on Wednesday last, while Mr. R. Herndon of New Salem, was preparing his rifle for a hunting excursion, it went off, and the ball, striking his wife in the neck, separated one of the principal arteries, and in a few moments she was a corpse. It is hardly possible to conceive the anguish of the husband on this melancholy catastrophe. The community in which he lives deeply sympathize with him in this afflicting event."

—*Sangamo Journal,*
January 26, 1833

The incident was shocking enough to generate newspaper coverage as far away as Galena[139] and is inherently of interest to us because of its impact on characters in our story, but it also provides an exact date documenting that Lincoln was already seeking out Ann. A week later, Abe went surety on a bond for her brother David, in a transaction presumably intended to finance Illinois College studies by David and Slicky Bill Greene, who had sold the Radford inventory to Berry and Lincoln.[140]

Ann's most junior sister, Sally, was quite young at the time but later recalled, "He was friendly with all of us girls, and while I knew that he cared especially for Ann, I have had to interpret what I saw and knew of their relations in the light of what my mother and my sister, Nan, told me."[141] The Rutledge home at the tavern was routinely filled with music, the family singing together from hymn books. When visiting there, Abe joined in. He teased Ann's younger sister Nancy with his version of "Legacy" from the *Missouri Harmony,* a rendition that made her flee the room blushing every time.[142] Sally agreed about Lincoln joining in *Missouri Harmony* songfests, though she said, "He could not sing very well."[143] "I can see him now, just as he looked," Nan said of Lincoln, "sitting by the big, old fashioned fireplace, absorbed in a book or chatting merrily with Annie or one of my brothers. He always came and went just as one of the family."[144] Such vignettes imply an atmosphere of gentle fun in the Rutledge home. Lincoln's family status among the Rutledges was documented by a patchwork quilt, held in the family for decades, that incorporated snips of Lincoln's garments.[145]

About the time Abe was appointed postmaster in May 1833, the Rutledges started to move from town to a farm in a nearby district called Sandridge.[146] This farm was the acreage McNamar had bought from James Cameron in December 1831. (It adjoined a farm once owned by the Rutledges; they had sold half to McNamar in July 1831 and the other half to Jack Armstrong's brother-in-law John "Fiddler" Jones in January 1833.[147]) McNamar later said that his intention was to settle his father on the property and while he was back East, his local business agent, the Rev. Dr. John Allen, "induced" the Rutledges "to occupy and take care of the place."[148] So the move doesn't necessarily indicate that the family still expected McNamar to marry into the clan. By implication, John Allen didn't think McNamar would return anytime soon, or else Allen would not have sought to establish the Rutledges on the property. I wouldn't be surprised if the arrangement was for them to stay there free of charge, their "rent" simply being upkeep of property that would otherwise be neglected and decline in value. The move to Sandridge was protracted, with Ann's mother going first and other family members following. When the mother first arrived in Sandridge, she kept house for her relative "Uncle Jimmy" Short until he got married in September 1833. According to Short, after that marriage and after Ann and the other Rutledges moved to the McNamar place, about a ten- or fifteen-minute walk from Short's, "Mr. Lincoln came over to see me and them every day or two."[149] That would seem to be the conduct of a courting man. Short and McNamar, by the way, eventually became brothers-in-law,[150] so McNamar thereby became a shirttail relative of Ann after her death.

In autumn 1833, after Short married and Lincoln began visiting him and the Rutledges frequently, Mary Owens showed up from Kentucky for a month's stay. She was Elizabeth Abell's sister and related to other New Salemites as well. Mrs. Bowling Green remembered Lincoln spending a fair amount of time with Owens, who was "living handy to Salem," as someone later said.[151] Lincoln described her as "intelligent and agreeable," adding, "no woman that I have seen, has a finer face."[152] In the words of someone who talked with Parthena Hill and Mrs. Bowling Green, "Lincoln went down into the neighborhood of Col. Rutledge's to do a job of surveying and remained there about three weeks." In consequence, "Miss Owens got miffed at his long stay there and left Abell's and went to Mentor Graham's," another Owens relative. Regarding Owens, the interviewer reported, "Lincoln never went to see her any more."[153] Note what all this says. For a week or so, he called on the visiting sister of his friend Elizabeth Abell, finding the stranger pleasant enough, but dropped her cold when opportunity arose to be near Ann Rutledge for three weeks. Judging from letters of Mary Owens and comments of her friends, Owens was a smart and level-headed person. She wouldn't have been irked if a man stopped coming over to visit because of a work assignment. Therefore, we may presume she saw some other reason, perhaps one that suddenly made his previous attention seem less flattering.

John "Fiddler" Jones, who lived on a farm adjoining the Rutledge place, claimed he personally knew of Lincoln making "regular visits" to Ann. Fiddler said Ann and Abe were "generally understood" to be betrothed.[154] "No one could have seen them together and not be convinced that they loved each other truly," sister Nancy said.[155] Mrs. Bowling Green and Parthena Hill were confident that Lincoln's courtship had been successful, and Mrs. Hill added that such was the belief around town.[156] Slicky Bill Greene, who knew both Lincoln and Ann, certainly had that understanding,[157] as did Isaac Cogdal, who claimed to have had his impression confirmed in an 1860 conversation with Lincoln.[158]

At what point the friendship shared by Abe Lincoln and Ann Rutledge shifted to mutual romance is hard for me to judge. I would not be surprised if such were the case by the end of 1834, regardless of whether a formal engagement occurred. By then McNamar's desertion must have seemed proved and permanent. Lincoln was no longer the flatboatman and rail-splitter who had arrived in town three years earlier, when McNamar was a prominent businessman. In contrast to the apparent mystery man who had absconded without a trace, Ann was now receiving attention from one of the county's most determined and prominent citizens, someone serving the people as an industrious and well-liked postmaster, surveyor, and now state legislator and law student—someone on whom the public print was bestowing the gentlemanly title of "Esq."

As Lincoln prepared to head for the state legislature convening in Vandalia, I like to think both those young folks looked forward to a life together, a future bright with hope.

⫸ NOTES ⫸

When a passage of text derives from multiple sources, portions of that text may be from source A, then source B, then source A again. Therefore, the order in which sources are listed in a note doesn't necessarily match the way sources are blended in the passage.

Chapter 1. KENTUCKY

1. Briggs and Briggs, *Nancy*, 79.
2. Barton, *Life*, 1:74.
3. Michaux, *Travels*, 213.
4. Oliver, *Eight*, 71–73. Oliver wrote of his experiences in Illinois dating from ca. 1840, demonstrating the widespread and long-lasting nature of such beliefs.
5. Examples of superstitions current among Lincoln's associates are from George U. Miles, statement to William H. Herndon, 1866, H-W Papers (transcript available in Wilson and Davis, *Herndon's*, 536); Lamon (Black), *Life*, 44. His Indiana neighbors had similar beliefs (Murr, "Lincoln," 336–39).
6. Bancroft, *Life*, 1:2.
7. Letter to editor of *Staunton Eagle*, dateline Jonesborough, Tennessee, clipped in *Vincennes Western Sun*, July 30, 1808.
8. Brooks, *Abraham*, 18.
9. "A foolish credulity seems quite as prevalent among the educated people of an enlightened time as among those who lacked the knowledge and intellectual training which are supposed to eradicate such credulity from the mind" (Eggleston, *First*, 90).
10. Luthin, *Real*, 4.
11. Briggs and Briggs, *Nancy*, 79.
12. Michaux, *Travels*, 217–18.
13. Browne, *Abraham*, 1:60, 71.
14. Quoted in Browne, *Abraham*, 1:72–73.
15. Erastus R. Burba to William H. Herndon, May 25, 1866, H-W Papers (transcript available in Wilson and Davis, *Herndon's*, 257).
16. Richard A. Creal to William H. Herndon, March 12, 1866, H-W Papers (transcript available in Wilson and Davis, *Herndon's*, 228).
17. Michaux, *Travels*, 220.
18. Beveridge, *Abraham*, 1:11–12; Herndon and Weik, *Herndon's Life of Lincoln*, 10–11; Thomas L. D. Johnston interview with William H. Herndon, ca. 1866, H-W Papers (transcript available in Wilson and Davis, *Herndon's*, 533); Lamon (Black), *Life*, 7; Warren, *Lincoln's Parentage*, 5, 297 (*see also* Barton, *Life*, 1:31–32); Augustus H. Chapman statement, ca. Sept. 1865, H-W Papers (transcript available in Wilson and Davis, *Herndon's*, 95–96); Augustus H. Chapman to William H. Herndon, Oct. 8, 1865, H-W Papers (transcript available in Wilson and Davis, *Herndon's*, 137); Augustus H. Chapman interview with William H. Herndon, ca. 1865–1866, H-W Papers (transcript available in Wilson and Davis, *Herndon's*, 439); William Clagett statement, ca. Feb. 22, 1866, H-W Papers (transcript available in Wilson and Davis, *Herndon's*, 219); Den-

nis Hanks interview with William H. Herndon, June 13, 1865, H-W Papers, (transcript available in Wilson and Davis, *Herndon's*, 36); Henry Pirtle to William H. Herndon, June 27, 1865, H-W Papers (transcript available in Wilson and Davis, *Herndon's*, 65); Henry Pirtle to William H. Herndon, July 4, 1865, H-W Papers (transcript available in Wilson and Davis, *Herndon's*, 71); Warren, *Lincoln's Youth*, 33. Stories from Denny Hanks merit close inspection for error, but the more reliable John Hanks declared that the "Indian story of Dennis Hanks is generally correct" and also vouched for the thrust of Chapman's account (John Hanks interview with William H. Herndon, ca. 1865–1866, H-W Papers (transcript available in Wilson and Davis, *Herndon's*, 454)). The date of pioneer Lincoln's death, like the date of Tom's birth, has been disputed. Some authorities (given in Beveridge, *Abraham*, 1:11 n. 2) even question the reality of the pioneer's murder, but that much discrepancy from family tradition is beyond belief.

19. Abraham Lincoln to Jesse Lincoln, April 1, 1854 (transcript available in *CW* 2:217).

20. Abraham Lincoln to Solomon Lincoln, March 6, 1848 (transcript available in *CW* 1:456); Abraham Lincoln, autobiography for Jesse Fell (transcript available in *CW* 3:511); Abraham Lincoln, autobiography for John L. Scripps (transcript available in *CW* 4:61); Herndon (Weik), *Life*, 10; Augustus H. Chapman to William H. Herndon, Oct. 8, 1865, H-W Papers (transcript available in Wilson and Davis, *Herndon's*, 137); William Clagett statement, ca. Feb. 22, 1866, H-W Papers (transcript available in Wilson and Davis, *Herndon's*, 219).

21. Mary Mitchell to Gov. Isaac Shelby, May 1, 1793, in Durrett Collection, Chronological Files, 1793, University of Chicago Library, quoted in Warren, *Lincoln's Parentage*, 311–12.

22. Sarah's general story of captivity and recovery may be found in the following sources, although they differ in many details: Kempf, *Abraham*, 29; Warren, *Lincoln's Parentage*, 63–67; Warren, *Lincoln's Youth*, 33–34; Warren, "Romance," 215; Charlotte S. Hobart Vawter newspaper clipping enclosed in Chauncey F. Black to William H. Herndon, April 30, 1874, H-W Papers (transcript available in Wilson and Davis, *Herndon's*, 585–86)—on p. 584, Chauncey Black harshly criticizes the subsequent material, but one is never quite sure of where Chauncey's head is. Warren's version of the 1874 newspaper clipping has puzzling differences from the Black version, although basic stories match. My account of Sarah Mitchell, of course, is only as reliable as these underlying sources. Not all Lincoln scholars accept them, but I don't find them unbelievable—which isn't the same as being certain of their accuracy.

23. Barton, *Life*, 1:11; Briggs and Briggs, *Nancy*, 26; Coleman, "Lincoln's," 82; Donald, *Lincoln*, 21–22; Tarbell, *Life*, 1:7; Warren, *Lincoln's Parentage*, 9; "Uncle," 2; Henry Pirtle to William H. Herndon, June 27, 1865, H-W Papers (transcript available in Wilson and Davis, *Herndon's*, 65); Henry Pirtle to William H. Herndon, July 4, 1865, H-W Papers (transcript available in Wilson and Davis, *Herndon's*, 71). Although Virginia repealed the British law governing inheritance when no will existed in 1785, the repeal didn't take effect until 1787. Regardless of when the pioneer Lincoln was killed between 1784 and 1786, the old law still ruled.

24. Quoted in Linder, *Reminiscences*, 38.

25. Warren, *Lincoln's Parentage*, 43, 270, 283; Warren, *Slavery*, unpaginated.

26. Warren, *Lincoln's Parentage*, 159.

27. Abraham Lincoln, autobiography for John L. Scripps (transcript available in *CW* 4:61); Abraham Lincoln to Solomon Lincoln, March 6, 1848 (transcript available in *CW* 1:456).

28. Abraham Lincoln to Jesse Lincoln, April 1, 1854 (transcript available in *CW* 2:217); Abraham Lincoln, autobiography for John L. Scripps (transcript available in *CW* 4:61); Barton, *Life*, 1:11; Barton, *Paternity*, 255; Brooks, *Abraham*, 5; Tarbell, *In the Footsteps*, 70–71; Warren, *Slavery*, unpaginated.

29. Warren, *Lincoln's Parentage*, 159.

30. Donald, *Lincoln*, 22, and Warren, *Lincoln's Parentage*, 43, maintain the £118 came from Tom's savings. Other authorities (Barton, *Life*, 1:11–12; Barton, "Lincoln's," 23; Barton, *Paternity*, 266–67; Beverage, *Abraham*, 1:12; Tarbell, *In the Footsteps*, 74; Thomas, *Abraham*, 5) have noted that brother Mordecai sold some family land about this time and might have given Tom a share of the proceeds, or perhaps the estate of his father was finally settled and yielded a lump

sum to Tom. We know he earned an income through years of hard work. The windfall theory rests on unproven assumption. *See also* Tim G. Needham to William H. Herndon, June 26, 1865, H-W Papers (transcript available in Wilson and Davis, *Herndon's*, 60) and Tim G. Needham to William H. Herndon, July 5, 1865, H-W Papers (transcript available in Wilson and Davis, *Herndon's*, 71).

31. Tarbell, *In the Footsteps*, 74, 117.
32. Beveridge, *Abraham*, 1:12; Warren, *Lincoln's Parentage*, 115.
33. Barton, *Life*, 1:35; Coleman, "Lincoln's," 63–64, 90; Warren, *Lincoln's Parentage*, 15–16, 129.
34. Beveridge, *Abraham*, 1:13; Warren, *Lincoln's Parentage*, 48–49, 182–84, 306 n. 35, 338 n. 14, 339 n. 14.
35. Beveridge, *Abraham*, 1:13; Warren, *Lincoln's Parentage*, 46–47, 182; Warren, "Romance," 217.
36. Beveridge, *Abraham*, 1:13–14; Furnas, *Goodbye*, 133; Warren, *Lincoln's Parentage*, 50, 185, 306 n. 40; Warren, "Romance," 217.
37. Warren, *Lincoln's Parentage*, 185.
38. Barton, *Life*, 1:13; Beveridge, *Abraham*, 1:21–22; Samuel Haycraft to William H. Herndon, ca. June 1865, H-W Papers (transcript available in Wilson and Davis, *Herndon's*, 67), Samuel Haycraft to John B. Helm, July 5, 1865, H-W Papers (transcript available in Wilson and Davis, *Herndon's*, 84); Warren, *Lincoln's Parentage*, 164–65.
39. John Hanks interview with William H. Herndon, ca. 1865, H-W Papers (transcript available in Wilson and Davis, *Herndon's*, 454); David Turnham interview with William H. Herndon, Sept. 15, 1865, H-W Papers (transcript available in Wilson and Davis, *Herndon's*, 122); Warren, "Romance," 217; Erastus Wright to Josiah G. Holland (enclosure), July 3, 1865 (transcript available in Guelzo, "Holland's," 34).
40. Ehrmann, *Missing*, 37; Anna O'Flynn in Ehrmann, *Missing*, 100; McMurtry, "Furniture"; McMurtry, "Thomas"; Tarbell, *In the Footsteps*, 133.
41. Warren, "Romance," 217.
42. Beveridge, *Abraham*, 1:13; Warren, *Lincoln's Parentage*, 116.
43. R. Gerald McMurtry, "The World of Tom and Nancy Lincoln," in Newman, *Lincoln*, 44; Tarbell, *Life*, 1:12; Warren, *Lincoln's Parentage*, 266–67; Warren, "Romance," 217.
44. Mentor Graham to William H. Herndon, July 15, 1865, H-W Papers (transcript available in Wilson and Davis, *Herndon's*, 76). Graham's account has been criticized for mistakes in dating and in Lincoln's childhood age, but errors in numbers after several decades are hardly enough to discredit the general memory.
45. William G. Green to William H. Herndon, Dec. 20, 1865, H-W Papers (transcript available in Wilson and Davis, *Herndon's*, 145).
46. Nancy's brother, Joseph Hanks, was a carpenter who eventually lived in Elizabethtown. He is sometimes incorrectly credited with teaching Tom Lincoln the carpenter's trade, an alleged connection that supposedly brought Tom and Nancy into contact. That story's error is shown by Briggs and Briggs, *Nancy*, 39–40; Warren, "June"; Warren, *Lincoln's Parentage*, 160.
47. Quoted in Whitney, *Life*, 149–50. Whitney attributes the story to Abraham Lincoln, but Whitney doesn't say that he heard it firsthand. And even if Abraham Lincoln told the story, that doesn't reveal whether Tom was telling a stretcher. The tale is of interest nonetheless.
48. Briggs and Briggs, *Nancy*, 31–32; William H. Herndon to Charles A. Hart, Dec. 28, 1866, in Hertz, *Hidden*, 52; William H. Herndon to Ward Hill Lamon, Feb. 24, 1869, in Hertz, *Hidden*, 59; William H. Herndon to Ward Hill Lamon, Feb. 25, 1870, in Hertz, *Hidden*, 63; William H. Herndon to Ward Hill Lamon, March 6, 1870, in Hertz, *Hidden*, 73–74; William H. Herndon, "Nancy Hanks" essay, Aug. 20, 1887, in Hertz, *Hidden*, 411–12; Herndon and Weik, *Herndon's Life of Lincoln*, 2–3; Charles B. Strozier and Stanley H. Cath, "Lincoln and the Fathers: Reflections on Idealization," in Cath, Gurwitt, and Gunsberg, *Fathers*, 297; Thomas, *Portrait*, 35. Abraham Lincoln's belief was consistent with what acquaintances of Nancy Hanks believed (Murr, "Lincoln," 333). In Kentucky, the conduct of Nancy's mother led to indictment for fornication (Barton, *Women*, 35; Beveridge, *Abraham*, 1:14 n. 5; Paul H. Verduin, "Appendix: Brief

Outline of the Joseph Hanks Family" in Wilson and Davis, *Herndon's*, 780; Warren, *Lincoln's Parentage*, 62). Nancy would "tell him [Abraham] stories about George Washington, an' say that Abe had jist as good Virginny blood in him as Washington. Mebbe she stretched things some, but it done Abe good" (Dennis Hanks, quoted in Atkinson, *Boyhood*, 18). The Atkinson interview with Hanks is questioned by some scholars. I have doubts about it but find it plausible enough to be worth mentioning.

49. Carter, *Turning*, 31.
50. William H. Herndon to Ward Hill Lamon, Feb. 25, 1870, in Hertz, *Hidden*, 63. *See also* Thomas, *Portrait*, 35.
51. Compare Tarbell, *Life*, 1:7–8 (McClure, Phillips & Co., 1902 ed.) with Barton, *Life*, 1:9 and Barton, *Paternity*, 267.
52. Jimmy Carter presented an example from his own experience: "One of the few Republicans who qualified to run outside the Atlanta area was my second cousin Perry Gordy, in Columbus, about whom I had heard but whom I had not met" (Carter, *Turning*, 65).
53. Kempf, *Abraham*, 33. Billy Herndon was another day counter (William H. Herndon to Truman Bartlett, Sept. 30, 1887, in Hertz, *Hidden*, 205–6). Entertaining and halfway plausible speculation exists about whether disease had rendered Tom Lincoln incapable of fathering a child, but halfway doesn't go far enough to convince me. *See* E. R. Burba to William H. Herndon, March 21, 1866, H-W Papers (transcript available in Wilson and Davis, *Herndon's*, 240); Charles Friend to William H. Herndon, July 31, 1889, H-W Papers (transcript available in Wilson and Davis, *Herndon's*, 674); Dennis Hanks interview with William H. Herndon, June 13, 1865, H-W Papers (transcript available in Wilson and Davis, *Herndon's*, 36); William H. Herndon to Ward Hill Lamon, Feb. 25, 1870, in Hertz, *Hidden*, 63; William H. Herndon to Jesse Weik, Jan. 1, 1886, in Hertz, *Hidden*, 118–19; William H. Herndon to Truman Bartlett, Sept. 30, 1887, in Hertz, *Hidden*, 205–7; Charles B. Strozier and Stanley H. Cath, "Lincoln and the Fathers: Reflections on Idealization," in Cath, Gurwitt, and Gunsberg, *Fathers*, 295.
54. Barton, *Life*, 1:484; Coleman, "A Preacher," 2–3, 5; Warren, *Lincoln's Parentage*, 228–29; Warren, "Rev. Jesse." *See also* Barton, *Life*, 1:18, 482–84; Coleman, "A Preacher," 5–6; E. B. Head (grandson of Jesse Head) in Tarbell, *Early*, 230.
55. Briggs and Briggs, *Nancy*, 68–69; Warren, "Romance," 220–22. Richard Berry's brother John was on the grand jury that indicted Nancy's mother for fornication (Barton, *Life*, 1:59, 62; Briggs and Briggs, *Nancy*, 37; Peterson, *Lucey Hanks*, 34).
56. Beveridge, *Abraham*, 1:21; Briggs and Briggs, *Nancy*, 75–76; R. Gerald McMurtry, "The World of Tom and Nancy Lincoln," in Newman, *Lincoln*, 45; McMurtry, "Bleakley"; Warren, *Lincoln's Parentage*, 51, 54.
57. Barton, *Women*, 67, 71; Kempf, *Abraham*, 29; Charlotte S. Hobart Vawter newspaper clipping enclosed in Chauncey F. Black to William H. Herndon, April 30, 1874, H-W Papers (transcript available in Wilson and Davis, *Herndon's*, 585–86).
58. Michaux, *Travels*, 248.
59. Numerous reports of her appearance exist, but they are contradictory and lack additional aspects, such as chronology, geography, or some incident supported by other reports, that I could use to evaluate them. Possibly they are describing different women named Nancy Hanks.
60. A. H. Chapman statement, ca. Sept. 1865, H-W Papers (transcript available in Wilson and Davis, *Herndon's*, 96–97); Harriet A. Chapman to William H. Herndon, Dec. 17, 1865, H-W Papers (transcript available in Wilson and Davis, *Herndon's*, 145); Harriet A. Chapman interview with Jesse Weik, ca. 1886–1887, Jesse W. Weik Papers (transcript available in Wilson and Davis, *Herndon's*, 646); W. H. Doak quoted in McMurtry, "Was," 24; William G. Greene to William H. Herndon, Dec. 20, 1865, H-W Papers (transcript available in Wilson and Davis, *Herndon's*, 145); William G. Greene, as quoted by H. C. Whitney in Chapman, *Latest*, 19; Nathaniel Grigsby interview with William H. Herndon, Sept. 12, 1865, H-W Papers (transcript available in Wilson and Davis, *Herndon's*, 111); Dennis Hanks interview with Erastus Wright,

June 8, 1865, H-W Papers (transcript available in Wilson and Davis, *Herndon's*, 28); Dennis Hanks interview with William H. Herndon, June 13, 1865, H-W Papers (transcript available in Wilson and Davis, *Herndon's*, 37); Dennis Hanks to William H. Herndon, ca. Dec. 1865, H-W Papers (transcript available in Wilson and Davis, *Herndon's*, 149); Dennis Hanks interview with Jesse Weik, ca. 1886, Jesse W. Weik Papers (transcript available in Wilson and Davis, *Herndon's*, 598); John Hanks interview with John Miles, May 25, 1865, H-W Papers (transcript available in Wilson and Davis, *Herndon's*, 5); John Hanks interview with William H. Herndon, ca. 1865–1866, H-W Papers (transcript available in Wilson and Davis, *Herndon's*, 454); John Hanks to Jesse Weik, June 12, 1887, Jesse W. Weik Papers (transcript available in Wilson and Davis, *Herndon's*, 615); Samuel Haycraft to William H. Herndon, ca. June 1865, H-W Papers (transcript available in Wilson and Davis, *Herndon's*, 67); David Turnham interview with William H. Herndon, Sept. 15, 1865, H-W Papers (transcript available in Wilson and Davis, *Herndon's*, 122); David Turnham to William H. Herndon, Dec. 6, 1865, H-W Papers (transcript available in Wilson and Davis, *Herndon's*, 142).

61. Dennis Hanks interview with Erastus Wright, June 8, 1865, H-W Papers (transcript available in Wilson and Davis, *Herndon's*, 28); Erastus Wright to Josiah G. Holland (enclosure), July 3, 1865 (transcript available in Guelzo, "Holland's," 34).

62. Atherton to Mather, June 20, 1924, in Beveridge, *Abraham*, 1:35 n. 5; A. H. Chapman statement, ca. Sept. 1865, H-W Papers (transcript available in Wilson and Davis, *Herndon's*, 97); Harriet A. Chapman interview with Jesse Weik, ca. 1886–1887, Jesse W. Weik Papers (transcript available in Wilson and Davis, *Herndon's*, 646); Nathaniel Grigsby interview with William H. Herndon, Sept. 12, 1865, H-W Papers (transcript available in Wilson and Davis, *Herndon's*, 113); Dennis Hanks interview with Erastus Wright, June 8, 1865, H-W Papers (transcript available in Wilson and Davis, *Herndon's*, 27); Dennis Hanks interview with William H. Herndon, June 13, 1865, H-W Papers (transcript available in Wilson and Davis, *Herndon's*, 37); Dennis Hanks interview with Jesse Weik, ca. 1886, Jesse W. Weik Papers (transcript available in Wilson and Davis, *Herndon's*, 598); John Hanks interview with William H. Herndon, ca. 1865–1866, H-W Papers (transcript available in Wilson and Davis, *Herndon's*, 454); John Hanks to Jesse Weik, June 12, 1887, Jesse W. Weik Papers (transcript available in Wilson and Davis, *Herndon's*, 615); William H. Herndon to Truman Bartlett, Oct. 1887, in Hertz, *Hidden*, 208; Herndon and Weik, *Herndon's Life of Lincoln*, 14; J. Edward Murr in Ehrmann, *Missing*, 98; unnamed source, quoted in Petersen, *Lincoln-Douglas*, 175–76 n. 20; William Wood interview with William H. Herndon, Sept. 15, 1865, H-W Papers (transcript available in Wilson and Davis, *Herndon's*, 124).

63. William H. Herndon to Ward Hill Lamon, Feb. 25, 1870, in Hertz, *Hidden*, 63; Herndon and Weik, *Herndon's Life of Lincoln*, 14. Indiana neighbor William Wood also called her "intellectual" (William Wood interview with William H. Herndon, Sept. 15, 1865, H-W Papers (transcript available in Wilson and Davis, *Herndon's*, 124)).

64. E. R. Burba to William H. Herndon, March 31, 1866, H-W Papers (transcript available in Wilson and Davis, *Herndon's*, 240); A. H. Chapman statement, ca. Sept. 1865, H-W Papers (transcript available in Wilson and Davis, *Herndon's*, 97); R. A. Creal to William H. Herndon, Feb. 18, 1866, H-W Papers (transcript available in Wilson and Davis, *Herndon's*, 214); Richard W. Creal in Barton, *Paternity*, 173; William G. Green to William H. Herndon, Dec. 20, 1865, H-W Papers (transcript available in Wilson and Davis, *Herndon's*, 145); Nathaniel Grigsby interview with William H. Herndon, Sept. 12, 1865, H-W Papers (transcript available in Wilson and Davis, *Herndon's*, 111,113); Dennis Hanks interview with Erastus Wright, June 8, 1865, H-W Papers (transcript available in Wilson and Davis, *Herndon's*, 28); Dennis Hanks to William H. Herndon, Jan. 26, 1866, H-W Papers (transcript available in Wilson and Davis, *Herndon's*, 176); Dennis Hanks interview with Jesse Weik, ca. 1886, Jesse W. Weik Papers (transcript available in Wilson and Davis, *Herndon's*, 598); John Hanks interview with William H. Herndon, ca. 1865–1866, H-W Papers (transcript available in Wilson and Davis, *Herndon's*, 454); Samuel Haycraft to William H. Herndon, ca. June 1865, H-W Papers (transcript available in Wilson and

Davis, *Herndon's*, 67); Samuel Haycraft to William H. Herndon, Dec. 7, 1866, H-W Papers (transcript available in Wilson and Davis, *Herndon's*, 503); informant quoted in Browne, *Abraham*, 1:83; Thomas L. D. Johnston interview with William H. Herndon, ca. 1866, H-W Papers (transcript available in Wilson and Davis, *Herndon's*, 533); Murr, "Lincoln," 322.

65. Quoted in Browne, *Abraham*, 1:82–83.

66. Mrs. Dowling, quoted in Atkinson, *Boyhood*, 44–45. Indiana neighbor Elizabeth Crawford said the Lincolns were "hospitable and very, very sociable" (Elizabeth Crawford interview with William H. Herndon, Sept. 16, 1865, H-W Papers (transcript available in Wilson and Davis, *Herndon's*, 126)).

67. Hobson, *Footprints*, 22. This was an Indiana neighbor, demonstrating Tom's continuing fondness for children after he left Kentucky.

68. Dennis Hanks, quoted in Atkinson, *Boyhood*, 9.

69. Barton, *Life*, 1:88; Warren, *Lincoln's Parentage*, 114. A full-size truck wagon "was made by cutting four wheels from a large tree, usually a black gum. A four-in hole was made in the middle of the wheels in which axles fitted. . . . They were very musical as well, for the more grease one put on the wooden axle to make it run lighter, the more it would squeak and squeal, making a noise that could be heard a mile" (Cockrum, *Pioneer*, 320–21).

70. Dennis Hanks quoted in Browne, *Every-Day*, 55.

71. Warren, *Lincoln's Parentage*, 114, 173.

72. George Balch interview with Jesse Weik, ca. 1886, Jesse W. Weik Papers (transcript available in Wilson and Davis, *Herndon's*, 597); Augustus H. Chapman statement, ca. Sept. 1865, H-W Papers (transcript available in Wilson and Davis, *Herndon's*, 97); Harriet A. Chapman interview with Jesse Weik, ca. 1886–1887, Jesse W. Weik Papers (transcript available in Wilson and Davis, *Herndon's*, 646); John Hanks to Jesse Weik, June 12, 1887, Jesse W. Weik Papers (transcript available in Wilson and Davis, *Herndon's*, 615); Townsend, *Lincoln and Liquor*, 6–7.

73. Dennis Hanks interview with William H. Herndon, June 13, 1865, H-W Papers (transcript available in Wilson and Davis, *Herndon's*, 37). *See also* his trivially different version in Dennis Hanks interview with Erastus Wright, June 8, 1865, H-W Papers (transcript available in Wilson and Davis, *Herndon's*, 28). Augustus H. Chapman also remembered the encounter, noting that it was atypical for Tom (Augustus H. Chapman statement, ca. Sept. 1865, H-W Papers (transcript available in Wilson and Davis, *Herndon's*, 96)). *See also* Erastus Wright to Josiah G. Holland (enclosure), July 3, 1865 (transcript available in Guelzo, "Holland's," 34).

74. A. H. Chapman statement, ca. Sept. 1865, H-W Papers (transcript available in Wilson and Davis, *Herndon's*, 97); Nathaniel Grigsby interview with William H. Herndon, Sept. 12, 1865, H-W Papers (transcript available in Wilson and Davis, *Herndon's*, 113); Dennis Hanks, quoted in Atkinson, *Boyhood*, 11. The survey, by Richard W. Creal, is in Barton, *Paternity*, 171–75. Rumors that emerged in distant places years afterward count for nothing. Keep in mind, too, that the mother of Denny Hanks was named Nancy Hanks and lived in the same region as Abraham Lincoln's mother; apparently the two kinswomen, who were of similar age, were of very different character in sexual conduct, and later rumors about Abraham's mother may have resulted from confused memories about Denny's. Billy Herndon, who received much of this gossip both in writing and in conversation, at one time believed that it applied to Abraham's mother but later changed his mind (William H. Herndon to Truman Bartlett, Sept. 30, 1887, in Hertz, *Hidden*, 205–7). A twentieth-century physician adroitly noted that according to psychological understandings of his own era, the observed conduct of Abraham's parents was inconsistent with promiscuity by Nancy before or after marriage (Kempf, *Abraham*, 76).

75. Beveridge, *Abraham*, 1:17–19; "Uncle," 6; Warren, *Lincoln's Parentage*, 256–57, 261–71, 297.

76. Warren, "Thomas."

77. Quoted in Browne, *Abraham*, 1:83.

78. Briggs and Briggs, *Nancy*, 65; Warren, "Romance," 217.

79. Augustus H. Chapman statement, ca. Sept. 8, 1865, H-W Papers (transcript available in Wilson and Davis, *Herndon's*, 100, 102).

80. Augustus H. Chapman statement, ca. Sept. 8, 1865, H-W Papers (transcript available in Wilson and Davis, *Herndon's*, 102).
81. Briggs and Briggs, *Nancy*, 75; Warren, *Lincoln's Parentage*, 54.
82. Warren, *Lincoln's Parentage*, 56, 310–11.
83. Barton, *Paternity*, 252–54; Beveridge, *Abraham*, 1:22–23; Briggs and Briggs, *Nancy*, 65; Warren, *Lincoln's Parentage*, 52, 161–64.
84. Barton, *Life*, 1:76–77; Barton, *Paternity*, 253; Barton, *Women*, 80; Beveridge, *Abraham*, 1:23; Warren, *Lincoln's Parentage*, 54, 56.
85. Barton, *Paternity*, 173, 182–83, 309, 315–16; Barton, *Women*, 82–84; Shutes, *Lincoln and the Doctors*, 3; Tarbell, *In the Footsteps*, 93.
86. Peggy Walters in Barton, *Women*, 83–84. Apparently quite a few women claimed to have been present at Abraham's birth, but I find the Walters claim plausible because of the context in which it arose and because she mentioned the birth being on a Sunday, an uncommonly noted detail that might be unlikely to occur in an impromptu fabrication.
87. Dennis Hanks, quoted in Atkinson, *Boyhood*, 6–7. A Western newspaper of the time described weather as "the severest cold of our winters" (*Vincennes Western Sun*, Feb. 4, 1809), perhaps adding credibility to Denny's alleged recollection of Tom's concern about cabin temperature. *See also* Dennis Hanks interview with William H. Herndon, June 13, 1865, H-W Papers (transcript available in Wilson and Davis, *Herndon's*, 38); Dennis Hanks in Browne, *Every-Day*, 51.
88. Weik, *Real*, 44.
89. Warren, *Lincoln's Parentage*, 106.
90. Barton, *Life*, 1:74; Beveridge, *Abraham*, 1:3.
91. Browne, *Abraham*, 1:75.
92. Nicolay and Hay, *Abraham*, 1:25.
93. Dennis Hanks, quoted in Atkinson, *Boyhood*, 10–11.
94. Quoted in George Borrett, *Letters from Canada and the United States* (London: Printed for private circulation by J. E. Adlard, 1865), 249–56, as given in Segal, *Conversations*, 348.
95. Faragher, *Sugar*, 41; Warren, *Lincoln's Parentage*, 189.
96. F. A. Michaux, *Travels*, 226–27.
97. Warren, *Lincoln's Parentage*, 189–90.
98. Warren, *Lincoln's Parentage*, 87.
99. Warren, *Lincoln's Parentage*, 265.
100. Beveridge, *Abraham*, 1:23–26, 41; Warren, *Lincoln's Parentage*, 117–18, 122, 315–16, 323–28.
101. Abraham Lincoln to Samuel Haycraft, June 4, 1860 (transcript available in *CW* 4:70).
102. Dennis Hanks interview with William H. Herndon, June 13, 1865, H-W Papers (transcript available in Wilson and Davis, *Herndon's*, 38).
103. Barton, *Women*, 85; Judge Otis M. Mather statement, June 14, 1924, in *Lincoln Herald*, 48 (Feb. 1946): 18.
104. Reynolds, *My Own Times*, 124–25. For a contemporary description of the comet, *see Lexington Kentucky Gazette*, March 17, 1812.
105. Dennis Hanks interview with William H. Herndon, June 13, 1865, H-W Papers (transcript available in Wilson and Davis, *Herndon's*, 36).
106. Quoted in Nicolay and Hay, *Abraham*, 1:27.
107. John Ewing, *Vincennes Western Sun*, Aug. 24, 1816.
108. Drake, *Pioneer*, 49; Johnson, *Illinois*, 112–13.
109. Barton, *Life*, 1:87–88; Drake, *Pioneer*, 47.
110. Quoted in Tarbell, *Life*, 1:20. Slightly different versions of the quotation can be found in Fehrenbacher and Fehrenbacher, *Recollected*, 508; Tarbell, *In the Footsteps*, 105; Warren, *Lincoln's Parentage*, 143. Tarbell (and the Fehrenbachers, who cite Tarbell's papers) credits J. J. Wright with reporting Lincoln's words. Warren credits Jesse Rodman.
111. Warren, *Lincoln's Parentage*, 144.

112. Beveridge, *Abraham*, 1:27, 30–31; Charles Friend to William H. Herndon, Aug. 20, 1889, H-W Papers (transcript available in Wilson and Davis, *Herndon's*, 676); Warren, *Lincoln's Parentage*, 143.

113. Otis M. Mather statement, June 14, 1924, in *Lincoln Herald*, 48 (Feb. 1946):18.

114. Dennis Hanks, quoted in Atkinson, *Boyhood*, 9, 12–13.

115. John Duncan to William H. Herndon, Feb. 21, 1867, H-W Papers (transcript available in Wilson and Davis, *Herndon's*, 557); John Duncan cited in Charles Friend to William H. Herndon, March 19, 1866, H-W Papers (transcript available in Wilson and Davis, *Herndon's*, 234–35); John Duncan cited in Charles Friend to William H. Herndon, Aug. 20, 1889, H-W Papers (transcript available in Wilson and Davis, *Herndon's*, 676).

116. Dennis Hanks interview with William H. Herndon, Sept. 8, 1865, H-W Papers (transcript available in Wilson and Davis, *Herndon's*, 103). A Lincoln comment can be read as implying that he was considered too young to handle an axe in Kentucky (Abraham Lincoln, autobiography for John L. Scripps, ca. June 1860 (transcript available in *CW* 4:62)), but such a tool was more physically demanding than a rifle. Denny purportedly told of young Lincoln carrying a rifle during the family's migration from Kentucky to Indiana (Dennis Hanks, quoted in Atkinson, *Boyhood*, 14).

117. E. R. Burba to William H. Herndon, March 31, 1866, H-W Papers (transcript available in Wilson and Davis, *Herndon's*, 241).

118. Austin Gollaher in Tarbell, *Life*, 1:17; Herndon and Weik, *Herndon's Life of Lincoln*, 18; Charles Friend to William H. Herndon, March 19, 1866, H-W Papers (transcript available in Wilson and Davis, *Herndon's*, 235). Gollaher's credibility has been questioned (Barton, *Life*, 1:78, 80–81; Warren, *Lincoln's Parentage*, 101–2, 147–49), but I include the story because the authoritative Miers, *Lincoln Day by Day*, finds it credible (1816 autumn) and because Lincoln is quoted as speaking fondly of his childhood friendship with Gollaher, thus indicating that the two did routinely play together. Denny Hanks also claimed to have saved Lincoln from drowning (Barton, *Life*, 1:80; Warren, *Lincoln's Parentage*, 148). Whether the boy had two lucky escapes, one, or none is unclear.

119. Barton, *Life*, 1:90–91.

120. Beveridge, *Abraham*, 1:23. *See also* John Hanks interview with William H. Herndon, ca. 1865–1866, H-W Papers (transcript available in Wilson and Davis, *Herndon's*, 454).

121. Barton, *Women*, 85. *See also* Tarbell, *Life*, 1:16.

122. John B. Helm to William H. Herndon, Aug. 1, 1865, H-W Papers (transcript available in Wilson and Davis, *Herndon's*, 82).

123. Presley Haycraft in Weik, *Real*, 15.

124. E. R. Burba to William H. Herndon, March 31, 1866, H-W Papers (transcript available in Wilson and Davis, *Herndon's*, 241).

125. John Hanks, notes of interview by William H. Herndon, H-W Papers (transcript available in Wilson and Davis, *Herndon's*, 454).

126. Dennis Hanks, quoted in Atkinson, *Boyhood*, 9.

127. E. R. Burba to William H. Herndon, March 31, 1866, H-W Papers (transcript available in Wilson and Davis, *Herndon's*, 241).

128. Quoted in Browne, *Abraham*, 1:276.

129. Quoted in Browne, *Abraham*, 1:83.

130. Alexander Sympson in Whitney, *Life*, 36–37.

131. E. R. Burba to William H. Herndon, March 31, 1866, H-W Papers (transcript available in Wilson and Davis, *Herndon's*, 241).

132. E. R. Burba to William H. Herndon, March 31, 1866, H-W Papers (transcript available in Wilson and Davis, *Herndon's*, 241).

133. Dennis Hanks interview with William H. Herndon, Sept. 8, 1865, H-W Papers (transcript available in Wilson and Davis, *Herndon's*, 104).

134. Quoted by Jesse H. Rodman via Charles Friend to William H. Herndon, Aug. 20, 1889, H-W Papers (transcript available in Wilson and Davis, *Herndon's*, 676). A genteel version of this story, in which fruit is substituted for feces, was published in Weik, *Real*, 17–18.

135. Dennis Hanks in William H. Herndon interview, Sept. 13, 1865, H-W Papers (transcript available in Wilson and Davis, *Herndon's*, 39). Dennis Hanks Indiana-sounding variant is quoted in Atkinson, *Boyhood*, 28–29. Still another variant is in Browne, *Every-Day*, 53. *See also* Dennis Hanks to William H. Herndon, Jan. 26, 1866, H-W Papers (transcript available in Wilson and Davis, *Herndon's*, 176).

136. Austin Gollaher in Tarbell, *Life*, 1:17.

137. Dennis Hanks in William H. Herndon interview, Sept. 13, 1865, H-W Papers (transcript available in Wilson and Davis, *Herndon's*, 39).

138. Dennis Hanks to William H. Herndon, Jan. 26, 1866, H-W Papers (transcript available in Wilson and Davis, *Herndon's*, 176).

139. Quoted by Usher F. Linder in Josiah G. Holland to William H. Herndon, Aug. 19, 1867, H-W Papers (transcript available in Wilson and Davis, *Herndon's*, 569). A similar White House–era quotation is given by Isaac N. Arnold in Oldroyd, *Lincoln*, 33. A prepresidential expression of the same sentiments is found in Herndon and Weik, *Herndon's Life of Lincoln*, 3.

140. Shutes, *Lincoln's*, 14, citing Townsend, *Lincoln and His Wife's Home Town*, 158.

141. Sarah Bush Johnston Lincoln interview with William H. Herndon, Sept. 8, 1865, H-W Papers (transcript available in Wilson and Davis, *Herndon's*, 107); Leonard Swett in Rice, *Reminiscences*, 458.

142. Warren, *Lincoln's Parentage*, 45.

143. Warren, *Lincoln's Parentage*, 45, 307 n. 42, 325–26, 346.

144. George Balch interview with Jesse Weik, ca. 1886, H-W Papers (transcript available in Wilson and Davis, *Herndon's*, 597); A. H. Chapman statement ca. Sept. 8, 1865, H-W Papers (transcript available in Wilson and Davis, *Herndon's*, 97); Harriet A. Chapman interview with Jesse Weik, Jesse W. Weik Papers (transcript available in Wilson and Davis, *Herndon's*, 646); Thomas Goodwin in Barton, *Paternity*, 271; Nathaniel Grigsby interview with William H. Herndon, Sept. 12, 1865, H-W Papers (transcript available in Wilson and Davis, *Herndon's*, 111); John Hanks to Jesse Weik, June 12, 1887, Jesse W. Weik Papers (transcript available in Wilson and Davis, *Herndon's*, 615); Samuel Haycraft to John B. Helm, July 5, 1865, H-W Papers (transcript available in Wilson and Davis, *Herndon's*, 84); Sarah Bush Johnston Lincoln interview with William H. Herndon, Sept. 8, 1865, H-W Papers (transcript available in Wilson and Davis, *Herndon's*, 107).

145. Abraham Lincoln, autobiography for John L. Scripps, ca. June 1860 (transcript available in *CW* 4:61).

146. Sarah Bush Johnston Lincoln interview with William H. Herndon, Sept. 8, 1865, H-W Papers (transcript available in Wilson and Davis, *Herndon's*, 107).

147. Those who say she could read and write include Barton, *Life*, 1:9, 14; Dennis Hanks, quoted in Atkinson, *Boyhood*, 11; Hill, *Lincoln*, 7; Nicolay and Hay, *Abraham*, 1:24. Those who say she could read but are silent about writing include Dennis Hanks interview with William H. Herndon, June 13, 1865, H-W Papers (transcript available in Wilson and Davis, *Herndon's*, 37, 40); Dennis Hanks interview with Jesse Weik, ca. 1886, Jesse W. Weik Papers (transcript available in Wilson and Davis, *Herndon's*, 598); Warren, "Lincoln's Hoosier," 106 (who cites Herndon). Those who say she could read but not write include Scripps, *Life*, 10. Those who say she was unable to write include Beveridge, *Abraham*, 1:16; Warren, *Lincoln's Parentage*, 115, 322. Straddling authorities include Briggs and Briggs, *Nancy*, 53; Tarbell, *Early*, 43 caption.

148. Beveridge, *Abraham*, 1:16; Ehrmann, *Missing*, 142; Tarbell, *Early*, 43 caption; Warren, *Lincoln's Parentage*, 115, 322.

149. Mary Todd Lincoln to John Todd Stuart, Dec. 15, 1873, ALPL (transcript available in Turner and Turner, *Mary*, 603–4). Wolf, *Almost*, 35, quotes Abraham as saying the same. In Brooks, *Abraham*, 6, Noah Brooks, who had close access to President Lincoln in the White House

years, seemingly reports that Lincoln said his mother was a voracious reader who read all sorts of stories to him and his sister, a surprising report, but one that—because of Brooks's good reputation for credibility—cannot be disregarded. His phraseology, however, permits an interpretation that Nancy was telling stories from memory.

150. Dennis Hanks interview with William H. Herndon, June 13, 1865, H-W Papers (transcript available in Wilson and Davis, *Herndon's*, 40).

151. Dennis Hanks interview with William H. Herndon, June 13, 1865, H-W Papers (transcript available in Wilson and Davis, *Herndon's*, 37, 40).

152. Dennis Hanks in Browne, *Every-Day*, 52; Dennis Hanks interview with William H. Herndon, June 13, 1865, H-W Papers (transcript available in Wilson and Davis, *Herndon's*, 37).

153. David Turnham interview with William H. Herndon, Sept. 15, 1865, H-W Papers (transcript available in Wilson and Davis, *Herndon's*, 122).

154. Warren, *Lincoln's Parentage*, 206. A similar 1831 contract in Illinois shows how stable such arrangements were over a span of years and miles (see "Education," 368).

155. Tarbell, *Life*, 1:18.

156. Sherman, *Recollections*, 33.

157. Joseph Gillespie, quoted in Prickett, "Joseph," 95.

158. Donald F. Tingley, "Anti-Intellectualism on the Illinois Frontier," in Tingley, *Essays*, 8.

159. "Country School Keeping," *SJ*, Dec. 21, 1833. This article gives a vivid portrayal of a typical and seemingly hopeless class session, introduced with the observation that "if there ever was anything which could approach a description of Bedlam, it was this school."

160. "Abraham Lincoln's First School Teacher," *Lincoln Lore* (April 7, 1930, no. 52); Barrett, *Life*, 19; Briggs and Briggs, *Nancy*, 60–61, 89; Nightingale, "Joseph," 254–55; Warren, "Environs," 126; Warren, *Lincoln's Parentage*, 210–13.

161. "Caleb Hazel, Lincoln's Neighbor and Teacher," *Lincoln Lore* (May 5, 1930, no. 56); Warren, *Lincoln's Parentage*, 215; J. Edward Murr in Ehrmann, *Missing*, 91; Warren, "Environs," 126.

162. Tarbell, *In the Footsteps*, 106.

163. Briggs and Briggs, *Nancy*, 89; "Caleb Hazel, Lincoln's Neighbor and Teacher," *Lincoln Lore* (May 5, 1930, no. 56); Townsend, *Lincoln and Liquor*, 9–10; Warren, *Lincoln's Parentage*, 214. Some doubt exists about the liquor prosecution. There were two Caleb Hazels, father and son, and confusion of their identities exists among authorities.

164. Drake, *Pioneer*, 66.

165. Barton, *Life*, 1:112; Warren, *Lincoln's Parentage*, 268.

166. Confusion exists about whether the teacher was the son or the fifty-five-year-old father, but most authorities consider the father to be the teacher.

167. "Caleb Hazel, Lincoln's Neighbor and Teacher," *Lincoln Lore* (May 5, 1930, no. 56).

168. Samuel Haycraft to William H. Herndon, ca. June 1865, H-W Papers (transcript available in Wilson and Davis, *Herndon's*, 67).

169. Francis X. Rapier in Barton, *Life*, 1:79. See also Beveridge, *Abraham*, 1:28–29.

170. Drake, *Pioneer*, 145.

171. Barton, *Life*, 1:321; Barton, *Soul*, 32; Brooks, *Abraham*, 26; William H. Herndon quoted in Weik, *Real*, 105; William H. Herndon to Isaac N. Arnold, Oct. 24, 1883, printed in *Letter from*, unpaginated; Frances Todd Wallace interview with William H. Herndon, ca. 1865–1866, H-W Papers (transcript available in Wilson and Davis, *Herndon's*, 485); Tarbell, *In the Footsteps*, 140.

172. Drake, *Pioneer*, 149.

173. John Hanks interview with William H. Herndon, ca. 1865, H-W Papers (transcript available in Wilson and Davis, *Herndon's*, 454).

174. Austin Gollaher in Tarbell, *Life*, 1:18.

175. Barrett, *Life*, 19.

176. Greeley, *Recollections*, 45. Greeley cited Murray's explanations of grammar for particular criticism but didn't seem to limit overall judgment to that one aspect.

177. Barton, *Life*, 1:120; Monaghan, "Literary," 413; Weik, *Real*, 22. The quotation, from Weik, appears to be from Lincoln, but ambiguity in Weik's introductory prose presents the possibility that the quotation is Billy Herndon's description of Lincoln's attitude.
178. Quoted in Warren, "Murray's."
179. *Vincennes Western Sun*, Sept. 3, 1808.
180. Lincoln quoted in John B. Weber to William H. Herndon, Nov. 5, 1866, H-W Papers (transcript available in Wilson and Davis, *Herndon's*, 396).
181. Barton, *Life*, 1:110; Bunbry B. Lloyd interview with William H. Herndon, ca. 1866, H-W Papers (transcript available in Wilson and Davis, *Herndon's*, 533); E. R. Burba to William H. Herndon, May 25, 1866, H-W Papers (transcript available in Wilson and Davis, *Herndon's*, 257); Warren, *Lincoln's Parentage*, 254.
182. Briggs and Briggs, *Nancy*, 60; Nightingale, "Joseph," 240–41; Ostendorf, "Lincoln," 130–31; Whitney, *Life*, 46.
183. Beveridge, *Abraham*, 1:37 n.; Briggs and Briggs, *Nancy*, 95–96; Warren, *Lincoln's Parentage*, 288–89; Warren, *Slavery*, unpaginated.
184. *Vincennes Western Sun*, Dec. 7, 1816.
185. "Caleb Hazel, Lincoln's Neighbor and Teacher," *Lincoln Lore* (May 5, 1930, no. 56); Warren, "Environs," 127; Warren, *Lincoln's Parentage*, 217, 240–44; Warren, *Slavery*, unpaginated; Warren, "William." The antislavery attitude of this congregation wasn't the only aspect of Separates that distinguished them from other Baptists, but such details are beyond the scope of this book.
186. Beveridge, *Abraham*, 1:36; A. H. Chapman, ca. Sept. 8, 1865, H-W Papers (transcript available in Wilson and Davis, *Herndon's*, 97); Dennis Hanks interview with Erastus Wright, June 8, 1865, H-W Papers (transcript available in Wilson and Davis, *Herndon's*, 28). Charles Friend said Tom was baptized in the Rolling Fork stream, which Knob Creek flows into (Charles Friend to William H. Herndon, March 19, 1866, H-W Papers (transcript available in Wilson and Davis, *Herndon's*, 234)).
187. Harriet A. Chapman interview with Jesse Weik, ca. 1886–1887, Jesse W. Weik Papers (transcript available in Wilson and Davis, *Herndon's*, 646); Warren, "Log."
188. Dennis Hanks interview with William H. Herndon, June 13, 1865, H-W Papers (transcript available in Wilson and Davis, *Herndon's*, 38); Warren, *Lincoln's Parentage*, 240–41, 245; Warren, *Slavery*, unpaginated.
189. Barton, *Life*, 1:104–105; John Hanks interview with William H. Herndon, H-W Papers (transcript available in Wilson and Davis, *Herndon's*, 454); Warren, "William."
190. N. W. Miner, "Personal Recollections of Abraham Lincoln," p. 16 (1882 version), N. W. Miner Small Collection 1052. Miner was a Baptist preacher and neighbor of Abraham Lincoln in the late 1850s.
191. Scripps, *Life*, 11. A Springfield neighbor gives a similar report of Nancy reading to the family, but not of the children reading (N. W. Miner, "Personal Recollections of Abraham Lincoln," p. 16 (1882 version), N. W. Miner Small Collection 1052).
192. A Springfield neighbor of Lincoln said that Nancy read the Bible to Tom (N. W. Miner, "Personal Recollections of Abraham Lincoln," p. 16 (1882 version), N. W. Miner Small Collection 1052).
193. Wolf, *Almost*, 35–36.
194. N. W. Miner, "Personal Recollections of Abraham Lincoln," p. 16 (1882 version), N. W. Miner Small Collection 1052.
195. Holland, *Life*, 436.
196. Reynolds, *My Own Times*, 102.
197. Onstot, *Pioneers*, 106.
198. John B. Helm to William H. Herndon, Aug. 1, 1865, H-W Papers (transcript available in Wilson and Davis, *Herndon's*, 83). Helm was told that the couple was unmarried but engaged and the woman's name was Hanks. Weik incorrectly dated the occasion as 1806 and asked whether

Abraham's parents were the unmarried couple (Herndon and Weik, *Herndon's Life of Lincoln*, 14–16). Tom and Nancy had been married for about ten years when the camp meeting occurred. Herndon has been harshly criticized for this inaccuracy, but Weik wrote the book based on Herndon's information, and the Helm account furnished by Herndon clearly dated the camp meeting as ca. 1816. Weik also made deletions from the account without indicating those deletions with ellipses, made additions of his own, and changed the sequence of some words.

199. Beveridge, *Abraham*, 1:26.
200. Barton, *Life*, 1:92, 99–100; Beveridge, *Abraham*, 1:34–35; Warren, *Lincoln's Parentage*, 120–22, 167, 190, 329, 330 n. 24, 335.
201. Current, *Speaking*, 162; Warren, *Lincoln's Parentage*, 288–90, 356 n. 18; Warren, "Lincolns' Removal"; Warren, *Slavery*, unpaginated.
202. Barton, *Paternity*, 183.
203. Warren, "Environs," 129; Warren, *Slavery*, unpaginated.
204. Beveridge, *Abraham*, 1:28 n. 5; Warren, "Environs," 129; Warren, *Lincoln's Parentage*, caption on illustration opposite 288; Warren, *Slavery*, unpaginated.
205. Warren, *Slavery*, unpaginated.
206. Warren, "Lincolns' Removal"; Warren, *Slavery*, unpaginated.
207. Warren, *Slavery*, unpaginated.
208. Donald, *Lincoln*, 22. According to family tradition, Tom had "quite a little stock of hogs, horses, and cattle" at Knob Creek (A. H. Chapman statement, ca. Sept. 8, 1865, H-W Papers (transcript available in Wilson and Davis, *Herndon's*, 97)).
209. Barton, *Paternity*, 262; Beveridge, *Abraham*, 1:35–36; Judge Otis M. Mather statement, June 14, 1924, in *Lincoln Herald*, 48 (Feb. 1946): 18; Warren, *Lincoln's Parentage*, 119, 186–87.
210. Abraham Lincoln, autobiography for John L. Scripps, ca. June 1860 (transcript available in *CW* 4:61–62). *See also* Dennis Hanks interview with William H. Herndon, June 13, 1865, H-W Papers (transcript available in Wilson and Davis, *Herndon's*, 36); J. Edward Murr in Ehrmann, *Missing*, 84. Tom Lincoln wasn't alone in such feelings. Daniel Drake's relatives were enthusiastic about Kentucky land but decided not to move there. Factors against the move included "existence of slavery in Kentucky" and "uncertainty of land titles" (Drake, *Pioneer*, 209). Later, a family named Thompson moved to Illinois because the father could no longer stand living in the slave culture of Kentucky (Duis, *Good*, 137). In 1835, Jim Miller left Kentucky for the same reason and settled in Illinois (Duis, *Good*, 309), where in 1856 he would become the first Republican elected as state treasurer.
211. McConnel, *Western*, 108–9, 111.
212. Beveridge, *Abraham*, 1:34; Tarbell, *Early*, 53; Warren, *Lincoln's Youth*, 44.
213. Warren, "Environs," 131–32; Warren, "Factors"; Warren, *Lincoln's Parentage*, 291; Warren, *Lincoln's Youth*, 44.

Chapter 2. INDIANA

1. A. H. Chapman statement, ca. Sept. 8, 1865, H-W Papers (transcript available in Wilson and Davis, *Herndon's*, 97); Charles Friend to William H. Herndon, March 19, 1866, H-W Papers (transcript available in Wilson and Davis, *Herndon's*, 234); Dennis Hanks interview with William H. Herndon, June 13, 1865, H-W Papers (transcript available in Wilson and Davis, *Herndon's*, 38); Dennis Hanks to William H. Herndon, March 7, 1866, H-W Papers (transcript available in Wilson and Davis, *Herndon's*, 226); Dennis Hanks to William H. Herndon, March 19, 1866, H-W Papers (transcript available in Wilson and Davis, *Herndon's*, 233).

Controversy exists about whether the cargo included barrels of whiskey. Denny Hanks said yes, that Tom had bartered the Knob Creek place for $300 worth of whiskey (Dennis Hanks interview with William H. Herndon, June 13, 1865, H-W Papers (transcript available in Wilson and Davis, *Herndon's*, 38); Dennis Hanks, quoted in Atkinson, *Boyhood*, 14–15, which mentions four hundred gallons of whiskey). Other family tradition said Tom traded Knob Creek for four hundred gallons (A. H. Chapman statement, ca. Sept. 8, 1865, H-W Papers (transcript available in Wilson and Davis, *Herndon's*, 97). *See also* Arthur Ernest Morgan, "New Light on Lincoln's Early Years," in Wilson, *Lincoln*, 48. Fine students of Lincoln's life said Tom was carrying four hundred gallons (Barton, *Life*, 1:112; Nicolay and Hay, *Abraham*, 1:28). Another fine student believed that if the cargo included whiskey, it was distilled from Tom's own corn crop (Warren, *Lincoln's Parentage*, 168–69). This same student also stated that Tom did not barter the Knob Creek place for whiskey and concluded that no bulky barrels had to be moved, so no water voyage was necessary (Warren, *Lincoln's Parentage*, 291). Regardless of the barrel situation, I believe a water voyage would have been sensible, particularly for one person trying to move a large load. Floating a cargo was much easier than lugging it overland on roads whose existence was more apparent on the map than on the ground.

2. Howells, *Recollections*, 84–85.

3. Barton, *Life*, 1:112; Brooks, *Abraham*, 9–10; A. H. Chapman statement, ca. Sept. 8, 1865, H-W Papers (transcript available in Wilson and Davis, *Herndon's*, 97); Dennis Hanks interview with William H. Herndon, June 13, 1865, H-W Papers (transcript available in Wilson and Davis, *Herndon's*, 38); Nicolay and Hay, *Abraham*, 1:28; Tarbell, *In the Footsteps*, 112, 114.

4. Barton, *Life*, 1:112; Brooks, *Abraham*, 9–10; A. H. Chapman statement, ca. Sept. 8, 1865, H-W Papers (transcript available in Wilson and Davis, *Herndon's*, 98); Dennis Hanks interview with William H. Herndon, June 13, 1865, H-W Papers (transcript available in Wilson and Davis, *Herndon's*, 38); Nicolay and Hay, *Abraham*, 1:28; Murr, "Lincoln," 319.

5. Nicolay and Hay, *Abraham*, 1:28–29.

6. Quoted in Browne, *Abraham*, 1:83.

7. Barton, *Women*, 88; Barton, *Life*, 1:105; A. H. Chapman statement, ca. Sept. 8, 1865, H-W Papers (transcript available in Wilson and Davis, *Herndon's*, 97); John Duncan to William H. Herndon, Feb. 21, 1867, H-W Papers (transcript available in Wilson and Davis, *Herndon's*, 558); Dennis Hanks interview with Erastus Wright, June 8, 1865, H-W Papers (transcript available in Wilson and Davis, *Herndon's*, 27); Holland, *Life*, 26; Abraham Lincoln, autobiography for John L. Scripps, ca. June 1860 (transcript available in *CW* 4:61); McMurtry, "Re-Discovering," 12–13, 15, 17; Tarbell, *Life*, 1:30; Warren, "Environs," 122; Warren, *Lincoln's Parentage*, 81, 247; Warren, *Lincoln's Youth*, 18; Erastus Wright to Josiah G. Holland (enclosure), July 3, 1865 (transcript available in Guelzo, "Holland's," 33–34).

8. Barton, *Life*, 1:75; Tim G. Needham to William H. Herndon, June 26, 1865, H-W Papers (transcript available in Wilson and Davis, *Herndon's*, 60); Tarbell, *In the Footsteps*, 111–12.

9. Brooks, *Abraham*, 9; Dennis Hanks interview with William H. Herndon, June 13, 1865, H-W Papers (transcript available in Wilson and Davis, *Herndon's*, 38).

10. Nicolay and Hay, *Abraham*, 1:18.

11. Francis X. Rapier in Barton, *Life*, 1:78–79.

12. Hobson, *Footprints*, 15.

13. Dennis Hanks, quoted in Atkinson, *Boyhood*, 14. *See also* Dennis Hanks interview with William H. Herndon, June 13, 1865, H-W Papers (transcript available in Wilson and Davis, *Herndon's*, 39); Dennis Hanks to William H. Herndon, March 19, 1866, H-W Papers (transcript available in Wilson and Davis, *Herndon's*, 233).

14. A. H. Chapman statement, ca. Sept. 8, 1865, H-W Papers (transcript available in Wilson and Davis, *Herndon's*, 98).

15. Dennis Hanks interview with William H. Herndon, June 13, 1865, H-W Papers (transcript available in Wilson and Davis, *Herndon's*, 39).

16. A. H. Chapman statement, ca. Sept. 8, 1865, H-W Papers (transcript available in Wilson and Davis, *Herndon's*, 98); Beveridge, *Abraham*, 1:41; Warren, *Lincoln's Parentage*, 290.

17. Dennis Hanks interview with William H. Herndon, Sept. 8, 1865, H-W Papers (transcript available in Wilson and Davis, *Herndon's*, 104). Beveridge, *Abraham*, 1:41, reverses the seating order, but the point is not worth contention.

18. Barton, *Life*, 1:113; Briggs and Briggs, *Nancy*, 107; Warren, *Lincoln's Parentage*, 292, 294.

19. Beveridge, *Abraham*, 1:89–90, 90 n. 1.

20. Abraham Lincoln, speech at Lafayette, Indiana, Feb. 11, 1861 (transcript available in *CW* 4:192).

21. A. H. Chapman statement, ca. Sept. 8, 1865, H-W Papers (transcript available in Wilson and Davis, *Herndon's*, 98); Dennis Hanks to William H. Herndon, March 7, 1866, H-W Papers (transcript available in Wilson and Davis, *Herndon's*, 226); Nicolay and Hay, *Abraham*, 1:29.

22. Barton, *Life*, 1:112; Nathaniel Grigsby to William H. Herndon, Sept. 4, 1865, H-W Papers (transcript available in Wilson and Davis, *Herndon's*, 93); Nathaniel Grigsby interview with William H. Herndon, Sept. 12, 1865, H-W Papers (transcript available in Wilson and Davis, *Herndon's*, 111); Dennis Hanks to William H. Herndon, March 7, 1866, H-W Papers (transcript available in Wilson and Davis, *Herndon's*, 226); Murr, "Lincoln," 319; J. Edward Murr in Ehrmann, *Missing*, 85. Purportedly Carter had encouraged Tom's move to the vicinity, but as noted in the previous chapter, Tom's brother, Josiah, and their relative Austin Lincoln also may deserve credit.

23. *SJ*, March 1, 1834.

24. Browne, *Every-Day*, 45.

25. A. H. Chapman statement, ca. Sept. 8, 1865, H-W Papers (transcript available in Wilson and Davis, *Herndon's*, 98); Nicolay and Hay, *Abraham*, 1:29.

26. Fordham, *Personal*, 182.

27. Oliver, *Eight*, 154.

28. Dennis Hanks, quoted in Atkinson, *Boyhood*, 15. In Hanks's interview with Erastus Wright, June 8, 1865, H-W Papers (transcript available in Wilson and Davis, *Herndon's*, 28), and in Dennis Hanks to William H. Herndon, ca. Dec. 1865, H-W Papers (transcript available in Wilson and Davis, *Herndon's*, 149), Hanks mentions the half-faced camp but does not indicate how long the Lincolns lived in it.

29. A. H. Chapman statement, ca. Sept. 8, 1865, H-W Papers (transcript available in Wilson and Davis, *Herndon's*, 98); Arthur Ernest Morgan, "New Light on Lincoln's Early Years," in Wilson, *Lincoln*, 50.

30. Mrs. James Parkinson and Mrs. Sarah King in *History of Sangamon*, 187.

31. Power, *History*, 695.

32. Ewbank, "Building," 113–15.

33. Miller, *History*, 196.

34. Cockrum, *Pioneer*, 161.

35. Faragher, *Sugar*, 58, 88.

36. Faragher, *Sugar*, 136; Oliver, *Eight*, 236–37; Parrish, "Pioneer," 427.

37. Abraham Lincoln, autobiography for John L. Scripps, ca. June 1860 (transcript available in *CW* 4:62). *See also* Nathaniel Grigsby to William H. Herndon, Sept. 4, 1865, H-W Papers (transcript available in Wilson and Davis, *Herndon's*, 93).

38. Johnson, "Home," 149.

39. Warren, *Lincoln's Youth*, 21.

40. Parrish, "Pioneer," 427.

41. Dennis Hanks interview with William H. Herndon, June 13, 1865, H-W Papers (transcript available in Wilson and Davis, *Herndon's*, 39–40).

42. Coleman, "Half-Faced," 140; Warren, "Half-Faced Camp."

43. Abraham Lincoln, autobiography for John L. Scripps, ca. June 1860 (transcript available in *CW* 4:62).

44. Indeed, Lincoln's words demonstrate Denny Hanks's confusion. Seemingly on at least three occasions, Hanks said Lincoln killed the turkey while the family resided in the half-faced camp: Dennis Hanks interview with William H. Herndon, June 13, 1865, H-W Papers (transcript available in Wilson and Davis, *Herndon's*, 39); Dennis Hanks to William H. Herndon, March 7, 1866, H-W Papers (transcript available in Wilson and Davis, *Herndon's*, 226); Dennis Hanks to William H. Herndon, March 12, 1866, H-W Papers (transcript available in Wilson and Davis, *Herndon's*, 229). But Lincoln said they were living in their cabin at the time. Given the

content of these statements, all seem to speak of the same incident. Denny also said that the turkey kill occurred in autumn 1817 on the day that *he arrived* with Thomas and Betsy Sparrow to reside near the Lincolns, not the day *the Lincolns arrived* in 1816 (quoted in Browne, *Every-Day*, 51). So Denny was confused about the half-faced camp.

45. Quoted by Leonard Swett in Rice, *Reminiscences*, 457.
46. Dennis Hanks interview with William H. Herndon, June 13, 1865, H-W Papers (transcript available in Wilson and Davis, *Herndon's*, 38). Concurrence can be found in Barton, *Life*, 1:113; Warren, *Lincoln's Youth*, 41; Winkle, *Young*, 12–13.
47. Dennis Hanks interview with William H. Herndon, June 13, 1865, H-W Papers (transcript available in Wilson and Davis, *Herndon's*, 38); A. H. Chapman statement, ca. Sept. 8, 1865, H-W Papers (transcript available in Wilson and Davis, *Herndon's*, 98). *See also* Warren, *Lincoln's Youth*, 42.
48. Beveridge, *Abraham*, 1:47, 70, 95; Briggs and Briggs, *Nancy*, 107; James Long statement, ca. 1865, H-W Papers (transcript available in Wilson and Davis, *Herndon's*, 469); Tarbell, *Early*, 47 caption; Warren, *Lincoln's Youth*, 158–59; J. W. Wartmann to William H. Herndon, July 21, 1865, H-W Papers (transcript available in Wilson and Davis, *Herndon's*, 79); Joseph S. Wilson to James Harlan, June 27, 1865, H-W Papers (transcript available in Wilson and Davis, *Herndon's*, 62); Wilson and Davis, *Herndon's*, 38 n. 12.
49. Donald, *Lincoln*, 26.
50. Beveridge, *Abraham*, 1:44–45.
51. J. Edward Murr in Ehrmann, *Missing*, 91.
52. Dennis Hanks interview with William H. Herndon, June 13, 1865, H-W Papers (transcript available in Wilson and Davis, *Herndon's*, 39). Here Denny said they cleared six acres. Elsewhere, he said they used about twenty acres for farming (Dennis Hanks to William H. Herndon, Jan. 26, 1866, H-W Papers (transcript available in Wilson and Davis, *Herndon's*, 176)), but seemingly that refers to a few years later.
53. J. W. Wartmann to William H. Herndon, Nov. 1, 1866, H-W Papers (transcript available in Wilson and Davis, *Herndon's*, 392).
54. Oliver, *Eight*, 144.
55. Dennis Hanks, quoted in Atkinson, *Boyhood*, 14. *See also* Dennis Hanks interview with William H. Herndon, June 13, 1865, H-W Papers (transcript available in Wilson and Davis, *Herndon's*, 39); Dennis Hanks to William H. Herndon, March 12, 1866, H-W Papers (transcript available in Wilson and Davis, *Herndon's*, 229); Abraham Lincoln, autobiography for John L. Scripps, ca. June 1860 (transcript available in *CW* 4:62). Denny said the kill was the first or second day after the family arrived, but Lincoln dated it as February 1817.
56. Arthur Ernest Morgan, "New Light on Lincoln's Early Years," in Wilson, *Lincoln*, 52.
57. Hobson, *Footprints*, 29.
58. David Turnham to William H. Herndon, Feb. 21, 1866, H-W Papers (transcript available in Wilson and Davis, *Herndon's*, 217).
59. Nathaniel Grigsby interview with William H. Herndon, Sept. 12, 1865, H-W Papers (transcript available in Wilson and Davis, *Herndon's*, 113); David Turnham interview with William H. Herndon, Sept. 15, 1865, H-W Papers (transcript available in Wilson and Davis, *Herndon's*, 121). In New Salem days, he was still called not much of a hunter (Caleb Carman interview with William H. Herndon, Oct. 12, 1866, H-W Papers (transcript available in Wilson and Davis, *Herndon's*, 374)).
60. Oliver, *Eight*, 137–38.
61. J. Rowan Herndon to William H. Herndon, June 21, 1865, H-W Papers (transcript available in Wilson and Davis, *Herndon's*, 51). *See also* Herndon and Weik, *Herndon's Life of Lincoln*, 23, which may include invention from Weik. A fice dog was a small, feisty mutt.
62. Abraham Lincoln, "The Bear Hunt," 1846 (transcript available in *CW* 1:386). I have cast Lincoln's words in prose form, but he wrote them as verse.
63. Cockrum, *Pioneer*, 432.

64. Abraham Lincoln, "The Bear Hunt," 1846 (transcript available in *CW* 1:386–88). I have cast Lincoln's words in prose form, but he wrote them as verse.

65. Duis, *Good*, 172.

66. Fordham, *Personal*, 96.

67. Harris, *Journal*, 359.

68. Dennis Hanks to William H. Herndon, Jan. 6, 1866, H-W Papers (transcript available in Wilson and Davis, *Herndon's*, 154); Dennis Hanks to William H. Herndon, March 22, 1866, H-W Papers (transcript available in Wilson and Davis, *Herndon's*, 235); Dennis Hanks to William H. Herndon, May 4, 1866, H-W Papers (transcript available in Wilson and Davis, *Herndon's*, 252).

69. Elizabeth Crawford to William H. Herndon, May 3, 1866, H-W Papers (transcript available in Wilson and Davis, *Herndon's*, 248–49).

70. Elizabeth Crawford to William H. Herndon, July 22, 1866, H-W Papers (transcript available in Wilson and Davis, *Herndon's*, 261); Elizabeth Crawford to William H. Herndon, Sept. 7, 1866, H-W Papers (transcript available in Wilson and Davis, *Herndon's*, 335). *See also* J. W. Wartmann to William H. Herndon, June 19, 1866, H-W Papers (transcript available in Wilson and Davis, *Herndon's*, 260–61).

71. David Turnham to William H. Herndon, Feb. 21, 1866, H-W Papers (transcript available in Wilson and Davis, *Herndon's*, 217).

72. Fordham, *Personal*, 153–54.

73. Johnson, "Home," 147–48.

74. *Vincennes Western Sun*, Dec. 23, 1809.

75. Dennis Hanks to William H. Herndon, Jan. 6, 1866, H-W Papers (transcript available in Wilson and Davis, *Herndon's*, 154); Tarbell, *Early*, 57; A. H. Chapman statement, ca. Sept. 8, 1865, H-W Papers (transcript available in Wilson and Davis, *Herndon's*, 98); Tarbell, *Life*, 1:23.

76. Faux, *Memorable*, 236–37.

77. Briggs and Briggs, *Nancy*, 123–24; Warren, "The Lincolns and Audubon."

78. Dennis Hanks, quoted in Atkinson, *Boyhood*, 15.

79. Beveridge, *Abraham*, 1:40–41; Murr, "Lincoln," 319.

80. Matilda Johnston Hall Moore interview with William H. Herndon, Sept. 8, 1865, H-W Papers (transcript available in Wilson and Davis, *Herndon's*, 109).

81. Beveridge, *Abraham*, 1:41; A. H. Chapman statement, ca. Sept. 8, 1865, H-W Papers (transcript available in Wilson and Davis, *Herndon's*, 98); Dennis Hanks interview with William H. Herndon, June 13, 1865, H-W Papers (transcript available in Wilson and Davis, *Herndon's*, 39). *See also* Johnson, *Illinois*, 23.

82. Dennis Hanks interview with William H. Herndon, June 13, 1865, H-W Papers (transcript available in Wilson and Davis, *Herndon's*, 39). *See also* Beveridge, *Abraham*, 1:40; Briggs and Briggs, *Nancy*, 115.

83. Abraham Lincoln to Mrs. Orville H. Browning, April 1, 1838 (transcript available in *CW* 1:118). Judging from Lincoln's autobiography for John L. Scripps, which refers to Nancy Hanks Lincoln as "mother" (transcript available in *CW* 4:61) and Sarah Bush Johnston Lincoln as "stepmother" (transcript available in *CW* 4:63), the 1838 description refers to Nancy. A knowledgeable authority (Donald, *Lincoln*, 610 n. for p. 68) argues that Lincoln's memory of his mother's appearance would have been insufficient to allow him to give such details, so the description must have been of his stepmother. When I recall my mother's appearance in my childhood, however, I am clearly able to remember whether she looked weatherbeaten with missing teeth. Admittedly, Lincoln is quoted in conversation as referring to his stepmother as "mother" (Whitney, *Life*, 47), "mammy" (Atkinson, *Boyhood*, 55; Randall, *Mary*, 133), and "mama" (Augustus H. Chapman to William H. Herndon, Oct. 8, 1865, H-W Papers (transcript available in Wilson and Davis, *Herndon's*, 137)). Acknowledging lack of certainty, I believe the 1838 description referred to Nancy.

84. McCulloch, *Men*, 81.

85. Fordham, *Personal*, 201, 231.

86. Cockrum, *Pioneer*, 401.
87. William Taylor to Mr. Tucker, Aug. 19, 1833, in *SJ*, June 25, 1841.
88. *SJ*, May 19, 1838.
89. Levering, *Historic*, 91.
90. A. H. Chapman statement, ca. Sept. 8, 1865, H-W Papers (transcript available in Wilson and Davis, *Herndon's*, 98); Dennis Hanks interview with William H. Herndon, June 13, 1865, H-W Papers (transcript available in Wilson and Davis, *Herndon's*, 40).
91. Jordan, "Death," 110.
92. Beveridge, *Abraham*, 1:47–48; A. H. Chapman statement, ca. Sept. 8, 1865, H-W Papers (transcript available in Wilson and Davis, *Herndon's*, 98).
93. Beveridge, *Abraham*, 1:47–48; Hobson, *Footprints*, 17–19; Tarbell, *Early*, 75 caption.
94. William Wood interview with William H. Herndon, Sept. 15, 1865, H-W Papers (transcript available in Wilson and Davis, *Herndon's*, 123–24).
95. William H. Herndon to Ward Hill Lamon, March 6, 1870 (transcript available in Hertz, *Hidden*, 74).
96. Morris Birkbeck, quoted in Angle, *Prairie*, 65–66.
97. Dennis Hanks interview with William H. Herndon, June 13, 1865, H-W Papers (transcript available in Wilson and Davis, *Herndon's*, 40).
98. Dennis Hanks, quoted in Atkinson, *Boyhood*, 16–17.
99. Dennis Hanks, quoted in Atkinson, *Boyhood*, 8.
100. Hobson, *Footprints*, 17–18.
101. Abraham Lincoln to Fanny McCullough, Dec. 23, 1862 (transcript available in *CW* 6:16–17).
102. Dennis Hanks interview with William H. Herndon, June 13, 1865, H-W Papers (transcript available in Wilson and Davis, *Herndon's*, 40). *See also* A. H. Chapman statement, ca. Sept. 8, 1865, H-W Papers (transcript available in Wilson and Davis, *Herndon's*, 97); Dennis Hanks to William H. Herndon, Jan. 6, 1866, H-W Papers (transcript available in Wilson and Davis, *Herndon's*, 154); William H. Herndon to Ward Hill Lamon, March 6, 1870 (transcript available in Hertz, *Hidden*, 74); Warren, *Lincoln's Parentage*, 246–47; Warren, *Lincoln's Youth*, 55–56; Warren, "Reverend."
103. Beveridge, *Abraham*, 1:49.
104. Oliver, *Eight*, 133.
105. Dennis Hanks, quoted in Atkinson, *Boyhood*, 19.
106. Beveridge, *Abraham*, 1:49; Dennis Hanks interview with William H. Herndon, June 13, 1865, H-W Papers (transcript available in Wilson and Davis, *Herndon's*, 40).
107. Dennis Hanks interview with William H. Herndon, June 13, 1865, H-W Papers (transcript available in Wilson and Davis, *Herndon's*, 40).
108. Nathaniel Grigsby, Silas Richardson, Nancy Richardson, and John Romine interview with William H. Herndon, Sept. 14, 1865, H-W Papers (transcript available in Wilson and Davis, *Herndon's*, 116). *See also* David Turnham interview with William H. Herndon, Sept. 15, 1865, H-W Papers (transcript available in Wilson and Davis, *Herndon's*, 122).
109. Dennis Hanks interview with William H. Herndon, June 13, 1865, H-W Papers (transcript available in Wilson and Davis, *Herndon's*, 40). Lincoln's stepmother recalled the same peg-climbing arrangement (Sarah Bush Johnston Lincoln interview with William H. Herndon, Sept. 8, 1865, H-W Papers (transcript available in Wilson and Davis, *Herndon's*, 106)).
110. Beveridge, *Abraham*, 1:57.
111. Fordham, *Personal*, 216.
112. Faux, *Memorable*, 213.
113. Dennis Hanks, quoted in Atkinson, *Boyhood*, 19–20. According to one account (Barton, *Women*, 98), during this sojourn, Denny's two half-brothers, Squire and William Hall, were visiting at the Indiana homestead, helping make up in numbers whatever the cabin residents lacked in maturity while Tom was away.

114. Presley Nevil Haycraft to John Helm, July 19, 1865, H-W Papers (transcript available in Wilson and Davis, *Herndon's*, 87); John Helm to William H. Herndon, Aug. 1, 1865, H-W Papers (transcript available in Wilson and Davis, *Herndon's*, 82); Arthur Ernest Morgan, "New Light on Lincoln's Early Years," in Wilson, *Lincoln*, 49; Warren, "Widower."

115. Dennis Hanks interview with William H. Herndon, June 13, 1865, H-W Papers (transcript available in Wilson and Davis, *Herndon's*, 41).

116. Harriet A. Chapman to William H. Herndon, Dec. 17, 1865, H-W Papers (transcript available in Wilson and Davis, *Herndon's*, 145); Sarah Bush Johnston Lincoln interview with William H. Herndon, Sept. 8, 1865, H-W Papers (transcript available in Wilson and Davis, *Herndon's*, 109).

117. A. H. Chapman statement, ca. Sept. 8, 1865, H-W Papers (transcript available in Wilson and Davis, *Herndon's*, 99).

118. Samuel Haycraft to William H. Herndon, June 1865, H-W Papers (transcript available in Wilson and Davis, *Herndon's*, 68).

119. A. H. Chapman statement, ca. Sept. 8, 1865, H-W Papers (transcript available in Wilson and Davis, *Herndon's*, 99); Coleman, "Sarah," 13; Presley Nevil Haycraft to John Helm, July 19, 1865, H-W Papers (transcript available in Wilson and Davis, *Herndon's*, 87); John B. Helm to William H. Herndon, Aug. 1, 1865, H-W Papers (transcript available in Wilson and Davis, *Herndon's*, 82); Warren, "Lincoln's Hoosier," 107; Warren, *Lincoln's Parentage*, 150; Warren, *Lincoln's Youth*, 61–63, 190; Warren, "Sarah," 82–83; Warren, "Widower."

120. Arthur Ernest Morgan, "New Light on Lincoln's Early Years," in Wilson, *Lincoln*, 49–50; Warren, "Sarah," 84. *See also* Samuel Haycraft to John Helm, July 5, 1865, H-W Papers (transcript available in Wilson and Davis, *Herndon's*, 85); Samuel Haycraft to William H. Herndon, Dec. 7, 1866, H-W Papers (transcript available in Wilson and Davis, *Herndon's*, 503); Warren, *Lincoln's Youth*, 63–64; Warren, "Widower."

121. A. H. Chapman statement, ca. Sept. 8, 1865, H-W Papers (transcript available in Wilson and Davis, *Herndon's*, 98).

122. Samuel Haycraft to John Helm, July 5, 1865, H-W Papers (transcript available in Wilson and Davis, *Herndon's*, 85); Samuel Haycraft to William H. Herndon, Dec. 7, 1866, H-W Papers (transcript available in Wilson and Davis, *Herndon's*, 503); Arthur Ernest Morgan, "New Light on Lincoln's Early Years," in Wilson, *Lincoln*, 50; Tarbell, *Early*, 52; Tarbell, *In the Footsteps*, 129; Warren, "Sarah," 84; Warren, "Widower."

123. A. H. Chapman statement, ca. Sept. 8, 1865, H-W Papers (transcript available in Wilson and Davis, *Herndon's*, 99).

124. A. H. Chapman statement, ca. Sept. 8, 1865, H-W Papers (transcript available in Wilson and Davis, *Herndon's*, 99); Sarah Bush Johnston Lincoln interview with William H. Herndon, Sept. 8, 1865, H-W Papers (transcript available in Wilson and Davis, *Herndon's*, 106).

125. Dennis Hanks, quoted in Atkinson, *Boyhood*, 20.

126. Beveridge, *Abraham*, 1:61 n. 4; Matilda Johnston Hall Moore interview with William H. Herndon, Sept. 8, 1865, H-W Papers (transcript available in Wilson and Davis, *Herndon's*, 109).

127. Dennis Hanks, quoted in Atkinson, *Boyhood*, 22.

128. Dennis Hanks interview with William H. Herndon, June 13, 1865, H-W Papers (transcript available in Wilson and Davis, *Herndon's*, 41).

129. Dennis Hanks, quoted in Atkinson, *Boyhood*, 22–23.

130. Dennis Hanks, quoted in Atkinson, *Boyhood*, 21. *See also* A. H. Chapman statement, ca. Sept. 8, 1865, H-W Papers (transcript available in Wilson and Davis, *Herndon's*, 99). Whip sawing was a loathsome two-person job. One stood in a pit under the log, with sawdust showering on him, while pulling the blade up and down in rhythm with the sawyer standing on ground level (Cockrum, *Pioneer*, 331). One can easily understand why Tom Lincoln had been willing to forgo a plank floor for so long.

131. Elizabeth Crawford to William H. Herndon, July 22, 1866, H-W Papers (transcript available in Wilson and Davis, *Herndon's*, 262).

132. Beveridge, *Abraham*, 1:61; Dennis Hanks interview with William H. Herndon, Sept. 8, 1865, H-W Papers (transcript available in Wilson and Davis, *Herndon's*, 105).

133. Barton, *Life*, 1:118. *See also* Arthur Ernest Morgan, "New Light on Lincoln's Early Years," in Wilson, *Lincoln*, 50.

134. A. H. Chapman statement, ca. Sept. 8, 1865, H-W Papers (transcript available in Wilson and Davis, *Herndon's*, 99).

135. Sarah Bush Johnston Lincoln interview with William H. Herndon, Sept. 8, 1865, H-W Papers (transcript available in Wilson and Davis, *Herndon's*, 106).

136. Coffin, *Reminiscences*, 85.

137. Quoted in Carpenter, *Six*, 129–30 (apparently citing Henry Raymond's *A History of the Administration of President Lincoln*). In Carpenter, the incident is ascribed to Lincoln's Kentucky years, but the presence of a "brother" indicates the Indiana years.

138. Joseph C. Richardson interview with William H. Herndon, ca. Sept. 14, 1865, H-W Papers (transcript available in Wilson and Davis, *Herndon's*, 119). The lads were fortunate to have encountered a genial owner. Outcomes were not always benign: "Two men were shot on the 15th ult. in Scott County, Iowa, while robbing a watermelon patch. Two of them immediately expired" (*Galena North Western Gazette & Galena Advertiser*, Sept. 18, 1841).

139. Abraham Lincoln, quoted in Stevens, *Reporter's*, 68.

140. Wesley Hall in Murr, "Lincoln," 323–25. Beveridge cites this article often. He notes caution on details of Hall's snowstorm story but has "no reasonable doubt that something of the sort happened" (Beveridge, *Abraham*, 1:78 n. 3). Allowing for lapses and distortions of memory, I am inclined to accept the snowstorm story as generally correct and indeed cannot point to any obvious error. My main hesitation is that Hall's story makes the cabin's population smaller than is commonly believed, but depending on the year and who was hired out elsewhere, a base population of three is plausible.

141. William H. Herndon to Isaac N. Arnold, Oct. 24, 1883, printed in *Letter from*, unpaginated.

142. Daniel Burner in Temple, "Lincoln and the Burners," 69.

143. Dennis Hanks to William H. Herndon, April 2, 1866, H-W Papers (transcript available in Wilson and Davis, *Herndon's*, 242).

144. Elizabeth Crawford to William H. Herndon, May 3, 1866, H-W Papers (transcript available in Wilson and Davis, *Herndon's*, 249); Dennis Hanks interview with William H. Herndon, June 13, 1865, H-W Papers (transcript available in Wilson and Davis, *Herndon's*, 42); Dennis Hanks interview with William H. Herndon, Sept. 8, 1865, H-W Papers (transcript available in Wilson and Davis, *Herndon's*, 105).

145. Dennis Hanks to William H. Herndon, Dec. 24, 1865, H-W Papers (transcript available in Wilson and Davis, *Herndon's*, 146). I've altered the last line of Hanks's excerpt in order to use the meter that Lincoln surely used. Here Lincoln expressed a theme then common in public discourse, for example: "*Hard times!—Hard times!*—is reiterated from every quarter. Money scarce—Provisions dear—and a prospect of light crops" *Vincennes Western Sun*, Sept. 21, 1816.

146. Dennis Hanks to William H. Herndon, Dec. 27, 1865, H-W Papers (transcript available in Wilson and Davis, *Herndon's*, 147).

147. Dennis Hanks to William H. Herndon, Dec. 24, 1865, H-W Papers (transcript available in Wilson and Davis, *Herndon's*, 146). For lyrics see Lair, *Songs*, 19.

148. David Turnham to William H. Herndon, Dec. 30, 1865, H-W Papers (transcript available in Wilson and Davis, *Herndon's*, 148). For lyrics see Lair, *Songs*, 9. The Roman Catholic hierarchy had no monopoly on such ruthlessness; an Indiana newspaper offered this item in 1816: "On Sunday the 25th of May last, as the priest of the parish of Drumrudy, in the county of Cavan, was celebrating mass in the church, a number of Orangemen with arms, rushed into the church and fired upon the congregation. . . . Killed all numbers of the congregation . . . men, women and children. The remainder of them that was not killed made their address to the magistrates for justice; but their reply was to 'go off for a damned set of papist rascals; it was the Orangemen's duty if they murdered every man of you'" (Letter, clipped in *Vincennes Western Sun*, Oct. 19, 1816).

149. Elizabeth Crawford to William H. Herndon, Feb. 21, 1866, H-W Papers (transcript available in Wilson and Davis, *Herndon's*, 215). For lyrics see Lair, *Songs*, 5.

150. Dennis Hanks to William H. Herndon, Dec. 24, 1865, H-W Papers (transcript available in Wilson and Davis, *Herndon's*, 146). "The Morning Trumpet," composer B. F. White, words by John Leland. "Bound for Canaan" version lyrics in Lair, *Songs*, 8. "How Tedious and Tasteless," words by John Newton. "Greenfields" version lyrics in Lair, *Songs*, 7.

151. *CW* 1:xxxiii (photo from Oliver R. Barrett Collection, transcript available on p. 1); Isaac Watts, "The shortness of life, and the goodness of God," Hymn II:58; Wilson, *Lincoln before Washington*, 140. Accessibility of Watts's hymns is mentioned by Matilda Johnston Moore interview with William H. Herndon, Sept. 8, 1865, H-W Papers (transcript available in Wilson and Davis, *Herndon's*, 109); David Turnham interview with William H. Herndon, Sept. 15, 1865, H-W Papers (transcript available in Wilson and Davis, *Herndon's*, 121); David Turnham to William H. Herndon, Dec. 30, 1865, H-W Papers (transcript available in Wilson and Davis, *Herndon's*, 148).

152. Nathaniel Grigsby interview with William H. Herndon, Sept. 12, 1865, H-W Papers (transcript available in Wilson and Davis, *Herndon's*, 112).

153. Bestor, Mearns, and Daniels, *Three*, 73; Abraham Lincoln, "Temperance Address," Feb. 22, 1842 (transcript available in *CW* 1:276); Isaac Watts, "Life the day of grace and hope," Hymn I:88.

154. Isaac Watts, "Our frail bodies, and God our preserver," Hymn II:19; H.C. Whitney to William H. Herndon, June 23, 1887, H-W Papers (transcript available in Wilson and Davis, *Herndon's*, 617).

155. Dennis Hanks, quoted in Atkinson, *Boyhood*, 35–36.

156. Dennis Hanks interview with William H. Herndon, June 13, 1865, H-W Papers (transcript available in Wilson and Davis, *Herndon's*, 42).

157. Nathaniel Grigsby interview with William H. Herndon, Sept. 12, 1865, H-W Papers (transcript available in Wilson and Davis, *Herndon's*, 114).

158. Dennis Hanks interview with William H. Herndon, June 13, 1865, H-W Papers (transcript available in Wilson and Davis, *Herndon's*, 42).

159. Arnold, *Life*, 26–27; Brooks, *Abraham*, 33; John Hanks interview with William H. Herndon, June 13, 1865, H-W Papers (transcript available in Wilson and Davis, *Herndon's*, 45); Holland, *Life*, 33; Nicolay and Hay, *Abraham*, 1:36; David Turnham interview with William H. Herndon, Sept. 15, 1865, H-W Papers (transcript available in Wilson and Davis, *Herndon's*, 122).

160. Dennis Hanks, quoted in Lamon (Black), *Life*, 56. Reportedly, Tom would give the household's children a small quantity of whiskey each morning for medicinal purposes (son of Sophie Hanks, quoted in Arthur Ernest Morgan, "New Light on Lincoln's Early Years," in Wilson, *Lincoln*, 52).

161. Arthur Ernest Morgan, "New Light on Lincoln's Early Years," in Wilson, *Lincoln*, 52. John Hanks said, however, that this was the only time he saw Lincoln use beverage alcohol.

162. Nathaniel Grigsby interview with William H. Herndon, Sept. 12, 1865, H-W Papers (transcript available in Wilson and Davis, *Herndon's*, 112).

163. David Turnham interview with William H. Herndon, Sept. 15, 1865, H-W Papers (transcript available in Wilson and Davis, *Herndon's*, 121).

164. William Wood interview with William H. Herndon, Sept. 15, 1865, H-W Papers (transcript available in Wilson and Davis, *Herndon's*, 123).

165. Cartwright, *Autobiography*, 212.

166. Elizabeth Crawford to William H. Herndon, Feb. 21, 1866, H-W Papers (transcript available in Wilson and Davis, *Herndon's*, 216); Lair, *Songs*, 26; Alan Lomax, "The Gospel Ship Baptist Hymns and White Spirituals from the Southern Mountains," *Gospel Ship*, New World Records 80294.

167. Hobson, *Footprints*, 80–81; Abraham Lincoln, Aug. 21, 1858 (transcript available in *CW* 3:16); Townsend, *Lincoln and Liquor*, 22.

168. Townsend, *Lincoln and Liquor*, 20. *See also* Percy Wells Bidwell, "A History of Northern Agriculture 1620 to 1840," in Bidwell and Falconer, *History*, 169.

169. *Niles Register*, clipped in *Vincennes Western Sun*, Nov. 8, 1817.

170. Dennis Hanks, quoted in Atkinson, *Boyhood*, 29–32; Houser, *Lincoln's Education*, 172 n. 19; Shutes, *Lincoln's*, 28; Ida M. Tarbell, quoted in Atkinson, *Boyhood*, 34 n.; Warren, "Environs," 139–40; *Vandalia Illinois Intelligencer*, June 13, 1829; *Western Monthly Review* clipped in *Vandalia Illinois Intelligencer*, May 30, 1829.

171. Warren, "Lincoln's Hoosier," 107–8.

172. Abraham Lincoln, autobiography for John L. Scripps, ca. June 1860 (transcript available in *CW* 4:62).

173. Abraham Lincoln, autobiography for John L. Scripps, ca. June 1860 (transcript available in *CW* 4:62). *See also* Dennis Hanks interview with William H. Herndon, Sept. 8, 1865, H-W Papers (transcript available in Wilson and Davis, *Herndon's*, 104).

174. Abraham Lincoln, autobiography for Jesse Fell, Dec. 20, 1859 (transcript available in *CW* 3:511).

175. Drake, *Pioneer*, 149–50.

176. Anna Caroline Roby Gentry interview with William H. Herndon, Sept. 17, 1865, H-W Papers (transcript available in Wilson and Davis, *Herndon's*, 131).

177. The general story of this schooling is in Beveridge, *Abraham*, 1:53–56; Nathaniel Grigsby to William H. Herndon, Sept. 4, 1865, H-W Papers (transcript available in Wilson and Davis, *Herndon's*, 93); Nathaniel Grigsby interview with William H. Herndon, Sept. 12, 1865, H-W Papers (transcript available in Wilson and Davis, *Herndon's*, 112); Herndon and Weik, *Herndon's Life of Lincoln*, 33–34; David Turnham interview with William H. Herndon, Sept. 15, 1865, H-W Papers (transcript available in Wilson and Davis, *Herndon's*, 121); Warren, "Environs," 133–34; Warren, "Lincoln's Hoosier," 108–10; Warren, *Lincoln's Youth*, 81–83.

178. Abraham Lincoln, address to the New Jersey Senate, Feb. 21, 1861 (transcript available in *CW* 4:235–36).

179. Nathaniel Grigsby to William H. Herndon, Sept. 4, 1865, H-W Papers (transcript available in Wilson and Davis, *Herndon's*, 94); John Oskins interview with William H. Herndon, Sept. 16, 1865, H-W Papers (transcript available in Wilson and Davis, *Herndon's*, 128); Warren, "Lincoln's Hoosier," 111–13. The general story of this schooling is in Warren, *Lincoln's Youth*, 99–103.

180. The general story of this schooling is in Nathaniel Grigsby to William H. Herndon, Sept. 4, 1865, H-W Papers (transcript available in Wilson and Davis, *Herndon's*, 94); Houser, *Lincoln's Education*, 19; Thomas L. D. Johnston interview with William H. Herndon, ca. 1866, H-W Papers (transcript available in Wilson and Davis, *Herndon's*, 532); Abraham Lincoln, arithmetic exercise book pages (photos available in *CW* 1:xxix-xlviii); Sarah Bush Johnston Lincoln interview with William H. Herndon, Sept. 8, 1865, H-W Papers (transcript available in Wilson and Davis, *Herndon's*, 107); Warren, "Azel"; Warren, "Environs," 135; Warren, "Lincoln's Hoosier," 111, 113–16; Warren, *Lincoln's Youth*, 102, 125–33. Persons wishing to ponder Lincoln's schoolboy arithmetic writings may wish to consult Dorfman, "Lincoln's" (Part I) and Dunlap, "Lincoln's." I suppose it possible that the arithmetic book referred to by Dorsey was the homemade one, but a homemade one would indicate just as much interest in education as a regular textbook would.

181. William H. Herndon to Jesse Weik, Oct. 8, 1881 (transcript available in Hertz, *Hidden*, 85).

182. Jefferson Davis, quoted in Davis, *Jefferson*, 18–19.

183. Elizabeth Crawford interview with William H. Herndon, Sept. 16, 1865, H-W Papers (transcript available in Wilson and Davis, *Herndon's*, 126).

184. Elizabeth Crawford to William H. Herndon, April 19, 1866, H-W Papers (transcript available in Wilson and Davis, *Herndon's*, 245).

185. Quoted in Townsend, *Lincoln and the Bluegrass*, 15.

186. Nathaniel Grigsby to William H. Herndon, Sept. 4, 1865, H-W Papers (transcript available in Wilson and Davis, *Herndon's*, 94).

187. Joseph C. Richardson interview with William H. Herndon, ca. Sept. 14, 1865, H-W Papers (transcript available in Wilson and Davis, *Herndon's*, 119).

188. David Turnham interview with William H. Herndon, Sept. 15, 1865, H-W Papers (transcript available in Wilson and Davis, *Herndon's*, 121).

189. Nathaniel Grigsby interview with William H. Herndon, Sept. 12, 1865, H-W Papers (transcript available in Wilson and Davis, *Herndon's*, 112–13).

190. Sarah Bush Johnston Lincoln interview with William H. Herndon, Sept. 8, 1865, H-W Papers (transcript available in Wilson and Davis, *Herndon's*, 107).

191. David Turnham interview with William H. Herndon, Sept. 15, 1865, H-W Papers (transcript available in Wilson and Davis, *Herndon's*, 121).

192. John Hanks interview with William H. Herndon, June 13, 1865, H-W Papers (transcript available in Wilson and Davis, *Herndon's*, 43).

193. Abraham Lincoln, autobiography for Jesse Fell, Dec. 20, 1859 (transcript available in *CW* 3:511).

194. Abraham Lincoln, autobiography for John L. Scripps, ca. June 1860 (transcript available in *CW* 4:62).

195. Anna Caroline Roby Gentry interview with William H. Herndon, Sept. 17, 1865, H-W Papers (transcript available in Wilson and Davis, *Herndon's*, 132). Browne, *Every-Day*, 70 and Barton, *Women*, 138 (both probably relying on Lamon (Black), *Life*, 70), changed "moon" to "sun."

196. Gilbert J. Greene, quoted in Chapman, *Latest*, 524.

197. William H. Herndon personal notes in Nathaniel Grigsby, Silas Richardson, Nancy Richardson, and John Romine interview with William H. Herndon, Sept. 14, 1865, H-W Papers (transcript available in Wilson and Davis, *Herndon's*, 117–18); Houser, *Lincoln's Education*, 155; J. W. Lamar in Hobson, *Footprints*, 22; Murr, "Lincoln," 342; Warren, "Environs," 140; Warren, *Lincoln's Youth*, 86–87, 121–22; Warren, "Pigeon."

198. Warren, "Lincoln the Sexton"; Warren, *Lincoln's Youth*, 121–22; Wolf, *Almost*, 37–38.

199. Nathaniel Grigsby to William H. Herndon, Jan. 21, 1866, H-W Papers (transcript available in Wilson and Davis, *Herndon's*, 169).

200. Elizabeth Crawford to William H. Herndon, Feb. 21, 1866, H-W Papers (transcript available in Wilson and Davis, *Herndon's*, 215). *See also* Beveridge, *Abraham*, 1:71.

201. John Hanks interview with William H. Herndon, ca. 1865, H-W Papers (transcript available in Wilson and Davis, *Herndon's*, 455).

202. Dennis Hanks interview with William H. Herndon, June 13, 1865, H-W Papers (transcript available in Wilson and Davis, *Herndon's*, 37). *See also* Dennis Hanks interview with Jesse Weik, ca. 1886, H-W Papers (transcript available in Wilson and Davis, *Herndon's*, 598). For another example see Dennis Hanks, quoted in Atkinson, *Boyhood*, 34–35.

203. Warren, *Lincoln's Youth*, 213; Warren, "Pigeon."

204. Matilda Johnston Hall Moore interview with William H. Herndon, Sept. 8, 1865, H-W Papers (transcript available in Wilson and Davis, *Herndon's*, 109). Nat Grigsby said that torturing turtles was a common pastime among boys and that Lincoln took them to task for it (Nathaniel Grigsby interview with William H. Herndon, Sept. 12, 1865, H-W Papers (transcript available in Wilson and Davis, *Herndon's*, 112)).

205. Sarah Bush Johnston Lincoln interview with William H. Herndon, Sept. 8, 1865, H-W Papers (transcript available in Wilson and Davis, *Herndon's*, 108).

206. Nathaniel Grigsby to William H. Herndon, Sept. 4, 1865, H-W Papers (transcript available in Wilson and Davis, *Herndon's*, 94); Nathaniel Grigsby interview with William H. Herndon, Sept. 12, 1865, H-W Papers (transcript available in Wilson and Davis, *Herndon's*, 112).

207. Faragher, *Sugar*, 153.

208. Dennis Hanks, quoted in Browne, *Every-Day*, 54.

209. Wolf, *Almost*, 37.
210. Barton, *Soul*, 66.
211. Dennis Hanks, quoted in Atkinson, *Boyhood*, 18–19.
212. Dennis Hanks interview with William H. Herndon, Sept. 8, 1865, H-W Papers (transcript available in Wilson and Davis, *Herndon's*, 106).
213. John Hanks, quoted in Arthur Ernest Morgan, "New Light on Lincoln's Early Years," in Wilson, *Lincoln*, 54.
214. Sarah Bush Johnston Lincoln interview with William H. Herndon, Sept. 8, 1865, H-W Papers (transcript available in Wilson and Davis, *Herndon's*, 107).
215. Nathaniel Grigsby to William H. Herndon, Jan. 21, 1866, H-W Papers (transcript available in Wilson and Davis, *Herndon's*, 169).
216. Dennis Hanks to William H. Herndon, April 2, 1866, H-W Papers (transcript available in Wilson and Davis, *Herndon's*, 242).
217. Matilda Johnston Hall Moore interview with William H. Herndon, Sept. 8, 1865, H-W Papers (transcript available in Wilson and Davis, *Herndon's*, 110). *See also* A. H. Chapman statement, ca. Sept. 8, 1865, H-W Papers (transcript available in Wilson and Davis, *Herndon's*, 102); Dennis Hanks, quoted in Browne, *Every-Day*, 54.
218. Sarah Bush Johnston Lincoln interview with William H. Herndon, Sept. 8, 1865, H-W Papers (transcript available in Wilson and Davis, *Herndon's*, 107).
219. Elizabeth Crawford to William H. Herndon, April 19, 1866, H-W Papers (transcript available in Wilson and Davis, *Herndon's*, 246).
220. Martin L. Bundy to James R. B. Van Cleave, July 16, 1908, Lincoln Centennial Association Papers.
221. Dennis Hanks to William H. Herndon, March 19, 1866, H-W Papers (transcript available in Wilson and Davis, *Herndon's*, 233); Wolf, *Almost*, 37. *See also* Joseph Gillespie to William H. Herndon, Jan. 31, 1866, H-W Papers (transcript available in Wilson and Davis, *Herndon's*, 181); Dennis Hanks to William H. Herndon, Dec. 24, 1865, H-W Papers (transcript available in Wilson and Davis, *Herndon's*, 146).
222. Elizabeth Crawford to William H. Herndon, April 19, 1866, H-W Papers (transcript available in Wilson and Davis, *Herndon's*, 245–46).
223. Dennis Hanks interview with William H. Herndon, June 13, 1865, H-W Papers (transcript available in Wilson and Davis, *Herndon's*, 39); Dennis Hanks quoted in Browne, *Every-Day*, 54; David Turnham interview with William H. Herndon, Sept. 15, 1865, H-W Papers (transcript available in Wilson and Davis, *Herndon's*, 122); Warren, "Accident."
224. Johnson, "Home," 189. *See also* West, "Memoirs," 223–24; Johnson, *Illinois*, 21–22.
225. Herndon and Weik, *Herndon's Life of Lincoln*, 25.
226. Dennis Hanks, quoted in Atkinson, *Boyhood*, 37.
227. Dennis Hanks interview with William H. Herndon, June 13, 1865, H-W Papers (transcript available in Wilson and Davis, *Herndon's*, 39).
228. Donald, *Lincoln's*, 53; Herndon's notes at end of interview with Nathaniel Grigsby, Silas Richardson, Nancy Richardson, and John Romine, Sept. 14, 1865, H-W Papers (transcript available in Wilson and Davis, *Herndon's*, 118); Dennis Hanks interview with William H. Herndon, June 13, 1865, H-W Papers (transcript available in Wilson and Davis, *Herndon's*, 42); Dennis Hanks, quoted in Atkinson, *Boyhood*, 37; Dennis Hanks in Browne, *Every-Day*, 54; William H. Herndon to Ward Hill Lamon, March 6, 1870 (transcript available in Hertz, *Hidden*, 72–73); Herndon and Weik, *Herndon's Life of Lincoln*, 51–52; Kempf, *Abraham*, 9–10, 11 n., 58–59, 81; Abraham Lincoln, autobiography for John L. Scripps, ca. June 1860 (transcript available in *CW* 4:62). Shutes, *Lincoln's*, 195 disagrees with the findings of Kempf, finding no permanent malformation of skull or lasting brain injury. I believe Herndon's letter to Lamon is a reliable source for what Lincoln was saying to the horse, and I suspect Weik has massaged the quotation in the biography he ghosted for Herndon.
229. Beveridge, *Abraham*, 1:59.

230. Beveridge, *Abraham*, 1:70–71, 84 n. 1; M. L. Houser comment in Scripps, *Life*, 19 n. 2; Warren, *Lincoln's Youth*, 84. The 1820 census listed eight (Miers, *Lincoln*, 1820).

231. Dennis Hanks to William H. Herndon, Jan. 26, 1866, H-W Papers (transcript available in Wilson and Davis, *Herndon's*, 176).

232. Harriet Chapman to William H. Herndon, Dec. 10, 1866, H-W Papers (transcript available in Wilson and Davis, *Herndon's*, 513).

233. A. H. Chapman statement, ca. Sept. 8, 1865, H-W Papers (transcript available in Wilson and Davis, *Herndon's*, 98, 100, 102); Nathaniel Grigsby to William H. Herndon, Sept. 4, 1865, H-W Papers (transcript available in Wilson and Davis, *Herndon's*, 94); Dennis Hanks interview with Erastus Wright, June 8, 1865, H-W Papers (transcript available in Wilson and Davis, *Herndon's*, 27–28); Dennis Hanks interview with William H. Herndon, June 13, 1865, H-W Papers (transcript available in Wilson and Davis, *Herndon's*, 40); J. W. Lamar in Hobson, *Footprints*, 23; John Romine interview with William H. Herndon, Sept. 14, 1865, H-W Papers (transcript available in Wilson and Davis, *Herndon's*, 118); David Turnham interview with William H. Herndon, Sept. 15, 1865, H-W Papers (transcript available in Wilson and Davis, *Herndon's*, 122); J. W. Wartmann to William H. Herndon, July 21, 1865, H-W Papers (transcript available in Wilson and Davis, *Herndon's*, 79).

234. Dennis Hanks, quoted in Atkinson, *Boyhood*, 16.

235. Tarbell, *Early*, 67 caption.

236. William Wood interview with William H. Herndon, Sept. 15, 1865, H-W Papers (transcript available in Wilson and Davis, *Herndon's*, 123).

237. Elizabeth Crawford to William H. Herndon, Sept. 7, 1866, H-W Papers (transcript available in Wilson and Davis, *Herndon's*, 335); Elizabeth Crawford to William H. Herndon, Jan. 4, 1866, H-W Papers (transcript available in Wilson and Davis, *Herndon's*, 150); Nathaniel Grigsby to William H. Herndon, Sept. 4, 1865, H-W Papers (transcript available in Wilson and Davis, *Herndon's*, 94); Nathaniel Grigsby to William H. Herndon, Oct. 25, 1865, H-W Papers (transcript available in Wilson and Davis, *Herndon's*, 140); J. W. Wartmann to William H. Herndon, July 21, 1865, H-W Papers (transcript available in Wilson and Davis, *Herndon's*, 79).

238. Browne, *Abraham*, 1:86.

239. As an attorney, Lincoln typically represented the pregnant daughter's father in such cases. *See* "Anderson v. Ryan," L00698; "Berry v. Cagle," L01515; "Dunn v. Carle," L01340; "Grable v. Margrave," L00935; "Hicks v. Meeker," L01079; "Keenan v. Price," L01928; "Matthews v. Turley," L00954; "Patterson v. Winkler," L00738; "Tipton v. Browning," L04711. All these files in Benner and Davis, *Law*.

240. Abraham Lincoln to Albert G. Hodges, April 4, 1864 (transcript available in *CW* 7:281).

241. Elizabeth Crawford to William H. Herndon, Sept. 7, 1866, H-W Papers (transcript available in Wilson and Davis, *Herndon's*, 335). *See also* Elizabeth Crawford interview with William H. Herndon, Sept. 16, 1865, H-W Papers (transcript available in Wilson and Davis, *Herndon's*, 125–26).

McLean County, Illinois, in the 1820s, "was thickly inhabited by snakes, and the settlers tell great stories of the number they killed. Nevertheless the settlers often went to the field and did their ploughing barefooted. Mr. Peasley of Down says that while ploughing around a patch of ground, the snakes continually crawled away from the furrow to the center of the unplowed patch, and when it became very small the grass was fairly alive with the wriggling, squirming reptiles, and they would at last break in every direction" (Duis, *Good*, 6–7).

242. Tarbell, *In the Footsteps*, 105.

243. Dennis Hanks interview with William H. Herndon, June 13, 1865, H-W Papers (transcript available in Wilson and Davis, *Herndon's*, 41).

244. Sarah Bush Johnston Lincoln interview with William H. Herndon, Sept. 8, 1865, H-W Papers (transcript available in Wilson and Davis, *Herndon's*, 108).

245. Nathaniel Grigsby interview with William H. Herndon, Sept. 12, 1865, H-W Papers (transcript available in Wilson and Davis, *Herndon's*, 113).

246. Joseph C. Richardson interview with William H. Herndon, ca. Sept. 14, 1865, H-W Papers (transcript available in Wilson and Davis, *Herndon's*, 119).

247. Dennis Hanks interview with William H. Herndon, June 13, 1865, H-W Papers (transcript available in Wilson and Davis, *Herndon's*, 42); Dennis Hanks to William H. Herndon, Dec. 24, 1865, H-W Papers (transcript available in Wilson and Davis, *Herndon's*, 146).

248. William Wood interview with William H. Herndon, Sept. 15, 1865, H-W Papers (transcript available in Wilson and Davis, *Herndon's*, 124–25).

249. Dennis Hanks, quoted in Browne, *Every-Day*, 53.

250. Joseph C. Richardson statement, ca. 1865, H-W Papers (transcript available in Wilson and Davis, *Herndon's*, 474).

251. Joseph C. Richardson interview with William H. Herndon, ca. Sept. 14, 1865, H-W Papers (transcript available in Wilson and Davis, *Herndon's*, 120).

252. John Romine interview with William H. Herndon, Sept. 14, 1865, H-W Papers (transcript available in Wilson and Davis, *Herndon's*, 118).

253. Sarah Bush Johnston Lincoln interview with William H. Herndon, Sept. 8, 1865, H-W Papers (transcript available in Wilson and Davis, *Herndon's*, 106–7). Her granddaughter's husband may not have been old enough to observe this trait personally in Indiana but agreed that "Lincoln was not industrious as a worker on the farm or at any other kind of manual labor. He only showed industry in attainment of knowledge" (A. H. Chapman interview with William H. Herndon, ca. Sept. 8, 1865, H-W Papers (transcript available in Wilson and Davis, *Herndon's*, 102)).

254. For examples of pioneer contemporaries describing Lincoln as lazy, see Dennis Hanks interview with William H. Herndon, Sept. 8, 1865, H-W Papers (transcript available in Wilson and Davis, *Herndon's*, 104); Matilda Johnston Hall Moore interview with William H. Herndon, Sept. 8, 1865, H-W Papers (transcript available in Wilson and Davis, *Herndon's*, 109). An exception, notable for its rarity, is David Turnham's declaration that Lincoln "didn't love physical work" but "taking all in all he was not a lazy man" (David Turnham interview with William H. Herndon, Sept. 15, 1865, H-W Papers (transcript available in Wilson and Davis, *Herndon's*, 121)). Another neighbor agreed, "Abe was always an industrious lad, worked at something or was reading, not loitering away his time" (Absolom Roby interview with William H. Herndon, Sept. 17, 1865, H-W Papers (transcript available in Wilson and Davis, *Herndon's*, 132)).

255. Tillson, *Woman's*, 82.

256. Sarah Bush Johnston Lincoln interview with William H. Herndon, Sept. 8, 1865, H-W Papers (transcript available in Wilson and Davis, *Herndon's*, 107).

257. Dennis Hanks interview with William H. Herndon, June 13, 1865, H-W Papers (transcript available in Wilson and Davis, *Herndon's*, 41).

258. Joseph C. Richardson statement, ca. 1865, H-W Papers (transcript available in Wilson and Davis, *Herndon's*, 474).

259. Sarah Bush Johnston Lincoln interview with William H. Herndon, Sept. 8, 1865, H-W Papers (transcript available in Wilson and Davis, *Herndon's*, 107).

260. Leonard Swett in Rice, *Reminiscences*, 459.

261. Dennis Hanks interview with William H. Herndon, June 13, 1865, H-W Papers (transcript available in Wilson and Davis, *Herndon's*, 41). *See also* A. H. Chapman statement, ca. Sept. 8, 1865, H-W Papers (transcript available in Wilson and Davis, *Herndon's*, 101).

262. Dennis Hanks interview with William H. Herndon, Sept. 8, 1865, H-W Papers (transcript available in Wilson and Davis, *Herndon's*, 105).

263. Sarah Bush Johnston Lincoln interview with William H. Herndon, Sept. 8, 1865, H-W Papers (transcript available in Wilson and Davis, *Herndon's*, 107). Stepsister Tilda spoke of Lincoln writing not only on boards, but also on walls (Matilda Johnston Hall Moore interview with William H. Herndon, Sept. 8, 1865, H-W Papers (transcript available in Wilson and Davis, *Herndon's*, 109)).

264. Sarah Bush Johnston Lincoln interview with William H. Herndon, Sept. 8, 1865, H-W Papers (transcript available in Wilson and Davis, *Herndon's*, 107).

265. Abraham Lincoln, quoted in Gulliver, "Talk," 1. Billy Herndon wrote a thorough critique of Gulliver's article (Herndon, "Lincoln and Strangers" in Hertz, *Hidden*, 401–3), one accepted by Fehrenbacher and Fehrenbacher, *Recollected*, 189–90. Rather few reported conversations with Lincoln are dependable as verbatim transcriptions, but errors in the quoted passage seem more attributable to a lapse of Gulliver's memory than to fabrication; Gulliver said the conversation was published four years after it occurred. I doubt that Lincoln referred to his sleeping loft as a "bedroom," nor (as in a passage I omitted) was he likely to have paced back and forth in the loft, though he may have walked restlessly somewhere. Given, however, that Gulliver's report cannot have been contaminated by what Lincoln's stepmother told Herndon a year later, and given the match with what both Gulliver and the stepmother reported, I think Gulliver's article is credible.

266. Sarah Bush Johnston Lincoln interview with William H. Herndon, Sept. 8, 1865, H-W Papers (transcript available in Wilson and Davis, *Herndon's*, 107). Denny Hanks agreed that Lincoln read the Bible some but not "half as much as said" (Dennis Hanks interview with Willam H. Herndon, Sept. 8, 1865, H-W Papers (transcript available in Wilson and Davis, *Herndon's*, 106)).

267. Nathaniel Grigsby interview with William H. Herndon, Sept. 12, 1865, H-W Papers (transcript available in Wilson and Davis, *Herndon's*, 112); William Fortune in Ehrmann, *Missing*, 75–76; Dennis Hanks interview with William H. Herndon, June 13, 1865, H-W Papers (transcript available in Wilson and Davis, *Herndon's*, 41); Dennis Hanks interview with William H. Herndon, Sept. 8, 1865, H-W Papers (transcript available in Wilson and Davis, *Herndon's*, 105); Dennis Hanks to William H. Herndon, Dec. 27, 1865, H-W Papers (transcript available in Wilson and Davis, *Herndon's*, 146–47); Dennis Hanks to William H. Herndon, March 12, 1866, H-W Papers (transcript available in Wilson and Davis, *Herndon's*, 229); John Hanks interview with William H. Herndon, June 13, 1865, H-W Papers (transcript available in Wilson and Davis, *Herndon's*, 43); John Hanks interview with William H. Herndon, ca. 1865, H-W Papers (transcript available in Wilson and Davis, *Herndon's*, 455); John Hougland interview with William H. Herndon, Sept. 17, 1865, H-W Papers (transcript available in Wilson and Davis, *Herndon's*, 130); Matilda Johnston Hall Moore interview with William H. Herndon, Sept. 8, 1865, H-W Papers (transcript available in Wilson and Davis, *Herndon's*, 109–10); Speed, *Reminiscences*, 38; David Turnham interview with William H. Herndon, Sept. 15, 1865, H-W Papers (transcript available in Wilson and Davis, *Herndon's*, 121); David Turnham to William H. Herndon, Sept. 16, 1865, H-W Papers (transcript available in Wilson and Davis, *Herndon's*, 129); David Turnham to William H. Herndon, Oct. 12, 1865, H-W Papers (transcript available in Wilson and Davis, *Herndon's*, 138); Warren, "Dr. Franklin." The stepmother couldn't remember titles but noted his retentive memory (Sarah Bush Johnston Lincoln interview with William H. Herndon, Sept. 8, 1865, H-W Papers (transcript available in Wilson and Davis, *Herndon's*, 108)). A cottage industry exists in identifying books read by young Lincoln, but such a list seems unnecessary here. The point is that he read as much as he could.

268. Dennis Hanks, quoted in Atkinson, *Boyhood*, 24–25.

269. Sarah Bush Johnston Lincoln interview with William H. Herndon, Sept. 8, 1865, H-W Papers (transcript available in Wilson and Davis, *Herndon's*, 107). *See also* Warren, "Early Newspapers"; William Wood interview with William H. Herndon, Sept. 15, 1865, H-W Papers (transcript available in Wilson and Davis, *Herndon's*, 123).

270. Dennis Hanks, quoted in Atkinson, *Boyhood*, 25.

271. William Wood interview with William H. Herndon, Sept. 15, 1865, H-W Papers (transcript available in Wilson and Davis, *Herndon's*, 124).

272. John Hanks interview with William H. Herndon, ca. 1865, H-W Papers (transcript available in Wilson and Davis, *Herndon's*, 455).

273. Dennis Hanks, quoted in Atkinson, *Boyhood*, 27.

274. Elizabeth Crawford interview with William H. Herndon, Sept. 16, 1865, H-W Papers (transcript available in Wilson and Davis, *Herndon's*, 126).

275. Elizabeth Crawford to William H. Herndon, Sept. 7, 1866, H-W Papers (transcript available in Wilson and Davis, *Herndon's*, 335).

276. Barton, *Life*, 1:122; Bestor, Mearns, and Daniels, *Three*, 75; A. H. Chapman statement, ca. Sept. 8, 1865, H-W Papers (transcript available in Wilson and Davis, *Herndon's*, 101); Elizabeth Crawford interview with William H. Herndon, Sept. 16, 1865, H-W Papers (transcript available in Wilson and Davis, *Herndon's*, 125); Dennis Hanks interview with William H. Herndon, June 13, 1865, H-W Papers (transcript available in Wilson and Davis, *Herndon's*, 41); John Hanks interview with William H. Herndon, ca. 1865, H-W Papers (transcript available in Wilson and Davis, *Herndon's*, 455); Mitgang, *Abraham*, 187–88; Oliver Terry to Jesse Weik, July 1888, H-W Papers (transcript available in Wilson and Davis, *Herndon's*, 662–63); J. W. Wartmann to William H. Herndon, July 21, 1865, H-W Papers (transcript available in Wilson and Davis, *Herndon's*, 79).

277. A. H. Chapman statement, ca. Sept. 8, 1865, H-W Papers (transcript available in Wilson and Davis, *Herndon's*, 101); Joseph C. Richardson interview with William H. Herndon, ca. Sept. 14, 1865, H-W Papers (transcript available in Wilson and Davis, *Herndon's*, 119). *See also* William Fortune in Ehrmann, *Missing*, 73–74.

278. William Fortune in Ehrmann, *Missing*, 73–74; Herndon and Weik, *Herndon's Life of Lincoln*, 36. Crawford did have a blue nose (Joseph Richardson interview with William H. Herndon, ca. Sept. 14, 1865, H-W Papers (transcript available in Wilson and Davis, *Herndon's*, 119–20)). Richardson's account raises the possibility that the rhyme was part of "The Chronicles of Reuben." The double infare inspiring the "Chronicles" was in 1829, and Crawford's wife dated the book incident as 1829 (Elizabeth Crawford interview with William H. Herndon, Sept. 16, 1865, H-W Papers (transcript available in Wilson and Davis, *Herndon's*, 125)).

279. Dennis Hanks interview with William H. Herndon, June 13, 1865, H-W Papers (transcript available in Wilson and Davis, *Herndon's*, 41). I assume here that Lincoln wrote and distributed only one poem about Blue Nose and acknowledge that my assumption may be plausible but is unverified.

280. Ehrmann, *Missing*, 144–46; Hobson, *Footprints*, 29. For mention of Abraham's cabinetmaking *see also* Nathaniel Grigsby to William H. Herndon, Sept. 4, 1865, H-W Papers (transcript available in Wilson and Davis, *Herndon's*, 94). The book meant enough to Lincoln that he quoted its frontispiece caption, "firm as the surge-repelling rock," when referring to himself as resolute (Abraham Lincoln to Mrs. O. H. Browning, April 1, 1838 (transcript available in *CW* 1:118)), an observation from Warren, *Lincoln's Youth*, 162, 255 n. 11.

281. Ehrmann, *Missing*, 144.

282. Beveridge, *Abraham*, 1:95 n. 3; Houser, *Lincoln's Education*, 17–18.

283. John W. Lamar in Hobson, *Footprints*, 23; Anna O'Flynn in Ehrmann, *Missing*, 100; Tarbell, *Early*, 71–72.

284. John W. Lamar to William H. Herndon, May 18, 1867, H-W Papers (transcript available in Wilson and Davis, *Herndon's*, 560).

285. Nathaniel Grigsby interview with William H. Herndon, Sept. 12, 1865, H-W Papers (transcript available in Wilson and Davis, *Herndon's*, 114).

286. Absolom Roby interview with William H. Herndon, Sept. 17, 1865, H-W Papers (transcript available in Wilson and Davis, *Herndon's*, 132).

287. Elizabeth Crawford interview with William H. Herndon, Sept. 16, 1865, H-W Papers (transcript available in Wilson and Davis, *Herndon's*, 126–27). *See also* Elizabeth Crawford to William H. Herndon, Jan. 4, 1866, H-W Papers (transcript available in Wilson and Davis, *Herndon's*, 151).

288. Arnold, *Life*, 25.

289. Lamon, *Recollections*, 182.

290. Sarah Bush Johnston Lincoln interview with William H. Herndon, Sept. 8, 1865, H-W Papers (transcript available in Wilson and Davis, *Herndon's*, 107; *see also* 108).

291. Matilda Johnston Hall Moore interview with William H. Herndon, Sept. 8, 1865, H-W Papers (transcript available in Wilson and Davis, *Herndon's*, 110).

292. Dennis Hanks interview with William H. Herndon, Sept. 8, 1865, H-W Papers (transcript available in Wilson and Davis, *Herndon's*, 104). *See also* Sarah Bush Johnston Lincoln interview with William H. Herndon, Sept. 8, 1865, H-W Papers (transcript available in Wilson and Davis, *Herndon's*, 108). Matilda Johnston Hall Moore noted the political nature of some Lincoln speeches (interview with William H. Herndon, Sept. 8, 1865, H-W Papers (transcript available in Wilson and Davis, *Herndon's*, 110)).

293. William Fortune in Ehrmann, *Missing*, 75; John Hanks interview with William H. Herndon, June 13, 1865, H-W Papers (transcript available in Wilson and Davis, *Herndon's*, 43); John Hanks interview with William H. Herndon, ca. 1865–1866, H-W Papers (transcript available in Wilson and Davis, *Herndon's*, 455). *See also* A. H. Chapman statement, ca. Sept. 8, 1865, H-W Papers (transcript available in Wilson and Davis, *Herndon's*, 102); David Turnham interview with William H. Herndon, Sept. 15, 1865, H-W Papers (transcript available in Wilson and Davis, *Herndon's*, 123).

294. A. H. Chapman statement, ca. Sept. 8, 1865, H-W Papers (transcript available in Wilson and Davis, *Herndon's*, 102); Murr, "Lincoln," 344–46.

295. William Greene to William H. Herndon, May 29, 1865, H-W Papers (transcript available in Wilson and Davis, *Herndon's*, 11).

296. William Wood interview with William H. Herndon, Sept. 15, 1865, H-W Papers (transcript available in Wilson and Davis, *Herndon's*, 124).

297. William Greene to William H. Herndon, Jan. 23, 1866, H-W Papers (transcript available in Wilson and Davis, *Herndon's*, 175); Nathaniel Grigsby interview with William H. Herndon, Sept. 16, 1865, H-W Papers (transcript available in Wilson and Davis, *Herndon's*, 128). Despite details inconsistent with the preceding, what may be a reference to this poem is in Murr, "Lincoln," 345, although it may be to a different poem.

298. Tarbell, *Life*, 1:29–30. A variant with trivial differences is in Barton, *Women*, 118–19. Although Abraham is quoted as saying the woman read the first stories he ever heard, the incident surely occurred in Indiana; the literary creation sounds more like a teenage fantasy than one from a boy aged seven years or younger. The location of the broken wagon is unclear. It was not necessarily on a road, but even if it was, a road did exist in the Indiana farm's vicinity (Warren, *Lincoln's Youth*, 122), so a road would not necessarily date the incident as a Kentucky occurrence.

299. Kempf, *Abraham*, 46–47.

300. William Wood interview with William H. Herndon, Sept. 15, 1865, H-W Papers (transcript available in Wilson and Davis, *Herndon's*, 123–24). *See also* Beveridge, *Abraham*, 1:77, 82; Ehrmann, *Missing*, 10; Oliver Terry to Jesse Weik, July 14, 1888, H-W Papers (transcript available in Wilson and Davis, *Herndon's*, 658); Oliver Terry to Jesse Weik, July 1888, H-W Papers (transcript available in Wilson and Davis, *Herndon's*, 662); David Turnham to William H. Herndon, Sept. 5, 1866, H-W Papers (transcript available in Wilson and Davis, *Herndon's*, 334); Weik, *Real*, 130. "Pitcher" has also been spelled "Pritcher." When interrogated about the topic at the age of ninety-two, Pitcher said Lincoln borrowed books sixty years earlier, but he could not remember absolutely that they included law books. That at least some were law books seems a safe assumption. Reverend Farmer has also been identified as affiliated with the United Brethren church (Hobson, *Footprints*, 51–52).

301. *Vincennes Western Sun*, March 16, 1816.

302. Mentor Graham to William H. Herndon, July 15, 1865, H-W Papers (transcript available in Wilson and Davis, *Herndon's*, 76).

303. Mentor Graham interview with William H. Herndon, ca. 1865–1866, H-W Papers (transcript available in Wilson and Davis, *Herndon's*, 450).

304. Joseph C. Richardson statement, ca. 1865, H-W Papers (transcript available in Wilson and Davis, *Herndon's*, 473); Tarbell, *Early*, 84.

305. Sampson Mason, quoted in Smith, *Early*, 56. Smith was on the scene and thought Mason's description was exaggerated.

306. Smith, *Early*, 285.

307. *History of Warwick*, 616–17.
308. Brackenridge to Jesse Weik, Dec. 15, 1914, Jesse W. Weik Papers; Inglehart, "Environment," 163–64; S. T. Johnson interview with William H. Herndon, Sept. 14, 1865, H-W Papers (transcript available in Wilson and Davis, *Herndon's*, 115). See also Arnold, *Life*, 25; Browne, *Every-Day*, 56–57; Houser, *Lincoln's Education*, 37 n. 12. The attorney's name has also been spelled "Breckenridge." A few details of his life are in Isaac Moore to William H. Herndon, Sept. 27, 1866, H-W Papers (transcript available in Wilson and Davis, *Herndon's*, 354). Johnson dated the murder trial as 1828, but Beveridge and Warren found that to be incorrect (Beveridge, *Abraham*, 1:91 n. 2; Warren, *Lincoln's Youth*, 198–99).
309. S. T. Johnson interview with William H. Herndon, Sept. 14, 1865, H-W Papers (transcript available in Wilson and Davis, *Herndon's*, 115). *See also* Dennis Hanks interview with William H. Herndon, Sept. 8, 1865, H-W Papers (transcript available in Wilson and Davis, *Herndon's*, 104).
310. Nathaniel Grigsby to William H. Herndon, Oct. 25, 1865, H-W Papers (transcript available in Wilson and Davis, *Herndon's*, 140); Dennis Hanks interview with William H. Herndon, Sept. 8, 1865, H-W Papers (transcript available in Wilson and Davis, *Herndon's*, 104); Hobson, *Footprints*, 30; Nicolay and Hay, *Abraham*, 1:35; Tarbell, *Early*, 167; Townsend, *Lincoln the Litigant*, 41; David Turnham to William H. Herndon, Sept. 16, 1865, H-W Papers (transcript available in Wilson and Davis, *Herndon's*, 129); David Turnham to William H. Herndon, Oct. 12, 1865, H-W Papers (transcript available in Wilson and Davis, *Herndon's*, 138); Warren, "Environs," 142.
311. Beveridge, *Abraham*, 1:74; Hill, *Lincoln*, 10, 12 n. 1; Hobson, *Footprints*, 30; Tarbell, *Early*, 166–67; Warren, *Lincoln's Youth*, 201.
312. Oliver Terry to Jesse Weik, July 1888, H-W Papers (transcript available in Wilson and Davis, *Herndon's*, 662); Weik, *Real*, 130.
313. A. H. Chapman, statement ca. Sept. 8, 1865, H-W Papers (transcript available in Wilson and Davis, *Herndon's*, 102).
314. Hill, *Lincoln*, 57.
315. J. Edward Murr in Ehrmann, *Missing*, 89–90.
316. J. Edward Murr in Ehrmann, *Missing*, 94; McConnel, *Western*, 125–26.
317. Dennis Hanks interview with William H. Herndon, Sept. 8, 1865, H-W Papers (transcript available in Wilson and Davis, *Herndon's*, 104).
318. Cockrum, *Pioneer*, 189.
319. Beveridge, *Abraham*, 1:83–84; William Fortune in Ehrmann, *Missing*, 76; Thomas, "Lincoln's Humor," 83; Warren, *Lincoln's Youth*, opposite 162, 194–95.
320. Abner Y. Ellis statement to William H. Herndon, ca. Jan. 23, 1866, H-W Papers (transcript available in Wilson and Davis, *Herndon's*, 173).
321. Nathaniel Grigsby interview with William H. Herndon, Sept. 12, 1865, H-W Papers (transcript available in Wilson and Davis, *Herndon's*, 114–15).
322. Anna Caroline Roby Gentry interview with William H. Herndon, Sept. 17, 1865, H-W Papers (transcript available in Wilson and Davis, *Herndon's*, 132).
323. Absolom Roby interview with William H. Herndon, Sept. 17, 1865, H-W Papers (transcript available in Wilson and Davis, *Herndon's*, 132).
324. Dennis Hanks interview with William H. Herndon, Sept. 8, 1865, H-W Papers (transcript available in Wilson and Davis, *Herndon's*, 105).
325. Dennis Hanks interview with William H. Herndon, June 13, 1865, H-W Papers (transcript available in Wilson and Davis, *Herndon's*, 41).
326. Sarah Bush Johnston Lincoln interview with William H. Herndon, Sept. 8, 1865, H-W Papers (transcript available in Wilson and Davis, *Herndon's*, 108).
327. Joseph C. Richardson interview with William H. Herndon, ca. Sept. 14, 1865, H-W Papers (transcript available in Wilson and Davis, *Herndon's*, 120).
328. Nathaniel Grigsby interview with William H. Herndon, Sept. 12, 1865, H-W Papers (transcript available in Wilson and Davis, *Herndon's*, 112).

329. John Hanks in Weik, *Real*, 276.

330. Elizabeth Crawford to William H. Herndon, Jan. 4, 1866, H-W Papers (transcript available in Wilson and Davis, *Herndon's*, 151).

331. Dennis Hanks interview with Jesse Weik, ca. 1886, H-W Papers (transcript available in Wilson and Davis, *Herndon's*, 598).

332. Matilda Johnston Moore interview with William H. Herndon, Sept. 8, 1865, H-W Papers (transcript available in Wilson and Davis, *Herndon's*, 110).

333. William H. Herndon, "Honest Abe: A Story of Lincoln's Youth" (transcript available in Hertz, *Hidden*, 422–23).

334. Herndon and Weik, *Herndon's Life of Lincoln*, 30–31.

335. Strozier, *Lincoln's*, 22–23, 238–39 n. 88.

336. Matilda Johnston Moore interview with William H. Herndon, Sept. 8, 1865, H-W Papers (transcript available in Wilson and Davis, *Herndon's*, 110).

337. David Turnham interview with William H. Herndon, Sept. 15, 1865, H-W Papers (transcript available in Wilson and Davis, *Herndon's*, 122); Wilson and Davis, *Herndon's*, 134 n. 1.

338. Beveridge, *Abraham*, 1:80.

339. Nathaniel Grigsby to William H. Herndon, Jan. 21, 1866, H-W Papers (transcript available in Wilson and Davis, *Herndon's*, 169).

340. Sarah Bush Johnston Lincoln interview with William H. Herndon, Sept. 8, 1865, H-W Papers (transcript available in Wilson and Davis, *Herndon's*, 108). *See also* Dennis Hanks interview with William H. Herndon, Sept. 8, 1865, H-W Papers (transcript available in Wilson and Davis, *Herndon's*, 105); Joseph C. Richardson interview with Willima H. Herndon, ca. Sept. 14, 1865, H-W Papers (transcript available in Wilson and Davis, *Herndon's*, 120); David Turnham interview with William H. Herndon, Sept. 15, 1865, H-W Papers (transcript available in Wilson and Davis, *Herndon's*, 122); David Turnham to William H. Herndon, Dec. 17, 1866, H-W Papers (transcript available in Wilson and Davis, *Herndon's*, 518).

341. Tarbell, *Life*, 1:29. *See also* J. W. Wartmann to William H. Herndon, Sept. 4, 1866, H-W Papers (transcript available in Wilson and Davis, *Herndon's*, 330). A richly detailed example is given in Barton, *Women*, 148–56, but Barton acknowledges that part of it is his own invention. Barton also speaks of Lincoln's continuing interest in socializing with girls after moving to Illinois (Barton, *Women*, 161, 163–65).

342. John Hanks interview with William H. Herndon, ca. 1865, H-W Papers (transcript available in Wilson and Davis, *Herndon's*, 455).

343. Anna Caroline Roby Gentry interview with William H. Herndon, Sept. 17, 1865, H-W Papers (transcript available in Wilson and Davis, *Herndon's*, 131).

344. George Balch interview with Jesse Weik, ca. 1886, H-W Papers (transcript available in Wilson and Davis, *Herndon's*, 597).

345. Ehrmann, *Missing*, 38; Warren, "Lincoln's Memories"; Shutes, *Lincoln's*, 26.

346. John Hanks interview with William H. Herndon, ca. 1865–1866, H-W Papers (transcript available in Wilson and Davis, *Herndon's*, 456).

347. Austin Gollaher, interviewed by D. J. Thomas, quoted in Tarbell, *Early*, 46.

348. David Turnham interview with William H. Herndon, Sept. 15, 1865, H-W Papers (transcript available in Wilson and Davis, *Herndon's*, 121).

349. Nathaniel Grigsby interview with William H. Herndon, Sept. 12, 1865, H-W Papers (transcript available in Wilson and Davis, *Herndon's*, 113). *See also* John Hanks interview with William H. Herndon, ca. 1865–1866, H-W Papers (transcript available in Wilson and Davis, *Herndon's*, 456).

350. Barton, *Women*, 111–12; Nathaniel Grigsby interview with William H. Herndon, Sept. 12, 1865, H-W Papers (transcript available in Wilson and Davis, *Herndon's*, 112).

351. Dennis Hanks, quoted in Atkinson, *Boyhood*, 19.

352. Elizabeth Crawford interview with William H. Herndon, Sept. 16, 1865, H-W Papers (transcript available in Wilson and Davis, *Herndon's*, 126).

353. Tarbell, *Early*, 67 caption.

354. Beveridge, *Abraham*, 1:84.

355. Lair, *Songs*, 24.

356. Elizabeth Crawford to William H. Herndon, May 3, 1866, H-W Papers (transcript available in Wilson and Davis, *Herndon's*, 249–50); Donald, *Lincoln Reconsidered*, 157; Lamon, *Recollections*, 152–53.

357. Hobson, *Footprints*, 22. Given Kentucky wedding customs, the Lincoln song might have been performed at the infare instead of the wedding (*see* Drake, *Pioneer*, 184).

358. Drake, *Pioneer*, 184.

359. Hobson, *Footprints*, 21.

360. Samuel E. Kercheval to Jesse Weik, Dec. 2, 1887, H-W Papers (transcript available in Wilson and Davis, *Herndon's*, 645).

361. Beveridge, *Abraham*, 1:84; Samuel Crawford to William H. Herndon, Jan. 8, 1866, H-W Papers (transcript available in Wilson and Davis, *Herndon's*, 154); Samuel E. Kercheval to Jesse Weik, Dec. 2, 1887, H-W Papers (transcript available in Wilson and Davis, *Herndon's*, 645); Joseph C. Richardson interview with William H. Herndon, ca. Sept. 14, 1865, H-W Papers (transcript available in Wilson and Davis, *Herndon's*, 119).

362. A. H. Chapman statement, ca. Sept. 8, 1865, H-W Papers (transcript available in Wilson and Davis, *Herndon's*, 100, 102); Hobson, *Footprints*, 22, 24; Petersen, *Lincoln-Douglas*, 177 n. 27; Shutes, *Lincoln and the Doctors*, 59; Shutes, *Lincoln's*, 31; Townsend, *Lincoln and Liquor*, 21. The niece relationship of Mrs. J. W. Lamar to Nancy Grigsby is noted in Wilson and Davis, *Herndon's*, 598 n. 2.

363. Hobson, *Footprints*, 24; Shutes, *Lincoln's*, 32.

364. Nathaniel Grigsby to William H. Herndon, Sept. 4, 1865, H-W Papers (transcript available in Wilson and Davis, *Herndon's*, 94); Warren, "Environs," 140.

365. Dennis Hanks, quoted in Atkinson, *Boyhood*, 21–22.

366. Barton, *Women*, 111; Weik, *Real*, 34.

367. Petersen, *Lincoln-Douglas*, 177 n. 27.

368. Dec. 28, 1816.

369. Samuel Crawford to William H. Herndon, Jan. 8, 1866, H-W Papers (transcript available in Wilson and Davis, *Herndon's*, 154); Samuel E. Kercheval to Jesse Weik, Dec. 2, 1887, H-W Papers (transcript available in Wilson and Davis, *Herndon's*, 645); Joseph C. Richardson to William H. Herndon, ca. Sept. 14, 1865, H-W Papers (transcript available in Wilson and Davis, *Herndon's*, 119).

370. Quoted in Warren, *Lincoln's Youth*, 196. *See also* Lair, *Songs*, 23.

371. Beveridge, *Abraham*, 1:92; William H. Herndon to Jesse Weik, Jan. 8, 1887 (transcript available in Hertz, *Hidden*, 155). Another version says the switch happened, but through inadvertence rather than at Lincoln's instigation (Joseph C. Richardson interview with William H. Herndon, ca. Sept. 14, 1865, H-W Papers (transcript available in Wilson and Davis, *Herndon's*, 119–20). John W. Lamar to J. W. Wartmann, Jan. 3, 1887, H-W Papers (transcript available in Wilson and Davis, *Herndon's*, 598), and Samuel Crawford to William H. Herndon, Jan. 8, 1865, H-W Papers (transcript available in Wilson and Davis, *Herndon's*, 154), are neutral on whether the switch was a prank or accidental, but Lamar's declaration that the event did happen has particular credibility, as he says he often heard the story from his father-in-law, who was the brother of the bridegrooms' mother. Lamar's wife attended the infare and recalled hearing talk about what happened.

372. Quoted in Barton, *Life*, 1:126 n., and in Warren, *Lincoln's Youth*, 196.

373. Joseph C. Richardson interview with William H. Herndon, Sept. 14, 1865, H-W Papers (transcript available in Wilson and Davis, *Herndon's*, 120). *See also* mention by Thomas Bunton that he remembered hearing the "Chronicles" (Hobson, *Footprints*, 28).

374. Elizabeth Crawford interview with William H. Herndon, Sept. 16, 1865, H-W Papers (transcript available in Wilson and Davis, *Herndon's*, 127); Elizabeth Crawford to William H. Herndon,

Jan. 4, 1866, H-W Papers (transcript available in Wilson and Davis, *Herndon's*, 152). Her daughter Ruth once said, "Lord, yes; I've heard mother tell it a thousand times" (Hobson, *Footprints*, 29). John Romine offered a fragment differing in detail, but it was so close to what Elizabeth Crawford dictated as to demonstrate a strong folk memory of the "Chronicles" (John Romine interview with William H. Herndon, Sept. 14, 1865, H-W Papers (transcript available in Wilson and Davis, *Herndon's*, 118). *See also* Nathaniel Grigsby interview with William H. Herndon, Sept. 12, 1865, H-W Papers (transcript available in Wilson and Davis, *Herndon's*, 114); Nathaniel Grigsby to William H. Herndon, Jan. 21, 1866, H-W Papers (transcript available in Wilson and Davis, *Herndon's*, 169); Joseph C. Richardson interview with William H. Herndon, Sept. 14, 1865, H-W Papers (transcript available in Wilson and Davis, *Herndon's*, 120); J. W. Wartmann to William H. Herndon, July 21, 1865, H-W Papers (transcript available in Wilson and Davis, *Herndon's*, 79); William Wood interview with William H. Herndon, Sept. 15, 1865, H-W Papers (transcript available in Wilson and Davis, *Herndon's*, 123). Herndon said the manuscript existed when he did his 1865 research in Indiana (William H. Herndon to Jesse Weik, Dec. 22, 1886 (transcript available in Hertz, *Hidden*, 150). Weik implied that he relied on Lincoln's original holograph manuscript in Herndon and Weik, *Herndon's Life of Lincoln*, 44–47, but I am skeptical, as that document was missing as the twenty-first century began. Barton reported that after Herndon and Weik's book was published, the original manuscript was possessed by Edmond Grigsby, and a newspaper intended to print it (Barton, *Life*, 1:126 n.). Grigsby in-law John Lamar said that the document did exist and was once in the possession of a carpenter who found it while working in the house of the bridegrooms' parents (John W. Lamar to J. W. Wartmann, Jan. 3, 1887, H-W Papers (transcript available in Wilson and Davis, *Herndon's*, 598–99)). Aaron Grigsby's brother Red claimed to have possessed the manuscript at one time and said it no longer existed (Hobson, *Footprints*, 28). The parody of King James Bible language was by no means unique to Lincoln, of course. For example, see a satire actually entitled "Chronicles" in *Edwardsville Illinois Advocate*, Jan. 12, 1832. *See also* first and second "Epistle of Zaccheus to the Americans," *Belleville Advocate*, Sept. 10, 17, 24, Oct. 1, Nov. 11, 1841; Peter Cartwright, "First Chronicle Concerning the Rulers of My People," *Vandalia Illinois Intelligencer*, Jan. 17, 1829; "Chronicles," *Tazewell Whig*, Dec. 5, 1846.

375. Elizabeth Crawford to William H. Herndon, Jan. 4, 1866, H-W Papers (transcript available in Wilson and Davis, *Herndon's*, 151–52); Elizabeth Crawford to William H. Herndon, Feb. 21, 1866, H-W Papers (transcript available in Wilson and Davis, *Herndon's*, 215–16). Compare with Carl Sandburg, *Carl Sandburg's New American Songbag* (New York: Broadcast Music, 1950), 52; http://user.txcyber.com/~james/Munnerlyn/benjamin2/poem_bh_skinner_bible.htm.

376. Beveridge, *Abraham*, 1:92; Joseph C. Richardson interview with William H. Herndon, Sept. 14, 1865, H-W Papers (transcript available in Wilson and Davis, *Herndon's*, 120); J. W. Wartmann to William H. Herndon, July 21, 1865, H-W Papers (transcript available in Wilson and Davis, *Herndon's*, 79).

377. Beveridge, *Abraham*, 1:92.

378. Nathaniel Grigsby to William H. Herndon, Feb. 12, 1866, H-W Papers (transcript available in Wilson and Davis, *Herndon's*, 209).

379. Samuel Crawford to William H. Herndon, Jan. 8, 1866, H-W Papers (transcript available in Wilson and Davis, *Herndon's*, 154–55).

380. Beveridge, *Abraham*, 1:93–94; Nathaniel Grigsby interview with William H. Herndon, Sept. 12, 1865, H-W Papers (transcript available in Wilson and Davis, *Herndon's*, 113–14); Nathaniel Grigsby to William H. Herndon, Sept. 19, 1865, H-W Papers (transcript available in Wilson and Davis, *Herndon's*, 345); Samuel E. Kercheval to Jesse Weik, Dec. 2, 1887, H-W Papers (transcript available in Wilson and Davis, *Herndon's*, 645); John W. Lamar to J. W. Wartmann, Jan. 3, 1887, H-W Papers (transcript available in Wilson and Davis, *Herndon's*, 598); Joseph C. Richardson interview with William H. Herndon, ca. Sept. 14, 1865, H-W Papers (transcript available in Wilson and Davis, *Herndon's*, 120); Green Taylor interview with William H. Herndon, Sept. 16, 1865, H-W Papers (transcript available in Wilson and Davis, *Herndon's*, 130);

David Turnham interview with William H. Herndon, Sept. 15, 1865, H-W Papers (transcript available in Wilson and Davis, *Herndon's*, 122); David Turnham to William H. Herndon, Sept. 5, 1866, H-W Papers (transcript available in Wilson and Davis, *Herndon's*, 334); Warren, *Lincoln's Youth*, 196–97. In another variant of the story, John Johnston related a tale about the bride and groom mixup, which resulted in the fight, with either the tale or the fight or both resulting in Lincoln writing the "Chronicles" (Elizabeth Ray Grigsby in Hobson, *Footprints*, 26–27), but that version sounds like a memory mixup. Still another version says the fight grew out of a disgreement between Lincoln and William Grigsby over ownership of a puppy, to be settled by outcome of the physical trial, with the fight leading to Lincoln's being snubbed at the Grigsby brothers' infare, then resulting in composition of the "Chronicles" (Beveridge, *Abraham*, 1:93 n. 4–94 n. 4). Such an argument between the two young men is plausible, but not the notion of Lincoln's agreeing to establish ownership of a puppy through a fight.

381. Nathaniel Grigsby to William H. Herndon, Oct. 25, 1865, H-W Papers (transcript available in Wilson and Davis, *Herndon's*, 140).

382. Cockrum, *Pioneer*, 506.

383. Abraham Lincoln to Andrew Johnston, Sept. 6, 1846 (transcript available in *CW* 1:384); Abraham Lincoln, "My Childhood-Home I See Again" (transcript available in *CW* 1:368–69). I have cast Lincoln's words in prose form, but he wrote them as verse. *See also* variant in Abraham Lincoln to Andrew Johnston, April 18, 1846 (transcript available in *CW* 1:378–79).

384. Abraham Lincoln, "The Maniac," 1846 (transcript available in *CW* 1:385–86). I have cast Lincoln's words in prose form, but he wrote them as verse.

385. Woods, *Two*, 248–49.

386. Barton, *Women*, 147; Barton, *Life*, 1:130; Herndon and Weik, *Herndon's Life of Lincoln*, 52; Joseph C. Richardson interview with William H. Herndon, ca. Sept. 14, 1865, H-W Papers (transcript available in Wilson and Davis, *Herndon's*, 119); Green Taylor interview with William H. Herndon, Sept. 16, 1865, H-W Papers (transcript available in Wilson and Davis, *Herndon's*, 129–30); Dennis Hanks interview with William H. Herndon, June 13, 1865, H-W Papers (transcript available in Wilson and Davis, *Herndon's*, 42); A. H. Chapman statement, ca. Sept. 8, 1865, H-W Papers (transcript available in Wilson and Davis, *Herndon's*, 100); Tarbell, *Early*, 61 caption, 83 caption; Tarbell, *In the Footsteps*, 134; Weik, *Real*, 25; Warren, "Lincoln the Clerk." Authorities conflict over whether Taylor's ferry operation crossed the Anderson River or the Ohio River, and his son said it crossed both. Because (as we shall see) a Kentucky outfit had a legal monopoly on Ohio River ferry traffic and was willing to enforce the monopoly in court, Taylor's operation seemingly would have been taking a chance if it crossed the Ohio. Weik says Taylor paid Lincoln 37 cents a day (Herndon and Weik, *Herndon's Life of Lincoln*, 52), a calculation perhaps including both wages and board.

387. Tarbell, *In the Footsteps*, 135.

388. Quoted by William D. Kelley in Rice, *Reminiscences*, 279–80. Variants of the story are in Conant, "Portrait," 514; Leonard Swett in Rice, *Reminiscences*, 457–58. A portion of the Kelley version not quoted here refers to Lincoln's building a flatboat, which he rowed to transport passengers midway across the river to a steamer, and a similar detail is in Conant. I believe those segments are garbled, as flatboats were not rowed, especially by one person. In my opinion, that glitch does not invalidate the Kelley quotation's thrust.

389. Barton, *Women*, 141–47; Beveridge, *Abraham*, 1:85; Townsend, *Lincoln the Litigant*, 36–38. Authorities conflict over whether Lincoln or the judge found the point differentiating between travel midway or all the way across the Ohio River. Barton, who is a knowledgeable authority, credits Lincoln, but in the cited account, he acknowledges that he has massaged the historical record to fill in some blanks. This Barton account also seems to be the basis for the Dill brothers' ambush story. As Barton claims to be drawing from local tradition, the story cannot be dismissed, but we don't know how much of the story comes from local tradition and how much from Barton's imagination.

390. Barton, *Life*, 1:132–33; Barton, *Women*, 147–48; Beveridge, *Abraham*, 1:85.

391. Anna O'Flynn in Ehrmann, *Missing*, 99–100; Green Taylor interview with William H. Herndon, Sept. 16, 1865, H-W Papers (transcript available in Wilson and Davis, *Herndon's*, 130).

392. Beveridge, *Abraham*, 1:84–85; Green Taylor interview with William H. Herndon, Sept. 16, 1865, H-W Papers (transcript available in Wilson and Davis, *Herndon's*, 129–30). Taylor's neighborhood was not the only place where Lincoln did pork cutting (Elizabeth Crawford to William H. Herndon, Sept. 7, 1865, H-W Papers (transcript available in Wilson and Davis, *Herndon's*, 335); John R. Dougherty interview with William H. Herndon, Sept. 17, 1865, H-W Papers (transcript available in Wilson and Davis, *Herndon's*, 133); John S. Houghland interview with William H. Herndon, Sept. 17, 1865, H-W Papers (transcript available in Wilson and Davis, *Herndon's*, 130)).

393. Bigelow, *Retrospections*, 12.

394. Eggleston, *First*, 54–55.

395. A. H. Chapman statement, ca. Sept. 8, 1865, H-W Papers (transcript available in Wilson and Davis, *Herndon's*, 100–102); Kempf, *Abraham*, 92; Townsend, *Lincoln and Liquor*, 21; Townsend, *Lincoln and the Bluegrass*, 124; Weik, *Real*, 25–26. Kempf says that Lincoln worked with Denny Hanks; the other sources say the companion was John D. Johnston.

396. Howells, *Recollections*, 139.

397. One story says eighteen-year-old Lincoln constructed a small boat to carry produce from the family farm to a nearby river trading post (Brooks, *Abraham*, 36, 38; Holland, *Life*, 33). Supposedly the farm barely produced enough for home consumption (*see* William H. Herndon to Ward Hill Lamon, March 6, 1870 (transcript available in Hertz, *Hidden*, 74); John Romine interview with William H. Herndon, Sept. 14, 1865, H-W Papers (transcript available in Wilson and Davis, *Herndon's*, 118), but Lincoln is quoted as saying that enough surplus for sale was raised at least once (quoted by William D. Kelley in Rice, *Reminiscences*, 279). Indeed, one relative declared that in 1820, the "farm was well stocked with hogs, horses, and cattle, and that year he [Tom] had raised a fine crop of wheat, corn, and vegetables," and spoke of Tom making more than one flatboat trip to sell surplus produce (A. H. Chapman statement, ca. Sept. 8, 1865, H-W Papers (transcript available in Wilson and Davis, *Herndon's*, 99–100)). As noted elsewhere in this chapter, Abe Lincoln at least once took wool to be carded, presumably from the farm's sheep. Another story says Abe raised a tobacco crop on someone else's land and paid for its shipment to Memphis by serving as a crew member on the boat (J. Edward Murr in Ehrmann, *Missing*, 86). I doubt that he had time to raise tobacco in addition to his other activities.

398. Anna Caroline Roby Gentry interview with William H. Herndon, Sept. 17, 1865, H-W Papers (transcript available in Wilson and Davis, *Herndon's*, 131); James Gentry Jr., cited in Warren, "Lincoln's Return"; Nathaniel Grigsby to William H. Herndon, Sept. 4, 1865, H-W Papers (transcript available in Wilson and Davis, *Herndon's*, 94); Nathaniel Grigsby interview with William H. Herndon, Sept. 12, 1865, H-W Papers (transcript available in Wilson and Davis, *Herndon's*, 114); John Romine interview with William H. Herndon, Sept. 14, 1865, H-W Papers (transcript available in Wilson and Davis, *Herndon's*, 118). Authorities are unclear about whether James Sr., or his son Allen hired Lincoln.

399. Abraham Lincoln, quoted by William D. Kelley in Rice, *Reminiscences*, 279. Kelley conflates the flatboat with a rowboat.

400. Abraham Lincoln, quoted by William D. Kelley in Rice, *Reminiscences*, 279.

401. David Turnham to William H. Herndon, Feb. 21, 1866, H-W Papers (transcript available in Wilson and Davis, *Herndon's*, 217).

402. Fordham, *Personal*, 195–96.

403. Woods in Thwaites 10:255, quoted in Townsend, *Lincoln and Liquor*, 22.

404. Bullard, "Abe," 3–4; Anna Caroline Roby Gentry interview with William H. Herndon, Sept. 17, 1865, H-W Papers (transcript available in Wilson and Davis, *Herndon's*, 131); Herndon and Weik, *Herndon's Life of Lincoln*, 54; Absolom Roby interview with William H. Herndon, Sept.

17, 1865, H-W Papers (transcript available in Wilson and Davis, *Herndon's*, 132); Warren, "Lincoln, Miss"; Warren, "Most." Credible authorities say the trip started in December, but I'm inclined to think a crew member's wife (and her father) had the correct memory. The date is unimportant to our story anyway.

405. Woods, *Two*, 252–53.
406. Charles Lyell quoted in Bullard, "Abe," 4.
407. Bullard, "Abe," 7.
408. Details of a leisurely flatboat trip from Peoria to New Orleans, with many trading stops, can be found in *Peoria Register and North-Western Gazetteer*, July 2, 1841.
409. Turpie, *Sketches*, 32.
410. Anna Caroline Roby Gentry interview with William H. Herndon, Sept. 17, 1865, H-W Papers (transcript available in Wilson and Davis, *Herndon's*, 131). *See also* William G. Greene to William H. Herndon, June 7, 1865, H-W Papers (transcript available in Wilson and Davis, *Herndon's*, 26); Herndon and Weik, *Herndon's Life of Lincoln*, 54.
411. John Romine intereview with William H. Herndon, Sept. 14, 1865, H-W Papers (transcript available in Wilson and Davis, *Herndon's*, 118). *See also* Leonard Swett recalling 1853 reminiscence by Lincoln, in Rice, *Reminiscences*, 462, bearing in mind that Swett confuses this trip with Lincoln's later New Orleans trip.
412. John R. Dougherty interview with William H. Herndon, Sept. 17, 1865, H-W Papers (transcript available in Wilson and Davis, *Herndon's*, 133).
413. Abraham Lincoln, autobiography for John L. Scripps, ca. June 1860 (transcript available in *CW* 4:62).
414. Herndon and Weik, *Herndon's Life of Lincoln*, 54.
415. Howells, *Life*, 22–23; Abraham Lincoln, autobiography for John L. Scripps, ca. June 1860 (transcript available in *CW* 4:62). River pirates perennially preyed on flatboat men; *see* an account in *Vicksburg Sentinel*, Nov. 13, 1839, clipped in *Galena North Western Gazette and Galena Advertiser*, Dec. 21, 1839 (interior date Dec. 17). Even steamboats weren't immune: "On the night of Friday the 26th ult. the steamboats *Winnebago*, *Otto*, and *Orion*, lying at the wharf in St. Louis, Mo. were boarded by a gang of thieves or robbers, and plundered" (*Vandalia Illinois Advocate and State Register*, May 4, 1833).
416. Bullard, "Abe," 5.
417. Quoted by Josiah Blackburn of the *London Free Press*, clipped in *New York Times*, Aug. 1, 1864, and *Sacramento Daily Union*, Aug. 23, 1864, as given in Segal, *Conversations*, 336 and slightly abridged in Fehrenbacher and Fehrenbacher, *Recollected*, 31.
418. John Baillie, quoted in Warren, "Lincoln in New Orleans."
419. Abraham Lincoln to Alexander Stephens, January 9, 1860, quoted in Warren, *Slavery*, unpaginated. Although not included in the *Collected Works*, the editors of that canon did not cite this letter as questionable either.
420. Turpie, *Sketches*, 33.
421. A friend of Lincoln's later said the two young men "disposed very successfully of their cargo" but gave no grounds for the statement (Arnold, *Life*, 26).
422. *Peoria Register and North-Western Gazetteer*, July 2, 1841.
423. Ford, *History*, 64–65.
424. *Galena North Western Gazette and Galena Advertiser*, May 6, 1837.
425. George H. Yeaman, cited in Warren, "Lincoln's Return." Possibly Lincoln referred to his 1831 trip.
426. Anna Caroline Roby Gentry interview with William H. Herndon, Sept. 17, 1865, H-W Papers (transcript available in Wilson and Davis, *Herndon's*, 131).
427. Howells, *Recollections*, 85.
428. Nicolay and Hay, *Abraham*, 1:44; William Wood interview with William H. Herndon, Sept. 15, 1865, H-W Papers (transcript available in Wilson and Davis, *Herndon's*, 124). "Uncle" here was a term of familiar respect to an elder, not an indication of genealogy.
429. Dennis Hanks, quoted in Atkinson, *Boyhood*, 39.

430. John R. Dougherty interview with William H. Herndon, Sept. 17, 1865, H-W Papers (transcript available in Wilson and Davis, *Herndon's*, 133); John S. Houghland interview with William H. Herndon, Sept. 17, 1865, H-W Papers (transcript available in Wilson and Davis, *Herndon's*, 130); Tarbell, *Early*, 79 caption; Francis Marion Van Natter, quoted in Houser, *Lincoln's Education*, 48; Warren, "Lincoln's Early," 624; Warren, "Early Newspapers"; J. W. Wartmann to William H. Herndon, June 8, 1865, H-W Papers (transcript available in Wilson and Davis, *Herndon's*, 29). Miers, *Lincoln*, 1829, says Lincoln worked at James Gentry's store, not that of Jones.

431. John R. Dougherty interview with William H. Herndon, Sept. 17, 1865, H-W Papers (transcript available in Wilson and Davis, *Herndon's*, 133).

432. Nathaniel Grigsby interview with William H. Herndon, Sept. 16, 1865, H-W Papers (transcript available in Wilson and Davis, *Herndon's*, 127); Dennis Hanks interview with William H. Herndon, Sept. 8, 1865, H-W Papers (transcript available in Wilson and Davis, *Herndon's*, 103).

433. A. H. Chapman statement, ca. Sept. 8, 1865, H-W Papers (transcript available in Wilson and Davis, *Herndon's*, 100).

434. Nathaniel Grigsby interview with William H. Herndon, Sept. 12, 1865, H-W Papers (transcript available in Wilson and Davis, *Herndon's*, 114).

435. Dennis Hanks interview with William H. Herndon, Sept. 8, 1865, H-W Papers (transcript available in Wilson and Davis, *Herndon's*, 103). John Hanks said, "Abe never was a Democrat: He was always a Whig—so was his father before him" (John Hanks interview with William H. Herndon, ca. 1865, H-W Papers (transcript available in Wilson and Davis, *Herndon's*, 457)), but this testimony should probably be read in the context of John's acquaintance with Lincoln in Illinois from 1830 forward, rather than as a commentary on the immediately preceding years in Indiana, when John (who was then residing in Illinois) probably had little or no knowledge of Lincoln's political views or their reported transformation. Denny Hanks also said that the transformation occurred in Illinois rather than Indiana (Dennis Hanks to William H. Herndon, March 12, 1866, H-W Papers (transcript available in Wilson and Davis, *Herndon's*, 229); Dennis Hanks to William H. Herndon, Sept. 10, 1866, H-W Papers (transcript available in Wilson and Davis, *Herndon's*, 337)), and David Turnham concurred in that chronology (David Turnham to William H. Herndon, Sept. 29, 1865, H-W Papers (transcript available in Wilson and Davis, *Herndon's*, 356); David Turnham to William H. Herndon, Oct. 19, 1866, H-W Papers (transcript available in Wilson and Davis, *Herndon's*, 376)). I'm inclined to think the change started in Indiana. Regardless, a change occurred in the late Indiana or early Illinois years.

436. Nathaniel Grigsby interview with William H. Herndon, Sept. 12, 1865, H-W Papers (transcript available in Wilson and Davis, *Herndon's*, 114).

437. Dennis Hanks interview with William H. Herndon, Sept. 8, 1865, H-W Papers (transcript available in Wilson and Davis, *Herndon's*, 105).

438. Elizabeth Crawford to William H. Herndon, Feb. 21, 1866, H-W Papers (transcript available in Wilson and Davis, *Herndon's*, 216). John Palmer sang a tougher version (*Personal*, 7) in the 1824 campaign:

> Ladies, you are much mistaken,
> And I can tell you why,
> For General Jackson will be elected,
> And Clay will surely die!

439. Dennis Hanks to William H. Herndon, March 7, 1866, H-W Papers (transcript available in Wilson and Davis, *Herndon's*, 226); Barton, *Life*, 1:138; Paul H. Verduin, "Appendix: Brief Outline of the Joseph Hanks Family," in Wilson and Davis, *Herndon's*, 781; Warren, "Other."

440. Dennis Hanks to William H. Herndon, March 7, 1866, H-W Papers (transcript available in Wilson and Davis, *Herndon's*, 226). *See also* Coleman, *Abraham*, 3; Tarbell, *In the Footsteps*, 154.

441. William H. Herndon, 1881 speech in *History of Sangamon*, 211–12.

442. Dennis Hanks, quoted in Atkinson, *Boyhood*, 41; John Hanks interview with William H. Herndon, ca. 1865, H-W Papers (transcript available in Wilson and Davis, *Herndon's*, 456); Warren, *Lincoln's Youth*, 204.

443. Simeon Francis to Allen Francis, 1831, Simeon Francis Papers.
444. Dennis Hanks to William H. Herndon, March 7, 1866, H-W Papers (transcript available in Wilson and Davis, *Herndon's*, 226); Warren, *Lincoln's Youth*, 204.
445. Dennis Hanks, quoted in Atkinson, *Boyhood*, 41.
446. Coleman, *Abraham*, 2–4.
447. Tarbell, *In the Footsteps*, 83.
448. Ehrmann, *Missing*, 144; J. W. Wartmann to William H. Herndon, July 21, 1865, H-W Papers (transcript available in Wilson and Davis, *Herndon's*, 79).
449. Beveridge, *Abraham*, 1:95; Tarbell, *In the Footsteps*, 154–55; Warren, *Lincoln's Youth*, 204.
450. Tarbell, *In the Footsteps*, 155; David Turnham interview with William H. Herndon, Sept. 15, 1865, H-W Papers (transcript available in Wilson and Davis, *Herndon's*, 122); Warren, *Lincoln's Youth*, 205.
451. Nathaniel Grigsby, Silas Richardson, Nancy Richardson, and John Romine interviews with William H. Herndon, Sept. 14, 1865, H-W Papers (transcript available in Wilson and Davis, *Herndon's*, 116); Hobson, *Footprints*, 33; William Wood interview with William H. Herndon, Sept. 15, 1865, H-W Papers (transcript available in Wilson and Davis, *Herndon's*, 124).
452. William Wood interview with William H. Herndon, Sept. 15, 1865, H-W Papers (transcript available in Wilson and Davis, *Herndon's*, 124). *See also* Nathaniel Grigsby, Silas Richardson, Nancy Richardson, and John Romine interviews with William H. Herndon, Sept. 14, 1865, H-W Papers (transcript available in Wilson and Davis, *Herndon's*, 116).
453. David Turnham interview with William H. Herndon, Sept. 15, 1865, H-W Papers (transcript available in Wilson and Davis, *Herndon's*, 121).
454. Barton, *Life*, 1:128; Barton, *Women*, 109–10; Warren, *Youth*, 207. There were two Nancy Grigsbys, Aaron's mother and sister, who married Elizabeth Crawford's son, but the difference in ages means that the church records referred to the mother.
455. Allen Brooner, quoted in Tarbell, *Early*, 75 caption.
456. Hobson, *Footprints*, 32.
457. Warren, *Lincoln's Youth*, 207.
458. J. Edward Murr in Ehrmann, *Missing*, 93–94; Hobson, *Footprints*, 32–34; Tarbell, *Early*, 79 caption, 99. In a cabinet meeting, Lincoln spoke of this peddling operation. His details are probably unreliable, as he was telling the story as an autobiographical yarn to illustrate a point under discussion, but the fact of his peddling seems attested by him (*"Abe" Lincoln's Yarns and Stories*, 342–43, cited in Zall, *Abe*, 124).
459. Warren, *Lincoln's Youth*, 205–6.
460. J. Edward Murr in Ehrmann, *Missing*, 93.
461. Browne, *Every-Day*, 80; J. Edward Murr in Ehrmann, *Missing*, 93–94.
462. Charles B. Strozier and Stanley H. Cath, "Lincoln and the Fathers: Reflections on Idealization," in Cath, Gurwitt, and Gunsberg, *Fathers*, 292.
463. Joseph Gillespie to William H. Herndon, Jan. 31, 1866, H-W Papers (transcript available in Wilson and Davis, *Herndon's*, 181).
464. N. W. Miner, "Personal Recollections of Abraham Lincoln," p. 12, N. W. Miner Small Collection 1052.
465. John L. Scripps to William H. Herndon, June 24, 1865, H-W Papers (transcript available in Wilson and Davis, *Herndon's*, 57).
466. Leonard Swett in Rice, *Reminiscences*, 457.
467. Swett quoted in Tarbell, *Early*, 96.
468. Nathaniel Grigsby to William H. Herndon, Jan. 21, 1866, H-W Papers (transcript available in Wilson and Davis, *Herndon's*, 169); Dennis Hanks interview with William H. Herndon, Sept. 8, 1865, H-W Papers (transcript available in Wilson and Davis, *Herndon's*, 105); Joseph C. Richardson statement, ca. 1865, H-W Papers (transcript available in Wilson and Davis, *Herndon's*, 474); David Turnham interview with William H. Herndon, Sept. 15, 1865, H-W Papers

(transcript available in Wilson and Davis, *Herndon's*, 121); David Turnham to William H. Herndon, Dec. 17, 1866, H-W Papers (transcript available in Wilson and Davis, *Herndon's*, 518).

469. Harriet A. Chapman to William H. Herndon, Dec. 10, 1866, H-W Papers (transcript available in Wilson and Davis, *Herndon's*, 512).

470. Dennis Hanks to William H. Herndon, March 22, 1866, H-W Papers (transcript available in Wilson and Davis, *Herndon's*, 236).

471. Abraham Lincoln, "My Childhood-Home I See Again," 1846 (transcript available in *CW* 1:367–68). *See also* variant in Abraham Lincoln to Andrew Johnston, April 18, 1846 (transcript available in *CW* 1:378–79).

Chapter 3. ILLINOIS

1. *Galena Advertiser*, Feb. 1, 1830.
2. *Galena Advertiser*, March 1, 1830.
3. *Galena Miners' Journal*, March 13, 1830.
4. A. H. Chapman statement, ca. Sept. 8, 1865, H-W Papers (transcript available in Wilson and Davis, *Herndon's*, 103).
5. Abraham Lincoln quoted in Peter Smith to J. Warren Keifer, July 17, 1860, printed in Smith, *When*, 49 and also in Warren, "The Lincolns Crossing."
6. Browne, *Abraham*, 1:124–25; Coleman, *Abraham*, 6; Jesse K. Dubois interview with John Nicolay, July 4, 1875 (transcript available in Burlingame, *Oral*, 29–30). The version in Browne has Lincoln giving incorrect dating, but I believe such an error by the relater does not negate the anecdote's credibility. Even Nicolay and Hay (*Abraham*, 1:45), whose general accuracy cannot be surpassed, possibly err in dating the trip (depending on how one interprets the words "streams swollen by the February thaws").
7. *SJ*, March 9, 1833.
8. A standing committee of the jocular statehouse Lobby was named "on the improvement made in the road through Purgatory Swamp, and to report what further improvements are necessary" to make it passable (*Daily Chicago American*, Dec. 31, 1839).
9. Dickens, *American*, 281–82.
10. *Quincy Whig* clipped in *Shawneetown Illinois Republican*, Feb. 5, 1842.
11. Jesse K. Dubois interview with William H. Herndon, Dec. 1, 1888, H-W Papers (transcript available in Wilson and Davis, *Herndon's*, 718–19); William H. Herndon to Jesse Weik, Dec. 1, 1888 (transcript available in Hertz, *Hidden*, 227–28); Johnson, *Illinois*, 109; Abraham Lincoln, autobiography for John L. Scripps, ca. June 1860 (transcript available in *CW* 4:63); Miers, *Lincoln*, 1830; Abraham Lincoln quoted in Peter Smith to J. Warren Keifer, July 17, 1860, printed in Smith, *When*, 49, and also in Warren, "The Lincolns Crossing." The Smith book version says "fice dog," and Warren's version says "fist dog." Regardless of which quotation is correct, the two terms are variants referring to a small, feisty mutt.
12. Davis, "Lincoln," 83; Dennis Hanks, quoted in Atkinson, *Boyhood*, 41–42; John Hanks interview with William H. Herndon, ca. 1865, H-W Papers (transcript available in Wilson and Davis, *Herndon's*, 456); Hobson, *Footprints*, 34; Miers, *Lincoln*, 1830; Whitney, *Life*, 465–66.
13. Stuart, *Three*, 2:360.
14. A. H. Chapman statement, ca. Sept. 8, 1865, H-W Papers (transcript available in Wilson and Davis, *Herndon's*, 100); Dennis Hanks interview with William H. Herndon, June 13, 1865, H-W Papers (transcript available in Wilson and Davis, *Herndon's*, 42–43); Dennis Hanks, quoted in Atkinson, *Boyhood*, 42; John Hanks interview with William H. Herndon, ca. 1865, H-W Papers (transcript available in Wilson and Davis, *Herndon's*, 456); John Hanks interview with William H. Herndon, June 13, 1865, H-W Papers (transcript available in Wilson and Davis, *Herndon's*, 43); John Hanks, in *The Rail Splitter* (Cincinnati), Aug. 15, 1860, quoted in Temple, "Lincoln's Fence Rails," 33; John Hanks in Weik, *Real*, 276; Davis, "Lincoln," 83; Lansden, "Abraham," 57; Nicolay and Hay, *Abraham*, 1:46.

15. Drake, *Pioneer*, 69–70.
16. Oliver, *Eight*, 239.
17. Joseph Suppiger, dateline Highland, Illinois, March 19, 1832, "Letters," 435–36.
18. Davis, "Hanks," 114–16; John Hanks interview with William H. Herndon, ca. 1865, H-W Papers (transcript available in Wilson and Davis, *Herndon's*, 456); Abraham Lincoln to John Hanks, Aug. 24, 1860 (transcript available in *CW* 4:100); Tarbell, *In the Footsteps*, 159.
19. George Close interview with James Quay Howard (transcript available in Basler, "James," 391); Davis, "Lincoln," 91–92; Howells, *Life*, 24 n.; Temple, "Lincoln's Fence Rails," 33.
20. Davis, "Lincoln," 101; Dennis Hanks, quoted in Atkinson, *Boyhood*, 42; Tarbell, *In the Footsteps*, 160; Abraham Lincoln, autobiography for John L. Scripps, ca. June 1860 (transcript available in *CW* 4:63).
21. *History of Sangamon*, 66.
22. Fordham, *Personal*, 230.
23. Schoolcraft, *Travels*, 301.
24. Petition to Macon County Commissioners' Court, May 26, 1830 (transcript in *CW* 1:2); Wilson, *Uncollected*, 1:29–30.
25. Ford, *History*, 68.
26. Barton, *Women*, 157–59; John G. Bergen to David B. Ayres, Jan. 1, 1830, in Van Fenstermaker, "Description," 137; George Close interview with James Quay Howard (transcript available in Basler, "James," 391); Davis, "Lincoln," 97; Sarah Powers Durfee in Johns, *Personal*, 61; William Greene to William H. Herndon, May 29, 1865, H-W Papers (transcript available in Wilson and Davis, *Herndon's*, 11); Dennis Hanks, quoted in Atkinson, *Boyhood*, 42; John Hanks interview with William H. Herndon, ca. 1865, H-W Papers (transcript available in Wilson and Davis, *Herndon's*, 456); Howells, *Life*, xv, 28 (1938 ed.). I have doubts about the Durfee account, though it is based on conversation with a purported eyewitness to the speech. Details conflict with the recollection of eyewitness John Hanks, which I do consider reliable, and Slicky Bill Greene speaks of hearing Lincoln talk about the experience. In addition to the George Close interview above, mention of his rail-splitting collaboration with Lincoln is in Stevens, *Reporter's*, 11.
27. Linder, *Reminiscences*, 62; Snyder, *Adam*, 172.
28. Letter to editor, *Galena Miners' Journal*, Feb. 20, 1830.
29. Davis, "Lincoln," 99.
30. Levering, *Historic*, 145.
31. Appraisal of an Estray, Dec. 16, 1830 (transcript in *CW* 1:3); Warren, "A. Lincoln—Appraiser"; Wilson, *Uncollected*, 1:32.
32. Chandler, "New," 507; John Hanks interview with William H. Herndon, ca. 1865, H-W Papers (transcript available in Wilson and Davis, *Herndon's*, 456); Abraham Lincoln, quoted in Volk, "Lincoln," 247.
33. *Vandalia Illinois Advocate and State Register*, Dec. 7, 1833. For another example, *see Quincy Whig*, March 28, 1840.
34. Davis, "Lincoln," 103–4; Miers, *Lincoln*, Feb. 1831; Robert Warnick in Barton, *Women*, 163, 165–66. The account of the accident given by Barton in *Women* and in *Life* (1:143–44) is clearly incorrect—Lincoln was not paddling a canoe across a frozen stream—but I accept the Robert Warnick material as authentic and as being quoted accurately enough.
35. Angle, *"Here,"* 33.
36. Angle, *"Here,"* 33; Davis, "Lincoln," 102; Duis, *Good*, 9, 179; Nicolay and Hay, *Abraham*, 1:47; Onstot, *Pioneers*, 352; Power, *History*, 62–63; James McGrady Rutledge, quoted in Pond, "Memoirs," 82; Stringer, *History*, 89.
37. James McGrady Rutledge, quoted in Pond, "Memoirs," 82–83.
38. Duis, *Good*, 463.
39. Duis, *Good*, 9; Onstot, *Pioneers*, 352; Power, *History*, 64.

40. Onstot, *Pioneers*, 135. *See also* Duis, *Good*, 9.
41. Power, *History*, 64.
42. Brooks, *Abraham*, 47; Nicolay and Hay, *Abraham*, 1:48.
43. Stringer, *History*, 90.
44. John G. Bergen quoted in Angle, *"Here,"* 34.
45. Angle, *"Here,"* 34.
46. *Galena Miners' Journal*, Dec. 4, 1830; Stringer, *History*, 89.
47. Davis, "Lincoln," 106.
48. Brooks, *Abraham*, 47. *See also* Nicolay and Hay, *Abraham*, 1:48.
49. Duis, *Good*, 179.
50. Barton, *Life*, 1:146; John Hanks interview with William H. Herndon, ca. 1865, H-W Papers (transcript available in Wilson and Davis, *Herndon's*, 456); Townsend, *Lincoln and the Bluegrass*, 34.
51. James Hall to William H. Herndon, Sept. 17, 1875, H-W Papers (transcript available in Wilson and Davis, *Herndon's*, 580); Townsend, *Lincoln and the Bluegrass*, 32, 150–51, 153, 184.
52. Townsend, *Lincoln and the Bluegrass*, 31.
53. Townsend, *Lincoln and the Bluegrass*, 31–32.
54. Townsend, *Lincoln and the Bluegrass*, 36.
55. Townsend, *Lincoln and the Bluegrass*, 32.
56. James Short to William H. Herndon, July 7, 1865, H-W Papers (transcript available in Wilson and Davis, *Herndon's*, 73).
57. William Greene interview with William H. Herndon, May 30, 1865, H-W Papers (transcript available in Wilson and Davis, *Herndon's*, 18).
58. Mentor Graham interview with William H. Herndon, May 29, 1865, H-W Papers (transcript available in Wilson and Davis, *Herndon's*, 9).
59. Hardin Bale interview with William H. Herndon, H-W Papers (transcript available in Wilson and Davis, *Herndon's*, 13).
60. John Purcell in *Vincennes Western Sun and General Advertiser*, Dec. 27, 1834, quoted in Wilson, *Honor's*, 336 n. 15.
61. Gerhard, *Illinois*, 67. *See also* Krenkel, *Illinois*, 10; Scheiber, *Ohio*, 9–10.
62. Duis, *Good*, 128.
63. Barton, *Life*, 1:147, 147 n.; Brooks, *Abraham*, 47–48; Davis, "Lincoln," 106; John Hanks interview with William H. Herndon, ca. 1865, H-W Papers (transcript available in Wilson and Davis, *Herndon's*, 456); John Hanks interview with William H. Herndon, June 13, 1865, H-W Papers (transcript available in Wilson and Davis, *Herndon's*, 44); Abraham Lincoln, autobiography for John L. Scripps, ca. June 1860 (transcript available in *CW* 4:63); Townsend, *Lincoln and the Bluegrass*, 34. I don't accept all that Davis says, but I accept that the $60 was combined wages for all three men. An account of a similar flatboat trip ten years later said ordinary deckhands received $15 a month (*Peoria Register and North-Western Gazetteer*, July 2, 1841).
64. Duis, *Good*, 10; Wesley Elliott interview with William H. Herndon, ca. 1865, H-W Papers (transcript available in Wilson and Davis, *Herndon's*, 447–48); John Hanks interview with William H. Herndon, ca. 1865, H-W Papers (transcript available in Wilson and Davis, *Herndon's*, 456); Abraham Lincoln, autobiography for John L. Scripps, ca. June 1860 (transcript available in *CW* 4:63). Some authorities deny that John Johnston accompanied the other two men in the canoe. Lincoln says the three "purchased a large canoe and came down the Sangamon River in it." Hanks says Lincoln accompanied him in the canoe, but does not say Johnston was absent. One participant says all three men rode together; another participant does not deny it.
65. John Hanks interview with William H. Herndon, ca. 1865, H-W Papers (transcript available in Wilson and Davis, *Herndon's*, 457); Oliver, *Eight*, 241. A clever variation stayed within the law: A lumber operator could make the minimum down payment on a tract, strip it of trees, and then make no more payments (Dick, *Lure*, 11). Title would be forfeited for nonpayment, but the goal

of harvesting the land's timber would have been achieved. *See also Beardstown Gazette*, Jan. 28, 1852; *Chicago American*, Feb. 25, May 27, 1837; Faragher, *Sugar*, 132–33; *Vandalia Illinois State Register and People's Advocate*, March 24, 1837.

66. David Newsom and Samuel Huston, *SJ*, March 23, 1833.

67. *Vandalia Illinois Intelligencer*, March 20, 1830. Even stealing privately owned timber was prevalent enough to attract attention from churches as "open violation of the law of God, truly dishonoring God, impairing the moral sense of communities, and hindering the progress of the Gospel . . . not only inexcusable but as truly sinful as any of the acts of trespass" (Proceedings Congregational Association of Illinois, semi-annual meeting, April 16, 1840, in *Quincy Whig*, June 6, 1840).

68. John Roll quoted in Turner, "John," 104; Caleb Carman interview with William H. Herndon, Oct. 12, 1866, H-W Papers (transcript available in Wilson and Davis, *Herndon's*, 373); John Hanks interview with William H. Herndon, ca. 1865, H-W Papers (transcript available in Wilson and Davis, *Herndon's*, 457); Daniel Burner quoted in Temple, "Lincoln and the Burners," 67; Reynolds, *My Own Times*, 82. *See also* Lynn McNulty Greene to William H. Herndon, July 30, 1865, H-W Papers (transcript available in Wilson and Davis, *Herndon's*, 81).

69. John McNamar to William H. Herndon, Nov. 25, 1866, H-W Papers (transcript available in Wilson and Davis, *Herndon's*, 420).

70. Daniel Burner in Temple, "Lincoln and the Burners," 67; Caleb Carman interview with William H. Herndon, Oct. 12, 1866, H-W Papers (transcript available in Wilson and Davis, *Herndon's*, 373 (possibly including comments by Jacob Carman)); Caleb Carman to William H. Herndon, Nov. 30, 1866, H-W Papers (transcript available in Wilson and Davis, *Herndon's*, 429); Caleb Carman interview with William H. Herndon, March 1887, H-W Papers (transcript available in Wilson and Davis, *Herndon's*, 607); William Greene to William H. Herndon, May 29, 1865, H-W Papers (transcript available in Wilson and Davis, *Herndon's*, 11); John Hanks interview with William H. Herndon, ca. 1865, H-W Papers (transcript available in Wilson and Davis, *Herndon's*, 456–57); John Hanks interview with William H. Herndon, June 13, 1865, H-W Papers (transcript available in Wilson and Davis, *Herndon's*, 44); Howells, *Life*, 26–27 (including marginal notes by Abraham Lincoln); Abraham Lincoln, autobiography for John L. Scripps, ca. June 1860 (transcript available in *CW* 4:63); Roll, "Sangamo," 154–58; John Roll in Turner, "John," 104–105; Erastus Wright in "Lincoln in 1831," 9. *See also* Erastus Wright to J. G. Holland, July 10, 1865 (transcript available in Guelzo, "Holland's," 40).

John Hanks is cited as saying the pay for building the boat was $18 a month, but the interviewer's notes may have confused this with the pay rate for taking the boat to New Orleans (Erastus Wright to Josiah G. Holland (enclosure), July 3, 1865 (transcript available in Guelzo, "Holland's," 35)).

71. "Petition to Sangamon County Commissioners' Court for Appointment of a Constable," ca. March 11, 1831 (transcript available in *CW* 1:3; Wilson, *Uncollected*, 1:34).

72. Petition to county commissioners concerning Benjamin Elmore, Feb. 9, 1833 (transcript available in *CW* 1:17–18).

73. Coleman Smoot to William H. Herndon, May 7, 1866, H-W Papers (transcript available in Wilson and Davis, *Herndon's*, 254); Townsend, *Lincoln and the Bluegrass*, 36.

74. George Harrison to William H. Herndon, ca. summer 1866, H-W Papers (transcript available in Wilson and Davis, *Herndon's*, 330).

75. Caleb Carman in Oldroyd, *Lincoln*, 518. Carman's testimony is unreliable on several points, but if he erred about the cargo's size and price, such error is harmless.

76. John Bennett in Oldroyd, *Lincoln*, 559; William Butler interview with John Nicolay, June 13, 1875 (transcript available in Burlingame, *Oral*, 19); Mentor Graham interview with James Quay Howard (transcript available in Basler, "James," 389); William Greene interview with William H. Herndon, May 30, 1865, H-W Papers (transcript available in Wilson and Davis, *Herndon's*, 17); William Greene interview with James Quay Howard (transcript available in

Basler, "James," 397); John Hanks interview with William H. Herndon, ca. 1865, H-W Papers (transcript available in Wilson and Davis, *Herndon's*, 457); John Hanks interview with William H. Herndon, June 13, 1865, H-W Papers (transcript available in Wilson and Davis, *Herndon's*, 44); John Rowan Herndon to William H. Herndon, June 11, 1865, H-W Papers (transcript available in Wilson and Davis, *Herndon's*, 34); Howells, *Life*, 27 (including marginal notation by Abraham Lincoln); Hurie, "Early," 595; Kempf, *Abraham*, 101; Abraham Lincoln, "Communication to the People of Sangamo County," March 9, 1832 (transcript available in *CW* 1:6); *Lincoln and New Salem*, 18–19; John Roll in Tarbell, *Early*, 106; John Roll in Turner, "John," 104; Tarbell, *Early*, 108–9; Tarbell, *In the Footsteps*, 166–67; Thomas, *Lincoln's*, 41; Townsend, *Lincoln and the Bluegrass*, 35; Richard Yates, speech June 7, 1860, quoted in Scripps, *Life*, 31.

Eyewitness Slicky Bill Greene says no hole was bored in the bow, that Offutt proposed it but Lincoln rejected the idea (William Greene interview with William H. Herndon, May 30, 1865, H-W Papers (transcript available in Wilson and Davis, *Herndon's*, 21), but Greene is also credited with saying Lincoln did bore a hole (William Greene in Browne, *Every-Day*, 92; Holland, *Life*, 61). The attribution in Browne and Holland, however, seems to be from the Yates speech. Yates didn't directly state that Greene said Lincoln bored a hole.

77. "Clark v. Lake," file L03023 in Benner and Davis, *Law*.
78. Barton, *Life*, 1:159; Hurie, "Early," 595; *Lincoln and New Salem*, 11; Sale, "Old," 1057; Tarbell, *Early*, 103 caption.
79. Abraham Lincoln, "Communication to the People of Sangamo County," March 9, 1832 (transcript available in *CW* 1:6).
80. Lynn McNulty Greene to William H. Herndon, July 30, 1865, H-W Papers (transcript available in Wilson and Davis, *Herndon's*, 80); William Greene to William H. Herndon, May 29, 1865, H-W Papers (transcript available in Wilson and Davis, *Herndon's*, 11–12).
81. Oliver, "Hog," 345. *See also* Oliver, *Eight*, 80.
82. Howells, *Recollections*, 64–65.
83. Duis, *Good*, 424.
84. Bidwell and Falconer, *History*, 167; John Hanks interview with William H. Herndon, ca. 1865, H-W Papers (transcript available in Wilson and Davis, *Herndon's*, 457); John Hanks interview with William H. Herndon, June 13, 1865, H-W Papers (transcript available in Wilson and Davis, *Herndon's*, 44); Abraham Lincoln, autobiography for John L. Scripps, ca. June 1860 (transcript available in *CW* 4:63–64); Coleman Smoot to William H. Herndon, May 7, 1866, H-W Papers (transcript available in Wilson and Davis, *Herndon's*, 254). *See also* Herndon and Weik, *Herndon's Life of Lincoln*, 63; Holland, *Life*, 42; *Lincoln and New Salem*, 19; Stevens, *Reporter's*, 5–6.
85. Jason Duncan to William H. Herndon, ca. 1866, H-W Papers (transcript available in Wilson and Davis, *Herndon's*, 542).
86. Schoolcraft, *Travels*, 300–301, 305.
87. John Hanks interview with William H. Herndon, ca. 1865, H-W Papers (transcript available in Wilson and Davis, *Herndon's*, 457).
88. Duis, *Good*, 511.
89. Duis, *Good*, 511.
90. Abraham Lincoln, autobiography for John L. Scripps, ca. June 1860 (transcript available in *CW* 4:64).
91. John Hanks interview with William H. Herndon, ca. 1865, H-W Papers (transcript available in Wilson and Davis, *Herndon's*, 457–58); John Hanks interview with William H. Herndon, June 13, 1865, H-W Papers (transcript available in Wilson and Davis, *Herndon's*, 44). *See also* John Hanks to Jesse Weik, April 19, 1888, H-W Papers (transcript available in Wilson and Davis, *Herndon's*, 656).
92. For example, Lincoln indicated that all three young men took a canoe from Decatur, but Hanks maintaned silence about whether Johnston was aboard (John Hanks interview with William H.

Herndon, ca. 1865, H-W Papers (transcript available in Wilson and Davis, *Herndon's*, 456); Abraham Lincoln, autobiography for John L. Scripps, ca. June 1860 (transcript available in *CW* 4:63)). In the same autobiography, Lincoln said, speaking of himself in the third person, "Returning from the [Indian war] campaign, and encouraged by his great popularity among his immediate neighbors, he, the same year [1832], ran for the legislature" (transcript available in *CW* 4:64). Here the implied chronology is that he decided to run after coming back from the war, but in fact he had announced his candidacy before the war. Admittedly he may have referred to *resuming* his campaign rather than *starting* it, but an ordinary interpretation of the language is that he decided to run after the war. One would think he would vividly remember whether he became a candidate before or after a war—just as vividly as remembering whether John Hanks left the flatboat party in St. Louis on the way to New Orleans or on the way back. A mistake in one memory suggests the possibility of mistake in the other.

93. Stuart, *Three*, 2:198.

94. Simon Cameron to Sheldon Potter, Dec. 20, 1831, quoted in Warren, "Lincoln in New Orleans" and in Warren, *Lincoln's Youth*, 182–83.

95. Stuart, *Three*, 2:202.

96. A. W. Snyder to Hiram Snyder, March 29, 1839, J. F. Snyder Papers.

97. Copy of Leonard Swett (dateline Bloomington, describing recent trip to New Orleans) to Sister, Aug. 11, 1848, Leonard Swett Papers.

98. Stuart, *Three*, 2:201–202.

99. G. M., "South Carolina," *New England Magazine*, reprinted in *Illinois Monthly Magazine* (Nov. 1831): 66–77. I resist temptation to present eyewitness accounts refuting G. M.'s observations and shall simply offer comments made by an observer in the 1830s: "The great shrewdness and tact exhibited by slaves in *keeping themselves out of difficulty*, when close questioned by strangers as to their treatment, cannot fail to strike every accurate observer. . . . If these northern visitors derived their information that the slaves are *not* cruelly treated from *their own observation*, it amounts to this, *they did not see* cruelties inflicted on the slaves" (*American Slavery*, 128–29).

100. *Portland Advertiser*, clipped in *SJ*, June 1, 1833.

101. *Vandalia Illinois Intelligencer*, May 8, 1830.

102. Bullard, "Abe," 11.

103. A. W. Snyder to Hiram Snyder, March 29, 1839, J. F. Snyder Papers.

104. John Hanks interview with William H. Herndon, ca. 1865, H-W Papers (transcript available in Wilson and Davis, *Herndon's*, 457).

105. Herndon and Weik, *Herndon's Life of Lincoln*, 64. *See also* William H. Herndon to Isaac Arnold, Oct. 21, 1882 (transcript available in Arnold, *Life*, 31 n. 1). "Trio" here would surely be the hired hands, excluding their boss, Offutt. If so, however, this was an error by Weik, as Hanks seemingly said he wasn't present at this slave sale. William Jayne, who was well acquainted with Lincoln, gave an account similar to the one in Herndon and Weik, *Herndon's Life of Lincoln* (Jayne, *Abraham*, 20–21), but Jayne's account may well be based on that source rather than on conversation with Lincoln. An eyewitness described an 1842 New Orleans slave sale sounding much like the one that Lincoln witnessed, though not as raunchy: "She was very sprucely dressed in a dark bombazine gown, which set off her waist and shoulders to great advantage, while the apron in front, whiter than the new fallen snow, greatly heightened her appearance" (*Peoria Register and North-Western Gazetteer*, Sept. 16, 1842).

106. John Hanks quoted in Browne, *Abraham*, 1:140.

107. John Hanks to Jesse Weik, June 12, 1887, H-W Papers (transcript available in Wilson and Davis, *Herndon's*, 615).

108. Current, *Lincoln Nobody*, 217; Paul Angle in Herndon and Weik, *Herndon's Life of Lincoln*, 64 n. 1; Warren, "Most"; Warren, *Slavery*.

109. *Vandalia Illinois Intelligencer*, Feb. 19, 1831.

110. "An Act respecting free Negroes and Mulattoes, Servants, and Slaves," Illinois, *Revised Laws* (1833), "Negroes, &c.," 463–64 and (1839), "Negroes, &c.," 506–7. In force January 17, 1829. In addition to paying informants, the law also gave rewards to apprehenders.

111. "An Act to amend an act, entitled 'An act respecting free Negroes, Mulattoes, Servants, and Slaves,' approved January 17, 1829," Illinois, *Revised Laws* (1839), "Negroes, &c.," 506. In force February 1, 1831.

112. Koerner, *Memoirs*, 1:296.

113. Correspondent to Brother, July 6, 1831, Simeon Francis Papers. The letter writer may have been Simeon Francis, who would become a close political ally of Lincoln in Springfield.

114. John Hanks interview with William H. Herndon, ca. 1865, H-W Papers (transcript available in Wilson and Davis, *Herndon's*, 458); John Hanks interview with William H. Herndon, June 13, 1865, H-W Papers (transcript available in Wilson and Davis, *Herndon's*, 44); John G. Nicolay in Wilson, *Intimate*, 411.

115. Duis, *Good*, 10–11.

116. Stephen T. Logan interview with John Nicolay, July 6, 1875, Abraham Lincoln Papers, LOC 1959 microfilm, 97:43645ff (transcript available in Burlingame, *Oral*, 34).

117. Coleman, *Abraham*, 19–20; Howells, *Life*, 27; Abraham Lincoln, autobiography for John L. Scripps, ca. June 1860 (transcript available in *CW* 4:63–64); Nicolay and Hay, *Abraham*, 1:190.

118. Abraham Lincoln, autobiography for John L. Scripps, ca. June 1860, H-W Papers (transcript available in Wilson and Davis, *Herndon's*, 64).

119. Robert B. Rutledge to William H. Herndon, Dec. 4, 1866, H-W Papers (transcript available in Wilson and Davis, *Herndon's*, 497).

120. James Short to William H. Herndon, July 7, 1865, H-W Papers (transcript available in Wilson and Davis, *Herndon's*, 72).

121. Royal Clary interview with William H. Herndon, ca. Oct. 1866, H-W Papers (transcript available in Wilson and Davis, *Herndon's*, 370).

122. Abraham Lincoln, autobiography for John L. Scripps, ca. June 1860 (transcript available in *CW* 4:64).

123. Robert B. Rutledge to William H. Herndon, ca. Nov. 1866, H-W Papers (transcript available in Wilson and Davis, *Herndon's*, 382); Tarbell, *In the Footsteps*, 172.

124. Store license fee receipt, July 7, 1831, Denton Offutt, 86–46–7 (filed with 85–51–7), ALPL; Tarbell, *Life*, 1:72.

125. Mrs. Brown in Holland, *Life*, 40–41; William Butler interview with John Nicolay, June 13, 1875 (transcript available in Burlingame, *Oral*, 20); Albert Hale to Josiah G. Holland, June 22, 1865 (transcript available in Guelzo, "Holland's," 30–31). The quotation is from the Hale version. Slicky Bill Greene, who was in a position to know, said that Lincoln never worked on a Sangamon County farm (William Greene to William H. Herndon, June 11, 1865, H-W Papers (transcript available in Wilson and Davis, *Herndon's*, 33)). I am inclined to think Slicky Bill was mistaken on this point; he was occasionally mistaken on others. Lincoln had to make a living somehow after coming to New Salem in the summer of 1831, and farmwork sounds plausible. The chronology of his life would have allowed him to make a Galena trip in February 1832 to market the crop. Mr. and Mrs. Brown and Holland all must be wrong in their dating of this farmwork. The Browns dated it from a time when Lincoln was still in Indiana; seemingly Butler and Holland dated it when Lincoln was in Macon County. Such dating errors, however, do not impair the story's plausibility. Indeed, were it not for Slicky Bill's protest, the story would probably be accepted without question. Leonard Swett reports that Lincoln said in 1853 that he had done hired farm labor in Sangamon County (Leonard Swett in Rice, *Reminiscences*, 460), and Butler's testimony agrees. Mrs. Brown said the farm's owner was a Mr. Taylor, but her memory may be mistaken on that point; presumably Butler was correct in saying he owned the farm.

126. Quoted from *Northwestern Christian Advocate* in Chapman, *Latest*, 528.

127. Warren, "Rev. Jesse."

128. Bray, "Cartwright," 113.
129. Nicolay and Hay, *Abraham*, 1:101–2; Bray, "Cartwright," 112–13; William Butler interview with John Nicolay, June 13, 1875 (transcript available in Burlingame, *Oral*, 20). I say Butler was a skeptical listener to Reverend Cartwright not because of direct testimony about this occasion, but because of Butler's general political outlook.
130. Mentor Graham interview with William H. Herndon, May 29, 1865, H-W Papers (transcript available in Wilson and Davis, *Herndon's*, 8–9); "Lincoln's First Vote"; Thomas, "Lincoln: Voter" (Sept. 1934), 4. Lincoln served as clerk in the September 30, 1832, constable election (election return, Sept. 20, 1832 (transcript available in *CW* 1:13)); perhaps that is how the tradition originated about his clerkship at the summer 1831 election.
131. *Belleville Advocate*, June 6, 1840; Beveridge, *Abraham*, 1:137 n. 2; "Candidates for Congress"; James M. Duncan, "Address to the People of Illinois," June 3, 1830, in *Vandalia Illinois Intelligencer*, June 12, 1830; Bowling Green, *Courier Extra*, July 26, 1830, Broadside Collection, ALPL (transcript available in *Galena Trail and Coach Road Newsletter* (Dec. 30, 2004): 6); "Lincoln's First Vote"; Linder, *Reminiscences*, 376; Tarbell, *Early*, 127 n.; Alexander Trent to editor, July 3, 1830, in *Vandalia Illinois Intelligencer*, July 17, 1830. The William Green referred to by Trent may have been the father of Slicky Bill Greene (spellings of some names routinely varied). I'm unaware of any connection with the murderer Green referred to in the passage about Turney's oratory; the exasperated judge in that murder case was John Reynolds. In his remarks, Reynolds also made clear that he wanted Green's friends to understand that the death sentence was required by the law, not by the judge; in other words, they should not seek out Reynolds for revenge (Ford, *History*, 54; Koerner, *Memoirs*, 1:336; Snyder, *Adam*, 310). Turney was apparently brother to Hopkins Lacy Turney, a member of the Tennessee legislature in 1831 and later a U.S. Representative and Senator (*Madisonian*, Feb. 5, 1839, clipped in *Quincy Whig*, Feb. 23, 1839; *Illinois Journal*, Aug. 30, Sept. 6, 1848).
132. "Candidates for Constable"; Poll book New Salem precinct, Aug. 1, 1831, photo in Tarbell, *Life*, 1:opposite 70; Tarbell, *Early*, 127 n.; Thomas, "Lincoln: Voter" (Sept. 1934), 4. Voters could make two choices in the magistrate election, and Lincoln also voted for Edmund Greer.
133. J. Rowan Herndon in Findley, *A. Lincoln*, 3. *See also* Murr, "Lincoln," 344. Lincoln would tell a story on different occasions, tweaked for a particular audience. Row Herndon remembered also hearing this one in a political speech "in reply to some of the opposite candidates who had represented themselves as something extra" (J. Rowan Herndon to William H. Herndon, July 3, 1865, H-W Papers (transcript available in Wilson and Davis, *Herndon's*, 69)), the story's point thereby shifting from simple ridicule of a minister to a more general ridicule of pomposity. Lincoln's deft ability to adapt seemingly numberless stories to a current situation made him a feared opponent in debate. The preacher and lizard motif wasn't unique to Lincoln: *See* "Parson Bullin's Lizards" in George W. Harris, *Sut Lovingood*.
134. License fee receipt, July 7, 1831, Denton Offutt, 86–46–7 (filed with 85–51–7), ALPL; Royal Clary interview with James Quay Howard (transcript available in Basler, "James," 394); Henry McHenry interview with William H. Herndon, May 29, 1865, H-W Papers (transcript available in Wilson and Davis, *Herndon's*, 14). According to Tarbell, *Early*, 118–19, and Tarbell, *Life*, 1:71–72, Lincoln traveled to Beardstown and found Offutt's store goods there. Walking back to New Salem, Lincoln crossed paths with two wagoners heading toward Beardstown to pick up the goods. Characteristically, Offutt had made an assumption without factual backing, the assumption being that Lincoln would wait around in Beardstown and come back with the merchandise. Offutt therefore had not bothered to give the teamsters any written authorization to receive the items. Lincoln remedied that on the spot, writing out an authorization as Offutt's agent. They went on their way, and eventually the store's stock arrived in New Salem. The Beardstown trip recounted by Tarbell occurred after November 1832, but the teamster encounter may have occurred on a different trip. I wonder whether a Beardstown warehouse would have accepted Lincoln's authorization, but perhaps he or the teamsters were known to proper persons in Beardstown. The story is plausible but questionable.

135. Miers, *Lincoln*, Sept. 13, 1831; Wilson, *Uncollected*, 1:547, 2:147. Offutt borrowed from politician William Porter, who assigned the note to William Brown. More than one William Brown was a politician, leaving uncertainty about who held Offutt's note (and of course, note holder Brown may have been a nonpolitician).

136. Barton, *Women*, 169; Maltby, *Life*, 26; Miers, *Lincoln*, Sept. 2, 1831. The deed was from William Batterton, likely kin to the Batterton cited by Alexander Trent as authority for the story of Bowling Green's agreement with Governor Reynolds. Barton is knowledgeable but tends to fill in blanks by using his imagination, and Maltby's memory is obviously flawed; I am cautious in evaluating how far to trust what they say.

137. Howells, *Life*, 28; Howells, *Life*, xv (1938 ed.). Charles Maltby claimed to have been assistant clerk at $15 a month, with chief clerk Lincoln getting $25 a month and board (Maltby, *Life*, 26). That pay rate is not impossible but is inconsistent with Howells, who says Lincoln received a straight $15. Maltby may have been on the scene, and indeed, Jimmy Short remembered him clerking at the Offutt store (James Short to William H. Herndon, July 7, 1865, H-W Papers (transcript available in Wilson and Davis, *Herndon's*, 74)), but see the previous note. He was right, apparently, about Lincoln boarding with Offutt (Robert B. Rutledge to William H. Herndon, ca. Nov. 1866, H-W Papers (transcript available in Wilson and Davis, *Herndon's*, 382)). The Howells account was reviewed for accuracy by Lincoln, who made no change to the $15 pay claim, but he may have viewed the point as too small for comment. I find Howells to be the more plausible account.

138. William Greene interview with William H. Herndon, May 30, 1865, H-W Papers (transcript available in Wilson and Davis, *Herndon's*, 17–18).

139. Henry McHenry interview with William H. Herndon, May 29, 1865, H-W Papers (transcript available in Wilson and Davis, *Herndon's*, 14).

140. Mentor Graham interview with William H. Herndon, May 29, 1865, H-W Papers (transcript available in Wilson and Davis, *Herndon's*, 9).

141. Hobson, *Footprints*, 35; Nicolay and Hay, *Abraham*, 1:83; Tarbell, *Early*, 123; Tarbell, *Life*, 1:75–76; Thomas, *Lincoln's*, 95–96. These authorities are reliable, but Basler, *Lincoln Legend*, 123–24, found that the tea and change incidents lack "even the usual authority of some old friend of New Salem." Even so, such stories illustrate what people believed about Lincoln.

142. Onstot, *Pioneers*, 85–86. *See also Lincoln and New Salem*, 56; Nicolay and Hay, *Abraham*, 1:83; Tarbell, *Life*, 1:75. Confusion exists about whether the incident occurred during Lincoln's service for Offutt or while Lincoln ran his own store, but I accept the Offutt designation.

143. Townsend, *Lincoln and the Bluegrass*, 38.

144. H. B. Fearon, *Sketches of America* (London: Longman, Hurst, Rees, Orme, and Browne, 1818), p. 201, quoted in Bidwell and Falconer, *History*, 174.

145. Mentor Graham interview with William H. Herndon, May 29, 1865, H-W Papers (transcript available in Wilson and Davis, *Herndon's*, 9).

146. Jason Duncan to William H. Herndon, ca. 1866, H-W Papers (transcript available in Wilson and Davis, *Herndon's*, 539). *See also* William Greene interview with William H. Herndon, May 30, 1865, H-W Papers (transcript available in Wilson and Davis, *Herndon's*, 17); Howells, *Life*, 28; Hurie, "Early," 596; John McNamar to William H. Herndon, June 4, 1866, H-W Papers (transcript available in Wilson and Davis, *Herndon's*, 259); Sale, "Old," 1057; Tarbell, *Early*, 103 caption; Erastus Wright to Josiah G. Holland, July 10, 1865 (transcript available in Guelzo, "Holland's," 38–39).

147. Robert B. Rutledge to William H. Herndon, ca. Nov. 1866, H-W Papers (transcript available in Wilson and Davis, *Herndon's*, 382).

148. List in *CW* 8:430–32; Wilson, *Uncollected*, 1:35.

149. Denton Offutt, quoted in William Greene interview with William H. Herndon, May 30, 1865, H-W Papers (transcript available in Wilson and Davis, *Herndon's*, 18). *See also* Maltby, *Life*, 28; L. M. Smith interview with James Quay Howard (transcript available in Basler, "James," 390).

150. Nicolay and Hay, *Abraham*, 1:79–80.

151. James Short to William H. Herndon, July 7, 1865, H-W Papers (transcript available in Wilson and Davis, *Herndon's*, 73).

152. John Potter in Stevens, *Reporter's*, 7.

153. Levering, *Historic*, 185. Levering was talking about Indiana toughs bearing generic similarity to the Clary's Grove Boys.

154. Mr. Goff in Onstot, *Pioneers*, 83 ("Goff" appears to be a misidentification of Slicky Bill Greene). *See also* Daniel Burner in Temple, "Lincoln and the Burners," 68; Royal Clary interview with William H. Herndon, ca. Oct. 1866, H-W Papers (transcript available in Wilson and Davis, *Herndon's*, 371); Henry Hohimer interview with William H. Herndon, March 7, 1887, H-W Papers (transcript available in Wilson and Davis, *Herndon's*, 604); Nicolay and Hay, *Abraham*, 1:79; James Short to William H. Herndon, July 7, 1865, H-W Papers (transcript available in Wilson and Davis, *Herndon's*, 74). A similar story with different identification of the barrel's passenger is told in the Johnson Gaines Greene interview with William H. Herndon, Oct. 5, 1866, H-W Papers (transcript available in Wilson and Davis, *Herndon's*, 366). I don't believe versions that have Lincoln stuffing the victim in a barrel (James Gourley interview with William H. Herndon, ca. 1865, H-W Papers (transcript available in Wilson and Davis, *Herndon's*, 451); Stevens, *Reporter's*, 5). Such activity wasn't limited to New Salem (Reynolds, *My Own Times*, 69).

155. Daniel Burner in Temple, "Lincoln and the Burners," 68.

156. James Short to William H. Herndon, July 7, 1865, H-W Papers (transcript available in Wilson and Davis, *Herndon's*, 74). *See also* William Greene to William H. Herndon, Nov. 27, 1865, H-W Papers (transcript available in Wilson and Davis, *Herndon's*, 141).

157. James Taylor interview with William H. Herndon, ca. 1865, H-W Papers (transcript available in Wilson and Davis, *Herndon's*, 482).

158. William Greene interview with James Quay Howard (transcript available in Basler, "James," 399).

159. Ross, *Lincoln's*, 39.

160. Abraham Lincoln quoted in Brooks, "Lincoln," 886; Abraham Lincoln quoted in Brooks, *Washington*, 258–59; Abraham Lincoln quoted in Frank Moore, *Anecdotes, Poetry and Incidents of the War* (1866), as given in Zall, *Abe*, 63. By using ellipses, I have combined the Brooks and Moore versions; this is a nonstandard use of ellipses, but it maintains the story's flow. Variants of the story are in Abraham Lincoln, quoted in Browne, *Every-Day*, 616–17; Abraham Lincoln, quoted in Hertz, *Abraham*, 1:295; Owen T. Reeves, "Personal Recollections and Estimates of Lincoln," in Angle, ed., *Abraham Lincoln by Some Men*, 23–24.

161. Chandler, "New," 510; Onstot, *Pioneers*, 53. A variant gander pulling, with the bird tied to a post, is described in *American Turf Register*, clipped in *Galena North Western Gazette and Galena Advertiser*, Aug. 20, 1836.

162. Pythagoras to editor, *Quincy Whig*, Jan. 18, 1840. Given Lincoln's earlier protests against cruelty toward animals and later examples of going out of his way to be kind to animals, including birds, his participation in gander pullings and cockfights is curious. Most folks viewed animals as tools, however, rather than living beings with rights. From the *Sangamo Journal*, March 15, 1832: "To prevent rabbits from injuring trees.—In the fall, before the rabbits commence their work, kill some of them and tear them in pieces, and rub them on the trees. This will prevent the rabbits from eating them for that winter. One rabbit will be sufficient for thirty or forty trees."

163. Barton, *Soul*, 46; *Lincoln and New Salem*, 70; Arthur Ernest Morgan, "New Light on Lincoln's Early Years," in Wilson, *Lincoln*, 52.

164. Miller, *History*, 711; Robert B. Rutledge to William H. Herndon, ca. Nov. 1866, H-W Papers (transcript available in Wilson and Davis, *Herndon's*, 386).

165. Reynolds, *My Own Times*, 84.

166. Quoted in Henry McHenry interview with William H. Herndon, May 29, 1865, H-W Papers (transcript available in Wilson and Davis, *Herndon's*, 14).

167. Speed, *Reminiscences*, 20 (also Speed, quoted in Wilson, *Intimate*, 17). Miller, *History*, 711, concurs. I find those authorities persuasive for the nickname's origin. Beveridge (*Abraham*, 1:114, citing *Lincoln and New Salem*, 35–36) and Tarbell (*Early*, 123, and *Life*, 1:76) credit Lincoln's honesty as an Offutt store clerk. New Salem–era acquaintance John Bennett said Lincoln simply earned the nickname then and afterward through general honesty (quoted in Browne, *Every-Day*, 149). Lincoln's later associate Paul Selby said the nickname was prevalent by 1854 (quoted in "Glimpses of Lincoln in the Fifties," as given in Wilson, *Lincoln*, 162).

168. Robert B. Rutledge to William H. Herndon, ca. Nov. 1866, H-W Papers (transcript available in Wilson and Davis, *Herndon's*, 387).

169. Daniel Burner, in Temple, "Lincoln and the Burners," 68.

170. *Lincoln and New Salem*, 26; Mr. Goff in Onstot, *Pioneers*, 84 ("Goff" appears to be a misidentification of Slicky Bill Greene); William Greene to William H. Herndon, June 11, 1865, H-W Papers (transcript available in Wilson and Davis, *Herndon's*, 33, 33 n. 2). *See also* William Greene interview with James Quay Howard (transcript available in Basler, "James," 399); Stevens, *Black*, 283. The Mr. Estep who was fleecing Slicky Bill may or may not have been a local real estate owner, but using a trick repeatedly to win bets against the same victim rates the perpetrator as a confidence man. Daniel Burner claimed he watched Lincoln win the bet and that Lincoln won by lifting the barrel with his hands (Daniel Burner, in Temple, "Lincoln and the Burners," 68). Burner here said Lincoln won the bet *from* Greene rather than *for* Greene, but I consider that a misspeaking.

171. J. Rowan Herndon to William H. Herndon, May 28, 1865, H-W Papers (transcript available in Wilson and Davis, *Herndon's*, 7).

172. James Short to William H. Herndon, July 7, 1865, H-W Papers (transcript available in Wilson and Davis, *Herndon's*, 73).

173. Hardin Bale interview with William H. Herndon, May 29, 1865, H-W Papers (transcript available in Wilson and Davis, *Herndon's*, 13). *See also* Hardin Bale interview with William H. Herndon, 1866, H-W Papers (transcript available in Wilson and Davis, *Herndon's*, 528).

174. William Greene interview with William H. Herndon, May 30, 1865, H-W Papers (transcript available in Wilson and Davis, *Herndon's*, 19).

175. Probably Josiah Blackburn of the *London Free Press*, reprinted in *Sacramento Daily Union*, Aug. 23, 1864, quoted in Segal, *Conversations*, 335.

176. James M. Stradling to John W. Gilbert, March 6, 1863, quoted in Segal, *Conversations*, 249.

177. Carpenter, *Six*, 287–89. *See also* pp. 113–14.

178. Chapman, *Latest*, 46.

179. Lynn McNulty Greene to William H. Herndon, July 30, 1865, H-W Papers (transcript available in Wilson and Davis, *Herndon's*, 80); John M. Rutledge to William H. Herndon, Nov. 18, 1866, H-W Papers (transcript available in Wilson and Davis, *Herndon's*, 402); Robert B. Rutledge to William H. Herndon, ca. Nov. 1866, H-W Papers (transcript available in Wilson and Davis, *Herndon's*, 386); James Short to William H. Herndon, July 7, 1865, H-W Papers (transcript available in Wilson and Davis, *Herndon's*, 73).

180. Nathaniel Branson to William H. Herndon, Aug. 3, 1865, H-W Papers (transcript available in Wilson and Davis, *Herndon's*, 91); Royal Clary interview with William H. Herndon, ca. Oct. 1866, H-W Papers (transcript available in Wilson and Davis, *Herndon's*, 370); James Gourley interview with William H. Herndon, H-W Papers (transcript available in Wilson and Davis, *Herndon's*, 451); William Miller(?) statement for William H. Herndon, ca. Sept. 1866, H-W Papers (transcript available in Wilson and Davis, *Herndon's*, 363).

181. Abner Y. Ellis statement to William H. Herndon, ca. Jan. 23, 1866, H-W Papers (transcript available in Wilson and Davis, *Herndon's*, 174). I suspect the name "Royal Armstrong" may be misspoken and that Jack's companion was Royal Clary.

182. James Short to William H. Herndon, July 7, 1865, H-W Papers (transcript available in Wilson and Davis, *Herndon's*, 73).

183. Robert B. Rutledge to William H. Herndon, ca. Nov. 1866, H-W Papers (transcript available in Wilson and Davis, *Herndon's*, 386).

184. James Short to William H. Herndon, July 7, 1865, H-W Papers (transcript available in Wilson and Davis, *Herndon's*, 73).

185. Henry McHenry interview with William H. Herndon, Oct. 10, 1866, H-W Papers (transcript available in Wilson and Davis, *Herndon's*, 369).

186. James Gourley interview with William H. Herndon, ca. 1865, H-W Papers (transcript available in Wilson and Davis, *Herndon's*, 451).

187. Wilson, *Honor's*, 35–36. Wilson's chapter on the wrestling match is unsurpassed, meriting perusal by anyone who seeks more information on the topic. *See also* Hannah Armstrong interview with William H. Herndon, 1866, H-W Papers (transcript available in Wilson and Davis, *Herndon's*, 526); Henry Clark interview with William H. Herndon, 1866, H-W Papers (transcript available in Wilson and Davis, *Herndon's*, 528); Royal Clary interview with James Quay Howard (transcript available in Basler, "James," 394); Lynn McNulty Greene to William H. Herndon, July 30, 1865, H-W Papers (transcript available in Wilson and Davis, *Herndon's*, 80); William Greene interview with James Quay Howard (transcript available in Basler, "James," 399); Howells, *Life*, xxii, 34–35; Howells, *Life* (1938 ed.), xvi; John M. Rutledge to William H. Herndon, Nov. 18, 1866, H-W Papers (transcript available in Wilson and Davis, *Herndon's*, 402); James Short to William H. Herndon, July 7, 1865, H-W Papers (transcript available in Wilson and Davis, *Herndon's*, 73–74).

188. Robert B. Rutledge to William H. Herndon, ca. Nov. 1866, H-W Papers (transcript available in Wilson and Davis, *Herndon's*, 386).

189. Lynn McNulty Greene to William H. Herndon, July 30, 1865, H-W Papers (transcript available in Wilson and Davis, *Herndon's*, 80); Volney Hickox, *Illinois State Journal*, Oct. 15, 1874, quoted in Wilson, *Honor's*, 33.

190. John Potter in Stevens, *Reporter's*, 7.

191. Lynn McNulty Greene to William H. Herndon, July 30, 1865, H-W Papers (transcript available in Wilson and Davis, *Herndon's*, 80); *Lincoln and New Salem*, 26; Ross, *Lincoln's*, 39; Robert B. Rutledge to William H. Herndon, ca. Nov. 1866, H-W Papers (transcript available in Wilson and Davis, *Herndon's*, 386); Wilson, *Honor's*, 37.

192. Jason Duncan to William H. Herndon, ca. 1866, H-W Papers (transcript available in Wilson and Davis, *Herndon's*, 539).

193. Enclosure with Abner Ellis to William H. Herndon, Jan. 23, 1866, H-W Papers (transcript available in Wilson and Davis, *Herndon's*, 170).

194. Nicolay and Hay, *Abraham*, 1:81.

195. Document drawn for James Eastep, Nov. 12, 1831 (transcript available in *CW* 1:3–4).

196. Bill of sale drawn for John Ferguson, Jan. 25, 1832 (transcript available in *CW* 1:4); file N04998 in Benner and Davis, *Law.*

197. Onstot, *Pioneers*, 153.

198. Onstot, *Pioneers*, 46, 114; Thomas, *Lincoln's*, 26.

199. Daniel Burner in Temple, "Lincoln and the Burners," 69; Mentor Graham interview with William H. Herndon, May 29, 1865, H-W Papers (transcript available in Wilson and Davis, *Herndon's*, 10).

200. Caleb Carman interview with William H. Herndon, Oct. 12, 1866, H-W Papers (transcript available in Wilson and Davis, *Herndon's*, 374); Caleb Carman to William H. Herndon, Nov. 30, 1866, H-W Papers (transcript available in Wilson and Davis, *Herndon's*, 430).

201. Jason Duncan to William H. Herndon, ca. Nov. 1866, H-W Papers (transcript available in Wilson and Davis, *Herndon's*, 540).

202. William G. Greene interview with William H. Herndon, May 30, 1865, H-W Papers (transcript available in Wilson and Davis, *Herndon's*, 20).

203. Hill, *Lincoln*, 57.
204. Chandler, "New," 514; William Greene to William H. Herndon, May 29, 1865, H-W Papers (transcript available in Wilson and Davis, *Herndon's*, 12); William Greene to William H. Herndon, May 30, 1865, H-W Papers (transcript available in Wilson and Davis, *Herndon's*, 18). Chandler said Lincoln and Slicky Bill studied grammar together, but Slicky Bill said Lincoln studied it on his own, though Slicky Bill acknowledged the possibility that Lincoln might have asked other people occasional questions. Jason Duncan, below, states that he was one such person, and Slicky Bill's brother Nult makes the same claim. Long afterward, at a White House visit, Lincoln embarrassed Greene by introducing the man as his grammar teacher, Greene denying that he merited such credit (*Lincoln and New Salem*, 31–32).
205. Mentor Graham interview with William H. Herndon, May 29, 1865, H-W Papers (transcript available in Wilson and Davis, *Herndon's*, 10); Howells, *Life* (1938 ed.), xv, 29; Thomas, *Lincoln's*, 48.
206. Mentor Graham interview with William H. Herndon, May 29, 1865, H-W Papers (transcript available in Wilson and Davis, *Herndon's*, 10); Lynn McNulty Greene to William H. Herndon, July 30, 1865, H-W Papers (transcript available in Wilson and Davis, *Herndon's*, 80); Lynn McNulty Greene interview with James Quay Howard (transcript available in Basler, "James," 393).
207. Maltby, *Life*, 27, 31. *See also* statement by Daniel Burner in Temple, "Lincoln and the Burners," 67, and Temple commentary on 70–71 n. 29.
208. Jason Duncan to William H. Herndon, ca. 1866, H-W Papers (transcript available in Wilson and Davis, *Herndon's*, 539).
209. Bestor, Mearns, and Daniels, *Three*, 57; William G. Greene interview with James Quay Howard (transcript available in Basler, "James," 398); Holland, *Life*, 46.
210. Maltby, *Life*, 31.
211. Mentor Graham interview with William H. Herndon, May 29, 1865, H-W Papers (transcript available in Wilson and Davis, *Herndon's*, 10). Graham implies the conversation was in 1833, but if such an exchange occurred, it couldn't have been that late, as Lincoln had begun his study of the topic much earlier. Nicolay and Hay (*Abraham*, 1:84) date the conversation as during Lincoln's clerkship at the Offutt store. I don't address the question of how much Graham ever taught Lincoln about anything.
212. Wilson, *Honor's*, 63.
213. Maltby, *Life*, 28.
214. Arnold, *Life*, 33.
215. Lynn McNulty Greene interview with James Quay Howard (transcript available in Basler, "James," 393).
216. Orville H. Browning interview with John Nicolay, June 17, 1875 (transcript available in Burlingame, *Oral*, 6–7).
217. Caleb Carman in Oldroyd, *Lincoln*, 519.
218. Chandler, "New," 513; Donald, *Lincoln*, 41; John Rowan Herndon to William H. Herndon, Aug. 16, 1865, H-W Papers (transcript available in Wilson and Davis, *Herndon's*, 91); Simon, *Lincoln's*, 5; Walsh, *Shadows*, 161 n. 99; Strozier, *Lincoln's*, 240 n. 2; Wolf, *Almost*, 41.
219. William McNeely in Oldroyd, *Lincoln*, 393.
220. Robert B. Rutledge to William H. Herndon, Nov. 30, 1866, H-W Papers (transcript available in Wilson and Davis, *Herndon's*, 426). *See also* Robert B. Rutledge to William H. Herndon, ca. Nov. 1866, H-W Papers (transcript available in Wilson and Davis, *Herndon's*, 384).
221. Mentor Graham interview with William H. Herndon, May 29, 1865, H-W Papers (transcript available in Wilson and Davis, *Herndon's*, 9); Mentor Graham to William H. Herndon, July 15, 1865, H-W Papers (transcript available in Wilson and Davis, *Herndon's*, 76); Maltby, *Life*, 27. "The first book I ever saw in Lincoln's hand was Blackstone, in 1832" (Isaac Cogdal interview with William H. Herndon, ca. 1865, H-W Papers (transcript available in Wilson and Davis, *Herndon's*, 440)). Row Herndon remembered Lincoln reading statutes and books on contracts as well,

but the dating of that memory is uncertain (John Rowan Herndon to William H. Herndon, Aug. 16, 1865, H-W Papers (transcript available in Wilson and Davis, *Herndon's*, 91)). At some point in the New Salem years, Lincoln acquired his own copy of Blackstone, but the manner and time of acquisition are disputed (Arnold, *Life*, 40; Barton, *Life*, 1:194; Bestor, Mearns, and Daniels, *Three*, 60, citing Mearns, *Lincoln*, 1:158; Bestor, Mearns, and Daniels, *Three*, 61, quoting Allan Jaspar Conant, "My Acquaintance with Abraham Lincoln," in Authors Club, *Liber Scriptorum: The First Book of the Authors Club* (New York: The Author's Club, 1893), 172; Conant, "Portrait," 514 (Conant's version critiqued in Fehrenbacher and Fehrenbacher, *Recollected*); Jason Duncan to William H. Herndon, ca. 1866, H-W Papers (transcript available in Wilson and Davis, *Herndon's*, 540); Lynn McNulty Greene to William H. Herndon, July 30, 1865, H-W Papers (transcript available in Wilson and Davis, *Herndon's*, 81); Hapgood, *Abraham*, 36–37; Howells, *Life* (1938 ed.), xvii, 31; *Lincoln and New Salem*, 54; Peterson, *Lincoln*, 92).

222. Hardin Bale interview with William H. Herndon, May 29, 1865, H-W Papers (transcript available in Wilson and Davis, *Herndon's*, 13).

223. Maltby, *Life*, 27.

224. Robert B. Rutledge to William H. Herndon, Dec. 4, 1866, H-W Papers (transcript available in Wilson and Davis, *Herndon's*, 497).

225. Unidentified "credible witness" quoted in Beveridge, *Abraham*, 1:134. The source is perhaps Mentor Graham; compare, "I have known him down here in Menard [to] study for hours the best way of any of three to express an idea" (Mentor Graham quoted by William H. Herndon in Hertz, *Hidden*, 132).

226. Caleb Carman to William H. Herndon, Nov. 30, 1866, H-W Papers (transcript available in Wilson and Davis, *Herndon's*, 430).

227. Maltby, *Life*, 28.

228. Mentor Graham to William H. Herndon, July 15, 1865, H-W Papers (transcript available in Wilson and Davis, *Herndon's*, 76).

229. Dennis Hanks quoted in Browne, *Abraham*, 1:174.

230. John Allen interview with James Quay Howard (transcript available in Basler, "James," 388); Chandler, "New," 523; Maltby, *Life*, 28; John M. Rutledge to William H. Herndon, Nov. 18, 1866, H-W Papers (transcript available in Wilson and Davis, *Herndon's*, 402); Robert B. Rutledge to William H. Herndon, ca. Nov. 1866, H-W Papers (transcript available in Wilson and Davis, *Herndon's*, 384). Two knowledgeable persons say that no such club existed (William G. Greene to William H. Herndon, Dec. 3, 1865, H-W Papers (transcript available in Wilson and Davis, *Herndon's*, 142), and George U. Miles to William H. Herndon, Dec. 8, 1865, H-W Papers (transcript available in Wilson and Davis, *Herndon's*, 143)), but I think they are mistaken.

231. Jason Duncan to William H. Herndon, ca. 1866, H-W Papers (transcript available in Wilson and Davis, *Herndon's*, 539).

232. Daniel Burner in Temple, "Lincoln and the Burners," 68.

233. Robert B. Rutledge to William H. Herndon, ca. Nov. 1866, H-W Papers (transcript available in Wilson and Davis, *Herndon's*, 384–85).

234. Dennis Hanks, quoted in Atkinson, *Boyhood*, 40.

235. Maltby, *Life*, 32.

236. Pond, "New Salem Community Activities," 90.

237. Wilson, *Honor's*, 70–71.

238. *SJ*, Dec. 21, 1833.

239. Maltby, *Life*, 32–33.

240. Wilson, *Honor's*, 71. *See also* Basler, *Touchstone*, 170; the 1837 journal of Rock Creek debating society reproduced in Bone, "Rock," 63–76; Pond, "New Salem Community Activities," 84–91; Strozier, *Lincoln's*, 240 n. 1.

241. John Allen interview with James Quay Howard (transcript available in Basler, "James," 388); Lynn McNulty Greene interview with James Quay Howard (transcript available in Basler, "James," 393).

Chapter 4. POLITICS OF 1832

1. Robert B. Rutledge to William H. Herndon, ca. Nov. 1866, H-W Papers (transcript available in Wilson and Davis, *Herndon's*, 385).
2. I say this from Butler's language: "When we first ran Lincoln for the legislature" (William Butler interview with John Nicolay (transcript available in Burlingame, *Oral*, 19)).
3. John Rowan Herndon to William H. Herndon, May 28, 1865, H-W Papers (transcript available in Wilson and Davis, *Herndon's*, 6). Row Herndon incorrectly dated the calls for Lincoln to run as midsummer rather than the previous winter, but Row said he was more certain about *what* happened than *when* (p. 8). The May 28 account has errors and must be used cautiously.
4. John T. Stuart interview with John Nicolay, June 23, 1875 (transcript available in Burlingame, *Oral*, 10).
5. Letter to editor, *Galena Miners' Journal*, Feb. 20, 1830. This analysis, of which the quoted material is but a small portion, is so similar to the one in Ford, *History*, 56–58, as to make me wonder whether Ford might be the letter writer. *See also* the description in McConnel, *Western*, 373–75, which includes the tactic of preventing an opponent's supporters from voting.
6. Robert B. Rutledge to William H. Herndon, ca. Nov. 1866, H-W Papers (transcript available in Wilson and Davis, *Herndon's*, 385).
7. *SJ*, Jan. 19, 1832.
8. *SJ*, Feb. 2, 1832.
9. *Cincinnati Daily Gazette*, Jan. 19, 1832, clipped in *SJ*, Feb. 16, 1832.
10. Vincent Bogue in *SJ*, Jan. 26, 1832.
11. Angle, *"Here,"* 36. Rorabaugh, *Alcoholic*, 83, offers an early-nineteenth-century comparison of passenger rates for steamboat (2 cents per mile) and stagecoach service (23 cents per mile).
12. *SJ*, Jan. 26, 1832.
13. *SJ*, Feb. 9, 16, 1832.
14. *SJ*, March 8, 1832.
15. *SJ*, March 29, 1832; July 12, 1832.
16. Maltby, *Life*, 29; *SJ*, March 8, 1832.
17. *Edwardsville Illinois Advocate*, March 23, 1832.
18. *SJ*, March 29, 1832.
19. D. in *SJ*, July 12, 1832. In speaking of necessary boat design for the Sangamon, the observer clearly had the sidewheeler *Talisman*'s experience in mind.
20. John Rowan Herndon to William H. Herndon, June 11, 1865, H-W Papers (transcript available in Wilson and Davis, *Herndon's*, 34); Wilson, *Uncollected*, 1:47; interview with Mrs. Bergen in Roberts, "'We,'" 23. Row Herndon's phraseology can be interpreted as saying Lincoln helped guide the craft, rather than serving as the upstream pilot.
21. Maltby, *Life*, 29.
22. Onstot, *Pioneers*, 158. Onstot here confuses trips made by the *Talisman* and the *Utility* but captures the enthusiasm created by the *Talisman*.
23. Herndon and Weik, *Herndon's Life of Lincoln*, 72–73.
24. Miller, *History*, 249–50; Onstot, *Pioneers*, 222.
25. Herndon and Weik, *Herndon's Life of Lincoln*, 73.
26. Pratt, "Lincoln Pilots," 325–26. For more on trip, *see* John Rowan Herndon to William H. Herndon, June 11, 1865, H-W Papers (transcript available in Wilson and Davis, *Herndon's*, 34); Maltby, *Life*, 29.
27. *SJ*, March 29, 1832.
28. William Cullen Bryant, quoted in Tarbell, *Early*, 157; Josiah Francis to Charles Francis, May 4, 1832, Simeon Francis Papers, Small Collection 525.
29. *SJ*, April 26, 1832.
30. H. E. Dummer interview with William H. Herndon, ca. 1865, H-W Papers (transcript available in Wilson and Davis, *Herndon's*, 442).
31. *St. Louis Missouri Republican*, April 3, 1832, quoted in Pratt, "Lincoln Pilots," 327.

32. Quoted in Herndon and Weik, *Herndon's Life of Lincoln*, 74.

33. Interview with Mrs. Bergan in Roberts, "'We,'" 22–23.

34. John Lightfoot interview with William H. Herndon, Sept. 13, 1887, H-W Papers (transcript available in Wilson and Davis, *Herndon's*, 639).

35. H. E. Dummer interview with William H. Herndon, ca. 1865, H-W Papers (transcript available in Wilson and Davis, *Herndon's*, 442).

36. *SJ*, April 26, 1832.

37. John Rowan Herndon to William H. Herndon, June 11, 1865, H-W Papers (transcript available in Wilson and Davis, *Herndon's*, 34); Herndon and Weik, *Herndon's Life of Lincoln*, 75; Stephen T. Logan interview with John Nicolay, July 6, 1875, Abraham Lincoln Papers, LOC 1959 microfilm, 97:43645ff (transcript available in Burlingame, *Oral*, 34, and in "Stephen T. Logan," 1); Maltby, *Life*, 29; Power, *History*, 43; Sheahan, *Life*, 12.

38. Herndon and Weik, *Herndon's Life of Lincoln*, 75; *Lincoln and New Salem*, 36.

39. John Rowan Herndon to William H. Herndon, June 11, 1865, H-W Papers (transcript available in Wilson and Davis, *Herndon's*, 34).

40. Maltby, *Life*, 29–30.

41. Hapgood, *Abraham*, 31; John Rowan Herndon to William H. Herndon, June 11, 1865, H-W Papers (transcript available in Wilson and Davis, *Herndon's*, 34); Pratt, "Lincoln Pilots," 328. See below, however, the contemporary statement by George Forquer about the pilot, which raises question about Row Herndon's (and thereby Lincoln's) piloting role. Note, too, silence in Lincoln's campaign platform about any involvement with the *Talisman*, though he readily refers to his flatboating experience.

42. *St. Louis Times*, clipped in *SJ*, May 3, 1832.

43. Mitchell, *Illinois*, 36, 104.

44. Onstot, *Pioneers*, 222–23. *See also* p. 158, which, however, mixes the *Utility* with the *Talisman*. *See also Lincoln and New Salem*, 36; Miller, *History*, 250; *SJ*, April 19, 26, 1834. Thomas Harris was in an excellent position to have precise information about both the *Talisman* and *Utility* and said the latter boat made two trips in 1834, not surviving its second one (Thomas L. Harris to William Walters and George R. Weber, Jan. 27, 1845, *Illinois State Register*, Feb. 14, 1845).

45. Abraham Lincoln, autobiography for John L. Scripps, ca. June 1860 (transcript available in *CW* 4:64).

46. *SJ*, April 5, 12, 19, 26, 1832.

47. *SJ*, April 19, 1832.

48. *SJ*, May 10, 1832.

49. Thomas, *Lincoln's*, 12.

50. Miers, *Lincoln*, Sept. 13, 1831.

51. Abraham Lincoln, "Communication to the People of Sangamo County," March 9, 1832 (transcript available in *CW* 1:5–9).

52. This New Salem businessman, John McNamar (also known as McNeil), said, "I corrected at his request some of the grammatical errors in his first address to the voters of Sangamon County" (John McNamar to G. U. Miles, May 5, 1866, H-W Papers (transcript available in Wilson and Davis, *Herndon's*, 253)).

53. *SJ*, Dec. 22, 1832.

54. *SJ*, March 29, 1832.

55. *SJ*, Feb. 16, 1832.

56. *SJ*, March 29, 1832.

57. D. in *SJ*, July 12, 1832.

58. Quoted in *SJ*, Feb. 9, 1832.

59. George Forquer, *SJ*, July 12, 1832.

60. George Forquer, *SJ*, July 12, 1832.

61. Thomas M. Neale, *SJ*, July 12, 1832.

62. Edward Robison statement of candidacy, *SJ*, June 21, 1832.

63. Anson G. Henry, speaking of that era in *Illinois State Journal*, Sept. 17, 1860, as given in "'The Journal Paper,'" 182. Thomas Ford remembered double that rate as routine and knew instances of 200 and 300 percent (Ford, *History*, 160).

64. Joseph Suppiger, March 19, 1832, in "Letters from New Switzerland," 436.

65. *SJ*, Feb. 23, 1832. *See also* a brief review of situation in Ford, *History*, 159–60.

66. Memorial by officers of the Bank of Illinois at Shawneetown to Legislature, Dec. 8, 1834, printed in *Vandalia Illinois Advocate and State Register*, Dec. 17, 1834.

67. Stephen A. Douglas to Julius N. Granger, Nov. 14, 1834 (transcript available in Douglas, *Letters*, 11).

68. Robert L. Wilson to William H. Herndon, Feb. 10, 1866, H-W Papers (transcript available in Wilson and Davis, *Herndon's*, 201).

69. Nov. 28, 1835.

70. Mercator, "Usury in Illinois," *Galena Advertiser*, March 1, 1830.

71. Junius reply to Mercator, *Galena Advertiser*, March 22, 1830; *SJ*, Aug. 2, 1834.

72. The principle, though not my hypothetical example, is given in "Osborn v. McCowen," (25 Ill. 218 (1861)), file L00881 in Benner and Davis, *Law*. I suspect the practice was used successfully in other instances before this case arose.

73. "Partlow v. Williams," (19 Ill. 132 (1857)), file L01994 in Benner and Davis, *Law*.

74. Edward Robison, *SJ*, June 21, 1832.

75. Thomas M. Neale, *SJ*, July 12, 1832.

76. John Dawson, *SJ*, Jan. 26, 1832.

77. *SJ*, Feb. 9, 1832.

78. Feb. 3, 1836.

79. George Forquer, *SJ*, July 12, 1832. Forquer's language may also have meant that speculators were able to resell land at such a big price that a high interest rate on the initial purchase could be comfortably absorbed, but given that speculators surely didn't finance their operations through loan sharks, I doubt that such reading of Forquer's language would be correct.

80. D. T. to Editor, *Galena Miners' Journal*, March 27, 1830.

81. Boritt, *Lincoln*, 122.

82. Wayland, *Elements of Political*, 132, 134.

83. George Forquer, *SJ*, July 12, 1832.

84. Erastus Wright, *SJ*, Dec. 14, 1833.

85. Edward Robison, *SJ*, June 21, 1832.

86. Thomas M. Neale, *SJ*, July 12, 1832.

87. George Forquer, *SJ*, July 12, 1832.

88. John T. Stuart interview with John Nicolay, June 23, 1875 (transcript available in Burlingame, *Oral*, 11).

89. *Vandalia Free Press* clipped in *Jacksonville Illinoian*, Jan. 20, 1838.

90. The explanation in the following paragraphs is from J. M. Early, Aug. 9, 1832, B-40, Broadside Collection, ALPL.

91. Peter Cartwright in J. M. Early, Aug. 9, 1832, B-40, Broadside Collection, ALPL.

92. Thomas J. Pickett in Wilson, *Intimate*, 190; John T. Stuart interview with John Nicolay, June 23, 1875 (transcript available in Burlingame, *Oral*, 10); Third District, *SJ*, April 25, 1835. The switch is alluded to in a comment about Big Red, apparently by Whig leader Dr. Anson G. Henry: "Who of the party does not know how difficult it was to make 'the Boys' swallow him?" (One Who Knows, *SJ*, May 2, 1835). "One Who Knows" appears to have been Dr. Anson G. Henry (*SJ*, May 23, June 6, 13, 1835).

93. *SJ*, Feb. 2, 1832.

94. *Vandalia Illinois Intelligencer*, May 3, 1828.

95. *SJ*, Feb. 2, 1832.

96. John T. Stuart interview with John Nicolay, June 23, 1875 (transcript available in Burlingame, *Oral*, 10–11).

97. Archer G. Herndon in J. M. Early, Aug. 9, 1832, B-40, Broadside Collection, ALPL.

98. One Who Knows, *SJ*, May 2, 1835. In the One Who Knows account, Taylor was "the Hon. Receiver at Chicago."

99. John T. Stuart interview with John Nicolay, June 23, 1875 (transcript available in Burlingame, *Oral*, 7).

100. Brooks, *Abraham*, 74; "Bulletin No. 4," *Vandalia Illinois Intelligencer*, June 5, 1830; Edwards, *History*, 217; "Fayette, Junior" in *Vandalia Illinois Intelligencer*, Nov. 7, 1829; Pease, *Frontier*, 149.

101. One Who Knows, *SJ*, May 2, 1835. Forquer disputed the One Who Knows version, but One Who Knows claimed that what he said about Forquer's switch to the Democrats could be confirmed by Democratic activist Robert Allen, Dr. Elias H. Merryman, Forquer's old law partner Edward Jones, and Andy Orr (One Who Knows, *SJ*, May 16, 1835). Details of confirmations are in Anson G. Henry, *SJ*, June 13, 1835.

102. John T. Stuart interview with John Nicolay, June 23, 1875 (transcript available in Burlingame, *Oral*, 10). *SJ*, April 27, 1843, has a list of Democratic leaders who came from Whig origins: Thomas Ford, George Forquer, Sidney Breese, Alfred W. Cavarly, James Ralston, William Richardson, Murray McConnel, Josiah Lamborn, John "Candlebox" Calhoun, Robert Smith, J. M. Strode, and O. B. Ficklin. A similar list is in *SJ*, Jan. 11, 1844, clipped in *Illinois State Register*, Jan. 19, 1844, and still another similar list includes W. L. D. Ewing, Jesse Thomas the Younger, and William Walters (*Alton Telegraph*, Jan. 13, 1844, clipped in *Illinois State Register*, Jan. 19, 1844). The original anti-Jackson stance of Edward Coles, Forquer, Ford, and Breese is demonstrated by their 1827 correspondence reprinted in *SJ*, May 30, 1844; *see also* June 13, 1844 (this correspondence was intended for public consumption in 1827, and they wouldn't have released it then without intending to harm Jackson). For Calhoun, *see also* anonymous letter in *SJ*, April 25, 1835; Archer Herndon, *SJ*, Aug. 1, 1835; Third District, *SJ*, April 25, 1835; *SJ*, July 25, 1835 (in *SJ*, Aug. 1, Anson G. Henry acknowledged authorship of the anonymous July 25 item), *SJ*, May 20, 1837; Calhoun's Clay background is implied in Third District, *SJ*, May 2, 1835. For Forquer, *see also* anonymous letter in *SJ*, April 25, 1835; Third District, *SJ*, April 25, 1835; One Who Knows, *SJ*, May 2, 1835. Cartwright's Clay background is briefly mentioned by A Spectator in *SJ*, Aug. 29, 1835 (reference to Arabian pony running against "Sir Archy" Herndon). That is a satirical letter but can be accepted as literally correct about the Clay background. Cartwright's Clay background is implied in Third District, *SJ*, May 2, 1835, and stated outright in One Who Knows, *SJ*, May 2, 1835. Regarding Democratic editor William Walters, *see* A Whig of Illinois to Editor, *Vandalia Free Press and Illinois Whig*, Aug. 21, 1841; *see also SJ*, Feb. 1, 1844. Regarding Breese, *see also Illinois Daily Journal*, Jan. 3, 1851.

103. J. M. Early, Aug. 9, 1832, B-40, Broadside Collection, ALPL.

104. Jason Duncan to William H. Herndon, ca. 1866, H-W Papers (transcript available in Wilson and Davis, *Herndon's*, 541–42).

Chapter 5. INDIAN WAR

1. John T. Stuart interview with John Nicolay, June 23, 1875 (transcript available in Burlingame, *Oral*, 8). In that era, "frolic" meant a drunken binge by a group of persons, and as we shall see, Stuart wasn't exaggerating. Although combatants commonly resort to alcohol for coping with fear, both Stuart's choice of the term "frolic" and the general conduct of Illinois militia persuade me that Black Hawk War personnel were partying or, at the least, simply engaging in the kind of alcohol abuse seen at barn raisings and other group activities. The alcohol abuse doesn't strike me as self-medication to reduce stress of combat.

2. Elizabeth Therese Baird in Reuben Gold Thwaites, ed., *Collections of the State Historical Society of Wisconsin* 14 (1898): 17–18, quoted in *Galena Trail and Coach Road* 3 (July 25, 2003): 3.

3. "Indians Were Frequent Callers," *Reflections of Pioneers of Lee County* (1893): 91–92, quoted in *Galena Trail and Coach Road* 3 (July 25, 2003): 3.

4. Illinois Indians, however, engaged in practices that disturbed whites' sensibilities and would have impeded efforts to form an integrated society. For example:

> One of their ceremonies was to burn a dog to death. They would select a small white dog and make his feet fast with four wooden pins, which they would drive in the ground and then pile wood and burn [*sic*] over him until he was covered four or five feet deep. They would set fire to the pile and then gather in a ring around it. When the dog commenced to burn he would set up the most terrific and awful howling that was ever heard. His cries would ring through the woods for half a mile. When the dog commenced howling the Indians would set up some doleful, dismal cries and keep it up as long as the dog kept howling (Onstot, *Pioneers*, 397).

We should remember, however, that settlers delighted in pastimes such as gander pulling and cockfighting. What seems barbarous to some may be ordinary and even reverent to others.

5. Quoted in Tarbell, *Early*, 135.

6. Quoted in Bennett, "Building," 339.

7. Duis, *Good*, 98.

8. Stevens, *Black*.

9. Resolution, Illinois house of representatives, Jan. 19, 1831, in *Vandalia Illinois Intelligencer*, Jan. 22, 1831. From dating of this resolution and Lincoln's New Orleans trip, note that Black Hawk's presence in Illinois was no brief excursion.

10. John J. Hardin to Sarah Hardin, dateline headquarters near Rushville, June 19, 1831, John J. Hardin Papers.

11. Ford, *History*, 74.

12. Snyder, *Adam*, 303 n.

13. George Archibald McCall letter of July 1, 1831 (transcript available in McCall, *Letters*, 237–38).

14. Joseph Duncan to John J. Hardin, Feb. 7, 1832, John J. Hardin Papers, Hardin Family Collection.

15. Davidson and Stuvé, *Complete*, 380. Such action didn't mean Reynolds was at all sympathetic to Indian rights. In his Dec. 8, 1830, message to the legislature, he declared: "The general good of the present, and future population, seems to require the permanent establishment of three public roads in this state, extending from its southern, to its northern limits. . . . I am aware, that some of these roads may, probably pass in the northern part of the state, over a section of country to which the Indian claim has not been extinguished. This Indian claim ought not, in my opinion, to prevent the state from exercising her sovereignty over it" (quoted in *Vandalia Illinois Intelligencer*, Dec. 11, 1830).

16. Davidson and Stuvé, *Complete*, 380.

17. *Edwardsville Illinois Advocate*, Dec. 16, 1831.

18. *Edwardsville Illinois Advocate*, Feb. 17, 1832.

19. Correspondent to Brother [Josiah Francis to Charles Francis], May 4, 1832, Simeon Francis Papers.

20. *Edwardsville Illinois Advocate*, May 8, 1832.

21. Petersen, *Lincoln-Douglas*, 59.

22. Illinois house of representatives, Jan. 19, 1831, in *Vandalia Illinois Intelligencer*, Jan. 22, 1831.

23. John Reynolds to Gen. William Clark (U.S. Superintendent of Indian Affairs, St. Louis), Jan. 25, 1832 (transcript available in Greene and Alvord, *Governors'*, 200).

24. *Edwardsville Illinois Advocate* clipped in *Sangamon Journal*, Dec. 8, 1831; William Thomas and John T. Stuart to John Reynolds, Nov. 4, 1831 (transcript available in Greene and Alvord, *Governors'*, 188–90).

25. Rorabaugh, *Alcoholic*, 14. *See also* Drake, *Pioneer*, 187.

26. *Lincoln and New Salem*, 38; Miers, *Lincoln*, April 7, 1832.

27. John Reynolds, proclamation, April 16, 1832, *Edwardsville Illinois Advocate*, Extra, B-386, Broadside Collection, ALPL; John Reynolds, April 17, 1832, *Illinois Herald*—Extra, Springfield, April 20, 1832, B-70, Broadside Collection, ALPL. *See also* Onstot, *Pioneers*, 17.

28. West, "Memoirs," 233. *See also* Onstot, *Pioneers*, 17.

29. April 12, 1832.

30. *SJ*, April 19, 1832.

31. George Davenport to Gen. Henry Atkinson, April 13, 1832, printed in *SJ*, April 26, 1832.

32. George Davenport to editors of *The Republican*, April 19, 1832, clipped in *SJ*, May 3, 1832.

33. Felix St. Vrain, Indian agent, to Superintendent of Indian Affairs, St. Louis, letter printed in *SJ*, May 3, 1832.

34. McHarry, "John," 40.

35. Henry Dodge, quoted in Ioway, "Reminiscences of a Volunteer," *Galena North Western Gazette and Galena Advertiser*, May 16, 1835.

36. *Illinois Herald*—Extra, Springfield, April 20, 1832, B-70, Broadside Collection, ALPL; Orr, "Indian," 67–70, 76. The *Illinois Herald* includes General Atkinson's message to Governor Reynolds.

37. Thus a logical time for Black Hawk's band to plant corn, and therefore evidence that their intention was exactly as they stated—to raise crops, not go to war.

38. *SJ*, April 26, 1832.

39. *Edwardsville Illinois Advocate*, June 19, 1832.

40. Moses, *Illinois*, 1:364.

41. March 23, 1833.

42. Josiah Francis to Charles Francis, May 4, 1832, Simeon Francis Papers.

43. Ioway, "Reminiscences of a Volunteer," *Galena North Western Gazette and Galena Advertiser*, May 16, 1835. *See also* Ioway's article of June 13, in which a trader is indiscreet enough to express hope for a British Band victory.

44. Moses, *Illinois*, 1:364.

45. McConnel, *Western*, 121.

46. William Clagett statement enclosed with Charles Friend to William H. Herndon, Feb. 22, 1866, H-W Papers (transcript available in Wilson and Davis, *Herndon's*, 220).

47. McConnel, *Western*, 118–19.

48. Townsend, *Lincoln and Liquor*, 9.

49. George M. Harrison to William H. Herndon, ca. 1866, H-W Papers (transcript available in Wilson and Davis, *Herndon's*, 327).

50. McConnel, *Western*, 116.

51. William Miller (?) statement for William H. Herndon, ca. Sept. 1866, H-W Papers (transcript available in Wilson and Davis, *Herndon's*, 363–64).

52. Orr, "Indian," 78–79.

53. Stephen A. Douglas to Gehazi Granger, Nov. 9, 1835 (transcript available in Douglas, *Letters*, 21).

54. McConnel, *Western*, 115.

55. John Allen interview with James Quay Howard (transcript available in Basler, "James," 388); Luthin, *Real*, 27; Nicolay and Hay, *Abraham*, 1:89. Reportedly (*Lincoln and New Salem*, 38; William G. Greene interview with William H. Herndon, Oct. 9, 1866, H-W Papers (transcript available in Wilson and Davis, *Herndon's*, 368); William G. Greene interview with James Quay Howard (transcript available in Basler, "James," 398); Tarbell, *Early*, 137–38) Kirkpatrick had formerly employed Lincoln. As the story goes, Lincoln had engaged in brutal work at Kirkpatrick's sawmill, moving logs by using a handspike instead of a cant hook. Using an inadequate tool increased such work's difficulty and danger, but Lincoln volunteered to do it that way in return for Kirkpatrick paying him the $2 that a cant hook cost, on top of regular pay. Supposedly Kirkpatrick reneged on the agreement, and when he ran for captain of New Salem's com-

pany, Lincoln decided to run against him. Allegedly, "when Lincoln beat Kirkpatrick, Lincoln said, 'Damn him, I've beat him. He used me badly.'" The story is entertaining and plausible, and it ultimately comes from William G. "Slicky Bill" Greene, who was in a good position to know and seems supported by John Allen. Slicky Bill's stories, however, don't always pan out. This one has the minor problem of why a sawmill operator would lack a cant hook and the major problem of Lincoln denying that he ever worked for Kirkpatrick (Lincoln's notation in Howells, *Life*, 38). Barton's version (*Life*, 1:176) of the sawmill incident says it occurred while Offutt's flatboat was under construction. This would place it at Sangamo Town, which then opens the possibility that Lincoln was not necessarily working for Kirkpatrick, but was instead investing sweat equity in transforming the logs into boards at the mill, a plausible reason why Kirkpatrick wouldn't have a cant hook for use by an extra person. Layers of supposition, however, are no substitute for evidence.

56. William Miller (?) statement for William H. Herndon, ca. Sept. 1866, H-W Papers (transcript available in Wilson and Davis, *Herndon's*, 361).

57. Abraham Lincoln, autobiography for John L. Scripps, ca. June 1860 (transcript available in *CW* 4:64). *See also* Abraham Lincoln, autobiography for Jesse Fell, Dec. 20, 1859 (transcript available in *CW* 3:512).

58. Abraham Lincoln, "Speech in U.S. House of Representatives on the Presidential Question," July 27, 1848 (transcript available in *CW* 1:510).

59. "Black Hawk War Payroll," 413; David Pantier to William H. Herndon, July 21, 1865, H-W Papers (transcript available in Wilson and Davis, *Herndon's*, 78).

60. Ioway, "Reminiscences of a Volunteer," *Galena North Western Gazette and Galena Advertiser*, Aug. 1, 1835.

61. Benjamin F. Irwin to William H. Herndon, Sept. 22, 1866, H-W Papers (transcript available in Wilson and Davis, *Herndon's*, 353). *See also* William Miller (?) statement for William H. Herndon, ca. Sept. 1866, H-W Papers (transcript available in Wilson and Davis, *Herndon's*, 363).

62. John T. Stuart interview with John Nicolay, June 23, 1875 (transcript available in Burlingame, *Oral*, 9).

63. Benjamin F. Irwin to William H. Herndon, Sept. 22, 1866, H-W Papers (transcript available in Wilson and Davis, *Herndon's*, 353).

64. John T. Stuart interview with John Nicolay, June 23, 1875 (transcript available in Burlingame, *Oral*, 8).

65. William Butler interview with John Nicolay, June 13, 1875 (transcript available in Burlingame, *Oral*, 19). Reuben Brown, who was also present at the farm debate between Reverend Cartwright and Lincoln, was a militia captain.

66. Benjamin F. Irwin to William H. Herndon, Sept. 22, 1866, H-W Papers (transcript available in Wilson and Davis, *Herndon's*, 353). Irwin doesn't purport to give Miller's words verbatim. *See also* William Miller (?) statement for William H. Herndon, ca. Sept. 1866, H-W Papers (transcript available in Wilson and Davis, *Herndon's*, 363).

67. William G. Greene to William H. Herndon, May 29, 1865, H-W Papers (transcript available in Wilson and Davis, *Herndon's*, 12); Lincoln quoted in Fehrenbacher and Fehrenbacher, *Recollected*, 333.

68. William G. Greene interview with William H. Herndon, May 30, 1865, H-W Papers (transcript available in Wilson and Davis, *Herndon's*, 19). *See also* William G. Greene to William H. Herndon, Nov. 1, 1866, H-W Papers (transcript available in Wilson and Davis, *Herndon's*, 390); William G. Greene in Oldroyd, *Lincoln*, 516; Joseph Gillespie to William H. Herndon, Jan. 31, 1866, H-W Papers (transcript available in Wilson and Davis, *Herndon's*, 186); Joseph Gillespie in Oldroyd, *Lincoln*, 461; Joseph Gillespie in Prickett, "Joseph," 105; John M. Rutledge to William H. Herndon, Nov. 18, 1866, H-W Papers (transcript available in Wilson and Davis, *Herndon's*, 401); Robert B. Rutledge to William H. Herndon, ca. Nov. 1866, H-W Papers (transcript available in Wilson and Davis, *Herndon's*, 387 and in Hertz, *Hidden*, 317).

69. Arnold, *Life*, 36–37; J. Rowan Herndon to William H. Herndon, May 28, 1865, H-W Papers

(transcript available in Wilson and Davis, *Herndon's*, 7); George M. Harrison to William H. Herndon, Jan. 29, 1867, H-W Papers (transcript available in Wilson and Davis, *Herndon's*, 555–56); Howells, *Life*, 40; Benjamin F. Irwin to William H. Herndon, Sept. 22, 1866, H-W Papers (transcript available in Wilson and Davis, *Herndon's*, 353); John T. Stuart interview with John Nicolay, June 23, 1875 (transcript available in Burlingame, *Oral*, 8).

70. William G. Greene to William H. Herndon, May 29, 1865, H-W Papers (transcript available in Wilson and Davis, *Herndon's*, 12).

71. Henry McHenry interview with William H. Herndon, May 29, 1865, H-W Papers (transcript available in Wilson and Davis, *Herndon's*, 15).

72. Benjamin F. Irwin to William H. Herndon, Sept. 22, 1866, H-W Papers (transcript available in Wilson and Davis, *Herndon's*, 353).

73. John T. Stuart interview with John Nicolay, June 23, 1875 (transcript available in Burlingame, *Oral*, 8–9). Bill Greene had a higher estimate of Captain Lincoln's military abilities: "He had a considerable eye for military affairs" (William G. Greene to William H. Herndon, May 30, 1865, H-W Papers (transcript available in Wilson and Davis, *Herndon's*, 19)).

74. Orr, "Indian," 67–68.

75. Bonham, *Fifty*, 36.

76. Bonham, *Fifty*, 37.

77. Benjamin Perley Poore in Rice, *Reminiscences*, 218–19. I have silently deleted an interpolation by Poore, namely, "said he." Whether Lincoln actually related that anecdote has been questioned, and if he did relate it, he may simply have been adapting a tale already in circulation but having nothing to do with him. *See* Fehrenbacher and Fehrenbacher, *Recollected*, 363. Weik's presentation of the story (Herndon and Weik, *Herndon's Life of Lincoln*, 77–78) implies that William H. Herndon heard it from Lincoln, but such implication may be a fudge by which Weik presented an anecdote he got from some source other than Herndon.

78. Quoted in Stevens, *Black*, 117.

79. Quoted in Stevens, *Black*, 117.

80. Miers, *Lincoln*, April 27, 1832; Pratt, "Lincoln in the Black Hawk War," 5.

81. John J. Hardin, "Special Order No. 7" (transcript available in *CW* 1:10); Miers, *Lincoln*, April 28, 1832; "Receipt for Arms" (transcript available in *CW* 1:9); Temple, "Lincoln's Arms," 147.

82. Miers, *Lincoln*, April 30, 1832; William Miller (?) statement for William H. Herndon, ca. Sept. 1866, H-W Papers (transcript available in Wilson and Davis, *Herndon's*, 361); Stevens, *Black*, 280.

83. Snyder, *Adam*, 122–23.

84. Quoted in Stevens, *Black*, 118; Miers, *Lincoln*, May 2, 1832.

85. William Miller (?) statement for William H. Herndon, ca. Sept. 1866, H-W Papers (transcript available in Wilson and Davis, *Herndon's*, 361).

86. Orr, "Indian," 77–78.

87. Brown, "Major," 110.

88. William G. Greene to William H. Herndon, Nov. 1, 1866, H-W Papers (transcript available in Wilson and Davis, *Herndon's*, 390).

89. Barton, *Life*, 1:178; William G. Greene to William H. Herndon, May 30, 1865, H-W Papers (transcript available in Wilson and Davis, *Herndon's*, 18–19); William G. Greene interview with James Quay Howard (transcript available in Basler, "James," 398–99); Howells, *Life*, 39; Stevens, *Black*, 285–86.

90. Howells, *Life*, xvii (1938 ed.); Howells, *Life*, xxiii (editor's introduction to 1960 ed.).

91. William Miller (?) statement for William H. Herndon, ca. Sept. 1866, H-W Papers (transcript available in Wilson and Davis, *Herndon's*, 363).

92. George M. Harrison to William H. Herndon, Dec. 20, 1866, H-W Papers (transcript available in Wilson and Davis, *Herndon's*, 520).

93. George M. Harrison to William H. Herndon, Jan. 29, 1867, H-W Papers (transcript available in Wilson and Davis, *Herndon's*, 553–55).

94. Quoted in Miers, *Lincoln*, May 3, 1832.

95. William Miller (?) statement for William H. Herndon, ca. Sept. 1866, H-W Papers (transcript available in Wilson and Davis, *Herndon's*, 361–62); Browning quoted in Stevens, *Black*, 118.

96. William Miller (?) statement for William H. Herndon, ca. Sept. 1866, H-W Papers (transcript available in Wilson and Davis, *Herndon's*, 361–62); Nicolay and Hay, *Abraham*, 1:90; Miers, *Lincoln*, May 3, 1832.

97. Orr, "Indian," 73.

98. Davidson and Stuvé, *Complete*, 384; Miers, *Lincoln*, May 5–7, 1832.

99. *SJ*, May 17, 1832. Governor Reynolds took a brighter view, later writing: "Many of the volunteers were enabled by the payments they received from the Government for the military services to purchase homes for themselves of the public lands. This war had the effect to circulate much money throughout the state. The whole expenses of the war were eight or ten millions of dollars, and the greater portion of it was paid out to the Illinois volunteers" (Reynolds, *My Own Times*, 443). I find the governor's claim hard to believe. If a miltiaman served sixty days in federal service, that would earn him $12.60 before deductions, hardly enough to buy ten acres, let alone a homestead. If the millions Reynolds spoke of existed, that money surely went to contractors.

100. William G. Greene interview with William H. Herndon, May 30, 1865, H-W Papers (transcript available in Wilson and Davis, *Herndon's*, 19).

101. David Pantier to William H. Herndon, July 21, 1865, H-W Papers (transcript available in Wilson and Davis, *Herndon's*, 78). I rely on standard chronology of Lincoln's movements rather than conflicting dates given by Pantier. Pantier's claim that Lincoln had to carry a wooden sword has been challenged, primarily on grounds that Lincoln didn't have a metal sword. That lack, however, doesn't mean he wasn't forced to don a symbol of humiliation.

102. Pratt, "Lincoln in the Black Hawk War," 7.

103. John T. Stuart interview with William H. Herndon, ca. 1865, H-W Papers (transcript available in Wilson and Davis, *Herndon's*, 481).

104. Miers, *Lincoln*, May 12, 1832; Pratt, "Lincoln in the Black Hawk War," 7.

105. Ioway, "Reminiscences of a Volunteer," *Galena North Western Gazette and Galena Advertiser*, June 13, 1835.

106. Orr, "Indian," 70.

107. Duis, *Good*, 102.

108. Quoted in Duis, *Good*, 111.

109. Miers, *Lincoln*, May 13 and 14, 1832; Nicolay and Hay, *Abraham*, 1:91.

110. Duis, *Good*, 103, 222.

111. Nicolay and Hay, *Abraham*, 1:91.

112. Davidson and Stuvé, *Complete*, 385; Duis, *Good*, 761.

113. John Hanks interview with William H. Herndon, ca. 1865, H-W Papers (transcript available in Wilson and Davis, *Herndon's*, 458, and in Hertz, *Hidden*, 349).

114. Duis, *Good*, 223.

115. *SJ*, June 14, 1832.

116. Davidson and Stuvé, *Complete*, 386; Moses, *Illinois*, 367; Harry E. Pratt, "Lincoln in the Black Hawk War," in Ander, *John*, 22. *See also* Miers, *Lincoln*, May 14, 1832.

117. Ford, *History*, 78–79.

118. William Miller (?) statement for William H. Herndon, ca. Sept. 1866, H-W Papers (transcript available in Wilson and Davis, *Herndon's*, 362).

119. Linder, *Reminiscences*, 220–21. In this passage, I believe Linder has confused Stillman's Run with the battle at Kellogg's Grove; the quoted passage is an apt description of Stillman's Run and inconsistent with Kellogg's Grove (where Indians chased Americans to a fort and laid siege).

120. Nicolay and Hay, *Abraham*, 1:91–93.

121. Reynolds, *My Own Times*, 364–68.

122. John Hanks interview with William H. Herndon, ca. 1865, H-W Papers (transcript available in Wilson and Davis, *Herndon's*, 458 and in Hertz, *Hidden*, 349).
123. Duis, *Good*, 763.
124. Moses, *Illinois*, 367.
125. Linder, *Reminiscences*, 220.
126. Quoted in Palmer, *Bench*, 621. *See also* James Strode, quoted in *Illinois State Register*, Sept. 19, 1845.
127. Quoted in Ford, *History*, 80.
128. Thomas Hoyne in Palmer, *Bench*, 620–21.
129. William Miller (?) statement for William H. Herndon, ca. Sept. 1866, H-W Papers (transcript available in Wilson and Davis, *Herndon's*, 362).
130. Duis, *Good*, 467–68.
131. Orr, "Indian," 74; Royal Clary interview with William H. Herndon, ca. Oct. 1866, H-W Papers (transcript available in Wilson and Davis, *Herndon's*, 371).
132. Orr, "Indian," 75.
133. William Miller (?) statement for William H. Herndon, ca. Sept. 1866, H-W Papers (transcript available in Wilson and Davis, *Herndon's*, 362).
134. Davidson and Stuvé, *Complete*, 386–87. *See also* Royal Clary interview with William H. Herndon, ca. Oct. 1866, H-W Papers (transcript available in Wilson and Davis, *Herndon's*, 371).
135. Stevens, *Black*, 140.
136. William Miller (?) statement for William H. Herndon, ca. Sept. 1866, H-W Papers (transcript available in Wilson and Davis, *Herndon's*, 362).
137. William Miller (?) statement for William H. Herndon, ca. Sept. 1866, H-W Papers (transcript available in Wilson and Davis, *Herndon's*, 362).
138. Quoted in Stevens, *Black*, 128.
139. Jefferson Davis quoted in Davis, *Jefferson*, 75; Jefferson Davis remarks on John Dixon, *Congressional Globe* 36:1 (June 8, 1860): 2751; Stevens, *Black*, 294–95, 299–302, 305. Evidently the statement of "Rev. Dr. Harsha, of Omaha," quoted in Varina Davis's book is the origin of an incorrect story that Jefferson Davis swore Lincoln into federal service during the war. The story is in Varina Davis's book but is not told by her (Davis, *Jefferson*, 131–32). Whether Davis and Lincoln knew each other in Illinois and whether Davis swore him into federal service are two separate questions.
140. Robert Anderson to Elihu B. Washburne, May 10, 1870, printed in "Letter," 426; Davis, *Jefferson*, 77, 561.
141. Hay, "Colonel," 105.
142. Davis, *Jefferson*, 77.
143. Davis, *Jefferson*, 64; Pratt, "Lincoln in the Black Hawk War," 8. Harney's ability to run down a wolf is plausible; Crow Indians called him "Man-Who-Runs-like-the-Deer" (http://freepages .genealogy.rootsweb.com/~harney2/General/military.htm).
144. Davis, *Jefferson*, 69–70, 74, 76. These incidents weren't necessarily during the Black Hawk War.
145. Pratt, "Lincoln in the Black Hawk War," 8.
146. Stevens, *Black*, 149–50, 155–57; Duis, *Good*, 171; Ford, *History*, 82.
147. Duis, *Good*, 464.
148. Royal Clary interview with William H. Herndon, ca. Oct. 1866, H-W Papers (transcript available in Wilson and Davis, *Herndon's*, 372).
149. Stevens, *Black*, 180. More details in Davidson and Stuvé, *Complete*, 388 n.; Onstot, *Pioneers*, 377–78.
150. Theophilus W. Smith, June 5, 1832, *Edwardsville Illinois Advocate*, June 26, 1832.
151. Ford, *History*, 84; Snyder, *Adam*, 121–22 (including Jones quotation); Stevens, *Black*, 170; Elijah Iles quoted in Arnold, *Address*, 20; Elijah Iles quoted in Tarbell, *Early*, 147.
152. Davidson and Stuvé, *Complete*, 389; Luthin, *Real*, 27–28; Miers, *Lincoln*, May 23, 1832; Pratt, "Lincoln in the Black Hawk War," 8; Stevens, *Black*, 162.

153. Quoted in Stevens, *Black*, 163.
154. William Miller (?) statement for William H. Herndon, ca. Sept. 1866, H-W Papers (transcript available in Wilson and Davis, *Herndon's*, 363).
155. Nicolay and Hay, *Abraham*, 1:93; Davidson and Stuvé, *Complete*, 389; Miers, *Lincoln*, May 26, 1832.
156. Quoted in Herndon and Weik, *Herndon's Life of Lincoln*, 82.
157. John T. Stuart interview with John Nicolay, June 23, 1875 (transcript available in Burlingame, *Oral*, 8–9).
158. Robert Anderson to Elihu B. Washburne, May 10, 1870, printed in "Letter," 423. Miers, *Lincoln*, May 29, 1832, reports that the weapons were valued at $10.
159. Temple, "Lincoln's Arms," 147.
160. Cartwright, *Autobiography*, 283; Stevens, *Black*, 167–68.
161. Taylor quoted in Miers, *Lincoln*, June 7, 1832; Elijah Iles quoted in Arnold, *Address*, 20; Elijah Iles quoted in Tarbell, *Early*, 147, and in Stevens, *Black*, 173. Although the preceding sources say Colonel Taylor dispatched a militia company, those reports are contradicted by Stevens in *Black*.
162. Elijah Iles to Isaac N. Arnold, Dec. 7, 1868, printed in Arnold, *Address*, 20.
163. Quoted in Tarbell, *Early*, 147.
164. Miers, *Lincoln*, June 7, 1832; John T. Stuart interview with John Nicolay, June 23, 1875 (transcript available in Burlingame, *Oral*, 9).
165. Quoted in Tarbell, *Early*, 147.
166. John T. Stuart interview with John Nicolay, June 23, 1875 (transcript available in Burlingame, *Oral*, 9).
167. Arnold, *Life*, 36.
168. Quoted in Tarbell, *Early*, 148–50, and in Stevens, *Black*, 174. *See also* Elijah Iles to Isaac N. Arnold, Dec. 7, 1868, printed in Arnold, *Address*, 20–21.
169. Arnold, *Life*, 36.
170. Addison Philleo statement in *SJ*, July 26, 1834.
171. Ford, *History*, 85.
172. "Henry" in *Jacksonville News* clipped in *Chicago Democrat*, June 25, 1834.
173. John T. Stuart interview with William H. Herndon, ca. 1865, H-W Papers (transcript available in Wilson and Davis, *Herndon's*, 481).
174. Brunson, *Western*, 2:36.
175. A Looker On to editor, *Galena North Western Gazette and Galena Advertiser*, Dec. 24, 1836.
176. N***** to editor, *Galena North Western Gazette and Galena Advertiser*, Jan. 31, 1835.
177. Proceedings of citizens meeting, Dubuque, *Galena North Western Gazette and Galena Advertiser*, Aug. 29, 1835.
178. *Edwardsville Illinois Advocate*, May 22, 1832.
179. *SJ*, May 31, 1832.
180. Miers, *Lincoln*, June 10, 1832; Pratt, "Lincoln in the Black Hawk War," 10.
181. John T. Stuart interview with John Nicolay, June 23, 1875 (transcript available in Burlingame, *Oral*, 8–9).
182. Miers, *Lincoln*, June 16, 1832; Pratt, "Lincoln in the Black Hawk War," 11. I accept those authorities' statement about Early serving as a private under Lincoln, although the muster roll prepared by Captain Lincoln does not list Early (transcript available in *CW* 1:11–12).
183. George M. Harrison to William H. Herndon, ca. 1866, H-W Papers (transcript available in Wilson and Davis, *Herndon's*, 327).
184. George M. Harrison to William H. Herndon, ca. 1866, H-W Papers (transcript available in Wilson and Davis, *Herndon's*, 327).
185. Abraham Lincoln, "Speech in U.S. House of Representatives on the Presidential Question," July 27, 1848 (transcript available in *CW* 1:510).
186. Miers, *Lincoln*, June 17, 1832.
187. Rorabaugh, *Alcoholic*, 15.

188. Order No. 16, Aug. 28, 1832 (transcript available in Stevens, *Black*, 249).
189. Bryant, *Prose*, 2:20.
190. Pratt, "Lincoln in the Black Hawk War," 11.
191. Tarbell, *Early*, 152.
192. Abraham Lincoln, "Speech in U.S. House of Representatives on the Presidential Question," July 27, 1848 (transcript available in *CW* 1:510).
193. Lambert, "Black," 473.
194. Royal Clary interview with William H. Herndon, ca. Oct. 1866, H-W Papers (transcript available in Wilson and Davis, *Herndon's*, 372).
195. Linder, *Reminiscences*, 220–21. Linder says he is describing Dement's conduct at Stillman's Run. Having found no other reference to Dement's presence there, I think Linder has confused Stillman's Run with Kellogg's Grove. *See also* next two source notes.
196. William Miller (?) statement for William H. Herndon, ca. Sept. 1866, H-W Papers (transcript available in Wilson and Davis, *Herndon's*, 363). *See also* next source note.
197. Davidson and Stuvé, *Complete*, 392–93; Jacob M. Early, quoted in Miers, *Lincoln*, June 26, 1832 and in Pratt, "Lincoln in the Black Hawk War," 11–12; Ford, *History*, 86–87; George M. Harrison to William H. Herndon, ca. 1866, H-W Papers (transcript available in Wilson and Davis, *Herndon's*, 327–28); Abraham Lincoln quoted in Brooks, "Personal Reminiscences," 563; John T. Stuart interview with John Nicolay, June 23, 1875 (transcript available in Burlingame, *Oral*, 8); Stevens, *Black*, 199–201. Harrison here and elsewhere (e.g., George M. Harrison to Abraham Lincoln, May 29, 1860 (transcript available in Burlingame, *Oral*, 100)) refers to this encounter as a battle at Gratiot's Grove, but his details demonstrate that he confused the name of that Wisconsin border location with Kellogg's Grove. Gratiot's Grove, north of Kellogg's Grove and about twenty miles northeast of Galena, had a Black Hawk War fort just as Kellogg's Grove did. John T. Stuart also spoke of a battle at Gratiot's Grove (John T. Stuart interview with William H. Herndon, ca. 1865, H-W Papers (transcript available in Wilson and Davis, *Herndon's*, 481)), but his details point to Kellogg's Grove. I believe the conversation between Noah Brooks and Lincoln was about Kellogg's Grove. I doubt that Lincoln had another opportunity to view such a scene. Although Brooks's introductory remarks can be interpreted as describing a different incident, I think Brooks simply made assumptions regarding what Lincoln was talking about. Such assumptions are common enough in reports of conversations with Lincoln, in which people exhibit misunderstanding because they lacked detailed knowledge of what he was talking about, even though they may have his words basically correct.
198. Orr, "Indian," 70, 73.
199. *New Haven Advertiser*, clipped in *SJ*, Sept. 8, 1832.
200. Ford, *History*, 89; Pratt, "Lincoln in the Black Hawk War," 12.
201. Luthin, *Real*, 28; Miers, *Lincoln*, July 8, 1832; Pratt, "Lincoln in the Black Hawk War," 12.
202. Abraham Lincoln, "Speech in U.S. House of Representatives on the Presidential Question," July 27, 1848 (transcript available in *CW* 1:510).
203. Ford, *History*, 89.
204. Pratt, "Lincoln in the Black Hawk War," 12.
205. Miers, *Lincoln*, May 18, June 13, 1832; Pratt, "Lincoln in the Black Hawk War," 11; Stevens, *Black*, 131, 291.
206. Ford, *History*, 89–90; Miers, *Lincoln*, July 9, 1832; Pratt, "Lincoln in the Black Hawk War," 13.

Chapter 6. POLITICIAN, MERCHANT, POSTMASTER, SURVEYOR
1. George M. Harrison to William H. Herndon, ca. 1866, H-W Papers (transcript available in Wilson and Davis, *Herndon's*, 328–29); John T. Stuart interview with William H. Herndon, ca. June 1865, H-W Papers (transcript available in Wilson and Davis, *Herndon's*, 64); John T. Stuart interview with John Nicolay, June 23, 1875 (transcript available in Burlingame, *Oral*, 9–10).
2. George M. Harrison to William H. Herndon, ca. 1866, H-W Papers (transcript available in Wilson and Davis, *Herndon's*, 329); Tarbell, *Early*, 155.

3. Patrick Shirreff, 1833 (transcript available in Angle, *Prairie*, 136).

4. Daniel Burner, quoted in Temple, "Lincoln and the Burners," 66.

5. George M. Harrison to Abraham Lincoln, May 29, 1860 (transcript available in Burlingame, *Oral*, 100); Nicolay, *Personal*, 138–39.

6. Edward Robison, *SJ*, June 21, 1832.

7. Miers, *Lincoln*, June 4, 1832; Pratt, "Lincoln in the Black Hawk War," 9–10.

8. *Chicago Democrat*, Nov. 18, 1835.

9. George M. Harrison to William H. Herndon, Jan. 29, 1867, H-W Papers (transcript available in Wilson and Davis, *Herndon's*, 555).

10. Orr, "Indian," 73–74; Ioway, "Reminiscences of a Volunteer," *Galena North Western Gazette and Galena Advertiser*, May 16, 1835.

11. Orr, "Indian," 67, 73–74.

12. *Edwardsville Illinois Advocate*, June 19, 1832.

13. Thomas Neale, *SJ*, July 12, 1832.

14. John Dawson, *SJ*, July 12, 1832.

15. *SJ*, July 19, 1832; Miers, *Lincoln*, July 19, 1832.

16. John T. Stuart interview with John Nicolay, June 23, 1875 (transcript available in Burlingame, *Oral*, 10). For additional comment on the handbill war, *see* John T. Stuart, "Reply of John T. Stuart to an Anonymous Hand Bill Signed 'A Citizen of Sangamon,'" B-401, Broadside Collection, ALPL.

17. J. M. Early, Aug. 9, 1832, B-40, Broadside Collection, ALPL.

18. Lincoln later specifically noted that he didn't run as a supporter of former President John Quincy Adams, but as a solid opponent of Andrew Jackson and supporter of Clay. Lincoln observed that no Adams party existed in Illinois; one Illinois party supported Jackson, and the other simply opposed Jackson (Howells, *Life*, 40).

19. Beveridge, *Abraham*, 1:126.

20. John T. Stuart interview with John Nicolay, June 23, 1875 (transcript available in Burlingame, *Oral*, 10).

21. Henry McHenry interview with William H. Herndon, May 29, 1865, H-W Papers (transcript available in Wilson and Davis, *Herndon's*, 15).

22. William Greene interview with William H. Herndon, May 30, 1865, H-W Papers (transcript available in Wilson and Davis, *Herndon's*, 20).

23. Abner Y. Ellis statement for William H. Herndon, ca. Jan. 23, 1866, H-W Papers (transcript available in Wilson and Davis, *Herndon's*, 171). Ellis has ambiguity in dating his account but seems to mean the 1832 campaign.

24. James A. Herndon to William H. Herndon, May 29, 1865, H-W Papers (transcript available in Wilson and Davis, *Herndon's*, 16). In this letter, James Herndon wrote a few lines giving his memory of Lincoln's speech. I doubt that he intended it as a verbatim report, but he probably captured the spirit of Lincoln's remarks. Earlier, he had given a similar version to William H. Herndon, who got it printed in the *Illinois State Journal* (Nov. 5, 1864), a version reproduced in Herndon and Weik, *Herndon's Life of Lincoln*, 86, and in Wilson, *Uncollected*, 1:43. *See also* James A. Herndon to William H. Herndon, June 20, 1865, H-W Papers (transcript available in Wilson and Davis, *Herndon's*, 49); James A. Herndon interview with William H. Herndon, ca. 1865, H-W Papers (transcript available in Wilson and Davis, *Herndon's*, 460–61).

25. James A. Herndon interview with William H. Herndon, ca. 1865, H-W Papers (transcript available in Wilson and Davis, *Herndon's*, 460).

26. John Rowan Herndon to William H. Herndon, June 21, 1865, H-W Papers (transcript available in Wilson and Davis, *Herndon's*, 51). *See also* John Rowan Herndon to William H. Herndon, May 28, 1865, H-W Papers (transcript available in Wilson and Davis, *Herndon's*, 7).

27. Stephen T. Logan, July 6, 1875, Abraham Lincoln Papers, LOC 1959 microfilm, 97:43645ff (transcript available in Burlingame, *Oral*, 35 and in "Stephen T. Logan," 2).

28. *SJ*, April 12, 1832.

29. Ford, *History*, 68–69.

30. John Rowan Herndon to William H. Herndon, May 28, 1865, H-W Papers (transcript available in Wilson and Davis, *Herndon's*, 7).

31. William G. Greene interview with James Quay Howard (transcript available in Basler, "James," 399).

32. *SJ*, July 26, Aug. 2, 1832.

33. *Niles' Weekly Register*, given in Benton, *Thirty*, 1:281. The weekly edited by Hezekiah Niles is considered one of the most accurate sources of information about life in the era.

34. *New York Sunday Times* clipped in *Illinois Daily Journal*, Jan. 23, 1850.

35. Philip Clark, quoted in *Chicago Times-Herald*, March 13, 1901, reprinted in Wilson, *Lincoln*, 63–64. Clark remembers that the exchange between Cartwright and Lincoln was in one of Lincoln's early campaigns and was about the Bank of the United States, but he is less certain about the specific issue. Clark thought the two candidates might have talked about Jackson's removal of deposits, but that occurred after the 1832 campaign. Cartwright started but dropped out from the 1834 legislature campaign, thereby limiting opportunity for a debate that year about the 1833 withdrawal of deposits. (A dozen candidates ran for representative in 1834. I doubt that any campaign event would have featured just Lincoln and Cartwright, and the big summer political gatherings of 1834 began after Cartwright withdrew.) If Lincoln asked about some controversial action of Jackson's regarding the Bank, the only such action in 1832 would have been the veto, and likely the only opportunity to pose such a question would have been the August 4 speech-making in Springfield, as the veto wasn't announced in the *Sangamo Journal* until July 26, and Jackson's veto message didn't appear in the newspaper until August 2. I acknowledge the possibility that the two men encountered each other and discussed the Bank in a later campaign, either before Cartwright abandoned his 1834 campaign or afterward when he might have appeared as a Democratic activist rather than a candidate.

36. Stephen T. Logan, July 6, 1875, Abraham Lincoln Papers, LOC 1959 microfilm, 97:43645ff (transcript available in Burlingame, *Oral*, 35, and in "Stephen T. Logan," 1–2); Miers, *Lincoln*, Aug. 4, 1832. As we shall see, Logan's description of himself as a Whig was misleading. He would say, with understatement, "In the years 1835 and 1836 there was not a good understanding between several of the prominent Whigs and myself, particularly Lincoln, [Simeon] Francis, A. G. Henry, and A. G. Herndon" (Logan interrogatory in William Butler deposition, Nov. 5, 1838, document 3496, "Logan v. Adams" in Benner and Davis, *Law*. Logan made that remark as part of a question he asked, and Butler concurred about Logan's relations with those Whigs). Logan also said harsh things about Governor Duncan, an ostensible Democrat but allied with the Whigs (Stephen T. Logan item for publication, document 120626, marked "C" in deposition document 3463, Benner and Davis, *Law*). Around Springfield, Logan was considered a Whig (*see* comments by Jacob C. Planck, Archer G. Herndon, and Garrett Elkin in "Logan v. Adams," depositions, document 3499 in Benner and Davis, *Law*), but a maverick one—maverick enough that his Whig allegiance was unapparent to Simeon Francis until 1837 (Simeon Francis, "Logan v. Adams," depositions, document 3499 in Benner and Davis, *Law*).

37. John T. Stuart interview with John Nicolay, June 23, 1875 (transcript available in Burlingame, *Oral*, 10).

38. Stephen T. Logan, July 6, 1875, quoted in Nicolay and Hay, *Abraham*, 1:102–3 n. 1; Tarbell, *Early*, 155. Although these authorities can be interpreted as presenting Logan's remarks as referring to the 1832 election, he may be speaking of 1834 (compare Stephen T. Logan interview with John Nicolay, July 6, 1875, transcript in Burlingame, *Oral*, 36). Even if Logan's words literally speak of 1834, they capture the spirit of 1832, so I quote them here.

39. Jason Duncan to William H. Herndon, ca. 1866, H-W Papers (transcript available in Wilson and Davis, *Herndon's*, 540).

40. John T. Stuart interview with John Nicolay, June 23, 1875 (transcript available in Burlingame, *Oral*, 10).

41. *SJ*, Aug. 11, 1832; Tarbell, *Early*, 158.

42. William Butler interview with John Nicolay, June 13, 1875 (transcript available in Burlingame, *Oral*, 20).

43. Jason Duncan to William H. Herndon, ca. 1866, H-W Papers (transcript available in Wilson and Davis, *Herndon's*, 540).
44. Stephen T. Logan, July 6, 1875, Abraham Lincoln Papers, LOC 1959 microfilm, 97:43645ff (transcript available in Burlingame, *Oral*, 36 and in "Stephen T. Logan," 2–3).
45. John T. Stuart interview with John Nicolay, June 23, 1875 (transcript available in Burlingame, *Oral*, 10–11).
46. Robert B. Rutledge to William H. Herndon, ca. Nov. 1866, H-W Papers (transcript available in Wilson and Davis, *Herndon's*, 385).
47. George Close interview with James Quay Howard (transcript available in Basler, "James," 391). The rail-splitting angle is also mentioned by John Potter in Stevens, *Reporter's*, 11.
48. Browne, *Every-Day*, 115.
49. Abner Y. Ellis statement to William H. Herndon, ca. Jan. 23, 1866, H-W Papers (transcript available in Wilson and Davis, *Herndon's*, 172–73).
50. Paul Pry, *Belleville Great Western*, March 14, 1840.
51. A Soldier, *SJ*, Aug. 25, 1832.
52. *Vandalia Illinois Advocate*, March 23, 1833.
53. Linder, *Reminiscences*, 49, referring to John Randolph's characterization of Hardin. *See also* McMurtry, *Ben*, 4; Townsend, "Lincoln's," 4.
54. Elizabeth Duncan biographical sketch of John J. Hardin, Folder 31, Duncan Family Papers. *See also* A Lobby Member, dateline Springfield, Dec. 31, 1840, in *Quincy Whig*, Jan. 16, 1841.
55. Snyder, *Adam*, 201 n.
56. Gillespie, *Recollections*, 38. Koerner, *Memoirs*, 1:499, says the eyes were "jet-black."
57. Onstot, *Pioneers*, 375. *See also* Charles Hardin to John J. Hardin, Jan. 7, 1843, Hardin Family Papers.
58. Gillespie, *Recollections*, 38.
59. Koerner, *Memoirs*, 1:499.
60. Epler, "History," 171.
61. Stephen A. Douglas to Julius N. Granger, May 9, 1835 (transcript in Douglas, *Letters*, 17–18).
62. John J. Hardin to John McHenry, Feb. 11, 1832, John J. Hardin Papers, Hardin Family Collection.
63. M. McHenry to John H. McHenry, June 20, 1834, John J. Hardin Papers, Hardin Family Collection (transcript available in Johannsen, *Stephen*, 22).
64. John J. Hardin to Robert W. Scott, Sept. 24, 1830 (transcript available in Helm, *True*, 69–70).
65. Helm, *True*, 67.
66. V. McKnight to John J. Hardin, June 29, 1831, John J. Hardin Papers, Hardin Family Collection.
67. John J. Hardin to Sarah Hardin, June 30, 1831, John J. Hardin Papers, Hardin Family Collection.
68. Sarah Hardin to John J. Hardin, Sept. 23, [1831?], John J. Hardin Papers, Hardin Family Collection. This apparent date is eight months after the marriage began. An infant might have been on the scene by then, but not a child that could walk. So the letter must be from a later year.
69. Sarah Hardin to John J. Hardin, April 2, 1832, John J. Hardin Papers, Hardin Family Collection.
70. Elizabeth Duncan, biographical sketch of John J. Hardin, Folder 31, Duncan Family Papers.
71. Henry Clay to John J. Hardin, July 24, 1833 (transcript in John J. Hardin Papers, Hardin Family Collection (original in Henry Clay Collection)); Henry Clay to John J. Hardin, Feb. 11, 1834 (transcript in John J. Hardin Papers, Hardin Family Collection (original in Henry Clay Collection)).
72. Porter Clay to John J. Hardin, Aug. 20, 1833, John J. Hardin Papers, Hardin Family Collection. I am reading the signature as "P" Clay, although the handwriting and condition of the manuscript allow the initial to be read as "E."
73. Porter Clay to John J. Hardin, Aug. 25, 1832, John J. Hardin Papers, Hardin Family Collection.
74. Hickey, "Lincoln the Real Estate," 71.
75. "John Todd to Maria L. Todd, Bill of Sale," Nov. 24, 1832, John J. Hardin Papers, Hardin Family Collection. This was the same date on which Maria acquired title to land that John Todd lost

to her via foreclosure of a mortgage he had given her on the property; Hardin acted as Maria's attorney in suing John Todd for the real estate (Hickey, "Lincoln the Real Estate," 71). I suspect these land and slave deals were connected.

76. Art. VI, § 3; *Boon* v. *Juliet*, Illinois Reports, 1 Scammon 258, 259 (1836); *Choisser* v. *Hargrave*, Illinois Reports, 1 Scammon 317, 318 (1836).

77. *SJ*, May 4, 1833.

78. Illinois, *Revised Laws*, 1833, "Apprentices," 68–73.

79. Wade, *Slavery*, 220.

80. William H. Brown, "Early History of Illinois," *Galena North Western Gazette and Galena Advertiser*, Jan. 11, 1841 (internal date Jan. 6), and also as lecture to Chicago Lyceum, Dec. 8, 1840, in *Daily Chicago American*, Dec. 22, 1840; Aldrich, "Slavery," 122; Allen, "Slavery," 413, 418–19; Stephen Douglas to Edward Coles, Feb. 18, 1854 (transcript available in Douglas, *Letters*, 293–96); Finkelman, "Slavery," 250; Harris, "Negro," 51. Finkelman may be referring to Indiana contracts, but Illinois adopted Indiana's indentured servant regulations.

81. Quoted in Harris, "Negro," 50.

82. William H. Brown, "Early History of Illinois," *Galena North Western Gazette and Galena Advertiser*, Jan. 11, 1841 (internal date Jan. 6), and also as lecture to Chicago Lyceum, Dec. 8, 1840, in *Daily Chicago American*, Dec. 22, 1840. *See also* Krug, *Lyman*, 60.

83. Cockrum, *Pioneer*, 142–45. As we shall see, Illinois law forbade selling indentured servants into perpetual slavery at an out-of-state slave market, but if any owners chose to violate that law, I doubt that the victims were in a position to file charges.

84. Allen, "Slavery," 411–12, 416–17, 419–23.

85. Illinois, *Revised Laws*, 1833, "Negroes, &c.," §19.

86. Illinois, *Revised Laws*, 1833, "Negroes, &c.," §21.

87. Illinois, *Revised Laws*, 1833, "Negroes, &c.," §22.

88. Illinois, *Revised Laws*, 1833, "Negroes, &c.," §24–25.

89. Copy of indenture, Oct. 7, 1839, John J. Hardin Papers, Hardin Family Collection.

90. Ford, *History*, 18.

91. "An Act providing for the valuation of Lands and other property, and laying a tax thereon," March 27, 1819, Illinois, *Session Laws*, 1819, 313; "An Act for levying and collecting a Tax on Land and other Property," Feb. 18, 1823, Illinois, *Session Laws*, 1823, 203; Haig, *History*, 39–40.

92. Illinois house of representatives, *Journal*, 9:1 (1834–1835), 429–30.

93. John T. Stuart to John J. Hardin, Aug. 30, 1833, John J. Hardin Papers, Hardin Family Collection. I suspect Stuart refers to John Hardin's brother Charles.

94. Maria Todd to John J. Hardin, Nov. 23, 1833(?), John J. Hardin Papers, Hardin Family Collection. Because of the letter's content, I read the date as 1833.

95. Maria Todd to John J. Hardin, Dec. 15, 1833, John J. Hardin Papers, Hardin Family Collection.

96. Maria Todd to John J. Hardin, Dec. 27, 1833, John J. Hardin Papers, Hardin Family Collection.

97. Hart, "Springfield's," 41, notes that John Todd owned five slaves in 1830 but also states that census records allowed blacks to be described only as either free or slave. Therefore, he may have owned *indentured* slaves. One of Dr. Todd's indentured servants was publicly described as "a female slave" who became indentured when he brought her to Illinois. When she "was advanced in years—perhaps fifty" and her indenture contract neared its end, Dr. Todd pointed out "that in her advanced age she would find it difficult to sustain herself by hard labor" and offered to extend her contract so she could have an easier life as his house servant. She declined the offer and chose to take her chances in the cold world of freedom (*Illinois Daily Journal*, July 18, 1850).

98. The adult African American woman Phoebe has been described as a slave in 1836 by someone who distinguished between slaves and indentured servants (Hart, "Springfield's," 44), but the 1832 document calls her an indentured servant. In 1836, she allowed Dr. Todd to make her daughter Elizabeth his indentured servant (Hart, "Springfield's," 44).

99. Illinois, *Revised Laws*, 1833, Criminal Code, § 150.

100. As we saw above, the ban on selling an indentured servant into perpetual slavery didn't necessarily apply to selling a slave imported into Illinois who thereupon refused to sign an indenture. Seemingly, a slave who was thereby temporarily in Illinois could legally be sent to an out-of-state slave market, but an indentured servant couldn't legally be sold in an out-of-state slave market.

101. Lemuel Smith to John J. Hardin, July 7, 1835, John J. Hardin Papers, Hardin Family Collection.

102. Indenture agreement among Dolly Smith, John J. Hardin, and Sarah E. Hardin, Nov. 4, 1837, John J. Hardin Papers, Hardin Family Collection.

103. On Jan. 24, 1839, John Stuart prepared documentation to indenture "a girl of color" (file N05020 in Benner and Davis, *Law*).

104. Abraham Lincoln, autobiography for John L. Scripps, ca. June 1860 (transcript available in *CW* 4:64–65).

105. James A. Herndon to William H. Herndon, May 29, 1865, H-W Papers (transcript available in Wilson and Davis, *Herndon's*, 16); Tarbell, *Early*, 116; Thomas, *Lincoln's*, 60.

106. Thomas, *Lincoln's*, 6.

107. Henry Clark interview with William H. Herndon, 1866, H-W Papers (transcript available in Wilson and Davis, *Herndon's*, 528).

108. William G. Greene to William H. Herndon, June 7, 1865, H-W Papers (transcript available in Wilson and Davis, *Herndon's*, 26); John Rowan Herndon to William H. Herndon, Oct. 28, 1866, H-W Papers (transcript available in Wilson and Davis, *Herndon's*, 378).

109. James A. Herndon to William H. Herndon, ca. 1865, H-W Papers (transcript available in Wilson and Davis, *Herndon's*, 460); John Rowan Herndon to William H. Herndon, Oct. 28, 1866, H-W Papers (transcript available in Wilson and Davis, *Herndon's*, 378).

110. Miers, *Lincoln*, August 1832; Thomas, *Lincoln's New Salem*, 12.

111. John Rowan Herndon to William H. Herndon, May 28, 1865, H-W Papers (transcript available in Wilson and Davis, *Herndon's*, 7). *See also* Chandler, "New," 531; James A. Herndon to William H. Herndon, ca. 1865, H-W Papers (transcript available in Wilson and Davis, *Herndon's*, 460); John Rowan Herndon to William H. Herndon, Oct. 28, 1866, H-W Papers (transcript available in Wilson and Davis, *Herndon's*, 378).

112. John Rowan Herndon to William H. Herndon, May 28, 1865, H-W Papers (transcript available in Wilson and Davis, *Herndon's*, 7); Thomas, *Lincoln's*, 60, 70.

113. Onstot, *Pioneers*, 233.

114. William G. Greene in Onstot, *Pioneers*, 82.

115. Tarbell, *Early*, 160.

116. Herndon and Weik, *Herndon's Life of Lincoln*, 88.

117. George Spears to William H. Herndon, Oct. 17, 1866, H-W Papers (transcript available in Wilson and Davis, *Herndon's*, 375).

118. Chandler, "New," 528; Ross, *Lincoln's*, 38.

119. Oliver, *Eight*, 124.

120. Fordham, *Personal*, 121.

121. Ford, *History*, 63.

122. Stephen A. Douglas to Julius N. Granger, May 24, 1835 (transcript available in Douglas, *Letters*, 19).

123. Ross, *Lincoln's*, 8–9.

124. James Davis interview with William H. Herndon, 1866, H-W Papers (transcript available in Wilson and Davis, *Herndon's*, 529–30). *See also* William G. Greene interview with William H. Herndon, May 30, 1865, H-W Papers (transcript available in Wilson and Davis, *Herndon's*, 20).

125. James McGrady Rutledge in Tarbell, *Early*, 172–74.

126. Johnson, *Frontier*, 13; Johnson, *Illinois*, 64; Ross, *Lincoln's*, 9.

127. Abraham Lincoln, debate with Stephen A. Douglas, Aug. 21, 1858 (transcript available in *CW* 3:16).

128. Nelson Alley and Abraham Lincoln, promissory note to James D. Henry, Oct. 30, 1832 (transcript available in *CW* 1:13); attachment, foreclosure, and sale notices, *SJ*, Aug. 18, Nov. 24, Dec. 1, 1832, March 23, 1833; Beveridge, *Abraham*, 1:119 n. 5; Pratt, "Lincoln Pilots," 328–29; Sheriff's sale notice, *SJ*, Oct. 20, Oct. 27, 1832; Townsend, *Lincoln the Litigant*, 46–48, 52–53. Suggestion has been made that the note was residue from Lincoln and Alley signing as Bogue's sureties during the *Talisman* project. I feel otherwise, because any creditor suspicious of Bogue's wealth would have found no reassurance in Lincoln's pledge, and because the phrase "value received" indicates the note's origin was a transfer of property in October. Bill Greene had an uncertain memory of Nelson Alley buying a stock of goods from the Herndon brothers when they sold out their store and may well have been thinking of the purchase from Bogue's creditors (William G. Greene to William H. Herndon, Oct. 24, 1866, H-W Papers (transcript available in Wilson and Davis, *Herndon's*, 377)). Or maybe Alley bought from both sources, goods from Bogue's creditors and from the Herndons.

129. Barrett, *Life*, 49; Jason Duncan to William H. Herndon, ca. 1866, H-W Papers (transcript available in Wilson and Davis, *Herndon's*, 540); election return, Nov. 5, 1832 (transcript available in *CW* 1:14); Abraham Lincoln, autobiography for John L. Scripps, ca. June 1860 (transcript available in *CW* 4:64); Luthin, "Abraham," 610; Miers, *Lincoln*, Nov. 5, 6, 1832; Thomas, "Lincoln the Postmaster," 3–4; Thomas, "Lincoln: Voter" (Sept. 1934), 5.

130. "CASH continued to be advanced by the undersigned for the claims of the late Volunteers. T. M. Neale," *SJ*, June 21, 1832; "Cash paid for the claims of the late volunteers. Call at my office. T. M. Neale," *SJ*, Jan. 19, 1833.

131. Abraham Lincoln, certificate of discharge for Nathan Drake, with assignment of pay to John Taylor (transcript available in *CW* Supp. 1–2).

132. "Earliest," 545; "A Volunteer" letter, *Edwardsville Illinois Advocate*, March 16, 1832; *SJ*, Jan. 12, March 22, April 12, 1832. Paymaster visit notices in *SJ*, June 21, 28, July 5, 12, Oct. 27, Nov. 3, 10, 17, Dec. 15, 22, 1832; April 13, 1833. Lincoln was involved in paperwork for veterans selling their pay claims (*CW* Supp. 1–2; file N05438 in Benner and Davis, *Law*). Campbell & Britton dry goods in Springfield advertised their willingness to trade merchandise for Black Hawk war pay claims (*SJ*, Dec. 29, 1831).

133. "Black Hawk War Payroll," 412–13; Pratt, *Personal*, 11; Warren, "Lincoln's Financial."

134. *SJ*, Jan. 12, 26, Feb. 23, March 9, 16, 23, April 13, July 20, 27, Aug. 31, 1833, and Feb. 1, March 8, May 10, July 19, Aug. 23, Oct. 4, 1834; *Shawneetown Illinois Journal and State Intelligencer*, Nov. 22, 1834. Thomas Neale advertised his willingness to help gain compensation for loss of horses (*SJ*, June 8, 1833). The Henry Eddy Papers, ALPL, have much correspondence about such efforts. Lincoln's law practice included representing veterans seeking this kind of recompense; as with pay claims, horse claims could be sold to third parties, who would then collect (files N05019, N05048, N05055, in Benner and Davis, *Law*; Wilson, *Uncollected*, 1:585).

135. *SJ*, June 8, 1833.

136. Henry Clark interview with William H. Herndon, 1866, H-W Papers (transcript available in Wilson and Davis, *Herndon's*, 528); William G. Greene in Onstot, *Pioneers*, 81–82; William G. Greene to William H. Herndon, Oct. 24, 1866, H-W Papers (transcript available in Wilson and Davis, *Herndon's*, 377); William H. Herndon to Jesse Weik, June 13, 1888 (transcript available in Hertz, *Hidden*, 213); *Lincoln and New Salem*, 44; Miller, *History*, 710–11; Henry McHenry interview with William H. Herndon, 1866, H-W Papers (transcript available in Wilson and Davis, *Herndon's*, 534); Miers, *Lincoln*, July 10, 1833; Mortgage drawn for William Greene Jr. to Reuben Radford, Jan. 15, 1833 (transcript available in *CW* 1:15–16).

137. William G. Greene in Onstot, *Pioneers*, 82; *Lincoln and New Salem*, 44.

138. Hardin Bale interview with William H. Herndon, May 29, 1865, H-W Papers (transcript available in Wilson and Davis, *Herndon's*, 13); William G. Greene in Onstot, *Pioneers*, 82; *Lincoln and New Salem*, 44–45; William G. Greene interview with William H. Herndon, May 30, 1865, H-W Papers (transcript available in Wilson and Davis, *Herndon's*, 20); Henry McHenry to

William H. Herndon, ca. 1866, H-W Papers (transcript available in Wilson and Davis, *Herndon's*, 534); Miller, *History*, 711; Pratt, *Personal*, 12; Thomas, *Lincoln's*, 61, 70.

139. Chandler, "New," 529; Tarbell, *Early*, 160, 169. *See also* Herndon and Weik, *Herndon's Life of Lincoln*, 89; *Lincoln and New Salem*, 15, 42; Nicolay and Hay, *Abraham*, 1:111; Robert Rutledge to William H. Herndon, ca. Nov. 1866, H-W Papers (transcript available in Wilson and Davis, *Herndon's*, 383–84); Thomas, *Lincoln's New Salem*, 6; Winkle, *Young*, 103.

140. Ross, *Lincoln's*, 4–5. Ross says Lincoln was working as a clerk for merchant Sam Hill, but I think he is mixed up about that, although Lincoln may have worked for Hill later. *See also* slight variant of Ross quoted in Onstot, *Pioneers*, 76.

141. Abner Ellis statement, ca. Jan. 23, 1866, H-W Papers (transcript available in Wilson and Davis, *Herndon's*, 170).

142. D. L. Dix, "An Account of the Jails and Poor Houses in Illinois—No. 4," *SJ*, April 8, 1847.

143. Petition to county commissioners concerning Benjamin Elmore, Feb. 9, 1833 (transcript available in *CW* 1:17–18); file N05001 in Benner and Davis, *Law*.

144. Robert B. Rutledge to William H. Herndon, ca. Nov. 1866, H-W Papers (transcript available in Wilson and Davis, *Herndon's*, 385). *See also Lincoln and New Salem*, 64–65; James Taylor interview with William H. Herndon, ca. 1865, H-W Papers (transcript available in Wilson and Davis, *Herndon's*, 482). Confusion exists about the barefoot boy's name. Taylor's version indicates the boy was chopping for Ann Rutledge's father. In that version, although Rutledge was enabling the lad to acquire shoes, Lincoln felt more charity was needed. I wonder why Rutledge didn't let the fellow acquire shoes first and then do the chore in payment. Rutledge gave this denouement: "'Ab' remembered this act with the liveliest gratitude. Once, he, being a cast iron Democrat, determined to vote against his party and for Mr. Lincoln; but the friends, as he afterwards said with tears in eyes, made him drunk, and he had voted against Abe."

145. Angle, "Lincoln and Liquor" (June 1932), 3; Bond, March 6, 1833, document 130274, file N05304 in Benner and Davis, *Law*; Hamm, "Prohibitionists'," 113; Pease, *Frontier*, 45; Tarbell, *Early*, 169; Warren, "Tavern"; Wilson, *Uncollected*, 1:576.

146. *History of Sangamon*, 297.

147. Daniel Burner in Temple, "Lincoln and the Burners," 66. *See also* Daniel Burner in Hapgood, *Abraham*, 37. Burner was the brother-in-law of Dr. Jason Duncan (Burner in Tarbell, *Early*, 195), who had campaigned for Lincoln in the 1832 election.

148. License prices in Luthin, *Real*, 31.

149. Thompson Ware McNeely to William H. Herndon, Nov. 12, 1866, H-W Papers (transcript available in Wilson and Davis, *Herndon's*, 397); George Spears to William H. Herndon, Nov. 3, 1866, H-W Papers (transcript available in Wilson and Davis, *Herndon's*, 393).

150. James Davis interview with William H. Herndon, 1866, H-W Papers (transcript available in Wilson and Davis, *Herndon's*, 530).

151. John Rowan Herndon to William H. Herndon, Oct. 28, 1866, H-W Papers (transcript available in Wilson and Davis, *Herndon's*, 379); Onstot, *Pioneers*, 78; Ross, *Lincoln's*, 8.

152. Royal Clary interview with William H. Herndon, ca. Oct. 1866, H-W Papers (transcript available in Wilson and Davis, *Herndon's*, 371).

153. Jones A. Mendall, *SJ*, May 11, 1833.

154. *New York Observer*, clipped in *St. Louis Observer*, Oct. 30, 1834.

155. *Vandalia Illinois Advocate*, March 30, 1833.

156. Moses Stuart, "On the Use of Tobacco," *Illinois Monthly Magazine* (Feb. 1831): 209, 213, 214.

157. *Vandalia Illinois Advocate and State Register*, May 25, 1833.

158. Stephen A. Douglas to Julius N. Granger, May 24, 1835 (transcript available in Douglas, *Letters*, 19).

159. Abraham Lincoln, "Communication to the People of Sangamo County," March 9, 1832 (transcript available in *CW* 1:7).

160. *Lincoln and New Salem*, 21; John McNamar (McNeil) to William H. Herndon, June 4, 1866, H-W Papers (transcript available in Wilson and Davis, *Herndon's*, 259); James Short to William

H. Herndon, July 7, 1865, H-W Papers (transcript available in Wilson and Davis, *Herndon's*, 73). The incident sounds authentic, but its dating is questionable. *See also* Ross, *Lincoln's*, 57, for tendency of Sangamon River to spread out of its channel. *Lincoln and New Salem* and Nicolay and Hay, *Abraham*, 1:78, say it occurred while Lincoln was waiting for Offutt's store goods in summer 1831, and Beveridge (*Abraham* 1:109) accepts that dating, but Short dates it more toward 1833. Tarbell, *Early*, 118, and Tarbell, *Life*, 1:71, date the incident as following the August 1, 1831, election. A summer trip down the Sangamon was hardly likely to encounter flooding conditions. Short seems right; documentation proves that the migrant (Dr. David Nelson) was still at New Salem in March 1832 (Draft drawn on James Rutledge, March 8, 1832 (transcript available in *CW* 1:4)), and immediately after March 1832, Lincoln was supposedly piloting the *Talisman* and definitely serving in the Black Hawk War.

161. "Alley v. Duncan," file L05903 in Benner and Davis, *Law*; "Close v. Ritter," file L04874 in Benner and Davis, *Law*; Miers, *Lincoln*, entries for April 1833; Pratt, "Genesis," 3–8; "State Bank of Illinois v. Bowling," document 124290, file L04573 in Benner and Davis, *Law*; "State Bank of Illinois v. Parkinson," document 124318, file L04576 in Benner and Davis, *Law*.

162. "People v. Edwards & Edwards," file L04235 in Benner and Davis, *Law* (including affidavit, Sept. 19, 1832, document 122823; affidavit, April 16, 1833, document 122827; data bar; deposition, April 6, 1831, document 820; order, April 16, 1833, document 122828; order, June 10, 1834, document 131751); "People v. Edwards et al.," file L04236 in Benner and Davis, *Law* (including data bar). Other defendants included James Edwards and James Hodgepeth. Identifications of William Carpenter as the politician and "William Green" as Bill are based on my personal assumptions, and I acknowledge the possibility that further investigation may fail to support them. Part of my assumption about Bill is based on supposition that the party attracted a crowd younger than his father, William Greene. I acknowledge the possibility that Bowling Green was surety only for James Edwards or James Hodgepeth, or both, but he definitely was surety for one or more defendants.

163. John Holt, U.S. Army Judge Advocate General during Civil War, interview with John Nicolay, Oct. 29, 1875 (transcript available in Burlingame, *Oral*, 69–70). Lincoln's attitude also lends credibility to his reported outrage at the New Orleans slave auction, a detail that in turn lends credibility to the report of his presence at the sale.

164. Barton, *Life*, 1:212; Chandler, "New," 531; Jason Duncan to William H. Herndon, ca. 1866, H-W Papers (transcript available in Wilson and Davis, *Herndon's*, 540); Houser, *Lincoln's Education*, 21; Johnson, *Illinois*, 63; Abraham Lincoln, autobiography for John L. Scripps, ca. June 1860 (transcript available in *CW* 4:65); *Lincoln and New Salem*, 13, 50; *New York Morning Herald*, clipped in *Vandalia Illinois Intelligencer*, April 25, 1829; Onstot, *Pioneers*, 87–88; Rufus Rockwell Wilson, "Editor's Introduction" in Ross, *Lincoln's*, xxii; Thomas, "Lincoln the Postmaster," 3–4. Illinois politician Benjamin Mills claimed that Jackson did pay attention to politics of rural postmasters (*Galena North Western Gazette and Galena Advertiser*, Jan. 31, 1835).

165. Pratt, *Personal*, 15; Thomas, "Lincoln the Postmaster," 4. Miers, *Lincoln*, May 7, 1833, says shoemaker Alexander Ferguson (also spelled Furgeson) was the surety with Alley, but I believe that report is mistaken.

166. Tarbell, *Early*, 176 caption.

167. Holland, *Life*, 55; Kempf, *Abraham*, 117; *Lincoln and New Salem*, 50, 56; Thomas, "Lincoln the Postmaster," 8.

168. Colby, "Jonathan," 431.

169. Illinois constitution of 1818, art. II, § 25.

170. Pratt, *Personal*, 16–17.

171. Patrick Shirreff, quoted in Angle, *Prairie*, 138–39; Thomas, *Lincoln's*, 63–64.

172. Pratt, *Personal*, 17. Some postmasters might accept a barter arrangement from a mail recipient who lacked specie (Angle, "*Here*," 23), but this was an arrangement between those two individuals. The postmaster had to furnish specie to the federal government.

173. John Allen interview with James Quay Howard (transcript available in Basler, "James," 388); Brooks, *Abraham*, 68–69; Holland, *Life*, 55; Howells, *Life*, 32.

174. Onstot, *Pioneers*, 46–50; Ross, *Lincoln's*, 18–22. Ross said Lincoln was already surveying in the summer of 1833, but I believe that memory is mistaken. Dr. Henry was appointed Sangamon Town postmaster that spring (*SJ*, May 18, 1833) and apparently resigned in the autumn (*SJ*, Oct. 12, 1833), although a distinguished student says he left the postmastership in August (Pratt, *Dr.*, 3).

175. Ross, *Lincoln's*, 2.

176. Percy Wells Bidwell, "A History of Northern Agriculture 1620 to 1840," in Bidwell and Falconer, *History*, 247–48, conveniently summarizes the financial scene of Western store business, illustrating that the Berry & Lincoln operation's practices were typical.

177. Duis, *Good*, 266.

178. Carson, "Cracker," 8–9; Curti, *Making*, 226; Hammond, *Banks*, 608.

179. McGrady Rutledge in Tarbell, *Early*, 174. For the general practice, *see* Bigelow, *Retrospections*, 1:11; Carson, "Cracker," 8–9; Faragher, *Sugar*, 134–35; Howells, *Recollections*, 137–38.

180. Duden, *Report* (1824–27), quoted in W. G. Bek, *Missouri Historical Review* 13 (1918): 273, as given in Percy Wells Bidwell, "A History of Northern Agriculture 1620 to 1840," in Bidwell and Falconer, *History*, 174. *See also* Percy Wells Bidwell, "A History of Northern Agriculture 1620 to 1840," in Bidwell and Falconer, *History*, 249. The double-profit aspect may be why in Springfield of the 1830s, "all the merchants advertised that they would take country produce in exchange for goods, and some even preferred it to cash" (Angle, *"Here,"* 47).

181. Ross, *Lincoln's*, 5. Ross says this incident occurred in 1832, while Lincoln was clerking in Sam Hill's store. I think Ross is mixed up about Lincoln working for Hill then, although there is testimony that Lincoln worked for Hill in 1834 after the Berry & Lincoln store folded (Robert L. Wilson to William H. Herndon, Feb. 10, 1866, H-W Papers (transcript available in Wilson and Davis, *Herndon's*, 201)). Ross's memory appears incorrect to me, but I acknowledge he may be right about referring the incident to Hill's store. Even if the conversation didn't occur in the Berry & Lincoln store, it illustrates the economic principle I discuss.

182. Daniel Burner in Temple, "Lincoln and the Burners," 66.

183. Daniel Burner in Temple, "Lincoln and the Burners," 66.

184. Abner Ellis statement for William H. Herndon, ca. Jan. 23, 1866, H-W Papers (transcript available in Wilson and Davis, *Herndon's*, 170); Daniel Burner in Hapgood, *Abraham*, 37, and in Tarbell, *Early*, 172; Winkle, *Young*, 109.

185. Miers, *Lincoln*, April 29, 1833; Pratt, *Personal*, 14.

186. Henry Clark interview with William H. Herndon, 1866, H-W Papers (transcript available in Wilson and Davis, *Herndon's*, 528); James Davis interview with William H. Herndon, 1866, H-W Papers (transcript available in Wilson and Davis, *Herndon's*, 530); John Rowan Herndon to William H. Herndon, June 21, 1865, H-W Papers (transcript available in Wilson and Davis, *Herndon's*, 51); John Rowan Herndon to William H. Herndon, Oct. 28, 1866, H-W Papers (transcript available in Wilson and Davis, *Herndon's*, 378); George Spears to William H. Herndon, Oct. 17, 1866, H-W Papers (transcript available in Wilson and Davis, *Herndon's*, 375).

187. Beveridge, *Abraham*, 1:119 n. 5; Miers, *Lincoln*, Aug. 20, Sept. 13, 1833, and March 17, 1834; Townsend, *Lincoln the Litigant*, 46–48, 52–53; Wilson, *Uncollected*, 1:47–48. Pratt, *Personal*, 10, says that the judgment was satisfied by money from several people, but Lincoln paid nothing on it. Why anyone other than Alley or Lincoln would pay to satisfy judgment against them is unclear. In October 1833, Lincoln and two other persons appraised some New Salem town lots owned by Henry Sinco, being auctioned to pay a debt Sinco owed to Alley (*CW* 1:20). That transaction might have allowed Alley to help Lincoln pay the debt they owed on Bogue's store goods, but there were no bidders and thus no sale (Baber, *A. Lincoln*, 7; Wilson, *Uncollected*, 1:57).

188. Declaration by Henry E. Dummer on behalf of Stuart & Dummer, filed April 9, 1834, document 125927 in Benner and Davis, *Law*; Promissory note to Reuben Radford, Oct. 19, 1833

(transcript in *CW* 1:20); promissory note, Oct. 19, 1833, document 125928 in Benner and Davis, *Law.*

189. *SJ*, April 13, 20, 27, May 4, 11, 1833.
190. Abraham Lincoln, autobiography for John L. Scripps, ca. June 1860 (transcript available in *CW* 4:65).
191. Angle, "Lincoln and Liquor" (June 1932), 4; Peterson, *Lincoln*, 249; Leonard Swett in Chapman, *Latest*, 153–54, and in Rice, *Reminiscences*, 462–63.
192. Hardin Bale interview with William H. Herndon, May 29, 1865, H-W Papers (transcript available in Wilson and Davis, *Herndon's*, 13); William G. Greene interview with William H. Herndon, May 30, 1865, H-W Papers (transcript available in Wilson and Davis, *Herndon's*, 20); George Spears to William H. Herndon, Oct. 17, 1866, H-W Papers (transcript available in Wilson and Davis, *Herndon's*, 375).
193. *Lincoln and New Salem*, 62; Robert Rutledge to William H. Herndon, ca. Nov. 1866, H-W Papers (transcript available in Wilson and Davis, *Herndon's*, 384); Ross, *Lincoln's*, 38; Townsend, *Lincoln and Liquor*, 33, 36.
194. Daniel Burner in Temple, "Lincoln and the Burners," 66–67.
195. Miers, *Lincoln*, Aug. 26, Sept. 16, 1833; Trent & Trent v. Rutledge et al., file L04682 in Benner and Davis, *Law.* Townsend, *Lincoln the Litigant*, 62, says John Stuart acted as the Trents' attorney, but this isn't confirmed by Benner and Davis.
196. "Watkins v. Lincoln & Berry," file L04766 in Benner and Davis, *Law* (including appeal bond, Dec. 25, 1833, document 125918). This data indicates that Berry admitted the plaintiff's claim, that Lincoln contested it, and that Berry and Lincoln both appealed. It's unclear how Berry could say the plaintiff was right and then appeal judgment favoring the plaintiff.
197. Beveridge, *Abraham*, 1:128; Chandler, "New," 531; *Lincoln and New Salem*, 62; John Rowan Herndon to William H. Herndon, May 28, 1865, H-W Papers (transcript available in Wilson and Davis, *Herndon's*, 7); John Rowan Herndon to William H. Herndon, June 21, 1865, H-W Papers (transcript available in Wilson and Davis, *Herndon's*, 51); John Rowan Herndon to William H. Herndon, Oct. 28, 1866, H-W Papers (transcript available in Wilson and Davis, *Herndon's*, 378); Tarbell, *Early*, 187; Tarbell, *Life*, 1:120–21; Thomas, *Lincoln's*, 13; Winkle, *Young*, 99, 104–5. I'm disinclined to think much connection existed between the Rutledge lot litigation and the Trents' acquisition of the Berry & Lincoln store. If Berry and Lincoln turned over the store to satisfy the $150 bond that Lincoln had given the Trents (in which Berry had no obligation), Lincoln and Berry would be left responsible for the much larger store debt. More plausibly, if Lincoln and Berry were looking for buyers, sale of the store might have been offered to the Trents as a matter of goodwill for abandoning the Rutledge litigation. Tarbell identifies Alexander's brother as William. A story tells of Lincoln representing the Trent brothers in a lawsuit against Lincoln's good friend Jack Kelso over ownership of a pig, in which Lincoln presented witnesses on behalf of the Trents. Kelso presented no witnesses, and Lincoln argued that the preponderance of evidence was in the Trents' favor. Justice Bowling Green ruled in favor of Kelso, saying that the witnesses were liars and that Green was well aware that the pig in question was Kelso's (*Lincoln and New Salem*, 77; Townsend, *Lincoln the Litigant*, 62–63). If true, the story would be telling commentary on the Trents, but in order to be true, Lincoln would have had to knowingly present witnesses committing perjury. I say "knowingly" because Green's knowledge of the pig surely would have been shared by much of the community. Lincoln's entire law career argues against his attempting such a trick. Moreover, in another version of the story, Lincoln represents John Ferguson instead of the Trents (Hill, *Lincoln*, 29; Tarbell, *Early*, 200 (citing James McGrady Rutledge, cousin of Ann)). The authorities are good, but their stories conflict and, to me, seem unbelievable as recorded.
198. *SJ*, May 31, 1832.
199. Quoted in *American Atheists*, no. 977 (Nov. 15, 2001), citing conversation related by Walt Whitman.

200. Dole, "Pioneer," 118. *See also* Benjamin Lakin, dateline Clermont County, Ohio, Nov. 27, 1833, in *Christian Advocate and Journal*, Dec. 20, 1833.

201. Quoted in *American Atheists*, no. 977 (Nov. 15, 2001), citing conversation related by Walt Whitman.

202. *Galenian*, Nov. 15, 1833.

203. J. Duncan to Editor, *Beardstown Chronicle*, March 8, 1834.

204. *SJ*, Nov. 16, 1833.

205. *Cincinnati Gazette* clipped in *SJ*, Nov. 30, 1833.

206. *Frankfort Commonwealth* clipped in *SJ*, Dec. 14, 1833.

207. *New York Commercial Adv.* clipped in *SJ*, Dec. 7, 1833.

208. *Hartford Times* clipped in *SJ*, Dec. 14, 1833.

209. *Portsmouth Journal* clipped in *SJ*, Dec. 14, 1833.

210. *SJ*, Dec. 21, 1833.

211. *Frankfort Commonwealth* clipped in *SJ*, Dec. 14, 1833.

212. Johnson, *Frontier*, 106.

213. *Frankfort Commonwealth* clipped in *SJ*, Dec. 14, 1833. *See also* Faragher, *Sugar*, 91.

214. "A young man from western Virginia," *American Slavery as It Is*, 69.

215. Tarbell, *Early*, 191; Thomas, "Lincoln the Postmaster," 8; Robert L. Wilson to William H. Herndon, Feb. 10, 1866, H-W Papers (transcript available in Wilson and Davis, *Herndon's*, 201).

216. Abner Ellis statement for William H. Herndon, ca. Jan. 23, 1866, H-W Papers (transcript available in Wilson and Davis, *Herndon's*, 170); Nicolay and Hay, *Abraham*, 1:113; Wilson, *Uncollected*, 1:171.

217. Beveridge, *Abraham*, 1:133; *Chicago American*, May 28, 1839; Herndon and Weik, *Herndon's Life of Lincoln*, 98; Nichols, *Disruption*, 109; *SJ*, July 30, 1836.

218. John Calhoun, July 25, 1835, B-20, Broadside Collection, ALPL. *See also SJ*, July 25, 1835 (in *SJ*, Aug.1, Anson G. Henry acknowledged authorship of the anonymous July 25 item).

219. *SJ*, July 30, 1836.

220. *SJ*, Dec. 8, 1832.

221. *SJ*, July 30, 1836.

222. *SJ*, March 9, 1833.

223. "Springfield" pseudonym, letter in *SJ*, June 6, 1835.

224. Accounts vary on whether he was Receiver of Public Moneys or Register, but John Taylor was appointed Receiver when Big Red was appointed Register (*Vandalia Illinois Intelligencer*, Aug. 1, 1829).

225. Examples are in Rohrbough, *Land*, 284, 290–91. As Lincoln's close friend Dr. Anson Henry put it, "It was not thought wrong or disreputable for a government officer to use the money in his possession, *provided*, he had a reasonable prospect for raising it when it was wanted for disbursement" (quoted in *Illinois State Journal*, Sept. 17, 1860, as given in "'The Journal Paper,'" 182).

226. Dick, *Lure*, 42; Erickson, *Banking*, 55.

227. Dick, *Lure*, 43; Rohrbough, *Land*, 290.

228. Erickson, *Banking*, 55–56. In the 1840s, Illinois real estate loan rates were seldom under 20 percent, sometimes reaching 100 percent (p. 56).

229. Stephen A. Douglas to William L. May, Jan. 20, 1841 (transcript available in Douglas, *Letters*, 94).

230. "A Countryman," *SJ*, July 28, 1838. Yes, this date is a few years after 1833, but I doubt that the letter speaks of an innovation.

231. *Public and General Statute Laws of the State of Illinois*, "Surveyors," 669, §3 (1839). This is the 1829 statute in effect when Calhoun became county surveyor.

232. Nicolay and Hay, *Abraham*, 1:117. Private surveyors existed. They wouldn't have existed if county surveyors were needed to establish boundaries for private transactions. As Lincoln

retained some payments made by clients for surveys, and some payment was in barter rather than cash, that shows he was doing private survey work in addition to county assignments. Although state statute specified fees the county surveyor charged for establishing town lots (Illinois, *Revised Laws*, 1833, "Fees," 296), that doesn't necessarily preclude the possibility of private surveyors performing such a function for some special purpose of a town developer. For horse-race track, see William G. Greene interview with William H. Herndon, May 30, 1865, H-W Papers (transcript available in Wilson and Davis, *Herndon's*, 20); Henry McHenry interview with William H. Herndon, 1866, H-W Papers (transcript available in Wilson and Davis, *Herndon's*, 534).

233. Nicolay and Hay, *Abraham*, 1:114–15. Baber, *A. Lincoln*, 1, and Beveridge, *Abraham*, 1:132, concur.

234. Fee schedule in Baber, *A. Lincoln*, 11; Illinois, *Revised Laws*, 1833, "Fees," 296. For examples of Lincoln's per diem charges, *see* Michael Killion, Hugh Armstrong, and Abraham Lincoln to the county commissioners' court, June 2, 1834 (transcript available in *CW* 1:24); James Strawbridge, Levi Cantrall, and Abraham Lincoln to the county commissioners court, Nov. 4, 1834 (transcript available in *CW* 1:26). By statute (Illinois, *Revised Laws*, 1833, "Fees," 296), both fees and per diem went to the county surveyor, but surely the deputy surveyor got a substantial share. Otherwise there was little reason for someone to accept a deputy position.

235. John Moore Fisk interview with William H. Herndon, Feb. 18, 1887, H-W Papers (transcript available in Wilson and Davis, *Herndon's*, 715); William H. Herndon to Jesse Weik, Feb. 18, 1887 (transcript available in Hertz, *Hidden*, 176); *Lincoln and New Salem*, 59; Onstot, *Pioneers*, 249; Tarbell, *In the Footsteps*, 195. Accounts conflict on whether the reassurance came from Simmons or Calhoun.

236. Quoted in Carpenter, *Six*, 111–12.

237. Quoted in Tarbell, *Early*, 190 caption. *See also Lincoln and New Salem*, 59.

238. Isaac N. Arnold in Oldroyd, *Lincoln*, 35; Chandler, "New," 514; William Greene to William H. Herndon, May 29, 1865, H-W Papers (transcript available in Wilson and Davis, *Herndon's*, 12); William Greene to William H. Herndon, May 30, 1865, H-W Papers (transcript available in Wilson and Davis, *Herndon's*, 18); Houser, *Lincoln's Education*, 47, 80. Ross, *Lincoln's*, 6–7, refers to Lincoln studying Greene's books to prepare for surveying. None is specified as a surveying text, and Ross seems to confuse Lincoln's earlier use of Greene's books with later surveying study. Although Ross was in a position to have firsthand knowledge, here he may be relying on (and garbling) previously published material.

239. Baber, *A. Lincoln*, 2; Beveridge, *Abraham*, 1:132; Herndon and Weik, *Herndon's Life of Lincoln*, 99; *Lincoln and New Salem*, 59; Nicolay and Hay, *Abraham*, 1:115.

240. Henry McHenry interview with William H. Herndon, May 29, 1865, H-W Papers (transcript available in Wilson and Davis, *Herndon's*, 14); Tarbell, *Early*, 182; Thomas, *Lincoln's New Salem*, 69. *See also* Mentor Graham interview with William H. Herndon, May 29, 1865, H-W Papers (transcript available in Wilson and Davis, *Herndon's*, 11).

241. Caleb Carman interview with William H. Herndon, Oct. 12, 1866, H-W Papers (transcript available in Wilson and Davis, *Herndon's*, 374); Mentor Graham interview with William H. Herndon, May 29, 1865, H-W Papers (transcript available in Wilson and Davis, *Herndon's*, 10); Henry McHenry interview with William H. Herndon, May 29, 1865, H-W Papers (transcript available in Wilson and Davis, *Herndon's*, 14); Nicolay and Hay, *Abraham*, 1:115; Thomas, *Lincoln's New Salem*, 69. Some authorities question or outright reject claims that Graham provided assistance (Baber, *A. Lincoln*, 1; Dorfman, "Lincoln's" (Part 2), 110), but I'm willing to accept reports that the two men consulted—although I'm confident Graham had no special expertise to offer. Regarding Graham's limited teaching capacities and his claims to have taught Lincoln, *see* Houser, *Lincoln's Education*, 108–9; William G. Greene to William H. Herndon, June 7, 1865, H-W Papers (transcript available in Wilson and Davis, *Herndon's*, 26); Temple, *Abraham Lincoln: From*, 20 n. 2.

242. Henry McHenry interview with William H. Herndon, May 29, 1865, H-W Papers (transcript available in Wilson and Davis, *Herndon's*, 14); *Lincoln and New Salem*, 59. McHenry noted that Lincoln "continued reading law at the same time."

243. *Lincoln and New Salem*, 59.

244. Abraham Lincoln, autobiography for John L. Scripps, ca. June 1860 (transcript available in *CW* 4:65). *See also* Arnold, *Life*, 26 n. 1.

245. Edward Tiffin to Josiah Meigs, Oct. 9, 1817 (transcript available in Rohrbough, *Land*, 101).

246. Caton, *Early*, 12–13.

247. Miller, *History*, 334–35.

248. Elizabeth Abell to William H. Herndon, Feb. 15, 1867, H-W Papers (transcript available in Wilson and Davis, *Herndon's*, 557). For Lincoln taking some fees in trade, *see also* Russell Godbey to William H. Herndon, Aug. 17, 1887, H-W Papers (transcript available in Wilson and Davis, *Herndon's*, 624); Tarbell, *In the Footsteps*, 197. Controversy exists about who did the foxing and other foxing details, but the issue isn't worth documenting here.

249. Mitchell, *Illinois*, 39.

250. Baber, *A. Lincoln*, 49; Chandler, "New," 545; Pond, "Memoirs," 84.

251. Baber, *A. Lincoln*, 12, 19.

252. Baber, *A. Lincoln*, xvi–xvii, 157.

253. Robert L. Wilson to William H. Herndon, Feb. 10, 1866, H-W Papers (transcript available in Wilson and Davis, *Herndon's*, 201). Later expert opinion concurs: Baber, *A. Lincoln*, 65; Dorfman, "Lincoln's" (Part 2), 110.

254. Henry McHenry interview with William H. Herndon, May 29, 1865, H-W Papers (transcript available in Wilson and Davis, *Herndon's*, 14–15).

255. Baber, *A. Lincoln*, 15.

256. Onstot, *Pioneers*, 151.

257. John Weber to William H. Herndon, Nov. 5, 1866, H-W Papers (transcript available in Wilson and Davis, *Herndon's*, 395–96). A variant of the story gives the banter as between Lincoln and Coleman Smoot in 1832 (Coleman Smoot to William H. Herndon, May 7, 1866, H-W Papers (transcript available in Wilson and Davis, *Herndon's*, 253–54)).

258. This is my own conclusion, but other authorities concur (Arnold, *Life*, 41; Nicolay and Hay, *Abraham*, 1:117). For mention of real estate speculation by Western surveyors, *see* McGrane, *Panic*, 56–57.

259. Baber, *A. Lincoln*, 35.

Chapter 7. POLITICS OF 1834: GOVERNOR AND LEGISLATORS

1. George Forquer, *SJ*, July 12, 1832.

2. William L. May to George Forquer, May 18, 1835, printed in *SJ*, Feb. 13, 1836.

3. *Galenian*, Nov. 15, 1833.

4. Illinois, *Revised Laws* 1833, "Seat of Government," 572–73.

5. *SJ*, May 4, 1833. Indeed, eventually the law committing the legislature to the plebiscite's result would be repealed, but we'll come to that later.

6. *Alton Spectator* article commented upon in *SJ*, June 15, 1833; transcript of A. P. Field (dateline Vandalia) to Henry Eddy, June 25, 1834, Henry Eddy Papers; *SJ*, Aug. 23, 1834; *Vandalia Whig and Illinois Intelligencer*, July 10, 1834.

7. *SJ*, Dec. 7, 28, 1833; Jan. 11, 1834.

8. "Justice," in *Chicago Democrat*, Dec. 17, 1833.

9. *Chicago Democrat*, Feb. 4, 1834; *SJ*, Jan. 11, 1834. *See also* Justice, "Catching Whales," *Beardstown Chronicle*, April 5, 1834.

10. *SJ*, Feb. 8, 15, March 1, 8, 22, 29, April 12, 1834.

11. *Beardstown Chronicle*, March 22, 1834; *Chicago Democrat*, March 4, 1834; *Galenian*, Jan. 3, 10, 17, 1834.

12. *Galenian*, Feb. 7, 1834.
13. *Beardstown Chronicle*, March 22, 1834.
14. *Chicago Democrat*, Feb. 25, 1834.
15. *Vandalia Illinois Advocate and State Register*, Jan. 18, 1834. *See also SJ*, June 15, 1833.
16. *SJ*, Sept. 27 (two articles), Nov. 15, 1834. *See also* Beveridge, *Abraham*, 1:175, 175 n. 3. This was neither the first (for example, *see SJ*, July 27, 1833) nor the last accusation of skulduggery for Springfield's benefit.
17. Petition to county commissioners, Feb. 25, 1834 (transcript available in *CW* 1:21).
18. Baber, *A. Lincoln*, 83.
19. Baber, *A. Lincoln*, 84.
20. *SJ*, March 15, 1834 (transcript available in *CW* 1:21).
21. "A Voter of Tazewell" to Editor, *SJ*, May 10, 1834.
22. *SJ*, March 15, 1834 (transcript available in *CW* 1:21–22).
23. *SJ*, March 22, 1834.
24. Baringer, *Lincoln's Vandalia*, 42; Davidson and Stuvé, *Complete*, 416 n.; Moses, *Illinois*, 422. These authorities disagree on whether Duncan's hair was straight or curly; I have chosen the majority's description.
25. William Linn to Editor, *Vandalia Illinois Advocate and State Register*, March 1, 1834.
26. "Plebian" in *Jacksonville Sentinel* clipped in *Chicago Democrat*, Sept. 2, 1835.
27. Reuben Harrison, James Shepherd, Alonzo Holcomb, and A. G. Henry, "Address to the People of Illinois," *Beardstown Chronicle*, March 22, 1834; declaration of Sangamon County meeting, *SJ*, March 15, 1834.
28. Linder, *Reminiscences*, 109; William Walters, *Illinois State Register*, April 29, 1842.
29. *SJ*, Nov. 16, 23, 30, Dec. 14, 1833; Jan. 25, 1834. The June 7, 1834, *SJ* mentions defense by the *Jacksonville Illinois Patriot*. Defense was also seen in the Democratic press, e.g. *Galenian*, Nov. 22, 1833.
30. Baringer, *Lincoln's Vandalia*, 42.
31. *Vandalia Illinois Advocate and State Register*, Feb. 8, 1834.
32. *St. Clair Gazette*, clipped in *Chicago Democrat*, March 4, 1834. *See also* "To the Voters of Illinois," B-156, Broadside Collection, ALPL.
33. *SJ*, Aug. 2, 1832.
34. Joseph Duncan to Editor, *Vandalia Free Press*, clipped in *Chicago American*, Feb. 4, 1837; *Vandalia Illinois State Register and People's Advocate*, Jan. 27, 28, 1837.
35. Handbill signed by "Citizen," B-25, Broadside Collection, ALPL.
36. Burlingame, *Oral*, 142 n. 122; William Butler interview with John Nicolay, June 13, 1875 (transcript available in Burlingame, *Oral*, 21); Jesse Dubois interview with John Nicolay, July 4, 1875 (transcript available in Burlingame, *Oral*, 31); *Missouri Reporter* clipped in *Illinois State Register*, July 1, 1842; *SJ*, June 24, 1837. Dubois includes Robert Wilson as an Illiopolis investor, but Wilson was a member of Sangamon County's later "Long Nine" delegation in the legislature, a delegation that worked hard to make Springfield the seat of government.
37. Jockey Club, "Great Political Horse Race," B-239, Broadside Collection, ALPL.
38. Snyder, *Adam*, 96.
39. Pease, *Frontier*, 130; Reynolds, *My Own Times*, 263. John Messinger is also credited with teaching Kinney to read and write (Snyder, *Adam*, 95).
40. Illinois Servitude and Emancipation Records, 1722–1863, an Index Compiled from the Illinois State Archives, published May 5, 2002, www.webroots.org/library/usahist/ilsaer0.txt.
41. Ford, *History*, 68. *See also* Reynolds, *My Own Times*, 295–96.
42. "Truth" to Editor, *Galena Miners' Journal*, July 24, 1830.
43. Koerner, *Memoirs*, 1:309.
44. James Shields to Gustave Koerner, Dec. 22, 1838, J. F. Snyder Papers.
45. Koerner, *Memoirs*, 1:475.
46. Reynolds, *My Own Times*, 263.

47. Koerner, *Memoirs*, 1:70.
48. Barnhart, "Southern," 362, 362 n. 7; Harris, *History*, 112; Howard, *Illinois*, 131; Illinois Servitude and Emancipation Records, 1722–1863, an Index Compiled from the Illinois State Archives, published May 5, 2002, http://www.webroots.org/library/usahist/ilsaer0.txt. "He was always driven from place to place in a magnificent carriage drawn by very spirited horses, with two colored servants on the box" (Brown, "Springfield," 479).
49. Davidson and Stuvé, *Complete*, 339; Edwards, *History*, 186; Huston, *Financing*, 1:69; Snyder, *Adam*, 79. Apparently more than one loan involving more than one bank officer was involved, but I use the term "loan" in a generic sense rather than referring to a particular transaction. As Edwards was one of the most brutal opponents of Treasury Secretary Crawford's hopes to become President, and Kinney was one of Crawford's strong supporters, that difference of opinion surely helped fuel the charges that Edwards made against bank president Kinney. The state bank "was founded without money, and wholly on the credit of the State" (Ford, *History*, 25). Thus loans were based on state credit, ultimately making the state government the source of financing for the proslavery newspaper.
50. *Vandalia Illinois Advocate and State Register*, May 17, 1834.
51. William Kinney in *St. Clair Gazette*, clipped in *Vandalia State Register and People's Advocate*, Friday, Feb. 17(?), 1837.
52. Ford, *History*, 69.
53. Reynolds, *My Own Times*, 263.
54. "Dionicias" in *Vandalia Illinois Intelligencer*, May 15, 1830.
55. Printed in *Chicago Democrat*, Jan. 21, 1834.
56. Reynolds, *My Own Times*, 290.
57. "Fayette, Junior," in *Vandalia Illinois Intelligencer*, Nov. 7, 1829.
58. Pease, *Frontier*, 131.
59. Reynolds, *My Own Times*, 290–91. For a contemporary report of the phrase, *see* "Timon" in *Vandalia Illinois Intelligencer*, Oct. 24, 1829. *See also Belleville Advocate*, June 6, 1840.
60. "Fayette, Junior," in *Vandalia Illinois Intelligencer*, Nov. 7, 1829.
61. Reynolds, *My Own Times*, 296.
62. *Beardstown Chronicle*, clipped in *Chicago Democrat*, Sept. 3, 1834.
63. William Kinney in *Chicago Democrat*, July 16, 1834; William Kinney in *SJ*, July 26, 1834.
64. Koerner, *Memoirs*, 1:475.
65. John Taylor to Editors, July 20, 1830, in *Vandalia Illinois Intelligencer*, July 31, 1830. Hamilton's father was President Washington's Treasury Secretary. This is the same William Hamilton we encountered in the Black Hawk War. By 1834, Taylor was associated with Joseph Duncan in real estate speculation.
66. Snyder, *Adam*, 97.
67. *Vandalia Illinois Intelligencer*, July 31, 1830. Possibly Forquer was trying to deter a follower of *code duello*, which allowed a gentleman to whip or cane a defenseless offender whose conduct made him unworthy of being invited to a gentleman's field of honor. Anson G. Henry claimed that in 1832, Big Red May "wrote to Judge Hall, at Vandalia, 'that Geo. Forquer, was walking the streets *belted to a horseman's pistol*,' in anticipation of a visit from him [Big Red] with a cowhide" (Anson G. Henry in *SJ*, June 13, 1835).
68. In this geopolitical analysis, I basically accept the thinking of Ford, *History*, 9, but he may insufficiently credit the Ohio River's encouragement of Eastern linkage (*see* Pease, *Frontier*, 387–88).
69. William Elliot, *SJ*, June 21, 1834.
70. "Fayette, Junior," in *Vandalia Illinois Intelligencer*, Nov. 7, 1829, Feb. 6, 1830; William Kinney circular to voters, *Chicago Democrat*, July 16, 1834, and *Galenian*, July 21, 1834; William Kinney to Elias Kent Kane, Nov. 10, 1825 (transcript available in *Vandalia Illinois Advocate and State Register*, June 14, 1834); letter in *St. Clair Gazette* clipped in *Chicago Democrat*, May 21, 1834; *SJ*, July 26, 1834.

71. Bonham, *Fifty*, 36; Davidson and Stuvé, *Complete*, 364; *Galena Advertiser*, Feb. 15, 1830; John Hacker to R. K. Fleming, April 24, 1830, in *The Crisis—Extra*, July 13, 1830 (transcript available in *Galena Trail and Coach Road Newsletter* (Dec. 30, 2004): 6; Reynolds, *My Own Times*, 296.

72. William Kinney in *Chicago Democrat*, July 16, 1834; William Kinney in *SJ*, July 26, 1834.

73. Speech of Felix Grundy, quoted in "To the Voters of Illinois" handbill, B-156, Broadside Collection, ALPL.

74. Reynolds, *My Own Times*, 291.

75. Kinney campaign circular to voters, *Galena Miners' Journal*, April 24, 1830; "Victory," dateline Nov. 4, 1829, in *Illinois Courier*, clipped in *Galena Advertiser*, Feb. 22, 1830.

76. Declaration of Sangamon County meeting, *SJ*, March 15, 1834; Reuben Harrison, James Shepherd, Alonzo Holcomb, and A. G. Henry, "Address to the People of Illinois," *Beardstown Chronicle*, March 22, 1834.

77. *Vandalia Illinois Advocate and State Register*, May 17, 1834.

78. Jockey Club, "Great Political Horse Race," B-239, Broadside Collection, ALPL.

79. Snyder, *Adam*, 36; *Vincennes Western Sun*, Aug. 27, Sept. 3, 9, Oct. 1, 8, Nov. 5, 1808, and April 29, 1809; www.randolphcountyillinois.net/sub33.htm; Barnhart, "Southern," 362, 362 n. 7; Illinois Servitude and Emancipation Records, 1722–1863, an Index Compiled from the Illinois State Archives, published May 5, 2002, www.webroots.org/library/usahist/ilsaer0.txt.

80. *Vandalia Illinois Intelligencer*, June 20, 1829.

81. Illinois Servitude and Emancipation Records, 1722–1863, an Index Compiled from the Illinois State Archives, published May 5, 2002, www.webroots.org/library/usahist/ilsaer0.txt; Tillson, *Woman's*, 138 n. 18.

82. Tillson, *Woman's*, 137–41.

83. Joseph Gillespie to William H. Herndon, Dec. 8, 1866, H-W Papers (transcript available in Wilson and Davis, *Herndon's*, 509); Ford, *History*, 103; Gillespie, *Recollections*, 36; Linder, *Reminiscences*, 107.

84. *Alton Spectator* clipped in *SJ*, Feb. 22, 1834.

85. Statement of Madison County meeting, in *SJ*, March 22, 1834.

86. Declaration of Sangamon County meeting, in *SJ*, March 15, 1834.

87. Reuben Harrison, James Shepherd, Alonzo Holcomb, and A. G. Henry, "Address to the People of Illinois," *Beardstown Chronicle*, March 22, 1834.

88. Pratt, *Dr.*, 5. *See also SJ* clipped in *Beardstown Chronicle*, March 22, 1834.

89. *SJ*, Sept. 7, 1833.

90. *SJ*, July 12, 1834.

91. Ford, *History*, 103. Ford's statement can be read as saying that Henry's *majority*, not his *total*, would be 20,000 votes, but I have taken the more conservative interpretation. To me, Ford's use of "majority" here is ambiguous. When Ford wrote, he knew that the vote total in that election had turned out to be about 33,000, so a projected majority of 20,000 over all competitors in such a total would have been impressive indeed. The winner, Joseph Duncan, received 17,500 votes.

92. Power, *History*, 369.

93. Gillespie, *Recollections*, 35.

94. Reynolds, *My Own Times*, 399.

95. Gillespie, *Recollections*, 35. *See also* Reynolds, *My Own Times*, 397.

96. Reynolds, *My Own Times*, 398.

97. Joseph Gillespie in Prickett, "Joseph," 103.

98. *SJ*, Aug. 11, 1832.

99. *SJ*, Sep. 1, 1832.

100. Reynolds, *My Own Times*, 397.

101. Gillespie, *Recollections*, 35–36.

102. James Short to William H. Herndon, July 7, 1865, H-W Papers (transcript available in Wilson and Davis, *Herndon's*, 74).

103. William H. Herndon, undated, H-W Papers (transcript available in Wilson and Davis, *Herndon's*, 66).

104. Abner Ellis in Browne, *Every-Day*, 124.

105. Hardin Bale interview with William H. Herndon, 1866, H-W Papers (transcript available in Wilson and Davis, *Herndon's*, 528).

106. James Short to William H. Herndon, July 7, 1865, H-W Papers (transcript available in Wilson and Davis, *Herndon's*, 74).

107. Royal Clary interview with William H. Herndon, ca. Oct. 1866, H-W Papers (transcript available in Wilson and Davis, *Herndon's*, 370).

108. Caleb Carman interview with William H. Herndon, Oct. 12, 1866, H-W Papers (transcript available in Wilson and Davis, *Herndon's*, 374).

109. Onstot, *Pioneers*, 155, 196, 199. For more, *see* Pond, "New Salem's Miller," 29–31.

110. Baber, *A. Lincoln*, 63, 85–87; Russell Godbey to William H. Herndon, Aug. 17, 1887, H-W Papers (transcript available in Wilson and Davis, *Herndon's*, 624); Michael Killion, Hugh Armstrong, and Abraham Lincoln to the County Commissioners Court, June 2, 1834 (transcript available in *CW* 1:24–25). Baber analyzed Lincoln's work, and Baber's work regarding the Musick road has been analyzed by Doug Criner, "Lincoln's Musick Ford Survey" (http://enginova.com/lincoln.htm) and "New Info on Abe's Survey" (http://enginova.com/New%20Info .htm).

111. Baber, *A. Lincoln*, 57–58, 84–85, 101, 105; "Survey for Jesse Gum," March 3, 1834 (transcript available in *CW* 1:22–23).

112. *SJ*, April 19, 26, 1834.

113. Davidson and Stuvé, *Complete*, 408; Power, *History*, 370; *SJ*, April 5, 12, 26, 1834.

114. "VanBergen v. Lincoln et al.," file L04767 in Benner and Davis, *Law*.

115. Palmer, *Bench*, 166.

116. Praecipe by Henry in Dummer, April 7, 1834, document 125925 in Benner and Davis, *Law*; summons by Sangamon County coroner to William F. Berry, Abraham Lincoln, and William Greene, April 7, 1834, document 125926 in Benner and Davis, *Law*; declaration by Henry E. Dummer on behalf of Stuart & Dummer, filed April 9, 1834, document 125927 in Benner and Davis, *Law*; Thomas, *Lincoln's New Salem*, 72.

117. Enos, "Description," 205–6.

118. *Working Man's Advocate*, clipped in *Galenian*, April 11, 1834.

119. *Alton Spectator*, clipped in *Vandalia Illinois Advocate and State Register*, April 26, 1834; *Beardstown Chronicle*, March 8, April 12, 1834; *Beardstown Chronicle*, clipped in *Chicago Democrat*, April 30, 1834; *Beardstown Chronicle*, clipped in *Vandalia Illinois Advocate and State Register*, April 26, 1834; *Chicago Democrat*, March 18, April 23, 1834; *SJ*, April 19, 1834; *Jacksonville Patriot* clipped in *Galenian*, March 21, 1834. In addition to newspaper coverage, convention proceedings were printed up and distributed as a handbill ("'Seat of Government,'" B-403, Broadside Collection, ALPL).

120. *Vandalia Illinois Advocate and State Register*, April 26, 1834.

121. *SJ*, July 12, 1834.

122. *SJ*, June 14, 1834.

123. Court order, April 29, 1834, document 125929 in Benner and Davis, *Law*; Miers, *Lincoln*, April 29, 1834; Schwartz, *Finding*, 9; summons, April 7, 1834, document 125926 in Benner and Davis, *Law*; Wilson, *Uncollected*, 1:56. *See also* William G. Greene interview with James Quay Howard (transcript available in Basler, "James," 400). Some authorities say $69 of this amount was owed to Reuben Radford and $154 in principal and damages to Peter Van Bergen. Such a joint award would indicate that Radford hadn't assigned the entirety of the note to Van Bergen. I suspect that Radford assigned the whole note and the $154 is an amount Van Bergen decided

to seek (reduced from his original demand of $550 for a $254 debt). As mentioned below, however, there are notations from Radford about a $35 credit to the note and an assignment of the note back to Berry by Radford; such notations would indicate Radford retained an interest in the note.

124. *Lincoln and New Salem*, 62–63; Miers, *Lincoln*, April 26, 1834; Pratt, *Personal*, 13; Stevens, *Reporter's*, 8; Thomas, *Lincoln's New Salem*, 72; Schwartz, *Finding*, 7–9; Thomas Watkins, quoted in Tarbell, *Early*, 186, and Tarbell, *Life*, 1:120; "Watkins v. Lincoln & Berry," file L04766 in Benner and Davis, *Law*. Case data of Watkins v. Lincoln & Berry indicate that Berry joined in Lincoln's appeal, a confusing action given that earlier Berry had admitted the plaintiff's claim was correct. Schwartz argues that the Watkins horse debt story is a garbled commingling of the Watkins suit on the Knapp and Pogue note and the Van Bergen suit on the Radford note. Schwartz says that the horse was bought from stock raiser William Watkins, not stock raiser Thomas Watkins—as said by *Lincoln and New Salem*, 62–63, and Townsend, *Lincoln the Litigant*, 70. Those last two sources may well have been wrong about the name, but the dogskin glove story by a New Salem resident (Ross, *Lincoln's*, 5) also refers to a stock raiser Thomas Watkins, as do Wilson and Davis (*Herndon's*, 534 n. 1) and Slicky Bill Greene (William G. Greene interview with William H. Herndon, May 30, 1865, H-W Papers (transcript available in Wilson and Davis, *Herndon's*, 20)). Given the level of complexity, my conclusion that there were two lawsuits, one by Thomas Watkins and one by William Watkins, is less strong than many of my other beliefs.

125. Election return, May 5, 1834 (transcript available in *CW* 1:23–24); Thomas, "Lincoln: Voter" (Sept. 1934), 5; Wilson, *Uncollected* 1:63.

126. Writ of execution, June 2, 1834, document 124931 in Benner and Davis, *Law*.

127. Testimony exists that Greene paid this judgment and that Lincoln eventually repaid him (William G. Greene interview with William H. Herndon, May 30, 1865, H-W Papers (transcript available in Wilson and Davis, *Herndon's*, 20); James Short to William H. Herndon, July 7, 1865, H-W Papers (transcript available in Wilson and Davis, *Herndon's*, 74)), but those recollections seem mistaken. Given the intricacies of Lincoln's store debts, however, possibility exists that transactions occurred that have been lost in the documentary record.

128. Henderson, "Rough," 366.

129. Benjamin Horace Hibbard, *History of Agriculture in Dane County, Wisconsin*, 96, quoted in Hibbard, *History*, 207.

130. For examples, *see Chicago American*, June 8, 1835 (two items); *Chicago Democrat* clipped in *SJ*, April 8, 1837; Crombie to Editor, *Chicago American*, April 23, 1836; William L. D. Ewing, speech to U.S. Senate, Feb. 1, 1837, in *Vandalia Illinois State Register and People's Advocate*, June 9, 1837; *Galena North Western Gazette and Galena Advertiser*, May 21, 1841, and May 14, 21, 1842.

131. Brunson, *Western*, 2:34.

132. *Chicago Democrat*, Dec. 24, 1834.

133. Charles Chandler interview with William H. Herndon, ca. 1885, H-W Papers (transcript available in Wilson and Davis, *Herndon's*, 719–21); Miers, *Lincoln*, June 4, 1834. Variants of the story can be found in Chandler, "New," 545–49; *Lincoln and New Salem*, 65–67; Shutes, *Lincoln and the Doctors*, 13–14.

134. Abraham Lincoln to George Spears, July 1, 1834 (transcript available in *CW* 1:25); *Lincoln and New Salem*, 35 caption, 58, 69 caption.

135. Onstot, *Pioneers*, 195.

136. Rufus Rockwell Wilson, "Editor's Introduction" in Ross, *Lincoln's*, xx.

137. Dowrie, "Development," 7.

138. Abner Ellis statement to William H. Herndon, ca. Jan. 23, 1866, H-W Papers (transcript available in Wilson and Davis, *Herndon's*, 171).

139. Tarbell, *In the Footsteps*, 202.

140. Herndon and Weik, *Herndon's Life of Lincoln*, 103.
141. Maltby, *Life*, 44–45.
142. *Lincoln and New Salem*, 28.
143. Russell Godbey interview with William H. Herndon, ca. 1865, H-W Papers (transcript available in Wilson and Davis, *Herndon's*, 449). Although this interview speaks of the 1834 election, the reference to fighting isn't explicitly to 1834. I am comfortable assuming that such did happen then. Herndon's notes are unclear about the extent of Godbey's quotation of Lincoln; Lincoln may have said, "Let's go and break up the row with a laugh." *See also* Russell Godbey interview with William H. Herndon, ca. 1865, H-W Papers (transcript available in Wilson and Davis, *Herndon's*, 450). Seemingly, Denny Hanks also spoke of Lincoln's having the talent to stop a fight by using words (Hanks in Browne, *Every-Day*, 53–54).
144. John R. Herndon to William H. Herndon, May 28, 1865, H-W Papers (transcript available in Wilson and Davis, *Herndon's*, 8).
145. Winkle, *Young*, 116.
146. Dennis Hanks, quoted in Browne, *Abraham*, 1:174. Hanks wasn't necessarily speaking about the 1834 campaign, but Lincoln was definitely knowledgeable on the topic.
147. William H. Herndon to Ward Hill Lamon, Feb. 25, 1870 (transcript available in Hertz, *Hidden*, 64).
148. John Hill, "A Romance of Reality," *Menard Axis*, Feb. 15, 1862 (reprinted in Monaghan, "New," 144, and in Wilson and Davis, *Herndon's*, 25).
149. Stevens, *Reporter's*, 8. *See also* 13.
150. Pratt, "Lincoln and the Division," 399; Stevens, *Reporter's*, 8, 13.
151. Stringer, *History*, 213–14; John T. Stuart interview with John Nicolay, June 23, 1875 (transcript available in Burlingame, *Oral*, 11).
152. James Matheny interview with William H. Herndon, Nov. 1866, H-W Papers (transcript available in Wilson and Davis, *Herndon's*, 432).
153. Son of Sophie Hanks, quoted in Arthur Ernest Morgan, "New Light on Lincoln's Early Years," in Wilson, *Lincoln*, 54.
154. Wolf, *Almost*, 40.
155. Russell Godbey interview with William H. Herndon, ca. 1865, H-W Papers (transcript available in Wilson and Davis, *Herndon's*, 449). *See also* Russell Godbey interview with William H. Herndon, ca. 1865, H-W Papers (transcript available in Wilson and Davis, *Herndon's*, 450).
156. William H. Herndon to Francis E. Abbott, Feb. 18, 1870, printed in clipping, *Abraham Lincoln Scrapbook* (ALPL), 49 (apparently from *The Index* 1 (April 2, 1870), 5).
157. Peter Cartwright, *Vandalia Illinois Intelligencer*, Jan. 17, 1829. An argument can be made that Cartwright was speaking metaphorically, but he was never known for sophisticated preaching to intellectuals.
158. Peter Cartwright, *Vandalia Illinois Intelligencer*, Jan. 10, 1829 (and reprinted Jan. 17).
159. *Vandalia Illinois Intelligencer*, Jan. 31, 1829.
160. William Kinney campaign circular to voters in *Galena Miners' Journal*, April 24, 1830. For text of bill, *see Vandalia Illinois Intelligencer*, Jan. 31, 1829. Cartwright gives his take on the controversy in *Vandalia Illinois Intelligencer*, Jan. 17, 31, 1829.
161. "Newlight" to editor, *Galena Miners' Journal*, July 31, 1830.
162. Whitney, *Life*, 12. The entire quotation is italicized in the original.
163. Hardin Bale interview with William H. Herndon, May 29, 1865, H-W Papers (transcript available in Wilson and Davis, *Herndon's*, 13).
164. Isaac Cogdal interview with William H. Herndon, ca. 1865, H-W Papers (transcript available in Wilson and Davis, *Herndon's*, 441).
165. James Matheny interview with William H. Herndon, Nov. 1866, H-W Papers (transcript available in Wilson and Davis, *Herndon's*, 432); James Matheny interview with William H. Herndon, ca. March 1870, H-W Papers (transcript available in Wilson and Davis, *Herndon's*, 577).

166. John Hill, "A Romance of Reality," *Menard Axis*, Feb. 15, 1862 (reprinted in Monaghan, "New," 143, and in Wilson and Davis, *Herndon's*, 24).

167. John Hill to William H. Herndon, June 27, 1865, H-W Papers (transcript available in Wilson and Davis, *Herndon's*, 61–62).

168. William H. Herndon to Francis E. Abbott, Feb. 18, 1870, printed in clipping, *Abraham Lincoln Scrapbook* (ALPL), 49 (apparently from *The Index* 1 (April 2, 1870), 5).

169. Henry McHenry to William H. Herndon, Jan. 8, 1866, H-W Papers (transcript available in Wilson and Davis, *Herndon's*, 156).

170. Mentor Graham to B. F. Irwin, March 17, 1874 (transcript available in "Lincoln's Religious Belief," printed in clipping apparently from letter of B. F. Irwin in *Illinois State Journal*, May 15 or 16, 1874, in *Abraham Lincoln Scrapbook* (ALPL), 64 and reverse side of 64; also in Barton, *Soul*, 346–47, and Wolf, *Almost*, 46–47).

171. What Sam Hill burned has been questioned as well. Mentor Graham said, "About the burning of a paper by Hill, I have some recollection of his snatching a letter from Lincoln and putting it into the fire. It was a letter written by Hill to McNamar. His real name was Neal. Some of the schoolchildren had picked up the letter, and handed it to Lincoln. Neal and Lincoln were talking about it, when Hill snatched the letter from Lincoln and put it into the fire. The letter was respecting a young lady, Miss Ann Rutledge, for whom all three of these gentlemen seemed to have respect." "Respect" in that context meant "love." Graham says this memory is uncertain (Mentor Graham to B. F. Irwin, March 17, 1874 (transcript available in "Lincoln's Religious Belief," printed in clipping apparently from letter of B. F. Irwin in *Illinois State Journal*, April 20 or May 16, 1874, in *Abraham Lincoln Scrapbook* (ALPL), 64 and reverse side of 64; also in Wolf, *Almost*, 46–47). Graham's account has errors and multiple implausibilities. McNamar arrived in town under the alias of McNeil, but McNamar and not Neal was his real name. As the common school system wasn't yet established, could there have been schoolchildren? Such minor objections are easily disregarded as trivial imperfections in a memory recalling an event from decades earlier. A more important objection is that McNamar left town in the summer of 1832 and didn't return until autumn 1835 after Ann Rutledge had died. So the scene remembered by Graham would have occurred at the latest in winter months of early 1832 (the stove being in use and Lincoln having left for the Black Hawk War in April). No contemporary witness dates the infidel manuscript as early 1832, and I've seen no evidence of Lincoln having a romantic interest in Ann in 1832.

  Lincoln and New Salem (50 n., 56) gives a similar but more detailed account, attributed as "it is said," but for a controversial situation, I need a more specific attribution. In that account, supposedly the letter dealt in part with closing out the McNamar-Hill partnership on Hill's initiative because of jealousy over Ann Rutledge, but another authority denies that mutual interest in Ann caused any trouble between McNamar and Hill (Chandler, "New," 525). The business partnership continued through the summer of 1832 and more likely was closed out as a result of McNamar's leaving town, an action involving McNamar's initiative and not Hill's. Perhaps the two men made their close-out arrangements six months early; perhaps the letter burning was an incident separate from the infidel manuscript. Perhaps Hill wrote a letter to his business partner whom Hill would routinely see face-to-face in their store, and perhaps it was possible that Lincoln and McNamar would discuss it. But why would Hill grab the letter and burn it—unless perhaps he had second thoughts about it? Or perhaps he was just in an irate or embarrassed mood. Barton, *Soul*, 151, seems to extrapolate further yet from Mentor Graham's report. These letter-burning accounts involve too many perhapses for me. I've found no attribution for this letter-burning story other than Graham. In contrast, more than one Lincoln acquaintance speaks of Hill burning an infidel manuscript written by Lincoln.

  John Hill said of Graham, "It was quite natural that history should have caught from the interviews with him a good deal of romance" (John Hill to Fern Nance Pond, Feb. 6, 1896 (transcript available in Houser, *Lincoln's Education*, 108)), but Hill's own statements merit close scrutiny. Temple, *Abraham Lincoln: From*, 20 n. 2 presents evidence raising questions about Graham's accuracy and veracity.

172. Robert B. Rutledge to William H. Herndon, ca. Nov. 1, 1866, H-W Papers (transcript available in Wilson and Davis, *Herndon's*, 384). *See also* Nancy Prewitt in Margaret Flindt, "Lincoln as a Lover [etc.], An Interview with Nancy, Sister of Ann Rutledge," *Chicago Inter-Ocean* (Feb. 12, 1886), as given in Walsh, *Shadows*, 43; Tarbell, *In the Footsteps*, 215–16.

173. Charles Maltby, quoted in Temple, *Abraham Lincoln: From*, 16.

174. Quoted in Stevens, *Reporter's*, 12.

175. William H. Herndon to Abbott, Feb. 18, 1870, printed in clipping, *Abraham Lincoln Scrapbook* (ALPL), 49.

176. Herndon and Weik, *Herndon's Life of Lincoln*, 355.

177. Abner Y. Ellis statement for William H. Herndon, ca. Jan. 23, 1866, H-W Papers (transcript available in Wilson and Davis, *Herndon's*, 172); Abner Y. Ellis to William H. Herndon, Jan. 30, 1866, H-W Papers (transcript available in Wilson and Davis, *Herndon's*, 179); Abner Y. Ellis to William H. Herndon, Feb. 14, 1866, H-W Papers (transcript available in Wilson and Davis, *Herndon's*, 210); Abner Y. Ellis to William H. Herndon, Dec. 11, 1866, H-W Papers (transcript available in Wilson and Davis, *Herndon's*, 513).

178. Paine, *Age*, 31–33, 62.

179. Cartwright, *Autobiography*, 288–89.

180. Volney, *Ruins*, 181–82.

181. Volney, *Ruins*, 59.

182. William H. Herndon to Abbott, Feb. 18, 1870, printed in clipping, *Abraham Lincoln Scrapbook* (ALPL), 49.

183. Dr. William Ellery Channing, *Vandalia Illinois Intelligencer*, Sept. 18, 1830.

184. *Christian Advocate and Journal*, Jan. 10, 1834.

185. *Phil. Liberalist*, clipped in *Galenian*, Jan. 31, 1834.

186. *Quincy Whig*, Sept. 5, 1840. The same article noted that argument for religious candidates was made by abolitionists, evidence of their danger to American institutions.

187. James H. Matheny interview with William H. Herndon, ca. March 1870, H-W Papers (transcript available in Wilson and Davis, *Herndon's*, 576–77). *See also* James H. Matheny interview with William H. Herndon, ca. 1865, H-W Papers (transcript available in Wilson and Davis, *Herndon's*, 472).

188. Beveridge, *Abraham*, 1:300–301. *See also* James H. Matheny interview with William H. Herndon, May 3, 1866, H-W Papers (transcript available in Wilson and Davis, *Herndon's*, 251).

189. James H. Matheny interview with William H. Herndon, ca. March 1870, H-W Papers (transcript available in Wilson and Davis, *Herndon's*, 576).

190. Milton Hay to John Hay, Feb. 8, 1887, quoted in "Recollections of Lincoln," 9.

191. James H. Matheny interview with William H. Herndon, ca. March 1870, H-W Papers (transcript available in Wilson and Davis, *Herndon's*, 576). *See also* James H. Matheny interview with William H. Herndon, Nov. 1866, H-W Papers (transcript available in Wilson and Davis, *Herndon's*, 432).

192. William H. Herndon to Ward Hill Lamon, Feb. 25, 1870 (transcript available in Hertz, *Hidden*, 64–65).

193. Speed, *Reminiscences*, 32 (reprinted in Wilson, *Intimate*, 22).

194. John T. Stuart interview with William H. Herndon, Dec. 20, 1866, H-W Papers (transcript available in Wilson and Davis, *Herndon's*, 519); John T. Stuart interview with William H. Herndon, ca. March 1870, H-W Papers (transcript available in Wilson and Davis, *Herndon's*, 576).

195. Speed, *Reminiscences*, 32 (reprinted in Wilson, *Intimate*, 22).

196. David Davis interview with William H. Herndon, Sept. 20, 1866, H-W Papers (transcript available in Wilson and Davis, *Herndon's*, 348); David Davis interview with William H. Herndon, 1866, H-W Papers (transcript available in Wilson and Davis, *Herndon's*, 529).

197. William H. Herndon, "Lincoln's Philosophy and Religion," in Hertz, *Hidden*, 407–8. *See also* William H. Herndon to Abbott, Feb. 18, 1870, printed in clipping, *Abraham Lincoln Scrapbook* (ALPL), 49–50; Herndon, "Analysis," 415–17.

198. William H. Herndon to Truman H. Bartlett, Oct. 1887 (transcript available in Hertz, *Hidden*, 209).

199. Elizabeth Abell to William H. Herndon, Feb. 15, 1867, H-W Papers (transcript available in Wilson and Davis, *Herndon's*, 557).

200. William H. Herndon in *History of Sangamon*, 211.

201. *SJ*, July 12, 1834.

202. William Alvey statement, B-4, Broadside Collection, ALPL; *SJ*, July 19, 1834.

203. Richard Quinton, June 21, 1834, B-116, Broadside Collection, ALPL.

204. Jehu Durley, *SJ*, July 19, 1834. Durley's name is also given as John (Thomas, "Lincoln: Voter" (Sept. 1934), 6).

205. Francis Arenz to John J. Hardin, dateline Beardstown, July [Aug.] 5, 1834, Hardin Family Papers.

206. Sidney Breese to A. F. Grant, June 16, 1834 (transcript available in Henry Eddy Papers).

207. Russell Godbey interview with William H. Herndon, ca. 1865, H-W Papers (transcript available in Wilson and Davis, *Herndon's*, 449).

208. Stephen T. Logan interview with John Nicolay, July 6, 1875, Abraham Lincoln Papers, LOC microfilm, 97:43648ff (transcript available in Burlingame, *Oral*, 36, and in "Stephen T. Logan," *Bulletin of the Abraham Lincoln Association*, 2).

209. John T. Stuart interview with John Nicolay, June 23, 1875 (transcript available in Burlingame, *Oral*, 11–12). Fifteen years before this interview, John Stuart told the story to James Quay Howard, with the significant change that the deal offered to Lincoln came from Whigs who were disgruntled with John Stuart (John T. Stuart interview with James Quay Howard in Burlingame, *Oral*, 134 n. 50; *see also* Howells, *Life*, 47, derived from that interview). I find either version plausible but have quoted the more detailed one. *See also* Baringer, *Lincoln's Vandalia*, 9; Ninian W. Edwards interview with William H. Herndon, ca. 1865, H-W Papers (transcript available as #333 in Wilson and Davis, *Herndon's*, 446); and John T. Stuart interview with William H. Herndon, ca. 1865, H-W Papers (transcript available as #374 in Wilson and Davis, *Herndon's*, 480), which all say the offer was from Democrats.

210. A Citizen of Sangamon, "To John T. Stuart," B-400, Broadside Collection, ALPL.

211. Joseph Klein to John J. Hardin, dateline Springfield, July 29, 1834, Hardin Family Papers.

212. John T. Stuart, "Reply of John T. Stuart to an Anonymous Hand Bill Signed 'A Citizen of Sangamon,'" B-401, Broadside Collection, ALPL.

213. William Kinney in *Chicago Democrat*, July 16, 1834. Compare to slightly different version, probably because of newspaper editorial garbling, William Kinney in *SJ*, July 26, 1834.

214. A. G. Herndon, July 30, 1834, B-58, Broadside Collection, ALPL.

215. John T. Stuart, "To the Voters of Sangamon County," Aug. 1, 1834, B-147, Broadside Collection, ALPL.

216. Peter Cartwright in *SJ*, July 12, 1834.

217. Robert Stuart to John T. Stuart, Aug.(?) 9, 1834, Stuart-Hay Family Papers.

218. Cartwright, *Autobiography*, 262.

219. Letter by "Justice," *SJ*, July 19, 1834.

220. *SJ*, July 26, 1834.

221. Charles James Fox Clarke to Mother, dateline New Salem, Aug. 3, 1834 (transcript available in Clarke, "Sketch," 562).

222. *SJ*, July 26, 1834. "*Bill*-ious eructations" is a pun about handbills.

223. Hawkins Taylor in "Lincoln Carries," 330–31, and in Wilson, *Intimate*, 9–10.

224. *SJ*, Aug. 16, Sept. 6, Nov. 15, 1834. I have used totals from *SJ*, Sept. 27, 1834, which conflict with those in Simon, *Lincoln's*, 18.

225. *SJ*, Aug. 30, 1834.

226. "State Pride" in *St. Clair Gazette*, clipped in *Chicago Democrat*, July 9, 1834.
227. *Chicago Democrat*, June 4, 1834.
228. Rev. William Kinney to Joseph Duncan, (transcript available in Snyder, *Adam*, 172).
229. Linder, *Reminiscences*, 90–91.
230. Wilson, *Uncollected*, 1:255.
231. The accounts cited below differ in details but clearly refer to the same case.
232. Caton, *Early*, 55.
233. Caton, *Early*, 56. *See also* Linder, *Reminiscences*, 90.
234. Erastus Wright to Samuel Wright, Nov. 26, 1826 (transcript available in "He Had His," 92).
235. Erastus Wright to Samuel Wright, Nov. 26, 1826 (transcript available in "He Had His," 92).
236. Enos, "Description," 204–5.
237. Caton, *Early*, 57; Enos, "Description," 205; *History of Sangamon*, 224; Linder, *Reminiscences*, 91.
238. Erastus Wright to Samuel Wright, Nov. 26, 1826 (transcript available in "He Had His," 92). Years later, newspapers printed accounts of alleged success at using electricity to revive a hanged murderer whose neck was not broken by the drop, who was able to sit up and walk briefly with assistance, but then died for good a few minutes later (*Louisville City Gazette*, April 10, 1841, clipped in *Sangamo Journal*, April 30, 1841; *Baltimore Sun* clipped in *Illinois State Register*, May 7, 1841).
239. Caton, *Early*, 58. *See also* Linder, *Reminiscences*, 91.
240. Abraham Lincoln, "To the Public," Oct. 18, 1837, in *SJ*, Oct. 28, 1837 (printed as document 120620 in Benner and Davis, *Law*, and transcript available in *CW* 1:102).
241. Enos, "Description," 205.
242. Palmer, *Bench*, 158–59; Power, *History*, 76; *SJ*, Nov. 30, 1833.
243. His platform (James Adams circular to voters, dateline Springfield, July 3, 1830, in *Vandalia Illinois Intelligencer*, July 17, 1830) was scarcely different from his 1834 gubernatorial platform.
244. *Chicago Democrat*, March 18, 1834; *SJ*, March 29; June 14, 21, 1834; *SJ* clipped in *Chicago Democrat*, July 2, 1834. Gen. James D. Henry of Sangamon County was still viewed as a candidate when the public effort to boom Adams started, but Adams didn't announce his own candidacy until after word arrived of Henry's death.
245. Pease, *Frontier*, 149.
246. *Vandalia Illinois Intelligencer*, July 12, 19, 1828.
247. James Adams circular to voters, dateline Springfield, July 3, 1830, in *Vandalia Illinois Intelligencer*, July 17, 1830.
248. James Adams in *SJ*, July 12, 1834; Krenkel, *Illinois*, 54.

Chapter 8. POLITICS OF 1834: CONGRESSIONAL
1. This may have been an open seat. I've seen no reference to incumbent Charles Slade seeking reelection. Indeed, he died during the 1834 campaign.
2. A. W. Snyder to James Semple, Aug. 8, 1837, J. F. Snyder Papers.
3. Letter, *Jacksonville Illinoisian*, quoted in *Galena North Western Gazette and Galena Advertiser*, Aug. 10, 1839 (interior date Aug. 8).
4. Orr, "Indian," 67.
5. Edwards quoted by "Fayette, Junior," *Vandalia Illinois Intelligencer*, Nov. 7, 1829.
6. Quoted by "Q," *Vandalia Illinois Intelligencer*, Jan. 9, 1830.
7. Scott, *Supreme*, 172, quoted in McHarry, "John," 24. Another observer remarked, "It is a matter of no astonishment whatever to me, nor to those who are at all conversant with the governor's former course in politics, that he should not only be ready but willing at all times to betray and sacrifice the best friends he had" (*SJ*, July 18, 1835).
8. Reynolds, *My Own Times*, 79.
9. Miner to Editor, *Galena Miners' Journal*, July 24, 1830.

10. Illinois Servitude and Emancipation Records, 1722–1863, an Index Compiled from the Illinois State Archives, published May 5, 2002, www.webroots.org/library/usahist/ilsaer0.txt; Snyder, "Pen," 122–23; Davidson and Stuvé, *Complete*, 365; Koerner, *Memoirs*, 1:336; Linder, *Reminiscences*, 149–50; McHarry, "John," 29–33; Reynolds, *My Own Times*, 107, 111–19; Snyder, *Adam*, 299, 302–305, 313–14, 317–18.

11. "Fayette, Junior," *Vandalia Illinois Intelligencer*, Nov. 14, 1829; Reynolds, *My Own Times*, 151; Snyder, *Adam*, 304–305; "Victory," dateline Nov. 4, 1829, *Illinois Courier*, clipped in *Galena Advertiser*, Feb. 22, 1830; Benjamin Willis to Artemas Hale, Dec. 26, 1834, printed in "Early Settlers," 268.

12. Koerner, *Memoirs*, 1:335–36; Moses, *Illinois*, 353; Palmer, *Bench*, 19; Reynolds, *My Own Times*, 173; Snyder, *Adam*, 32, 306, 310.

13. Ford, *History*, 71.

14. Snyder, *Adam*, 307–8, 317, 328; Snyder, "Pen," 122–23.

15. Reynolds, *My Own Times*, 296–97.

16. Reynolds, *My Own Times*, 296.

17. J. L. G., dateline June 1, 1830, in *Vandalia Illinois Intelligencer*, July 3, 1830.

18. Snyder, *Adam*, 313.

19. "Bulletin No. 6," *Vandalia Illinois Intelligencer*, July 3, 1830.

20. Reynolds, *My Own Times*, 316.

21. Quoted in Snyder, *Adam*, 327.

22. *Belleville Great Western*, March 14, 1840.

23. Quoted in Snyder, *Adam*, 298. See also Gillespie, *Recollections*, 19–20; Moses, *Illinois*, 383 n.

24. Linder, *Reminiscences*, 277.

25. James Dill to Electors and People of the County of Dearborn, in *Vincennes Western Sun*, May 13, 1809.

26. James Dill to Editor, dateline Laurenceburgh, Oct. 18, 1809, in *Vincennes Western Sun*, Dec. 2, 1809.

27. Illinois Servitude and Emancipation Records, 1722–1863, an Index Compiled from the Illinois State Archives, published May 5, 2002, www.webroots.org/library/usahist/ilsaer0.txt.

28. Snyder, *Adam*, 14–15, 20–22.

29. Snyder, *Adam*, 30, 33–35, 46.

30. Snyder, *Adam*, 50.

31. Gillespie, *Recollections*, 20.

32. Reynolds, *My Own Times*, 444.

33. *History of St. Clair County* (1881), quoted in Snyder, *Adam*, 397.

34. Reynolds, *My Own Times*, 444.

35. Linder, *Reminiscences*, 277; Snyder, *Adam*, 99.

36. Koerner, *Memoirs*, 1:329; Snyder, *Adam*, 160.

37. Koerner, *Memoirs*, 1:428.

38. Snyder, *Adam*, 65.

39. Snyder, *Adam*, 99.

40. *Chicago Democrat*, Jan. 21, 1834; *Galenian*, Jan. 24, 1834.

41. Quoted in Snyder, *Adam*, 250 n.

42. Snyder, *Adam*, 250.

43. Snyder, *Adam*, 202, 204.

44. Adam Snyder, *Vandalia Illinois Advocate and State Register*, April 5, 1834.

45. *The Jour.*, clipped in *Galenian*, April 4, 1834.

46. *Western Hemisphere*, clipped in *Galenian*, Aug. 9, 1833.

47. *Galena Advertiser*, March 29, 1830.

48. Reynolds, *My Own Times*, 444.

49. Snyder, *Adam*, 169–70.

50. Palmer quoted in Snyder, *Adam*, 170.

51. Snyder, *Adam*, 398.

52. Snyder, *Adam*, 399. Despite leniency about atheist members elsewhere in a later time, the chance of a professed atheist joining an Illinois lodge in Lincoln's time was slim.

53. Jockey Club, "Great Political Horse Race," B-239, Broadside Collection, ALPL; Reynolds, *My Own Times*, 444–45; Adam W. Snyder to James Semple, Aug. 12, 1834, J. F. Snyder Papers.

54. Koerner, *Memoirs*, 1:407.

55. John Reynolds to Henry Eddy, Aug. 13, 1834, Henry Eddy Papers.

56. Hart, "Springfield's," 42; "Kane v. May & Eastham," file L03727 in Benner and Davis, *Law*. I acknowledge that Big Red might not have owned any slaves during the congressional campaign, but during his lifetime, he owned more than one. He also had at least one apprentice ("Logan v. Adams," deposition, Sept. 4, 1838, document 3462 in Benner and Davis, *Law*).

57. Feb. 8, 1834.

58. Benjamin Willis to Artemas Hale, Dec. 26, 1834, quoted in "Early Settlers," 268.

59. Correspondent report, Dec.11, 1836, in *SJ*, Dec. 17, 1836.

60. Thomas J. Pickett in Wilson, *Intimate*, 190. In the 1840 campaign, Whigs claimed Van Buren had fancy gold plates and other extravagances in the White House. The *Illinois State Register* printed denials (May 15, 22, 1840). Reportedly, President Tyler told a visitor that Van Buren's infamous gold spoons didn't exist and never had (*Indiana Sentinal* clipped in *Illinois State Register*, June 16, 1843).

61. *See* Anonymous letter in *SJ*, April 25, 1835; *Galena North Western Gazette and Galena Advertiser*, May 30, 1835; "Third District" letter in *SJ*, April 25, 1835; "A True and Steadfast Friend of General Jackson" letter in *SJ*, May 2, 1835.

62. Benjamin Willis to Artemas Hale, Dec. 26, 1834, quoted in "Early Settlers," 268, and in Simon, *Lincoln's*, 19.

63. The partnership's existence is undisputed, but because of incorrect dating from a fine authority, I point out mention of the partnership in *SJ*, Nov. 30, 1833. *See also* Palmer, *Bench*, 173.

64. Palmer, *Bench*, 173.

65. Thomas J. Pickett in Wilson, *Intimate*, 190.

66. *Galena Miners' Journal*, Feb. 13, 1830.

67. Gillespie, *Recollections*, 39. *See also* Palmer, *Bench*, 161.

68. Moses, *Illinois*, 381 n.

69. Angle, "*Here*," 60; *Galenian*, Dec. 23, 1834; Gillespie, *Recollections*, 39; Roberts, "Reminiscence," 968.

70. "To the Voters of the Third Congressional District," B-389, Broadside Collection, ALPL.

71. *Vandalia Illinois Intelligencer*, Aug. 1, 1829.

72. *Quincy Whig*, Dec. 10, 1842.

73. *Genius of Liberty* clipped in *Peoria Register and North-Western Gazetteer*, Jan. 22, 1841; H. Warren in *Genius of Liberty* clipped in *Daily Chicago American*, Dec. 31, 1840.

74. Moses O. Bledsoe public letter to Smith in *Vandalia Illinois Intelligencer*, July 31, 1830. *See also* Conkling, *Recollections*, 47; James Hall in *Vandalia Illinois Intelligencer*, Aug. 21, 1830; Scott, *Supreme*, 288; Snyder, *Adam*, 156.

75. Davidson and Stuvé, *Complete*, 368–69; Thomas Gillham, et al., "To the Senators and Representatives in the Eighth General Assembly," Dec. 5, 1832, B-741, Broadside Collection, ALPL; Moses, *Illinois*, 380–81; *SJ*, Jan. 12, Feb. 16, 1833; *Vandalia Illinois Advocate*, Jan. 12, 19, 26, Feb. 2, 16, 23, 1833.

76. Ninian Edwards, "To the People of Illinois," Nov. 16, 1832, in *Alton Spectator*, Nov. 20, 1832; *SJ*, Nov. 24, 1832.

77. Theophilus Smith, *Edwardsville Illinois Advocate*, Dec. 4, 1832. *See also SJ*, Dec. 15, 1832; Theophilus Smith to Editor, *Edwardsville Illinois Advocate*, Nov. 27, 1832. Smith is obviously incorrect when saying the encounter took place in Belleville, as the U.S. Land Office was in Edwardsville.

78. George Kelley, *SJ*, Dec. 15, 1832.

79. Samuel D. Lockwood to Mary Lockwood, Feb. 7, 1833, Lockwood Family Papers.

80. Gillespie, *Recollections*, 39. *See also SJ*, Feb. 23, 1833.

81. Tammany's enemies in the legislature worked on finding other means to throw him out of office, but he continued to prevail. Details are beyond this book's scope, but a leader in the continuing efforts was Rep. Cyrus Edwards, whom Smith had been threatening to kill (*SJ*, Feb. 23, 1833). The impeachment is summarized in Ford, *History*, 112–13.

82. *Galenian*, July 28, 1834.

83. *SJ*, April 26, 1834, also clipped in *Chicago Democrat*, May 7, 1834.

84. Aristides in *Chicago Democrat*, May 21, 1834. Sunday mail service was another issue pitting organized religion against defenders of civil liberties. The *Galena Miners' Journal* noted: "Memorials from many parts of this union against the transportation of the mails, and the opening of the post offices on the Sabbath, are presented to Congress. . . . Does not the occasion call for every republican to raise his voice against any measure, though small in its commencement, which might in the end lead to a union of church and state! We fear that the prevention of transporting the mails on the Sabbath, by an act of Congress, would be a stepping stone to greater calamities!" (March 13, 1830). The March 20 issue of the newspaper also reprinted an article from *Phil. Friend* about Sunday mail:

> The danger anticipated from the efforts now making, in relation to the suspension of the mail, is far from being imaginary. Those who are thus determined to invade the privileges of their fellow citizens are an organized body. . . .
>
> The alarm and jealousy which have pervaded the country, lest an ascendency in the government should be obtained by a religious party, must continue to exist until their cause shall be removed.
>
> . . . Every description of force is foreign to the religion of Christ, neither sanctioned by his precepts, nor authorized by his example.
>
> It is, therefore, worth the consideration of those who are favorable to the views of an aspiring priesthood, whether the measures they are now pursuing will not have a result different from what they anticipate.

85. Roberts, "Reminiscence," 958.

86. Doyle, "Address," 446.

87. Palmer, *Bench*, 181.

88. Stephen A. Douglas, "Autobiographical Sketch," Sept. 1, 1838 (transcript available in Douglas, *Letters*, 62–63). *See also* Stephen A. Douglas to Julius N. Granger, May 9, 1835 (transcript available in Douglas, *Letters*, 15–16); Milton, *Eve*, 18.

89. Milton, *Eve*, 18.

90. Sheahan, *Life*, 19.

91. Sheahan, *Life*, 18–20. *See also* Johannsen, *Stephen*, 25–26; Stevens, "Life," 285.

92. Stephen A. Douglas, "Autobiographical Sketch," Sept. 1, 1838 (transcript available in Douglas, *Letters*, 63–64). *See also* Stephen A. Douglas to Julius N. Granger, May 9, 1835 (transcript available in Douglas, *Letters*, 15–16).

93. Stephen A. Douglas, "Autobiographical Sketch," Sept. 1, 1838 (transcript available in Douglas, *Letters*, 64).

94. Quoted in Justice, "To the Electors in the Third Congressional District," B-388, Broadside Collection, ALPL.

95. William May, advertisement in *SJ*, June 28, 1834.

96. Salt tariffs really were an issue in Illinois congressional competition. *See* John Reynolds, *Vandalia Illinois Advocate and State Register*, March 22, 1834; John Reynolds to Henry Eddy and R. W. Clark, July 6, 1834, transcript in Henry Eddy Papers.

97. Although Sim Francis wasn't the only person who made editorial decisions, and I don't absolutely know that he wasn't ill or otherwise out of the office when Big Red submitted his defense, harsh things Big Red's law partner Stephen Logan said about Simeon (noted later) satisfy me that Simeon was working against Big Red.

98. Editorial, *SJ*, June 28, 1834.

99. William May, advertisement in *SJ*, June 28, 1834.

100. *SJ*, July 26, 1834; handbill, which says it is reprinted from *Jacksonville Illinois Patriot*, July 12, 1834, B-390, Broadside Collection, ALPL; handbill that says it is reprinted from *Jacksonville Illinois Patriot*, July 19, 1834, B-392, Broadside Collection, ALPL; handbill "Illinois Patriot, Extra. Jacksonville, July 16, 1834," B-685, Broadside Collection, ALPL. *See also* Benjamin Willis to Artemas Hale, Dec. 26, 1834, printed in "Early Settlers," 268.

101. *SJ*, July 26, 1834; William May handbill to "Fellow Citizens," B-402, Broadside Collection, ALPL. May spells the name Van Burgen but clearly means Van Bergen. At some point, May sued Van Bergen for slander; May's attorney in that action was Stephen Logan (deposition, Sept. 4, 1838, document 3462 in Benner and Davis, *Law*).

102. Philo-Agricola, "No. IV. To Wm. L. May, Esq.," [July 1834], B-395, Broadside Collection, ALPL.

103. *Illinois Herald*—Extra, Springfield, April 20, 1832, B-70, Broadside Collection, ALPL.

104. Henry, in *Jacksonville News*, clipped in *Chicago Democrat*, June 25, 1834.

105. A Volunteer of 1832, "To the Electors of the 3d Congressional District," B-387, Broadside Collection, ALPL. Col. Strode said, "As to compensation for bearing the letter, I have no personal knowledge, but was informed by a respectable gentleman of Galena that Mr. Mills received from the government some 300 dollars for it" (*SJ*, July 26, 1834).

106. Benjamin Mills, "To the Electors of the Third Congressional District of the State of Illinois," B-244, Broadside Collection, ALPL; Benjamin Mills, *Chicago Democrat*, July 23, 1834; Benjamin Mills, *SJ*, July 26, 1834. These statements are similar but not all duplicates.

107. "To Benj. Mills, Esq.," B-398, Broadside Collection, ALPL; *SJ*, July 26, 1834.

108. Benjamin Mills, *Chicago Democrat*, July 23, 1834; Benjamin Mills, *SJ*, July 26, 1834.

109. *SJ*, July 26, 1834; William May, "Fellow Citizens," B-402, Broadside Collection, ALPL. Sim Francis's affirmation demonstrates that the handbill was printed at the *Sangamo Journal* office.

110. Justice, "To the Electors in the Third Congressional District," B-388, Broadside Collection, ALPL.

111. "Committee of Vigilance" of Galena, *Chicago Democrat*, Aug. 6, 1834; *Galenian*, July 28, 1834; H. Newhall et al., "Report," adopted by public meeting in Galena, July 18, 1834, B-137, Broadside Collection, ALPL. Trivial difference exists among these three versions.

112. Justice, "To the Electors in the Third Congressional District," B-388, Broadside Collection, ALPL.

113. *SJ*, July 26, 1834; William May, handbill "Fellow Citizens," B-402, Broadside Collection, ALPL.

114. "To Benj. Mills, Esq.," B-398, Broadside Collection, ALPL; *SJ*, July 26, 1834.

115. "To Benj. Mills, Esq.," B-398, Broadside Collection, ALPL; *SJ*, July 26, 1834.

116. Justice, "To the Electors in the Third Congressional District," B-388, Broadside Collection, ALPL; "To Benj. Mills, Esq.," B-398, Broadside Collection, ALPL; *SJ*, July 26, 1834.

117. "To Benj. Mills, Esq.," B-398, Broadside Collection, ALPL; *SJ*, July 26, 1834.

118. "To Benj. Mills, Esq.," B-398, Broadside Collection, ALPL; *SJ*, July 26, 1834.

119. *Galena North Western Gazette and Galena Advertiser*, Feb. 14, 1835; "To the Voters of the Third Congressional District," B-389, Broadside Collection, ALPL.

120. "To the Voters of the Third Congressional District," B-389, Broadside Collection, ALPL.

121. Gillespie, *Recollections*, 38.

122. Benjamin Mills editorial, *Galena North Western Gazette and Galena Advertiser*, Jan. 17, 1835.

123. John Bergen to David Ayres, Jan. 1, 1830 (transcript available in Van Fenstermaker, "Description," 137).

124. Sangamon, "Congressional Election.—To the Voters of Sangamon County," [July 1834], B-397, Broadside Collection, ALPL. The need for congressional authorization of such diversion is also noted in *SJ*, March 22, 1834.

125. Benjamin Mills, *Galena North Western Gazette and Galena Advertiser*, Feb. 14, 1835.

126. Jockey Club, "Great Political Horse Race," B-239, Broadside Collection, ALPL; *SJ*, Aug. 2, 1834; "To the Voters of the State of Illinois," B-391, Broadside Collection, ALPL.

127. *SJ*, Feb. 23, March 9, 1833.

128. A Man of Morgan, "To the Voters of Morgan County," B-393 and B-396 (same item), Broadside Collection, ALPL.
129. *SJ*, March 8, 1834.
130. *SJ*, March 8, 1834.
131. Pease, *Frontier*, 261; *SJ*, March 22, 1834.
132. Peter Cartwright to Mr. Lamb, dateline Vandalia, Jan. 1, 1833, Peter Cartwright Photostat File, ALPL.
133. Richard Quinton, June 21, 1834, B-116, Broadside Collection, ALPL.
134. *SJ*, Sept. 27, 1834. Citations about Reverend Cartwright's plan will be given later in context of Lincoln's attack against it.
135. Sangamon, "Congressional Election.—To the Voters of Sangamon County," [July 1834], B-397, Broadside Collection, ALPL.
136. Stephen A. Douglas to Julius N. Granger, Sept. 21, 1834 (transcript available in Douglas, *Letters*, 9).

Chapter 9. LAW STUDIES, REVENGE, ROMANCE
1. Arnold, *Life*, 40; Abraham Lincoln, autobiography for John L. Scripps, ca. June 1860 (transcript available in *CW* 4:65); Maltby, *Life*, 44.
2. William G. Greene to William H. Herndon, May 29, 1865, H-W Papers (transcript available in Wilson and Davis, *Herndon's*, 12).
3. Henry McHenry interview with William H. Herndon, 1866, H-W Papers (transcript available in Wilson and Davis, *Herndon's*, 534); Burner quoted in Temple, "Lincoln and the Burners," 67.
4. John Roll in Turner, "John," 104.
5. James Gourley interview with William H. Herndon, ca. 1865, H-W Papers (transcript available in Wilson and Davis, *Herndon's*, 451); William G. Greene interview with William H. Herndon, May 30, 1865, H-W Papers (transcript available in Wilson and Davis, *Herndon's*, 18); John Rowan Herndon to William H. Herndon, May 28, 1865, H-W Papers (transcript available in Wilson and Davis, *Herndon's*, 7); Holland, *Life*, 65. With Gourley, compare Weik, *Real*, 119–20, for a possible example of Weik's harmless conversion of interview notes into prose that an interviewee didn't necessarily speak.
6. *Lincoln and New Salem*, 68.
7. Henry E. Dummer interview with William H. Herndon, ca. 1865, H-W Papers (transcript available in Wilson and Davis, *Herndon's*, 442).
8. Angle, "Record," 127. Testimony exists that Lincoln also received encouragement from Springfield lawyer Stephen T. Logan: Logan "and his partner were sitting one afternoon in their office, unemployed, door open, when Lincoln appeared with compass and staff. 'Well how now, Abe, what's up?' 'I'm dead broke. Enough surveying but all on tick, no pay.' 'Well, better study law—you see how busy we are.' 'If you'll lend me books I will.'" (James Hall to William H. Herndon (apparently citing testimony from Josephus Hewitt), Sept. 17, 1873, H-W Papers (transcript available in Wilson and Davis, *Herndon's*, 581)). I haven't noticed Logan credited anywhere else with promoting Lincoln's early law study. Lincoln's complaint here about surveying on credit, rather than for cash, raises further question about this testimony. Although he did do private surveying, surely much of his work was for the county, and I suspect he must have been paid within reasonable time for county work.
9. Abraham Lincoln to Isham Reavis, Nov. 5, 1855 (transcript available in *CW* 2:327).
10. Russell Godbey to William H. Herndon, ca. 1865, H-W Papers (transcript available in Wilson and Davis, *Herndon's*, 449).
11. Henry McHenry interview with William H. Herndon, 1866, H-W Papers (transcript available in Wilson and Davis, *Herndon's*, 534).
12. Robert B. Rutledge to William H. Herndon, Nov. 30, 1866, H-W Papers (transcript available in Wilson and Davis, *Herndon's*, 426).
13. Henry McHenry interview with William H. Herndon, 1866, H-W Papers (transcript available in Wilson and Davis, *Herndon's*, 534). *See also* Henry McHenry interview with William H. Hern-

don, May 29, 1865, H-W Papers (transcript available in Wilson and Davis, *Herndon's*, 14); Henry McHenry interview with James Quay Howard (transcript available in Basler, "James," 390).

14. Henry McHenry interview with William H. Herndon, May 29, 1865, H-W Papers (transcript available in Wilson and Davis, *Herndon's*, 14).

15. Henry McHenry interview with James Quay Howard (transcript available in Basler, "James," 390).

16. McConnel, *Western*, 125–26.

17. Speed, *Reminiscences*, 21 (also printed in Wilson, *Intimate*, 18).

18. Abraham Lincoln to Isham Reavis, Nov. 5, 1855 (transcript available in *CW* 2:327).

19. Abraham Lincoln to William H. Grigsby, Aug. 3, 1858 (transcript available in *CW* 2:535).

20. Abraham Lincoln to John M. Brockman, Sept. 25, 1860 (transcript available in *CW* 4:121).

21. Robert B. Rutledge to William H. Herndon, Nov. 30, 1866, H-W Papers (transcript available in Wilson and Davis, *Herndon's*, 426).

22. *Lincoln and New Salem*, 68.

23. Caleb Carman interview with William H. Herndon, Oct. 12, 1866, H-W Papers (transcript available in Wilson and Davis, *Herndon's*, 374–75).

24. *SJ*, Dec. 13, 1834.

25. Writ of execution, Aug. 25, 1834, document 125924 in Benner and Davis, *Law.*

26. Writ of scire facias (notation of execution on Abraham Lincoln, Aug. 20, 1834), document 125932 in Benner and Davis, *Law.*

27. Peter Van Bergen interview with John Nicolay, July 7, 1875 (transcript available in Burlingame, *Oral*, 33); *Chicago Democrat*, July 1, 1835.

28. Quoted in Hibbard, *History*, 222–23.

29. Stephen A. Douglas to Julius N. Granger, Nov. 14, 1834 (transcript available in Douglas, *Letters*, 10–11).

30. Baber, *A. Lincoln*, 114–15; "Lincoln's Association," 201; *SJ*, Sept. 6, 13, 20, 27, Oct. 4, 1834; Peter Van Bergen interview with John Nicolay, July 7, 1875 (transcript available in Burlingame, *Oral*, 33).

31. Miers, *Lincoln*, Nov. 19, 1834; receipt and assignment, document 125934 in Benner and Davis, *Law*; Pratt, *Personal*, 13; Thomas, *Lincoln's New Salem*, 72; Townsend, *Lincoln the Litigant*, 69. On the back of the document in which Van Bergen agreed to collect the note is this notation: "Received of the within obligation $ thirty five dollars in part pay of a horse beast October the 11 1834. R. Radford." Townsend, *Lincoln the Litigant*, 68–69, indicates this is evidence Slicky Bill Greene gave his horse to Radford (Baber, *A. Lincoln*, 116, is consistent with Townsend's version but doesn't mention the document). Pratt, *Personal*, 13, Schwartz, *Finding*, 10, and Thomas, *Lincoln's New Salem*, 72, say this notation refers to a horse from Berry. Does the notation mean Berry bartered a horse in part payment of the note, or that Radford was buying a horse from Berry and allowing a credit on the note in partial payment, in addition to paying Berry cash? Does it mean that Berry, who isn't named, did anything? Or does the payment refer to Greene or Lincoln? The notation seems to mean that Van Bergen didn't own the note and was simply acting as Radford's collection agent (otherwise, how could Radford say the obligation was reduced?), yet Van Bergen's lawsuit certainly indicates that he owned the note outright.

32. *Galenian*, Sept. 29, 1834.

33. William May circular to voters, dateline Springfield, *SJ*, Sept. 27, 1834; *Chicago Democrat*, Oct. 8, 1834.

34. *Chicago Democrat*, Oct. 8 (two articles), 22, 29, 1834; *SJ*, Oct. 4, 24, Nov. 15, 1834. James Turney (reputedly pro-Jackson) was briefly a candidate for the short term, but he allowed his name to be put forward with the understanding that no one else would run. When May and Mills entered the race, he dropped out (*Chicago Democrat*, Oct. 22, 1834). This was the same Turney who had captured Lincoln's vote in 1830.

35. *Galenian*, Oct. 6, 1834.

36. Election return, Oct. 27, 1834 (transcript available in *CW* 1:25–26).

37. Hart, "Springfield's," 42–43; Thomas, "Lincoln: Voter" (Sept. 1934), 6–7.

38. Colby, "Jonathan," 429–30.

39. Ford, *History*, 15.

40. Peter Cartwright, dateline April 15,1834, in *Christian Advocate and Journal*, May 30, 1834, 158. I use the version as quoted in "Rev. Peter Cartwright's Letter," handbill B-385, Broadside Collection, ALPL, because that version probably had wider circulation in Sangamon County. With the possible exception of a numeral in a passage I haven't quoted ("0 children baptized" in *Christian Advocate* and "9 children baptized" in the handbill), which may simply be a case of broken type, the only differences are typographical design (such as brackets rather than parentheses around "Illinois"); verbal content is the same. The letter was one of his periodic reports about how the church was faring in Illinois. *See* examples in *Christian Advocate and Journal*, Dec. 20, 1833 (two letters); Jan. 3, Oct. 31, 1834.

41. W. Fisk, dateline March 18, 1834, *Christian Advocate and Journal*, April 4, 1834. From this letter, we may infer that the teachers Cartwright wanted to import would be from New England, an importation that would hardly go down well in Illinois, but I've seen no records from the era indicating that Cartwright was challenged on that point.

42. Samuel Hill [Abraham Lincoln] to Editor, dateline New Salem, Sept. 7, 1834, in *Beardstown Chronicle*, Nov. 1, 1834. According to statements of both Cartwright and Lincoln (Peter Cartwright, *SJ*, Aug. 30, 1834; Samuel Hill [Abraham Lincoln], *Beardstown Chronicle*, Nov. 1, 1834), a portion of Cartwright's *Christian Advocate* letter and a commentary about it were published by Ashford Smith in the *Rock Spring Pioneer* (though not necessarily written by him), in far-distant St. Clair County. In contrast, the critic who produced the handbill had the fairness and self-confidence to present Cartwright's entire letter. Cartwright claimed the full letter would substantially reduce criticisms against him, but as we shall see presently, the handbill commentator found plenty to criticize. Given the existence of two different items (*Pioneer* and handbill), published in places far away from each other, with dissimilar manners of quoting Cartwright's letter, odds are that the commentaries in the two items were also different. I believe that the *Pioneer* article (which seems lost) and the handbill were two different items, produced by different persons. In "Moral Waste," Cartwright also said the *Christian Advocate* itself printed only part of his letter, but the context of that statement indicates he probably misspoke and meant the *Pioneer* (or the statement could be an editorial error of the *Sangamo Journal*).

43. "Rev. Peter Cartwright's Letter," handbill B-385, Broadside Collection, ALPL.

44. Caleb Carman to William H. Herndon, Nov. 30, 1866, H-W Papers (transcript available in Wilson and Davis, *Herndon's*, 429–30).

45. Peter Cartwright, *SJ*, Dec. 6, 1834.

46. Peter Cartwright, *SJ*, Aug. 30, 1834. The phrase "moral waste" wasn't unique to Cartwright. For example, *see* William G. Grownlow, *Christian Advocate and Journal*, May 9, 1834.

47. *SJ*, Sept. 27, 1834.

48. Joseph Rogers, *SJ*, Oct. 4, 1834.

49. *SJ*, Sept. 27, 1834.

50. Peter Cartwright, *SJ*, Dec. 6, 1834.

51. Peter Cartwright, dateline Quincy district, Sept. 22, 1834, *Christian Advocate and Journal*, Oct. 31, 1834.

52. John McNamar to William H. Herndon, Dec. 1, 1866, H-W Papers (transcript available in Wilson and Davis, *Herndon's*, 493).

53. Onstot, *Pioneers*, 114. *See also* 46, 152.

54. That delightful phrase is from Johnson, *Frontier*, 226.

55. Cartwright, *Autobiography*, 133.

56. Cartwright, *Autobiography*, 189, 306.

57. Onstot, *Pioneers*, 46, 114; Thomas, *Lincoln's*, 26; Wilson, *Lincoln*, 58, 67, 72.

58. Onstot, *Pioneers*, 114.

59. Samuel Hill [Abraham Lincoln] to Editor, dateline New Salem, Sept. 7, 1834, in *Beardstown Chronicle*, Nov. 1, 1834.

60. Bray, "Cartwright," 116; One Who Knows, *SJ*, May 2, 1835; Wilson, *Lincoln*, 58. "One Who Knows" appears to have been Dr. Anson G. Henry (*SJ*, May 23, June 6, 13, 1835).

61. John McNamar to William H. Herndon, Dec. 1, 1866, H-W Papers (transcript available in Wilson and Davis, *Herndon's*, 493).

62. *Galena North Western Gazette and Galena Advertiser*, Nov. 29, 1834.

63. *Quincy Illinois Bounty Land Register*, April 17, 1835.

64. James Strawbridge, Levi Cantrall, and Abraham Lincoln to the county commissioners' court, Nov. 4, 1834 (transcript available in *CW* 1:26).

65. Baber, *A. Lincoln*, 93.

66. Beekman, "Reminiscences," 90–91; Kempf, *Abraham*, 115; *Lincoln and New Salem*, 76; Pond, "Memoirs," 84–85.

67. Court order, Nov. 19, 1834, document 125933 in Benner and Davis, *Law*; Thomas, *Lincoln's New Salem*, 72.

68. Receipt and assignment, document 125934 in Benner and Davis, *Law*.

69. The abbreviation is read as "Oct" by Thomas, *Lincoln's New Salem*, 72, accepted by Miers, *Lincoln*, Nov. 19, 1834. In the October 11 notation, the final "t" is crossed in "part" and "beast," a handwriting characteristic supporting my reading of "Nov" (in which the final letter isn't crossed). Townsend, *Lincoln the Litigant*, 69, and the data bar in Benner and Davis, *Law*, concur with my reading of the month.

70. *Lincoln and New Salem*, 62; Robert Rutledge to William H. Herndon, ca. Nov. 1866, H-W Papers (transcript available in Wilson and Davis, *Herndon's*, 384). Details of the debt are a little obscure.

71. Mentor Graham interview with William H. Herndon, April 2, 1866, H-W Papers (transcript available in Wilson and Davis, *Herndon's*, 242). *See also* Esther Summers Bale interview with William H. Herndon, 1866, H-W Papers (transcript available in Wilson and Davis, *Herndon's*, 527); Henry McHenry interview with William H. Herndon, 1866, H-W Papers (transcript available in Wilson and Davis, *Herndon's*, 534); Robert B. Rutledge to William H. Herndon, ca. Nov. 1, 1866, H-W Papers (transcript available in Wilson and Davis, *Herndon's*, 383). Sam Hill's wife remembered Ann's hair as brown (Parthena Nance Hill interview with William H. Herndon, ca. March 1887, H-W Papers (transcript available in Wilson and Davis, *Herndon's*, 604)), and John McNamar and Slicky Bill Greene's brother called it blond (Lynn McNulty Greene to William H. Herndon, May 3, 1866, H-W Papers (transcript available in Wilson and Davis, *Herndon's*, 250) and John McNamar to G. U. Miles, May 5, 1866, H-W Papers (transcript available in Wilson and Davis, *Herndon's*, 253)), but some red hair varies in shade from brown to red to blondish day by day.

72. John McNamar to George Miles, May 5, 1866, H-W Papers (transcript available in Wilson and Davis, *Herndon's*, 253).

73. *Lincoln and New Salem*, 83.

74. Mentor Graham interview with William H. Herndon, April 2, 1866, H-W Papers (transcript available in Wilson and Davis, *Herndon's*, 242–43).

75. Esther Summers Bale interview with William H. Herndon, 1866, H-W Papers (transcript available in Wilson and Davis, *Herndon's*, 527).

76. Tarbell, *Early*, 211.

77. Henry McHenry interview with William H. Herndon, 1866, H-W Papers (transcript available in Wilson and Davis, *Herndon's*, 534).

78. Sarah Saunders, quoted in *San Diego Sun*, Jan. 11, 1922, as given in Walsh, *Shadows*, 45–46.

79. John McNamar to William H. Herndon, Nov. 25, 1866, H-W Papers (transcript available in Wilson and Davis, *Herndon's*, 420).

80. Herndon and Weik, *Herndon's Life of Lincoln*, 108; Kempf, *Abraham*, 123; Tarbell, *Early*, 211.

81. Parthena Hill interview with William H. Herndon, ca. March 1887, H-W Papers (transcript available in Wilson and Davis, *Herndon's*, 605).

82. For McNeil's (McNamar's) feelings toward Lincoln, *see* John McNamar to George Miles, May 5, 1866, H-W Papers (transcript available in Wilson and Davis, *Herndon's*, 252–53); *Illinois*

State Journal, Oct. 15, 1874, as given in Walsh, *Shadows*, 168 n. 137. For Lincoln's feelings, *see* John McNamar to William H. Herndon, June 4, 1866, H-W Papers (transcript available in Wilson and Davis, *Herndon's*, 259); salutations and closings in Abraham Lincoln to John McNamar, Dec. 24, 1836 (transcript available in *CW* 1:60); Abraham Lincoln to John McNamar, ca. Nov. 9, 1843 (transcript available in *CW* 1:330 and along with incoming correspondence in Wilson, *Uncollected*, 2:476–77). The 1843 matter is seemingly mentioned in John McNamar to William H. Herndon, Dec. 1, 1866, H-W Papers (transcript available in Wilson and Davis, *Herndon's*, 493).

83. Robert B. Rutledge to William H. Herndon, Nov. 21, 1866, H-W Papers (transcript available in Wilson and Davis, *Herndon's*, 409).

84. Esther Summers Bale interview with William H. Herndon, 1866, H-W Papers (transcript available in Wilson and Davis, *Herndon's*, 527); Benjamin Irwin to William H. Herndon, Sept. 22, 1866, H-W Papers (transcript available in Wilson and Davis, *Herndon's*, 352–53); Thompson McNeely to William H. Herndon, Nov. 12, 1866, H-W Papers (transcript available in Wilson and Davis, *Herndon's*, 397).

85. Robert B. Rutledge to William H. Herndon, Nov. 18, 1866, H-W Papers (transcript available in Wilson and Davis, *Herndon's*, 402).

86. Winkle, *Young*, 107.

87. Robert B. Rutledge to William H. Herndon, ca. Nov. 1866, H-W Papers (transcript available in Wilson and Davis, *Herndon's*, 383); Robert B. Rutledge to William H. Herndon, Nov. 18, 1866, H-W Papers (transcript available in Wilson and Davis, *Herndon's*, 402); Robert B. Rutledge to William H. Herndon, Nov. 21, 1866, H-W Papers (transcript available in Wilson and Davis, *Herndon's*, 409).

88. Daniel G. Burner in Temple, "Lincoln and the Burners," 69; Jason Duncan to William H. Herndon, ca. 1866, H-W Papers (transcript available in Wilson and Davis, *Herndon's*, 541).

89. George U. Miles to William H. Herndon, March 23, 1866, H-W Papers (transcript available in Wilson and Davis, *Herndon's*, 236–37).

90. John McNamar to William H. Herndon, June 4, 1866, H-W Papers (transcript available in Wilson and Davis, *Herndon's*, 258).

91. Jasper Rutledge interview with William H. Herndon, March 9, 1887, H-W Papers (transcript available in Wilson and Davis, *Herndon's*, 606).

92. John McNamar to William H. Herndon, Jan. 20, 1867, H-W Papers (transcript available in Wilson and Davis, *Herndon's*, 545); "McNamar" named in deed record, Dec. 9, 1831, document 130375, and deed record Dec. 9, 1831, document 130374 in file N05446 in Benner and Davis, *Law*. The legal documents spell the seller's name as "Camron." Lincoln also surveyed the property (John McNamar to William H. Herndon, June 4, 1866), H-W Papers (transcript available in Wilson and Davis, *Herndon's*, 258). An 1842 writ of execution in a Menard County circuit court case (document 4797 in Allen v. Patterson, file L00151, Benner and Davis, *Law*; also in Wilson, *Uncollected*, 2:287–88) says it was signed in the presence of "John McNeil," raising the possibility that McNamar was using his old alias again. More plausible to me, especially since McNamar had served as Menard County assessor by then and was well known to the courthouse crowd, perhaps clerk Nathan Dresser by force of old habit simply hurriedly jotted down the name by which he used to know McNamar.

93. Herndon and Weik, *Herndon's Life of Lincoln*, 108–9.

94. John McNamar to George Miles, May 5, 1866, H-W Papers (transcript available in Wilson and Davis, *Herndon's*, 252).

95. Robert B. Rutledge to William H. Herndon, ca. Nov. 1866, H-W Papers (transcript available in Wilson and Davis, *Herndon's*, 383).

96. For example, *Galena North Western Gazette and Galena Advertiser*, Sept. 23, Nov. 25, 1842; *Galenian*, Jan. 3, 1834 (transcript available in *Galena Trail and Coach Road Newsletter* (Jan. 30, 2005): 6); *Illinois State Register*, Sept. 6, Nov. 8, 1844; *Quincy Argus and Illinois Bounty Land Register*, Aug. 9, 1836; *Quincy Whig*, Oct. 20, 1838. *See also SJ*, May 2, 1844, June 5,

1845; *Shawneetown Illinois Advertiser*, Feb. 25, 1837; *Shawneetown Illinois Republican*, Sept. 17, 1842.

97. For example, April 4, 1834: "INFORMATION WANTED. John Thomas, son of the Rev. Wm. Thomas, of the M.E. Church, went westward three or more years since, and when last heard from was living near Smithfield, Fayette county, Pa. Any person having knowledge of the said John, whether he be living or dead, would confer a great favor by directing a line to Philip Thomas, near Cecilton, Cecil county, Md. The National Gazette and papers of the west would confer a favor by inserting the above."

98. Sarah Saunders, in *San Diego Sun*, Jan. 11, 1922, as given in Walsh, *Shadows*, 46.

99. John McNamar to William H. Herndon, June 4, 1866, H-W Papers (transcript available in Wilson and Davis, *Herndon's*, 259).

100. Jason Duncan to William H. Herndon, ca. 1866, H-W Papers (transcript available in Wilson and Davis, *Herndon's*, 541).

101. Herndon and Weik, *Herndon's Life of Lincoln*, 108; *SJ*, Jan. 5, 1833 (transcript available in Walsh, *Shadows*, 157 n. 76). The *SJ* announcement refers to a dissolution dated Sept. 4, 1832. I'm inclined to think that the announcement was Hill's work and the September date reflects the point at which new debts to the store become owed entirely to Hill. McNamar had to have been out of New Salem by early August if he hadn't seen Lincoln after the Black Hawk War.

102. John McNamar to George Miles, May 5, 1866, H-W Papers (transcript available in Wilson and Davis, *Herndon's*, 252).

103. John McNamar to George Miles, May 5, 1866, H-W Papers (transcript available in Wilson and Davis, *Herndon's*, 252).

104. John McNamar to William H. Herndon, Jan. 20, 1867, H-W Papers (transcript available in Wilson and Davis, *Herndon's*, 546). The quotation is an adaptation from *Hamlet*, Act 5, scene 2.

105. Walsh, *Shadows*, 132–33.

106. Walsh, *Shadows*, 134.

107. George U. Miles to William H. Herndon, March 23, 1866, H-W Papers (transcript available in Wilson and Davis, *Herndon's*, 237).

108. Herndon and Weik, *Herndon's Life of Lincoln*, 110.

109. Daniel G. Burner, quoted in Temple, "Lincoln and the Burners," 69.

110. Parthena Hill interview with William H. Herndon, ca. March 1887, H-W Papers (transcript available in Wilson and Davis, *Herndon's*, 604–5).

111. Sarah Saunders, quoted in *San Diego Sun*, Jan. 11, 1922, as given in Walsh, *Shadows*, 46.

112. Kempf, *Abraham*, 123.

113. John R. Herndon to William H. Herndon, Aug. 16, 1865, H-W Papers (transcript available in Wilson and Davis, *Herndon's*, 92).

114. Jason Duncan to William H. Herndon, ca. 1866, H-W Papers (transcript available in Wilson and Davis, *Herndon's*, 541).

115. Jack Armstrong's brother-in-law Henry McHenry said (interview with William H. Herndon, May 29, 1865, H-W Papers (transcript available in Wilson and Davis, *Herndon's*, 15)) that Lincoln didn't "seduce women." Slicky Bill Greene said Lincoln did no "running after women" (William G. Greene to William H. Herndon, Nov. 27, 1865, H-W Papers (transcript available in Wilson and Davis, *Herndon's*, 142)).

116. Nathaniel Branson to William H. Herndon, Aug. 3, 1865, H-W Papers (transcript available in Wilson and Davis, *Herndon's*, 90–91).

117. John Hill to William H. Herndon, June 6, 1865, H-W Papers (transcript available in Wilson and Davis, *Herndon's*, 23).

118. Johnson G. Greene interview with William H. Herndon, Oct. 5, 1866, H-W Papers (transcript available in Wilson and Davis, *Herndon's*, 365); Johnson Greene interview with William H. Herndon, Oct. 10, 1866, H-W Papers (transcript available in Wilson and Davis, *Herndon's*, 370); William G. Greene interview with William H. Herndon, Oct. 9, 1866, H-W Papers (transcript available in Wilson and Davis, *Herndon's*, 367); John McNamar to William H. Herndon,

Nov. 25, 1866, H-W Papers (transcript available in Wilson and Davis, *Herndon's*, 421); Tarbell, *Early*, 195. Two of the male "youngsters" seemingly referred to here, the townsman and Duncan, were in their thirties.

119. Robert B. Rutledge to William H. Herndon, Nov. 30, 1866, H-W Papers (transcript available in Wilson and Davis, *Herndon's*, 426).

120. John R. Herndon to William H. Herndon, July 3, 1865, H-W Papers (transcript available in Wilson and Davis, *Herndon's*, 69).

121. James Miles to James R. B. Van Cleave, July 12, 1908, Lincoln Centennial Association Papers.

122. Mentor Graham interview with William H. Herndon, May 29, 1865, H-W Papers (transcript available in Wilson and Davis, *Herndon's*, 10).

123. Caleb Carman interview with William H. Herndon, Oct. 12, 1866, H-W Papers (transcript available in Wilson and Davis, *Herndon's*, 374).

124. Riley Potter, quoted in Stevens, *Reporter's*, 8.

125. Abner Ellis to William H. Herndon, Dec. 6, 1866, H-W Papers (transcript available in Wilson and Davis, *Herndon's*, 501). The comment from Ellis can be read as referring to ribald jokes, but such is unlikely. In the 1830s, it went without saying that refined ladies wouldn't enjoy hearing a ribald story from a man.

126. Abner Ellis statement, ca. Jan. 23, 1866, H-W Papers (transcript available in Wilson and Davis, *Herndon's*, 170).

127. Mentor Graham interview with James Quay Howard (transcript available in Basler, "James," 389).

128. Caleb Carman in Oldroyd, *Lincoln*, 519; Caleb Carman interview with William H. Herndon, Oct. 12, 1866, H-W Papers (transcript available in Wilson and Davis, *Herndon's*, 373–74).

129. Tarbell, *Early*, 191–92. *See also* John Q. Spears interview with William H. Herndon, H-W Papers (transcript available in Wilson and Davis, *Herndon's*, 705).

130. Travis Elmore interview with Jesse Weik, ca. 1883, H-W Papers (transcript available in Wilson and Davis, *Herndon's*, 593).

131. Maltby, *Life*, 27–28. *See also* Tarbell, *Early*, 192.

132. Travis Elmore interview with Jesse Weik, ca. 1883, H-W Papers (transcript available in Wilson and Davis, *Herndon's*, 593).

133. William Butler interview with John Nicolay, June 13, 1875 (transcript available in Burlingame, *Oral*, 19).

134. John Rowan Herndon to William H. Herndon, July 3, 1865, H-W Papers (transcript available in Wilson and Davis, *Herndon's*, 69); Walsh, *Shadows*, 67.

135. Hannah Armstrong interview with William H. Herndon, 1866, H-W Papers (transcript available in Wilson and Davis, *Herndon's*, 525–27).

136. James Taylor interview with William H. Herndon, ca. 1865, H-W Papers (transcript available in Wilson and Davis, *Herndon's*, 482).

137. George U. Miles to William H. Herndon, March 23, 1866, H-W Papers (transcript available in Wilson and Davis, *Herndon's*, 236).

138. Nancy Prewitt, quoted in Margaret Flindt, "Lincoln as a Lover [etc.], An Interview with Nancy, Sister of Ann Rutledge," *Chicago Inter-Ocean* (Feb. 12, 1886), as given in Walsh, *Shadows*, 67. *See also* Walsh, *Shadows*, 67–68, 156 n. 67.

139. *Galenian*, Feb. 27, 1833. These sorts of accidents weren't routine, but neither were they unheard of. For examples, *see Nauvoo Wasp*, Aug. 13, 1842; *Quincy Whig*, Dec. 11, 1841.

140. Beveridge, *Abraham*, 1:150 n. 5; Townsend, *Lincoln the Litigant*, 56.

141. Sarah Saunders, quoted in *San Diego Sun*, Jan. 11, 1922, as given in Walsh, *Shadows*, 45.

142. Nancy Prewitt in Margaret Flindt, "Lincoln as a Lover [etc.], An Interview with Nancy, Sister of Ann Rutledge," *Chicago Inter-Ocean* (Feb. 12, 1886), as given in Walsh, *Shadows*, 43; Tarbell, *In the Footsteps*, 215–16. *See also* Robert B. Rutledge to William H. Herndon, ca. Nov. 1, 1866, H-W Papers (transcript available in Wilson and Davis, *Herndon's*, 384). Barton (*Life*,

1:196, 197 n.) expresses skepticism about the story because of flaws in its details. Thomas Moore's "Legacy," also known as "When in death I shall calm recline," goes like this:

> When in death I shall calm recline
>   O bear my heart to my mistress dear;
> Tell her it lived upon smiles and wine,
>   Of brightest hue while it lingered here.
> Bid her not shed one tear of sorrow
>   To sully a heart so brilliant and light;
> But balmy drops of the red grape borrow
>   To bathe the relic from morn to night.

In Lincoln's parody, he substituted "old gray" for "red grape" (*Lincoln and New Salem*, 32).

143. Sarah Saunders, quoted in Walsh, *Shadows*, 45.

144. Nancy Prewitt, quoted in Margaret Flindt, "Lincoln as a Lover [etc.], An Interview with Nancy, Sister of Ann Rutledge," *Chicago Inter-Ocean* (Feb. 12, 1886), as given in Walsh, *Shadows*, 42.

145. Walsh, *Shadows*, 45. A story tells of Lincoln attending a quilting bee, normally thought of as a female enclave, and sitting with Ann (Elizabeth Herndon Bell interview with Jesse Weik, Aug. 24, 1883, H-W Papers (transcript available in Wilson and Davis, *Herndon's*, 591); Elizabeth Herndon Bell interviews with William H. Herndon, March 1887, H-W Papers (transcripts available in Wilson and Davis, *Herndon's*, 605–6), and perhaps relied on by Jayne in *Abraham*, 29, and in his February 12, 1907, speech to Daughters of the American Revolution in Wilson, *Lincoln*, 80, also by Kempf, *Abraham*, 126. Bell seems to be unreliable, and Ann's sister Sally dismissed such a tale as ridiculous (Sarah Saunders letter in ALPL, quoted in Walsh, *Shadows*, 152 n. 45). New Salem's vicinity did, however, have quilting bees at which both genders were welcome, both sewing and partying (Charles James Fox Clarke to Mother, Jan. 15, 1837 (transcript available in Clarke, "Sketch," 575)).

146. The dating of this move seems reliable (Walsh, *Shadows*, 70), as does the date that Nelson Alley bought the Rutledge tavern (late November 1832 according to Thomas, *Lincoln's New Salem*, 12). Good authorities seem to conflict over when the Rutledges ran the tavern; perhaps they continued running it while Alley owned it.

147. Beveridge, *Abraham*, 1:148.

148. John McNamar to William H. Herndon, Jan. 20, 1867, H-W Papers (transcript available in Wilson and Davis, *Herndon's*, 545); John McNamar to William H. Herndon, June 4, 1866, H-W Papers (transcript available in Wilson and Davis, *Herndon's*, 258); George U. Miles to William H. Herndon, March 23, 1866, H-W Papers (transcript available in Wilson and Davis, *Herndon's*, 236–37); John M. Rutledge to William H. Herndon, Nov. 25, 1866, H-W Papers (transcript available in Wilson and Davis, *Herndon's*, 423); Robert B. Rutledge to William H. Herndon, Nov. 21, 1866, H-W Papers (transcript available in Wilson and Davis, *Herndon's*, 409).

149. James Short to William H. Herndon, July 7, 1865, H-W Papers (transcript available in Wilson and Davis, *Herndon's*, 73–74); Walsh, *Shadows*, 70.

150. John McNamar to William H. Herndon, Dec. 1, 1866, H-W Papers (transcript available in Wilson and Davis, *Herndon's*, 493).

151. George U. Miles to William H. Herndon, March 23, 1866, H-W Papers (transcript available in Wilson and Davis, *Herndon's*, 237).

152. Abraham Lincoln to Eliza Browning, April 1, 1838 (transcript available in *CW* 1:117–18).

153. George U. Miles to William H. Herndon, March 23, 1866, H-W Papers (transcript available in Wilson and Davis, *Herndon's*, 237). Mrs. Bowling Green remembered the Owens visit as longer than it was, perhaps confusing it with a later visit.

154. John Jones statement, Oct. 22, 1866, H-W Papers (transcript available in Wilson and Davis, *Herndon's*, 387).

155. Nancy Prewitt, quoted in Margaret Flindt, "Lincoln as a Lover [etc.], An Interview with Nancy, Sister of Ann Rutledge," *Chicago Inter-Ocean* (Feb. 12, 1886), as given in Walsh, *Shadows*, 43.

156. George U. Miles to William H. Herndon, March 23, 1866, H-W Papers (transcript available in Wilson and Davis, *Herndon's*, 236–37).

157. William G. Greene to William H. Herndon, May 30, 1866, H-W Papers (transcript available in Wilson and Davis, *Herndon's*, 21).

158. Isaac Cogdal interview with William H. Herndon, ca. 1865, H-W Papers (transcript available in Wilson and Davis, *Herndon's*, 440); Isaac Cogdal interview with William H. Herndon, ca. 1865, H-W Papers (transcript available in Wilson and Davis, *Herndon's*, 441). Cogdal's account has been often questioned and defended. The debate can be found elsewhere; here I simply note that I find Cogdal's account believable.

⊱ SOURCES ⊰

If a chapter note has all necessary information for locating a source, that information is not duplicated here.

ABBREVIATIONS

ALPL   Abraham Lincoln Presidential Library.
CW   *Collected Works of Abraham Lincoln.*
H-W Papers Herndon-Weik Papers.
LOC   Library of Congress.
SJ   *Sangamo Journal.*

MANUSCRIPT COLLECTIONS CITED

Abraham Lincoln Scrapbook: Photostats of Newspaper Clippings. ALPL.

Duncan Family Papers. ALPL.

Eddy, Henry, Papers. ALPL.

Francis, Simeon, Papers. Small Collection 525, ALPL.

Hardin, John J., Papers. Hardin Family Collection, Chicago Historical Society.

Herndon-Weik Papers. The two great archival repositories of this material are the LOC and the Huntington Library. Most readers wishing to examine the Herndon-Weik Papers will be satisfied with printed transcripts in Wilson and Davis, *Herndon's.* Readers needing to examine originals can find location data in Wilson and Davis. In Herndon's interview notes, some language sounds more like his mode of expression than a verbatim transcript, but I assume he faithfully preserved the spirit of what persons told him even if their exact words are lost. Some of his materials disappeared before reaching the LOC, and I'm confident he relied on his memory for some things he said about Lincoln. Lack of documentation in the H-W Papers doesn't imply that Herndon fabricated anything.

Lincoln, Abraham, Papers. LOC.

Lincoln Centennial Association Papers. ALPL.

Lockwood Family Papers. ALPL.

Miner, N. W., Small Collection 1052, ALPL.

Snyder, J. F., Papers. ALPL.

Stuart-Hay Family Papers. ALPL.

Swett, Leonard, Papers. ALPL.

Weik, Jesse W., Papers. ALPL. Transcripts of some items may be found in Wilson and Davis, *Herndon's.*

NEWSPAPERS

As full citations are given in notes or accompany the quotes, newspapers aren't listed here. Occasional discrepancies occur between the dates on a particular issue's front page and on its masthead. Dates on internal pages may differ from that on the front page. Such possibilities should be remembered when tracing a citation. Normally citations include the place of publication in a newspaper's name, but for a few titles, such as *Sangamo Journal* and *Illinois State Register*, where the place of publication became Springfield, the town is omitted.

JOURNALS AND PERIODICALS

Aldrich, O. W. "Slavery or Involuntary Servitude in Illinois Prior to and After Its Admission as a State." *Journal of the Illinois State Historical Society* 9 (1916): 109–32.

Allen, John W. "Slavery and Negro Servitude in Pope County, Illinois." *Journal of the Illinois State Historical Society* 42 (1949): 411–23.

Angle, Paul M. "Lincoln and Liquor." *Bulletin of the Abraham Lincoln Association*, no. 27 (June 1932): 3–9.

———. "The Record of a Friendship: A Series of Letters from Lincoln to Henry E. Dummer." *Journal of the Illinois State Historical Society* 31 (1938): 125–37.

Barnhart, John D. "The Southern Influence in the Formation of Illinois." *Journal of the Illinois State Historical Society* 32 (1939): 358–78.

Basler, Roy P., ed. "James Quay Howard's Notes on Lincoln." *Abraham Lincoln Quarterly* 4 (Dec. 1947): 386–400.

Beekman, Colby. "Reminiscences of P. P. Grosboll." *Journal of the Illinois State Historical Society* 14 (1921): 90–91.

Bennett, A. Milo. "The Building of a State: The Story of Illinois." *Journal of the Illinois State Historical Society* 13 (1920): 324–54.

"A Black Hawk War Payroll." *Journal of the Illinois State Historical Society* 47 (1954): 411–13.

Bone, Robert E. "Rock Creek Lyceum." *Journal of the Illinois State Historical Society* 19, nos. 1–2 (1926): 63–76.

Bray, Robert. "The Cartwright-Lincoln Acquaintance." *The Old Northwest* 13 (Summer 1987): 111–30.

Brooks, Noah. "Lincoln." *Scribner's Monthly* 15 (April 1878): 884–86.

———. "Personal Reminiscences of Lincoln." *Scribner's Monthly* 15 (Feb.–March 1878): 561–69, 673–81.

Brown, C. C. "Major John T. Stuart." *Transactions of the Illinois State Historical Society* 7 (1902): 109–14.

Brown, Caroline Owsley. "Springfield Society before the Civil War." *Journal of the Illinois State Historical Society* 15 (1922): 477–500.

Bullard, F. Lauriston. "Abe Goes down the River." *Lincoln Herald* 50 (Feb. 1948): 2–14.

"Candidates for Congress," *Lincoln Lore*, no. 17 (Aug. 5, 1929).

"Candidates for Constable," *Lincoln Lore*, no. 17 (Aug. 5, 1929).

Carson, Gerald. "Cracker Barrel Days in Old Illinois Stores." *Journal of the Illinois State Historical Society* 47 (1954): 7–19.

Chandler, Josephine Craven. "New Salem: Early Chapter in Lincoln's Life." *Journal of the Illinois State Historical Society* 22 (1930): 501–58. Chandler claimed family connections with several New Salem residents.

Clarke, Charles R. "Sketch of Charles James Fox Clarke with Letters to His Mother." *Journal of the Illinois State Historical Society* 22 (1930): 559–81.

Colby, Lydia. "Jonathan Colby, Pioneer of 1834 in Menard County, Illinois." *Journal of the Illinois State Historical Society* 17 (1924): 428–35.

Coleman, Charles H. "Lincoln's Lincoln Grandfather." *Journal of the Illinois State Historical Society* 52 (1959): 59–90.

———. "Sarah Bush Lincoln, the Mother Who Survived Him." *Lincoln Herald* 54 (Summer 1952): 13–19.

Coleman, J. Winston, Jr. "A Preacher and a Shrine." *Lincoln Herald* 46 (Dec. 1944): 2–9.

Conant, Alban Jasper. "A Portrait Painter's Reminiscences of Lincoln." *McClure's Magazine* 32 (1909): 512–16.

Davis, Edwin D. "The Hanks Family in Macon County, Illinois (1838–1939)." *Transactions of the Illinois State Historical Society [Papers in Illinois History]* (1939): 112–52.

———. "Lincoln and Macon County, Illinois, 1830–1831." *Journal of the Illinois State Historical Society* 25 (1932): 63–107.

Dole, Mrs. Joseph C. "Pioneer Days in Coles County, Illinois." *Journal of the Illinois State Historical Society* 14 (1921): 107–21.

Dorfman, Maurice. "Lincoln's Arithmetic Education: Influence on His Life." Part 1. *Lincoln Herald* 68 (1966): 61–80.

———. "Lincoln's Arithmetic Education: Influence on His Life." Part 2. *Lincoln Herald* 68 (1966): 108ff.

Dowrie, George William. "The Development of Banking in Illinois, 1817–1863." *University of Illinois Studies in the Social Sciences* 2 (Dec. 1913): 1–181.

Doyle, Cornelius J. "Address." *Journal of the Illinois State Historical Society* 23 (1930): 439–58.

Dunlap, Lloyd A. "Lincoln's Sum Book." *Lincoln Herald* 61 (1959): 6–10.

"Earliest Known Lincoln-Black Hawk War Discharge." *Journal of the Illinois State Historical Society* 52 (1959): 544–46.

"The Early Settlers: A Realistic Picture." *Journal of the Illinois State Historical Society* 37 (1944): 266–69.

"Education in Early Illinois." *Journal of the Illinois State Historical Society* 37 (1944): 368ff.

Enos, Zimri. "Description of Springfield." *Transactions of the Illinois State Historical Society* 14 (1909): 190–208.

Epler, Cyrus. "History of the Morgan County Bar." *Journal of the Illinois State Historical Society* 19, nos. 3–4 (1926–1927): 163–75.

Ewbank, Louis B. "Building a Pioneer Home." *Indiana Magazine of History* 40 (1944): 111–28.

Finkelman, Paul. "Slavery, the 'More Perfect Union,' and the Prairie State." *Journal of the Illinois State Historical Society* 80 (1987): 248–69.

Guelzo, Allen C. "Holland's Informants: The Construction of Josiah Holland's 'Life of Abraham Lincoln.'" *Journal of the Abraham Lincoln Association* 23 (2002): 1–53.

Gulliver, John P. "A Talk with Abraham Lincoln." *The Independent* 16 (Sept. 1, 1864): 1.

Hamm, Richard F. "The Prohibitionists' Lincoln." *Illinois Historical Journal* 86 (1993): 99ff.

Harris, Newton D. "Negro Servitude in Illinois." *Transactions of the Illinois State Historical Society for the Year 1906*. Publication no. 11 (1906): 49–56.

Hart, Richard E. "Springfield's African Americans as a Part of the Lincoln Community." *Journal of the Abraham Lincoln Association* 20 (Winter 1999): 35–54.

Hay, John. "Colonel Baker." *Harper's New Monthly Magazine* 24 (1861): 103–10.

"He Had His 'Dish Right Side Up.'" *Journal of the Illinois State Historical Society* 47 (1954): 91–94.

Henderson, John G. "Rough Justice in Pioneer Days." *Journal of the Illinois State Historical Society* 33 (1940): 366–67.

Herndon, William H. "Analysis of the Character of Abraham Lincoln." *Abraham Lincoln Quarterly* 1 (Sept. 1941): 343–83; (Dec. 1941): 403–41.

Hickey, James T. "Lincoln the Real Estate Agent." *Journal of the Illinois State Historical Society* 53 (1960): 70–78.

Hurie, Anna Kathryn. "Early Mills in Illinois." *Journal of the Illinois State Historical Society* 22 (1930): 593–600.

Inglehart, John E. "The Environment of Abraham Lincoln in Indiana." *Indiana Historical Society Publications* 8 (1925): 147–70.

Johnson, Oliver. As related by Howard Johnson. "A Home in the Woods: Oliver Johnson's Reminiscences of Early Marion County." *Indiana Historical Publications* 16 (1951): 143–234. Johnson arrived in Marion County in 1822.

Jordan, Philip D. "The Death of Nancy Hanks Lincoln." *Indiana Magazine of History* 40 (1944): 103–10.

"'The Journal Paper Was Always My Friend.'" *Journal of the Illinois State Historical Society* 46 (1953): 178–86.

Lambert, Joseph I. "The Black Hawk War: A Military Analysis." *Journal of the Illinois State Historical Society* 32 (1939): 442–73.

Lansden, John M. "Abraham Lincoln, Judge David Davis and Judge Edward Bates." *Journal of the Illinois State Historical Society* 7 (April 1914): 56–58.

"Letter from General Robert Anderson to Elihu B. Washburne." *Journal of the Illinois State Historical Society* 10 (1917): 422–28.

"Letters from New Switzerland, 1831–1832." *Journal of the Illinois State Historical Society* 49 (1956): 431–44.

"Lincoln Carries Lake Fork Precinct." *Journal of the Illinois State Historical Society* 49 (1956): 329–31.

"Lincoln in 1831." *Bulletin of the Abraham Lincoln Association*, no. 50 (Dec. 1937): 9.

"Lincoln's Association with New Boston." *Journal of the Illinois State Historical Society* 51 (1958): 200–202.

"Lincoln's First Vote." *Lincoln Lore*, no. 17 (Aug. 5, 1929).

Luthin, Reinhard H. "Abraham Lincoln and the Tariff." *American Historical Review* 49 (1944): 609–29.

McHarry, Jessie. "John Reynolds." *Journal of the Illinois State Historical Society* 6 (1913): 7–57.

McMurtry, R. Gerald. "The Bleakley & Montgomery Ledgers." *Lincoln Lore*, no. 1479 (May 1961).

———. "Furniture Made by Thomas Lincoln." *Lincoln Lore*, no. 1512 (Feb. 1964).

———. "Re-Discovering the Supposed Grave of Lincoln's Brother." *Lincoln Herald* 48 (Feb. 1946): 12–19.

———. "Thomas Lincoln's Corner Cupboards." *Lincoln Lore*, no. 1476 (Feb. 1961).

———. "Was Thomas Lincoln Photographed?" *Lincoln Herald* 46 (Feb. 1944): 21–24.

Monaghan, Jay. "Literary Opportunities in Pioneer Times." *Journal of the Illinois State Historical Society* 33 (1940): 412–37.

———. "New Light on the Lincoln-Rutledge Romance." *Abraham Lincoln Quarterly* 3 (Sept. 1944): 138–45.

Murr, J. Edward. "Lincoln in Indiana." *Indiana Magazine of History* 13 (1917): 307–48.

Nightingale, Joseph R. "Joseph H. Barrett and John Locke Scripps, Shapers of Lincoln's Religious Image." *Journal of the Illinois State Historical Society* 92 (1999): 238–73.

Oliver, William. "Hog Killing, Pioneer Style." *Journal of the Illinois State Historical Society* 40 (1947): 343–45.

Orr, William. "The Indian War." *Journal of the Illinois State Historical Society* 5 (1912): 66–79.

Ostendorf, Lloyd. "Lincoln and the Sisters 'Back Home.'" *Lincoln Herald* 60 (1958): 130ff.

Parrish, Braxton. "Pioneer Preacher's Autobiography." *Journal of the Illinois State Historical Society* 49 (1956): 424–31.

"A Petition Signed by Lincoln." *Journal of the Illinois State Historical Society* 46 (1953): 190.

Pond, Fern Nance. "The Memoirs of James McGrady Rutledge." *Journal of the Illinois State Historical Society* 29 (1936–37): 76–88.

———. "New Salem Community Activities: Documentary." *Journal of the Illinois State Historical Society* 48 (1955): 82–101.

———. "New Salem's Miller and Kelso." *Lincoln Herald* 52 (Dec. 1950): 26–31.

Pratt, Harry E. "The Genesis of Lincoln the Lawyer." *Bulletin of the Abraham Lincoln Association*, no. 57 (Sept. 1939): 3–10.

———. "Lincoln and the Division of Sangamon County." *Journal of the Illinois State Historical Society* 47 (1954): 398–409.

———. "Lincoln in the Black Hawk War." *Bulletin of the Abraham Lincoln Association*, no. 54 (Dec. 1938): 3–13.

———. "Lincoln Pilots the Talisman." *Abraham Lincoln Quarterly* 2 (Sept. 1943): 319–29.

Prickett, Josephine Gillespie. "Joseph Gillespie." *Transactions of the Illinois State Historical Society* 17 (1912): 93–114.

"Recollections of Lincoln: Three Letters of Intimate Friends." *Bulletin of the Abraham Lincoln Association*, no. 25 (Dec. 1931): 3–9.

Roberts, Daniel. "A Reminiscence of Stephen A. Douglas." *Harper's New Monthly Magazine* 87 (1893): 957–59.

Roberts, Octavia. "'We All Knew Abr'ham.'" *Abraham Lincoln Quarterly* 4 (March 1946): 17–29.

Roll, John Linden. "Sangamo Town." *Journal of the Illinois State Historical Society* 19, nos. 3–4 (1926–27): 153–60.

Sale, Mrs. Anthony W. "The Old Mills of Sangamon County." *Journal of the Illinois State Historical Society* 18 (1926): 1056–58.

Snyder, John F. "Pen Portrait of a Governor." *Journal of the Illinois State Historical Society* 38 (1945): 122–23.

"Stephen T. Logan Talks about Lincoln." *Bulletin of the Abraham Lincoln Association*, no. 12 (Sept. 1928): 1–3, 5.

Stevens, Frank E. "Life of Stephen Arnold Douglas." *Journal of the Illinois State Historical Society* 16 (Oct. 1923–Jan. 1924): 247–673.

Temple, Wayne C. "Lincoln and the Burners at New Salem." *Lincoln Herald* 67 (1965): 59–71.

———. "Lincoln's Arms and Dress in the Black Hawk War." *Lincoln Herald* 72 (1969): 145–49.

———. "Lincoln's Fence Rails." *Journal of the Illinois State Historical Society* 47 (1954): 20–34.

Thomas, Benjamin P. "Lincoln the Postmaster." *Bulletin of the Abraham Lincoln Association*, no. 31 (June 1933): 3–9.

———. "Lincoln: Voter and Candidate." *Bulletin of the Abraham Lincoln Association*, no. 36 (Sept. 1934): 3–9.

———. "Lincoln's Humor: An Analysis." *Abraham Lincoln Association Papers 1935* (1936): 61–90.

Townsend, William H. "Lincoln's 'Rebel' Niece." *Lincoln Herald* 46 (Dec. 1944): 2–12.

Turner, Garda Ann. "John E. Roll Recalls Lincoln." *Lincoln Herald* 62 (1960): 103–5.

"Uncle Mordecai Lincoln: Only Lincoln Relative with Whom the President Was Familiar." *Lincoln Kinsman*, no. 12 (June 1939).

Van Fenstermaker, J. "A Description of Sangamon County, Illinois, in 1830." *Agricultural History* 39 (1965): 136–40.

Volk, Leonard W. "The Lincoln Life-Mask and How It Was Made." *Journal of the Illinois State Historical Society* 8 (1915): 238–48. (First published in *Century Magazine* 23 (Dec. 1881): 223–68; also reprinted in Whitney, *Life*, 471–77).

Warren, Louis A. "The Accident at the Mill." *Lincoln Lore*, no. 902 (July 22, 1946).

———. "Azel W. Dorsey, Lincoln Pedagogue." *Lincoln Lore*, no. 65 (July 7, 1930)

———. "Dr. Franklin Influences the Boy Lincoln." *Lincoln Lore*, no. 1310 (May 17, 1954).

———. "Early Newspapers Lincoln Read." *Lincoln Lore*, no. 629 (April 28, 1941).

———. "The Environs of Lincoln's Youth." *Abraham Lincoln Association Papers* (1932): 111–44.

———. "Factors Contributing to the 1816 Lincoln Migration." *Lincoln Lore*, no. 657 (Nov. 10, 1941).

———. "The Hoosier Home of Thomas Lincoln." *Lincoln Lore*, no. 137 (Nov. 23, 1931).

———. "A June Bride." *Lincoln Lore*, no. 112 (June 1, 1931).

———. "Lincoln in New Orleans." *Lincoln Lore*, no. 333 (Aug. 26, 1935).

———. "Lincoln, Miss Roby, and Astronomy." *Lincoln Lore*, no. 1349 (Feb. 14, 1955).

———. "Lincoln the Clerk." *Lincoln Lore*, no. 175 (Aug. 15, 1932).

———. "Lincoln the Sexton." *Lincoln Lore*, no. 87 (Dec. 8, 1930).

———. "Lincoln's Early Political Background." *Journal of the Illinois State Historical Society* 23 (1931): 618–29.

———. "Lincoln's Financial Income." *Lincoln Lore*, no. 1360 (May 2, 1955).

———. "Lincoln's Hoosier Schoolmasters." *Indiana Magazine of History* 27 (1931): 104–18.

———. "Lincoln's Memories of Princeton, Indiana." *Lincoln Lore*, no. 1193 (Feb. 18, 1952).

———. "Lincoln's Return Trip from New Orleans." *Lincoln Lore*, no. 472 (April 25, 1938).

———. "The Lincolns and Audubon." *Lincoln Lore*, no. 597 (Sept. 16, 1940).

———. "The Lincolns Crossing the Wabash." *Lincoln Lore*, no. 480 (June 20, 1938).

———. "The Lincolns' Removal from Kentucky." *Lincoln Lore*, no. 921 (Dec. 2, 1946).

———. "A Log Meeting House and a Deerskin Record Book." *Lincoln Lore*, no. 767 (Dec. 20, 1943).

———. "Most Important Venture of Lincoln's Youth." *Lincoln Lore*, no. 1276 (Sept. 21, 1953).

———. "Murray's English Reader." *Lincoln Lore*, no. 76 (Sept. 22, 1930).

————. "The Other Nancy Hanks." *Lincoln Lore*, no. 1366 (June 13, 1955).

————. "Pigeon Creek Church." *Lincoln Lore*, no. 661 (Dec. 8, 1941).

————. "Reverend David Elkin." *Lincoln Lore*, no. 69 (Aug. 4, 1930).

————. "Rev. Jesse Head, Pioneer Preacher." *Lincoln Lore*, no. 113 (June 8, 1931).

————. "The Romance of Thomas Lincoln and Nancy Hanks." *Indiana Magazine of History* 30 (1934): 213–22.

————. "Sarah Bush Lincoln: The Stepmother of Abraham Lincoln." *Transactions of the Illinois State Historical Society* 33 (1926): 80–88.

————. "A Significant December Wedding." *Lincoln Lore*, no. 817 (Dec. 4, 1944).

————. "The Tavern License Broadside." *Lincoln Lore*, no. 1251 (March 30, 1953).

————. "That Half-Faced Camp." *Lincoln Lore*, no. 557 (Dec. 11, 1939).

————. "Widower Lincoln Marries Widow Johnston." *Lincoln Lore*, no. 765 (Dec. 6, 1943).

————. "William Downs." *Lincoln Lore*, no. 74 (Sept. 8, 1930).

West, Edward William. "Memoirs." *Journal of the Illinois State Historical Society* 22 (1929): 215–95.

BOOKS

Abraham Lincoln Scrapbook. See Manuscript Collections Cited.

American Slavery as It Is: Testimony of a Thousand Witnesses. New York: American Anti-Slavery Society, 1839.

Ander, O. Fritof, ed. *The John H. Hauberg Historical Essays.* Augustana Library Publications, no. 26, edited by Lucien White. Rock Island, IL: Augustana College Library, 1954.

Angle, Paul M. *"Here I Have Lived": A History of Lincoln's Springfield, 1821–1865.* New Brunswick, NJ: Rutgers University Press, 1935. Reprint of Springfield, IL: Abraham Lincoln Association, 1935.

————, ed. *Abraham Lincoln by Some Men Who Knew Him.* Freeport, NY: Books for Libraries Press, 1969. Essay Index Reprint Series. Reprint of Chicago: Americana House, 1950 (which itself was a reprint of the first edition).

————, ed. *Prairie State: Impressions of Illinois, 1673–1967, by Travelers and Other Observers.* Chicago: University of Chicago Press, 1968.

Arnold, Isaac N. *Address to Chicago Historical Society, November 19, 1868.* Chicago: Fergus Printing Co., 1877.

————. *The Life of Abraham Lincoln.* 4th ed. Lincoln: University of Nebraska Press, Bison Books, 1994. Reprint of Chicago: A. C. McClurg & Co., 1884.

Atkinson, Eleanor. *The Boyhood of Lincoln.* New York: McClure Company, 1908. This book purports to be a January 1889 interview with ninety-year-old Dennis Hanks at his Charleston, Illinois, residence. The book was well received when it appeared ("Holiday Book Number," *New York Times*, Dec. 4, 1908, p. 716), and its authenticity is accepted by Warren (*Lincoln's Parentage*, 104; *Lincoln's Youth*, 190; "Hoosier"; "Significant"). Atkinson's segment on p. 37, in which Hanks describes the horse mill, uses language close to what Hanks used in a June 13, 1865, interview with William H. Herndon (H-W Papers, transcript available in Wilson and Davis, *Herndon's*, 39), which suggests the possibility of fabrication, but Hanks may have simply used similar language when talking more than once about the same subject. The same can be said when comparing Atkinson's report on pp. 28–29 with the passage in Browne, *Every-Day*, 53, where Hanks speaks of Lincoln throwing something at snowbirds. The occasional error (such as the assertion on pp. 14–15 that Tom Lincoln obtained his Indiana farm by bartering four hundred gallons of whiskey) may add overall credibility, suggesting that Atkinson was indeed simply reporting what Hanks said. Why there was a twenty-year gap between conducting the interview and publishing it and whether dialogue in the book was reconstructed rather than from verbatim notes are open questions. Nonetheless, in some ways the book sounds authentic, describing the setting of interviews in a good brick house of Charleston, along with interaction between Hanks and his daughter Mrs. Dowling during Atkinson's visit. Despite doubts about the book, I have used it for whatever it is worth. I don't utilize it for crucial information or to refute other accounts.

Baber, Adin. *A. Lincoln with Compass and Chain.* Hanks Family Historical Series, vol. 5. Kansas, IL: By the Author, 1968.

Bancroft, Frederic. *The Life of William Seward.* 2 vols. New York: Harper & Brothers, 1900.

Baringer, William E. *Lincoln's Vandalia: A Pioneer Portrait.* New Brunswick, NJ: Rutgers University Press, 1949.

Barrett, Joseph H. *Life of Abraham Lincoln.* New York: Moore, Wilstach & Baldwin, 1865. This early biography is praised by Nightingale, "Joseph," who notes Barrett had Lincoln's full cooperation.

Barton, William E. *The Life of Abraham Lincoln.* Vol. 1. Indianapolis: the Bobbs-Merrill Company, 1925. Barton is quite knowledgeable but freely admits to inventing material to fill in gaps of knowledge. His accounts are honest but must be used with caution.

————. *The Paternity of Abraham Lincoln: Was He the Son of Thomas Lincoln? An Essay on the Chastity of Nancy Hanks.* New York: George H. Doran Company, 1920.

————. *The Soul of Abraham Lincoln.* New York: George H. Doran Company, 1920.

————. *The Women Lincoln Loved.* Indianapolis: Bobbs-Merrill Company, 1927.

Basler, Roy P. *The Lincoln Legend: A Study in Changing Conceptions.* New York: Octagon Books, 1969. Reprint of Boston, 1935.

————. *A Touchstone for Greatness: Essays, Addresses, and Occasional Pieces about Abraham Lincoln.* Contributions in American Studies, no. 4, series editor Robert H. Walker. Westport, CT: Greenwood Press, 1973.

Benner, Martha L., and Cullom Davis, eds. *The Law Practice of Abraham Lincoln: Complete Documentary Edition.* Urbana: University of Illinois Press, 2000. Rather than referring to original documents that are nearly inaccessible in various court archives and elsewhere, I cite to this convenient DVD set of reproductions of those documents. Anyone needing to examine the originals can find location data in Benner and Davis.

Benton, Thomas Hart. *Thirty Years' View; or, A History of the Working of the American Government for Thirty Years, from 1820 to 1850.* 2 vols. New York: D. Appleton and Company, 1854–1856.

Bestor, Arthur, David C. Mearns, and Jonathan Daniels. *Three Presidents and Their Books.* Urbana: University of Illinois Press, 1955.

Beveridge, Albert Jeremiah. *Abraham Lincoln: 1809–1858.* 2 vols. Boston: Houghton Mifflin Company, 1928.

Bidwell, Percy Wells, and John I. Falconer. *History of Agriculture in the Northern United States, 1620–1860.* Carnegie Institution of Washington Publication no. 358. New York: Peter Smith, 1941. Reprint of Washington: Carnegie Institution of Washington, 1925.

Bigelow, John. *Retrospections of an Active Life.* 5 vols. New York: Baker & Taylor Co. (vols. 1–3) and Garden City, NY: Doubleday, Page, & Company, 1909–13.

Bonham, Jeriah. *Fifty Years' Recollections with Observations and Reflections on Historical Events, Giving Sketches of Eminent Citizens: Their Lives and Public Services.* Peoria, IL: J. W. Franks & Sons, 1883.

Boritt, Gabor S. *Lincoln and the Economics of the American Dream.* Memphis: Memphis State University Press, 1978.

Briggs, Harold E., and Ernestine B. Briggs. *Nancy Hanks Lincoln: A Frontier Portrait.* New York: Bookman Associates, 1952.

Brooks, Noah. *Abraham Lincoln and the Downfall of American Slavery.* New York: G. P. Putnam's Sons, 1897. This appears to be the same as Noah Brooks, *The Life of Lincoln*, vol. 8 in *The Writings of Abraham Lincoln*, edited by Arthur Brooks Lapsley (New York: G. P. Putnam's Sons, 1888).

Browne, Francis Fisher. *The Every-Day Life of Abraham Lincoln.* Lincoln: University of Nebraska Press, Bison Books, 1995. Reprint of Minneapolis: Northwestern Publishing Co., 1887, which was based on New York: N. D. Thompson Publishing Co., 1886.

Browne, Robert H. *Abraham Lincoln and the Men of His Time.* 2 vols. New York: Eaton & Mains, 1901.

Brunson, Alfred. *A Western Pioneer; or, Incidents of the Life and Times of Rev. Alfred Brunson, A.M., D.D., Embracing a Period of Over Seventy Years.* 2 vols. Cincinnati: Walden & Stowe, 1880.

Bryant, William Cullen. *Prose Writings of William Cullen Bryant.* Edited by Parke Godwin. Vol. 2, *Travels, Addresses, and Comments.* New York: Russell & Russell, 1964. Reprint of New York: D. Appleton and Co., 1884.

Burlingame, Michael, ed. *An Oral History of Abraham Lincoln: John G. Nicolay's Interviews and Essays.* Carbondale: Southern Illinois University Press, 1996.

Carpenter, Francis B. *Six Months at the White House with Abraham Lincoln: The Story of a Picture.* New York: Hurd and Houghton, 1866. The edition I used says 1867 on title page, 1866 on copyright page.

Carter, Jimmy. *Turning Point: A Candidate, a State, and a Nation Come of Age.* New York: Times Books, 1992.

Cartwright, Peter. *Autobiography of Peter Cartwright, the Backwoods Preacher.* W. P. Strickland, ed. Cincinnati: Jennings & Graham, 1856.

Cath, Stanley H., Alan Gurwitt, and Linda Gunsberg, eds. *Fathers and Their Families.* Hillsdale, NJ: Analytic Press, 1989.

Caton, John Dean. *Early Bench and Bar of Illinois.* Chicago: Chicago Legal News Company, 1893.

Chapman, Ervin. *Latest Light on Lincoln and War-Time Memories.* New York: Fleming H. Revell Company, 1917. Chapman must be used with particular caution. For example, he accepts Charles Chiniquy's account of conversations with Lincoln about religion and James B. Merwin's assertions of Lincoln's prohibition activities.

Cockrum, William Monroe. *Pioneer History of Indiana.* Oakland City, IN: Press of the Oakland City Journal, 1907.

Coffin, Levi. *Reminiscences of Levi Coffin: The Reputed President of the Underground Railroad.* New York: Augustus M. Kelley, 1968. Reprint of Cincinnati: Western Tract Society, 1876.

Coleman, Charles H. *Abraham Lincoln and Coles County, Illinois.* New Brunswick, NJ: Scarecrow Press, 1955.

Conkling, James C. *Recollections of the Bench and Bar.* Fergus Historical Series, no. 22. Chicago: Fergus Printing Company, 1882.

Current, Richard Nelson. *The Lincoln Nobody Knows.* New York: McGraw-Hill Book Company, 1958.

———. *Speaking of Abraham Lincoln: The Man and His Meaning for Our Times.* Urbana: University of Illinois Press, 1983.

Curti, Merle. *The Making of an American Community: A Case Study of Democracy in a Frontier County.* Stanford, CA: Stanford University Press, 1969. Reprint of 1959 edition.

Davidson, Alexander, and Bernard Stuvé. *A Complete History of Illinois from 1763–1873; Embracing the Physical Features of the Country; Its Early Explorations; Aboriginal Inhabitants; French and British Occupation; Conquest by Virginia; Territorial Condition and the Subsequent Civil, Military and Political Events of the State.* Springfield: Illinois Journal Company, 1874.

Davis, Varina. *Jefferson Davis, Ex-President of the Confederate States of America: A Memoir.* Vol. 1. Baltimore: Nautical & Aviation Publishing Company of America, 1990. Reprint of New York: Belford Co., 1890.

Dick, Everett. *The Lure of the Land: A Social History of the Public Lands from the Articles of Confederation to the New Deal.* Lincoln: University of Nebraska Press, 1970.

Dickens, Charles. *American Notes for General Circulation and Hunted Down.* Boston: Estes & Lauriat, 1890.

Donald, David Herbert. *Lincoln.* New York: Simon & Schuster, 1995.

———. *Lincoln Reconsidered: Essays on the Civil War Era.* 2nd ed. New York: Alfred A. Knopf, 1969.

———. *Lincoln's Herndon.* New York: Da Capo Press, 1989. Reprint of New York: Alfred A. Knopf, 1948.

Douglas, Stephen A. *The Letters of Stephen A. Douglas.* Robert W. Johannsen, ed. Urbana: University of Illinois Press, 1961.

Drake, Daniel. *Pioneer Life in Kentucky: 1785–1800.* New York: Henry Schuman, 1948.

Duis, Etzard. *Good Old Times in McLean County, Illinois.* Bloomington: Leader Publishing and Printing House, 1874.

Edwards, Ninian W. *History of Illinois from 1778 to 1833; and Life and Times of Ninian Edwards.* Springfield: Illinois State Journal Company, 1870.

Eggleston, George Cary. *The First of the Hoosiers.* Philadelphia: Drexel Biddle, 1903.

Ehrmann, Bess V. *The Missing Chapter in the Life of Abraham Lincoln.* Chicago: Walter M. Hill, 1938.

Erickson, Erling A. *Banking in Frontier Iowa, 1836–1865.* Ames: Iowa State University Press, 1971.

Faragher, John Mack. *Sugar Creek: Life on the Illinois Prairie.* New Haven, CT: Yale University Press, 1986.

Faux, William. *Memorable Days in America.* London: W. Simpkin and R. Marshall, 1823. Reprinted in *Early Western Travels, 1748–1846,* edited by Reuben Gold Thwaites, vols. 11 and 12. Cleveland: Arthur H. Clark Company, 1904.

Fehrenbacher, Don E., and Virginia Fehrenbacher, comps. *Recollected Words of Abraham Lincoln.* Stanford, CA: Stanford University Press, 1996.

Findley, Paul. *A. Lincoln: The Crucible of Congress.* New York: Crown Publishers, 1979.

Ford, Thomas. *A History of Illinois from Its Commencement as a State in 1818 to 1847.* Urbana: University of Illinois Press, 1995. Reprint.

Fordham, Elias Pym. *Personal Narrative of Travels in Virginia, Maryland, Pennsylvania, Ohio, Indiana, Kentucky; and of a Residence in the Illinois Territory, 1817–1818.* Edited by Frederic Austin Ogg. Cleveland: Arthur H. Clark Company, 1906.

Furnas, J. C. *Goodbye to Uncle Tom.* New York: Apollo Editions, 1968. Reprint of New York: William Sloane Associates, 1956.

Gerhard, Fred. *Illinois as It Is.* Chicago: Keen and Lee, and Philadelphia: Charles Desilver, 1857.

Gillespie, Joseph. *Recollections of Early Illinois, and Her Noted Men.* Fergus Historical Series, no. 13. Chicago: Fergus Printing Company, 1880.

Greeley, Horace. *Recollections of a Busy Life.* Miami, FL: Mnemosyne Publishing Co., 1969. Reprint of New York: J. B. Ford and Company, 1868.

Greene, Evarts Boutell, and Clarence Walworth Alvord, eds. *The Governors' Letter-Books, 1818–1834.* Executive Series, vol. 1. *Collections of the Illinois State Historical Library,* vol. 4. Springfield: Illinois State Historical Library, 1909.

Haig, Robert Murray. *A History of the General Property Tax in Illinois.* University of Illinois Studies in the Social Sciences, vol. 3. Urbana: University of Illinois, 1914.

Hammond, Bray. *Banks and Politics in America from the Revolution to the Civil War.* Princeton, NJ: Princeton University Press, 1957.

Hapgood, Norman. *Abraham Lincoln: The Man of the People.* New York: Macmillan Company, 1901.

Harris, Thaddeus Mason. *The Journal of a Tour into the Territory Northwest of the Alleghany Mountains. . . .* Boston: Manning & Loring, 1805. Reprinted in *Early Western Travels, 1748–1846,* edited by Reuben Gold Thwaites, vol. 3. Cleveland: The Arthur H. Clark Company, 1904.

Helm, Katherine. *The True Story of Mary, Wife of Lincoln.* New York: Harper & Brothers, 1928. Portions seem fictionalized, and in private conversations, Abraham Lincoln is quoted using language close to that found in his public statements. Nonetheless, reports of family traditions are useful, as are quotations from writings of family members and friends.

Herndon, William H., and Jesse W. Weik. *Herndon's Life of Lincoln.* New York: Da Capo Press, 1983. Reprint of Cleveland: World Pub. Co., 1942. Weik was the ghostwriter of this volume, which contained inaccuracies that anguished Herndon. Some failings in the volume for which Herndon has been blamed should more properly be ascribed to Weik. The book is a good starting place to learn about covered topics, but a person needing verified facts should consult additional sources of information.

Hertz, Emanuel. *Abraham Lincoln: A New Portrait.* 2 vols. New York: Horace Liveright, 1931.

———, ed. *The Hidden Lincoln, from the Letters and Papers of William H. Herndon.* New York: Blue Ribbon Books, 1940. Reprint of New York: Viking Press, 1938. Hertz has been criticized for errors in his collections of documents that are puzzling because he was obviously knowledgeable. Still, he is often cited, and even relied on, because access to his printed collections is so much more practical than examining the original items. Much of his work has been superseded by Wilson and Davis, *Herndon's*.

Hibbard, Benjamin Horace. *A History of the Public Land Policies*. Land Economics Series. New York: Peter Smith, 1939. Reprint of New York: Macmillan, 1924.

Hill, Frederick Trevor. *Lincoln the Lawyer*. New York: Century Co., 1906. This book should be used cautiously.

History of Sangamon County, Illinois: Together with Sketches of Its Cities, Villages and Townships, Educational, Religious, Civil, Military, and Political History; Portraits of Prominent Persons, and Biographies of Representative Citizens. Chicago: Inter-State Publishing Company, 1881.

History of Warwick, Spencer and Perry Counties. Evansville, IN: Unigraphic, 1965. Reprint of Chicago: Goodspeed, Bros. & Co., 1885.

Hobson, Jonathan Todd. *Footprints of Abraham Lincoln*. Dayton, 1909.

Holland, Josiah G. *The Life of Abraham Lincoln*. Springfield, MA: Gurdon Bill, 1866.

Houser, M. L. *Lincoln's Education and Other Essays*. New York: Bookman Associates, 1957.

Howard, Robert P. *Illinois: A History of the Prairie State*. Grand Rapids: William B. Eerdmans Publishing Company, 1972.

Howells, William Cooper. *Recollections of Life in Ohio from 1813 to 1840*. Cincinnati: Robert Clarke Company, 1895.

Howells, William Dean. *Life of Abraham Lincoln*. Springfield, IL: Abraham Lincoln Association, 1938.

———. *Life of Abraham Lincoln*. Bloomington: Indiana University Press, 1960. Facsimile ed. This edition reproduces Lincoln's emendations. Those corrections do not mean, however, that Lincoln approved everything else as accurate; he may have passed over items that did not seem important enough to correct or qualify. Introduction pagination apparently differs from that in the 1938 Abraham Lincoln Association edition. Originally published as *Lives and Speeches of Abraham Lincoln and Hannibal Hamlin*. Columbus, OH: Follett, Foster & Co., 1860.

Jayne, William. *Abraham Lincoln: Personal Reminiscences of the Martyred President*. Chicago: Grand Army Hall and Memorial Association, 1908. In this 1900 speech, Jayne does not always distinguish his firsthand recollections from material he acquired through other sources. Thus close reading is required to evaluate what he says.

Johannsen, Robert W. *Stephen A. Douglas*. New York: Oxford University Press, 1973.

Johnson, Charles A. *The Frontier Camp Meeting: Religion's Harvest Time*. Dallas: Southern Methodist University Press, 1955.

Johnson, Charles Beneulyn. *Illinois in the Fifties; or, A Decade of Development*. Champaign, IL: Flanigan-Pearson Co., 1918.

Kempf, Edward J. *Abraham Lincoln's Philosophy of Common Sense: An Analytical Biography of a Great Mind*. Special Publications of the New York Academy of Sciences, vol. 6. New York: The Academy, 1965. The physician author's grasp of historical detail is less sure than his style suggests, but he offers useful medical and mental observations.

Koerner, Gustave. *Memoirs of Gustave Koerner, 1809–1896*. 2 vols. Edited by Thomas J. McCormack. Cedar Rapids, IA: Torch Press, 1909.

Krenkel, John H. *Illinois Internal Improvements, 1818–1848*. Cedar Rapids, IA: Torch Press, 1958.

Krug, Mark M. *Lyman Trumbull: Conservative Radical*. New York: A. S. Barnes and Company, 1965.

Lair, John. *Songs Lincoln Loved*. New York: Duell, Sloan and Pearce, and Boston: Little, Brown and Company, 1954.

Lamon, Ward Hill. *Recollections of Abraham Lincoln, 1847–1865*. Edited by Dorothy Lamon Teillard. Lincoln: University of Nebraska Press, Bison Books, 1994. Reprint of 2nd ed., Washington, DC: Dorothy Lamon Teillard, 1911.

Lamon, Ward Hill. Ghostwritten by Chauncey Black. *The Life of Abraham Lincoln from His Birth to His Inauguration as President*. Boston: James R. Osgood and Company, 1872. Ostensibly written by Lincoln's friend Lamon, this controversial book was actually written by Black, whose hatred of Lincoln is evident throughout. The volume must be used cautiously.

A Letter from Wm. H. Herndon to Isaac N. Arnold Relating to Abraham Lincoln, His Wife, and Their Life in Springfield. Chicago and Springfield, IL: R. R. Donnelley & Sons Co., and Frye Printing Co., n.d. Reprint of privately printed 1937 ed.

Levering, Julia Henderson. *Historic Indiana.* New York: G. P. Putnam's Sons, 1916.

Lincoln, Abraham. *The Collected Works of Abraham Lincoln.* 8 vols. and index vol. Edited by Roy P. Basler. New Brunswick, NJ: Rutgers University Press, 1953–55.

———. *The Collected Works of Abraham Lincoln: Supplement, 1832–1865.* Edited by Roy P. Basler. Contributions in American Studies, edited by Robert H. Walker, no. 7. Westport, CT: Greenwood Press, 1974.

———. *The Collected Works of Abraham Lincoln: Second Supplement, 1848–1865.* Edited by Roy P. Basler and Christian O. Basler. New Brunswick, NJ: Rutgers University Press, 1990.

Lincoln and New Salem. Petersburg, IL: Old Salem Lincoln League, n.d. [ca. 1918].

Linder, Usher F. *Reminiscences of the Early Bench and Bar of Illinois.* Chicago: Chicago Legal News Company, 1879.

Luthin, Reinhard H. *The Real Abraham Lincoln: A Complete One Volume History of His Life and Times.* Englewood Cliffs, NJ: Prentice-Hall, 1960.

McCall, George Archibald. *Letters from the Frontiers.* Gainesville, FL: University Presses of Florida, 1974. Reprint of Philadelphia: J. B. Lippincott & Co., 1868.

McConnel, John L. *Western Characters.* New York: Redfield, 1853.

McCulloch, Hugh. *Men and Measures of Half a Century: Sketches and Comments.* The American Scene: Comments and Commentators. Edited by Wallace D. Farnham. New York: Da Capo Press, 1970. Reprint of New York: Charles Scribner's Sons, 1888.

McGrane, Reginald Charles. *The Panic of 1837: Some Financial Problems of the Jacksonian Era.* New York: Russell & Russell, 1965. Reprint of Chicago: University of Chicago Press, 1924.

McMurtry, R. Gerald. *Ben Hardin Helm: "Rebel" Brother-in-Law of Abraham Lincoln—with a Biographical Sketch of His Wife and an Account of the Todd Family of Kentucky.* Chicago: Civil War Round Table, 1943.

Maltby, Charles. *The Life and Public Services of Abraham Lincoln.* Stockton, CA: Daily Independent Steam Power Print, 1884.

Michaux, François André. *Travels to the West of the Alleghany Mountains. . . .* London: B. Crosby and Co. and J. P. Hughes, 1805. Reprinted in *Early Western Travels, 1748–1846,* edited by Reuben Gold Thwaites, vol. 3. Cleveland: Arthur H. Clark Company, 1904.

Miers, Earl Schenck, ed.-in-chief. *Lincoln Day by Day: A Chronology, 1809–1865.* Dayton: Morningside, 1991. Reprint of Washington, DC: Lincoln Sesquicentennial Commission, 1960.

Miller, R. D., et al. *The History of Menard and Mason Counties, Illinois.* Chicago: O. L. Baskin & Co., 1879.

Milton, George Fort. *The Eve of Conflict: Stephen A. Douglas and the Needless War.* Boston: Houghton Mifflin Company, 1934.

Mitchell, Samuel Augustus. *Illinois in 1837.* Philadelphia: S. Augustus Mitchell and Grigg & Elliot, 1837.

Mitgang, Herbert, ed. *Abraham Lincoln: A Press Portrait.* Chicago: Quadrangle Books, 1971.

Moses, John. *Illinois, Historical and Statistical.* 2 vols. Chicago: Fergus Printing Company, 1889–92.

Newman, Ralph G., ed. *Lincoln for the Ages.* Garden City, New York: Doubleday & Company, 1960.

Nichols, Roy Franklin. *The Disruption of American Democracy.* New York: Macmillan Company, 1948.

Nicolay, Helen. *Personal Traits of Abraham Lincoln.* New York: Century Co., 1912.

Nicolay, John G., and John Hay. *Abraham Lincoln: A History.* 10 vols. New York: Century Co., 1890.

Oldroyd, Osborn Hamiline. *The Lincoln Memorial: Album of Immortelles.* Nonsubscription ed. New York: G. W. Carleton & Co., 1882.

Oliver, William. *Eight Months in Illinois with Information to Immigrants.* Chicago: Walter M. Hill, 1924. Reprint of Newcastle upon Tyne, 1843.

Onstot, Thompson Gains. *Pioneers of Menard and Mason Counties*. Forest City, IL, 1902. Reprint by Church of Jesus Christ of Latter-Day Saints, 1986.

Paine, Thomas. *The Age of Reason*. Buffalo, NY: Prometheus Books, 1984. Reprint.

Palmer, John McAuley (1817–1900). *The Bench and Bar of Illinois: Historical and Reminiscent*. 2 vols. Chicago: Lewis Publishing Co., 1899.

Pease, Theodore Calvin. *The Frontier State, 1818–1848*. The Sesquicentennial History of Illinois, vol. 2. Urbana: University of Illinois Press, 1987. Reprint of Springfield: Illinois Centennial Commission, 1918.

Petersen, William F. *Lincoln-Douglas: The Weather as Destiny*. Springfield, IL: Charles C. Thomas, 1943.

Peterson, James A. *In re Lucey Hanks*. Yorkville, IL: Privately published, 1973.

Peterson, Merrill D. *Lincoln in American Memory*. New York: Oxford University Press, 1994.

Power, John Carroll, with Mrs. S. A. Power. *History of the Early Settlers of Sangamon County, Illinois*. Springfield, IL: Edwin A. Wilson & Co., 1876.

Pratt, Harry E. *Dr. Anson G. Henry: Lincoln's Physician and Friend*. Harrogate, TN: Lincoln Memorial University, 1944. Reprinted from *Lincoln Herald* 45, nos. 3 and 4 (1943).

———. *The Personal Finances of Abraham Lincoln*. Springfield, IL: Abraham Lincoln Association, 1943.

Randall, Ruth Painter. *Mary Lincoln: Biography of a Marriage*. Boston: Little, Brown and Company, 1953.

Reynolds, John. *My Own Times: Embracing Also the History of My Life*. Belleville, IL: B. H. Perryman and H. L. Davison, 1855.

———. *Pioneer History of Illinois*. Belleville, IL: N. A. Randall, 1852.

Rice, Allen Thorndike, ed. *Reminiscences of Abraham Lincoln by Distinguished Men of His Time*. New York: North American Review, 1888.

Rohrbough, Malcolm J. *The Land Office Business: The Settlement and Administration of American Public Lands, 1789–1837*. New York: Oxford University Press, 1968.

Rorabaugh, W. J. *The Alcoholic Republic: An American Tradition*. New York: Oxford University Press, 1979.

Ross, Harvey Lee. *Lincoln's First Years in Illinois*. Elmira, NY: Primavera Press, 1946. Reprint of *The Early Pioneers and Pioneer Events of the State of Illinois. . . .* Chicago: Eastman Brothers, 1899.

Scheiber, Harry N. *Ohio Canal Era: A Case Study of Government and the Economy, 1820–1861*. Athens: Ohio University Press, 1969.

Schoolcraft, Henry R. *Travels in the Central Portions of the Mississippi Valley*. New York: Collins and Hannay, 1825.

Schwartz, Thomas F. *Finding the Missing Link: A Promissory Note and the Lost Town of Pappsville*. Historical Bulletin, no. 51. Racine: Lincoln Fellowship of Wisconsin, 1996.

Scott, John M. *Supreme Court of Illinois, 1818: Its First Judges and Lawyers*. Bloomington, 1896.

Scripps, John L. *Life of Abraham Lincoln*. Annotated by M. L. Houser. Peoria: E. J. Jacob, 1931.

Segal, Charles M., ed. *Conversations with Lincoln*. New York: G. P. Putnam's Sons, 1961.

Sheahan, James W. *The Life of Stephen A. Douglas*. New York: Harper & Brothers, Publishers, 1860. This fine campaign biography is particularly useful for its articulate advocacy of Douglas's ideas. From the preface: "These pages have been prepared without having been submitted to Mr. Douglas, who, if he read them at all, will do so for the first time after the issue of the book. They have been written by one who agrees fully with Mr. Douglas in political views, and who, since the passage of the Kansas-Nebraska Act, has been engaged in maintaining before the people of Illinois the wisdom, justice, and expediency of the policy." Today explanations of Douglas's thought typically come either from his own words or from later analysts who have little, if any, experience in politics. Here, instead, is a vigorous advocacy produced by one of Douglas's Illinois colleagues. This is how Douglas appeared to one of the true believers, whose ranks numbered in the tens and hundreds of thousands. Here is their hero. In contrast to Sheahan's assertion, two acclaimed biographers of Douglas report that the Senator examined and had opportunity to change each chapter before publication (Johannsen, *Stephen*, 701, 733–34; Milton, *Eve*, 68 n. 8, 381). Milton says Douglas made numerous changes. His correspondence verifies his close involvement with writing the book (Stephen Douglas to James Sheahan, April 18, 1859, and autobiographical notes, April 17, 1859 (transcripts available in Douglas, *Letters*, 443–44, 446)).

Sherman, John. *Recollections of Forty Years in the House, Senate and Cabinet: An Autobiography.* Vol. 1. Chicago: Werner Company, 1895. Alternate title *John Sherman's Recollections.* . . .

Shutes, Milton H. *Lincoln and the Doctors: A Medical Narrative of the Life of Abraham Lincoln.* New York: Pioneer Press, 1933.

———. *Lincoln's Emotional Life.* Philadelphia: Dorrance, 1957.

Simon, Paul. *Lincoln's Preparation for Greatness: The Illinois Legislative Years.* Urbana: University of Illinois Press, 1971. Reprint of Norman: University of Oklahoma Press, 1965.

Smith, George Washington. *When Lincoln Came to Egypt.* Herrin, IL: Trovillion Private Press, 1940.

Smith, Oliver Hampton. *Early Indiana Trials and Sketches.* Cincinnati: Moore, Wilstach, Keys & Co., Printers, 1858.

Snyder, John Francis. *Adam W. Snyder and His Period in Illinois History, 1817–1842.* 2nd and rev. ed. Virginia, IL: E. Needham, 1906.

Speed, Joshua F. *Reminiscences of Abraham Lincoln and Notes of a Visit to California: Two Lectures.* Louisville, KY: John P. Morton and Co., 1884.

Stevens, Frank E. *The Black Hawk War, Including a Review of Black Hawk's Life.* Chicago: Frank E. Stevens, 1903.

Stevens, Walter Barlow. *A Reporter's Lincoln.* St. Louis: Missouri Historical Society, 1916.

Stringer, Lawrence Beaumont. *History of Logan County Illinois.* Chicago: Pioneer Publishing Company, 1911.

Strozier, Charles B. *Lincoln's Quest for Union: Public and Private Meanings.* New York: Basic Books, 1982.

Stuart, James. *Three Years in North America.* 2nd ed. Edinburgh: Robert Cadell, 1833.

Tarbell, Ida M. *The Early Life of Abraham Lincoln.* New York: S. S. McClure, 1896.

———. *In the Footsteps of the Lincolns.* New York: Harper & Brothers, 1924. Alternate title *In the Footsteps of Lincoln*, 1923.

———. *The Life of Abraham Lincoln.* 2 vols. New York: Macmillan Company, 1928. Unless stated otherwise in the source note, references to Tarbell's *Life* are for this edition.

Temple, Wayne C. *Abraham Lincoln: From Skeptic to Prophet.* Mahomet, IL: Mayhaven Publishing, 1995.

Thomas, Benjamin P. *Abraham Lincoln: A Biography.* New York: Modern Library, 1968. Reprint of 1952.

———. *Lincoln's New Salem.* Springfield, IL: Abraham Lincoln Association, 1934.

———. *Portrait for Posterity: Lincoln and His Biographers.* New Brunswick, NJ: Rutgers University Press, 1947.

Tillson, Christiana Holmes. *A Woman's Story of Pioneer Illinois.* Edited by Milo Milton Quaife. Chicago: Lakeside Press, 1919.

Tingley, Donald F., ed. *Essays in Illinois History in Honor of Glenn Huron Seymor.* Carbondale: Southern Illinois University Press, 1968.

Townsend, William H. *Lincoln and His Wife's Home Town.* Indianapolis: Bobbs-Merrill Company, 1929.

———. *Lincoln and Liquor.* New York: Press of the Pioneers, 1934.

———. *Lincoln and the Bluegrass: Slavery and Civil War in Kentucky.* Lexington: University of Kentucky Press, 1955.

———. *Lincoln the Litigant.* Boston: Houghton Mifflin Company, 1925.

Turpie, David. *Sketches of My Own Times.* Indianapolis: Bobbs-Merrill Company, 1903.

Volney, Constantine Francis. *The Ruins; or, Meditation on the Revolutions of Empires: And the Law of Nature.* New York: Truth Seeker Co., 1913. Reprint of 1890 ed.

Wade, Richard C. *Slavery in the Cities: The South, 1820–1860.* New York: Oxford University Press, 1964.

Walsh, John Evangelist. *The Shadows Rise: Abraham Lincoln and the Ann Rutledge Legend.* Urbana, IL: University of Chicago Press, 1993.

Warren, Louis A. *Lincoln's Parentage and Childhood: A History of the Kentucky Lincolns Supported by Documentary Evidence.* New York: Century Co., 1926.

———. *Lincoln's Youth: Indiana Years, Seven to Twenty-One, 1816–1830.* Indianapolis: Indiana Historical Society, 1991. Reprint of New York: Appleton, Century, Crofts, 1959.

———. *The Slavery Atmosphere of Lincoln's Youth.* Fort Wayne, IN: Lincolniana Publishers, 1933.

Wayland, Francis. *The Elements of Political Economy.* New York: Leavitt, Lord & Company, 1837.

Weik, Jesse William. *The Real Lincoln: A Portrait.* Boston: Houghton Mifflin Company, 1922.

Whitney, Henry Clay. *Life on the Circuit with Lincoln.* Caldwell, ID: Caxton Printers, 1940. Reprint of Boston, 1892. Whitney's book must be used cautiously. His veracity cannot be automatically dismissed or accepted. What he says must be compared with what is known from other sources.

Wilson, Douglas L. *Honor's Voice: The Transformation of Abraham Lincoln.* New York: Alfred A. Knopf, 1998.

———. *Lincoln before Washington: New Perspectives on the Illinois Years.* Urbana: University of Illinois Press, 1997.

Wilson, Douglas L., and Rodney O. Davis, eds. *Herndon's Informants: Letters, Interviews, and Statements about Abraham Lincoln.* Urbana: University of Illinois Press, 1998.

Wilson, Rufus Rockwell, ed. *Intimate Memories of Lincoln.* Elmira, NY: Primavera Press, 1945.

———. ed. *Uncollected Works of Abraham Lincoln: His Letters, Addresses and Other Papers.* 2 vols. Elmira, NY: Primavera Press, 1947–48.

Winkle, Kenneth J. *The Young Eagle: The Rise of Abraham Lincoln.* Dallas: Taylor Trade Publishing, 2001.

Wolf, William J. *The Almost Chosen People: A Study of the Religion of Abraham Lincoln.* Garden City, NY: Doubleday & Company, 1959. Alternate titles *The Religion of Abraham Lincoln*, 1963, and *Lincoln's Religion*, 1970. The 1963 version has a third appendix.

Woods, John. *Two Years' Residence in the Settlement on the English Prairie, in the Illinois Country of the United States.* London: Longman, Hurst, Rees, Orme, and Brown, 1822. Reprinted in *Early Western Travels, 1748–1846*, edited by Reuben Gold Thwaites, vol. 10. Cleveland: Arthur H. Clark Company, 1904.

Zall, P. M., ed. *Abe Lincoln Laughing: Humorous Anecdotes from Original Sources by and about Abraham Lincoln.* Berkeley: University of California Press, 1982.

➤ INDEX ➤